PARALLEL DISTRIBUTED PROCESSING

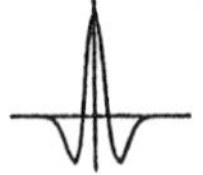

Computational Models of Cognition and Perception

Editors

Jerome A. Feldman
Patrick J. Hayes
David E. Rumelhart

Parallel Distributed Processing: Explorations in the Microstructure of Cognition. Volume 1: Foundations, by David E. Rumelhart, James L. McClelland, and the PDP Research Group

Parallel Distributed Processing: Explorations in the Microstructure of Cognition. Volume 2: Psychological and Biological Models, by James L. McClelland, David E. Rumelhart, and the PDP Research Group

Neurophilosophy: Toward a Unified Science of the Mind-Brain, by Patricia S. Churchland

Qualitative Reasoning About Physical Systems, edited by Daniel G. Bobrow

Visual Cognition, edited by Steven Pinker

PARALLEL DISTRIBUTED PROCESSING

Explorations in the Microstructure of Cognition

Volume 1: Foundations

David E. Rumelhart James L. McClelland
and the PDP Research Group

Chisato Asanuma
Francis H. C. Crick
Jeffrey L. Elman
Geoffrey E. Hinton
Michael I. Jordan
Alan H. Kawamoto
Paul W. Munro
Donald A. Norman
Daniel E. Rabin
Terrence J. Sejnowski
Paul Smolensky
Gregory O. Stone
Ronald J. Williams
David Zipser

Institute for Cognitive Science
University of California, San Diego

A Bradford Book

The MIT Press
Cambridge, Massachusetts
London, England

Ninth Printing, 1989

Printed and bound in the United States of America

Library of Congress Cataloging-in-Publication Data

Rumelhart, David E.
Parallel distributed processing.

(Computational models of cognition and perception)
Vol. 2 by James L. McClelland, David E. Rumelhart, and the PDP Research Group.
"A Bradford book."
Includes bibliographies and indexes.
Contents: v. 1. Foundations — v. 2. Psychological and biological models.
1. Human information processing. 2. Cognition.
I. McClelland, James L. II. University of California, San Diego. PDP Research Group. III. Title. IV. Series.
BF455.R853 1986 153 85-24073
ISBN 0-262-18120-7 (v. 1)
0-262-13218-4 (v. 2)
0-262-18123-1 (set)

Contents

VOLUME 1
FOUNDATIONS

Preface ix

Acknowledgments xv

Addresses of the PDP Research Group xix

Part I THE PDP PERSPECTIVE 1

1 **The Appeal of Parallel Distributed Processing** 3
J. L. MCCLELLAND, D. E. RUMELHART, and G. E. HINTON

2 **A General Framework for Parallel Distributed Processing** 45
D. E. RUMELHART, G. E. HINTON, and J. L. MCCLELLAND

3 **Distributed Representations** 77
G. E. HINTON, J. L. MCCLELLAND, and D. E. RUMELHART

4 **PDP Models and General Issues in Cognitive Science** 110
D. E. RUMELHART and J. L. MCCLELLAND

Part II BASIC MECHANISMS 147

5 Feature Discovery by Competitive Learning 151
D. E. RUMELHART and D. ZIPSER

6 Information Processing in Dynamical Systems: Foundations of Harmony Theory 194
P. SMOLENSKY

7 Learning and Relearning in Boltzmann Machines 282
G. E. HINTON and T. J. SEJNOWSKI

8 Learning Internal Representations by Error Propagation 318
D. E. RUMELHART, G. E. HINTON, and R. J. WILLIAMS

Part III FORMAL ANALYSES 363

9 An Introduction to Linear Algebra in Parallel Distributed Processing 365
M. I. JORDAN

10 The Logic of Activation Functions 423
R. J. WILLIAMS

11 An Analysis of the Delta Rule and the Learning of Statistical Associations 444
G. O. STONE

12 Resource Requirements of Standard and Programmable Nets 460
J. L. MCCLELLAND

13 P3: A Parallel Network Simulating System 488
D. ZIPSER and D. E. RABIN

References 507

Index 517

VOLUME 2
PSYCHOLOGICAL AND BIOLOGICAL MODELS

Preface to Volume 2 ix

Addresses of the PDP Research Group xi

Part IV PSYCHOLOGICAL PROCESSES 1

14 Schemata and Sequential Thought Processes in PDP Models 7
D. E. RUMELHART, P. SMOLENSKY, J. L. MCCLELLAND, and G. E. HINTON

15 Interactive Processes in Speech Perception: The TRACE Model 58
J. L. MCCLELLAND and J. L. ELMAN

16 The Programmable Blackboard Model of Reading 122
J. L. MCCLELLAND

17 A Distributed Model of Human Learning and Memory 170
J. L. MCCLELLAND and D. E. RUMELHART

18 On Learning the Past Tenses of English Verbs 216
D. E. RUMELHART and J. L. MCCLELLAND

19 Mechanisms of Sentence Processing: Assigning Roles to Constituents 272
J. L. MCCLELLAND and A. H. KAWAMOTO

Part V BIOLOGICAL MECHANISMS 327

20 Certain Aspects of the Anatomy and Physiology of the Cerebral Cortex 333
F. H. C. CRICK and C. ASANUMA

21 Open Questions About Computation in Cerebral Cortex 372
T. J. SEJNOWSKI

22 Neural and Conceptual Interpretation of PDP Models 390
P. SMOLENSKY

23 Biologically Plausible Models of Place Recognition and Goal Location 432
D. ZIPSER

24 State-Dependent Factors Influencing Neural Plasticity: A Partial Account of the Critical Period 471
P. W. MUNRO

25 Amnesia and Distributed Memory 503
J. L. MCCLELLAND and D. E. RUMELHART

Part VI CONCLUSION 529

---

26 Reflections on Cognition and Parallel Distributed Processing 531
D. A. NORMAN

Future Directions 547

References 553

Index 581

Preface

One of the great joys of science lies in the moment of shared discovery. One person's half-baked suggestion resonates in the mind of another and suddenly takes on a definite shape. An insightful critique of one way of thinking about a problem leads to another, better understanding. An incomprehensible simulation result suddenly makes sense as two people try to understand it together.

This book grew out of many such moments. The seeds of the book were sown in our joint work on the interactive activation model of word perception. Since then, each of us has worked with the other and with other collaborators. The results of these collaborations are reported in several of the chapters of this book. The book also contains many chapters by other colleagues whose explorations have become intertwined with ours. Each chapter has its own by-line, but each also reflects the influences of other members of the group. We hope the result reflects some of the benefits of parallel distributed processing!

The idea of parallel distributed processing—the notion that intelligence emerges from the interactions of large numbers of simple processing units—has come and gone before. The idea began to seem more and more attractive to us as the contrast between our convictions about basic characteristics of human perception, memory, language, and thought and the accepted formal tools for capturing mental processes became more apparent. Symbol-processing machines, for all their Turing equivalence, had failed to provide useful frameworks for capturing the simple insights about the interactive nature of processing that had lead to such models as the HEARSAY model of speech understanding. More generally, they had failed to provide a framework for representing knowledge in a way that allowed it to be accessed by content and effectively combined with other knowledge to produce useful automatic syntheses that would allow intelligence to be productive. And they made no contact with the real strengths and weaknesses of the hardware in the brain. A Cray computer can perform on the order of 100 million double-precision multiplications in a second, but it does not exhibit natural intelligence. How then are we to understand the capabilities of human thought, given the time constants and noisiness inherent in neural systems? It seemed obvious that to get any processing done in real time, the slow, noisy hardware in the brain would have to do massively parallel processing.

As our interest in parallel mechanisms developed, we began to study the work of others who shared our convictions and to build on their work. Particularly important in this regard was Hinton and J. A. Anderson's (1981) *Parallel Models of Associative Memory.* Indeed, we see our book as a descendant of their book on two accounts. First, the material presented here represents further developments on the work presented in Hinton and Anderson's book. Second, we owe a particular intellectual debt to both Hinton and Anderson. Our interest in distributed, associative memories goes back to interactions with Jim Anderson, beginning as early as 1968. Our interest in these topics began in earnest, however, during the period when we were developing the interactive activation model of word perception, in 1979, shortly after Geoffrey Hinton began a postdoctoral fellowship at UCSD. Geoffrey's crisp explanations showed us the potential power and generality of models created from connections among simple processing units, and fit together nicely with our own developing conviction that various aspects of perception, language processing, and motor control were best thought of in terms of massively parallel processing (see McClelland, 1979, and Rumelhart, 1977, for our earliest steps in this direction).

The project culminating in this book formally began in December, 1981 when the two of us and Geoffrey Hinton decided to work together exploring the implications of network models and to write a book outlining our conclusions. We expected the project to take about six months. We began in January 1982 by bringing a number of our colleagues together to form a discussion group on these topics. During the first six months we met twice weekly and laid the foundation for most of the work presented in these volumes. Our first order of business was to develop a name for the class of models we were investigating. It seemed to us that the phrase *parallel distributed processing* (PDP for short) best captured what we had in mind. It emphasized the parallel nature of the processing, the use of distributed representations and distributed control, and the fact that these were general processing systems, not merely memories we were studying, as the phrase *associative memory* suggests. Thus the PDP research group was born. Hinton and McClelland left after the first six months—Hinton to CMU and McClelland to MIT and later to CMU. The PDP research group, however, has continued regular meetings at UCSD up to the present time. The group has varied from five or six of us at times to as many as 15 or more at other times, and there is now a parallel group of about 15 or so psychologists and computer scientists at CMU.

Shortly after leaving UCSD in 1982, Hinton began working with Terrence Sejnowski on the Boltzmann machine (Chapter 7) and decided to drop from the role of organizer of the project to a contributor, so he could spend more time working on the implications of the Boltzmann machine. Thus, the primary responsibility for putting the book together fell to the two of us. At first we expected to complete the book within a year after we began our work. Soon, however, it became clear that there was much work to be done and many directions to explore. Thus, our work continued and expanded as we and our colleagues followed the implications of the PDP approach in many different ways.

A good deal has happened since we began this project. Though much of the initial groundwork was laid in early 1982, most of the material described in these volumes did not take its present form until much later.

The work has been interdisciplinary and represents what we consider a true cognitive science approach. Although the two of us have been trained as cognitive psychologists, the PDP group as a whole includes people from a wide range of backgrounds. It includes people trained in physics, mathematics, neuroscience, molecular biology, and computer sciences, as well as in psychology. We also envision an interdisciplinary audience for our book. We are cognitive psychologists and we hope, primarily, to present PDP models to the community of cognitive psychologists as alternatives to the models that have dominated cognitive psychology for the past decade or so. We also, however, see ourselves as studying architectures for computation and methods for artificial intelligence. Therefore, we hope that this book will be seen as relevant to researchers in computer science and artificial intelligence. Also, the PDP approach provides a set of tools for developing models of the neurophysiological basis of human information processing, and so we hope portions of these books will seem relevant to neuroscientists as well.

ORGANIZATION OF THE BOOK

Our book consists of six parts, three in each of the two volumes. The overall structure is indicated in the accompanying table. Part I provides an overview. Chapter 1 presents the motivation for the approach and describes much of the early work that lead to the developments reported in later sections. Chapter 2 describes the PDP framework in more formal terms. Chapter 3 focuses on the idea of distributed representation, and Chapter 4 provides a detailed discussion of several general issues that the PDP approach has raised and explains how these issues are addressed in the various later chapters of the book.

The remaining parts of the book present different facets of our explorations in parallel distributed processing. The chapters in Part II address central theoretical problems in the development of models of parallel distributed processing, focusing for the most part on fundamental problems in learning. The chapters in Part III describe various mathematical and computational tools that have been important in the development and analysis of PDP models. Part IV considers

A CONDENSED TABLE OF CONTENTS

VOLUME I

I. THE PDP PERSPECTIVE	II. BASIC MECHANISMS	III. FORMAL ANALYSES
1. The Appeal of PDP	5. Competitive Learning	9. Linear Algebra
2. A Framework for PDP	6. Harmony Theory	10. Activation Functions
3. Distributed Representations	7. Boltzmann Machines	11. The Delta Rule
4. General Issues	8. Learning by Error Propagation	12. Resource Requirements
		13. Parallel Network Simulator

VOLUME II

IV. PSYCHOLOGICAL PROCESSES	V. BIOLOGICAL MECHANISMS	VI. CONCLUSION
14. Schemata and PDP	20. Anatomy and Physiology	26. Reflections
15. Speech Perception	21. Computation in the Brain	Future Directions
16. Model of Reading	22. Neural and Conceptual Levels	
17. Learning and Memory	23. Place Recognition	
18. Morphology Acquisition	24. Neural Plasticity	
19. Sentence Processing	25. Amnesia	

applications and implications of PDP models to various aspects of human cognition, including perception, memory, language, and higher-level thought processes. Part V considers the relation between parallel distributed processing models and the brain, reviews relevant aspects of the anatomy and physiology, and describes several models that apply PDP models to aspects of the neurophysiology and neuropsychology of information processing, learning, and memory. Part VI contains two short pieces: a reflection on PDP models by Don Norman and a brief discussion of our thoughts about promising future directions.

How to read this book? It is too long to read straight through. Nor is it designed to be read this way. Chapter 1 is a good entry point for readers unfamiliar with the PDP approach, but beyond that the various parts of the book may be approached in various orders, as one might explore the different parts of a complex object or machine. The various facets of the PDP approach are interrelated, and each part informs the others; but there are few strict sequential dependencies. Though we have tried to cross-reference ideas that come up in several places, we hope that most chapters can be understood without reference to the rest of the book. Where dependencies exist they are noted in the introductory sections at the beginning of each part of the book.

This book charts the explorations we and our colleagues have made in the microstructure of cognition. There is a lot of terrain left to be explored. We hope this book serves as a guide that helps others join us in these ongoing explorations.

December 1985

James L. McClelland
PITTSBURGH, PENNSYLVANIA

David E. Rumelhart
LA JOLLA, CALIFORNIA

Acknowledgments

As we have already said, nearly all the ideas in this book were born out of interactions, and one of our most important acknowledgments is to the environment that made these interactions possible. The Institute for Cognitive Science at UCSD and the members of the Institute have made up the core of this environment.

Don Norman, our colleague and friend, the Founder and Director of the Institute, deserves special credit for making ICS an exciting and stimulating place, for encouraging our explorations in parallel distributed processing, and for his central role in arranging much of the financial support this book has benefited from (of which more below). The atmosphere depends as well on the faculty, visiting scholars, and graduate students in and around ICS. The members of the PDP Research Group itself, of course, have played the most central role in helping to shape the ideas found in this book. All those who contributed to the actual contents of the book are listed on the cover page; they have all contributed, as well, in many other ways. Several other participants in the group who do not have actual contributions to the book also deserve mention. Most prominent among these are Mike Mozer and Yves Chauvin, two graduate students in the Cognitive Science Lab, and Gary Cottrell, a recent addition to the group from the University of Rochester.

Several other members of the intellectual community in and around ICS have played very important roles in helping us to shape our thoughts. These include Liz Bates, Michael Cole, Steve Draper, Don

Gentner, Ed Hutchins, Jim Hollan, Jean Mandler, George Mandler, Jeff Miller, Guy van Orden, and many others, including the participants in Cognitive Science 200.

There are also several colleagues at other universities who have helped us in our explorations. Indeed, the annual connectionist workshops (the first of which resulted in the Hinton and Anderson book) have been important opportunities to share our ideas and get feedback on them from others in the field, and to learn from the contributions of others. Jim Anderson, Dana Ballard, Jerry Feldman, Geoff Hinton and Terry Sejnowski all had a hand in organizing different ones of these meetings; and we have learned a great deal from discussions with them and other participants, particularly Andy Barto, Scott Fahlman, Christof von der Malsburg, John Hopfield, Dave Touretzky, and more recently Mark Fanty and Gene Charniak. McClelland's discussions at MIT (particularly with Jerry Fodor and Molly Potter) helped in the clarification of several aspects of our thinking, and various colleagues at and around CMU—particularly John Anderson, Mark Derthick, Dave Klahr, Brian MacWhinney, and Jeff Sokolov—have contributed a great deal through discussions over the last year and a half or so, as we have worked toward the completion of the book. Others one or both of us have interacted with a great deal include Bill Brewer, Neal Cohen, Al Collins, Billy Salter, Ed Smith, and Walter Schneider. All of these people have contributed more or less directly to the development of the ideas presented in this book.

An overlapping group of colleagues deserves credit for helping us improve the book itself. Jim Anderson, Andy Barto, Larry Barsalou, Chris Reisbeck, Walter Schneider, and Mark Seidenberg all read several chapters of the book and sent useful comments and suggestions. Many other people read and commented on individual chapters, and we are sincerely grateful for their careful contributions, which we acknowledge in the appropriate chapters.

This project owes a tremendous amount to the help of the excellent staff of the Institute for Cognitive Science. Kathy Farrelly, in particular, has played an enormous role in all aspects of the production of the book; her cheerful, thoughtful, and very careful assistance made the production of the book run much more smoothly than we have had any right to hope and allowed us to keep working on the content of some of the chapters even as the final production was rolling forward on other sections. Eileen Conway's assistance with graphics and formatting has also been invaluable and we are very grateful to her as well. Mark Wallen kept the computers running, served as chief programming consultant and debugger par excellence, and tamed troff, the phototypesetter. Without him we would never have gotten all the formatting to come out right. Karol Lightner worked very hard toward the end of the project on final proofing and indexing, and Sondra Buffett, as the Administrative Director of ICS, held everything together and kept everything running throughout the entire four years of the project.

Our project has been supported by a number of different agencies and foundations. Primary support came from the System Development Foundation and the Office of Naval Research. The System Development Foundation has provided direct support for the PDP research group through a grant to Norman and Rumelhart, and has also supported several of the individual members of the group (Crick, Hinton, Sejnowski, and Zipser). ONR contracts that have contributed support include N00014-79-C-0323, NR 667-437; N00014-85-K-0450, NR 667-548; and N00014-82-C-0374, NR 667-483.

The people behind both SDF and ONR deserve acknowledgment too. The entire PDP enterprise owes a particular debt of gratitude to Charlie Smith, formerly of SDF, who appreciated the appeal of parallel distributed processing very early on, understood our need for computing resources, and helped provide the entire PDP research group with the funds and encouragement needed to complete such project. Henry Halff, formerly of ONR, was also an early source of support, encouragement, and direction. Charlie Smith has been succeeded by Carl York, and Henry Halff has been succeeded by Susan Chipman, Michael Shafto, and Harold Hawkins. We are grateful to all of these people for their commitment to the completion of this book and to the ongoing development of the ideas.

Several other sources have contributed to the support of individual members of the group. These include the National Institute of Mental Health, through a Career Development Award—PHS-MH-00385—to McClelland and post-doctoral fellowships to Paul Smolensky and Paul Munro under Grant PHS-MH-14268 to the Center for Human Information Processing at UCSD. Smolensky received support in the form of a fellowship from the Alfred P. Sloan Foundation, and some of McClelland's work was supported by a grant from the National Science Foundation (BNS-79-24062). These and other sources of support for specific individuals or projects are acknowledged in the appropriate chapters.

Finally, we would like to thank our wives, Heidi and Marilyn. Their understanding, encouragement, and support throughout the four years of this project helped to make the process of bringing this book to life much more rewarding than it might have been.

JLM/DER

Addresses of the PDP Research Group

Chisato Asanuma	Salk Institute P.O. Box 85800 San Diego, CA 92138
Francis H. C. Crick	Salk Institute P.O. Box 85800 San Diego, CA 92138
Jeffrey L. Elman	Department of Linguistics University of California, San Diego La Jolla, CA 92093
Geoffrey E. Hinton	Department of Computer Science Carnegie-Mellon University Pittsburgh, PA 15213
Michael I. Jordan	Department of Computer and Information Science University of Massachusetts Amherst, MA 01003
Alan H. Kawamoto	Department of Psychology Carnegie-Mellon University Pittsburgh, PA 15213

James L. McClelland	Department of Psychology Carnegie-Mellon University Pittsburgh, PA 15213
Paul W. Munro	Department of Information Science University of Pittsburgh Pittsburgh, PA 15260
Donald A. Norman	Institute for Cognitive Science University of California, San Diego La Jolla, CA 92093
Daniel E. Rabin	Intellicorp 1975 El Camino Real West Mountain View, CA 94040
David E. Rumelhart	Institute for Cognitive Science University of California, San Diego La Jolla, CA 92093
Terrence J. Sejnowski	Department of Biophysics Johns Hopkins University Baltimore, MD 21218
Paul Smolensky	Department of Computer Science University of Colorado Boulder, CO 80309
Gregory O. Stone	Center for Adaptive Systems Department of Mathematics Boston University Boston, MA 02215
Ronald J. Williams	Institute for Cognitive Science University of California, San Diego La Jolla, CA 92093
David Zipser	Insitute for Cognitive Science University of California, San Diego La Jolla, CA 92093

PART I

THE PDP PERSPECTIVE

CHAPTER 1

The Appeal of Parallel Distributed Processing

J. L. McCLELLAND, D. E. RUMELHART, and G. E. HINTON

What makes people smarter than machines? They certainly are not quicker or more precise. Yet people are far better at perceiving objects in natural scenes and noting their relations, at understanding language and retrieving contextually appropriate information from memory, at making plans and carrying out contextually appropriate actions, and at a wide range of other natural cognitive tasks. People are also far better at learning to do these things more accurately and fluently through processing experience.

What is the basis for these differences? One answer, perhaps the classic one we might expect from artificial intelligence, is "software." If we only had the right computer program, the argument goes, we might be able to capture the fluidity and adaptability of human information processing.

Certainly this answer is partially correct. There have been great breakthroughs in our understanding of cognition as a result of the development of expressive high-level computer languages and powerful algorithms. No doubt there will be more such breakthroughs in the future. However, we do not think that software is the whole story.

In our view, people are smarter than today's computers because the brain employs a basic computational architecture that is more suited to deal with a central aspect of the natural information processing tasks that people are so good at. In this chapter, we will show through examples that these tasks generally require the simultaneous consideration of many pieces of information or constraints. Each constraint may be imperfectly specified and ambiguous, yet each can play a potentially decisive role in determining the outcome of processing. After examining these points, we will introduce a computational framework for modeling cognitive processes that seems well suited to exploiting these constaints and that seems closer than other frameworks to the style of computation as it might be done by the brain. We will review several early examples of models developed in this framework, and we will show that the mechanisms these models employ can give rise to powerful emergent properties that begin to suggest attractive alternatives to traditional accounts of various aspects of cognition. We will also show that models of this class provide a basis for understanding how learning can occur spontaneously, as a by-product of processing activity.

Multiple Simultaneous Constraints

Reaching and grasping. Hundreds of times each day we reach for things. We nearly never think about these acts of reaching. And yet, each time, a large number of different considerations appear to jointly determine exactly how we will reach for the object. The position of the object, our posture at the time, what else we may also be holding, the size, shape, and anticipated weight of the object, any obstacles that may be in the way—all of these factors jointly determine the exact method we will use for reaching and grasping.

Consider the situation shown in Figure 1. Figure 1A shows Jay McClelland's hand, in typing position at his terminal. Figure 1B indicates the position his hand assumed in reaching for a small knob on the desk beside the terminal. We will let him describe what happened in the first person:

> On the desk next to my terminal are several objects—a chipped coffee mug, the end of a computer cable, a knob from a clock radio. I decide to pick the knob up. At first I hesitate, because it doesn't seem possible. Then I just reach for it, and find myself grasping the knob in what would normally be considered a very awkward position—but it solves all of the constraints. I'm not sure what all the details of the movement were, so I let myself try it a few times more. I observe that my right hand is carried up off the keyboard, bent at the elbow, until my forearm is at about a 30° angle to the desk top and parallel to the side of the terminal. The palm is facing downward through most of this. Then, my arm extends and lowers down more or less parallel to the edge of the desk and parallel to the side of the terminal and, as it drops, it turns about 90° so that the

A

B

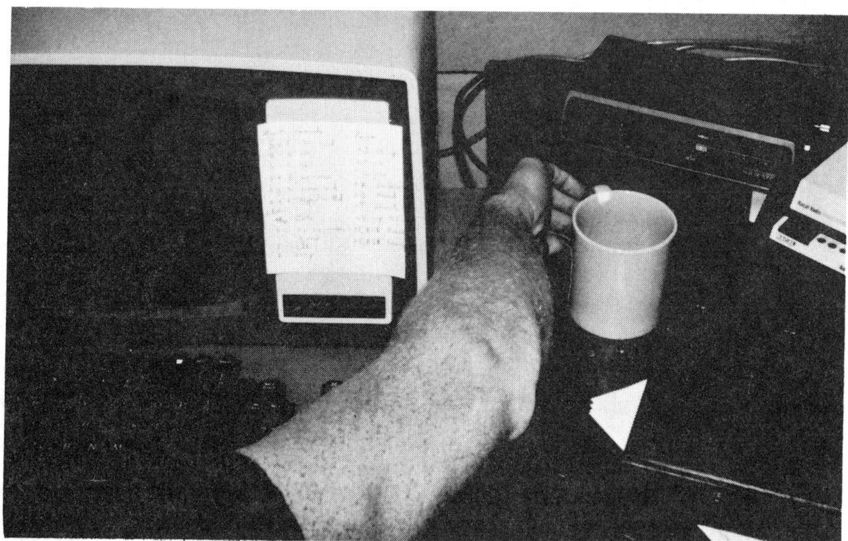

FIGURE 1. *A:* An everyday situation in which it is necessary to take into account a large number of constraints to grasp a desired object. In this case the target object is the small knob to the left of the cup. *B:* The posture the arm arrives at in meeting these constraints.

> palm is facing the cup and the thumb and index finger are below. The turning motion occurs just in time, as my hand drops, to avoid hitting the coffee cup. My index finger and thumb close in on the knob and grasp it, with my hand completely upside down.

Though the details of what happened here might be quibbled with, the broad outlines are apparent. The shape of the knob and its position on the table; the starting position of the hand on the keyboard; the positions of the terminal, the cup, and the knob; and the constraints imposed by the structure of the arm and the musculature used to control it—all these things conspired to lead to a solution which exactly suits the problem. If any of these constraints had not been included, the movement would have failed. The hand would have hit the cup or the terminal—or it would have missed the knob.

The mutual influence of syntax and semantics. Multiple constraints operate just as strongly in language processing as they do in reaching and grasping. Rumelhart (1977) has documented many of these multiple constraints. Rather than catalog them here, we will use a few examples from language to illustrate the fact that the constraints tend to be reciprocal: The example shows that they do not run only from syntax to semantics—they also run the other way.

It is clear, of course, that syntax constrains the assignment of meaning. Without the syntactic rules of English to guide us, we cannot correctly understand who has done what to whom in the following sentence:

> The boy the man chased kissed the girl.

But consider these examples (Rumelhart, 1977; Schank, 1973):

> I saw the grand canyon flying to New York.
> I saw the sheep grazing in the field.

Our knowledge of syntactic rules alone does not tell us what grammatical role is played by the prepositional phrases in these two cases. In the first, "flying to New York" is taken as describing the context in which the speaker saw the Grand Canyon—while he was flying to New York. In the second, "grazing in the field" could syntactically describe an analogous situation, in which the speaker is grazing in the field, but this possibility does not typically become available on first reading. Instead we assign "grazing in the field" as a modifier of the sheep (roughly, "who were grazing in the field"). The syntactic structure of each of these sentences, then, is determined in part by the semantic relations that the constituents of the sentence might plausibly bear to one another. Thus, the influences appear to run both ways, from the syntax to the semantics and from the semantics to the syntax.

In these examples, we see how syntactic considerations influence semantic ones and how semantic ones influence syntactic ones. We cannot say that one kind of constraint is primary.

Mutual constraints operate, not only between syntactic and semantic processing, but also within each of these domains as well. Here we consider an example from syntactic processing, namely, the assignment of words to syntactic categories. Consider the sentences:

> I like the joke.
> I like the drive.
> I like to joke.
> I like to drive.

In this case it looks as though the words *the* and *to* serve to determine whether the following word will be read as a noun or a verb. This, of course, is a very strong constraint in English and can serve to force a verb interpretation of a word that is not ordinarily used this way:

> I like to mud.

On the other hand, if the information specifying whether the function word preceding the final word is *to* or *the* is ambiguous, then the typical reading of the word that follows it will determine which way the function word is heard. This was shown in an experiment by Isenberg, Walker, Ryder, and Schweikert (1980). They presented sounds halfway between *to* (actually /tˆ/) and *the* (actually /ðˆ/) and found that words like *joke*, which we tend to think of first as nouns, made subjects hear the marginal stimuli as *the,* while words like *drive*, which we tend to think of first as verbs, made subjects hear the marginal stimuli as *to.* Generally, then, it would appear that each word can help constrain the syntactic role, and even the identity, of every other word.

Simultaneous mutual constraints in word recognition. Just as the syntactic role of one word can influence the role assigned to another in analyzing sentences, so the identity of one letter can influence the identity assigned to another in reading. A famous example of this, from Selfridge, is shown in Figure 2. Along with this is a second example in which none of the letters, considered separately, can be identified unambiguously, but in which the possibilities that the visual

FIGURE 2. Some ambiguous displays. The first one is from Selfridge, 1955. The second line shows that three ambiguous characters can each constrain the identity of the others. The third, fourth, and fifth lines show that these characters are indeed ambiguous in that they assume other identities in other contexts. (The ink-blot technique of making letters ambiguous is due to Lindsay and Norman, 1972).

information leaves open for each so constrain the possible identities of the others that we are capable of identifying all of them.

At first glance, the situation here must seem paradoxical: The identity of each letter is constrained by the identities of each of the others. But since in general we cannot know the identities of any of the letters until we have established the identities of the others, how can we get the process started?

The resolution of the paradox, of course, is simple. One of the different possible letters in each position fits together with the others. It appears then that our perceptual system is capable of exploring all these possibilities without committing itself to one until all of the constraints are taken into account.

Understanding through the interplay of multiple sources of knowledge. It is clear that we know a good deal about a large number of different standard situations. Several theorists have suggested that we store this knowledge in terms of structures called variously: *scripts* (Schank, 1976), *frames* (Minsky, 1975), or *schemata* (Norman & Bobrow, 1976; Rumelhart, 1975). Such knowledge structures are assumed to be the basis of comprehension. A great deal of progress has been made within the context of this view.

However, it is important to bear in mind that most everyday situations cannot be rigidly assigned to just a single script. They generally involve an interplay between a number of different sources of information. Consider, for example, a child's birthday party at a restaurant. We know things about birthday parties, and we know things about restaurants, but we would not want to assume that we have explicit knowledge (at least, not in advance of our first restaurant birthday party) about the conjunction of the two. Yet we can imagine what such a party might be like. The fact that the party was being held in a restaurant would modify certain aspects of our expectations for birthday parties (we would not expect a game of Pin-the-Tail-on-the-Donkey, for example), while the fact that the event was a birthday party would inform our expectations for what would be ordered and who would pay the bill.

Representations like scripts, frames, and schemata are useful structures for encoding knowledge, although we believe they only approximate the underlying structure of knowledge representation that emerges from the class of models we consider in this book, as explained in Chapter 14. Our main point here is that any theory that tries to account for human knowledge using script-like knowledge structures will have to allow them to interact with each other to capture the generative capacity of human understanding in novel situations. Achieving such interactions has been one of the greatest difficulties associated with implementing models that really think generatively using script- or frame-like representations.

PARALLEL DISTRIBUTED PROCESSING

In the examples we have considered, a number of different pieces of information must be kept in mind at once. Each plays a part, constraining others and being constrained by them. What kinds of mechanisms seem well suited to these task demands? Intuitively, these tasks seem to require mechanisms in which each aspect of the information in the situation can act on other aspects, simultaneously influencing other aspects and being influenced by them. To articulate these intuitions, we and others have turned to a class of models we call *Parallel Distributed Processing* (PDP) models. These models assume that information processing takes place through the interactions of a large number of simple processing elements called units, each sending excitatory and inhibitory signals to other units. In some cases, the units stand for possible hypotheses about such things as the letters in a particular display or the syntactic roles of the words in a particular sentence. In these cases, the activations stand roughly for the strengths associated with the different possible hypotheses, and the interconnections among the units stand for the constraints the system knows to exist between the hypotheses. In other cases, the units stand for possible goals and actions, such as the goal of typing a particular letter, or the action of moving the left index finger, and the connections relate goals to subgoals, subgoals to actions, and actions to muscle movements. In still other cases, units stand not for particular hypotheses or goals, but for aspects of these things. Thus a hypothesis about the identity of a word, for example, is itself distributed in the activations of a large number of units.

PDP Models: Cognitive Science or Neuroscience?

One reason for the appeal of PDP models is their obvious "physiological" flavor: They seem so much more closely tied to the physiology of the brain than are other kinds of information-processing models. The brain consists of a large number of highly interconnected elements (Figure 3) which apparently send very simple excitatory and inhibitory messages to each other and update their excitations on the basis of these simple messages. The properties of the units in many of the PDP models we will be exploring were inspired by basic properties of the neural hardware. In a later section of this book, we will examine in some detail the relation between PDP models and the brain.

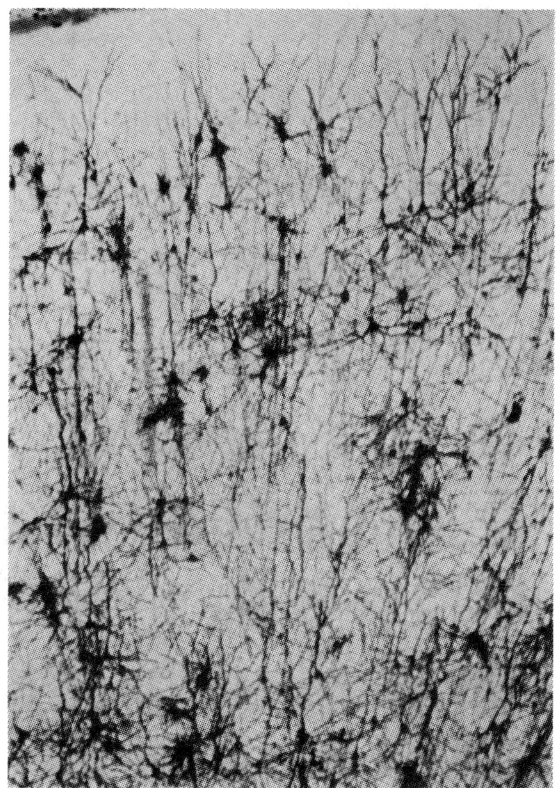

FIGURE 3. The arborizations of about 1 percent of the neurons near a vertica' slice through the cerebral cortex. The full height of the figure corresponds to the thickness of the cortex, which is in this instance about 2 mm. (From *Mechanics of the Mind*, p. 84, by C. Blakemore, 1977, Cambridge, England: Cambridge University Press. Copyright 1977 by Cambridge University Press. Reprinted by permission.)

Though the appeal of PDP models is definitely enhanced by their physiological plausibility and neural inspiration, these are not the primary bases for their appeal to us. We are, after all, cognitive scientists, and PDP models appeal to us for psychological and computational reasons. They hold out the hope of offering computationally sufficient and psychologically accurate mechanistic accounts of the phenomena of human cognition which have eluded successful explication in conventional computational formalisms; and they have radically altered the way we think about the time-course of processing, the nature of representation, and the mechanisms of learning.

The Microstructure of Cognition

The process of human cognition, examined on a time scale of seconds and minutes, has a distinctly sequential character to it. Ideas come, seem promising, and then are rejected; leads in the solution to a problem are taken up, then abandoned and replaced with new ideas. Though the process may not be discrete, it has a decidedly sequential character, with transitions from state-to-state occurring, say, two or three times a second. Clearly, any useful description of the overall organization of this sequential flow of thought will necessarily describe a sequence of states.

But what is the internal structure of each of the states in the sequence, and how do they come about? Serious attempts to model even the simplest macrosteps of cognition—say, recognition of single words—require vast numbers of microsteps if they are implemented sequentially. As Feldman and Ballard (1982) have pointed out, the biological hardware is just too sluggish for sequential models of the microstructure to provide a plausible account, at least of the microstructure of *human* thought. And the time limitation only gets worse, not better, when sequential mechanisms try to take large numbers of constraints into account. Each additional constraint requires more time in a sequential machine, and, if the constraints are imprecise, the constraints can lead to a computational explosion. Yet people get faster, not slower, when they are able to exploit additional constraints.

Parallel distributed processing models offer alternatives to serial models of the microstructure of cognition. They do not deny that there is a macrostructure, just as the study of subatomic particles does not deny the existence of interactions between atoms. What PDP models do is describe the internal structure of the larger units, just as subatomic physics describes the internal structure of the atoms that form the constituents of larger units of chemical structure.

We shall show as we proceed through this book that the analysis of the microstructure of cognition has important implications for most of the central issues in cognitive science. In general, from the PDP point of view, the objects referred to in macrostructural models of cognitive processing are seen as approximate descriptions of emergent properties of the microstructure. Sometimes these approximate descriptions may be sufficiently accurate to capture a process or mechanism well enough; but many times, we will argue, they fail to provide sufficiently elegant or tractable accounts that capture the very flexibility and open-endedness of cognition that their inventors had originally intended to capture. We hope that our analysis of PDP models will show how an examination of the microstructure of cognition can lead us closer to an adequate description of the real extent of human processing and learning capacities.

The development of PDP models is still in its infancy. Thus far the models which have been proposed capture simplified versions of the kinds of phenomena we have been describing rather than the full elaboration that these phenomena display in real settings. But we think there have been enough steps forward in recent years to warrant a concerted effort at describing where the approach has gotten and where it is going now, and to point out some directions for the future.

The first section of the book represents an introductory course in parallel distributed processing. The rest of this chapter attempts to describe in informal terms a number of the models which have been proposed in previous work and to show that the approach is indeed a fruitful one. It also contains a brief description of the major sources of the inspiration we have obtained from the work of other researchers. This chapter is followed, in Chapter 2, by a description of the quantitative framework within which these models can be described and examined. Chapter 3 explicates one of the central concepts of the book: *distributed representation*. The final chapter in this section, Chapter 4, returns to the question of demonstrating the appeal of parallel distributed processing models and gives an overview of our explorations in the microstructure of cognition as they are laid out in the remainder of this book.

EXAMPLES OF PDP MODELS

In what follows, we review a number of recent applications of PDP models to problems in motor control, perception, memory, and language. In many cases, as we shall see, parallel distributed processing mechanisms are used to provide natural accounts of the exploitation of multiple, simultaneous, and often mutual constraints. We will also see that these same mechanisms exhibit emergent properties which lead to novel interpretations of phenomena which have traditionally been interpreted in other ways.

Motor Control

Having started with an example of how multiple constraints appear to operate in motor programming, it seems appropriate to mention two models in this domain. These models have not developed far enough to capture the full details of obstacle avoidance and multiple constraints on reaching and grasping, but there have been applications to two problems with some of these characteristics.

Finger movements in skilled typing. One might imagine, at first glance, that typists carry out keystrokes successively, first programming one stroke and then, when it is completed, programming the next. However, this is not the case. For skilled typists, the fingers are continually anticipating upcoming keystrokes. Consider the word *vacuum.* In this word, the *v, a,* and *c* are all typed with the left hand, leaving the right hand nothing to do until it is time to type the first *u*. However, a high speed film of a good typist shows that the right hand moves up to anticipate the typing of the *u*, even as the left hand is just beginning to type the *v*. By the time the *c* is typed the right index finger is in position over the *u* and ready to strike it.

When two successive key strokes are to be typed with the fingers of the same hand, concurrent preparation to type both can result in similar or conflicting instructions to the fingers and/or the hand. Consider, in this light, the difference between the sequence *ev* and the sequence *er.* The first sequence requires the typist to move up from home row to type the *e* and to move down from the home row to type the *v,* while in the second sequence, both the *e* and the *r* are above the home row.

The hands take very different positions in these two cases. In the first case, the hand as a whole stays fairly stationary over the home row. The middle finger moves up to type the *e*, and the index finger moves down to type the *v*. In the second case, the hand as a whole moves up, bringing the middle finger over the *e* and the index finger over the *r*. Thus, we can see that several letters can simultaneously influence the positioning of the fingers and the hands.

From the point of view of optimizing the efficiency of the typing motion, these different patterns seem very sensible. In the first case, the hand as a whole is maintained in a good compromise position to allow the typist to strike both letters reasonably efficiently by extending the fingers up or down. In the second case, the need to extend the fingers is reduced by moving the whole hand up, putting it in a near-optimal position to strike either key.

Rumelhart and Norman (1982) have simulated these effects using PDP mechanisms. Figure 4 illustrates aspects of the model as they are illustrated in typing the word *very*. In brief, Rumelhart and Norman assumed that the decision to type a word caused activation of a unit for that word. That unit, in turn, activated units corresponding to each of the letters in the word. The unit for the first letter to be typed was made to inhibit the units for the second and following letters, the unit for the second to inhibit the third and following letters, and so on. As a result of the interplay of activation and inhibition among these units, the unit for the first letter was at first the most strongly active, and the units for the other letters were partially activated.

Each letter unit exerts influences on the hand and finger involved in typing the letter. The *v* unit, for example, tends to cause the index finger to move down and to cause the whole hand to move down with it. The *e* unit, on the other hand, tends to cause the middle finger on the left hand to move up and to cause the whole hand to move up also. The *r* unit also causes the left index finger to move up and the left hand to move up with it.

The extent of the influences of each letter on the hand and finger it directs depends on the extent of the activation of the letter. Therefore, at first, in typing the word *very*, the *v* exerts the greatest control.

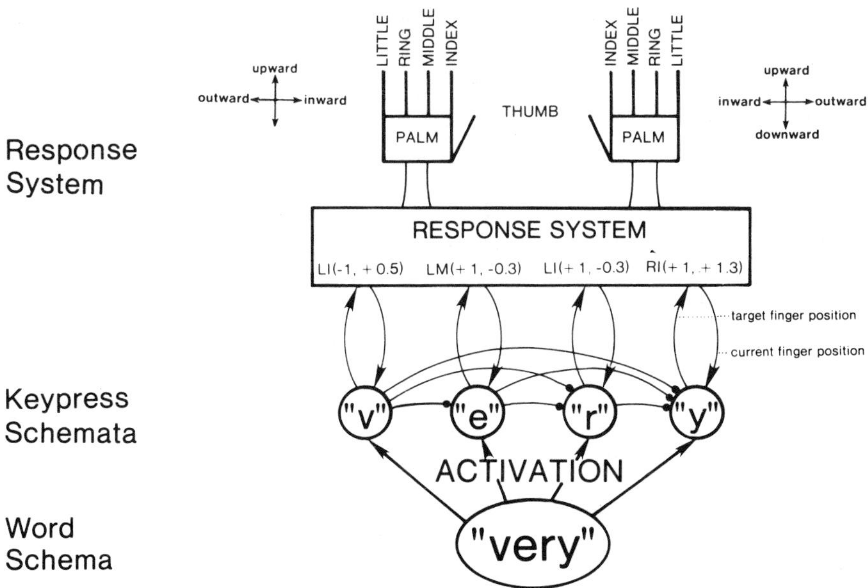

FIGURE 4. The interaction of activations in typing the word *very*. The *very* unit is activated from outside the model. It in turn activates the units for each of the component letters. Each letter unit specifies the target finger positions, specified in a keyboard coordinate system. L and R stand for the left and right hands, and I and M for the index and middle fingers. The letter units receive information about the current finger position from the response system. Each letter unit inhibits the activation of all letter units that follow it in the word: inhibitory connections are indicated by the lines with solid dots at their terminations. (From "Simulating a Skilled Typist: A Study of Skilled Motor Performance" by D. E. Rumelhart and D. A. Norman, 1982, *Cognitive Science, 6,* p. 12. Copyright 1982 by Ablex Publishing. Reprinted by permission.)

Because the *e* and *r* are simultaneously pulling the hand up, though, the *v* is typed primarily by moving the index finger, and there is little movement on the whole hand.

Once a finger is within a certain striking distance of the key to be typed, the actual pressing movement is triggered, and the keypress occurs. The keypress itself causes a strong inhibitory signal to be sent to the unit for the letter just typed, thereby removing this unit from the picture and allowing the unit for the next letter in the word to become the most strongly activated.

This mechanism provides a simple way for all of the letters to jointly determine the successive configurations the hand will enter into in the process of typing a word. This model has shown considerable success predicting the time between successive keystrokes as a function of the different keys involved. Given a little noise in the activation process, it can also account for some of the different kinds of errors that have been observed in transcription typing.

The typing model represents an illustration of the fact that serial behavior—a succession of key strokes—is not necessarily the result of an inherently serial processing mechanism. In this model, the sequential structure of typing emerges from the interaction of the excitatory and inhibitory influences among the processing units.

Reaching for an object without falling over. Similar mechanisms can be used to model the process of reaching for an object without losing one's balance while standing, as Hinton (1984) has shown. He considered a simple version of this task using a two-dimensional "person" with a foot, a lower leg, an upper leg, a trunk, an upper arm, and a lower arm. Each of these limbs is joined to the next at a joint which has a single degree of rotational freedom. The task posed to this person is to reach a target placed somewhere in front of it, without taking any steps and without falling down. This is a simplified version of the situation in which a real person has to reach out in front for an object placed somewhere in the plane that vertically bisects the body. The task is not as simple as it looks, since if we just swing an arm out in front of ourselves, it may shift our center of gravity so far forward that we will lose our balance. The problem, then, is to find a set of joint angles that simultaneously solves the two constraints on the task. First, the tip of the forearm must touch the object. Second, to keep from falling down, the person must keep its center of gravity over the foot.

To do this, Hinton assigned a single processor to each joint. On each computational cycle, each processor received information about how far the tip of the hand was from the target and where the center of gravity was with respect to the foot. Using these two pieces of information, each joint adjusted its angle so as to approach the goals of maintaining balance and bringing the tip closer to the target. After a number of iterations, the stick-person settled on postures that satisfied the goal of reaching the target and the goal of maintaining the center of gravity over the "feet."

Though the simulation was able to perform the task, eventually satisfying both goals at once, it had a number of inadequacies stemming from the fact that each joint processor attempted to achieve a solution in ignorance of what the other joints were attempting to do. This problem was overcome by using additional processors responsible for setting combinations of joint angles. Thus, a processor for flexion and extension of the leg would adjust the knee, hip, and ankle joints synergistically, while a processor for flexion and extension of the arm would adjust the shoulder and elbow together. With the addition of processors of this form, the number of iterations required to reach a solution was greatly reduced, and the form of the approach to the solution looked very natural. The sequence of configurations attained in one processing run is shown in Figure 5.

Explicit attempts to program a robot to cope with the problem of maintaining balance as it reaches for a desired target have revealed the difficulty of deriving explicitly the right combinations of actions for each possible starting state and goal state. This simple model illustrates that we may be wrong to seek such an explicit solution. We see here that a solution to the problem can emerge from the action of a number of simple processors each attempting to honor the constraints independently.

FIGURE 5. A sequence of configurations assumed by the stick "person" performing the reaching task described in the text, from Hinton (1984). The small circle represents the center of gravity of the whole stick-figure, and the cross represents the goal to be reached. The configuration is shown on every second iteration.

Perception

Stereoscopic vision. One early model using parallel distributed processing was the model of stereoscopic depth perception proposed by Marr and Poggio (1976). Their theory proposed to explain the perception of depth in random-dot stereograms (Julesz, 1971; see Figure 6) in terms of a simple distributed processing mechanism.

Julesz's random-dot stereograms present interesting challenges to mechanisms of depth perception. A stereogram consists of two random-dot patterns. In a simple stereogram such as the one shown here, one pattern is an exact copy of the other except that the pattern of dots in a region of one of the patterns is shifted horizontally with respect to the rest of the pattern. Each of the two patterns—corresponding to two retinal images—consists entirely of a pattern of random dots, so there is no information in either of the two views considered alone that can indicate the presence of different surfaces, let alone depth relations among those surfaces. Yet, when one of these dot patterns is projected to the left eye and the other to the right eye, an observer sees each region as a surface, with the shifted region hovering in front of or behind the other, depending on the direction of the shift.

FIGURE 6. Random-dot stereograms. The two patterns are identical except that the pattern of dots in the central region of the left pattern are shifted over with respect to those in the right. When viewed stereoscopically such that the left pattern projects to the left eye and the right pattern to the right eye, the shifted area appears to hover above the page. Some readers may be able to achieve this by converging to a distant point (e.g., a far wall) and then interposing the figure into the line of sight. (From *Foundations of Cyclopean Perception*, p. 21, by B. Julesz, 1971, Chicago: University of Chicago Press. Copyright 1971 by Bell Telephone Laboratories, Inc. Reprinted by permission.)

What kind of a mechanism might we propose to account for these facts? Marr and Poggio (1976) began by explicitly representing the two views in two arrays, as human observers might in two different retinal images. They noted that corresponding black dots at different perceived distances from the observer will be offset from each other by different amounts in the two views. The job of the model is to determine which points correspond. This task is, of course, made difficult by the fact that there will be a very large number of spurious correspondences of individual dots. The goal of the mechanism, then, is to find those correspondences that represent real correspondences in depth and suppress those that represent spurious correspondences.

To carry out this task, Marr and Poggio assigned a processing unit to each possible conjunction of a point in one image and a point in the other. Since the eyes are offset horizontally, the possible conjunctions occur at various offsets or disparities along the horizontal dimension. Thus, for each point in one eye, there was a set of processing units with one unit assigned to the conjunction of that point and the point at each horizontal offset from it in the other eye.

Each processing unit received activation whenever both of the points the unit stood for contained dots. So far, then, units for both real and spurious correspondences would be equally activated. To allow the mechanism to find the right correspondences, they pointed out two general principles about the visual world: (a) Each point in each view generally corresponds to one and only one point in the other view, and (b) neighboring points in space tend to be at nearly the same depth and therefore at about the same disparity in the two images. While there are discontinuities at the edges of things, over most of a two-dimensional view of the world there will be continuity. These principles are called the *uniqueness* and *continuity* constraints, respectively.

Marr and Poggio incorporated these principles into the interconnections between the processing units. The uniqueness constraint was captured by inhibitory connections among the units that stand for alternative correspondences of the same dot. The continuity principle was captured by excitatory connections among the units that stand for similar offsets of adjacent dots.

These additional connections allow the Marr and Poggio model to "solve" stereograms like the one shown in the figure. At first, when a pair of patterns is presented, the units for all possible correspondences of a dot in one eye with a dot in the other will be equally excited. However, the excitatory connections cause the units for the correct conjunctions to receive more excitation than units for spurious conjunctions, and the inhibitory connections allow the units for the correct conjunctions to turn off the units for the spurious connections. Thus, the model tends to settle down into a stable state in which only the correct correspondence of each dot remains active.

There are a number of reasons why Marr and Poggio (1979) modified this model (see Marr, 1982, for a discussion), but the basic mechanisms of mutual excitation between units that are mutually consistent and mutual inhibition between units that are mutually incompatible provide a natural mechanism for settling on the right conjunctions of points and rejecting spurious ones. The model also illustrates how general principles or rules such as the uniqueness and continuity principles may be embodied in the connections between processing units, and how behavior in accordance with these principles can emerge from the interactions determined by the pattern of these interconnections.

Perceptual completion of familiar patterns. Perception, of course, is influenced by familiarity. It is a well-known fact that we often misperceive unfamiliar objects as more familiar ones and that we can get by with less time or with lower-quality information in perceiving familiar items than we need for perceiving unfamiliar items. Not only does familiarity help us determine what the higher-level structures are when the lower-level information is ambiguous; it also allows us to fill in missing lower-level information within familiar higher-order patterns. The well-known *phonemic restoration effect* is a case in point. In this phenomenon, perceivers hear sounds that have been cut out of words as if they had actually been present. For example, Warren (1970) presented *legi#lature* to subjects, with a click in the location marked by the #. Not only did subjects correctly identify the word legislature; they also heard the missing /s/ just as though it had been presented. They had great difficulty localizing the click, which they tended to hear as a disembodied sound. Similar phenomena have been observed in visual perception of words since the work of Pillsbury (1897).

Two of us have proposed a model describing the role of familiarity in perception based on excitatory and inhibitory interactions among units standing for various hypotheses about the input at different levels of abstraction (McClelland & Rumelhart, 1981; Rumelhart & McClelland, 1982). The model has been applied in detail to the role of familiarity in the perception of letters in visually presented words, and has proved to provide a very close account of the results of a large number of experiments.

The model assumes that there are units that act as detectors for the visual features which distinguish letters, with one set of units assigned to detect the features in each of the different letter-positions in the word. For four-letter words, then, there are four such sets of detectors. There are also four sets of detectors for the letters themselves and a set of detectors for the words.

In the model, each unit has an activation value, corresponding roughly to the strength of the hypothesis that what that unit stands for is present in the perceptual input. The model honors the following important relations which hold between these "hypotheses" or activations: First, to the extent that two hypotheses are mutually consistent, they should support each other. Thus, units that are mutually consistent, in the way that the letter *T* in the first position is consistent with the word *TAKE*, tend to excite each other. Second, to the extent that two hypotheses are mutually inconsistent, they should weaken each other. Actually, we can distinguish two kinds of inconsistency: The first kind might be called between-level inconsistency. For example, the hypothesis that a word begins with a *T* is inconsistent with the hypothesis that the word is *MOVE*. The second might be called mutual exclusion. For example, the hypothesis that a word begins with *T* excludes the hypothesis that it begins with *R* since a word can only begin with one letter. Both kinds of inconsistencies operate in the word perception model to reduce the activations of units. Thus, the letter units in each position compete with all other letter units in the same position, and the word units compete with each other. This type of inhibitory interaction is often called *competitive inhibition*. In addition, there are inhibitory interactions between incompatible units on different levels. This type of inhibitory interaction is simply called *between-level inhibition*.

The set of excitatory and inhibitory interactions between units can be diagrammed by drawing excitatory and inhibitory links between them. The whole picture is too complex to draw, so we illustrate only with a fragment: Some of the interactions between some of the units in this model are illustrated in Figure 7.

Let us consider what happens in a system like this when a familiar stimulus is presented under degraded conditions. For example, consider the display shown in Figure 8. This display consists of the letters *W*, *O*, and *R*, completely visible, and enough of a fourth letter to rule out all letters other than *R* and *K*. Before onset of the display, the activations of the units are set at or below 0. When the display is presented, detectors for the features present in each position become active (i.e., their activations grow above 0). At this point, they begin to excite and inhibit the corresponding detectors for letters. In the first three positions, *W*, *O*, and *R* are unambiguously activated, so we will focus our attention on the fourth position where *R* and *K* are both equally consistent with the active features. Here, the activations of the detectors for *R* and *K* start out growing together, as the feature detectors below them become activated. As these detectors become active, they and the active letter detectors for *W*, *O*, and *R* in the other positions start to activate detectors for words which have these letters in

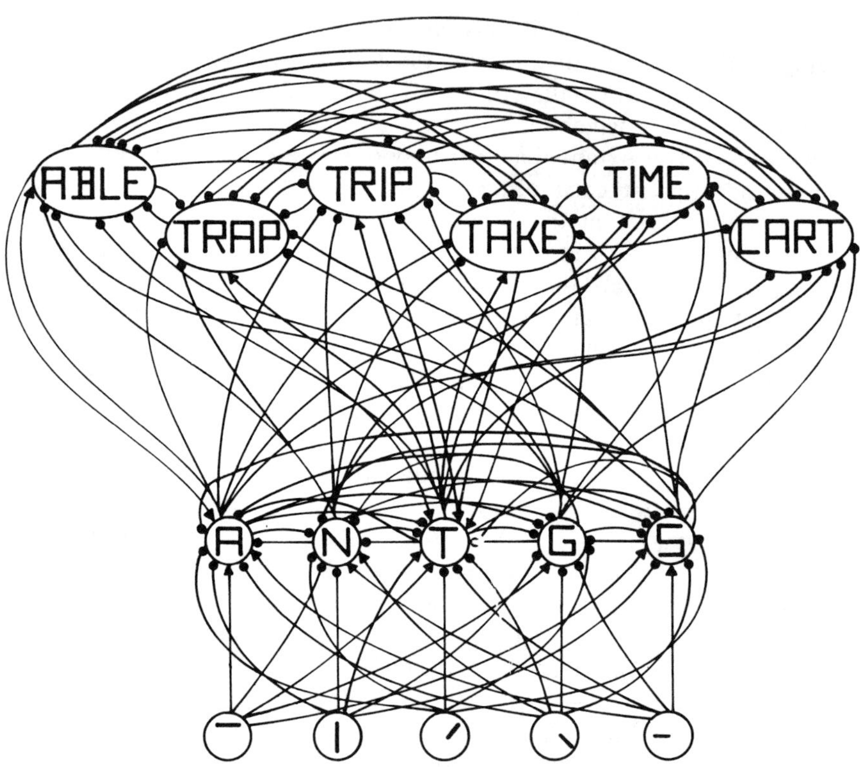

FIGURE 7. The unit for the letter *T* in the first position of a four-letter array and some of its neighbors. Note that the feature and letter units stand only for the first position; in a complete picture of the units needed from processing four-letter displays, there would be four full sets of feature detectors and four full sets of letter detectors. (From "An Interactive Activation Model of Context Effects in Letter Perception: Part 1. An Account of Basic Findings" by J. L. McClelland and D. E. Rumelhart, 1981, *Psychological Review, 88,* p. 380. Copyright 1981 by the American Psychological Association. Reprinted by permission.)

them and to inhibit detectors for words which do not have these letters. A number of words are partially consistent with the active letters, and receive some net excitation from the letter level, but only the word *WORK* matches one of the active letters in all four positions. As a result, *WORK* becomes more active than any other word and inhibits the other words, thereby successfully dominating the pattern of activation among the word units. As it grows in strength, it sends feedback to the letter level, reinforcing the activations of the *W, O, R,* and *K* in the corresponding positions. In the fourth position, this feedback gives *K* the upper hand over *R*, and eventually the stronger activation of the

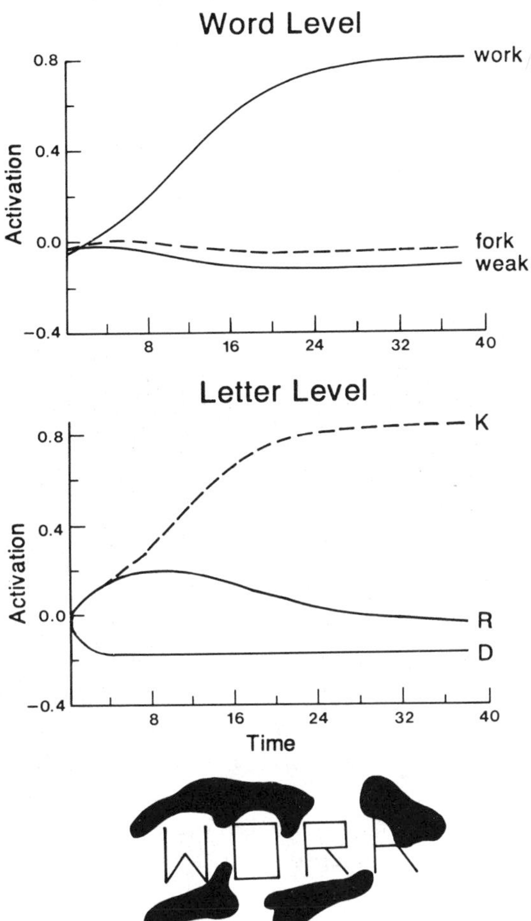

FIGURE 8. A possible display which might be presented to the interactive activation model of word recognition, and the resulting activations of selected letter and word units. The letter units are for the letters indicated in the fourth position of a four-letter display.

K detector allows it to dominate the pattern of activation, suppressing the *R* detector completely.

This example illustrates how PDP models can allow knowledge about what letters go together to form words to work together with natural constraints on the task (i.e., that there should only be one letter in one place at one time), to produce perceptual completion in a simple and direct way.

Completion of novel patterns. However, the perceptual intelligence of human perceivers far exceeds the ability to recognize familiar patterns and fill in missing portions. We also show facilitation in the perception of letters in unfamiliar letter strings which are word-like but not themselves actually familiar.

One way of accounting for such performances is to imagine that the perceiver possesses, in addition to detectors for familiar words, sets of detectors for regular subword units such as familiar letter clusters, or that they use abstract rules, specifying which classes of letters can go with which others in different contexts. It turns out, however, that the model we have already described needs no such additional structure to produce perceptual facilitation for word-like letter strings; to this extent it acts as if it "knows" the orthographic structure of English. We illustrate this feature of the model with the example shown in Figure 9, where the nonword *YEAD* is shown in degraded form so that the second letter is incompletely visible. Given the information about this letter, considered alone, either *E* or *F* would be possible in the second position. Yet our model will tend to complete this letter as an *E*.

The reason for this behavior is that, when *YEAD* is shown, a number of words are partially activated. There is no word consistent with *Y, E* or *F, A,* and *D*, but there are words which match *YEA_* (*YEAR*, for example) and others which match *_EAD* (*BEAD, DEAD, HEAD,* and *READ*, for example). These and other near misses are partially activated as a result of the pattern of activation at the letter level. While they compete with each other, none of these words gets strongly enough activated to completely suppress all the others. Instead, these units act as a group to reinforce particularly the letters *E* and *A*. There are no close partial matches which include the letter *F* in the second position, so this letter receives no feedback support. As a result, *E* comes to dominate, and eventually suppress, the *F* in the second position.

The fact that the word perception model exhibits perceptual facilitation to pronounceable nonwords as well as words illustrates once again how behavior in accordance with general principles or rules can emerge from the interactions of simple processing elements. Of course, the behavior of the word perception model does not implement exactly any of the systems of orthographic rules that have been proposed by linguists (Chomsky & Halle, 1968; Venesky, 1970) or psychologists (Spoehr & Smith, 1975). In this regard, it only approximates such rule-based descriptions of perceptual processing. However, rule systems such as Chomsky and Halle's or Venesky's appear to be only approximately honored in human performance as well (Smith & Baker, 1976). Indeed, some of the discrepancies between human performance data and rule systems occur in exactly the ways that we would predict from the word perception model (Rumelhart & McClelland, 1982). This illustrates the possibility that PDP models may provide more accurate accounts of the details of human performance than models

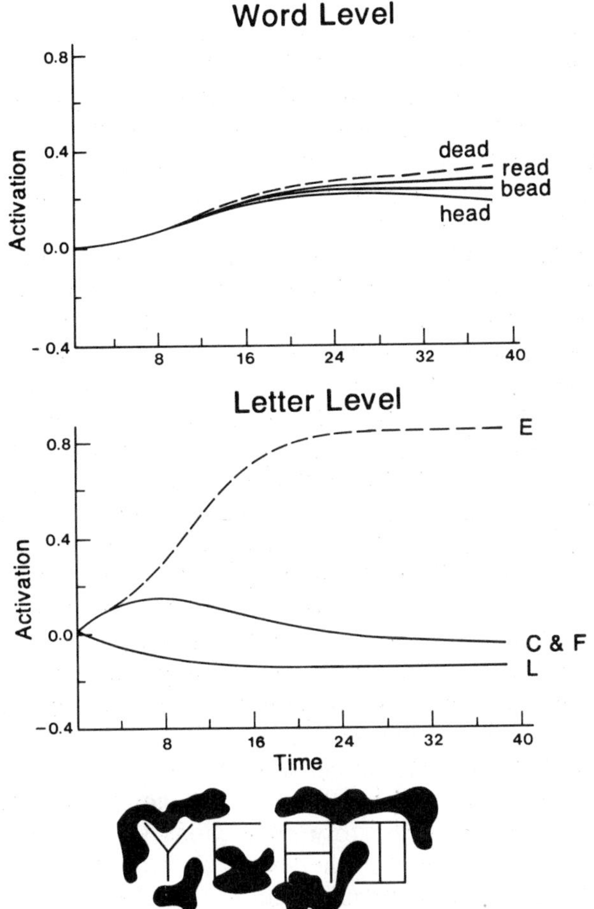

FIGURE 9. An example of a nonword display that might be presented to the interactive activation model of word recognition and the response of selected units at the letter and word levels. The letter units illustrated are detectors for letters in the second input position.

based on a set of rules representing human competence—at least in some domains.

Retrieving Information From Memory

Content addressability. One very prominent feature of human memory is that it is content addressable. It seems fairly clear that we can access information in memory based on nearly any attribute of the representation we are trying to retrieve.

Of course, some cues are much better than others. An attribute which is shared by a very large number of things we know about is not a very effective retrieval cue, since it does not accurately pick out a particular memory representation. But, several such cues, in conjunction, can do the job. Thus, if we ask a friend who goes out with several women, "Who was that woman I saw you with?", he may not know which one we mean—but if we specify something else about her—say the color of her hair, what she was wearing (in so far as he remembers this at all), where we saw him with her—he will likely be able to hit upon the right one.

It is, of course, possible to implement some kind of content addressability of memory on a standard computer in a variety of different ways. One way is to search sequentially, examining each memory in the system to find the memory or the set of memories which has the particular content specified in the cue. An alternative, somewhat more efficient, scheme involves some form of indexing—keeping a list, for every content a memory might have, of which memories have that content.

Such an indexing scheme can be made to work with error-free probes, but it will break down if there is an error in the specification of the retrieval cue. There are possible ways of recovering from such errors, but they lead to the kind of combinatorial explosions which plague this kind of computer implementation.

But suppose that we imagine that each memory is represented by a unit which has mutually excitatory interactions with units standing for each of its properties. Then, whenever any property of the memory became active, the memory would tend to be activated, and whenever the memory was activated, all of its contents would tend to become activated. Such a scheme would automatically produce content addressability for us. Though it would not be immune to errors, it would not be devastated by an error in the probe if the remaining properties specified the correct memory.

As described thus far, whenever a property that is a part of a number of different memories is activated, it will tend to activate all of the memories it is in. To keep these other activities from swamping the "correct" memory unit, we simply need to add initial inhibitory connections among the memory units. An additional desirable feature would be mutually inhibitory interactions among mutually incompatible property units. For example, a person cannot both be single and married at the same time, so the units for different marital states would be mutually inhibitory.

McClelland (1981) developed a simulation model that illustrates how a system with these properties would act as a content addressable memory. The model is obviously oversimplified, but it illustrates many of the characteristics of the more complex models that will be considered in later chapters.

Consider the information represented in Figure 10, which lists a number of people we might meet if we went to live in an unsavory neighborhood, and some of their hypothetical characteristics. A subset

The Jets and The Sharks

Name	Gang	Age	Edu	Mar	Occupation
Art	Jets	40's	J.H.	Sing.	Pusher
Al	Jets	30's	J.H.	Mar.	Burglar
Sam	Jets	20's	COL.	Sing.	Bookie
Clyde	Jets	40's	J.H.	Sing.	Bookie
Mike	Jets	30's	J.H.	Sing.	Bookie
Jim	Jets	20's	J.H.	Div.	Burglar
Greg	Jets	20's	H.S.	Mar.	Pusher
John	Jets	20's	J.H.	Mar.	Burglar
Doug	Jets	30's	H.S.	Sing.	Bookie
Lance	Jets	20's	J.H.	Mar.	Burglar
George	Jets	20's	J.H.	Div.	Burglar
Pete	Jets	20's	H.S.	Sing.	Bookie
Fred	Jets	20's	H.S.	Sing.	Pusher
Gene	Jets	20's	COL.	Sing.	Pusher
Ralph	Jets	30's	J.H.	Sing.	Pusher
Phil	Sharks	30's	COL.	Mar.	Pusher
Ike	Sharks	30's	J.H.	Sing.	Bookie
Nick	Sharks	30's	H.S.	Sing.	Pusher
Don	Sharks	30's	COL.	Mar.	Burglar
Ned	Sharks	30's	COL.	Mar.	Bookie
Karl	Sharks	40's	H.S.	Mar.	Bookie
Ken	Sharks	20's	H.S.	Sing.	Burglar
Earl	Sharks	40's	H.S.	Mar.	Burglar
Rick	Sharks	30's	H.S.	Div.	Burglar
Ol	Sharks	30's	COL.	Mar.	Pusher
Neal	Sharks	30's	H.S.	Sing.	Bookie
Dave	Sharks	30's	H.S.	Div.	Pusher

FIGURE 10. Characteristics of a number of individuals belonging to two gangs, the Jets and the Sharks. (From "Retrieving General and Specific Knowledge From Stored Knowledge of Specifics" by J. L. McClelland, 1981, *Proceedings of the Third Annual Conference of the Cognitive Science Society*, Berkeley, CA. Copyright 1981 by J. L. McClelland. Reprinted by permission.)

of the units needed to represent this information is shown in Figure 11. In this network, there is an "instance unit" for each of the characters described in Figure 10, and that unit is linked by mutually excitatory connections to all of the units for the fellow's properties. Note that we have included property units for the names of the characters, as well as units for their other properties.

Now, suppose we wish to retrieve the properties of a particular individual, say Lance. And suppose that we know Lance's name. Then we can probe the network by activating Lance's name unit, and we can see what pattern of activation arises as a result. Assuming that we know of no one else named Lance, we can expect the Lance name unit to be hooked up only to the instance unit for Lance. This will in turn activate the property units for Lance, thereby creating the pattern of

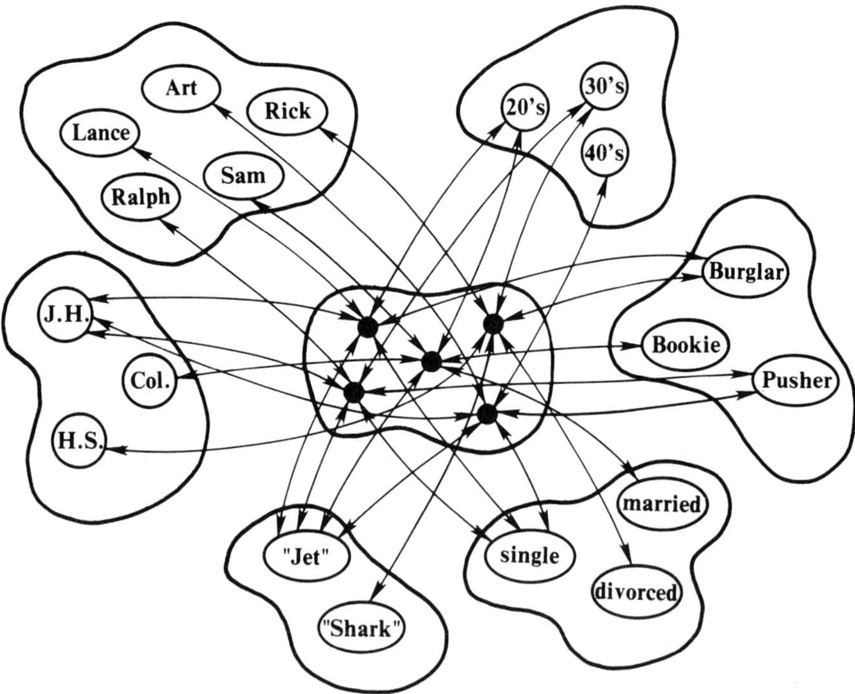

FIGURE 11. Some of the units and interconnections needed to represent the individuals shown in Figure 10. The units connected with double-headed arrows are mutually excitatory. All the units within the same cloud are mutually inhibitory. (From "Retrieving General and Specific Knowledge From Stored Knowledge of Specifics" by J. L. McClelland, 1981, *Proceedings of the Third Annual Conference of the Cognitive Science Society*, Berkeley, CA. Copyright 1981 by J. L. McClelland. Reprinted by permission.)

activation corresponding to Lance. In effect, we have retrieved a representation of Lance. More will happen than just what we have described so far, but for the moment let us stop here.

Of course, sometimes we may wish to retrieve a name, given other information. In this case, we might start with some of Lance's properties, effectively asking the system, say "Who do you know who is a Shark and in his 20s?" by activating the Shark and 20s units. In this case it turns out that there is a single individual, Ken, who fits the description. So, when we activate these two properties, we will activate the instance unit for Ken, and this in turn will activate his name unit, and fill in his other properties as well.

Graceful degradation. A few of the desirable properties of this kind of model are visible from considering what happens as we vary the set of features we use to probe the memory in an attempt to retrieve a particular individual's name. Any set of features which is sufficient to uniquely characterize a particular item will activate the instance node for that item more strongly than any other instance node. A probe which contains misleading features will most strongly activate the node that it matches best. This will clearly be a poorer cue than one which contains no misleading information—but it will still be sufficient to activate the "right answer" more strongly than any other, as long as the introduction of misleading information does not make the probe closer to some other item. In general, though the degree of activation of a particular instance node and of the corresponding name nodes varies in this model as a function of the exact content of the probe, errors in the probe will not be fatal unless they make the probe point to the wrong memory. This kind of model's handling of incomplete or partial probes also requires no special error-recovery scheme to work—it is a natural by-product of the nature of the retrieval mechanism that it is capable of graceful degradation.

These aspects of the behavior of the Jets and Sharks model deserve more detailed consideration than the present space allows. One reason we do not go into them is that we view this model as a stepping stone in the development of other models, such as the models using more distributed representations, that occur in other parts of this book. We do, however, have more to say about this simple model, for like some of the other models we have already examined, this model exhibits some useful properties which emerge from the interactions of the processing units.

Default assignment. It probably will have occurred to the reader that in many of the situations we have been examining, there will be other activations occurring which may influence the pattern of activation which is retrieved. So, in the case where we retrieved the properties of Lance, those properties, once they become active, can begin to activate the units for other individuals with those same properties. The memory unit for Lance will be in competition with these units and will tend to keep their activation down, but to the extent that they do become active, they will tend to activate their own properties and therefore fill them in. In this way, the model can fill in properties of individuals based on what it knows about other, similar instances.

To illustrate how this might work we have simulated the case in which we do not know that Lance is a Burglar as opposed to a Bookie or a Pusher. It turns out that there are a group of individuals in the set who are very similar to Lance in many respects. When Lance's properties become activated, these other units become partially activated, and they start activating their properties. Since they all share the same "occupation," they work together to fill in that property for Lance. Of course, there is no reason why this should necessarily be the right answer, but generally speaking, the more similar two things are in respects that we know about, the more likely they are to be similar in respects that we do not, and the model implements this heuristic.

Spontaneous generalization. The model we have been describing has another valuable property as well—it tends to retrieve what is common to those memories which match a retrieval cue which is too general to capture any one memory. Thus, for example, we could probe the system by activating the unit corresponding to membership in the Jets. This unit will partially activate all the instances of the Jets, thereby causing each to send activations to its properties. In this way the model can retrieve the typical values that the members of the Jets have on each dimension—even though there is no one Jet that has these typical values. In the example, 9 of 15 Jets are single, 9 of 15 are in their 20s, and 9 of 15 have only a Junior High School education; when we probe by activating the Jet unit, all three of these properties dominate. The Jets are evenly divided between the three occupations, so each of these units becomes partially activated. Each has a different name, so that each name unit is very weakly activated, nearly cancelling each other out.

In the example just given of spontaneous generalization, it would not be unreasonable to suppose that someone might have explicitly stored a generalization about the members of a gang. The account just given would be an alternative to "explicit storage" of the generalization. It has two advantages, though, over such an account. First, it does not require any special generalization formation mechanism. Second, it can provide us with generalizations on unanticipated lines, on demand.

Thus, if we want to know, for example, what people in their 20s with a junior high school education are like, we can probe the model by activating these two units. Since all such people are Jets and Burglars, these two units are strongly activated by the model in this case; two of them are divorced and two are married, so both of these units are partially activated.[1]

The sort of model we are considering, then, is considerably more than a content addressable memory. In addition, it performs default assignment, and it can spontaneously retrieve a general concept of the individuals that match any specifiable probe. These properties must be explicitly implemented as complicated computational extensions of other models of knowledge retrieval, but in PDP models they are natural by-products of the retrieval process itself.

REPRESENTATION AND LEARNING IN PDP MODELS

In the Jets and Sharks model, we can speak of the model's *active representation* at a particular time, and associate this with the pattern of activation over the units in the system. We can also ask: What is the stored knowledge that gives rise to that pattern of activation? In considering this question, we see immediately an important difference between PDP models and other models of cognitive processes. In most models, knowledge is stored as a static copy of a pattern. Retrieval amounts to finding the pattern in long-term memory and copying it into a buffer or working memory. There is no real difference between the stored representation in long-term memory and the active representation in working memory. In PDP models, though, this is not the case. In these models, the patterns themselves are not stored. Rather, what is stored is the *connection strengths* between units that allow these patterns to be re-created. In the Jets and Sharks model, there is an instance unit assigned to each individual, but that unit does not contain a copy of the representation of that individual. Instead, it is simply the case that the connections between it and the other units in the system are such that activation of the unit will cause the pattern for the individual to be reinstated on the property units.

---

[1] In this and all other cases, there is a tendency for the pattern of activation to be influenced by partially activated, near neighbors, which do not quite match the probe. Thus, in this case, there is a Jet Al, who is a Married Burglar. The unit for Al gets slightly activated, giving Married a slight edge over Divorced in the simulation.

This difference between PDP models and conventional models has enormous implications, both for processing and for learning. We have already seen some of the implications for processing. The representation of the knowledge is set up in such a way that the knowledge necessarily influences the course of processing. Using knowledge in processing is no longer a matter of finding the relevant information in memory and bringing it to bear; it is part and parcel of the processing itself.

For learning, the implications are equally profound. For if the knowledge is the strengths of the connections, learning must be a matter of finding the right connection strengths so that the right patterns of activation will be produced under the right circumstances. This is an extremely important property of this class of models, for it opens up the possibility that an information processing mechanism could learn, as a result of tuning its connections, to capture the interdependencies between activations that it is exposed to in the course of processing.

In recent years, there has been quite a lot of interest in learning in cognitive science. Computational approaches to learning fall predominantly into what might be called the "explicit rule formulation" tradition, as represented by the work of Winston (1975), the suggestions of Chomsky, and the ACT* model of J. R. Anderson (1983). All of this work shares the assumption that the goal of learning is to formulate explicit rules (propositions, productions, etc.) which capture powerful generalizations in a succinct way. Fairly powerful mechanisms, usually with considerable innate knowledge about a domain, and/or some starting set of primitive propositional representations, then formulate hypothetical general rules, e.g., by comparing particular cases and formulating explicit generalizations.

The approach that we take in developing PDP models is completely different. First, we do not assume that the goal of learning is the formulation of explicit rules. Rather, we assume it is the acquisition of connection strengths which allow a network of simple units to act *as though* it knew the rules. Second, we do not attribute powerful computational capabilities to the learning mechanism. Rather, we assume very simple connection strength modulation mechanisms which adjust the strength of connections between units based on information locally available at the connection.

These issues will be addressed at length in later sections of this book. For now, our purpose is to give a simple, illustrative example of the connection strength modulation process, and how it can produce networks which exhibit some interesting behavior.

Local vs. distributed representation. Before we turn to an explicit consideration of this issue, we raise a basic question about representation. Once we have achieved the insight that the knowledge is stored in the strengths of the interconnections between units, a question arises. Is there any reason to assign one unit to each pattern that we wish to learn? Another possibility—one that we explore extensively in this book—is the possibility that the knowledge about any individual pattern is not stored in the connections of a special unit reserved for that pattern, but is distributed over the connections among a large number of processing units. On this view, the Jets and Sharks model represents a special case in which separate units are reserved for each instance.

Models in which connection information is explicitly thought of as distributed have been proposed by a number of investigators. The units in these collections may themselves correspond to conceptual primitives, or they may have no particular meaning as individuals. In either case, the focus shifts to patterns of activation over these units and to mechanisms whose explicit purpose is to learn the right connection strengths to allow the right patterns of activation to become activated under the right circumstances.

In the rest of this section, we will give a simple example of a PDP model in which the knowledge is distributed. We will first explain how the model would work, given pre-existing connections, and we will then describe how it could come to acquire the right connection strengths through a very simple learning mechanism. A number of models which have taken this distributed approach have been discussed in this book's predecessor, Hinton and J. A. Anderson's (1981) *Parallel Models of Associative Memory*. We will consider a simple version of a common type of distributed model, a *pattern associator*.

Pattern associators are models in which a pattern of activation over one set of units can cause a pattern of activation over another set of units without any intervening units to stand for either pattern as a whole. Pattern associators would, for example, be capable of associating a pattern of activation on one set of units corresponding to the appearance of an object with a pattern on another set corresponding to the aroma of the object, so that, when an object is presented visually, causing its visual pattern to become active, the model produces the pattern corresponding to its aroma.

How a pattern associator works. For purposes of illustration, we present a very simple pattern associator in Figure 12. In this model, there are four units in each of two pools. The first pool, the A units, will be the pool in which patterns corresponding to the sight of various objects might be represented. The second pool, the B units, will be the pool in which the pattern corresponding to the aroma will be represented. We can pretend that alternative patterns of activation on

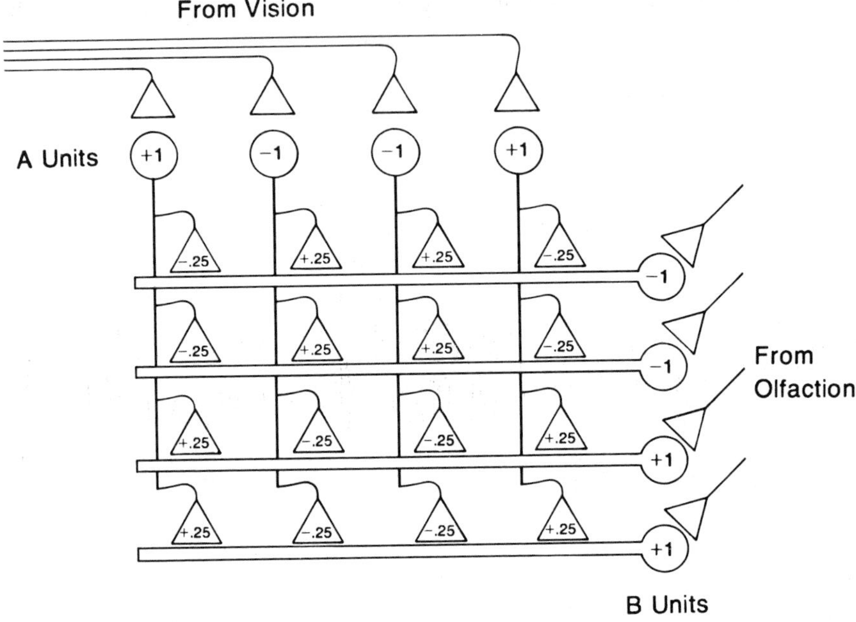

FIGURE 12. A simple pattern associator. The example assumes that patterns of activation in the A units can be produced by the visual system and patterns in the B units can be produced by the olfactory system. The synaptic connections allow the outputs of the A units to influence the activations of the B units. The synaptic weights linking the A units to the B units were selected so as to allow the pattern of activation shown on the A units to reproduce the pattern of activation shown on the B units without the need for any olfactory input.

the A units are produced upon viewing a rose or a grilled steak, and alternative patterns on the B units are produced upon sniffing the same objects. Figure 13 shows two pairs of patterns, as well as sets of interconnections necessary to allow the A member of each pair to reproduce the B member.

The details of the behavior of the individual units vary among different versions of pattern associators. For present purposes, we'll assume that the units can take on positive or negative activation values, with 0 representing a kind of neutral intermediate value. The strengths of the interconnections between the units can be positive or negative real numbers.

The effect of an A unit on a B unit is determined by multiplying the activation of the A unit times the strength of its synaptic connection with the B unit. For example, if the connection from a particular A unit to a particular B unit has a positive sign, when the A unit is

	+1	−1	−1	+1	
	−.25	+.25	+.25	−.25	−1
	−.25	+.25	+.25	−.25	−1
	+.25	−.25	−.25	+.25	+1
	+.25	−.25	−.25	+.25	+1

	−1	+1	−1	+1	
	+.25	−.25	+.25	−.25	−1
	−.25	+.25	−.25	+.25	+1
	−.25	+.25	−.25	+.25	+1
	+.25	−.25	+.25	−.25	−1

FIGURE 13. Two simple associators represented as matrices. The weights in the first two matrices allow the A pattern shown above the matrix to produce the B pattern shown to the right of it. Note that the weights in the first matrix are the same as those shown in the diagram in Figure 12.

excited (activation greater than 0), it will excite the B unit. For this example, we'll simply assume that the activation of each unit is set to the sum of the excitatory and inhibitory effects operating on it. This is one of the simplest possible cases.

Suppose, now, that we have created on the A units the pattern corresponding to the first visual pattern shown in Figure 13, the rose. How should we arrange the strengths of the interconnections between the A units and the B units to reproduce the pattern corresponding to the aroma of a rose? We simply need to arrange for each A unit to tend to excite each B unit which has a positive activation in the aroma pattern and to inhibit each B unit which has a negative activation in the aroma pattern. It turns out that this goal is achieved by setting the strength of the connection between a given A unit and a given B unit to a value proportional to the product of the activation of the two units. In Figure 12, the weights on the connections were chosen to allow the A pattern illustrated there to produce the illustrated B pattern according to this principle. The actual strengths of the connections were set to $\pm.25$, rather than ±1, so that the A pattern will produce the right magnitude, as well as the right sign, for the activations of the units in the B pattern. The same connections are reproduced in matrix form in Figure 13A.

Pattern associators like the one in Figure 12 have a number of nice properties. One is that they do not require a perfect copy of the input to produce the correct output, though its strength will be weaker in this case. For example, suppose that the associator shown in Figure 12 were presented with an A pattern of (1,−1,0,1). This is the A pattern shown in the figure, with the activation of one of its elements set to 0. The B pattern produced in response will have the activations of all of the B units in the right direction; however, they will be somewhat weaker than they would be, had the complete A pattern been shown. Similar effects are produced if an element of the pattern is distorted—or if the model is damaged, either by removing whole units, or random sets of connections, etc. Thus, their pattern retrieval performance of the model degrades gracefully both under degraded input and under damage.

How a pattern associator learns. So far, we have seen how we as model builders can construct the right set of weights to allow one pattern to cause another. The interesting thing, though, is that we do not need to build these interconnection strengths in by hand. Instead, the pattern associator can teach itself the right set of interconnections through experience processing the patterns in conjunction with each other.

A number of different rules for adjusting connection strengths have been proposed. One of the first—and definitely the best known—is due to D. O. Hebb (1949). Hebb's actual proposal was not sufficiently quantitative to build into an explicit model. However, a number of different variants can trace their ancestry back to Hebb. Perhaps the simplest version is:

> When unit A and unit B are simultaneously excited, increase the strength of the connection between them.

A natural extension of this rule to cover the positive and negative activation values allowed in our example is:

> Adjust the strength of the connection between units A and B in proportion to the product of their simultaneous activation.

In this formulation, if the product is positive, the change makes the connection more excitatory, and if the product is negative, the change makes the connection more inhibitory. For simplicity of reference, we will call this the *Hebb rule*, although it is not exactly Hebb's original formulation.

With this simple learning rule, we could train a "blank copy" of the pattern associator shown in Figure 12 to produce the B pattern for rose when the A pattern is shown, simply by presenting the A and B patterns together and modulating the connection strengths according to the Hebb rule. The size of the change made on every trial would, of course, be a parameter. We generally assume that the changes made on each instance are rather small, and that connection strengths build up gradually. The values shown in Figure 13A, then, would be acquired as a result of a number of experiences with the A and B pattern pair.

It is very important to note that the information needed to use the Hebb rule to determine the value each connection should have is *locally available* at the connection. All a given connection needs to consider is the activation of the units on both sides of it. Thus, it would be possible to actually implement such a connection modulation scheme locally, in each connection, without requiring any programmer to reach into each connection and set it to just the right value.

It turns out that the Hebb rule as stated here has some serious limitations, and, to our knowledge, no theorists continue to use it in this simple form. More sophisticated connection modulation schemes have been proposed by other workers; most important among these are the delta rule, discussed extensively in Chapters 8 and 11; the competitive learning rule, discussed in Chapter 5; and the rules for learning in stochastic parallel models, described in Chapters 6 and 7. All of these learning rules have the property that they adjust the strengths of connections between units on the basis of information that can be assumed to be locally available to the unit. Learning, then, in all of these cases, amounts to a very simple process that can be implemented locally at each connection without the need for any overall supervision. Thus, models which incorporate these learning rules train themselves to have the right interconnections in the course of processing the members of an ensemble of patterns.

Learning multiple patterns in the same set of interconnections. Up to now, we have considered how we might teach our pattern associator to associate the visual pattern for one object with a pattern for the aroma of the same object. Obviously, different patterns of interconnections between the A and B units are appropriate for causing the visual pattern for a different object to give rise to the pattern for its aroma. The same principles apply, however, and if we presented our pattern associator with the A and B patterns for steak, it would learn the right set of interconnections for that case instead (these are shown in Figure 13B). In fact, it turns out that we can actually teach the same pattern associator a number of different associations. The matrix representing the set of interconnections that would be learned if we taught the same pattern associator both the rose association and the steak association is shown in Figure 14. The reader can verify this by adding the two matrices for the individual patterns together. The reader can also verify that this set of connections will allow the rose A pattern to produce the rose B pattern, and the steak A pattern to produce the steak B pattern: when either input pattern is presented, the correct corresponding output is produced.

The examples used here have the property that the two different visual patterns are completely uncorrelated with each other. This being

$$\begin{bmatrix} - & + & + & - \\ - & + & + & - \\ + & - & - & + \\ + & - & - & + \end{bmatrix} + \begin{bmatrix} + & - & + & - \\ - & + & - & + \\ - & + & - & + \\ + & - & + & - \end{bmatrix} = \begin{bmatrix} & & ++ & -- \\ -- & ++ & & \\ & & -- & ++ \\ ++ & -- & & \end{bmatrix}$$

FIGURE 14. The weights in the third matrix allow either A pattern shown in Figure 13 to recreate the corresponding B pattern. Each weight in this case is equal to the sum of the weight for the A pattern and the weight for the B pattern, as illustrated.

the case, the rose pattern produces no effect when the interconnections for the steak have been established, and the steak pattern produces no effect when the interconnections for the rose association are in effect. For this reason, it is possible to add together the pattern of interconnections for the rose association and the pattern for the steak association, and still be able to associate the sight of the steak with the smell of a steak and the sight of a rose with the smell of a rose. The two sets of interconnections do not interact at all.

One of the limitations of the Hebbian learning rule is that it can learn the connection strengths appropriate to an entire ensemble of patterns only when all the patterns are completely uncorrelated. This restriction does not, however, apply to pattern associators which use more sophisticated learning schemes.

Attractive properties of pattern associator models. Pattern associator models have the property that uncorrelated patterns do not interact with each other, but more similar ones do. Thus, to the extent that a new pattern of activation on the A units is similar to one of the old ones, it will tend to have similar effects. Furthermore, if we assume that learning the interconnections occurs in small increments, similar patterns will essentially reinforce the strengths of the links they share in common with other patterns. Thus, if we present the same pair of patterns over and over, but each time we add a little random noise to each element of each member of the pair, the system will automatically learn to associate the central tendency of the two patterns and will learn to ignore the noise. What will be stored will be an average of the similar patterns with the slight variations removed. On the other hand, when we present the system with completely uncorrelated patterns, they will not interact with each other in this way. Thus, the same pool of units can extract the central tendency of each of a number of pairs of unrelated patterns. This aspect of distributed models is exploited extensively in Chapters 17 and 25 on distributed memory and amnesia.

Extracting the structure of an ensemble of patterns. The fact that similar patterns tend to produce similar effects allows distributed models to exhibit a kind of spontaneous generalization, extending behavior appropriate for one pattern to other similar patterns. This property is shared by other PDP models, such as the word perception model and the Jets and Sharks model described above; the main difference here is in the existence of simple, local, learning mechanisms that can allow the acquisition of the connection strengths needed to produce these generalizations through experience with members of the ensemble of patterns. Distributed models have another interesting property as well: If there are regularities in the correspondences between pairs of patterns, the model will naturally extract these regularities. This property allows distributed models to acquire patterns of interconnections that lead them to behave in ways we ordinarily take as evidence for the use of linguistic rules.

A detailed example of such a model is described in Chapter 18. Here, we describe the model very briefly. The model is a mechanism that learns how to construct the past tenses of words from their root forms through repeated presentations of examples of root forms paired with the corresponding past-tense form. The model consists of two pools of units. In one pool, patterns of activation representing the phonological structure of the root form of the verb can be represented, and, in the other, patterns representing the phonological structure of the past tense can be represented. The goal of the model is simply to learn the right connection strengths between the root units and the past-tense units, so that whenever the root form of a verb is presented the model will construct the corresponding past-tense form. The model is trained by presenting the root form of the verb as a pattern of activation over the root units, and then using a simple, local, learning rule to adjust the connection strengths so that this root form will tend to produce the correct pattern of activation over the past-tense units. The model is tested by simply presenting the root form as a pattern of activation over the root units and examining the pattern of activation produced over the past-tense units.

The model is trained initially with a small number of verbs children learn early in the acquisition process. At this point in learning, it can only produce appropriate outputs for inputs that it has explicitly been shown. But as it learns more and more verbs, it exhibits two interesting behaviors. First, it produces the standard *ed* past tense when tested with pseudo-verbs or verbs it has never seen. Second, it "overregularizes" the past tense of irregular words it previously completed correctly. Often, the model will blend the irregular past tense of the word with the regular *ed* ending, and produce errors like *CAMED* as the past of

COME. These phenomena mirror those observed in the early phases of acquisition of control over past tenses in young children.

The generativity of the child's responses—the creation of regular past tenses of new verbs and the overregularization of the irregular verbs—has been taken as strong evidence that the child has induced the rule which states that the regular correspondence for the past tense in English is to add a final *ed* (Berko, 1958). On the evidence of its performance, then, the model can be said to have acquired the rule. However, no special rule-induction mechanism is used, and no special language-acquisition device is required. The model learns to behave in accordance with the rule, not by explicitly noting that most words take *ed* in the past tense in English and storing this rule away explicitly, but simply by building up a set of connections in a pattern associator through a long series of simple learning experiences. The same mechanisms of parallel distributed processing and connection modification which are used in a number of domains serve, in this case, to produce implicit knowledge tantamount to a linguistic rule. The model also provides a fairly detailed account of a number of the specific aspects of the error patterns children make in learning the rule. In this sense, it provides a richer and more detailed description of the acquisition process than any that falls out naturally from the assumption that the child is building up a repertoire of explicit but inaccessible rules.

There is a lot more to be said about distributed models of learning, about their strengths and their weaknesses, than we have space for in this preliminary consideration. For now we hope mainly to have suggested that they provide dramatically different accounts of learning and acquisition than are offered by traditional models of these processes. We saw in earlier sections of this chapter that performance in accordance with rules can emerge from the interactions of simple, interconnected units. Now we can see how the aquisition of performance that conforms to linguistic rules can emerge from a simple, local, connection strength modulation process.

We have seen what the properties of PDP models are in informal terms, and we have seen how these properties operate to make the models do many of the kinds of things that they do. The business of the next chapter is to lay out these properties more formally, and to introduce some formal tools for their description and analysis. Before we turn to this, however, we wish to describe some of the major sources of inspiration for the PDP approach.

ORIGINS OF PARALLEL DISTRIBUTED PROCESSING

The ideas behind the PDP approach have a history that stretches back indefinitely. In this section, we mention briefly some of the people who have thought in these terms, particularly those whose work has had an impact on our own thinking. This section should not been seen as an authoritative review of the history, but only as a description of our own sources of inspiration.

Some of the earliest roots of the PDP approach can be found in the work of the unique neurologists, Jackson (1869/1958) and Luria (1966). Jackson was a forceful and persuasive critic of the simplistic localizationist doctrines of late nineteenth century neurology, and he argued convincingly for distributed, multilevel conceptions of processing systems. Luria, the Russian psychologist and neurologist, put forward the notion of the *dynamic functional system*. On this view, every behavioral or cognitive process resulted from the coordination of a large number of different components, each roughly localized in different regions of the brain, but all working together in dynamic interaction. Neither Hughlings-Jackson nor Luria is noted for the clarity of his views, but we have seen in their ideas a rough characterization of the kind of parallel distributed processing system we envision.

Two other contributors to the deep background of PDP were Hebb (1949) and Lashley (1950). We already have noted Hebb's contribution of the Hebb rule of synaptic modification; he also introduced the concept of cell assemblies—a concrete example of a limited form of distributed processing—and discussed the idea of reverberation of activation within neural networks. Hebb's ideas were cast more in the form of speculations about neural functioning than in the form of concrete processing models, but his thinking captures some of the flavor of parallel distributed processing mechanisms. Lashley's contribution was to insist upon the idea of distributed representation. Lashley may have been too radical and too vague, and his doctrine of equipotentiality of broad regions of cortex clearly overstated the case. Yet many of his insights into the difficulties of storing the "engram" locally in the brain are telling, and he seemed to capture quite precisely the essence of distributed representation in insisting that "there are no special cells reserved for special memories" (Lashley, 1950, p. 500).

In the 1950s, there were two major figures whose ideas have contributed to the development of our approach. One was Rosenblatt (1959, 1962) and the other was Selfridge (1955). In his *Principles of Neurodynamics* (1962), Rosenblatt articulated clearly the promise of a neurally inspired approach to computation, and he developed the *perceptron convergence procedure*, an important advance over the Hebb rule for changing synaptic connections. Rosenblatt's work was very controversial at the time, and the specific models he proposed were not up to all the hopes he had for them. But his vision of the human information processing system as a dynamic, interactive, self-organizing system lies at the core of the PDP approach. Selfridge's contribution was his insistence on the importance of interactive processing, and the development of *Pandemonium*, an explicitly computational example of a dynamic, interactive mechanism applied to computational problems in perception.

In the late 60s and early 70s, serial processing and the von Neumann computer dominated both psychology and artificial intelligence, but there were a number of researchers who proposed neural mechanisms which capture much of the flavor of PDP models. Among these figures, the most influential in our work have been J. A. Anderson, Grossberg, and Longuet-Higgins. Grossberg's mathematical analysis of the properties of neural networks led him to many insights we have only come to appreciate through extensive experience with computer simulation, and he deserves credit for seeing the relevance of neurally inspired mechanisms in many areas of perception and memory well before the field was ready for these kinds of ideas (Grossberg, 1978). Grossberg (1976) was also one of the first to analyze some of the properties of the competitive learning mechanism explored in Chapter 5. Anderson's work differs from Grossberg's in insisting upon distributed representation, and in showing the relevance of neurally inspired models for theories of concept learning (Anderson, 1973, 1977); the work in Chapters 17 and 25 on distributed memory and amnesia owes a great deal to Anderson's inspiration. Anderson's work also played a crucial role in the formulation of the *cascade* model (McClelland, 1979), a step away from serial processing down the road to PDP. Longuet-Higgins and his group at Edinburgh were also pursuing distributed memory models during the same period, and David Willshaw, a member of the Edinburgh group, provided some very elegant mathematical analyses of the properties of various distributed representation schemes (Willshaw, 1981). His insights provide one of the sources of the idea of coarse coding described at length in Chapter 3. Many of the contributions of Anderson, Willshaw, and others distributed modelers may be found in Hinton and Anderson (1981). Others who have made important contributions to learning in PDP models include Amari (1977a), Bienenstock, Cooper, and Munro (1982), Fukushima (1975), Kohonen (1977, 1984), and von der Malsburg (1973).

Toward the middle of the 1970s, the idea of parallel processing began to have something of a renaissance in computational circles. We have already mentioned the Marr and Poggio (1976) model of stereoscopic depth perception. Another model from this period, the *HEARSAY* model of speech understanding, played a prominent role in the development of our thinking. Unfortunately, HEARSAY's computational architecture was too demanding for the available computational resources, and so the model was not a computational success. But its basically parallel, interactive character inspired the interactive model of reading (Rumelhart, 1977), and the interactive activation model of word recognition (McClelland & Rumelhart, 1981; Rumelhart & McClelland, 1982).

The ideas represented in the interactive activation model had other precursors as well. Morton's *logogen* model (Morton, 1969) was one of the first models to capture concretely the principle of interaction of different sources of information, and Marslen-Wilson (e.g., Marslen-Wilson & Welsh, 1978) provided important empirical demonstrations of interaction between different levels of language processing. Levin's (1976) *Proteus* model demonstrated the virtues of activation-competition mechanisms, and Glushko (1979) helped us see how conspiracies of partial activations could account for certain aspects of apparently rule-guided behavior.

Our work also owes a great deal to a number of colleagues who have been working on related ideas in recent years. Many of these colleagues appear as authors or coauthors of chapters in this book. But there are others as well. Several of these people have been very influential in the development of the ideas in this book. Feldman and Ballard (1982) laid out many of the computational principles of the PDP approach (under the name of *connectionism*), and stressed the biological implausibility of most of the prevailing computational models in artificial intelligence. Hofstadter (1979, 1985) deserves credit for stressing the existence of a subcognitive—what we call microstructural—level, and pointing out how important it can be to delve into the microstructure to gain insight. A sand dune, he has said, is not a grain of sand. Others have contributed crucial technical insights. Sutton and Barto (1981) provided an insightful analysis of the connection modification scheme we call the *delta rule* and illustrated the power of the rule to account for some of the subtler properties of classical conditioning. And Hopfield's (1982) contribution of the idea that network models can be seen as seeking minima in energy landscapes played a prominent role in the development of the Boltzmann machine (Chapter 7), and in the crystallization of the ideas presented in Chapters 7 and 14 on harmony theory and schemata.

The power of parallel distributed processing is becoming more and more apparent, and many others have recently joined in the exploration of the capabilities of these mechanisms. We hope this book represents the nature of the enterprise we are all involved in, and that it does justice to the potential of the PDP approach.

ACKNOWLEDGMENTS

This research was supported by Contract N00014-79-C-0323, NR 667-437 with the Personnel and Training Research Programs of the Office of Naval Research, by grants from the System Development Foundation, and By a NIMH Career Development Award (MH00385) to the first author.

CHAPTER 2

A General Framework for Parallel Distributed Processing

D. E. RUMELHART, G. E. HINTON, and J. L. McCLELLAND

In Chapter 1 and throughout this book, we describe a large number of models, each different in detail—each a variation on the parallel distributed processing (PDP) idea. These various models, and indeed many in the literature, clearly have many features in common, but they are just as clearly distinct models. How can we characterize the general model of which these specific models are instances? In this chapter we propose a framework sufficiently general so that all of the various models discussed in the book and many models in the literature are special cases. We will proceed by first sketching the general framework and then by showing properties of certain specific realizations of the general model.[1]

The General Framework

It is useful to begin with an analysis of the various components of our models and then describe the various specific assumptions we can

[1] We are, of course, not the first to attempt a general characterization of this general class of models. Kohonen (1977, 1984), Amari (1977a), and Feldman and Ballard (1982) are papers with similarly general aims.

make about these components. There are eight major aspects of a parallel distributed processing model:

- A *set of processing units*
- A *state of activation*
- An *output function* for each unit
- A *pattern of connectivity* among units
- A *propagation rule* for propagating patterns of activities through the network of connectivities
- An *activation rule* for combining the inputs impinging on a unit with the current state of that unit to produce a new level of activation for the unit.
- A *learning rule* whereby patterns of connectivity are modified by experience
- An *environment* within which the system must operate

Figure 1 illustrates the basic aspects of these systems. There is a set of processing units generally indicated by circles in our diagrams; at each point in time, each unit u_i has an activation value, denoted in the diagram as $a_i(t)$; this activation value is passed through a function f_i to produce an output value $o_i(t)$. This output value can be seen as passing through a set of unidirectional connections (indicated by lines or arrows in our diagrams) to other units in the system. There is associated with each connection a real number, usually called the *weight* or *strength* of the connection designated w_{ij} which determines the amount of effect that the first unit has on the second. All of the inputs must then be combined by some operator (usually addition)—and the combined inputs to a unit, along with its current activation value, determine, via a function F, its new activation value. The figure shows illustrative examples of the function f and F. Finally, these systems are viewed as being plastic in the sense that the pattern of interconnections is not fixed for all time; rather, the weights can undergo modification as a function of experience. In this way the system can evolve. What a unit represents can change with experience, and the system can come to perform in substantially different ways. In the following sections we develop an explicit notation for each of these components and describe some of the alternate assumptions that have been made concerning each such component.

A set of processing units. Any parallel activation model begins with a set of processing units. Specifying the set of processing units and what they represent is typically the first stage of specifying a PDP model. In some models these units may represent particular conceptual objects such as features, letters, words, or concepts; in others they are

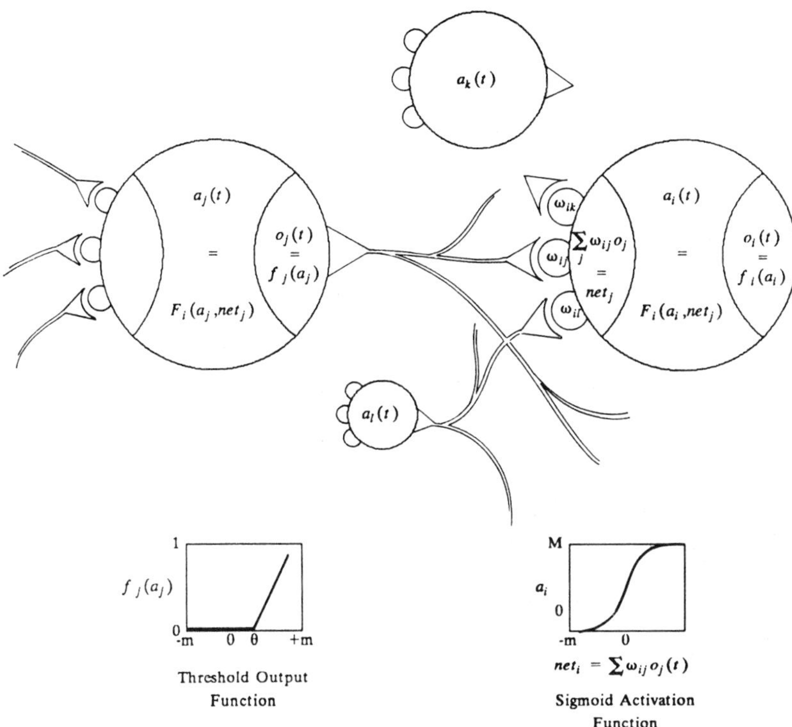

FIGURE 1. The basic components of a parallel distributed processing system.

simply abstract elements over which meaningful patterns can be defined. When we speak of a distributed representation, we mean one in which the units represent small, feature-like entities. In this case it is the pattern as a whole that is the meaningful level of analysis. This should be contrasted to a *one-unit–one-concept* representational system in which single units represent entire concepts or other large meaningful entities.

We let N be the number of units. We can order the units arbitrarily and designate the ith unit u_i. All of the processing of a PDP model is carried out by these units. There is no executive or other overseer. There are only relatively simple units, each doing it own relatively simple job. A unit's job is simply to receive input from its neighbors and, as a function of the inputs it receives, to compute an output value which it sends to its neighbors. The system is inherently parallel in that many units can carry out their computations at the same time.

Within any system we are modeling, it is useful to characterize three types of units: *input, output,* and *hidden*. Input units receive inputs from sources external to the system under study. These inputs may be either sensory input or inputs from other parts of the processing system in which the model is embedded. The output units send signals out of the system. They may either directly affect motoric systems or simply influence other systems external to the ones we are modeling. The hidden units are those whose only inputs and outputs are within the system we are modeling. They are not "visible" to outside systems.

The state of activation. In addition, to the set of units, we need a representation of the state of the system at time t. This is primarily specified by a vector of N real numbers, $\mathbf{a}(t)$, representing the pattern of activation over the set of processing units. Each element of the vector stands for the activation of one of the units at time t. The activation of unit u_i at time t is designated $a_i(t)$. It is the pattern of activation over the set of units that captures what the system is representing at any time. It is useful to see processing in the system as the evolution, through time, of a pattern of activity over the set of units.

Different models make different assumptions about the activation values a unit is allowed to take on. Activation values may be continuous or discrete. If they are continuous, they may be unbounded or bounded. If they are discrete, they may take binary values or any of a small set of values. Thus in some models, units are continuous and may take on any real number as an activation value. In other cases, they may take on any real value between some minimum and maximum such as, for example, the interval [0,1]. When activation values are restricted to discrete values they most often are binary. Sometimes they are restricted to the values 0 and 1 where 1 is usually taken to mean that the unit is active and 0 is taken to mean that it is inactive. In other models, activation values are restricted to the values $\{-1,+1\}$ (often denoted simply $\{-,+\}$). Other times nonbinary discrete values are involved. Thus, for example, they may be restricted to the set $\{-1,0,+1\}$, or to a small finite set of values such as $\{1,2,3,4,5,6,7,8,9\}$. As we shall see, each of these assumptions leads to a model with slightly different characteristics. It is part of the program of research represented in this book to determine the implications of these various assumptions.

Output of the units. Units interact. They do so by transmitting signals to their neighbors. The strength of their signals, and therefore the degree to which they affect their neighbors, is determined by their degree of activation. Associated with each unit, u_i, there is an output function, $f_i(a_i(t))$, which maps the current state of activation $a_i(t)$ to an output signal $o_i(t)$ (i.e., $o_i(t) = f_i(a_i(t))$). In vector notation, we represent the current set of output values by a vector, $\mathbf{o}(t)$. In some of our models the output level is exactly equal to the activation level of the unit. In this case f is the identity function $f(x)=x$. More often, however, f is some sort of threshold function so that a unit has no affect on another unit unless its activation exceeds a certain value. Sometimes the function f is assumed to be a stochastic function in which the output of the unit depends in a probabilistic fashion on its activation values.

The pattern of connectivity. Units are connected to one another. It is this pattern of connectivity that constitutes what the system knows and determines how it will respond to any arbitrary input. Specifying the processing system and the knowledge encoded therein is, in a parallel distributed processing model, a matter of specifying this pattern of connectivity among the processing units.

In many cases, we assume that each unit provides an additive contribution to the input of the units to which it is connected. In such cases, the total input to the unit is simply the weighted sum of the separate inputs from each of the individual units. That is, the inputs from all of the incoming units are simply multiplied by a weight and summed to get the overall input to that unit. In this case, the total pattern of connectivity can be represented by merely specifying the weights for each of the connections in the system. A positive weight represents an excitatory input and a negative weight represents an inhibitory input. As mentioned in the previous chapter, it is often convenient to represent such a pattern of connectivity by a weight matrix $\mathbf{W}$ in which the entry w_{ij} represents the strength and sense of the connection from unit u_j to unit u_i. The weight w_{ij} is a positive number if unit u_j excites unit u_i; it is a negative number if unit u_j inhibits unit u_i; and it is 0 if unit u_j has no direct connection to unit u_i. The absolute value of w_{ij} specifies the *strength of the connection.* Figure 2 illustrates the relationship between the connectivity and the weight matrix.

In the general case, however, we require rather more complex patterns of connectivity. A given unit may receive inputs of different kinds whose effects are separately summated. For example, in the previous paragraph we assumed that the excitatory and inhibitory connections simply summed algebraically with positive weights for excitation and negative weights for inhibition. Sometimes, more complex inhibition/excitation combination rules are required. In such cases it is convenient to have separate connectivity matrices for each kind of connection. Thus, we can represent the pattern of connectivity by a set of connectivity matrices, $\mathbf{W}_i$, one for each *type* of connection. It is common, for example, to have two types of connections in a model: an

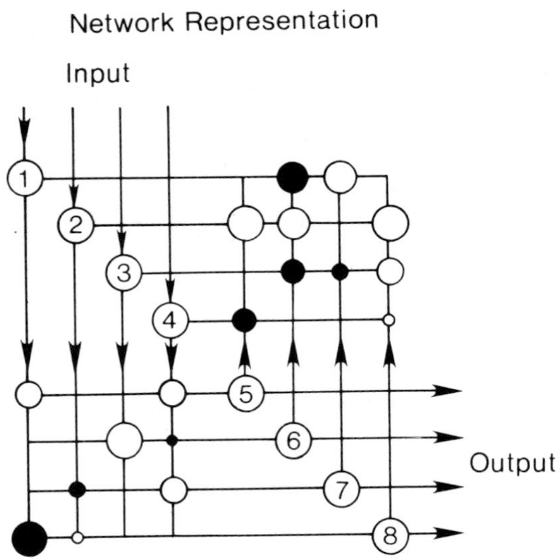

Network Representation

Matrix Representation

	u_1	u_2	u_3	u_4	u_5	u_6	u_7	u_8
u_1	0	0	0	0	0	−5	−5	0
u_2	0	0	0	0	+6	+5	0	+6
u_3	0	0	0	0	0	−3	−2	+3
u_4	0	0	0	0	−4	0	0	+1
u_5	+4	0	0	+4	0	0	0	0
u_6	0	0	+6	−1	0	0	0	0
u_7	0	−2	0	+4	0	0	0	0
u_8	−6	+1	0	0	0	0	0	0

FIGURE 2. The connectivity of a network represented by a network drawing and in a matrix. The figure shows an eight-unit network with units numbered from 1 to 8. Units 1 to 4 are input units. They receive inputs from the outside world and feedback from the output units—units 5 through 8. The connections among the units are indicated by the open and filled disks. The size of the disk indicates the strength of connection. Thus, the large black disk on the line connecting unit 1 to unit 8 indicates a strong inhibitory connection from 1 to 8. Similarly, the large open disk on the output line from unit 8 to unit 2 indicates that unit 8 strongly excites unit 2. The same connections are shown in the matrix representation on the left. The +6 in the column for u_8 and the row for u_2 indicates that unit 8 strongly excites unit 2. It should be noted that whenever there is a disk on a line connecting the output of one unit to the input of another in the network diagram there is a corresponding nonzero entry in the matrix. If the disk is filled, the entry in the matrix is negative. If the disk is open, the entry is positive. The larger the disk the greater the magnitude of the entry in the matrix. It might also be noted that the connections in the network have been laid out to correspond to the entries of the matrix. The black disk in the upper left corner of the network corresponds to the −6 in the upper left corner of the matrix. Each disk in the network is in the corresponding position of its location in the matrix. The network would not have to be drawn in this way, of course, and the matrix would still capture all of the connectivity information in the network. In general, because network drawings are difficult to work with we will often simply use the matrix representation to specify the pattern of connectivity.

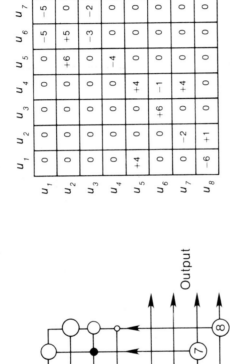

inhibitory connection and an excitatory connection. When the models assume simple addition of inhibition and excitation they do not constitute different *types* of connections in our present sense. They only constitute distinct types when they combine through some more complex rules.

The pattern of connectivity is very important. It is this pattern which determines what each unit represents. As we shall see below, many of the issues concerning whether *top-down* or *bottom-up* processing systems are correct descriptions or whether a system is hierarchical and if so how many levels it has, etc., are all issues of the nature of the connectivity matrix. One important issue that may determine both how much information can be stored and how much serial processing the network must perform is the *fan-in* and *fan-out* of a unit. The fan-in is the number of elements that either excite or inhibit a given unit. The fan-out of a unit is the number of units affected directly by a unit. Note, in some cases we need more general patterns of connectivity. Specifying such a pattern in the general case is complex and will be addressed in a later section of this chapter.

The rule of propagation. We also need a rule which takes the output vector, $\mathbf{o}(t)$, representing the output values of the units and combines it with the connectivity matrices to produce a *net input* for each type of input into the unit. We let net_{ij} be the net input of type i to unit u_j. Whenever only one type of connectivity is involved we suppress the first subscript and use net_j to mean the net input into unit u_j. In vector notation we can write $\mathbf{net}_i(t)$ to represent the net input vector for inputs of type i. The propagation rule is generally straightforward. For example, if we have two types of connections, inhibitory and excitatory, the net excitatory input is usually the weighted sum of the excitatory inputs to the unit. This is given by the vector product $\mathbf{net}_e = \mathbf{W}_e\mathbf{o}(t)$. Similarly, the net inhibitory effect can be written as $\mathbf{net}_i = \mathbf{W}_i\mathbf{o}(t)$. When more complex patterns of connectivity are involved, more complex rules of propagation are required. We treat this in the final section of the chapter.

Activation rule. We also need a rule whereby the net inputs of each type impinging on a particular unit are combined with one another and with the current state of the unit to produce a new state of activation. We need a function, $\mathbf{F}$, which takes $\mathbf{a}(t)$ and the vectors $\mathbf{net}_j$ for each different type of connection and produces a new state of activation. In the simplest cases, when $\mathbf{F}$ is the identity function and when all connections are of the same type, we can write $\mathbf{a}(t+1) = \mathbf{Wo}(t) = \mathbf{net}(t)$. Sometimes $\mathbf{F}$ is a threshold function so that the net input must exceed some value before contributing to the new state of activation. Often, the new state of activation depends on the old one as well as the current input. In general, however, we have

$$\mathbf{a}(t+1) = \mathbf{F}(\mathbf{a}(t),\mathbf{net}(t)_1,\mathbf{net}(t)_2,...);$$

the function **F** itself is what we call the activation rule. Usually, the function is assumed to be deterministic. Thus, for example, if a threshold is involved it may be that $a_i(t) = 1$ if the total input exceeds some threshold value and equals 0 otherwise. Other times it is assumed that **F** is stochastic. Sometimes activations are assumed to decay slowly with time so that even with no external input the activation of a unit will simply decay and not go directly to zero. Whenever $a_i(t)$ is assumed to take on continuous values it is common to assume that **F** is a kind of sigmoid function. In this case, an individual unit can *saturate* and reach a minimum or maximum value of activation.

Perhaps the most common class of activations functions is the *quasi-linear* activation function. In this case the activation function, **F**, is a nondecreasing function of a single *type* of input. In short,

$$a_i(t+1) = \mathbf{F}(net_i(t)) = \mathbf{F}(\sum_j w_{ij} o_j).$$

It is sometimes useful to add the constraint that **F** be a *differentiable* function. We refer to differentiable quasi-linear activation functions as *semilinear* functions (see Chapter 8).

Modifying patterns of connectivity as a function of experience. Changing the processing or knowledge structure in a parallel distributed processing model involves modifying the patterns of interconnectivity. In principle this can involve three kinds of modifications:

1. The development of new connections.
2. The loss of existing connections.
3. The modification of the strengths of connections that already exist.

Very little work has been done on (1) and (2) above. To a first order of approximation, however, (1) and (2) can be considered a special case of (3). Whenever we change the strength of connection away from zero to some positive or negative value, it has the same effect as growing a new connection. Whenever we change the strength of a connection to zero, that has the same effect as losing an existing connection. Thus, in this section we will concentrate on rules whereby *strengths* of connections are modified through experience.

Virtually all learning rules for models of this type can be considered a variant of the *Hebbian* learning rule suggested by Hebb in his classic book *Organization of Behavior* (1949). Hebb's basic idea is this: If a unit, u_i, receives a input from another unit, u_j; then, if both are highly active, the weight, w_{ij}, from u_j to u_i should be *strengthened.* This idea has been extended and modified so that it can be more generally stated as

$$\Delta w_{ij} = g(a_i(t), t_i(t)) h(o_j(t), w_{ij}),$$

where $t_i(t)$ is a kind of *teaching* input to u_i. Simply stated, this equation says that the change in the connection from u_j to u_i is given by the product of a function, $g()$, of the activation of u_i and its teaching input t_i and another function, $h()$, of the output value of u_j and the connection strength w_{ij}. In the simplest versions of Hebbian learning there is no teacher and the functions g and h are simply proportional to their first arguments. Thus we have

$$\Delta w_{ij} = \eta a_i o_j,$$

where η is the constant of proportionality representing the learning rate. Another common variation is a rule in which $h(o_j(t), w_{ij}) = o_j(t)$ and $g(a_i(t), t_i(t)) = \eta(t_i(t) - a_i(t))$. This is often called the *Widrow-Hoff* rule (Sutton & Barto, 1981). However, we call it the *delta rule* because the amount of learning is proportional to the *difference* (or delta) between the actual activation achieved and the target activation provided by a teacher. (The delta rule is discussed at length in Chapters 8 and 11.) In this case we have

$$\Delta w_{ij} = \eta(t_i(t) - a_i(t)) o_j(t).$$

This is a generalization of the *perceptron* learning rule for which the famous *perception convergence theorem* has been proved. Still another variation has

$$\Delta w_{ij} = \eta a_i(t)(o_j(t) - w_{ij}).$$

This is a rule employed by Grossberg (1976) and a simple variant of which has been employed in Chapter 5. There are many variations on this generalized rule, and we will describe some of them in more detail when we discuss various specific models below.

Representation of the environment. It is crucial in the development of any model to have a clear model of the environment in which this model is to exist. In PDP models, we represent the environment as a time-varying stochastic function over the space of input patterns. That is, we imagine that at any point in time, there is some probability that any of the possible set of input patterns is impinging on the input units. This probability function may in general depend on the history of inputs to the system as well as outputs of the system. In practice, most PDP models involve a much simpler characterization of the environment. Typically, the environment is characterized by a stable probability distribution over the set of possible input patterns independent of past inputs and past responses of the system. In this case, we can imagine listing the set of possible inputs to the system and numbering them from 1 to M. The environment is then characterized by a set of probabilities, p_i for $i = 1, \ldots, M$. Since each input pattern can be considered a vector, it is sometimes useful to characterize those patterns with nonzero probabilities as constituting *orthogonal* or *linearly independent* sets of vectors.[2] Certain PDP models are restricted in the kinds of patterns they are able to learn: some being able to learn to respond correctly only if the input vectors form an orthogonal set; others if they form a linearly independent set of vectors; and still others are able to learn to respond to essentially arbitrary patterns of inputs.

CLASSES OF PDP MODELS

There are many paradigms and classes of PDP models that have been developed. In this section we describe some general classes of assumptions and paradigms. In the following section we describe some specific PDP models and show their relationships to the general framework outlined here.

Paradigms of Learning

Although most learning rules have roughly the form indicated above, we can categorize the learning situation into two distinct sorts. These are:

- *Associative learning,* in which we learn to produce a particular pattern of activation on one set of units whenever another particular pattern occurs on another set of units. In general, such a learning scheme must allow an arbitrary pattern on one set of

[2] See Chapter 9 for explication of these terms.

units to produce another arbitrary pattern on another set of units.

- *Regularity discovery,* in which units learn to respond to "interesting" patterns in their input. In general, such a scheme should be able to form the basis for the development of feature detectors and therefore the basis for knowledge representation in a PDP system.

In certain cases these two modes of learning blend into one another, but it is valuable to see the different goals of the two kinds of learning. Associative learning is employed whenever we are concerned with storing patterns so that they can be re-evoked in the future. These rules are primarily concerned with storing the relationships among subpatterns. Regularity detectors are concerned with the *meaning* of a single units response. These kinds of rules are used when *feature discovery* is the essential task at hand.

The associative learning case generally can be broken down into two subcases—pattern association and auto-association. A *pattern association* paradigm is one in which the goal is to build up an association between patterns defined over one subset of the units and other patterns defined over a second subset of units. The goal is to find a set of connections so that whenever a particular pattern reappears on the first set of units, the associated pattern will appear on the second set. In this case, there is usually a *teaching input* to the second set of units during training indicating the desired pattern association. An *auto-association* paradigm is one in which an input pattern is associated with itself. The goal here is pattern completion. Whenever a *portion* of the input pattern is presented, the remainder of the pattern is to be filled in or completed. This is similar to simple pattern association, except that the input pattern plays both the role of the teaching input and of the pattern to be associated. It can be seen that simple pattern association is a special case of auto-association. Figure 3 illustrates the two kinds of learning paradigms. Figure 3A shows the basic structure of the pattern association situation. There are two distinct groups of units—a set of input units and a set of output units. Each input unit connects with each output unit and each output unit receives an input from each input unit. During training, patterns are presented to both the input and output units. The weights connecting the input to the output units are modified during this period. During a test, patterns are presented to the input units and the response on the output units is measured. Figure 3B shows the connectivity matrix for the pattern associator. The only modifiable connections are from the input units to the output units. All other connections are fixed at zero. Figure 3C shows the basic

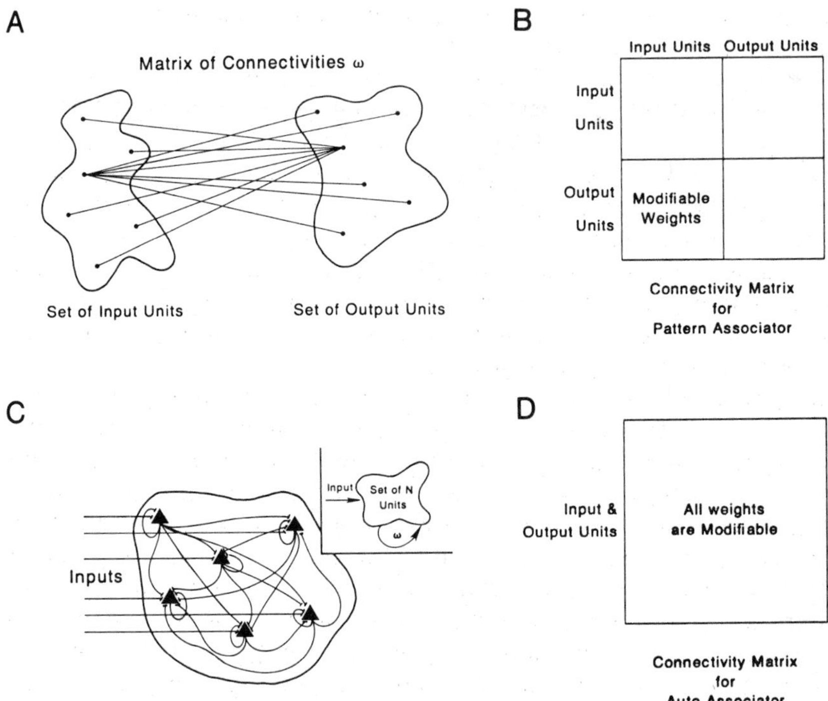

FIGURE 3. *A:* The basic structure of the pattern association situation. There are two distinct groups of units—a set of input units and a set of output units. Each input unit connects with each output unit and each output unit receives an input from each input unit. During training, patterns are presented to both the input and output units. The weights connecting the input to the output units are modified during this period. During a test, patterns are presented to the input units and the response on the output units is measured. (After Anderson, 1977.) *B:* The connectivity matrix for the pattern associator. The only modifiable connections are from the input units to the output units. All other connections are fixed at zero. *C:* The basic structure of the auto-association situation. All units are both input and output units. The figure shows a group of 6 units feeding back on itself through modifiable connections. Note that each unit feeds back on itself as well as on each of its neighbors. (After Anderson, Silverstein, Ritz, & Jones, 1977.) *D:* The connectivity matrix for the auto-associator. All units connect to all other units with modifiable weights.

structure of the auto-association situation. All units are both input and output units. The figure shows a group of 6 units feeding back on itself through modifiable connections. Note that each unit feeds back on itself as well as on each of its neighbors. Figure 3D shows the connectivity matrix for the auto-associator. All units connect to all other units with modifiable weights. In the case of auto-association, there is potentially a modifiable connection from every unit to every other unit. In the case of pattern association, however, the units are broken into two subpatterns, one representing the input pattern and another representing the teaching input. The only modifiable connections are those from the input units to the output units receiving the teaching input. In other cases of associative learning the teaching input may be more or less indirect. The problem of dealing with indirect feedback is difficult, but central to the development of more sophisticated models of learning. Barto and Sutton (1981) have begun a nice analysis of such learning situations.

In the case of regularity detectors, a teaching input is not explicitly provided; instead, the teaching function is determined by the unit itself. The form of the internal teaching function and the nature of its input patterns determine what features the unit will learn to respond to. This is sometimes called unsupervised learning. Each different kind of unsupervised learning procedure has its own evaluation function. The particular evaluation procedures are mentioned when we treat these models. The three unsupervised learning models discussed in this book are addressed in Chapters 5, 6, and 7.

Hierarchical Organizations of PDP Networks

It has become commonplace in cognitive science to describe such processes as *top-down*, *bottom-up*, and *interactive* to consist of many stages of processing, etc. It is useful to see how these concepts can be represented in terms of the patterns of connectivity in the PDP framework. It is also useful to get some feeling for the processing consequences of these various assumptions.

Bottom-Up Processing

The fundamental characteristic of a bottom-up system is that units at level i may not affect the activity of units at levels lower than i. To see how this maps onto the current formulation, it is useful to partition the coalitions of units into a set of discrete categories corresponding to the levels their inputs come from. There are assumed to be no coalitions with inputs from more than one level. Assume that there are L_i units at level i in the system. We then order the units such that those in level L_1 are numbered $u_1, \ldots, u_{L_1}$, those in level L_2 are numbered $u_{L_1+1}, \ldots, u_{L_1+L_2}$, etc. Then, the constraint that the system be a pure bottom-up system is equivalent to the constraint that the connectivity matrix, **W**, has zero entries for w_{ij} in which u_j is the member of a level no higher than u_i. This amounts to the requirement that the upper right-hand region of **W** contains zero entries. Table 1 shows this constraint graphically. The table shows an example of a three-level system with four units at each level.[3] This leads to a 12×12 connectivity matrix and an **a** vector of length 12. The matrix can be divided up into 9 regions. The upper-left region represents interactions among Level 1 units. The entries in the left-middle region of the matrix represents the effects of Level 1 units on Level 2 units. The lower-left region represents the effects of Level 1 units on Level 3 units. Often bottom-up models do not allow units at level i effect units at level $i+2$. Thus, in the diagram we have left that region empty representing no effect of Level 1 on Level 3. It is typical in a bottom-up system to assume as well that the lowest level units (Level 1) are input units and that the highest level units (Level 3) are output units. That is, the lowest level of the system is the only one to receive direct inputs from outside of this module and only the highest level units affect other units outside of this module.

TABLE 1

		Level 1 Input Units u1 u2 u3 u4	Level 2 Hidden Units u5 u6 u7 u8	Level 3 Output Units u9 u10 u11 u12
Level 1 Units	u1 u2 u3 u4	within Level 1 effects		
Level 2 Units	u5 u6 u7 u8	Level 1 affecting Level 2	within Level 2 effects	
Level 3 Units	u9 u10 u11 u12		Level 2 affecting Level 3	within Level 3 effects

[3] In general, of course, we would expect many levels and many units at each level.

Top-Down Processing

The generalization to a hierarchical top-down system should be clear enough. Let us order the units into levels just as before. A top-down model then requires that the lower-left regions of the weight matrix be empty—that is, no lower level unit affects a higher level unit. Table 2 illustrates a simple example of a top-down processing system. Note, in this case, we have to assume a top-down input or "message" that is propagated down the system from higher to lower levels as well as any data input that might be coming directly into Level 1 units.

Interactive Models

Interactive models are simply models in which there can be both top-down and bottom-up connections. Again the generalization is straightforward. In the general interactive model, any of the cells of the weight matrix could be nonzero. The more restricted models in which information flows both ways, but in which information only flows between adjacent levels, assume only that the regions of the matrix more than one region away from the main diagonal are zero. Table 3 illustrates a simple three-level interactive model with both top-down and bottom-up input. Most of the models that actually have been suggested count as interactive models in this sense.

TABLE 2

		Level 1 Input Units u1 u2 u3 u4	Level 2 Hidden Units u5 u6 u7 u8	Level 3 Output Units u9 u10 u11 u12
Level 1 Units	u1 u2 u3 u4	within Level 1 effects	Level 2 affecting Level 1	
Level 2 Units	u5 u6 u7 u8		within Level 2 effects	Level 3 affecting Level 2
Level 3 Units	u9 u10 u11 u12			within Level 3 effects

TABLE 3

		Level 1 Input Units u1 u2 u3 u4	Level 2 Hidden Units u5 u6 u7 u8	Level 3 Output Units u9 u10 u11 u12
Level 1 Units	u1 u2 u3 u4	within Level 1 effects	Level 2 affecting Level 1	
Level 2 Units	u5 u6 u7 u8	Level 1 affecting Level 2	within Level 2 effects	Level 3 affecting Level 2
Level 3 Units	u9 u10 u11 u12		Level 2 affecting Level 3	within Level 3 effects

It is sometimes supposed that a "single level" system with *no hierarchical structure* in which any unit can communicate with any other unit is somehow less powerful than these multilevel hierarchical systems. The present analysis shows that, on the contrary, the *existence* of *levels* amounts to a *restriction*, in general, of free communication among all units. Such *nonhierarchical* systems actually form a superset of the kinds of *layered* systems discussed above. There is, however, something to the view that having multiple levels can increase the power of certain systems. In particular, a "one-step" system consisting of only input and output units and no communication between them in which there is no opportunity for feedback or for hidden units is less powerful than systems with hidden units and with feedback. Since, in general, hierarchical systems involve many hidden units, some intralevel communication, and some feedback among levels, they are more powerful than systems not involving such hidden units. However, a system with an equal number of hidden units, but one not characterizable as hierarchical by the communication patterns is, in general, of more potential computational power. We address the issue of hidden units and "single-step" versus "multiple-step" systems in our discussion of specific models below.

Synchronous Versus Asynchronous Update

Even given all of the components of the PDP models we have described so far, there is still another important issue to be resolved in the development of specific models; that is the timing of the application of the activation rule. In some models, there is a kind of central timing pulse and after each such clock tick a new value is determined simultaneously for all units. This is a *synchronous update* procedure. It is usually viewed as a discrete, difference approximation to an underlying continuous, differential equation in which all units are continuously updated. In some models, however, units are updated *asynchronously* and at random. The usual assumption is that at each point in time each unit has a fixed probability of evaluating and applying its activation rule and updating its activation value. This later method has certain theoretical advantages and was developed by Hopfield (1982) and has been employed in Chapters 6, 7, and 14. The major advantage is that since the units are independently being updated, if we look at a short enough time interval, only one unit is updating at a time. Among other things, this system can help the stability of the network by keeping it out of oscillations that are more readily entered into with synchronous update procedures.

SPECIFIC VERSIONS OF THE GENERAL PARALLEL ACTIVATION MODEL

In the following sections we will show how specification of the particular functions involved produces various kinds of these models. There have been many authors who have contributed to the field and whose work might as well have been discussed. We discuss only a representative sample of this work.

Simple Linear Models

Perhaps the simplest model of this class is the simple linear model. In the simple linear model, activation values are real numbers without restriction. They can be either positive or negative and are not bounded. The output function, $f(a_i)$, in the linear model is just equal to the activation level a_i. Typically, linear models consist of two sets of units: a set of *input* units and a set of *output* units. (As discussed below, there is no need for hidden units since all computation possible with a multiple-step linear system can be done with a single-step linear system.) In general, any unit in the input layer may connect to any unit in the output layer. All connections in a linear model are of the same type. Thus, only a single connectivity matrix is required. The matrix consists of a set of positive, negative, and zero values, for excitatory values, inhibitory values, and zero connections, respectively. The new value of activation of each unit is simply given by the weighted sums of the inputs. For the simple linear model with connectivity matrix $\mathbf{W}$ we have

$$\mathbf{a}(t+1) = \mathbf{W}\mathbf{a}(t).$$

In general, it can be shown that a linear model such as this has a number of limitations. In particular, it can be shown that nothing can be computed from two or more steps that cannot be computed by a single step. This follows because the above equation implies

$$\mathbf{a}(t) = \mathbf{W}^t \mathbf{a}(0).$$

We can see this by proceeding step by step. Clearly,

$$\mathbf{a}(2) = \mathbf{W}\mathbf{a}(1) = \mathbf{W}(\mathbf{W}\mathbf{a}(0)) = \mathbf{W}^2\mathbf{a}(0).$$

It should be clear that similar arguments lead to $\mathbf{a}(t) = \mathbf{W}^t \mathbf{a}(0)$. From this, it follows that for every linear model with connectivity matrix $\mathbf{W}$ that can attain a particular state in t steps, there is another linear model with connectivity matrix $\mathbf{W}^t$ that can reach the same state in one step. This means, among other things, that there can never be any computational advantage in a linear model of multiple-step systems, nor can there ever be any advantage for allowing feedback.

The pattern association paradigm is the typical learning situation for a linear model. There is a set of input units and a set of output units. In general, each input unit may be connected to any output unit. Since this is a linear network, there is no feedback in the system nor are there hidden units between the inputs and outputs. There are two sources of input in the system. There are the input patterns that establish a pattern of activation on the input units, and there are the teaching units that establish a pattern of activation on the output units. Any of several learning rules could be employed with a linear network such as this, but the most common are the simple Hebbian rule and the delta rule. The linear model with the simple Hebbian rule is called the simple *linear associator* (cf. Anderson, 1970; Kohonen, 1977, 1984). In this case, the increment in weight w_{ij} is given by $\Delta w_{ij} = \eta a_j t_i$. In matrix notation, this means that $\Delta \mathbf{W} = \eta \mathbf{T} \mathbf{a}^T$. The system is then tested by presenting an input pattern without a teaching input and seeing how close the pattern generated on the output layer matches the original teaching input. It can be shown that if the input patterns are orthogonal,[4] there will be no interference and the system will perfectly produce the relevant associated patterns exactly on the output layer. If they are not orthogonal, however, there will be interference among the input patterns. It is possible to make a modification in the learning rule and allow a much larger set of possible associations. In particular, it is possible to build up correct associations among patterns whenever the set of input patterns are linearly independent. To achieve this, an error correcting rule must be employed. The delta rule is most commonly employed. In this case, the rule becomes $\Delta w_{ij} = \eta (t_i - a_i) a_j$. What is learned is essentially the difference between the desired response and that actually attained at unit u_i due to the input. Although it may take many presentations of the input pattern set, if the patterns are linearly independent the system will eventually be able to produce the desired outputs. Kohonen (1977, 1984) has provided an important analysis of this and related learning rules.

The examples described above were for the case of the pattern associator. Essentially the same results hold for the auto-associator version of the linear model. In this case, the input patterns and the teaching patterns are the same, and the input layer and the output layer are also the same. The tests of the system involve presenting a portion of the input pattern and having the system attempt to reconstruct the missing parts.

Linear Threshold Units

The weaknesses of purely linear systems can be overcome through the addition of nonlinearities. Perhaps the simplest of the nonlinear system consists of a network of linear threshold units. The linear threshold unit is a binary unit whose activation takes on the values $\{0,1\}$. The activation value of unit u_i is 1 if the weighted sum of its inputs is greater than some threshold θ_i and is 0 otherwise. The connectivity matrix for a network of such units, as in the linear system, is a matrix consisting of positive and negative numbers. The output function, f, is the identity function so that the output of a unit is equal to its activation value.

[4] See Chapter 9 for a discussion of orthogonality, linear independence , etc.

It is useful to see some of the kinds of functions that can be computed with linear threshold units that cannot be computed with simple linear models. The classic such function is the *exclusive or* (XOR) illustrated in Figure 4. The idea is to have a system which responds {1} if it receives a {0,1} or a {1,0} and responds {0} otherwise. The figure shows a network capable of this pattern. In this case we require two

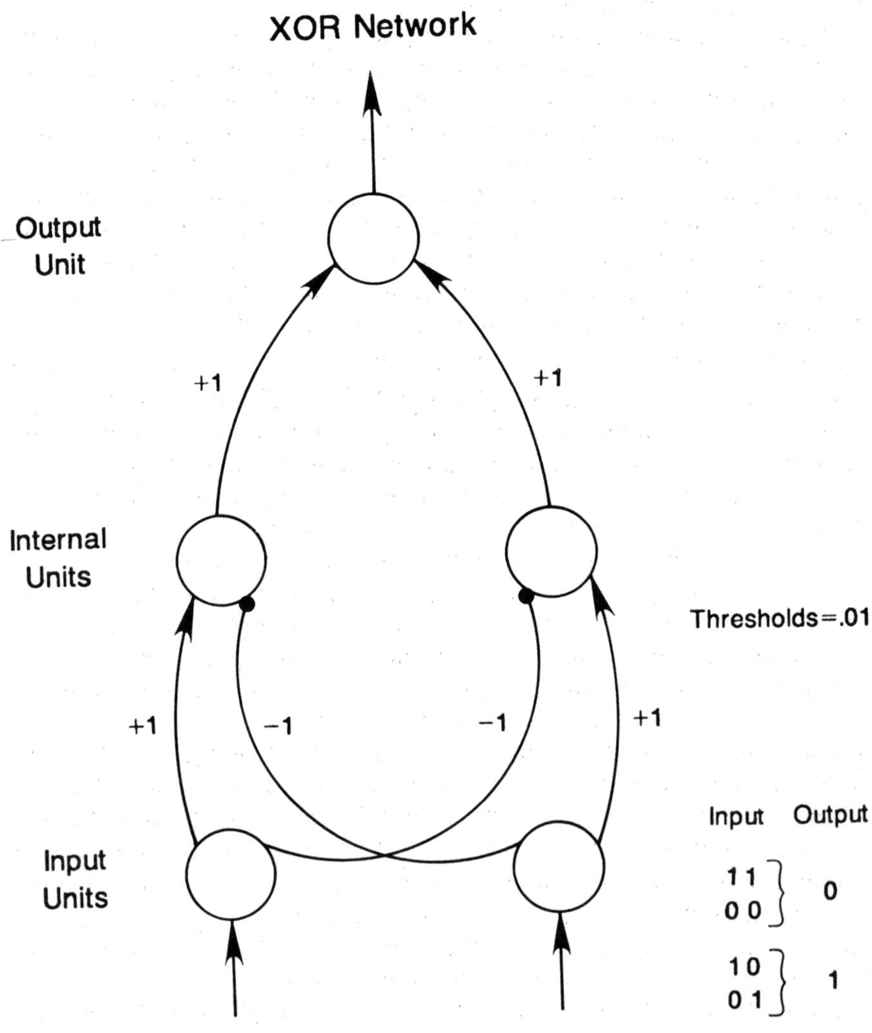

FIGURE 4. A network of linear threshold units capable of responding correctly on the XOR problem.

layers of units. Each unit has a zero threshold and responds just in case its input is greater than zero. The weights are ± 1. Since the set of stimulus patterns is not linearly independent, this is a discrimination that can never be made by a simple linear model and cannot be done in a single step by any network of linear threshold units.

Although multilayered systems of linear threshold units are very powerful and, in fact, are capable of computing any boolean function, there is no generally known learning algorithm for this general case (see Chapter 8). There is, however, a well-understood learning algorithm for the special case of the *perceptron*. A perceptron is essentially a single-layer network of linear threshold units without feedback. The learning situation here is exactly the same as that for the linear model. An input pattern is presented along with a teaching input. The perceptron learning rule is precisely of the same form as the delta rule for error correcting in the linear model, namely, $\Delta w_{ij} = \eta (t_i - a_i) a_j$. Since the teaching input and the activation values are only 0 or 1, the rule reduces to the statements that:

1. Weights are only changed on a given input line when that line is turned on (i.e., $a_j = 1$).

2. If the system is correct on unit i (i.e., $t_i = a_i$), make no change on any of the input weights.

3. If the unit j responds 0 when it should be 1, increase weights on all active lines by amount η.

4. If the unit j responds 1 when it should be 0, decrease weights on all active lines by amount η.

There is a theorem, the perceptron convergence theorem, that guarantees that if the set of patterns are learnable by a perceptron, this learning procedure will find a set of weights which allow it to respond correctly to all input patterns. Unfortunately, even though multilayer linear threshold networks are potentially much more powerful than the linear associator, the perceptron for which a learning result exists can learn no patterns not learnable by the linear associator. It was the limitations on what perceptrons could possibly learn that led to Minsky and Papert's (1969) pessimistic evaluation of the perceptron. Unfortunately that evaluation has incorrectly tainted more interesting and powerful networks of linear threshold and other nonlinear units. We have now developed a version of the delta rule—the generalized delta rule—which is capable of learning arbitrary mappings. It does not work for linear threshold units, but *does work* for the class of *semilinear* activation functions (i.e., differentiable activation functions). See Chapter 8 for a full discussion. As we shall see in the course of this book, the limitations of the one-step perceptron in no way apply to the more complex networks.

Brain State in a Box

The brain state in a box model was developed by J. A. Anderson (1977). This model too is a close relative of the simple linear associator. There is, however, a maximum and minimum activation value associated with each unit. Typically, units take on activation values in the interval [−1,1]. The brain state in a box (BSB) models are organized so that any unit can, in general, be connected to any other unit. The auto-associator illustrated in Figure 3 is the typical learning paradigm for BSB. Note that with this pattern of interconnections the system feeds back on itself and thus the activation can recycle through the system in a positive feedback loop. The positive feedback is especially evident in J. A. Anderson and Mozer's (1981) version. Their activation rule is given by

$$a_j(t+1) = a_j(t)+\sum w_{ij} a_i(t)$$

if a_j is less than 1 and greater than -1. Otherwise, if the quantity is greater than 1, $a_j = 1$ and if it is less than -1, $a_j = -1$. That is, the activation state at time $t+1$ is given by the sum of the state at time t and the activation propagated through the connectivity matrix provided that total is in the interval [−1,1]. Otherwise it simply takes on the maximum or minimum value. This formulation will lead the system to a state in which all of the units are at either a maximum or minimum value. It is possible to understand why this is called a brain state in a box model by considering a geometric representation of the system. Figure 5 illustrates the "activation space" of a simple BSB system consisting of three units. Each point in the box corresponds to a particular value of activation on each of the three units. In this case we have a three-dimensional space in which the first coordinate corresponds to the activation value of the first unit, the second coordinate corresponds to the activation value of the second unit, and the third coordinate corresponds to the activation value of the third unit. Thus, each point in the space corresponds to a possible state of the system. The feature that each unit is limited to the region [−1,1] means that all points must lie somewhere within the box whose vertices are given by the points (−1,−1,−1), (−1,−1,+1), (−1,+1,−1), (−1,+1,+1), (+1,−1,−1), (+1,−1,+1), (+1,+1,−1), and (+1,+1,+1). Moreover, since the

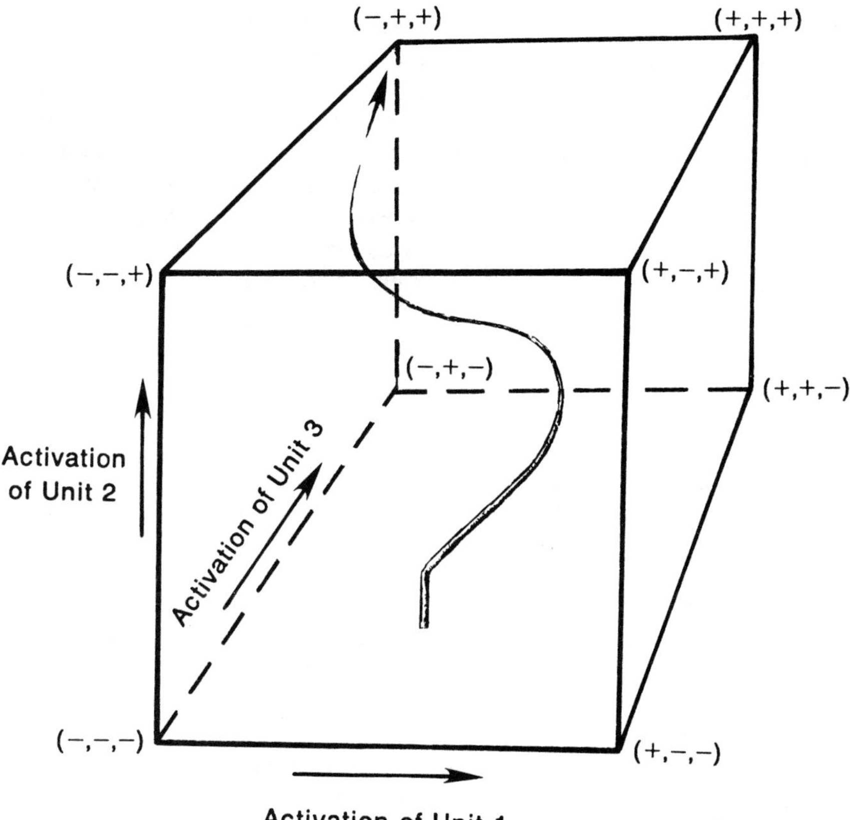

FIGURE 5. The state space for a three-unit version of a BSB model. Each dimension of the box represents the activation value of one unit. Each unit is bounded in activation between [−1,1]. The curving arrow in the box represents the sequence of states the system moved through. It began at the black spot near the middle of the box and, as processing proceeded, moved to the (−,+,+) corner of the box. BSB systems always end up in one or another of the corners. The particular corner depends on the start state of the network, the input to the system, and the pattern of connections among the units.

system involves positive feedback, it is eventually forced to occupy one of these vertices. Thus, the state of the system is constrained to lie within the box and eventually, as processing continues, is pushed to one of the vertices. Of course, the same geometric analogy carries over to higher dimensional systems. If there are N units, the state of the system can be characterized as a point within this N-dimensional hypercube and eventually the system ends up in one of the 2^N corners of the hypercube.

Learning in the BSB system involves auto-association. In different applications two different learning rules have been applied. J. A. Anderson and Mozer (1981) applied the simplest rule. They simply allowed the system to settle down and then employed the simple Hebbian learning rule. That is, $\Delta w_{ij} = \eta a_i a_j$. The error correction rule has also been applied to the BSB model. In this case we use the input as the teaching input as well as the source of activation to the system. The learning rule thus becomes $\Delta w_{ij} = \eta (t_i - a_i) a_j$ where t_i is the input to unit i and where a_i and a_j are the activation values of the system after it has stabilized in one of the corners of the hypercube.

Thermodynamic Models

Other more recent developments are the thermodynamic models. Two examples of such models are presented in the book. One, *harmony theory*, was developed by Paul Smolensky and is described in detail in Chapter 6. The other, the Boltzmann machine, was developed by Hinton and Sejnowski and is described in Chapter 7. Here we describe the basic idea behind these models and show how they relate to the general class of models under discussion. To begin, the thermodynamic models employ binary units which take on the values $\{0,1\}$. The units are divided into two categories: the *visible* units corresponding to our input and output units and the *hidden* units. In general, any unit may connect to any other unit. However, there is a constraint that the connections must be symmetric. That is, the $w_{ij} = w_{ji}$. In these models, there is no distinction between the output of the unit and its activation value. The activation values are, however, a stochastic function of the inputs. That is,

$$p(a_i(t)=1) = \frac{1}{1 + e^{-(\sum_j w_{ij} a_j + \eta_i - \theta_i)/T}}$$

where η_i is the input from outside of system into unit i, θ_i is the threshold for the unit, and T is a parameter, called *temperature*, which determines the slope of the probability function. Figure 6 shows how the probabilities vary with various values of T. It should be noted that as T approaches zero, the individual units become more and more like linear threshold units. In general, if the unit exceeds threshold by a great enough margin it will always attain value 1. If it is far enough below threshold, it always takes on value 0. Whenever the unit is above threshold, the probability that it will turn on is greater than 1/2.

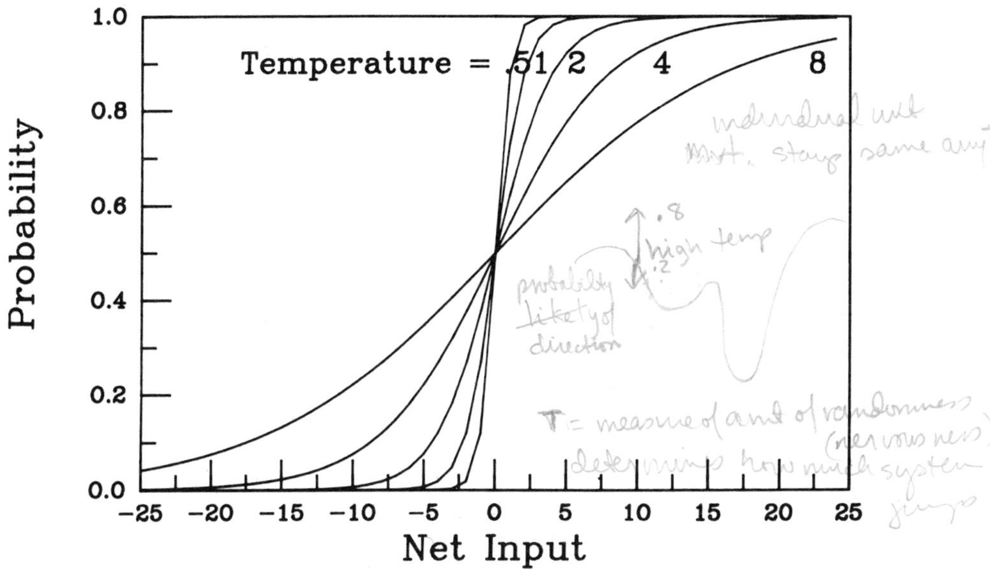

FIGURE 6. Probability of attaining value 1 as a function of the distance of the input of the unit from threshold. The function is plotted for several values of *T*.

Whenever it is below threshold, the probability that it will turn off is greater than 1/2. The temperature simply determines the range of uncertainty as to whether it will turn on or off. This particular configuration of assumptions allows a formal analogy between these models and thermodynamics and allows the proof of theorems concerning its performance as a function of the temperature of the system. This is not the place to discuss these theorems in detail, suffice it to say that this system, like the BSB system, can be viewed as attaining states on the corners of a hypercube. There is a global measure of the degree to which each state of the system is consistent with its input. The system moves into those states that are maximally consistent with the input and with the internal constraints represented by the weights. It can be shown that as the temperature approaches 0, the probability that the system attains the maximally consistent state approaches 1. These results are discussed in some detail in Chapters 6 and 7.

There is a learning scheme associated with the Boltzmann machine which is somewhat more complex than the others. In this case, the learning events are divided into two phases. During one phase, a set of patterns is randomly presented to the visible units and the system is allowed to respond to each in turn. During this phase of learning, the system is environmentally driven; a simple Hebbian rule is assumed to apply so that $\Delta w_{ij} = \eta a_i a_j$. Note, since activations take on values of 0 and 1 this says that the weight is incremented by an amount η whenever unit i and j are on, otherwise no change occurs. During the second phase of learning, the system is allowed to respond for an equal period of time in a so-called free-running state in which no inputs are presented. Since the system is stochastic, it will continue to respond even though no actual stimuli are presented. During this phase, a simple anti-Hebbian rule is employed, $\Delta w_{ij} = -\eta a_i a_j$. The intuition is roughly that the performance during the environmentally driven phase is determined by both the pattern of interconnections and by the environment. The performance during the free-running phase is determined only by the internal set of connections. To correctly reflect the environment, we should look at its performance due to the environment plus internal structure and then subtract out its performance due to internal structure alone. This is actually quite a powerful learning scheme. It can be shown that if a portion of the input units are turned on after the system has learned, it will complete the remaining portion of the visible units with the probability that those units had been present in the stimulus patterns given the subpattern that had been turned on. These issues are again addressed in Chapter 7.

Grossberg

Stephen Grossberg has been one of the major contributors to models of this class over the years. His work is complex and contains many important details which we cannot review here. We will instead describe some of the central aspects of his work and show how it relates to the general framework. Perhaps the clearest summary of Grossberg's work appears in Grossberg (1980). Grossberg's units are allowed to take on any real activation value between a minimum and a maximum value. The output function is, in many of Grossberg's applications, a threshold function so that a given unit will affect another unit only if its activation level is above its threshold. Moreover, Grossberg argues that the output function must be a *sigmoid* or S-shaped function of the activation value of the unit. Grossberg's activation rule is rather more complex than the others we have discussed thus far in that excitatory and inhibitory inputs don't simply sum, but appear separately in the activation rule. Grossberg has presented a number of possible activation rules, but they typically have the form

$$a_j(t+1) = a_j(t)(1-A) + (B-a_j(t))net_{ej}(t) - (a_j(t)+C)net_{ij}(t)$$

where A is the decay rate, B represents the maximal degree of excitation of the unit, and C is much smaller in magnitude than B and represents the maximal amount the unit can be inhibited below the resting value of 0. Grossberg generally assumes that the inhibitory inputs come from a kind of recurrent inhibitory field in which the unit is embedded and the excitatory inputs come from the unit itself and from another level of the system.

Grossberg has studied learning in these networks over a number of years and has studied several different learning schemes. The learning rule he has studied most, however, is similar to the one analyzed in Chapter 5 and is given by

$$\Delta w_{ij} = \eta a_i (o_j - w_{ij}).$$

Grossberg has applied this and similar learning rules in a number of cases, but a review of these applications is beyond the scope of the present discussion.

Interactive Activation Model

The interactive activation model of McClelland and Rumelhart (1981) and Rumelhart and McClelland (1982) had units which represented visual features, letters and words. Units could take on any value in the range [*min,max*]. The output function was a threshold function such that the output was 0 if the activation was below threshold and was equal to the difference of the activation value and the threshold if the activation was above threshold. The interactive activation model involves a connectivity pattern in which units are organized in layers, such that an element in a layer connects with excitatory connections with all elements in the layers above and below that are consistent with that unit, and connects negatively to all units in the layers above and below that are inconsistent with that unit. In addition, each unit inhibits all units in its own layer that are inconsistent with the unit in question. Thus, the interactive activation model is a kind of positive feedback system with maximum and minimum values for each unit, like the BSB model. The information coming into each unit is weighted (by the interconnection strengths) and summed algebraically to yield a "net input" to the unit. Let $net_j = \sum w_{ij} a_i$ be the net input to unit j. This net input is then combined with the previous activation value to produce the new activation value according to the following activation rule:

$$a_j(t+1) = a_j(t)(1-\Theta) + \begin{cases} net_j(max-a_j(t)) & net_j>0 \\ net_j(a_j(t)-min)) & \text{otherwise} \end{cases}$$

where Θ is the decay rate of the activation given no input. In other words, the new activation value is given by the old activation value properly decayed, plus (or minus) a factor that pushes toward the minimum or maximum value depending on the magnitude of the net input into the unit. This activation rule is similar to that employed by Grossberg, except in this formulation the excitation and inhibition are algebraically combined.

The interactive activation model was designed as a model for a processing system and our goals were to show how we could account for specific aspects of word perception. Thus, there was no specific model of learning proposed to explain where the particular network we assumed came from. As we shall see, much of the work on learning reported in this book has been aimed at giving plausible accounts of how such a network might have been learned. (See especially Chapters 5 and 6.)

Feldman and Ballard

Feldman and Ballard (1982) have proposed a framework they call *connectionist modeling*. The units have continuous activation values, which they call *potential* which can take on any value in the range [−10,10]. Their output function is a kind of threshold function which is allowed to take on a small number of discrete integer values ($0 \leqslant o_i \leqslant 9$). They have proposed a number of other unit types each with a somewhat different activation rule. Their simplest unit type is what they call the P-unit. In this case the activation rule is given by

$$a_j(t+1) = a_j(t) + \beta net_j(t).$$

Once the activation reaches its maximum or minimum value it is simply pinned to that value. Decay is implemented by self inhibition. Feldman and Ballard also have a *conjunctive* unit similar to our *sigma-pi* units described below. Feldman (1981) has also considered learning. In general, the approach to learning offers more machinery than is available within our current framework. In practice, however, the learning rules actually examined are of the same class we have already discussed.

SIGMA-PI UNITS

Before completing our section on a general framework, it should be mentioned that we have sometimes found it useful to postulate units that are more complex than those described up to this point in this chapter. In our descriptions thus far, we have assumed a simple additive unit in which the net input to the unit is given by $\sum w_{ij} a_i$. This is certainly the most common form in most of our models. Sometimes, however, we want multiplicative connections in which the output values of two (or possibly more) units are multiplied before entering into the sum. Such a multiplicative connection allows one unit to *gate* another. Thus, if one unit of a multiplicative pair is zero, the other member of the pair can have no effect, no matter how strong its output. On the other hand, if one unit of a pair has value 1, the output of the other is passed unchanged to the receiving unit. Figure 7 illustrates several such connections. In this case, the input to unit A is the weighted sum of the products of units B and C and units D and E. The pairs, BC and DE are called *conjuncts.* In this case we have conjuncts of size 2. In general, of course, the conjuncts could be of any size. We have no applications, however, which have required conjuncts larger than size 2. In general, then, we assume that the net input to a unit is given by the weighted sum of the products of a set of individual inputs. That is, the net input to a unit is given by $\sum w_{ij} \prod a_{i_1} a_{i_2} \cdots a_{i_k}$ where i indexes the conjuncts impinging on unit j and $u_{i_1}, u_{i_2}, \ldots, u_{i_k}$ are the k units in the conjunct. We call units such as these *sigma-pi units.*

In addition to their use as gates, sigma-pi units can be used to convert the output level of a unit into a signal that acts like a *weight* connecting two units. Thus, assume we have the pattern of connections illustrated in the figure. Assume further that the weights on those connections are all 1. In this case, we can use the output levels of units B and D to, in effect, set the weights from C to A and E to A respectively. Since, in general, it is the weights among the units that determine the behavior of the network, sigma-pi units allow for a dynamically programmable network in which the activation value of some units determine what another network can do.

In addition to its general usefulness in these cases, one might ask whether we might not sometime need still more complex patterns of interconnections. Interestingly, as described in Chapter 10, we will never be forced to develop any more complex interconnection type, since sigma-pi units are sufficient to mimic any function monotonic of its inputs.

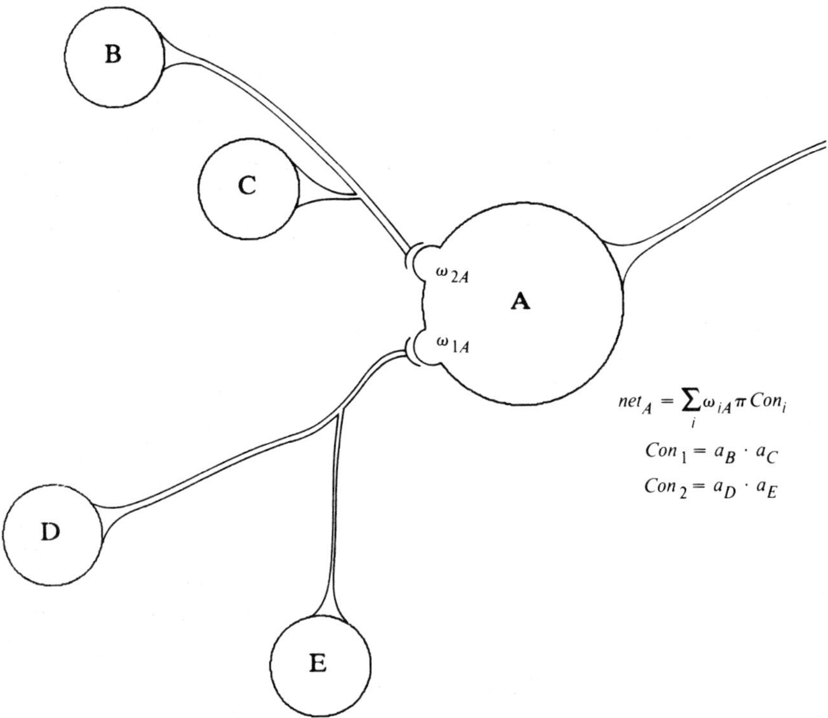

FIGURE 7. Two conjunctive inputs to unit A from the conjunct B and C and D and E. The input to unit A is the sum of the product of the outputs of units BC and DE.

CONCLUSION

We have provided a very general mathematical and conceptual framework within which we develop our models. This framework provides a language for expressing PDP models, and, though there is a lot of freedom within it, it is at least as constrained as most computational formalisms, such as production systems or high-level languages such as Lisp.

We must take note of the fact, however, that the framework does not specify *all* of the constraints we have imposed on ourselves in our model building efforts. For example, virtually any computing device, serial or parallel, can be described in the framework we have described here.

There is a further set of considerations which has guided our particular formulations. These further considerations arise from two sources: our beliefs about the nature of the hardware available for carrying out mental processes in the brain and our beliefs about the essential character of these mental processes themselves. We discuss below the additional constraints on our model building which arise from these two beliefs.

First, the operations in our models can be characterized as "neurally inspired." We wish to replace the "computer metaphor" as a model of mind with the "brain metaphor" as model of mind. This leads us to a number of considerations which further inform and constrain our model building efforts. Perhaps the most crucial of these is time. Neurons are remarkably slow relative to components in modern computers. Neurons operate in the time scale of milliseconds whereas computer components operate in the time scale of nanoseconds—a factor of 10^6 faster. This means that human processes that take on the order of a second or less can involve only a hundred or so time steps. Since most of the processes we have studied—perception, memory retrieval, speech processing, sentence comprehension, and the like—take about a second or so, it makes sense to impose what Feldman (1985) calls the "100-step program" constraint. That is, we seek explanations for these mental phenomena which do not require more than about a hundred elementary sequential operations. Given that the processes we seek to characterize are often quite complex and may involve consideration of large numbers of simultaneous constraints, our algorithms *must* involve considerable parallelism. Thus, although a serial computer could be created out of the kinds of components represented by our units, such an implementation would surely violate the 100-step program constraint for any but the simplest processes.

A second consideration differentiates our models from those inspired by the computer metaphor: that is, the constraint that all the knowledge is *in the connections.* From conventional programmable computers we are used to thinking of knowledge as being stored in the state of certain units in the system. In our systems we assume that only very short term storage can occur in the states of units; long term storage takes place in the connections among units. Indeed, it is the connections—or perhaps the rules for forming them through experience—which primarily differentiate one model from another. This is a profound difference between our approach and other more conventional approaches, for it means that almost all knowledge is *implicit* in the structure of the device that carries out the task rather than *explicit* in the states of units themselves. Knowledge is not directly accessible to interpretation by some separate processor, but it is built into the processor itself and directly determines the course of processing. It is acquired through tuning of connections as these are used in processing, rather than formulated and stored as declarative facts.

In addition to these two neurally inspired working assumptions, there are a number of other constraints that derive rather directly from our understanding of the nature of neural information processing. These assumptions are discussed more fully in Chapter 4.

The second class of constraints arises from our beliefs about the nature of human information processing considered at a more abstract, computational level of analysis. We see the kinds of phenomena we have been studying as products of a kind of constraint satisfaction procedure in which a very large number of constraints act simultaneously to produce the behavior. Thus, we see most behavior not as the product of a single, separate component of the cognitive system, but as the product of large set of interacting components, each mutually constraining the others and contributing in its own way to the globally observable behavior of the system. It is very difficult to use serial algorithms to implement such a conception, but very natural to use highly parallel ones. These problems can often be characterized as *best match* or *optimization* problems. As Minsky and Papert (1969) have pointed out, it is very difficult to solve best match problems serially. However, this is precisely the kind of problem that is readily implemented using highly parallel algorithms of the kind we consider in this book. See Kanerva (1984) for a discussion of the best match problem and its solution with parallel processing systems.

To summarize, the PDP framework consists not only of a formal language, but a perspective on our models. Other qualitative and quantitative considerations arising from our understanding of brain processing and of human behavior combine with the formal system to form what might be viewed as an aesthetic for our model building enterprises. The remainder of our book is largely a study of this aesthetic in practice.

ACKNOWLEDGMENTS

This research was supported by Contract N00014-79-C-0323, NR 667-437 with the Personnel and Training Research Programs of the Office of Naval Research, by grants from the System Development Foundation, and by a NIMH Career Development Award (MH00385) to the second author.

CHAPTER 3

Distributed Representations

G. E. HINTON, J. L. McCLELLAND, and D. E. RUMELHART

Given a network of simple computing elements and some entities to be represented, the most straightforward scheme is to use one computing element for each entity. This is called a *local* representation. It is easy to understand and easy to implement because the structure of the physical network mirrors the structure of the knowledge it contains. The naturalness and simplicity of this relationship between the knowledge and the hardware that implements it have led many people to simply assume that local representations are the best way to use parallel hardware. There are, of course, a wide variety of more complicated implementations in which there is no one-to-one correspondence between concepts and hardware units, but these implementations are only worth considering if they lead to increased efficiency or to interesting emergent properties that cannot be conveniently achieved using local representations.

This chapter describes one type of representation that is less familiar and harder to think about than local representations. Each entity is represented by a pattern of activity distributed over many computing elements, and each computing element is involved in representing many different entities. The strength of this more complicated kind of representation does not lie in its notational convenience or its ease of implementation in a conventional computer, but rather in the efficiency with which it makes use of the processing abilities of networks of simple, neuron-like computing elements.

Every representational scheme has its good and bad points. Distributed representations are no exception. Some desirable properties arise very naturally from the use of patterns of activity as representations. Other properties, like the ability to temporarily store a large set of arbitrary associations, are much harder to achieve. As we shall see, the best psychological evidence for distributed representations is the degree to which their strengths and weaknesses match those of the human mind.

The first section of this chapter stresses some of the virtues of distributed representations. The second section considers the efficiency of distributed representations, and shows clearly why distributed representations can be better than local ones for certain classes of problems. A final section discusses some difficult issues which are often avoided by advocates of distributed representations, such as the representation of constituent structure and the sequential focusing of processing effort on different aspects of a structured object.

Disclaimers. Before examining the detailed arguments in favor of distributed representations, it is important to be clear about their status within an overall theory of human information processing. It would be wrong to view distributed representations as an *alternative* to representational schemes like semantic networks or production systems that have been found useful in cognitive psychology and artificial intelligence. It is more fruitful to view them as one way of implementing these more abstract schemes in parallel networks, but with one proviso: Distributed representations give rise to some powerful and unexpected emergent properties. These properties can therefore be taken as primitives when working in a more abstract formalism. For example, distributed representations are good for content-addressable memory, automatic generalization, and the selection of the rule that best fits the current situation. So if one assumes that more abstract models are implemented in the brain using distributed representations, it is not unreasonable to treat abilities like content-addressable memory, automatic generalization, or the selection of an appropriate rule as primitive operations, even though there is no easy way to implement these operations in conventional computers. Some of the emergent properties of distributed representations are not easily captured in higher-level formalisms. For example, distributed representations are consistent with the simultaneous application of a large number of partially fitting rules to the current situation, each rule being applied to the degree that it is relevant. We shall examine these properties of distributed representations in the chapter on schemata (Chapter 14). There we will see clearly that schemata and other higher-level constructs provide only approximate characterizations of mechanisms which rely on distributed representations. Thus, the contribution that an analysis of distributed representations can make to these higher-level formalisms is to legitimize certain powerful, primitive operations which would otherwise appear to be an appeal to magic; to enrich our repertoire of primitive operations beyond those which can conveniently be captured in many higher-level formalisms; and to suggest that these higher-level formalisms may only capture the coarse features of the computational capabilities of the underlying processing mechanisms.

Another common source of confusion is the idea that distributed representations are somehow in conflict with the extensive evidence for localization of function in the brain (Luria, 1973). A system that uses distributed representations still requires many different modules for representing completely different kinds of thing at the same time. The distributed representations occur *within* these localized modules. For example, different modules would be devoted to things as different as mental images and sentence structures, but two different mental images would correspond to *alternative* patterns of activity in the same module. The representations advocated here are local at a global scale but global at a local scale.

VIRTUES OF DISTRIBUTED REPRESENTATIONS

This section considers three important features of distributed representations: (a) their essentially constructive character; (b) their ability to generalize automatically to novel situations; and (c) their tunability to changing environments. Several of these virtues are shared by certain local models, such as the interactive activation model of word perception, or McClelland's (1981) model of generalization and retrieval described in Chapter 1.

Memory as Inference

People have a very flexible way of accessing their memories: They can recall items from partial descriptions of their contents (Norman & Bobrow, 1979). Moreover, they can do this even if some parts of the partial description are wrong. Many people, for example, can rapidly retrieve the item that satisfies the following partial description: It is an actor, it is intelligent, it is a politician. This kind of *content-addressable* memory is very useful and it is very hard to implement on a conventional computer because computers store each item at a particular address, and to retrieve an item they must know its address. If all the combinations of descriptors that will be used for access are free of errors and are known in advance, it is possible to use a method called *hash coding* that quickly yields the address of an item when given part of its content. In general, however, content-addressable memory requires a massive search for the item that best fits the partial description. The central computational problem in memory is how to make this search efficient. When the cues can contain errors, this is very difficult because the failure to fit one of the cues cannot be used as a filter for quickly eliminating inappropriate answers.

Distributed representations provide an efficient way of using parallel hardware to implement best-fit searches. The basic idea is fairly simple, though it is quite unlike a conventional computer memory. Different items correspond to different patterns of activity over the very same group of hardware units. A partial description is presented in the form of a partial activity pattern, activating some of the hardware units.[1] Interactions between the units then allow the set of active units to influence others of the units, thereby completing the pattern, and generating the item that best fits the description. A new item is "stored" by modifying the interactions between the hardware units so as to create a new stable pattern of activity. The main difference from a conventional computer memory is that patterns which are not active do not exist anywhere. They can be re-created because the connection strengths between units have been changed appropriately, but each connection strength is involved in storing many patterns, so it is impossible to point to a particular place where the memory for a particular item is stored.

Many people are surprised when they understand that the connections between a set of simple processing units are capable of supporting a large number of different patterns. Illustrations of this aspect of distributed models are provided in a number of papers in the literature (e.g., Anderson, 1977; Hinton, 1981a); this property is illustrated in the model of memory and amnesia described in Chapters 17 and 25.

One way of thinking about distributed memories is in terms of a very large set of plausible inference rules. Each active unit represents a "microfeature" of an item, and the connection strengths stand for plausible "microinferences" between microfeatures. Any particular pattern

---

[1] This is easy if the partial description is simply a set of features, but it is much more difficult if the partial description mentions relationships to other objects. If, for example, the system is asked to retrieve John's father, it must represent John, but if John and his father are represented by mutually exclusive patterns of activity in the very same group of units, it is hard to see how this can be done without preventing the representation of John's father. A distributed solution to this problem is described in the text.

of activity of the units will satisfy some of the microinferences and violate others. A stable pattern of activity is one that violates the plausible microinferences less than any of the neighboring patterns. A new stable pattern can be created by changing the inference rules so that the new pattern violates them less than its neighbors. This view of memory makes it clear that there is no sharp distinction between genuine memory and plausible reconstruction. A genuine memory is a pattern that is stable because the inference rules were modified when it occurred before. A "confabulation" is a pattern that is stable because of the way the inference rules have been modified to store several different previous patterns. So far as the subject is concerned, this may be indistinguishable from the real thing.

The blurring of the distinction between veridical recall and confabulation or plausible reconstruction seems to be characteristic of human memory (Bartlett, 1932; Neisser, 1981). The reconstructive nature of human memory is surprising only because it conflicts with the standard metaphors we use. We tend to think that a memory system should work by storing literal copies of items and then retrieving the stored copy, as in a filing cabinet or a typical computer database. Such systems are not naturally reconstructive.

If we view memory as a process that constructs a pattern of activity which represents the most plausible item that is consistent with the given cues, we need some guarantee that it will converge on the representation of the item that best fits the description, though it might be tolerable to sometimes get a good but not optimal fit. It is easy to *imagine* this happening, but it is harder to make it actually work. One recent approach to this problem is to use statistical mechanics to analyze the behavior of groups of interacting *stochastic* units. The analysis guarantees that the better an item fits the description, the more likely it is to be produced as the solution. This approach is described in Chapter 7, and a related approach is described in Chapter 6. An alternative approach, using units with continuous activations (Hopfield, 1984) is described in Chapter 14.

Similarity and Generalization

When a new item is stored, the modifications in the connection strengths must not wipe out existing items. This can be achieved by modifying a very large number of weights very slightly. If the modifications are all in the direction that helps the pattern that is being stored, there will be a conspiracy effect: The total help for the intended pattern will be the sum of all the small separate modifications.

For unrelated patterns, however, there will be very little transfer of effect because some of the modifications will help and some will hinder. Instead of all the small modifications conspiring together, they will mainly cancel out. This kind of statistical reasoning underpins most distributed memory models, but there are many variations of the basic idea (See Hinton & Anderson, 1981, for several examples).

It is possible to prevent interference altogether by using orthogonal patterns of activity for the various items to be stored (a rudimentary example of such a case is given in Chapter 1). However, this eliminates one of the most interesting properties of distributed representations: They automatically give rise to generalizations. If the task is simply to remember accurately a set of unrelated items, the generalization effects are harmful and are called interference. But generalization is normally a helpful phenomenon. It allows us to deal effectively with situations that are similar but not identical to previously experienced situations.

People are good at generalizing newly acquired knowledge. If you learn a new fact about an object, your expectations about other similar objects tend to change. If, for example, you learn that chimpanzees like onions you will probably raise your estimate of the probability that gorillas like onions. In a network that uses distributed representations, this kind of generalization is automatic. The new knowledge about chimpanzees is incorporated by modifying some of the connection strengths so as to alter the causal effects of the distributed pattern of activity that represents chimpanzees.[2] The modifications automatically change the causal effects of all similar activity patterns. So if the representation of gorillas is a similar activity pattern over the same set of units, its causal effects will be changed in a similar way.

The very simplest distributed scheme would represent the concept of onion and the concept of chimpanzee by *alternative* activity patterns over the very same set of units. It would then be hard to represent chimps and onions at the same time. This problem can be solved by using separate modules for each possible role of an item within a larger structure. Chimps, for example, are the "agent" of the liking and so a pattern representing chimps occupies the "agent" module and the pattern representing onions occupies the "patient" module (see Figure 1).

[2] The internal structure of this pattern may also change. There is always a choice between changing the weights on the outgoing connections and changing the pattern itself so that different outgoing connections become relevant. Changes in the pattern itself alter its similarity to other patterns and thereby alter how generalization will occur in the future. It is generally much harder to figure out how to change the pattern that represents an item than it is to figure out how to change the outgoing connections so that a particular pattern will have the desired effects on another part of the network.

Each module can have alternative patterns for all the various items, so this scheme does not involve local representations of items. What is localized is the role.

If you subsequently learn that gibbons and orangutans do not like onions your estimate of the probability that gorillas like onions will fall, though it may still remain higher than it was initially. Obviously, the combination of facts suggests that liking onions is a peculiar quirk of chimpanzees. A system that uses distributed representations will automatically arrive at this conclusion, provided that the alternative patterns that represent the various apes are related to one another in a particular way that is somewhat more specific than just being similar to one another: There needs to be a part of each complete pattern that is identical for all the various apes. In other words, the group of units used for the distributed representations must be divided into two

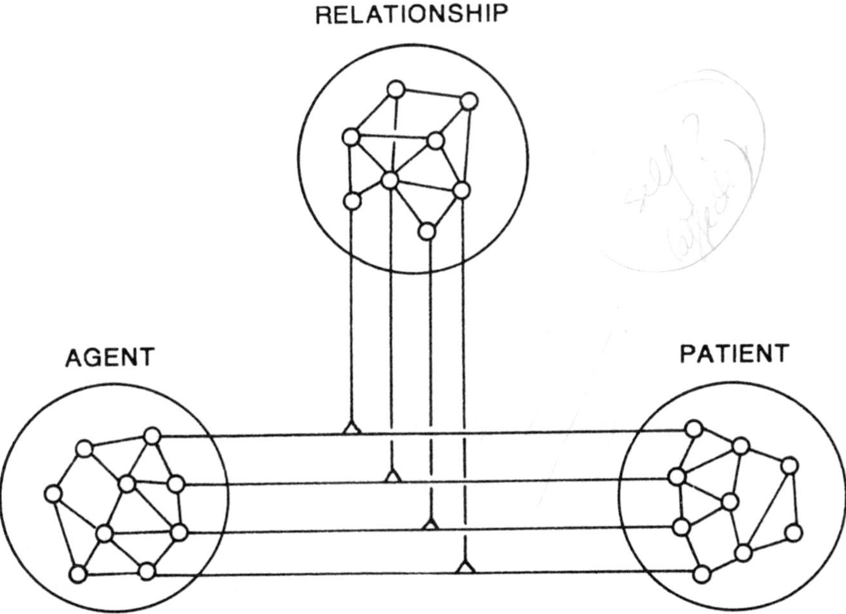

FIGURE 1. In this simplified scheme there are two different modules, one of which represents the agent and the other the patient. To incorporate the fact that chimpanzees like onions, the pattern for chimpanzees in one module must be associated with the pattern for onions in the other module. Relationships other than "liking" can be implemented by having a third group of units whose pattern of activity represents the relationship. This pattern must then "gate" the interactions between the agent and patient groups. Hinton (1981a) describes one way of doing this gating by using a fourth group of units.

subgroups, and all the various apes must be represented by the same pattern in the first subgroup, but by different patterns in the second subgroup. The pattern of activity over the first subgroup represents the *type* of the item, and the pattern over the second subgroup represents additional microfeatures that discriminate each instance of the type from the other instances. Note that any subset of the microfeatures can be considered to define a type. One subset might be common to all apes, and a different (but overlapping) subset might be common to all pets. This allows an item to be an instance of many different types simultaneously.

When the system learns a new fact about chimpanzees, it usually has no way of knowing whether the fact is true of all apes or is just a property of chimpanzees. The obvious strategy is therefore to modify the strengths of the connections emanating from *all* the active units, so that the new knowledge will be partly a property of apes in general and partly a property of whatever features distinguish chimps from other apes. If it is subsequently learned that other apes do not like onions, correcting modifications will be made so that the information about onions is no longer associated with the subpattern that is common to all apes. The knowledge about onions will then be restricted to the subpattern that distinguishes chimps from other apes. If it had turned out that gibbons and orangutans also liked onions, the modifications in the weights emanating from the subpattern representing apes would have reinforced one another, and the knowledge would have become associated with the subpattern shared by all apes rather than with the patterns that distinguish one ape from another.

A very simple version of this theory of generalization has been implemented in a computer simulation (Hinton, 1981a). Several applications that make use of this property can be found in Part IV of this book.

There is an obvious generalization of the idea that the representation of an item is composed of two parts, one that represents the type and another that represents the way in which this particular instance differs from others of the same type. Almost all types are themselves instances of more general types, and this can be implemented by dividing the pattern that represents the type into two subpatterns, one for the more general type of which this type is an instance, and the other for the features that discriminate this particular type from others instances of the same general type. Thus the relation between a type and an instance can be implemented by the relationship between a set of units and a larger set that includes it. Notice that the more general the type, the *smaller* the set of units used to encode it. As the number of terms in an *intensional* description gets smaller, the corresponding *extensional* set gets larger.

In traditional semantic networks that use local representations, generalization is not a direct consequence of the representation. Given that chimpanzees like onions, the obvious way of incorporating the new knowledge is by changing the strengths of connections belonging to the chimpanzee unit. But this does not automatically change connections that belong to the gorilla unit. So extra processes must be invoked to implement generalization in a localist scheme. One commonly used method is to allow activation to spread from a local unit to other units that represent similar concepts (Collins & Loftus, 1975; Quillian, 1968). Then when one concept unit is activated, it will partially activate its neighbors and so any knowledge stored in the connections emanating from these neighbors will be partially effective. There are many variations of this basic idea (Fahlman, 1979; Levin, 1976; McClelland, 1981).

It is hard to make a clean distinction between systems that use local representations plus spreading activation and systems that use distributed representations. In both cases the result of activating a concept is that many different hardware units are active. The distinction almost completely disappears in some models such as McClelland's (1981) generalization model, where the properties of a concept are represented by a pattern of activation over feature units and where this pattern of activation is determined by the interactions of a potentially very large number of units for instances of the concept. The main difference is that in one case there is a particular individual hardware unit that acts as a "handle" which makes it easy to attach purely conventional properties like the name of the concept and easier for the theorist who constructed the network to know what the individual parts of the network stand for.

If we construct our networks by hand-specifying the connections between the units in the network, a local representation scheme has some apparent advantages. First, it is easier to think one understands the behavior of a network if one has put in all the "knowledge"—all the connections—oneself. But if it is the entire, distributed pattern of interacting influences among the units in the network that is doing the work, this understanding can often be illusory. Second, it seems intuitively obvious that it is harder to attach an arbitrary name to a distributed pattern than it is to attach it to a single unit. What is intuitively harder, however, may not be more efficient. We will see that one can actually implement aribitrary associations with fewer units using distributed representations. Before we turn to such considerations, however, we examine a different advantage of distributed representations: They make it possible to create new concepts without allocating new hardware.

Creating New Concepts

Any plausible scheme for representing knowledge must be capable of learning novel concepts that could not be anticipated at the time the network was initially wired up. A scheme that uses local representations must first make a discrete decision about *when* to form a new concept, and then it must find a spare hardware unit that has suitable connections for implementing the concept involved. Finding such a unit may be difficult if we assume that, after a period of early development, new knowledge is incorporated by changing the strengths of the existing connections rather than by growing new ones. If each unit only has connections to a small fraction of the others, there will probably not be any units that are connected to just the right other ones to implement a new concept. For example, in a collection of a million units each connected at random to ten thousand others, the chance of there being *any* unit that is connected to a particular set of 6 others is only one in a million.

In an attempt to rescue local representations from this problem, several clever schemes have been proposed that use two classes of units. The units that correspond to concepts are not directly connected to one another. Instead, the connections are implemented by indirect pathways through several layers of intermediate units (Fahlman, 1980; Feldman, 1982). This scheme works because the number of *potential* pathways through the intermediate layers far exceeds the total number of physical connections. If there are k layers of units, each of which has a fan-out of n connections to randomly selected units in the following layer, there are n^k potential pathways. There is almost certain to be a pathway connecting any two concept-units, and so the intermediate units along this pathway can be dedicated to connecting those two concept-units. However, these schemes end up having to dedicate several intermediate units to each effective connection, and once the dedication has occurred, all but one of the actual connections emanating from each intermediate unit are wasted. The use of several intermediate units to create a single effective connection may be appropriate in switching networks containing elements that have units with relatively small fan-out, but it seems to be an inefficient way of using the hardware of the brain.

The problems of finding a unit to stand for a new concept and wiring it up appropriately do not arise if we use distributed representations. All we need to do is modify the interactions between units so as to create a new stable pattern of activity. If this is done by modifying a large number of connections very slightly, the creation of a new pattern need not disrupt the existing representations. The difficult problem is to choose an appropriate pattern for the new concept. The effects of the new representation on representations in other parts of the system will be determined by the units that are active, and so it is important to use a collection of active units that have roughly the correct effects. Fine-tuning of the effects of the new pattern can be achieved by slightly altering the effects of the active units it contains, but it would be unwise to choose a *random* pattern for a new concept because major changes would then be needed in the weights, and this would disrupt other knowledge. Ideally, the distributed representation that is chosen for a new concept should be the one that requires the least modification of weights to make the new pattern stable and to make it have the required effects on other representations.

Naturally, it is not necessary to create a new stable pattern all in one step. It is possible for the pattern to emerge as a result of modifications on many separate occasions. This alleviates an awkward problem that arises with local representations: The system must make a discrete all-or-none decision about when to create a new concept. If we view concepts as stable patterns, they are much less discrete in character. It is possible, for example, to differentiate one stable pattern into two closely related but different variants by modifying some of the weights slightly. Unless we are allowed to clone the hardware units (and all their connections), this kind of gradual, conceptual differentiation is much harder to achieve with local representations.

One of the central problems in the development of the theory of distributed representation is the problem of specifying the exact procedures by which distributed representations are to be learned. All such procedures involve connection strength modulation, following "learning rules" of the type outlined in Chapter 2. Not all the problems have been solved, but significant progress is being made on these problems. (See the chapters in Part II.)

DISTRIBUTED REPRESENTATIONS THAT WORK EFFICIENTLY

In this section, we consider some of the technical details about the implementation of distributed representations. First, we point out that certain distributed representation schemes can fail to provide a sufficient basis for differentiating different concepts, and we point out what is required to avoid this limitation. Then, we describe a way of using distributed representations to get the most information possible out of a simple network of connected units. The central result is a surprising one: If you want to encode features accurately using as few units as possible, it pays to use units that are very coarsely tuned, so that each feature activates many different units and each unit is activated by many different features. A specific feature is then encoded by a pattern of activity in many units rather than by a single active unit, so coarse coding is a form of distributed representation.

To keep the analysis simple, we shall assume that the units have only two values, on and off.[3] We shall also ignore the dynamics of the system because the question of interest, for the time being, is how many units it takes to encode features with a given accuracy. We start by considering the kind of feature that can be completely specified by giving a type (e.g., line-segment, corner, dot) and the values of some continuous parameters that distinguish it from other features of the same type (e.g., position, orientation, size.) For each type of feature there is a space of possible instances. Each continuous parameter defines a dimension of the feature space, and each particular feature corresponds to a point in the space. For features like dots in a plane, the space of possible features is two-dimensional. For features like stopped, oriented edge-segments in three-dimensional space, the feature space is six-dimensional. We shall start by considering two-dimensional feature spaces and then generalize to higher dimensionalities.

Suppose that we wish to represent the position of a single dot in a plane, and we wish to achieve high accuracy without using too many units. We define the accuracy of an encoding scheme to be the number of different encodings that are generated as the dot is moved a standard distance through the space. One encoding scheme would be to divide the units into an X group and a Y group, and dedicate each unit to encoding a particular X or Y interval as shown in Figure 2. A given dot would then be encoded by activity in two units, one from each group, and the accuracy would be proportional to the number of units used. Unfortunately, there are two problems with this. First, if two dots have to be encoded at the same time, the method breaks down. The two dots will activate two units in each group, and there will be no way of telling, from the active units, whether the dots were at $(x1, y1)$ and $(x2, y2)$ or at $(x1, y2)$ and $(x2, y1)$. This is called the *binding problem.* It arises because the representation does not specify what goes with what.

---

[3] Similar arguments apply with multivalued activity levels, but it is important not to allow activity levels to have arbitrary precision because this makes it possible to represent an infinite amount of information in a single activity level. Units that transmit a discrete impulse with a probability that varies as a function of their activation seem to approximate the kind of precision that is possible in neural circuitry (see Chapters 20 and 21).

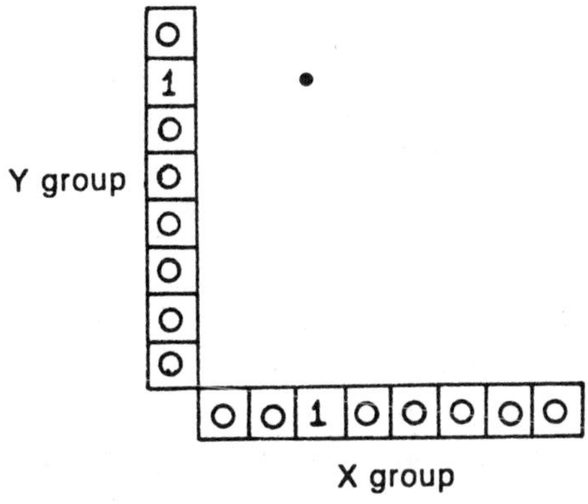

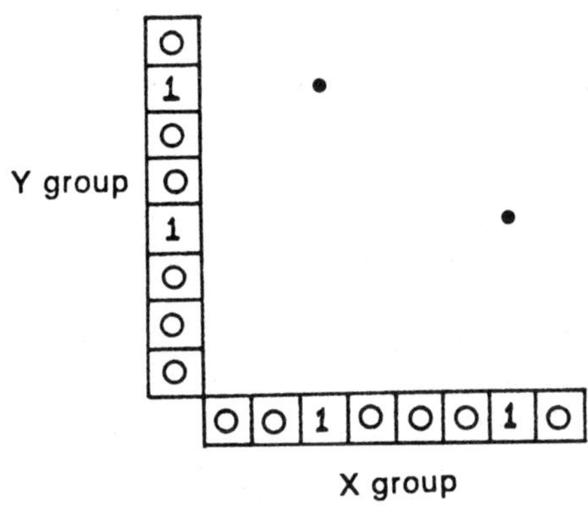

FIGURE 2. *A*: A simple way of using two groups of binary units to encode the position of a point in a two-dimensional space. The active units in the X and Y groups represent the x- and y-coordinates. *B*: When two points must be encoded at the same time, it is impossible to tell which x-coordinate goes with which y-coordinate.

The second problem arises even if we allow only one point to be represented at a time. Suppose we want certain representations to be associated with an overt response, but not others: We want $(x1, y1)$ and $(x2, y2)$ to be associated with a response, but not $(x1, y2)$ or $(x2, y1)$. We cannot implement this association using standard weighted connections to response units from units standing for the values on the two dimensions separately. For the unit for $x1$ and the unit for $x2$ would both have to activate the response, and the unit for ı and the unit for $y2$ would both have to activate the response. There would be no way of preventing the response from being activated when the unit for $x1$ and the unit for $y2$ were both activated. This is another aspect of the binding problem since, again, the representation fails to specify what must go with what.

In a conventional computer it is easy to solve the binding problem. We simply create two records in the computer memory. Each record contains a pair of coordinates that go together as coordinates of one dot, and the binding information is encoded by the fact that the two coordinate values are sitting in the same record (which usually means they are sitting in neighboring memory locations). In parallel networks it is much harder to solve the binding problem.

Conjunctive Encoding

One approach is to set aside, in advance, one unit for each possible *combination* of X and Y values. This amounts to covering the plane with a large number of small, nonoverlapping zones and dedicating a unit to each zone. A dot is then represented by activity in a single unit so this is a *local* representation. The use of one unit for each discriminable feature solves the binding problem by having units which stand for the conjunction of values on each of two dimensions. In general, to permit an arbitrary association between particular combinations of features and some output or other pattern of activation, some conjunctive representation may be required.

However, this kind of local encoding is very expensive. It is much less efficient than the previous scheme because the accuracy of pinpointing a point in the plane is only proportional to the square root of the number of units. In general, for a k-dimensional feature space, the local encoding yields an accuracy proportional to the kth root of the number of units. Achieving high accuracy without running into the binding problem is thus very expensive.

The use of one unit for each discriminable feature may be a reasonable encoding if a very large number of features are presented on each occasion, so that a large fraction of the units are active. However, it is a very inefficient encoding if only a very small fraction of the possible features are presented at once. The average amount of information conveyed by the state of a binary unit is 1 bit if the unit is active half the time, and it is much less if the unit is only rarely active.[4] It would

[4] The amount of information conveyed by a unit that has a probability of p of being on is $-p \log p - (1-p)\log(1-p)$.

therefore be more efficient to use an encoding in which a larger fraction of the units were active at any moment. This can be done if we abandon the idea that each discriminable feature is represented by activity in a single unit.

Coarse Coding

Suppose we divide the space into larger, overlapping zones and assign a unit to each zone. For simplicity, we will assume that the zones are circular, that their centers have a uniform random distribution throughout the space, and that all the zones used by a given encoding scheme have the same radius. The question of interest is how accurately a feature is encoded as a function of the radius of the zones. If we have a given number of units at our disposal is it better to use large zones so that each feature point falls in many zones, or is it better to use small zones so that each feature is represented by activity in fewer but more finely tuned units?

The accuracy is proportional to the number of different encodings that are generated as we move a feature point along a straight line from one side of the space to the other. Every time the line crosses the boundary of a zone, the encoding of the feature point changes because the activity of the unit corresponding to that zone changes. So the number of discriminable features along the line is just twice the number of zones that the line penetrates.[5] The line penetrates every zone whose center lies within one radius of the line (see Figure 3). This number is proportional to the radius of the zones, r, and it is also proportional to their number, n. Hence the accuracy, a, is related to the number of zones and to their radius as follows:

$$a \propto nr.$$

In general, for a k-dimensional space, the number of zones whose centers lie within one radius of a line through the space is proportional to the volume of a k-dimensional hypercylinder of radius r. This volume is equal to the length of the cylinder (which is fixed) times its $(k-1)$-dimensional cross-sectional area which is proportional to r^{k-1}.

---

[5] Problems arise if you enter and leave a zone without crossing other zone borders in between because you revert to the same encoding as before, but this effect is negligible if the zones are dense enough for there to be many zones containing each point in the space.

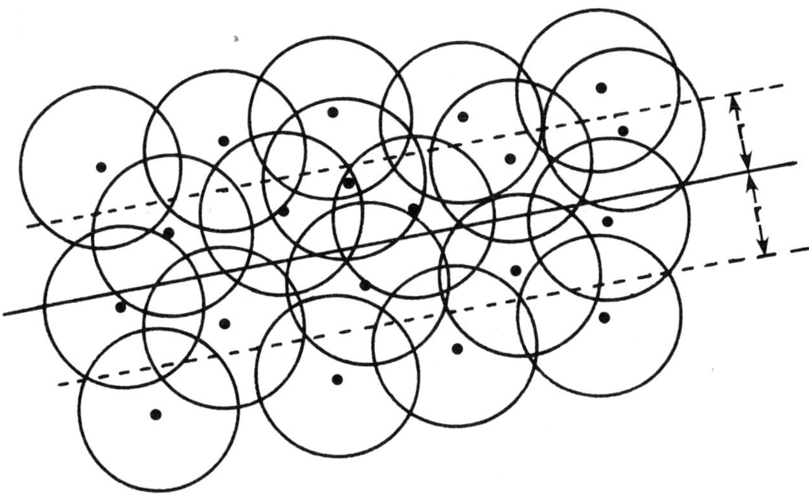

FIGURE 3. The number of zone boundaries that are cut by the line is proportional to the number of zone centers within one-zone radius of the line.

Hence, the accuracy is given by

$$a \propto nr^{k-1}.$$

So, for example, doubling the radius of the zones increases by a factor of 32, the *linear* accuracy with which a six-dimensional feature like a stopped oriented three-dimensional edge is represented. The intuitive idea that larger zones lead to sloppier representations is entirely wrong because distributed representations hold information much more efficiently than local ones. Even though each active unit is less specific in its meaning, the combination of active units is far more specific. Notice also that with coarse coding the accuracy is proportional to the number of units, which is much better than being proportional to the kth root of the number.

Units that respond to complex features in retinotopic maps in visual cortex often have fairly large receptive fields. This is often interpreted as the first step on the way to a translation invariant representation. However, it may be that the function of the large fields is not to achieve translation invariance but to pinpoint accurately where the feature is!

Limitations on coarse coding. So far, only the advantages of coarse coding have been mentioned, and its problematic aspects have been ignored. There are a number of limitations that cause the coarse coding strategy to break down when the "receptive fields" become too large. One obvious limitation occurs when the fields become comparable in size to the whole space. This limitation is generally of little interest because other, more severe, problems arise before the receptive fields become this large.

Coarse coding is only effective when the features that must be represented are relatively sparse. If many feature points are crowded together, each receptive field will contain many features and the activity pattern in the coarse-coded units will not discriminate between many alternative combinations of feature points. (If the units are allowed to have integer activity levels that reflect the number of feature points falling within their fields, a few nearby points can be tolerated, but not many.) Thus there is a resolution/accuracy trade-off. Coarse coding can give high accuracy for the parameters of features provided that features are widely spaced so that high resolution is not also required. As a rough rule of thumb, the diameter of the receptive fields should be of the same order as the spacing between simultaneously present feature points.[6]

The fact that coarse coding only works if the features are sparse should be unsurprising given that its advantage over a local encoding is that it uses the information capacity of the units more efficiently by making each unit active more often. If the features are so dense that the units would be active for about half the time using a local encoding, coarse coding can only make things worse.

A second major limitation on the use of coarse coding stems from the fact that the representation of a feature must be used to affect other representations. There is no point using coarse coding if the features have to be recoded as activity in finely tuned units before they can have the appropriate effects on other representations. If we assume that the effect of a distributed representation is the *sum* of the effects of the individual active units that constitute the representation, there is a strong limitation on the circumstances under which coarse coding can be used effectively. Nearby features will be encoded by similar sets of active units, and so they will inevitably tend to have similar effects. Broadly speaking, coarse coding is only useful if the required effect of a feature is the average of the required effects of its neighbors. At a fine enough scale this is nearly always true for spatial tasks. The scale at which it breaks down determines an upper limit on the size of the receptive fields.

---

[6] It is interesting that many of the geometric visual illusions illustrate interactions between features at a distance much greater than the uncertainty in the subjects' knowledge of the position of a feature. This is just what would be expected if coarse coding is being used to represent complex features accurately.

Another limitation is that whenever coarse-coded representations interact, there is a tendency for the coarseness to increase. To counteract this tendency, it is probably necessary to have lateral inhibition operating within each representation. This issue requires further research.

Extension to noncontinuous spaces. The principle underlying coarse coding can be generalized to noncontinuous spaces by thinking of a set of items as the equivalent of a receptive field. A local representation uses one unit for each possible item. A distributed representation uses a unit for a set of items, and it implicitly encodes a particular item as the intersection of the sets that correspond to the active units.

In the domain of spatial features there is generally a very strong regularity: Sets of features with similar parameter values need to have similar effects on other representations. Coarse coding is efficient because it allows this regularity to be expressed in the connection strengths. In other domains, the regularities are different, but the efficiency arguments are the same: It is better to devote a unit to a set of items than to a single item, provided that the set is chosen in such a way that membership in the set implies something about membership in other sets. This implication can then be captured as a connection strength. Ideally, a set should be chosen so that membership of this set has strong implications for memberships of other sets that are also encoded by individual units.

We illustrate these points with a very simple example. Consider a microlanguage consisting of the three-letter words of English made up of *w* or *l*, followed by *i* or *e*, followed by *g* or *r*. The strings *wig* and *leg* are words, but *weg*, *lig*, and all strings ending in *r* are not. Suppose we wanted to use a distributed representation scheme as a basis for representing the words, and we wanted to be able to use the distributed pattern as a basis for deciding whether the string is a word or a nonword. For simplicity we will have a single "decision" unit. The problem is to find connections from the units representing the word to the decision unit such that it fires whenever a word is present but does not fire when no word is present.[7]

[7] Note that the problem remains the same if the decision unit is replaced by a set of units and the task of the network is to produce a different pattern for the word and nonword decisions. For when we examine each unit, it either takes the same or a different value in the two patterns; in the cases where the value is the same, there is no problem, but neither do such units differentiate the two patterns. When the values are different, the unit behaves just like the single decision unit discussed in the text.

Figure 4 shows three representation schemes: a distributed scheme that does not work, a distributed scheme that does work, and a local scheme. In the first scheme, each letter/position combination is represented by a different unit. Since there are only five letter/position possibilities, only five units have connections to the output unit. Each word and nonword produces a different and unique pattern over these five units, but the connections from the five units to the decision unit cannot be set in such a way as to make the decision unit fire whenever one of the words is present and fail to fire whenever one of the nonwords is present.

The reason for the problem is simply that the connections between the letter/position units and the decision units can only capture the degree to which each letter indicates whether the string is a word or not. The *g* tends to indicate that a word is present, whereas the *r* indicates that the item is not a word; but each of the other letters, taken individually, has absolutely no predictive ability in this case.

Whether a letter string is a word or not cannot be determined conclusively from the individual letters it contains; it is necessary to consider also what *combinations* of letters it contains. Thus, we need a representation that captures what combinations of letters are present in a way that is sufficient for the purposes of the network. One could capture this by using local representations and assigning one node to each word, as in the third panel of Figure 4. However, it is important to see that one need not go all the way to local representations to solve the

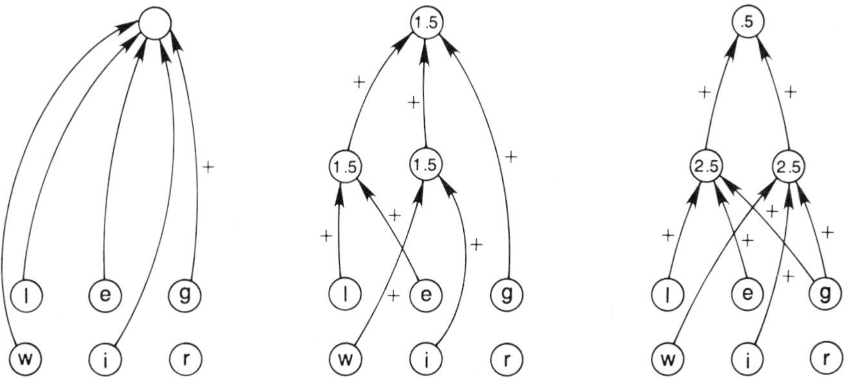

FIGURE 4. Three networks applied to the problem of determining which of the strings that can be made from *w* or *l*, followed by *i* or *e*, followed by *g* or *r* form words. Numbers on the connections represent connection strengths; numbers on the units represent the units' thresholds. A unit will take on an activation equal to 1 if its input exceeds it threshold; otherwise, its activation is 0.

problem facing our network. Conjunctive distributed representations will suffice.

The scheme illustrated in the second panel of the figure provides a conjunctive distributed representation. In this scheme, there are units for pairs of letters which, in this limited vocabulary, happen to capture the combinations that are essential for determining whether a string of letters is a word or not. These are, of course, the pairs *wi* and *le*. These conjunctive units, together with direct input to the decision unit from the *g* unit, are sufficient to construct a network which correctly classifies all strings consisting of a *w* or an *l*, followed by an *i* or an *e*, followed by a *g* or *r*.

This example illustrates that conjunctive coding is often necessary if distributed representations are to be used to solve problems that might easily be posed to networks. This same point could be illustrated with many other examples—the *exclusive or* problem is the classic example (Minsky & Papert, 1969). Other examples of problems requiring some sort of conjunctive encoding can be found in Hinton (1981a) and in Chapters 7 and 8. An application of conjunctive coding to a psychological model is found in Chapter 18.

Some problems (mostly very simple ones) can be solved without any conjunctive encoding at all, and others will require conjuncts of more than two units at a time. In general, it is hard to specify in advance just what "order" of conjunctions will be required. Instead, it is better to search for a learning scheme that can find representations that are adequate. The mechanisms proposed in Chapters 7 and 8 represent two steps toward this goal.

Implementing an Arbitrary Mapping Between Two Domains

The attentive reader will have noticed that a *local* representation can always be made to work in the example we have just considered. However, we have already discussed several reasons why distributed representations are preferable. One reason is that they can make more efficient use of parallel hardware than local representations.

This section shows how a distributed representation in one group of units can cause an appropriate distributed representation in another group of units. We consider the problem of implementing an *arbitrary* pairing between representations in the two groups, and we take as an example an extension of the previous one: the association between the visual form of a word and its meaning. The reason for considering an arbitrary mapping is that this is the case in which local representations seem most helpful. If distributed representations are better in this case, then they are certainly better in cases where there are underlying regularities that can be captured by regularities in the patterns of activation on the units in one group and the units in another. A discussion of the benefit distributed representations can provide in such cases can be found in Chapter 18.

If we restrict ourselves to monomorphemic words, the mapping from strings of graphemes onto meanings appears to be arbitrary in the sense that knowing what some strings of graphemes mean does not help one predict what a new string means.[8] This arbitrariness in the mapping from graphemes to meanings is what gives plausibility to models that have explicit word units. It is obvious that arbitrary mappings can be implemented if there are such units. A grapheme string activates exactly one word unit, and this activates whatever meaning we wish to associate with it (see Figure 5A). The semantics of similar grapheme strings can then be completely independent because they are mediated by separate word units. There is none of the automatic generalization that is characteristic of distributed representations.

Intuitively, it is not at all obvious that arbitrary mappings can be implemented in a system where the intermediate layer of units encodes the word as a distributed pattern of activity instead of as activity in a single local unit. The distributed alternative appears to have a serious drawback. The effect of a pattern of activity on other representations is the combined result of the individual effects of the active units in the pattern. So similar patterns tend to have similar effects. It appears that we are not free to make a given pattern have whatever effect we wish on the meaning representations without thereby altering the effects that other patterns have. This kind of interaction appears to make it difficult to implement arbitrary mappings from distributed representations of words onto meaning representations. We shall now show that these intuitions are wrong and that distributed representations of words can work perfectly well and may even be more efficient than single word units.

Figure 5B shows a three-layered system in which grapheme/position units feed into *word-set* units which, in turn, feed into *semantic* or *sememe* units. Models of this type, and closely related variants, have been analyzed by Willshaw (1981), V. Dobson (personal communication, 1984), and by David Zipser (personal communication, 1981); some further relevant analyses are discussed in Chapter 12. For simpli-

---

[8] Even for monomorphemic words there may be particular fragments that have associated meaning. For example, words starting with *sn* usually mean something unpleasant to do with the lips or nose (*sneer*, *snarl*, *snigger*), and words with long vowels are more likely to stand for large, slow things than words with short vowels (George Lakoff, personal communication). Much of Lewis Carroll's poetry relies on such effects.

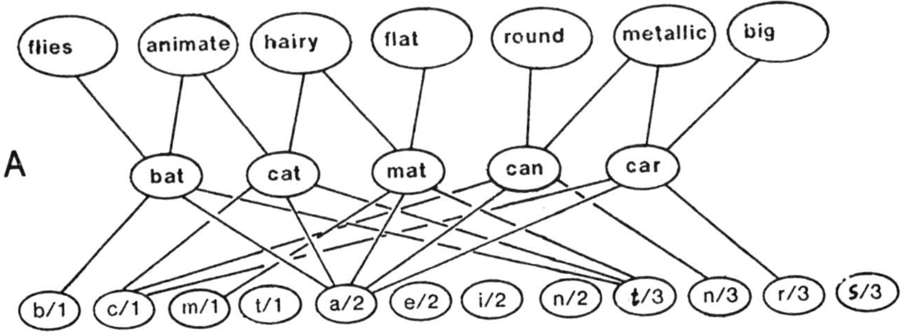

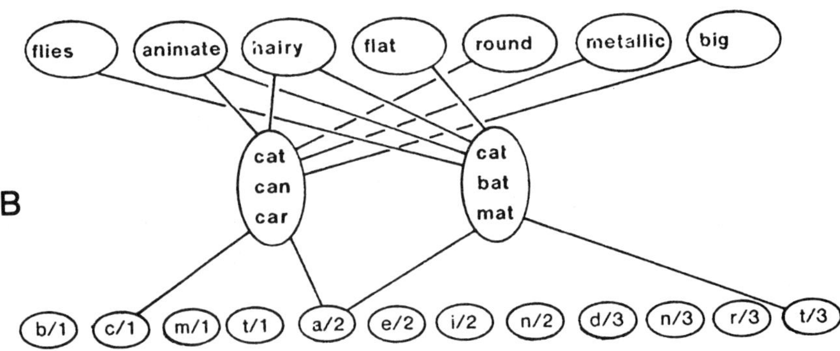

FIGURE 5. *A*: A three-layer network. The bottom layer contains units that represent particular graphemes in particular positions within the word. The middle layer contains units that recognize complete words, and the top layer contains units that represent semantic features of the meaning of the word. This network uses local representations of words in the middle layer. *B*: The top and bottom layers are the same as in (*A*), but the middle layer uses a more distributed representation. Each unit in this layer can be activated by the graphemic representation of any one of a whole set of words. The unit then provides input to every semantic feature that occurs in the meaning of *any* of the words that activate it. Only those word sets containing the word *cat* are shown in this example. Notice that the only semantic features which receive input from *all* these word sets are the semantic features of cat.

city, we shall assume that each unit is either active or inactive and that there is no feedback or cross-connections. These assumptions can be relaxed without substantially affecting the argument. A word-set unit is activated whenever the pattern of the grapheme/position units codes a word in a particular set. The set could be all the four-letter words starting with *HE*, for example, or all the words containing at least two *T*'s. All that is required is that it is possible to decide whether a word is in the set by applying a simple test to the activated grapheme/position units. So, for example, the set of all words meaning "nice" is *not* allowed as a word set. There is an implicit assumption that word meanings can be represented as sets of sememes. This is a contentious issue. There appears to be a gulf between the componential view in which a meaning is a set of features and the structuralist view in which the meaning of a word can only be defined in terms of its *relationships* to other meanings. Later in this chapter we consider one way of integrating these two views by allowing articulated representations to be built out of a number of different sets of active features.

Returning to Figure 5B, the question is whether it is possible to implement an arbitrary set of associations between grapheme/position vectors and sememe vectors when the word-set units are each activated by more than one word. It will be sufficient to consider just one of the many possible specific models. Let us assume that an active word-set unit provides positive input to all the sememe units that occur in the meaning of any word in the word set. Let us also assume that each sememe unit has a variable threshold that is dynamically adjusted to be just slightly less than the number of active word-set units. Only sememe units that are receiving input from every active word-set unit will then become active.

All the sememes of the correct word will be activated because each of these sememes will occur in the meaning of one of the words in the active word sets. However, additional sememes may also be activated because, just by chance, they may receive input from every active word-set unit. For a sememe to receive less input than its threshold, there must be at least one active word set that does not contain any word which has the sememe as part of its meaning. For each active word set the probability, i, of this happening is

$$i = (1 - p)^{(w - 1)}$$

where p is the proportion of words that contain the sememe and w is the number of words in the word set of the word-set unit. The reason for the term $w - 1$ is that the sememe is already assumed not to be part of the meaning of the correct word, so there are only $w - 1$ remaining words that could have it in their meaning.

Assume that when a word is coded at the graphemic level it activates u units at the word-set level. Each sememe that is not part of the word's meaning has a probability i of failing to receive input from each word-set unit. The probability, f, that all of these word-set units will provide input to it is therefore

$$f = (1 - i)^u$$
$$= [1 - (1 - p)^{(w-1)}]^u .$$

By inspection, this probability of a "false-positive" sememe reduces to zero when w is 1. Table 1 shows the value of f for various combinations of values of p, u, and w. Notice that if p is very small, f can remain negligible even if w is quite large. This means that distributed representations in which each word-set unit participates in the representation of many words do not lead to errors if the semantic features are relatively sparse in the sense that each word meaning contains only a small fraction of the total set of sememes. So the word-set units can be fairly nonspecific provided the sememe units are fairly specific (not shared by too many different word meanings). Some of the entries in the table make it clear that for some values of p, there can be a negligible chance of error even though the number of word-set units is considerably less than the number of words (the ratio of words to word-set units is w/u).

The example described above makes many simplifying assumptions. For example, each word-set unit is assumed to be connected to *every* relevant sememe unit. If any of these connections were missing, we could not afford to give the sememe units a threshold equal to the number of active word-set units. To allow for missing connections we could lower the threshold. This would increase the false-positive error rate, but the effect may be quite small and can be compensated by adding word-set units to increase the specificity of the word-level representations (Willshaw, 1981). Alternatively, we could make each word-set unit veto the sememes that do not occur in any of its words. This scheme is robust against missing connections because the absence of one veto can be tolerated if there are other vetos (V. Dobson, personal communication, 1984).

There are two more simplifying assumptions both of which lead to an underestimate of the effectiveness of distributed representations for the arbitrary mapping task. First, the calculations assume that there is no fine-tuning procedure for incrementing some weights and decrementing others to improve performance in the cases where the most frequent errors occur. Second, the calculations ignore cross-connections among the sememes. If each word meaning is a familiar stable pattern of sememes, there will be a strong "clean-up" effect which tends to suppress erroneous sememes as soon as the pattern of activation at the sememe level is sufficiently close to the familiar pattern for a particular word meaning. Interactions among the sememes also provide an explanation for the ability of a single grapheme string (e.g., *bank*) to elicit two quite different meanings. The *bottom-up* effect of the activated

TABLE 1

u	w	p	f	u	w	p	f	u	w	p	f
5	5	.2	0.071	5	5	.1	0.0048	5	5	.01	9.5×10^{-8}
5	10	.2	0.49	5	10	.1	0.086	5	10	.01	4.8×10^{-6}
5	20	.2	0.93	5	20	.1	0.48	5	20	.01	0.00016
5	40	.2	1.0	5	40	.1	0.92	5	40	.01	0.0036
5	80	.2	1.0	5	80	.1	1.0	5	80	.01	0.049
10	10	.2	0.24	10	10	.1	0.0074	10	10	.01	2.3×10^{-11}
10	20	.2	0.86	10	20	.1	0.23	10	20	.01	2.5×10^{-8}
10	40	.2	1.0	10	40	.1	0.85	10	40	.01	1.3×10^{-5}
10	80	.2	1.0	10	80	.1	1.0	10	80	.01	0.0024
10	160	.2	1.0	10	160	.1	1.0	10	160	.01	0.10
40	40	.2	0.99	40	40	.1	0.52	40	40	.01	2.7×10^{-20}
40	80	.2	1.0	40	80	.1	0.99	40	80	.01	3.5×10^{-11}
40	160	.2	1.0	40	160	.1	1.0	40	160	.01	0.00012
40	320	.2	1.0	40	320	.1	1.0	40	320	.01	0.19
40	640	.2	1.0	40	640	.1	1.0	40	640	.01	0.94
100	100	.2	1.0	10	100	.1	0.99	100	100	.01	9.0×10^{-21}
100	200	.2	1.0	10	200	.1	1.0	100	200	.01	4.8×10^{-7}
100	400	.2	1.0	100	400	.1	1.0	100	400	.01	0.16
100	800	.2	1.0	100	800	.1	1.0	100	800	.01	0.97

The probability, f, of a false-positive sememe as a function of the number of active word-set units per word, u, the number of words in each word-set, w, and the probability, p, of a sememe being part of a word meaning.

word-set units helps both sets of sememes, but as soon as *top-down* factors give an advantage to one meaning, the sememes in the other meaning will be suppressed by competitive interactions at the sememe level (Kawamoto & Anderson, 1984).

A simulation. As soon as there are cross-connections among the sememe units and fine-tuning of individual weights to avoid frequent errors, the relatively straightforward probabilistic analysis given above breaks down. To give the cross-connections time to clean up the output, it is necessary to use an iterative procedure instead of the simple "straight-through" processing in which each layer completely determines the states of all the units in the subsequent layer in a single, synchronous step. Systems containing cross-connections, feedback, and asynchronous processing elements are probably more realistic, but they are generally very hard to analyze. However, we are now beginning to discover that there are subclasses of these more complex systems that behave in tractable ways. One example of this subclass is described in more detail in Chapter 7. It uses processing elements that are inherently stochastic. Surprisingly, the use of stochastic elements makes these networks *better* at performing searches, *better* at learning, and *easier* to analyze.

A simple network of this kind can be used to illustrate some of the claims about the ability to "clean up" the output by using interactions among sememe units and the ability to avoid errors by fine-tuning the appropriate weights. The network contains 30 grapheme units, 20 word-set units, and 30 sememe units. There are no direct connections between grapheme and sememe units, but each word-set unit is connected to all the grapheme and sememe units. The grapheme units are divided into three sets of ten, and each three-letter word has one active unit in each group of ten (units can only have activity levels of 1 or 0). The "meaning" of a word is chosen at random by selecting each sememe unit to be active with a probability of 0.2. The network shown in Figure 6 has learned to associated 20 different grapheme strings with their chosen meanings. Each word-set unit is involved in the representation of many words, and each word involves many word-set units.

The details of the learning procedure used to create this network and the search procedure which is used to settle on a set of active sememes when given the graphemic input are described in Chapter 7. Here we simply summarize the main results of the simulation.

After a long period of learning, the network was able to produce the correct pattern of sememes 99.9% of the time when given a graphemic input. Removal of any one of the word-set units after the learning typically caused a slight rise in the error rate for several different words rather than the complete loss of one word. Similar effects have been observed in other distributed models (Wood, 1978). In our simulations, some of the erroneous responses were quite interesting. In 10,000 tests with a missing word-set unit there were 140 cases in which the model failed to recover the right sememe pattern. Some of these consisted of one or two missing or extra sememes, but 83 of the errors were exactly the pattern of sememes of some other word. This is a result of the cooperative interactions among the sememe units. If the input coming from the word-set units is noisy or underspecified as it may be when units are knocked out, the clean-up effect may settle on a similar but incorrect meaning.

This effect is reminiscent of a phenomenon called *deep dyslexia* which occurs with certain kinds of brain damage in adults. When shown a word and asked to read it, the subject will sometimes say a different word with a very similar meaning. The incorrect word sometimes has a very different sound and spelling. For example, when shown the word *PEACH*, the subject might say *APRICOT*. (See Coltheart, Patterson, & Marshall, 1980, for more information about acquired dyslexia.)

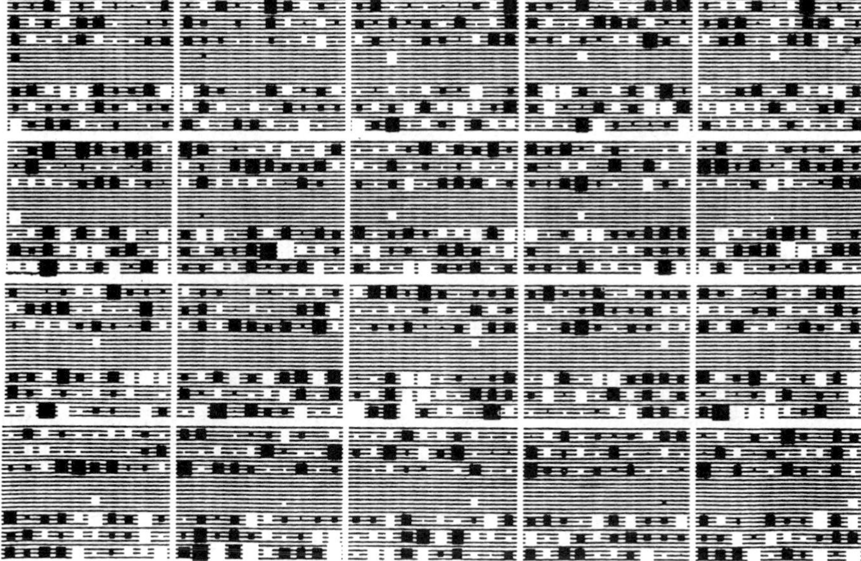

FIGURE 6. A compact display that shows all the connection strengths of the 20 units in the middle layer of a three-layer network. The network can map from a pattern of activity over the 30 units in the bottom layer (representing graphemes) to an associated pattern of activity over the 30 units of the top layer (representing sememes). Within each of the large rectangles that are used to depict middle-layer units, the 30 black and white rectangles at the top depict the weights of the connections to the top layer, and the 30 rectangles at the bottom depict the weights from the bottom layer. White rectangles are positive weights, black are negative, and the area of a rectangle depicts the magnitude of the weight. The single weight that occurs somewhere in the middle of a unit is its threshold (black means a positive threshold). The weights between the 30 units in the top layer are not shown in this display.

Semantic errors of this kind seem bizarre because it seems as if the subject must have accessed the lexical item *PEACH* in order to make the semantically related error, and if he can get to the lexical item why can't he say it? (These subjects may know and be able to say the words that they misread.) Distributed representations allow us to dispense with the rigid distinction between accessing a word and not accessing it. In a network that has learned the word *PEACH*, the graphemic representation of *PEACH* will cause approximately the right input to the sememe units, and interactions at the sememe level can then cause exactly the pattern of sememes for *APRICOT*. Another psychologically interesting effect occurs when the network relearns after it has been damaged. The network was damaged by adding noise to every connection that involved a word-set unit. This reduced the performance from 99.3% correct to 64.3%.[9] The network was then retrained and it exhibited very rapid relearning, much faster than its original rate of learning when its performance was 64.3% correct. This rapid recovery was predicted by a geometrical argument which shows that there is something special about a set of connection strengths that is generated by adding noise to a near-perfect set. The resulting set is very different from other sets of connection strengths that exhibit the same performance. (See Chapter 7 for further discussion.)

An even more surprising effect occurs if a few of the words are omitted from the retraining. The error rate for these words is substantially reduced as the retraining proceeds, even though the other grapheme-sememe pairings have no intrinsic relation to them because all the pairings were selected randomly. The "spontaneous" recovery of words that the network is not shown again is a result of the use of distributed representations. *All* the weights are involved in encoding the subset of the words that are shown during retraining, and so the added noise tends to be removed from *every* weight. A scheme that used a separate unit for each word would not behave in this way, so one can view spontaneous recovery of unrehearsed items as a qualitative signature of distributed representations.

STRUCTURED REPRESENTATIONS AND PROCESSES

In this section we consider two extensions of distributed representations. These extensions illustrate that the idea of distributed representations is consistent with some of the major insights from the field of artificial intelligence concerning the importance of structure in representations and processes. Perhaps because some proponents of distributed representations have not been particularly attuned to these issues, it is often unclear how structure is to be captured in a distributed representational scheme. The two parts of this section give some indication of the directions that can be taken in extending distributed representations to deal with these important considerations.

---

[9] The error rate was 99.3% rather than 99.9% in this example because the network was forced to respond faster, so the cooperative effects had less time to settle on the optimal output.

Representing Constituent Structure

Any system that attempts to implement the kinds of conceptual structures that people use has to be capable of representing two rather different kinds of hierarchy. The first is the "IS-A" hierarchy that relates types to instances of those types. The second is the part/whole hierarchy that relates items to the constituent items that they are composed of. The most important characteristics of the IS-A hierarchy are that known properties of the types must be "inherited" by the instances, and properties that are found to apply to all instances of a type must normally be attributed to the type. Earlier in this chapter we saw how the IS-A hierarchy can be implemented by making the distributed representation of an instance *include*, as a subpart, the distributed representation for the type. This representational trick automatically yields the most important characteristics of the IS-A hierarchy, but the trick can only be used for one kind of hierarchy. If we use the part/whole relationship between patterns of activity to represent the type/instance relationship between items, it appears that we cannot also use it to represent the part/whole relationship between items. We cannot make the representation of the whole be the sum of the representations of its parts.

The question of how to represent the relationship between an item and the constituent items of which it is composed has been a major stumbling block for theories that postulate distributed representations. In the rival, localist scheme, a whole is a node that is linked by labeled arcs to the nodes for its parts. But the central tenet of the distributed scheme is that different items correspond to *alternative* patterns of activity in the same set of units, so it seems as if a whole and its parts cannot both be represented at the same time.

Hinton (1981a) described one way out of this dilemma. It relies on the fact that wholes are not simply the sums of their parts. They are composed of parts that play particular roles within the whole structure. A shape, for example, is composed of smaller shapes that have a particular size, orientation, and position relative to the whole. Each constituent shape has its own spatial role, and the whole shape is composed of a set of shape/role pairs.[10] Similarly, a proposition is composed of objects that occupy particular semantic roles in the whole propositional

---

[10] Relationships between parts are important as well. One advantage of explicitly representing shape/role pairs is that it allows different pairs to support each other. One can view the various different locations within an object as slots and the shapes of parts of an object as the fillers of these slots. Knowledge of a whole shape can then be implemented by positive interactions between the various slot-fillers.

structure. This suggests a way of implementing the relationship between wholes and parts: The identity of each part should first be combined with its role to produce a single pattern that represents the *combination* of the identity and the role, and then the distributed representation for the whole should consist of the sum of the distributed representations for these identity/role combinations (plus some additional "emergent" features). This proposal differs from the simple idea that the representation of the whole is the sum of the representations of its parts because the subpatterns used to represent identity/role combinations are quite different from the patterns used to represent the identities alone. They do not, for example, contain these patterns as parts.

Naturally, there must be an access path between the representation of an item as a whole in its own right and the representation of that same item playing a particular role within a larger structure. It must be possible, for example, to generate the identity/role representation from two separate, explicit, distributed patterns one of which represents the identity and the other of which represents the role. It must also be possible to go the other way and generate the explicit representations of the identity and role from the single combined representation of the identity/role combination (see Figure 7).

The use of patterns that represent identity/role combinations allows the part/whole hierarchy to be represented in the same way as the type/instance hierarchy. We may view the whole as simply a particular instance of a number of more general types, each of which can be defined as the type that has a particular kind of part playing a particular role (e.g., men with wooden legs).

Sequential Symbol Processing

If constituent structure is implemented in the way described above, there is a serious issue about how many structures can be active at any one time. The obvious way to allocate the hardware is to use a group of units for each possible role within a structure and to make the pattern of activity in this group represent the identity of the constituent that is currently playing that role. This implies that only one structure can be represented at a time, unless we are willing to postulate multiple copies of the entire arrangement. One way of doing this, using units with programmable rather than fixed connections, is described in Chapter 16. However, even this technique runs into difficulties if more than a few modules must be "programmed" at once. However, people do seem to suffer from strong constraints on the number of structures of the same general type that they can process at once. The

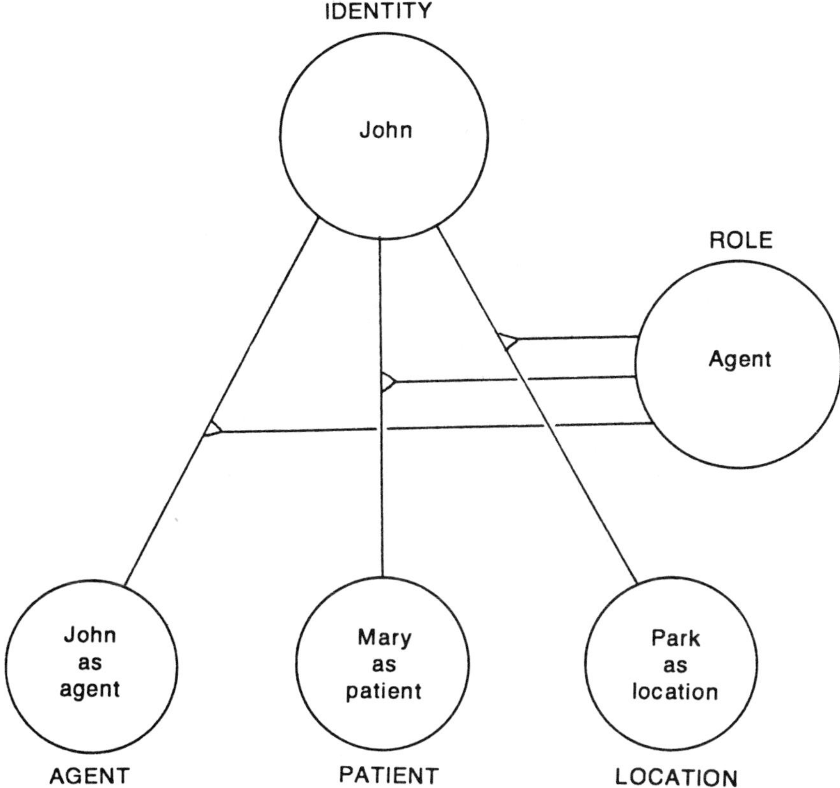

FIGURE 7. A sketch of the apparatus that might be necessary for combining separate representations of an identity and a role into a single pattern. Only one identity and only one role can be explicitly represented at a time because the identity and role groups can each have only one pattern of activity at a time. However, the various role groups allow many identity/role combinations to be encoded simultaneously. The small triangular symbols represent the ability of the pattern of activity in the group that explictly represents a role to determine which one of the many role groups is currently interacting with the identity group. This allows the identity occupying a particular role to be "read out" as well as allowing the reverse operation of combining an identity and a role.

sequentiality that they exhibit at this high level of description is initially surprising given the massively parallel architecture of the brain, but it becomes much easier to understand if we abandon our localist predelictions in favor of the distributed alternative which uses the parallelism to give each active representation a very rich internal structure that allows the right kinds of generalization and content-addressability. There may be some truth to the notion that people are sequential *symbol* processors if each "symbolic representation" is identified with a successive state of a large interactive network. See Chapter 14 for further discussion of these issues.

One central tenet of the sequential symbol processing approach (Newell, 1980) is the ability to focus on any part of a structure and to expand that into a whole that is just as rich in content as the original whole of which it was a part. The recursive ability to expand parts of a structure for indefinitely many levels and the inverse ability to package up whole structures into a reduced form that allows them to be used as constituents of larger structures is the essence of symbol processing. It allows a system to build structures out of things that refer to other whole structures without requiring that these other structures be represented in all their cumbersome detail.

In conventional computer implementations, this ability is achieved by using pointers. These are very convenient, but they depend on the use of addresses. In a parallel network, we need something that is functionally equivalent to arbitrary pointers in order to implement symbol processing. This is exactly what is provided by subpatterns that stand for identity/role combinations. They allow the full identity of the part to be accessed from a representation of the whole and a representation of the role that the system wishes to focus on, and they also allow explicit representations of an identity and a role to be combined into a less cumbersome representation, so that several identity/role combinations can be represented simultaneously in order to form the representation of a larger structure.

SUMMARY

Given a parallel network, items can be represented by activity in a single, local unit or by a pattern of activity in a large set of units with each unit encoding a microfeature of the item. Distributed representations are efficient whenever there are underlying regularities which can be captured by interactions among microfeatures. By encoding each piece of knowledge as a large set of interactions, it is possible to achieve useful properties like content-addressable memory and automatic generalization, and new items can be created without having to create new connections at the hardware level. In the domain of continuously varying spatial features it is relatively easy to provide a mathematical analysis of the advantages and drawbacks of using distributed represention.

Distributed representations *seem* to be unsuitable for implementing purely arbitrary mappings because there is no underlying structure and so generalization only causes unwanted interference. However, even for this task, distributed representations can be made fairly efficient and they exhibit some psychologically interesting effects when damaged.

There are several difficult problems that must be solved before distributed representations can be used effectively. One is to decide on the pattern of activity that is to be used for representing an item. The similarities between the chosen pattern and other existing patterns will determine the kinds of generalization and interference that occur. The search for good patterns to use is equivalent to the search for the underlying regularites of the domain. This learning problem is addressed in the chapters of Part II.

Another hard problem is to clarify the relationship between distributed representations and techniques used in artificial intelligence like schemas, or hierarchical structural descriptions. Existing artificial intelligence programs have great difficulty in rapidly finding the schema that best fits the current situation. Parallel networks offer the potential of rapidly applying a lot of knowledge to this best-fit search, but this potential will only be realized when there is a good way of implementing schemas in parallel networks. A discussion of how this might be done can be found in Chapter 14.

ACKNOWLEDGMENTS

This chapter is based on a technical report by the first author, whose work is supported by a grant from the System Development Foundation. We thank Jim Anderson, Dave Ackley, Dana Ballard, Francis Crick, Scott Fahlman, Jerry Feldman, Christopher Longuet-Higgins, Don Norman, Terry Sejnowski, and Tim Shallice for helpful discussions.

CHAPTER 4

PDP Models and General Issues in Cognitive Science

D. E. RUMELHART and J. L. MCCLELLAND

We are naturally optimistic about parallel distributed processing as a valuable framework for creating cognitive models. This does not mean, however, that there are no tough problems to be solved. Indeed, we have spent much of our effort convincing ourselves that PDP models could form a reasonable basis for modeling cognitive processes in general. In this chapter we shall address some of the objections that we and others have raised to the work and sketch our answers to these objections. However, we should like to say at the outset that we do not believe that any such general considerations as those discussed here will, in the end, bear much weight. The real proof is in the pudding. If PDP models are a valuable way to proceed, their usefulness will be proved in the added insights they bring to the particular substantive areas in which they are applied. The models we describe in later chapters are largely intended to constitute the beginnings of such a proof.

Many of the questions and issues raised below are addressed by material described in detail in other chapters in the book. For this reason, much of our present discussion is in the form of pointers to the relevant discussions. In this sense, this chapter serves not only as a discussion of our approach but as an overview of the issues and topics that are addressed in the chapters that follow.

SOME OBJECTIONS TO THE PDP APPROACH

PDP Models Are Too Weak

The one-layer perceptron. The most commonly heard objection to PDP models is a variant of the claim that PDP models cannot perform any interesting computations. One variant goes like this: "These PDP models sound a lot like perceptrons to me. Didn't Minsky and Papert show that perceptron-like models couldn't do anything interesting?" This comment represents a misunderstanding of what Minsky and Papert (1969) have actually shown. A brief sketch of the context in which Minsky and Papert wrote will help clarify the situation. (See Chapter 5 for a somewhat fuller account of this history.)

In the late 1950s and early 1960s there was a great deal of effort in the development of self-organizing networks and similar PDP-like computational devices. The best known of these was the *perceptron* developed by Frank Rosenblatt (see, for example, Rosenblatt, 1962). Rosenblatt was very enthusiastic about the perceptron and hopeful that it could serve as the basis both of artificial intelligence and the modeling of the brain. Minsky and Papert, who favored a *serial symbol processing* approach to artificial intelligence, undertook a very careful mathematical analysis of the perceptron in their 1969 book entitled, simply, *Perceptrons.*

The perceptron Minsky and Papert analyzed most closely is illustrated in Figure 1. Such machines consist of what is generally called a *retina*, an array of binary inputs sometimes taken to be arranged in a two-dimensional spatial layout; a set of *predicates*, a set of binary threshold units with fixed connections to a subset of units in the retina such that each predicate computes some local function over the subset of units to which it is connected; and one or more decision units, with modifiable connections to the predicates. This machine has only one layer of modifiable connections; for this reason we will call it a *one-layer* perceptron.

Minsky and Papert set out to show which functions can and cannot be computed by this class of machines. They demonstrated, in particular, that such perceptrons are unable to calculate such mathematical functions as parity (whether an odd or even number of points are on in the retina) or the topological function of connectedness (whether all points that are on are connected to all other points that are on either directly or via other points that are also on) without making use of absurdly large numbers of predicates. The analysis is extremely elegant and demonstrates the importance of a mathematical approach to analyzing computational systems.

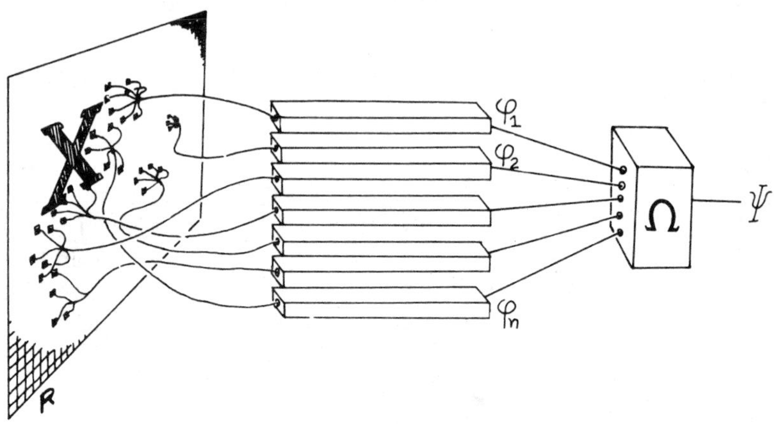

FIGURE 1. The one-layer perceptron analyzed by Minsky and Papert. (From *Perceptrons* by M. L. Minsky and S. Papert, 1969, Cambridge, MA: MIT Press. Copyright 1969 by MIT Press. Reprinted by permission.)

Minsky and Papert's analysis of the limitations of the one-layer perceptron, coupled with some of the early successes of the symbolic processing approach in artificial intelligence, was enough to suggest to a large number of workers in the field that there was no future in perceptron-like computational devices for artificial intelligence and cognitive psychology. The problem is that although Minsky and Papert were perfectly correct in their analysis, the results apply only to these simple one-layer perceptrons and not to the larger class of perceptron-like models. In particular (as Minsky and Papert actually conceded), it can be shown that a multilayered perceptron system, including several layers of predicates between the retina and the decision stage, can compute functions such as parity, using reasonable numbers of units each computing a very local predicate. (See Chapters 5 and 8 for examples of multilayer networks that compute parity). Similarly, it is not difficult to develop networks capable of solving the connectedness or inside/outside problem. Hinton and Sejnowski have analyzed a version of such a network (see Chapter 7).

Essentially, then, although Minsky and Papert were exactly correct in their analysis of the *one-layer perceptron,* the theorems don't apply to systems which are even a little more complex. In particular, it doesn't apply to multilayer systems nor to systems that allow feedback loops.

Minsky and Papert argued that there would not be much value to multilayer perceptrons. First, they argued that these systems are sufficiently unrestricted as to be vacuous. They pointed out, for example, that a universal computer could be built out of linear threshold units.

Therefore, restricting consideration of machines made out of linear threshold units is no restriction at all on what can be computed.

We don't, of course, believe that the class of models sketched in Chapter 2 is a small or restrictive class. (Nor, for that matter, are the languages of symbol processing systems especially restrictive.) The real issue, we believe, is that different algorithms are appropriate to different architectural designs. We are investigating an architecture in which cooperative computation and parallelism is natural. Serial symbolic systems such as those favored by Minsky and Papert have a natural domain of algorithms that differs from those in PDP models. Not everything can be done in one step without feedback or layering (both of which suggest a kind of "seriality"). We have been led to consider models that have both of these features. The real point is that we seek algorithms that are *as parallel as possible.* We believe that such algorithms are going to be closer in form to the algorithms which could be employed by the hardware of the brain and that the kind of parallelism we employ allows the exploitation of multiple information sources and cooperative computation in a natural way.

A further argument advanced by Minsky and Papert against perceptron-like models with hidden units is that there was no indication how such multilayer networks were to be trained. One of the appealing features of the one-layer perceptron is the existence of a powerful learning procedure, the perceptron convergence procedure of Rosenblatt. In Minsky and Papert's day, there was no such powerful learning procedure for the more complex multilayer systems. This is no longer true. Chapters 5, 6, 7, and 8 all provide schemes for learning in systems with hidden units. Indeed, Chapter 8 provides a direct generalization of the perceptron learning procedure which can be applied to arbitrary networks with multiple layers and feedback among layers. This procedure can, in principle, learn arbitrary functions including, of course, parity and connectedness.

The problem of stimulus equivalence. A second problem with early PDP models—and one that is not necessarily completely overcome by multilayer systems—is the problem of invariance or *stimulus equivalence*. An *A* is an *A* is an *A*, no matter where on the retina it appears or how large it is or how it is oriented; and people can, in general, recognize patterns rather well despite various transformations. It has always seemed elegant and natural to imagine that an *A*, no matter where it is presented, is normalized and then processed for recognition using stored knowledge of the appearance of the letter (Marr, 1982; Neisser, 1967).

In conventional computer programs this seems to be a rather straightforward matter requiring, first, normalization of the input, and, second, analysis of the normalized input. But in early PDP models it was never clear just how normalization could be made to work. Indeed, one of the main criticisms of perceptrons—one that is often leveled at more recent PDP models, too—is that they appear to provide no mechanism of attention, no way of focusing the machine on the analysis of a part of a larger whole and then switching to another part or back to the consideration of the whole.

While it is certainly true that certain PDP models lack explicit attentional mechanisms, it is far from true that PDP mechanisms are in principle incapable of exhibiting attentional phenomena. Likewise, while it is true that certain PDP models do not come to grips with the stimulus equivalence problem, it far from true that they are incapable of doing this in principle. To prove these points, we will describe a method for solving the stimulus equivalence problem that was described by Hinton (1981b). The idea is sketched in Figure 2. Essentially, it involves two sets of feature detectors. One (at the bottom of the figure) consists of *retinocentric* feature detectors and the other (above the retinocentric units) consists of canonical feature detectors. Higher order units that recognize canonical patterns (in this example, letters) sit above the canonical feature detectors and can have mutually excitatory connections to these feature detectors, just as in the interactive activation model of word recognition. What Hinton described was a method for mapping retinocentric feature patterns into canonical patterns. In general, for patterns in three-space, there are six degrees of freedom, but for present purposes we will consider only figures that are rotated around a fixed point in the plane. Here normalization simply amounts to a one-dimensional rotational transformation.

A fixed mapping from retinocentric units to canonical units would involve connecting each retinocentric feature detector to the corresponding canonical feature detector. Thus, to correct for a 90° clockwise rotation in the plane, we would want each retinal unit to project to the canonical unit corresponding to it at an offset of 90°.

How to implement variable mappings? Hinton proposed the use of a set of mapping units which act to switch on what amount to *dynamically programmable connections* from the retinocentric units to the canonical units. In the figure, three different mapping units are shown on the right: one that produces no rotation at all, one that produces a 90° clockwise rotation, and one that produces a 90° counterclockwise rotation. When one of these mapping units is active, it provides one of two inputs to a subset of the programmable connections. Thus, when the 90° clockwise mapping unit is active, it provides one of two inputs to the connection from each retinocentric unit to the central unit that corresponds to it under the 90° clockwise rotation. These connections are multiplicative—they pass the product of their two inputs on to the

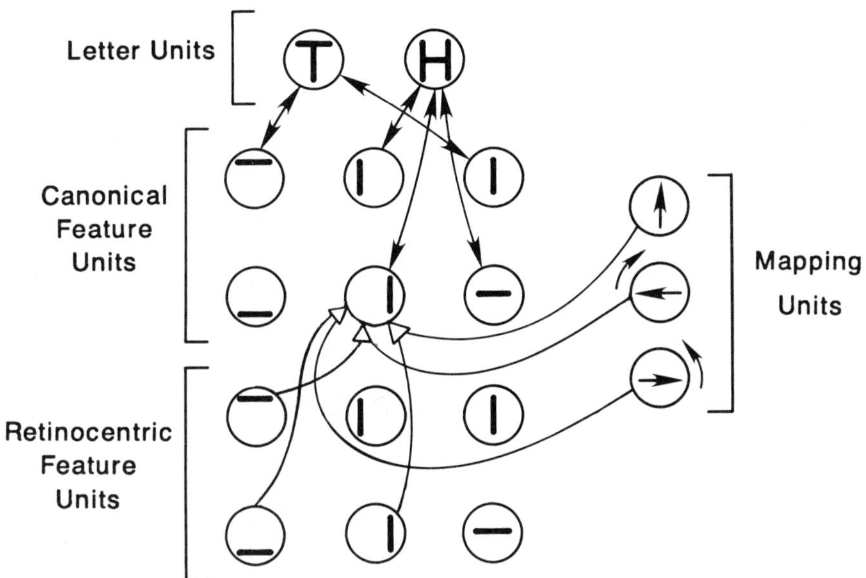

FIGURE 2. Hinton's (1981b) scheme for mapping patterns in one coordinate system into patterns in another coordinate system. At the top are two letter-detector units, with mutual excitatory connections to the six canonical feature units (the position and orientation of the line segment each of these detectors represents is indicated by the line segment in the "body" of each unit). At the bottom are six retinocentric feature units, and at the right are units corresponding to each of three different mappings from retinocentric to canonical features. (The arrows on the units indicate which direction in the retinocentric frame corresponds to upright in the canonical frame, and the arrow outside the unit indicates the nature of the transformation imposed on the retinocentric pattern). Each canonical unit receives three pairs of inputs, with each pair arriving at a multiplicative connection. These inputs are illustrated for one canonical unit only.

receiving unit. In this case, if a particular retinocentric feature is on and the 90° clockwise mapping unit is on, then the canonical feature corresponding to the active retinal feature will receive an excitatory input. If just one of the two inputs to the connection is on, no activation will flow to the central unit. In this way, when a mapping unit is active, it effectively programs the multiplicative connections needed to implement the corresponding mapping by activating one of the two inputs to each of the programmable connections.

Using this mechanism, it is possible to map from retinal to central coordinates if the mapping is known in advance. Object recognition can now proceed as follows: A mapping is chosen (perhaps on the basis of processing the preceding stimulus), and this is used to map a retinal input onto the canonical units. In a system involving variable *translational* mappings, in addition to the rotational mappings shown here, it would be possible to focus the attention of the system successively on each of several different patterns merely by changing the mapping. Thus it would not be difficult to implement a complete system for sequential processing of a series of patterns using Hinton's scheme (a number of papers have proposed mechanisms for performing a set of operations in sequence, including Grossberg, 1978, and Rumelhart & Norman, 1982; the latter paper is discussed in Chapter 1).

So far, we have described what amounts to a PDP implementation of a conventional pattern recognition system. First, map the pattern into the canonical frame of reference, then recognize it. Such is the procedure advocated, for example, by Neisser (1967) and Marr (1982). The demonstration shows that PDP mechanisms are in fact capable of normalization and of focusing attention successively on one pattern after another.

But the demonstration may also seem to give away too much. For it seems to suggest that the PDP network is simply a method for implementing standard sequential algorithms of pattern recognition. We seem to be left with the question, what has the PDP implementation added to our understanding of the problem?

It turns out that it has added something very important. It allows us to begin to see how we could solve the problem of recognizing an input pattern even in the case where we do not know in advance either what the pattern is or which mapping is correct. In a conventional sequential algorithm, we might proceed by serial search, trying a sequence of mappings and looking to see which mapping resulted in the best recognition performance. With Hinton's mapping units, however, we can actually perform this search in parallel. To see how this parallel search would work, it is first necessary to see how another set of multiplicative connections can be used to choose the correct mapping for a pattern given both the retinal input and the correct central pattern of activation.

In this situation, this simultaneous activation of a central feature and a retinal feature constitutes evidence that the mapping that connects them is the correct mapping. We can use this fact to choose the mapping by allowing central and retinal units that correspond under a particular mapping to project to a common multiplicative connection on the appropriate mapping unit. Spurious conjunctions will of course occur, but the correct mapping units will generally receive more conjunctions of canonical and retinal features than any other (unless there is an ambiguity due to a symmetry in the figure). If the mapping units compete so that the one receiving the most excitation is allowed to win, the network can settle on the correct mapping.

We are now ready to see how it may be possible to simultaneously settle on a mapping and a central representation using both sets of multiplicative connections. We simply need to arrange things so that when the retinal input is shown, each possible mapping we wish to consider is partially active. Each retinal feature then provides partial activation of the canonical feature corresponding to it under each of the mappings. The correct mapping allows the correct canonical pattern to be partially activated, albeit partially obscured by noise generated by the other partially activated mappings. Interactive activation between this central pattern and higher level detectors for the pattern then reinforces the elements of the pattern relative to the noise. This process by itself can be sufficient for correct recognition. Further cleanup of the central pattern can be achieved, though, by allowing the pattern emerging on the central units to work together with the input pattern to support the correct mapping over the other partially active mappings via the multiplicative connections onto the mapping units. This then results in further suppression of the noise. As this process continues, it eventually locks in the correct interpretation of the pattern, the correct canonical feature representation, *and* the correct mapping, all from the retinal input alone. Prior activation of the correct mapping facilitates the process of settling in, as do prior cues to the identity of the figure (see Rock, 1973, and Palmer, 1980, for evidence that these clues do facilitate performance), but are not, in general, essential unless the input is in fact ambiguous without them.

Hinton's mapping scheme allows us to make two points. First, that parallel distributed processing is in fact compatible with normalization and focusing of attention; and second, that a PDP implementation of a normalization mechanism can actually produce a computational advantage by allowing what would otherwise be a painful, slow, serial search to be carried out in a single settling of a parallel network. In general, Hinton's mapping system illustrates that PDP mechanisms are not restricted to fixed computations but are quite clearly capable of modulation and control by signals arising from other parts of an integrated processing system; and that they can, when necessary, be used to implement a serial process, in which each of several patterns is considered, one at a time.

The introduction of multiplicative or contingent connections (Feldman & Ballard, 1982) is a way of greatly increasing the power of PDP networks of fixed numbers of units (Marr, 1982; Poggio & Torre, 1978; see Chapter 10). It means, essentially, that each unit can perform computations as complex as those that could be performed by an entire one-layer perceptron, including both the predicates and the decision unit. However, it must also be noted that multiplicative connections are not strictly necessary to perform the required conjunctive computational operations. Nonlinear, quasi-multiplicative interactions can be implemented in a variety of ways. In the worst case, whole units could be dedicated to each multiplicative operation (as in the predicate layer of the perceptron).[1]

While Hinton's mapping mechanism indicates how attention might be implemented in PDP systems and imports some of the power of parallel distributed processing into the problem of simultaneously solving the mapping problem and the recognition problem, it does leave something to be desired. This is the fact that it allows only a single input pattern to be processed at one time since each pattern must be mapped separately onto the canonical feature units. Serial attention is sometimes required, but when we must resort to it, we lose the possibility of exploiting simultaneous, mutual constraints among several patterns. What has been processed before can still influence processing, but the ensemble of to-be-processed patterns cannot exert simultaneous, mutual influence on each other.

There is no doubt that sequentiality is forced upon us in some tasks—precisely those tasks in which the thought processes are extended over several seconds or minutes in time—and in such cases PDP mechanisms should be taken to provide potential accounts of the internal structure of a process evolving in time during the temporally extended structure of the thought process (see Chapter 14). But, in keeping with our general goals, we have sought to discover ways to maximally exploit simultaneous mutual constraints—that is, to maximize parallelism.

One mechanism which appears to make some progress in this direction is the connection information distribution mechanism described in Chapter 16. That mechanism uses multiplicative connections like those used in Hinton's model to send connection information out from a central knowledge store so that it can be used in local processing networks, each allocated to the contents of a different display location. The mechanism permits multiple copies of the same knowledge to be used at the same time, thereby effectively allowing tokens or local copies of patterns to be constructed from centrally stored knowledge of types in a parallel distributed processing system. These tokens then can interact with each other, allowing several patterns, all processed using the same centrally stored information, to exert simultaneous, mutual constraints on each other. Since these ideas, and their relation to attention, are discussed at length in Chapter 16, we will not elaborate on them further here.

---

[1] The linear threshold unit provides a quasi-multiplicative combination rule, and Sejnowski (1981) has described in detail how close approximation of the quantitative properties of multiplication of signals can be achieved by units with properties very much like those observed in real neurons.

Recursion. There are many other specific points that have been raised with respect to existing PDP models. Perhaps the most common one has to do with recursion. The ability to perform recursive function calls is a major feature of certain computational frameworks, such as augmented transition network (ATN) parsers (Woods, 1973; Woods & Kaplan, 1971), and is a property of such frameworks that gives them the capability of processing recursively defined structures such as sentences, in which embedding may produce dependencies between elements of a surface string that are indefinitely far removed from each other (Chomsky, 1957). It has often been suggested that PDP mechanisms lack the capacity to perform recursive computations and so are simply incapable of providing mechanisms for processing sentences and other recursively defined structures.

As before, these suggestions are simply wrong. As we have already seen, one can make an arbitrary computational machine out of linear threshold units, including, for example, a machine that can carry out all the operations necessary for implementing a Turing machine; the one limitation is that real biological systems cannot be Turing machines because they have finite hardware. In Chapter 14, however, we point out that with external memory aids (such as paper and pencil and a notational system) such limitations can be overcome as well.

We have not dwelt on PDP implementations of Turing machines and recursive processing engines because we do not agree with those who would argue that such capabilities are of the essence of human computation. As anyone who has ever attempted to process sentences like "The man the boy the girl hit kissed moved" can attest, our ability to process even moderate degrees of center-embedded structure is grossly impaired relative to that of an ATN parser. And yet, the human ability to use semantic and pragmatic contextual information to facilitate comprehension far exceeds that of any existing sentence processing machine we know of.

What is needed, then, is not a mechanism for flawless and effortless processing of center-embedded constructions. Compilers of computer languages generally provide such facilities, and they are powerful tools, but they have not demonstrated themselves sufficient for processing natural language. What is needed instead is a parser built from the kind of mechanism which facilitates the simultaneous consideration of large numbers of mutual and interdependent constraints. The challenge is to show how those processes that others have chosen to explain in terms of recursive mechanisms can be better explained by the kinds of processes natural for PDP networks.

This challenge is one that has not yet been fully met. However, some initial steps toward a PDP model of language processing are described in Chapter 19. The model whose implementation is described in that chapter illustrates how a variety of different constraints may be combined by PDP models to aid in the assignment of underlying roles to the constituents of sentences. The chapter also provides a discussion of three different ways in which the model could be extended to process embedded clauses in a way that is roughly consistent with human capabilities and limitations in this regard.

We do not claim to have solved these problems. Our existing models have limitations and much remains to be done. Our explorations have just begun. The question is not, is the job done—no computational framework can claim much on this score. The question instead is, can more progress be made through further exploration of the PDP perspective on the microstructure of cognition? The discovery of multilayer learning rules, the use of multiplicative connections to implement transformations of input patterns, the distribution of connection information, and the host of other developments described throughout this book, indicate to us that the answer to the question is "yes."

PDP Models Are Not Cognitive

We have observed that the cooperative character of parallel distributed processing often allows us to account for behavior which has previously been attributed to the application of specific rules of grammar or rules of thought. This has sometimes led us to argue that lawful behavior is not necessarily *rule-driven* behavior. Here, we must distinguish between *rules* and *regularities.* The bouncing ball and the orbiting planet exhibit regularities in their behavior, but neither is applying rules. We have demonstrated the power of this approach in our earlier work on word perception (McClelland & Rumelhart, 1981; Rumelhart & McClelland, 1982) and on the learning of English morphology (Chapter 18). In these cases we have been able to show how the apparent application of rules could readily *emerge* from interactions among simple processing units rather than from application of any higher level rules.

Some have viewed our argument against explicit rules as an argument against the cognitive approach to psychology. We do not agree. We believe that we are studying the *mechanisms* of cognition. The application of a rule (e.g., the firing of a production) is neither more nor less cognitive than the activation of our units. The real character of cognitive science is the attempt to explain mental phenomena through an understanding of the mechanisms which underlie those phenomena.

A related claim that some people have made is that our models appear to share much in common with behaviorist accounts of behavior. While they do involve simple mechanisms of learning, there is a crucial difference between our models and the radical behaviorism of Skinner and his followers. In our models, we are explicitly concerned with the problem of internal representation and mental processing, whereas the radical behaviorist explicitly denies the scientific utility and even the validity of the consideration of these constructs. The training of hidden units is, as is argued in Chapters 5 to 8, the construction of internal representations. The models described throughout the book all concern internal mechanisms for activating and acquiring the ability to activate appropriate internal representations. In this sense, our models must be seen as completely antithetical to the radical behaviorist program and strongly committed to the study of representation and process.

PDP Models Are the Wrong Level of Analysis

It is sometimes said that although PDP models are perfectly correct, they are at the wrong level of analysis and therefore not relevant to psychological data.[2] For example, Broadbent (1985) has argued that psychological evidence is irrelevant to our argument about distributed memory because the distribution assumption is only meaningful at what Marr (1982) has called the *implementational* (physiological) level and that the proper psychological level of description is the *computational* level.

The issues of levels of analysis and of theorizing is difficult and requires a good deal of careful thought. It is, we believe, largely an issue of scientific judgement as to what features of a lower level of analysis are relevant to a higher one. We are quite sure that it is not a matter for prescription. We begin our response to this objection with a review of Marr's analysis and his three levels of description. We then suggest that indeed our models are stated at the same level (in Marr's sense) as most traditional models from cognitive science. We then describe other senses of levels, including one in which higher level accounts can be said to be convenient approximations to lower level accounts. This sense comes closest to capturing our view of the

---

[2] The following discussion is based on a paper (Rumelhart & McClelland, 1985) written in response to a critique by Donald Broadbent (1985) on our work on distributed memory (cf. Chapter 17 and McClelland & Rumelhart, 1985).

relation between our PDP models and other traditional information processing models.

Marr's Notion of Levels

David Marr (1982) has provided an influential analysis of the issue of levels in cognitive science. Although we are not sure that we agree entirely with Marr's analysis, it is thoughtful and can serve as a starting point. Whereas Broadbent acknowledges only two levels of theory, the computational and the implementational, Marr actually proposes three, the *computational*, the *algorithmic*, and the *implementational* levels. Table 1 gives a description of Marr's three levels. We believe that PDP models are generally stated at the algorithmic level and are primarily aimed at specifying the representation of information and the processes or procedures involved in cognition. Furthermore, we agree with Marr's assertions that "each of these levels of description will have their place" and that they are "logically and causally related." Thus, no particular level of description is independent of the others. There is an implicit computational theory in PDP models as well as an appeal to certain implementational (physiological) considerations. We believe this to be appropriate. It is clear that different algorithms are more naturally implemented on different types of hardware and, therefore, information about the implementation can inform our hypotheses at the algorithmic level.

TABLE 1

THE THREE LEVELS AT WHICH ANY MACHINE CARRYING OUT INFORMATION PROCESSING TASKS MUST BE UNDERSTOOD

Computational Theory	Representation and Algorithm	Hardware Implementation
What is the goal of the computation, why is it appropriate, and what is the logic of the strategy by which it can be carried out?	How can this computational theory be implemented? In particular, what is the representation for the input and output, and what is the algorithm for the transformation?	How can the representation and algorithm be realized physically?

Note. From *Vision* by D. Marr, 1982, San Francisco: W. H. Freeman. Copyright 1982 by W. H. Freeman. Reprinted by permission.

Computational models, according to Marr, are focused on a formal analysis of the problem the system is solving—not the methods by which it is solved. Thus, in linguistics, Marr suggests that Chomsky's (1965) view of a *competence* model for syntax maps most closely onto a *computational* level theory, whereas a psycholinguistic theory is more of a *performance* theory concerned with how grammatical structure might actually be computed. Such a theory is concerned with the algorithmic level of description. It is the algorithmic level at which we are concerned with such issues as efficiency, degradation of performance under noise or other adverse conditions, whether a particular problem is easy or difficult, which problems are solved quickly and which take a long time to solve, how information is represented, etc. These are all questions to which psychological inquiry is directed and to which psychological data is relevant. Indeed, it would appear that this is the level to which psychological data speaks most strongly. At the computational level, it does not matter whether the theory is stated as a program for a Turing machine, as a set of axioms, or as a set of rewrite rules. It does not matter how long the computation takes or how performance of the computation is affected by "performance" factors such as memory load, problem complexity, etc. It doesn't matter how the information is represented, as long as the representation is rich enough, in principle, to support computation of the required function. The question is simply *what function* is being computed, not *how* is it being computed.

Marr recommends that a good strategy in the development of theory is to begin with a careful analysis of the goal of a particular computation and a formal analysis of the problem that the system is trying to solve. He believes that this top-down approach will suggest plausible algorithms more effectively than a more bottom-up approach. Thus, the computational level is given some priority. However, Marr certainly does not propose that a theory at the computational level of description is an adequate psychological theory.

As psychologists, we are committed to an elucidation of the algorithmic level. We have no quarrel with Marr's top-down approach as a strategy leading to the discovery of cognitive algorithms, though we have proceeded in a different way. We emphasize the view that the various levels of description are interrelated. Clearly, the algorithms must, at least roughly, compute the function specified at the computational level. Equally clearly, the algorithms must be computable in amounts of time commensurate with human performance, using the kind and amount of hardware that humans may reasonably be assumed to possess. For example, any algorithm that would require more specific events to be stored separately than there are synapses in the brain should be given a lower plausibility rating than those that require much less storage. Similarly, in the time domain, those algorithms that would require more than one serial step every millisecond or so would seem poor candidates for implementation in the brain (Feldman & Ballard, 1982).

In short, the claim that our models address a fundamentally different level of description than other psychological models is based on a failure to acknowledge the primary level of description to which much psychological theorizing is directed. At this level, our models should be considered as *competitors* of other models as a means of explaining psychological data.

Other notions of levels. Yet we do believe that in some sense PDP models are at a different level than other cognitive models such as prototype theories or schema theory. The reason is that there is more between the computational and the implementational levels than is dreamt of, even in Marr's scheme. Many of our colleagues have challenged our approach with a rather different conception of levels borrowed from the notion of levels of programming languages. It might be argued that a model such as, say, schema theory or the ACT* model of John R. Anderson (1983) is a statement in a "higher level" language analogous, let us say, to the Pascal or LISP programming languages and that our distributed model is a statement in a "lower level" theory that is, let us say, analogous to the assembly code into which higher level programs can be compiled. Both Pascal and assembler, of course, are considerably above the hardware level, though the latter may in some sense be closer to the hardware and more machine dependent than the former.

From this point of view one might ask why we are mucking around trying to specify our algorithms at the level of assembly code when we could state them more succinctly in a high-level language. We believe that most people who raise the levels issue with regard to our models have a relationship something like this in mind. People who adopt this notion have no objection to our models. They only believe that psychological models are more simply and easily stated in an equivalent higher level language—so why bother?

We believe that the programming language analogy is very misleading, unless it is analyzed more carefully. The relationship between a Pascal program and its assembly code counterpart is very special indeed. It is necessary for the Pascal and assembly language to map *exactly* onto one another only when the program was *written* in Pascal and the assembly code was compiled from the Pascal version. Had the original "programming" taken place in assembler, there is no guarantee that such a relationship would exist. Indeed, Pascal code will, in general, compile into only a small fraction of the possible assembly code programs that could be written. Since there is every reason to suppose that most of the programming that might be taking place in the brain is taking place at a "lower level" rather than a "higher level," it seems unlikely that some particular higher level description will be identical to some particular lower level description. We may be able to capture the actual code approximately in a higher level language—and it may often be useful to do so—but this does not mean that the higher level language is an adequate characterization.

There is still another notion of levels which illustrates our view. This is the notion of levels implicit in the distinction between Newtonian mechanics on the one hand and quantum theory on the other.[3] It might be argued that conventional symbol processing models are macroscopic accounts, analogous to Newtonian mechanics, whereas our models offer more microscopic accounts, analogous to quantum theory. Note, that over much of their range, these two theories make precisely the same predictions about behavior of objects in the world. Moreover, the Newtonian theory is often much simpler to compute with since it involves discussions of entire objects and ignores much of their internal structure. However, in some situations Newtonian theory breaks down. In these situations we must rely on the microstructural account of quantum theory. Through a thorough understanding of the relationship between the Newtonian mechanics and quantum theory we can understand that the macroscopic level of description may be *only an approximation* to the more microscopic theory. Moreover, in physics, we understand just when the macrotheory will fail and the microtheory must be invoked. We understand the macrotheory as a useful formal tool by virtue of its relationship to the microtheory. In this sense the objects of the macrotheory can be viewed as *emerging* from interactions of the particles described at the microlevel.

The basic perspective of this book is that many of the constructs of macrolevel descriptions such as schemata, prototypes, rules, productions, etc. can be viewed as emerging out of interactions of the microstructure of distributed models. These points are most explicitly considered in Chapters 6, 14, 17, and 18. We view macrotheories as approximations to the underlying microstructure which the distributed model presented in our paper attempts to capture. As approximations they are often useful, but in some situations it will turn out that an examination of the microstructure may bring much deeper insight. Note for example, that in a conventional model of language acquisition, one has to make very delicate decisions about the exact circumstances under which a new rule will be added to the rule system. In our PDP models no such decision need be made. Since the analog to a rule is

---

[3] This analogy was suggested to us by Paul Smolensky.

not necessarily discrete but simply something that may emerge from interactions among an ensemble of processing units, there is no problem with having the functional equivalent of a "partial" rule. The same observation applies to schemata (Chapter 14), prototypes and logogens (Chapter 18), and other cognitive constructs too numerous to mention. Thus, although we imagine that rule-based models of language acquisition—the logogen model, schema theory, prototype theory, and other macrolevel theories—may all be more or less valid approximate macrostructural descriptions, we believe that the actual algorithms involved cannot be represented precisely in any of those macrotheories.

It may also be, however, that some phenomena are too complex to be easily represented as PDP models. If these phenomena took place at a time frame over which a macrostructural model was an adequate approximation, there is no reason that the macrostructural model ought not be applied. Thus, we believe that the concepts of symbols and symbol processing can be very useful. Such models may sometimes offer the simplest accounts. It is, however, important to keep in mind that these models are approximations and should not be pushed too far. We suspect that when they are, some account similar to our PDP account will again be required. Indeed, a large part of our own motivation for exploring the PDP approach came from the failure of schema theory to provide an adequate account of knowledge application even to the task of understanding very simple stories.

Lest it may seem that we have given too much away, however, it should be noted that as we develop clearer understandings of the microlevel models, we may wish to formulate rather different macrolevel models. As pointed out in Chapter 3, PDP mechanisms provide a powerful alternative set of macrolevel primitives.[4]

Imagine a computational system that has as a primitive, "Relax into a state that represents an optimal global interpretation of the current input." This would be, of course, an extremely powerful place to begin building up a theory of higher level computations. Related primitives would be such things as "Retrieve the representation in memory best matching the current input, blending into it plausible reconstructions of details missing from the original memory trace," and "Construct a dynamic configuration of knowledge structures that captures the present situation, with variables instantiated properly." These sorts of primitives would be unthinkable in most conventional approaches to higher level cognition, but they are the kinds of emergent properties that PDP mechanisms give us, and it seems very likely that the availability of

---

[4] We thank Walter Schneider for stressing in his comments on an earlier draft of this chapter the importance of the differences between the computational primitives offered by PDP and those offered by other formalisms for modeling cognitive processes.

such primitives will change the shape of higher level theory considerably.

PDP mechanisms may also place some constraints on what we might realistically ask for in the way of computational primitives because of the costs of implementing certain kinds of computations in parallel hardware in a single relaxation search. The parallel matching of variablized productions is one case in point. Theories such as ACT* (J. R. Anderson, 1983) assume that this can be done without worrying about the implementation and, therefore, provide no principled accounts of the kinds of crosstalk exhibited in human behavior when processing multiple patterns simultaneously. However, it appears to be a quite general property of PDP mechanisms that they will exhibit crosstalk when processing multiple patterns in parallel (Hinton & Lang, 1985; Mozer, 1984; see Chapters 12 and 16).

High-level languages often preserve some of the character of the lower level mechanisms that implement them, and the resource and time requirements of algorithms drastically depends on the nature of the underlying hardware. Higher level languages that preserve the character of PDP mechanisms and exploit the algorithms that are effective descriptions of parallel networks are not here yet, but we expect such things to be coming along in the future. This will be a welcome development, in our view, since certain aspects of cognitive theory have been too strongly influenced by the discrete, sequential algorithms available for expression in most current high-level languages.

As we look closely, both at the hardware in which cognitive algorithms are implemented and at the fine structure of the behavior that these algorithms are designed to capture, we begin to see why it may be appropriate to formulate models which come closer to describing the microstructure of cognition. The fact that our microstructural models can account for many of the facts about the representation of general and specific information, for example, as discussed in Chapter 18, makes us ask why we should view constructs like logogens, prototypes, and schemata as anything other than convenient approximate descriptions of the underlying structure of memory and thought.

Reductionism and Emergent Properties

A slightly different, though related, argument is that the PDP enterprise is an exercise in reductionism—an exercise in which all of psychology is reduced to neurophysiology and ultimately to physics. It is argued that coherent phenomena which emerge at any level (psychology or physics or sociology) require their own language of description and explanation and that we are denying the essence of what is cognitive by reducing it to units and connections rather than adopting a more psychologically relevant language in our explanations.

We do not classify our enterprise as reductionist, but rather as interactional. We understand that new and useful concepts emerge at different levels of organization. We are simply trying to *understand* the essence of cognition as a property emerging from the *interactions* of connected units in networks.

We certainly believe in emergent phenomena in the sense of phenomena which could never be understood or predicted by a study of the lower level elements in isolation. These phenomena are functions of the particular kinds of groupings of the elementary units. In general, a new vocabulary is useful to talk about aggregate phenomena rather than the characteristics of isolated elements. This is the case in many fields. For example, we could not know about diamonds through the study of isolated atoms; we can't understand the nature of social systems through the study of isolated individuals; and we can't understand the behavior of networks of neurons from the study of isolated neurons. Features such as the hardness of the diamond is understandable through the interaction of the carbon atoms and the way they line up. The whole is different than the *sum* of the parts. There are nonlinear interactions among the parts. This does not, however, suggest that the nature of the lower level elements is irrelevant to the higher level of organization—on the contrary, the higher level is, we believe, to be understood primarily through the study of the interactions among lower level units. The ways in which units interact is not predictable from the lower level elements as isolated entities. It is, however, predictable *if* part of our study involves the interactions among these lower level units. We *can* understand why diamonds are hard, not as an isolated fact, but because we understand how the atoms of carbon can line up to form a perfect lattice. This is a feature of the aggregate, not of the individual atom, but the features of the atom are necessary for understanding the aggregate behavior. Until we understand that, we are left with the unsatisfactory statement that diamonds are hard, period. A useful fact, but not an explanation. Similarly, at the social level, social organizations cannot be understood without understanding the individuals which make up the organization. Knowing about the individuals tells us little about the structure of the organization, but we can't *understand* the structure of the higher level organizations without knowing a good deal about individuals and how they function. This is the sense of emergence we are comfortable with. We believe that it is entirely consistent with the PDP view of cognition.

There is a second, more practical reason for rejecting radical reductionism as a research strategy. This has nothing to do with emergence;

it has to do with the fact that we can't know everything and find out everything at once. The approach we have been arguing for suggests that to understand something thoroughly at some level requires knowledge at that level, plus knowledge of the lower levels. Obviously, this is impractical. In practice, even though there might be effects of lower levels on higher levels, one cannot always know them. Thus, attempting to formulate a description at this higher level as a first order of approximation is an important research strategy. We are forced into it if we are to learn anything at all. It is possible to learn a good deal about psychology without any reference whatsoever to any lower levels. This practical strategy is not, however, an excuse for ignoring what *is* known about the lower levels in the formulation of our higher level theories. Thus, the economist is wrong to ignore what we might know about individuals when formulating his theories. The chemist would be wrong to ignore what is known about the structure of the carbon atom in explaining the hardness of diamonds. We argued above that the view that the computational level is correct derives from experience with a very special kind of device in which the higher level was *designed* to give the right answers—exactly. In describing natural intelligence that can't, we suspect, be right—exactly. It can be a first order of approximation. As we learn more about a topic and as we look at it in more and more detail we are going to be forced to consider more and more how it might emerge (in the above sense) from the *interactions* among its constituents. Interaction is the key word here. Emergent properties occur whenever we have nonlinear interactions. In these cases the principles of interaction themselves must be formulated and the real theory at the higher level is, like chemistry, a theory of interactions of elements from a theory one level lower.

Not Enough Is Known From Neuroscience to Seriously Constrain Cognitive Theories

Many cognitive scientists believe that there will eventually be an understanding of the relationships between cognitive phenomena and brain functioning. Many of these same people feel, however, that the brain is such an exceptionally powerful computational device that it is capable of performing just about any computation. They suppose that facts now known from neuroscience place little or no restriction on what theories are possible at a cognitive level. In the meantime, they suppose, a top-down analysis of possible mechanisms of cognition can lead to an understanding of cognition that will stand independently of whatever might be discovered about brain functioning. Moreover, they believe that neuroscientists can be guided in their bottom-up search for an understanding of how the brain functions.

We agree with many of these sentiments. We believe that an understanding of the relationships between cognitive phenomena and brain functions will slowly evolve. We also believe that cognitive theories can provide a useful source of information for the neuroscientist. We do not, however, believe that current knowledge from neuroscience provides no guidance to those interested in the functioning of the mind. We have not, by and large, focused on the kinds of constraints which arise from detailed analysis of particular circuitry and organs of the brain. Rather we have found that information concerning *brain-style* processing has itself been very provocative in our model building efforts. Thus, we have, by and large, not focused on *neural modeling* (i.e., the modeling of neurons), but rather we have focused on *neurally inspired* modeling of cognitive processes. Our models have not depended strongly on the details of brain structure or on issues that are very controversial in neuroscience. Rather, we have discovered that if we take some of the most obvious characteristics of brain-style processing seriously we are led to postulate models which differ in a number of important ways from those postulated without regard for the hardware on which these algorithms are to be implemented. We have found that top-down considerations revolving about a need to postulate parallel, cooperative computational models (cf. Rumelhart, 1977) have meshed nicely with a number of more bottom-up considerations of brain style processing.

There are many brain characteristics which ought to be attended to in the formulation of our models (see Chapters 20 and 21). There are a few which we have taken most seriously and which have most affected our thinking. We discuss these briefly below.

Neurons are slow. One of the most important characteristics of brain-style processing stems from the speed of its components. Neurons are much slower than conventional computational components. Whereas basic operations in our modern serial computers are measured in the nanoseconds, neurons operate at times measured in the milliseconds—perhaps 10s of milliseconds. Thus, the basic hardware of the brain is some 10^6 times slower than that of serial computers. Imagine slowing down our conventional AI programs by a factor of 10^6. More remarkable is the fact that we are able to do very sophisticated processing in a few hundred milliseconds. Clearly, perceptual processing, most memory retrieval, much of language processing, much intuitive reasoning, and many other processes occur in this time frame. That means that these tasks must be done in no more than 100 or so serial steps. This is what Feldman (1985) calls the *100-step program constraint.* Moreover, note that individual neurons probably don't compute very complicated functions. It seems unlikely that a single neuron computes a function much more complex than a single instruction in a digital computer. Imagine, again, writing an interesting program in even 1000 operations of this limited complexity of a serial computer. Evidently, the brain succeeds through *massive parallelism.* Thus, we conclude, the mechanisms of mind are most likely best understood as resulting from the cooperative activity of very many relatively simple processing units operating in parallel.

There is a very large number of neurons. Another self-evident, but important, aspect of brain-style processing is the very large number of processing units involved. Conventional estimates hold that there are on the order of 10^{10} to 10^{11} neurons in the brain. Moreover, each neuron is an *active* processing unit. This suggests parallelism on a very large scale indeed. An understanding of parallel computation involving a few hundred reasonably complex processors provides the wrong model. It may well be that it is the massive scale of the parallelism of the brain that gives it its amazing power.

Although the human brain is large, the number of neurons is not unlimited. It happens that our models sometimes push the limits of plausibility because of the large number of units they require. This is a real constraint, one that we and others have begun to take into account in evaluating our models (see Chapter 12 for a discussion of this issue).

Neurons receive inputs from a large number of other neurons. Another important feature of brain processing is the large fan-in and fan-out to and from each unit. Estimates vary, but single cortical neurons can have from 1,000 to 100,000 synapses on their dendrites and, likewise, can make from 1,000 to 100,000 synapses on the dendrites of other neurons. Generally, one or a small number of action potentials received are not enough to generate an action potential (see, for example, Chapter 20). This suggests that human computation does not involve the kind of logic circuits out of which we make our digital computers, but that it involves a kind of statistical process in which the single units do not make decisions, but in which decisions are the product of the cooperative action of many somewhat independent processing units. Reliability derives from the stability of the statistical behavior of large numbers of units. Again, this degree of connectivity should be contrasted with the number of immediate neighbors of processors in current parallel computers. Usually these numbers are measured in the tens (or less) rather than in the thousands. Moreover, this large degree of connectivity suggests that no neuron is very many synapses away from any other neuron. If, for argument's sake, we assume that every cortical neuron is connected to 1,000 other neurons and that the system forms a lattice, all of the neurons in the brain would be within, at most, four synapses from one another. Thus, large fan-in and fan-out leads to shallow networks. It should finally be noted that even though the fan-in and fan-out is large, it is not unlimited. As described in Chapter 12, the limitations can cause problems for extending some simple ideas of memory storage and retrieval.

Learning involves modifying connections. Another key feature of our models which derives from our understanding of learning mechanisms in the brain is that the *knowledge is in the connections* rather than in the units themselves. Moreover, learning is generally assumed to involve modifying connection strengths. There are real computational advantages to such a simple learning procedure. Its simplicity and homogeneity allow us to develop powerful learning procedures which work simply and incrementally. (See Chapters 5, 6, 7, 8; Chapters 11, 17, 18, 24, and 25 consider the implications of this view.)

Neurons communicate by sending activation or inhibition through connections. Communication among neurons involves simple excitatory and inhibitory messages. Only a few bits can be communicated per second. Thus, unlike other parallel message passing systems such as Hewitt's (1975) ACTOR system which allows arbitrary symbolic messages to be passed among its units, we require simple, signed numbers of limited precision. This means that the currency of our systems is not symbols, but excitation and inhibition. To the degree that symbols are required, they must emerge from this subsymbolic level of processing (Hofstadter, 1979).

Connections in the brain seem to have a clear geometric and topological structure. There are a number of facts about the pattern of connections in the brain which, we believe, are probably important, but which have not yet had a large impact on our models. First, most connections are rather short. Some are long (these tend to be excitatory), but not most. There are rather strong geometric and topological constraints. There is a rough mapping in that input parameters (such as spatial location in vision or frequency in audition) are mapped onto spatial extent in the brain. In general it seems that nearby regions in one part of the brain map onto nearby regions in another part of the brain. Moreover, there is a general symmetry of connections. If there are connections from one region of the brain to another, there are usually connections in the reverse direction. Some of these features have been implemented in our models, though, interestingly, most often for computational reasons rather than for biological verisimilitude. For example, rough symmetry was a feature of our earlier work on word perception (cf. McClelland & Rumelhart, 1981), and it is a feature of the work described in Chapters 6, 7, 14, 15, and 16. The error propagation learning rule of Chapter 8 requires a back path for an error signal to be propagated back through. In general, reciprocally interacting systems are very important for the kind of processing we see as characteristic of PDP models. This is the defining feature of *interactive activation* models. We have also employed the view that connections between systems are excitatory and those within a region are inhibitory. This is employed to advantage in Chapters 5 and 15.

The geometric structure of connections in the brain have not had much impact on our work. We generally have not concerned ourselves with *where* the units might physically be with respect to one another. However, if we imagine that there is a constraint toward the conservation of connection length (which there must be), it is easy to see that those units which interact most should be the closest together. If you add to this the view that the very high-dimensional space determined by the *number* of interconnections must be embedded into the two- or three-dimensional space (perhaps two and a half dimensions) of the cortex, we can see the importance of mapping the major dimensions physically in the geometry of the brain (see Ballard, in press, for a discussion of embedding high-dimensional spaces into two dimensions).

Information is continuously available. Another important feature of neural information processing is that the neurons seem to provide *continuously available output* (Norman & Bobrow, 1975). That is, there does not seem to be an appreciable decision phase during which a unit provides no output. Rather it seems that the state of a unit reflects its current input. To the degree that a unit represents a hypothesis and its activation level (instantaneous firing rate or probability of firing) represents the degree to which evidence favors that hypothesis, the activation level of the unit provides continuous information about the current evaluation of that hypothesis. This hypothesis was incorporated into the precursors of our own work on parallel distributed processing, especially the *cascade* model (McClelland, 1979) and the interactive model of reading (Rumelhart, 1977), and it is a feature of virtually all of the PDP models in this book.[5] Interestingly, this contrasts starkly with what used to be the standard approach, namely, *stage* models of information processing (Sternberg, 1969), and thereby offers a very

[5] Though some PDP models use discrete binary units (e.g., Hinton, 1981a; Hopfield, 1982), they generally use large numbers of these to represent any object, so that when a few of the units that form part of a pattern are on, the pattern can be said to be partially active.

different perspective on decision-making processes and the basic notion of stages.

Graceful degradation with damage and information overload. From the study of brain lesions and other forms of brain damage, it seems fairly clear there is not some single neuron whose functioning is essential for the operation of any particular cognitive process. While reasonably circumscribed *regions* of the brain may play fairly specific roles, particularly at lower levels of processing, it seems fairly clear that within regions, performance is characterized by a kind of *graceful degradation* in which the system's performance gradually deteriorates as more and more neural units are destroyed, but there is no single critical point where performance breaks down. This kind of graceful degradation is characteristic of such global degenerative syndromes as Alzheimer's disease (cf. Schwartz, Marin, & Saffran, 1979). Again, this is quite different from many serial symbol processing models in which the disruption of a single step in a huge program can catastrophically impact the overall performance of the system. Imagine the operation of a computer in which a particular instruction did not work. So long as that instruction was not used, there would be no effect on the system. However, when that instruction was employed in some process, that process simply would not work. In the brain it seems that the system is highly redundant and capable of operating with a loss in performance roughly similar in magnitude to the magnitude of the damage (see Chapter 12 for details). This is a natural performance characteristic of PDP models.

Distributed, not central, control. There is one final aspect of our models which is vaguely derived from our understanding of brain functioning. This is the notion that there is *no central executive* overseeing the general flow of processing. In conventional programming frameworks it is easy to imagine an executive system which calls subroutines to carry out its necessary tasks. In some information processing models this notion of an executive has been carried over. In these models, all processing is essentially *top-down* or *executive-driven*; if there is no executive, then no processing takes place at all.

Neuropsychological investigation of patients with brain damage indicates that there is no part of the cortex on whose operation all other parts depend. Rather it seems that all parts work together, influencing one another, and each region contributes to the overall performance of the task and to the integration into it of certain kinds of constraints or sources of information. To be sure, brainstem mechanisms control vital bodily functions and the overall state of the system, and certain parts of the cortex are critical for receiving information in particular modalities. But higher level functions seem very much to be characterized by distributed, rather than central control.

This point has been made most clearly by the Russian neuropsychologist Luria (1966; 1973). Luria's investigations show that for every integrated behavioral function (e.g., visual perception, language comprehension or production, problem solving, reading), many different parts of the cortex play a role so that damage to any part influences performance but is not absolutely crucial to it. Even the frontal lobes, most frequently associated with executive functions, are not absolutely necessary in Luria's view, in that some residual function is generally observed even after massive frontal damage (and mild frontal damage may result in no detectable symptomatology at all). The frontal lobes have a characteristic role to play, facilitating strategy shifts and inhibiting impulsive responding, but the overall control of processing can be as severely impaired by damage to parietal lobe structures that appear to be responsible for maintaining organized representations that support coordinated and goal-directed activity.

Our view of the overall organization of processing is similar to Luria's. We have come to believe that the notion of subroutines with one system "calling" another is probably not a good way to view the operation of the brain. Rather, we believe that subsystems may *modulate* the behavior of other subsystems, that they may provide constraints to be factored into the relaxation computation. An elaboration of some aspects of these ideas may be found in Chapter 14.

Relaxation is the dominant mode of computation. Although there is no specific piece of neuroscience which compels the view that brain-style computation involves relaxation, all of the features we have just discussed have led us to believe that the primary mode of computation in the brain is best understood as a kind of *relaxation system* (cf. Chapters 6, 7, 14, 15, and 21) in which the computation proceeds by iteratively seeking to satisfy a large number of weak constraints. Thus, rather than playing the role of wires in an electric circuit, we see the connections as representing constraints on the co-occurrence of pairs of units. The system should be thought of more as *settling into a solution* than *calculating a solution*. Again, this is an important perspective change which comes out of an interaction of our understanding of how the brain must work and what kinds of processes seem to be required to account for desired behavior.

As can be seen, this list does not depend on specific discoveries from neuroscience. Rather, it depends on rather global considerations. Although none of these general properties of the brain tell us in any detail how the brain functions to support cognitive phenomena, together they lead to an understanding of how the brain works that serves as a set of constraints on the development of models of cognitive processes. We find that these assumptions, together with those that derive from the constraints imposed by the tasks we are trying to account for, strongly influence the form of our models of cognitive processes.

PDP Models Lack Neural Realism

On the one hand, it is sometimes said—as indicated in the previous section—that there is little or no constraint to be gained through looking at the brain. On the other hand, it is often said that we don't look closely enough. There are many facts of neuroscience that are not factored directly into our models. Sometimes we have failed to capture the fine structure of neural processing in our models. Other times we have assumed mechanisms that are not known to exist in brains (see Chapter 20). One prominent example is the near-ubiquitous assumption that units can have both excitatory and inhibitory connections when it seems reasonably clear that most cortical units are either excitatory or inhibitory. If, as we argued above, it is important to understand the microstructure of cognition, why do we ignore such detailed characteristics of the actual physical processes underlying that microstructure?

To be sure, to the extent that our models are directly relevant to brains, they are at best coarse approximations of the details of neurophysiological processing. Indeed, many of our models are clearly intended to fall at a level between the macrostructure of cognition and the details of neurophysiology. Now, we do understand that some of our approximations may have ramifications for the cognitive phenomena which form our major area of interest; by missing certain details of neurophysiology, we may be missing out on certain aspects of brain function that would make the difference between an accurate account of cognitive-level phenomena and a poor approximation. Our defense is simply that we see the process of model building as one of successive approximations. We try to be responsive to information from both the behavioral and the neural sciences. We also believe that the key to scientific progress is making the right approximations and the right simplifications. In this way the structure can be seen most clearly. This point is considered further in Chapter 21.

We have been pleased with the structure apparent through the set of approximations and simplifications we have chosen to make. There are, however, a number of other facts from neuroscience that we have not included in most of our models, but that we imagine will be important when we learn how to include them. The most obvious of these is the fact that we normally assume that units communicate via numbers. These are sometimes associated with mean firing rates. In fact, of course, neurons produce spikes and this spiking itself may have some computational significance (see Chapters 7 and 21 for discussions of the possible computational significance of neural spiking). Another example of possibly important facts of neuroscience which have not played a role in our models is the diffuse pattern of communication which occurs by means of the dispersal of chemicals into various regions of the brain through the blood stream or otherwise. We generally assume that communication is point-to-point from one unit to another. However, we understand that diffuse communication can occur through chemical means and such communication may play an important role in setting parameters and modulating the networks so that they can perform rather different tasks in different situations. We have employed the idea of diffuse distribution of chemicals in our account of amnesia (Chapter 25), but, in general, we have not otherwise integrated such assumptions into our models. Roughly, we imagine that we are studying networks in which there is a fixed setting of such parameters, but the situation may well be much more complex than that. (See Chapter 24 for some discussion of the role of norepinephrine and other neuromodulators.)

Most of our models are homogeneous with respect to the functioning of our units. Some of them may be designated as inhibitory and others as excitatory, but beyond that, they are rarely differentiated. We understand that there are perhaps hundreds of kinds of neurons (see Chapter 20). No doubt each of these kinds play a slightly different role in the information processing system. Our assumptions in this regard are obviously only approximate. Similarly, we understand that there are many different kinds of neurotransmitters and that there are different systems in which different of these neurotransmitters are dominant. Again, we have ignored this difference (except for excitatory and inhibitory connections) and presume that as more is understood about the information processing implications of such facts we will be able to determine how they fit into our class of models.

It is also true that we have assumed a number of mechanisms that are not known to exist in the brain (see Chapter 20). In general, we have postulated mechanisms which seemed to be required to achieve certain important functional goals, such as, for example, the development of internal representations in multilayer networks (see Chapter 8). It is possible that these hypothesized mechanisms do exist in the brain but have not yet been recognized. In that sense our work could be considered as a source of hypotheses for neuroscience. It is also possible that we are correct about the computations that are performed, but that they are performed by a different kind of neural mechanism than our formulations seem at first glance to suggest. If this is the case, it merely suggests that the most obvious mapping of our models onto neural structures is incorrect.

A neuroscientist might be concerned about the ambiguity inherent in the fact that many of the mechanisms we have postulated could be implemented in different ways. From our point of view, though, this is not a serious problem. We think it useful to be clear about how our mechanisms *might* be implemented in the brain, and we would certainly be worried if we proposed a process that could not be implemented in the brain. But since our primary concern is with the computations themselves, rather than the detailed neural implementation of these computations, we are willing to be instructed by neuroscientists on which of the possible implementations are actually employed. This position does have its dangers. We have already argued in this chapter that the mechanism whereby a function is computed often has strong implications about *exactly what* function is being computed. Nevertheless, we have chosen a level of approximation which seems to us the most fruitful, given our goal of understanding the human information processing system.

We close this section by noting two different ways in which PDP models can be related to actual neurophysiological processes, apart from the possibility that they might actually be intended to model what is known about the behavior of real neural circuitry (see Chapters 23 and 24 for examples of models of this class). First, they might be intended as idealizations. In this approach, the emergent properties of systems of real neurons are studied by idealizing the properties of the individual neurons, in much the same way that the emergent properties of real gasses can be studied by idealizing the properties of the individual gas molecules. This approach is described at the end of Chapter 21. An alternative is that they might be intended to provide a higher level of description, but one that could be mapped on to a real neurophysiological implementation. Our interactive activation model of word recognition has some of this flavor, as do most of the models described in Chapters 14 through 19. Specifically with regard to the word recognition model, we do not claim that there are individual neurons that stand for visual feature, letter, and word units, or that they are connected together just as we proposed in that model. Rather, we really suppose that the physiological substrate provides a mechanism whereby various abstract informational states—such as, for example, the state in which the perceptual system is entertaining the hypothesis that the second letter in a word is either an *H* or an *A*—can give rise to other informational states that are contingent upon them.

Nativism vs. Empiricism

Historically, perceptron-like models have been associated with the idea of "random self-organizing" networks, the learning of arbitrary associations, very general, very simple learning rules, and similar ideas which show the emergence of structure from the *tabula rasa*. We often find, especially in discussion with colleagues from linguistics surrounding issues of language aquisition (see Chapters 18 and 19), that PDP models are judged to involve learning processes that are too general and, all in all, give too little weight to innate characteristics of language or other information processing structures. This feeling is brought out even more by demonstrations that some PDP learning mechanisms are capable of learning to respond to symmetry and of learning how to deal with such basic perceptual problems as perceptual constancy under translation and rotation (see Chapter 8). In fact, however, PDP models are, in and of themselves, quite agnostic about issues of nativism versus empiricism. Indeed, they seem to us to offer a very useful perspective on the issue of innate versus acquired knowledge.

For the purposes of discussion let us consider an organism that consists of a very large set of very simple but highly interconnected processing units. The units are assumed to be homogeneous in their properties except that some are specialized to serve as "input" units because they receive inputs from the environment and some are specialized to serve as "output" units because they drive the effectors of the system. The behavior of such a system is thus entirely determined by the pattern of inputs, the pattern of interconnections among the units, and the nature of and connections to the effectors. Note, that interconnections can have various strengths—positive, negative, and zero. If the strength of connection is positive, then activity in one unit tends to increase the activity of the second unit. If the strength of connection is negative, then the activity in the first unit tends to decrease the activity of the second unit. If the strength is zero, then activity of the first unit has no effect on the activity of the second.

In such a system the radical nativism hypothesis would consist of the view that all of the interconnections are genetically determined at birth and develop only through a biologically driven process of maturation. If such were the case, the system could have any particular behavior entirely wired in. The system could be designed in such a way as to respond differentially to human speech from other acoustic stimuli, to perform any sort of computation that had proven evolutionarily adaptive, to mimic any behavior it might observe, to have certain stimulus dimensions to which it was pretuned to respond, etc. In short, if all of the connections were genetically predetermined, the system could perform *any* behavior that such a system of units, interconnections, and effectors might ever be capable of. The question of what behaviors it actually did carry out would presumably be determined by evolutionary processes. In this sense, this simple PDP model is clearly consistent with a rabidly nativist world view.

The radical empiricist hypothesis, on the other hand, suggests that there are no a priori limits on how the network of interconnections could be constituted. Any pattern of interconnections is possible. What determines the actual set of connections is the pattern of experiences the system gets. In this sense there is no prior limit on the nature of language; any language that could be processed by such a network could be learned by such an organism. The only limitations would be very general ones due to the nature of the learning rule in the system. With a sufficiently powerful learning rule, the organism could organize itself into whatever state proved maximally adaptive. Thus, there would be no limitation on the degree to which the behavior of the system could adapt to its environment. It could learn completely arbitrary associations. In short, if all connections in the system were modifiable by experience, the system could learn to perform any behavior at all that such a system of units, interconnections, and effectors might ever be capable of. The question of what behaviors it actually did carry out would presumably be determined by the learning process and the patterns of inputs the system actually experienced. In this sense, the simple PDP model is clearly consistent with a rabidly empiricist world view.

Obviously, it would be a straightforward matter to find a middle ground between the radical nativist view and the radical empiricist view as we have laid them out. Suppose, for sake of argument, that we have an organism whose initial state is wholly determined genetically. Suppose further that all of the connections were modifiable so that whatever the start state, any pattern of interconnections could emerge through interaction of the organism with its environment.[6] In such a system as this we have, it seems to us, the benefits of both nativism and empiricism. Like good nativists, we have given the organism a starting point that has been selected by its evolutionary history. We have not, however, strapped the organism with the rigid predeterminism that traditionally goes along with the nativist view. If there are

6 Obviously both of these views are overstatements. Clearly the genes do not determine *every* connection at birth. Probably some sort of random processes are also involved. Equally clearly, not *every* pattern of interconnectivity is possible since the spatial layout of the neurons in the cortex, for example, surely limit the connectivity. Still, there is probably a good deal of genetic specification of neural connection, and there is a good deal of plasticity in the pattern of connectivities after birth.

certain patterns of behavior which, in evolutionary time, have proven to be useful (such as sucking, reaching, or whatever) we can build them in, but we leave the organism free to modify or completely reverse any of these behavioral predispositions.[7] At the same time, we have the best of the empiricist view—namely, we place no a priori limitations on how the organism may adapt to its environment. We do, however, throw out the weakest aspect of the empiricist dogma—namely, the idea of the *tabula rasa* (or totally random net) as a starting point. The organism could start at whatever initial state its evolutionary history prepared it for.

Perhaps, at this stage, all of this seems painfully obvious. It seems obvious to us too, and nevertheless, it gives us a new perspective on the nativism/empiricism issue. The issue is not what is *the* set of predetermined modules as some would suggest (cf. Fodor, 1983). On this view it seems quite reasonable, we submit, that to the degree that there are modules, they are co-determined by the start state of the system (the genetic predisposition) and by the environment. (We take a module to be roughly a set of units which are powerfully interconnected among themselves and relatively weakly connected to units outside of the set; of course, this concept admits all gradations of modularity, just as our view of schemata allows all degrees of schematization of knowledge.) There is, on this view, no such thing as "hardwiring." Neither is there any such thing as "software." There are only connections. All connections are in some sense hardwired (in as much as they are physical entities) and all are software (in as much as they can be changed.) Thus, it may very well be that there is a part of the network prewired to deal with this or that processing task. If that task is not relevant in the organism's environment, that part of the network can be used for something else. If that part of the network is damaged, another part can come to play the role "normally" carried out by the damaged portion. These very properties have been noted characteristics of the brain since Hughlings-Jackson's work in the late 19th century (e.g., Jackson, 1869/1958); Jackson pointed them out as difficulties for the strict localizationist views then popular among students of the brain. Note too that our scheme allows for the organism to be especially sensitive to certain relationships (such as the relationship between nausea and eating, for which there might be stronger or more direct prewired

[7] Here again, our organism oversimplifies a bit. It appears that some parts of the nervous system—particularly lower level, reflexive, or regulatory mechanisms—seem to be prewired and subject only to control by trainable modulatory connections to higher level, more adaptive mechanisms, rather than to be directly modifiable themselves; for discussion see Teitelbaum (1967) and Gallistel (1980).

connections) while at the same time allowing quite arbitrary associations to be learned.

Finally, it should be mentioned that all of the learning schemes that have been proposed for networks of the sort we have studied are incremental (cf. Chapters 7, 8, 11, 18, 19, and 25), and therefore as an organism moves from its primarily genetically predetermined start state to its primarily environmentally determined final state, it will pass through a sequence of more or less intermediate states. There will be a kind of trajectory through the space of possible networks. This trajectory will constitute the developmental sequence for the organism. To the degree that different individuals share the same genetics (start state) and to the degree that their environments are similar, they will pass through similar trajectories. It should also be said that since, in PDP systems, what is learned is a product of both the current state of the organism and the current pattern of inputs, the start state will have an important effect on what is learned and the shape of the network following any given set of experiences. However, the greater the amount of experience, the more independent the system should be from its start state and the more dependent it should be on the structure of its environment.

Of course, not all connections may be plastic—certainly, many subcortical mechanisms are considerably less plastic than cortical ones. Also, plasticity may not continue throughout life (see Chapter 24). It would, of course, be a simple matter to suppose that certain connections are not modifiable. This is an issue about which our framework provides no answer. The major point is that there is no inconsistency between prewired, innate knowledge, and mutability and adaptability.

We cannot resist making one more point about the nativism/empiricism issue. This is that our PDP account of innate knowledge seems to provide a rather plausible account of how we can come to have innate "knowledge." To the extent that stored knowledge is assumed to be in the form of explicit, inaccessible rules of the kind often postulated by linguists as the basis for linguistic competence (see Chapter 18), it is hard to see how it could "get into the head" of the newborn. It seems to us implausible that the newborn possesses elaborate symbol systems and the systems for interpreting them required to put these explicit, inaccessible rules to use in guiding behavior. On our account, we do not need to attribute such complex machinery. If the innate knowledge is simply the prewired connections, it is encoded from the start in just the right way to be of use by the processing mechanisms.

Why Are People Smarter Than Rats?

Some have argued that since we claim that human cognition can be explained in terms of PDP networks and that the behavior of lower animals such as rats can also be described in terms of such networks we have no principled way of explaining why rats are not as smart as people. Given all of the above, the question does seem a bit puzzling. We are not claiming, in any way, that people and rats and all other organisms start out with the same prewired hardware. People have much more cortex than rats do or even than other primates do; in particular they have very much more prefrontal and parietal cortex—more brain structure not dedicated to input/output—and presumably, this extra cortex is strategically placed in the brain to subserve just those functions that differentiate people from rats or even apes. A case in point is the part of the brain known as the *angular gyrus*. This part of the brain does not exist even in chimpanzees. It sits at the intersection between the language areas of the temporal lobe and the visual areas of the parietal lobe, and damage to this area produces serious deficits in language and in the mapping of words onto meanings. While it is possible that structures like the angular gyrus possess some special internal wiring that makes them fundamentally different, somehow, in the kinds of cognitive operations they perform, their cytoarchitecture is not markedly different from that of other parts of the brain (see Chapters 20 and 21). Thus it seems to us quite plausible that some of the differences between rats and people lie in the potentiality for forming connections that can subserve the vital functions of language and thought that humans exhibit and other animals do not.

But there must be another aspect to the difference between rats and people as well. This is that the human environment includes other people and the cultural devices that they have developed to organize their thinking processes. Some thoughts on how we imagine these cultural devices are exploited in higher forms of intelligent behavior are presented in Chapter 14.

Conscious Knowledge and Explicit Reasoning

There may be cognitive scientists who accept some or all of what we have said up to this point, but still feel that something is missing, namely, an account of how we guide behavior using explicit, conscious knowledge, how we reason from what we know to new conclusions based on that knowledge, and how we find a path through a problem space through a series of sequential steps. Can parallel distributed processing have anything to say about these explicit, introspectively accessible, temporally extended acts of thinking? Some have suggested that the answer is no—that PDP models may be fine as accounts for perception, motor control, and other *low-level* phenomena, but that they are simply unable to account for the higher level mental processing of the kind involved in reasoning, problem solving, and other higher level aspects of thought.

We agree that many of the most natural applications of PDP models are in the domains of perception and memory (see, for example, Chapters 15, 16, and 17). However, we are convinced that these models are equally applicable to higher level cognitive processes and offer new insights into these phenomena as well. We must be clear, though, about the fact that we cannot and do not expect PDP models to handle complex, extended, sequential reasoning processes as a single settling of a parallel network. We think that PDP models describe the microstructure of the thought process, and the mechanisms whereby these processes come, through practice, to flow more quickly and run together into each other.

Partly because of the temporally extended nature of sequential thought processes—the fact that they involve many settlings of a network instead of just one—they are naturally more difficult to deal with, and our efforts in these areas are, as yet, somewhat tentative. Nevertheless, we have begun to develop models of language processing (Chapter 19), language acquisition (Chapter 18), sequential thought processes and consciousness (Chapter 14), and problem solving and thinking in general (Chapters 6, 8, and 14). We view this work as preliminary, and we firmly believe that other frameworks provide additional, important levels of description that can augment our accounts, but we are encouraged by the progress we have made in these areas and believe that the new perspectives that arise from these efforts are sufficiently provocative to be added to the pool of possible explanations of these higher level cognitive processes. Obviously, the extension of our explorations more deeply into these domains is high on our ongoing agenda. We see no principled reasons why these explorations cannot succeed, and every indication is that they will lead us somewhat further toward an understanding of the microstructure of cognition.

MANY MODELS OR JUST ONE?

Before concluding this chapter, some comment should be made about the status of the various models we and other members of the

PDP research group offer throughout the book. As the title of the book suggests, we understand our work as an *exploration*. We have been impressed with the potential of PDP models for changing our perspectives on the human information processing system. We have tried to maintain the kinds of general principles outlined in this chapter, but we have felt free to vary the details from application to application. Sometimes the variations are due to the fact that certain features of the models need to be elaborated to deal with certain phenomena but can be suppressed for other phenomena. Other times, we have simply made a different choice to explore a different part of the space of PDP models. We do not see ourselves capable as yet to produce the supermodel which would connect all of our areas of exploration together. Rather, we feel that the PDP framework which we are developing forms a kind of *metatheory* from which specific models can be generated for specific applications. The success of the particular models reflects indirectly on the metatheory, but we feel that the proper approach is to study detailed models of detailed applications while at the same time keeping one eye on the bigger picture. Thus, we don't really have a single model. Rather, we have a family of related models. In the best of all worlds each of our specific models may turn out to be a rough approximation to some unifying, underlying model as specialized to the problem area in question. More likely, however, each represents an exploration into a more or less uncharted region of the space of PDP models. Each application has lead to useful insights—both into the phenomena under study and into the behavior of the specific versions of the models used to account for them.

CONCLUSION

Some of the issues we have considered in this chapter are quite specific to our particular enterprise, but in the main, they are more general. They concern such questions as the scope of cognitive theory, the relation between levels, the question of nature vs. nurture, and the relevance of neural mechanisms to an analysis of cognition.

The present chapter has provided an overview of our views on a number of these central questions. In so doing, it has also provided an overview of the work that is described in the rest of the book, along with some of the reasons for doing it. Indeed, in many ways the rest of the book *is* our response to the issues we have touched on here. The chapters in Part II seek ways to overcome the computational limitations of earlier network models, and the chapters in Part III provide some of the formal tools that are crucial in pursuing these kinds of goals. The chapters in Part IV address themselves to cognitive constructs and attempt to redefine the cognitive structures of earlier theories in terms of emergent properties of PDP networks. The chapters in Part V consider the neural mechanisms themselves and their relation to the algorithmic level that is the focus of most of the work described in Parts II and IV.

ACKNOWLEDGMENTS

We would like to thank the many people who have raised the questions and the objections that we have attempted to discuss here. These people include John Anderson, Francis Crick, Steve Draper, Jerry Fodor, Jim Greeno, Allen Newell, Zenon Pylyshyn, Chris Riesbeck, Kurt van Lehn, and many others in San Diego, Pittsburgh, and elsewhere. In addition, we would like to thank Allan Collins, Keith Holyoak, and Walter Schneider for organizing seminars and symposia around these issues, and we would like to thank our many colleagues who have helped us formulate our answers to some of these questions, particularly Geoff Hinton, Paul Smolensky, and the other members of the PDP Research Group

Preparation of this chapter was supported by ONR contracts N00014-82-C-0374, NR 667-483 and N00014-79-C-0323, NR 667-437, by a grant from the System Development Foundation, and by a Research Scientist Career Development Award MH00385 to the second author from the National Institute of Mental Health.

PART II

BASIC MECHANISMS

The chapters of Part II represent explorations into specific architectures and learning mechanisms for PDP models. These explorations proceed through mathematical analysis coupled with results from simulations. The major theme which runs through all of these explorations is a focus on the learning problem. How can PDP networks evolve to perform the kinds of tasks we require of them? Since one of the primary features of PDP models in general is their ability to self-modify, these studies form an important base for the application of these models to specific psychological and biological phenomena.

In Chapter 5, Rumelhart and Zipser begin with a summary of the history of early work on learning in parallel distributed processing systems. They then study an unsupervised learning procedure called *competitive learning.* This is a procedure whereby feature detectors capable of discriminating among the members of a set of stimulus input patterns evolve without a specific teacher guiding the learning. The basic idea is to let pools of potential feature detector units *compete* among themselves to respond to each stimulus pattern. The winner within each pool—the one whose connections make it respond most strongly to the pattern—then adjusts its connections slightly toward the pattern that it won. Several earlier investigators have considered variants of the competitive learning idea (e.g., Grossberg, 1976; von der Malsberg, 1973). Rumelhart and Zipser show that when a competitive network is trained through repeated presentations of members of a set of patterns, each unit in a pool comes to respond when patterns with a particular attribute or property are presented. If there are two units in a pool, each comes to respond to opposite values of a binary feature which is useful in describing the stimulus set. If there are three units in the pool, each unit comes to respond to a value of a trinary feature, etc. It is shown through simulations and mathematical analysis that the competitive learning system can serve as a basis for the development of useful pattern descriptions.

Chapters 6 and 7 describe Smolensky's *harmony theory* and Hinton and Sejnowski's *Boltzmann machine*, respectively. These approaches were developed at the same time, and they have much in common. Both harmony theory and Boltzmann machines employ binary units whose values are determined probabilistically according to the Boltzmann equation. Each employs *simulated annealing* in which the *temperature* of the Boltzmann equation is moved slowly to zero as the system relaxes into its solution state where it finally freezes. Both systems apply mathematical formulations borrowed from physics to their systems to describe and analyze their behavior.

In spite of these similarities, the two systems were developed from very different perspectives. The similarities arose largely because both systems tapped mathematical physics as a tool for formalizing their ideas. Smolensky's harmony theory grew from an attempt to formalize the notion of *schema* and the ideas of schema theory. Hinton and Sejnowski's Boltzmann machine is based on the idea that stochastic units can be used as a mechanism of search—for finding globally good states of networks through simulated annealing. It combines insights on simulated annealing from Kirkpatrick, Gelatt, and Vecchi (1983) with the proof by Hopfield (1982) that there is a global energy function that can be locally minimized through a process of asynchronously updating individual units.

Chapter 6 provides a mathematical development of harmony theory and shows how a symbolic level of description can be seen as emerging from interactions among the individual processing units in harmony theory. It shows how harmony theory can be applied to a variety of phenomena, including intuitive problem solving and aspects of perception. It also provides a useful description of the mathematical relationships among harmony theory, Boltzmann machines, and the related mechanisms studied by S. Geman and D. Geman (1984).

Chapter 7 focuses on the issue of learning in Boltzmann machines. One of the most important contributions of the work on Boltzmann machines is the development of the two phase (wake/sleep) learning procedure. Hinton and Sejnowski show that if a Boltzmann machine runs under the influence of environmental inputs for a while and then runs "freely"—without inputs from the environment—there is a very simple learning rule which will allow the Boltzmann machine to pick up environmental regularities and develop its own internal representations for describing those regularities. The major part of Chapter 7 is an analysis of this learning procedure.

Chapter 8 is the study of still another learning procedure. In this chapter, Rumelhart, Hinton, and Williams show that it is possible to develop a generalization of the *delta rule* described in Chapter 2 so that arbitrary multilayered networks of units can be can be trained to do interesting tasks. Using this learning rule, the system can learn to associate arbitrary input/output pairs and in this way can learn to compute arbitrary input/output functions. The generalized delta rule is shown to provide a method of modifying any weight in any network, based on locally available information, so as to implement a gradient descent process that searches for those weights that minimize the error at the output units. Further, simulation work presented in the chapter shows that the problems of local minima often associated with gradient descent and other hill-climbing methods are suprisingly rare.

In general, the chapters in this section demonstrate that the barriers to progress in understanding learning in networks of simple neuron-like units have begun to crumble. There are still deep problems that remain unsolved, but the learning mechanisms described in these chapters make several inroads into some of the most challenging aspects of the theory of parallel distributed processing.

CHAPTER 5

Feature Discovery by Competitive Learning

D. E. RUMELHART and D. ZIPSER

This chapter reports the results of our studies with an unsupervised learning paradigm that we call *competitive learning*. We have examined competitive learning using both computer simulation and formal analysis and have found that when it is applied to parallel networks of neuron-like elements, many potentially useful learning tasks can be accomplished. We were attracted to competitive learning because it seems to provide a way to discover the salient, general features which can be used to classify a set of patterns. The basic components of the competitive learning scheme are:

- Start with a set of units that are all the same except for some randomly distributed parameter which makes each of them respond slightly differently to a set of input patterns.

- Limit the "strength" of each unit.

- Allow the units to compete in some way for the right to respond to a given subset of inputs.

The net result of correctly applying these three components to a learning paradigm is that individual units learn to specialize on sets of

This chapter originally appeared in *Cognitive Science*, 1985, 9, 75-112. Copyright 1985 by Ablex Publishing. Reprinted by permission.

similar patterns and thus become "feature detectors" or "pattern classifiers." In addition to Frank Rosenblatt, whose work will be discussed below, several others have exploited competitive learning in one form or another over the years. These include von der Malsburg (1973), Grossberg (1976), Fukushima (1975), and Kohonen (1982). Our analyses differ from many of these in that we focus on the development of feature detectors rather than pattern classification. We address these issues further below.

One of the central issues in the study of the processing capacities of neuron-like elements concerns the limitations inherent in a one-level system and the difficulty of developing learning schemes for multilayered systems. Competitive learning is a scheme in which important features can be discovered at one level that a multilayer system can use to classify pattern sets which cannot be classified with a single level system.

Thirty-five years of experience have shown that getting neuron-like elements to learn some easy things is often quite straightforward, but designing systems with powerful general learning properties is a difficult problem, and the competitive learning paradigm does not change this fact. What we hope to show is that competitive learning is a powerful strategy which, when used in a variety of situations, greatly expedites some difficult tasks. Since the competitive learning paradigm has roots which go back to the very beginnings of the study of artificial learning devices, it seems reasonable to put the whole issue into historical perspective. This is even more to the point, since one of the first simple learning devices, the perceptron, caused great furor and debate, the reverberations of which are still with us.

In the beginning, thirty-five or forty years ago, it was very hard to see how anything resembling a neural network could learn at all, so any example of learning was immensely interesting. Learning was elevated to a status of great importance in those days because it was somehow uniquely associated with the properties of animal brains. After McCulloch and Pitts (1943) showed how neural-like networks could compute, the main problem then facing workers in this area was to understand how such networks could learn.

The first set of ideas that really got the enterprise going were contained in Donald Hebb's *Organization of Behavior* (1949). Before Hebb's work, it was believed that some physical change must occur in a network to support learning, but it was not clear what this change could be. Hebb proposed that a reasonable and biologically plausible change would be to strengthen the connections between elements of the network only when both the presynaptic and postsynaptic units were active simultaneously. The essence of Hebb's ideas still persists today in many learning paradigms. The details of the rules for changing weight may be different, but the essential notion that the strength of connections between the units must change in response to some function of the correlated activity of the connected units still dominates learning models.

Hebb's ideas remained untested speculations about the nervous system until it became possible to build some form of simulated network to test learning theories. Probably the first such attempt occurred in 1951 when Dean Edmonds and Marvin Minsky built their learning machine. The flavor of this machine and the milieu in which it operated is captured in Minsky's own words which appeared in a wonderful *New Yorker* profile of him by Jeremy Bernstein (1981):

> In the summer of 1951 Dean Edmonds and I went up to Harvard and built our machine. It had three hundred tubes and a lot of motors. It needed some automatic electric clutches, which we machined ourselves. The memory of the machine was stored in the positions of its control knobs, 40 of them, and when the machine was learning, it used the clutches to adjust its own knobs. We used a surplus gyropilot from a B24 bomber to move the clutches. (p. 69)

This machine actually worked and was so fascinating to watch that Minsky remembers:

> We sort of quit science for awhile to watch the machine. We were amazed that it could have several activities going on at once in this little nervous system. Because of the random wiring it had a sort of fail safe characteristic. If one of the neurons wasn't working, it wouldn't make much difference and with nearly three hundred tubes, and the thousands of connections we had soldered there would usually be something wrong somewhere. . . . I don't think we ever debugged our machine completely, but that didn't matter. By having this crazy random design it was almost sure to work no matter how you built it. (p. 69)

In fact, the functioning of this machine apparently stimulated Minsky sufficiently to write his PhD thesis on a problem related to learning (Minsky, 1954). The whole idea must have generated rather wide interest; von Neumann, for example, was on Minsky's PhD committee and gave him encouragement. Although Minsky was perhaps the first on the scene with a learning machine, the real beginnings of meaningful neuron-like network learning can probably be traced to the work of Frank Rosenblatt, a Bronx High School of Science classmate of

Minsky's. Rosenblatt invented a class of simple neuron-like learning networks which he called perceptrons. In his book, *Principles of Neurodynamics* (1962), Rosenblatt brought together all of his results on perceptrons. In that book he gives a particularly clear description of what he thought he was doing:

> Perceptrons are not intended to serve as detailed copies of any actual nervous system. They're simplified networks, designed to permit the study of lawful relationships between the organization of a nerve net, the organization of its environment, and the "psychological" performances of which it is capable. Perceptrons might actually correspond to parts of more extended networks and biological systems; in this case, the results obtained will be directly applicable. More likely they represent extreme simplifications of the central nervous system, in which some properties are exaggerated and others suppressed. In this case, successive perturbations and refinements of the system may yield a closer approximation.
>
> The main strength of this approach is that it permits meaningful questions to be asked and answered about particular types of organizations, hypothetical memory mechanisms, and neural models. When exact analytical answers are unobtainable, experimental methods, either with digital simulation or hardware models, are employed. The model is not the terminal result, but a starting point for exploratory analysis of its behavior. (p. 28)

Rosenblatt pioneered two techniques of fundamental importance to the study of learning in neural-like networks: digital computer simulation and formal mathematical analysis, although he was not the first to simulate neural networks that could learn on digital computers (cf. Farley & Clark, 1954).

Since the paradigm of competitive learning uses concepts that appear in the work of Rosenblatt, it is worthwhile reviewing some of his ideas in this area. His most influential result was the "perceptron learning theorem" which boldly asserts:

> Given an elementary α-perceptron, a stimulus world W, and any classification $C(W)$ for which a solution exists; let all stimuli in W occur in any sequence, provided that each stimulus must reoccur in finite time; then beginning from an arbitrary initial state, an error correction procedure will always yield a solution to $C(W)$ in finite time, . . . (p. 596)

As it turned out, the real problems arose out of the phrase "for which a solution exists"—more about this later.

Less widely known is Rosenblatt's work on what he called "spontaneous learning." All network learning models require rules which tell how to present the stimuli and change the values of the weights in accordance with the response of the model. These rules can be characterized as forming a spectrum, at one end of which is learning with an error-correcting teacher, and at the other is completely spontaneous, unsupervised discovery. In between is a continuum of rules that depend on manipulating the content of the input stimulus stream to bring about learning. These intermediate rules are often referred to as "forced learning." Here we are concerned primarily with attempts to design a perceptron that would discover something interesting without a teacher because this is similar to what happens in the competitive learning case. In fact, Rosenblatt was able to build a perceptron that was able to spontaneously dichotomize a random sequence of input patterns into classes such that the members of a single class were similar to each other, and different from the members of the other class. Rosenblatt realized that any randomly initialized perceptron would have to dichotomize an arbitrary input pattern stream into a "1-set," consisting of those patterns that happened to produce a response of 1, and a "0-set," consisting of those that produced a response of 0. Of course one of these sets could be empty by chance and neither would be of much interest in general. He reasoned that if a perceptron could reinforce these sets by an appropriate rule based only on the perceptron's spontaneous response and not on a teacher's error correction, it might eventually end up with a dichotomization in which the members of each set were more like each other than like the members of the opposite set. What was the appropriate rule to use to achieve the desired dicotomization? The first rule he tried for these perceptrons, which he called C-type, was to increment weights on lines active with patterns in the 1-set, and decrement weights on lines active with patterns in the 0-set. The idea was to force a dichotomization into sets whose members were similar in the sense that they activated overlapping subsets of lines. The results were disastrous. Sooner or later all the input patterns were classified in one set. There was no dichotomy but there was stability. Once one of the sets won, it remained the victor forever.

Not to be daunted, he examined why this undesirable result occurred and realized that the problem lay in the fact that since the weights could grow without limit, the set that initially had a majority of the patterns would receive the majority of the reinforcement. This meant that weights on lines which could be activated by patterns in both sets would grow to infinite magnitudes in favor of the majority set, which in turn would lead to the capture of minority patterns by the majority set and ultimate total victory for the majority. Even where there was initial equality between the sets, inevitable fluctuations in the random presentation of patterns would create a majority set that would then go on to win. Rosenblatt overcame this problem by introducing mechanisms to limit weight growth in such a way that the set that was to be positively reinforced at active lines would compensate the other set by giving up some weight from all its lines. He called the modified perceptrons C'. An example of a C' rule is to lower the magnitude of all weights by a fixed fraction of their current value before specifically incrementing the magnitude of some of the weights on the basis of the response to an input pattern. This type of rule had the desired result of making an equal dichotomy of patterns a stable rather than an unstable state. Patterns in each of the sets were similar to each other in the sense that they depended on similar sets of input lines to produce a response. In Rosenblatt's initial experiment, the main feature of similarity was not so much the shape of the patterns involved, but their location on the retina. That is, his system was able to spontaneously learn something about the geometry of its input line arrangement. Later, we will examine this important property of spontaneous geometry learning in considerable detail. Depending on the desired learning task, it can be either a boon or a nuisance.

Rosenblatt was extremely enthusiastic about his spontaneous learning results. In fact, his response can be described as sheer ecstasy. To see what he thought about his achievements, consider his claim (Rosenblatt, 1959):

> It seems clear that the class C' perceptron introduces a new kind of information processing automaton: For the first time, we have a machine which is capable of having original ideas. As an analogue of the biological brain, the perceptron, more precisely, the theory of statistical separability, seems to come closer to meeting the requirements of a functional explanation of the nervous system than any system previously proposed. (p. 449)

Although Rosenblatt's results were both interesting and significant, the claims implied in the above quote struck his contemporaries as unfounded. What was also significant was that Rosenblatt appeared to be saying that the type of spontaneous learning he had demonstrated was a property of perceptrons, which could not be replicated by ordinary computers. Consider the following quote from the same source:

> As a concept, it would seem that the perceptron has established, beyond doubt, the feasibility and principle of

> non-human systems which may embody human cognitive functions at a level far beyond that which can be achieved through present day automatons. The future of information processing devices which operate on statistical, rather then logical principles seems to be clearly indicated. (p. 449)

It is this notion of Rosenblatt's—that perceptrons are in some way superior to computers—that ignited a debate in artificial intelligence that had significant effects on the development of neural-like network models for both learning and other cognitive processes. Elements of the debate are still with us today in arguments about what the brain can do that computers can't do. There is no doubt that this was an important issue in Rosenblatt's mind, and almost certainly contributed to the acrimonious debate at that time. Consider the following statement by Rosenblatt made at the important conference on Mechanization of Thought Processes back in 1959:

> Computers seem to share two main functions with the brain: (a) Decision making, based on logical rule, and (b) control, again based on logical rules. The human brain performs these functions, together with a third: interpretation of the environment. Why do we hold interpretation of the environment to be so important? The answer, I think, is to be found in the laws of thermodynamics. A system with a completely self contained logic can never spontaneously improve its ability to organize, and to draw valid conclusions from information. (Rosenblatt, 1959, p. 423)

Clearly in some sense, Rosenblatt was saying that there were things that the brain and perceptrons, because of their statistical properties, could do which computers could not do. Now this may seem strange since Rosenblatt knew that a computer program could be written that would simulate the behavior of statistical perceptrons to any arbitrary degree of accuracy. Indeed, he was one of the pioneers in the application of digital simulation to this type of problem. What he was actually referring to is made clear when we examine the comments of other participants at the conference, such as Minsky (1959) and McCarthy (1959), who were using the symbol manipulating capabilities of the computer to directly simulate the logical processes involved in decision making, theorem proving, and other intellectual activities of this sort. Rosenblatt believed the computer used in this way would be inadequate to mimic the brain's true intellectual powers. This task, he thought, could only be accomplished if the computer or other electronic devices were used to simulate perceptrons. We can summarize these divergent points of view by saying that Rosenblatt was concerned not only with what the brain did, but with how it did it, whereas others, such as Minsky and McCarthy, were concerned with simulating what the brain did, and didn't really care how it was done. The subsequent history of AI has shown both the successes and failures of the standard AI approach. We still have the problems today, and it's still not clear to what degree computational strategies similar to the ones used by the brain must be employed in order to simulate its performance.

In addition to producing fertilizer, as all debates do, this one also stimulated the growth of some new results on perceptrons, some of which came from Minsky. Rosenblatt had shown that a two layer perceptron could carry out any of the 2^{2^N} possible classifications of N binary inputs; that is, a solution to the classification problem had always existed in principle. This result was of no practical value however, because 2^N units were required to accomplish the task in the completely general case. Rosenblatt's approach to this problem was to use a much smaller number of units in the first layer with each unit connected to a small subset of the N inputs at random. His hope was that this would give the perceptron a high probability of learning to carry out classifications of interest. Experiments and formal analysis showed that these random devices could learn to recognize patterns to a significant degree but that they had severe limitations. Rosenblatt (1962) characterized his random perceptron as follows:

> It does not generalize well to similar forms occurring in new positions in the retinal field, and its performance in detection experiments, where a familiar figure appears against an unfamiliar background, is apt to be weak. More sophisticated psychological capabilities, which depend on the recognition of topological properties of the stimulus field, or on abstract relations between the components of a complex image, are lacking. (pp. 191-192)

Minsky and Papert worked through most of the sixties on a mathematical analysis of the computing powers of perceptrons with the goal of understanding these limitations. The results of their work are available in a book called *Perceptrons* (Minsky & Papert, 1969). The central theme of this work is that parallel recognizing elements, such as perceptrons, are beset by the same problems of scale as serial pattern recognizers. Combinatorial explosion catches you sooner or later, although sometimes in different ways in parallel than in serial. Minsky and Papert's book had a very dampening effect on the study of neuron-like networks as computational devices. Minsky has recently come to reconsider this negative effect:

> I now believe the book was overkill. . . . So after being irritated with Rosenblatt for overclaiming and diverting all those people along a false path, I started to realize that for what you get out of it — the kind of recognition it can do—it is such a simple machine that it would be astonishing if nature did not make use of it somewhere. (Bernstein, 1981, p. 103)

Perhaps the real lesson from all this is that it really is worthwhile trying to put things in perspective.

Once the problem of scale has been understood, networks of neuron-like elements are often very useful in practical problems of recognition and classification. These networks are somewhat analogous to computers, in that they won't do much unless programmed by a clever person; networks, of course, are not so much programmed as designed. The problem of finding networks of practical size to solve a particular problem is challenging because relatively small changes in network design can have very large effects on the scale of a problem. Consider networks of neuron-like units that determine the parity of their N binary inputs (see Figure 1). In the simple perceptrons studied by Minsky and Papert, units in the first layer output 1 only if all their inputs are 1 and output 0 otherwise. This takes 2^N units in the first layer, and a single linear threshold unit with a fan-in of 2^N in the second layer, to determine parity. If the units in the first layer are changed to linear threshold elements, then only N of them are required, but all must have a fan-in of N. If we allow a multilayer network to do the job, then about $3N$ units are needed, but none needs a fan-in of more than 2. The number of layers is of order $\log_2 N$. The importance of all this to the competitive learning paradigm, or any other for that matter, is that no network can learn what it is not capable of doing in principle. What any particular network can do is dependent on its structure and the computational properties of its component elements. Unfortunately, there is no canonical way to find the best network or to determine what it will learn, so the whole enterprise still has much of the flavor of an experimental science.

THE COMPETITIVE LEARNING MECHANISM

Paradigms of Learning

It is possible to classify learning mechanisms in several ways. One useful classification is in terms of the learning paradigm in which the

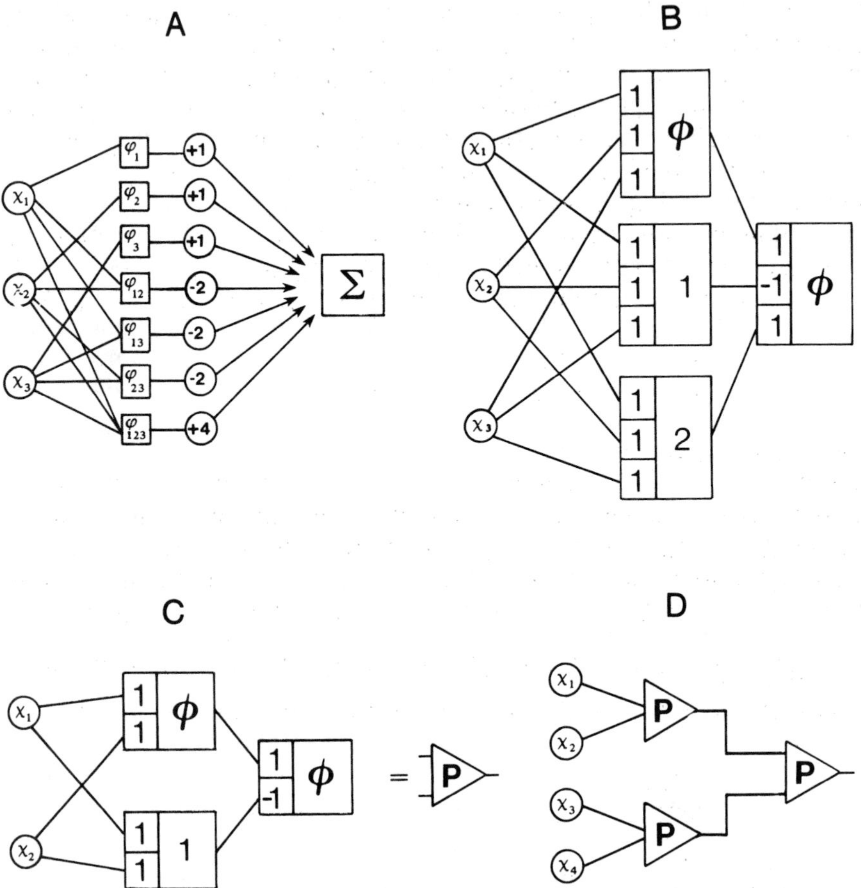

FIGURE 1. *A*: Parity network from Minsky and Papert (1969). Each ϕ unit has an output of 1 only if all of its inputs are 1. Σ is a linear threshold unit with threshold of 0, i.e., like all the other linear threshold units in the figure, it fires only when the sum of its weighted inputs is greater than the threshold. This and all the other networks signal odd parity with a 1 in the rightmost unit of the network. *B*: Parity network made from two layers of linear threshold units. *C*: Three-unit network for determining the parity of a pair of inputs. *D*: Two-layer network using the subnetwork described in *(C)*. In general, the number of *P*-units is of order N and the number of layers is of order $\log_2 N$.

model is supposed to work. There are at least four common learning paradigms in neural-like processing systems:

- *Auto Associator.* In this paradigm a set of patterns are repeatedly presented and the system is supposed to "store" the patterns. Then, later, parts of one of the original patterns or possibly a pattern similar to one of the original patterns is presented, and the task is to "retrieve" the original pattern through a kind of pattern completion procedure. This is an auto-association process in which a pattern is associated with itself so that a degraded version of the original pattern can act as a retrieval cue.

- *Pattern Associator.* This paradigm is really a variant on the auto-association paradigm. A set of *pairs* of patterns are repeatedly presented. The system is to learn that when one member of the pair is presented it is supposed to produce the other. In this paradigm one seeks a mechanism in which an essentially arbitrary set of input patterns can be paired with an arbitrary set of output patterns.

- *Classification Paradigm.* The classification paradigm also can be considered as a variant on the previous learning paradigms, although the goals are sufficiently different and it is sufficiently common that it deserves separate mention. In this case, there is a fixed set of categories into which the stimulus patterns are to be classified. There is a training session in which the system is presented with the stimulus patterns along with the categories to which each stimulus belongs. The goal is to learn to correctly classify the stimuli so that in the future when a particular stimulus or a slightly distorted version of one of the stimuli is presented, the system will classify it properly. This is the typical paradigm in which the perceptron is designed to operate and in which the perceptron convergence theorem is proved.

- *Regularity Detector.* In this paradigm there is a population of stimulus patterns and each stimulus pattern, S_k, is presented with some probability p_k. The system is supposed to *discover* statistically salient features of the input *population*. Unlike the classification paradigm, there is no a priori set of categories into which the patterns are to be classified; rather, the system must develop its own featural representation of the input stimuli which captures the most salient features of the population of input patterns.

Competitive learning is a mechanism well-suited for regularity detection, as in the environment described in above.

Competitive Learning

The architecture of a competitive learning system (illustrated in Figure 2) is a common one. It consists of a set of hierarchically layered units in which each layer connects, via excitatory connections, with the layer immediately above it. In the most general case, each unit of a layer receives an input from each unit of the layer immediately below and projects output to each unit in the layer immediately above it. Moreover, within a layer, the units are broken into a set of inhibitory clusters in which all elements within a cluster inhibit all other elements in the cluster. Thus the elements within a cluster at one level compete with one another to respond to the pattern appearing on the layer below. The more strongly any particular unit responds to an incoming stimulus, the more it shuts down the other members of its cluster.

There are many variations on the competitive learning theme. A number of researchers have developed variants of competitive learning mechanisms and a number of results already exist in the literature. We have already mentioned the pioneering work of Rosenblatt. In addition, von der Malsburg (1973), Fukushima (1975), and Grossberg (1976), among others, have developed models which are competitive learning models, or which have many properties in common with competitive learning. We believe that the essential properties of the competitive learning mechanism are quite general. However, for the sake of concreteness, in this paper we have chosen to study, in some detail, the simplest of the systems which seem to be representative of the essential characteristics of competitive learning. Thus, the system we have analyzed has much in common with the previous work, but wherever possible we have simplified our assumptions. The system that we have studied most is described below:

- The units in a given layer are broken into a set of nonoverlapping clusters. Each unit within a cluster inhibits every other unit within a cluster. The clusters are winner-take-all, such that the unit receiving the largest input achieves its maximum value while all other units in the cluster are pushed to their minimum value. [1] We have arbitrarily set the maximum value to 1 and the minimum value to 0.

[1] A simple circuit for achieving this result is attained by having each unit activate itself and inhibit its neighbors. Grossberg (1976) employs just such a network to *choose* the maximum value of a set of units.

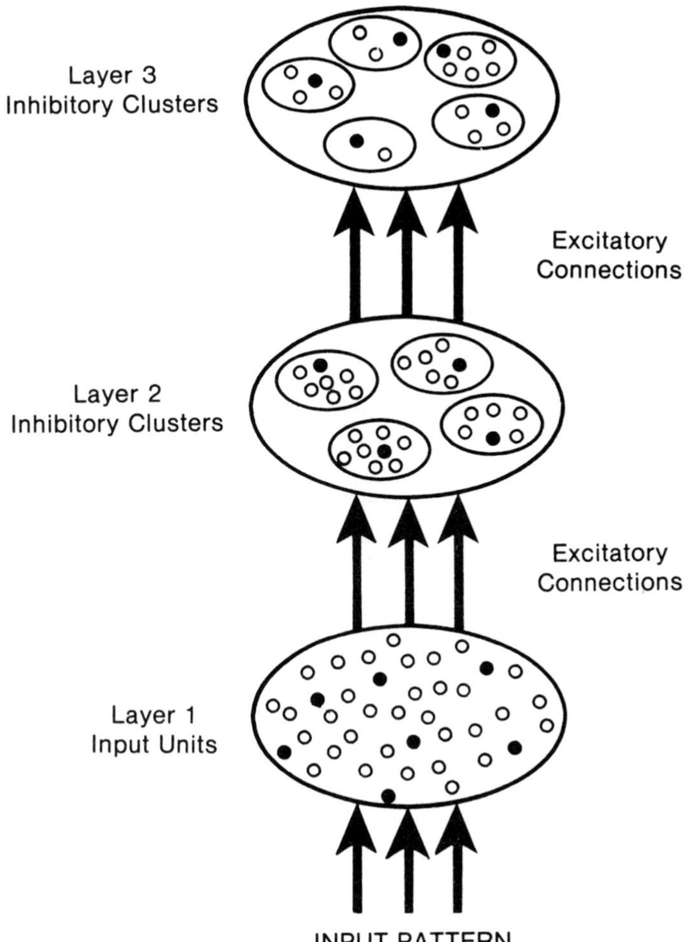

FIGURE 2. The architecture of the competitive learning mechanism. Competitive learning takes place in a context of sets of hierarchically layered units. Units are represented in the diagram as dots. Units may be active or inactive. Active units are represented by filled dots, inactive ones by open dots. In general, a unit in a given layer can receive inputs from all of the units in the next lower layer and can project outputs to all of the units in the next higher layer. Connections between layers are excitatory and connections within layers are inhibitory. Each layer consists of a set of clusters of mutually inhibitory units. The units within a cluster inhibit one another in such a way that only one unit per cluster may be active. We think of the configuration of active units on any given layer as representing the input pattern for the next higher level. There can be an arbitrary number of such layers. A given cluster contains a fixed number of units, but different clusters can have different numbers of units.

- Every element in every cluster receives inputs from the same lines.

- A unit learns if and only if it wins the competition with other units in its cluster.

- A stimulus pattern S_j consists of a binary pattern in which each element of the pattern is either *active* or *inactive*. An active element is assigned the value 1 and an inactive element is assigned the value 0.

- Each unit has a fixed amount of weight (all weights are positive) which is distributed among its input lines. The weight on the line connecting unit i on the lower (or input) layer to unit j on the upper layer, is designated w_{ij}. The fixed total amount of weight for unit j is designated $\sum_i w_{ij} = 1$. A unit learns by shifting weight from its inactive to its active input lines. If a unit does not respond to a particular pattern, no learning takes place in that unit. If a unit wins the competition, then each of its input lines give up some proportion g of its weight and that weight is then distributed equally among the active input lines.[2] More formally, the learning rule we have studied is:

$$\Delta w_{ij} = \begin{cases} 0 & \text{if unit } j \text{ loses on stimulus } k \\ g\frac{c_{ik}}{n_k} - g w_{ij} & \text{if unit } j \text{ wins on stimulus } k \end{cases}$$

where c_{ik} is equal to 1 if in stimulus pattern S_k, unit i in the lower layer is active and zero otherwise, and n_k is the number of active units in pattern S_k (thus $n_k = \sum_i c_{ik}$).

Figure 3 illustrates a useful geometric analogy to this system. We can consider each stimulus pattern as a vector. If all patterns contain the same number of active lines, then all vectors are the same length and each can be viewed as a point on an N-dimensional hypersphere,

---

2 This learning rule was proposed by von der Malsburg (1973). As Grossberg (1976) points out, renormalization of the weights is not necessary. The same result can be obtained by normalizing the input patterns and then assuming that the weights approach the values on the input lines. Normalizing weights is simpler to implement than normalizing patterns, so we chose that option. For most of our experiments, however, it does not matter which of these two rules we chose since all patterns were of the same magnitude.

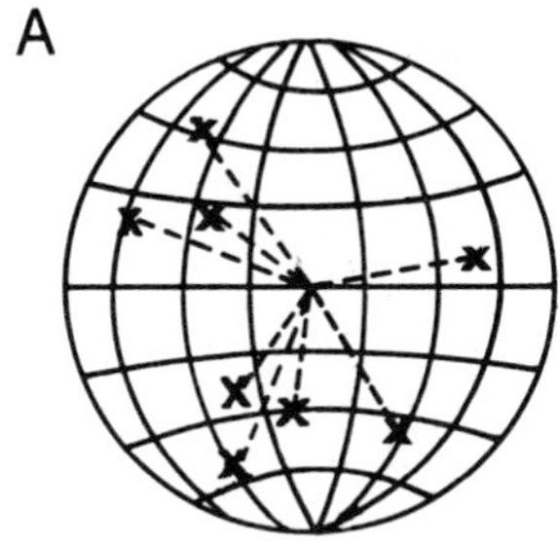

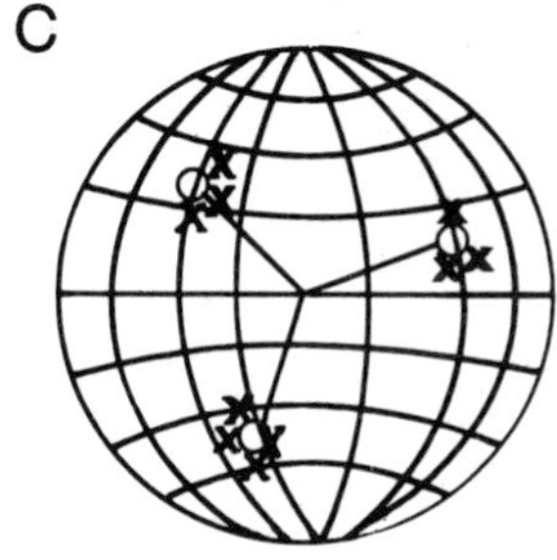

FIGURE 3. A geometric interpretation of competitive learning. *A*: It is useful to conceptualize stimulus patterns as vectors whose tips all lie on the surface of a hypersphere. We can then directly see the similarity among stimulus patterns as distance between the points on the sphere. In the figure, a stimulus pattern is represented as an ×. The figure represents a population of eight stimulus patterns. There are two clusters of three patterns and two stimulus patterns which are rather distinct from the others. *B*: It is also useful to represent the weights of units as vectors falling on the surface of the same hypersphere. Weight vectors are represented in the figure as o's. The figure illustrates the weights of two units falling on rather different parts of the sphere. The response rule of this model is equivalent to the rule that whenever a stimulus pattern is presented, the unit whose weight vector is closest to that stimulus pattern on the sphere wins the competition. In the figure, one unit would respond to the cluster in the northern hemisphere and the other unit would respond to the rest of the stimulus patterns. *C*: The learning rule of this model is roughly equivalent to the rule that whenever a unit wins the competition (i.e., is closest to the stimulus pattern), that weight vector is moved toward the presented stimulus. The figure shows a case in which there are three units in the cluster and three natural groupings of the stimulus patterns. In this case, the weight vectors for the three units will each migrate toward one of the stimulus groups.

where N is the number of units in the lower level, and therefore, also the number of input lines received by each unit in the upper level.

Each × in Figure 3A represents a particular pattern. Those patterns that are very similar are near one another on the sphere; those that are very different will be far from one another on the sphere. Now note that since there are N input lines to each unit in the upper layer, its weights can also be considered a vector in N-dimensional space. Since all units have the same total quantity of weight, we have N-dimensional vectors of approximately fixed length for each unit in the cluster.[3] Thus, properly scaled, the weights themselves form a set of vectors which (approximately) fall on the surface of the same hypersphere. In Figure 3B, the o's represent the weights of two units superimposed on the same sphere with the stimulus patterns. Now, whenever a stimulus pattern is presented, the unit which responds most strongly is simply the one whose weight vector is nearest that for the stimulus. The learning rule specifies that whenever a unit wins a competition for a stimulus pattern, it moves a percentage g of the way from its current location toward the location of the stimulus pattern on the hypersphere. Now, suppose that the input patterns fell into some number, M, "natural" groupings. Further, suppose that an inhibitory cluster receiving inputs from these stimuli contained exactly M units (as in Figure 3C). After sufficient training, and assuming that the stimulus groupings are sufficiently distinct, we expect to find one of the vectors for the M units placed roughly in the center of each of the stimulus groupings. In this case, the units have come to detect the grouping to which the input patterns belong. In this sense, they have "discovered" the structure of the input pattern sets.

Some Features of Competitive Learning

There are several characteristics of a competitive learning mechanism that make it an interesting candidate for further study, for example:

- Each cluster classifies the stimulus set into M groups, one for each unit in the cluster. Each of the units captures roughly an equal number of stimulus patterns. It is possible to consider a cluster as forming an M-ary feature in which every stimulus pattern is classified as having exactly one of the M possible

[3] It should be noted that this geometric interpretation is only approximate. We have used the constraint that $\sum_i w_{ij} = 1$ rather than the constraint that $\sum_i w_{ij}^2 = 1$. This latter constraint would ensure that all vectors are in fact the same length. Our assumption only assures that they will be approximately the same length.

values of this feature. Thus, a cluster containing 2 units acts as a binary feature detector. One element of the cluster responds when a particular feature is present in the stimulus pattern, otherwise the other element responds.

- If there is *structure* in the stimulus patterns, the units will break up the patterns along structurally relevant lines. Roughly speaking, this means that the system will find clusters if they are there. (A key problem, which we address below, is specifying the *nature* of the structure that this system discovers.)

- If the stimuli are highly structured, the classifications are highly stable. If the stimuli are less well-structured, the classifications are more variable, and a given stimulus pattern will be responded to first by one and then by another member of the cluster. In our experiments, we started the weight vectors in random directions and presented the stimuli randomly. In this case, there is rapid movement as the system reaches a relatively stable configuration (such as one with a unit roughly in the center of each cluster of stimulus patterns). These configurations can be more or less stable. For example, if the stimulus points don't actually fall into nice clusters, then the configurations will be relatively unstable, and the presentation of each stimulus will modify the pattern of responding so that the system will undergo continual evolution. On the other hand, if the stimulus patterns fall rather nicely into clusters, then the system will become very stable in the sense that the same units will always respond to the same stimuli.[4]

- The particular grouping done by a particular cluster depends on the starting value of the weights and the sequence of stimulus patterns actually presented. A large number of clusters, each receiving inputs from the same input lines can, in general, classify the inputs into a large number of different groupings, or alternatively, discover a variety of independent features present in the stimulus population. This can provide a kind of coarse coding of the stimulus patterns.[5]

---

[4] Grossberg (1976) has addressed this problem in his very similar system. He has proved that if the patterns are sufficiently sparse, and/or when there are enough units in the cluster, then a system such as this will find a perfectly stable classification. He also points out that when these conditions don't hold, the classification can be unstable. Most of our work is with cases in which there is *no* perfectly stable classification and the number of patterns is *much* larger than the number of units in the inhibitory clusters.

Formal Analysis

Perhaps the simplest mathematical analysis that can be given of the competitive learning model under discussion involves the determination of the sets of *equilibrium states* of the system—that is, states in which the average inflow of weight to a particular line is equal to the average outflow of weight on that line. Let p_k be the probability that stimulus S_k is presented on any trial. Let v_{jk} be the probability that unit j wins when stimulus S_k is presented. Now we want to consider the case in which $\sum_k \Delta w_{ij} v_{jk} p_k = 0$, that is, the case in which the average change in the weights is zero. We refer to such states as *equilibrium states.* Thus, using the learning rule and averaging over stimulus patterns we can write

$$0 = g \sum_k \frac{c_{ik}}{n_k} p_k v_{jk} - g \sum_k w_{ij} p_k v_{jk}$$

which implies that at equilibrium

$$w_{ij} \sum_k p_k v_{jk} = \sum_k \frac{p_k c_{ik} v_{jk}}{n_k}$$

and thus

$$w_{ij} = \frac{\sum_k \frac{p_k c_{ik} v_{jk}}{n_k}}{\sum_k p_k v_{jk}}.$$

There are a number of important observations to note about this equation. First, note that $\sum_k p_k v_{jk}$ is simply the probability that unit j wins averaged over all stimulus patterns. Note further that $\sum_k p_k c_{ik} v_{jk}$ is the probability that input line i is active and unit j wins. Thus, the ratio $\frac{\sum_k p_k c_{ik} v_{jk}}{\sum_k p_k v_{jk}}$ is the conditional probability that line i is active given unit j

---

[5] There is a problem in that one can't be certain that the different clusters will discover different features. A slight modification of the system in which clusters "repel" one another can insure that different clusters find different features. We shall not pursue that further in this paper.

wins, $p(\text{line}_i = 1 \mid \text{unit}_j \text{ wins})$. Thus, if all patterns are of the same size, i.e., $n_k = n$ for all k, then the weight w_{ij} becomes proportional to the probability that line i is active given unit j wins. That is,

$$w_{ij} \rightarrow \frac{1}{n} p(\text{line}_i = 1 \mid \text{unit}_j \text{ wins}).$$

We are now in a position to specify the response, at equilibrium, of unit j when stimulus S_l is presented. Let α_{jl} be the input to unit j in the face of stimulus S_l. This is simply the sum of weights on the active input lines. This can be written

$$\alpha_{jl} \rightarrow \sum_i w_{ij} c_{il} = \sum_i c_{il} \frac{\sum_k \frac{p_k c_{ik} v_{jk}}{n_k}}{\sum_k p_k v_{jk}}$$

which implies that at equilibrium

$$\alpha_{jl} = \frac{\sum_i p_i r_{li} v_{ji}}{\sum_i p_i v_{ji}}$$

where r_{li} represents the overlap between stimulus l and stimulus i, $r_{li} = \sum_k \frac{c_{ki} c_{kl}}{n_i}$. Thus, at equilibrium a unit responds most strongly to patterns that overlap other patterns to which the unit responds and responds most weakly to patterns that are far from patterns to which it responds. Finally, it should be noted that there is another set of restrictions on the value of v_{jk} — the probability that unit j responds to stimulus S_k. In fact, the competitive learning rule we have studied has the further restriction that

$$v_{jk} = \begin{cases} 1 & \alpha_{jk} > \alpha_{ik} \text{ for all } i \neq j \\ 0 & \text{otherwise.} \end{cases}$$

Thus, in general, there are many solutions to the equilibrium equations described above. The competitive learning mechanisms can only reach those equilibrium states in which the above-stated relationships between the v_{jk} and the α_{jk} also hold.

Whenever the system is in a state in which, on average, the weights are not changing, we say that the system has reached an *equilibrium state.* In such a state the values of α_{jk} become relatively stable, and therefore, the values of v_{ik} become stable. When this happens, the system always responds the same way to a particular stimulus pattern. However, it is possible that the weights will be pushed out of equilibrium by an unfortunate sequence of stimuli. In this case, the system can move toward a new equilibrium state (or possibly back to a previous one). Some equilibrium states are more stable than others in the sense that the v_{ik} become very unlikely to change values for long periods of time. In particular, this will happen whenever the largest α_{jk} is much larger than any other α_{ik} for all stimulus patterns S_k. In this case, small movements in the weight vector of one of the units is very unlikely to change which unit responds to which stimulus pattern. Such equilibrium states are said to be highly *stable.* We should expect, then, that after it has been learning for a period of time, the system will spend most of its time in the most highly stable of the equilibrium states. One good measure of the stability of an equilibrium state is given by the average amount by which the input to the winning units is greater than the response of all of the other units averaged over all patterns and all units in a cluster. This measure is given by T below:

$$T = \sum_k p_k \sum_{j,i} v_{jk} (\alpha_{jk} - \alpha_{ik}).$$

The larger the value of T, the more stable the system can be expected to be and the more time we can expect the system to spend in that state. Roughly, if we assume that the system moves into states which maximize T, we can show that this amounts to maximizing the overlap among patterns within a group while minimizing the overlap among patterns between groups. In the geometric analogy above, this will occur when the weight vectors point toward maximally compact stimulus regions that are as distant as possible from other such regions.

SOME EXPERIMENTAL RESULTS

Dipole Experiments

The essential structure that a competitive learning mechanism can discover is represented in the overlap of stimulus patterns. The simplest stimulus population in which stimulus patterns can overlap with one another is one constructed out of *dipoles*—stimulus patterns consisting of exactly two active elements and the rest inactive. If we have a total of N input units there are $N(N-1)/2$ possible dipole stimuli. Of course, if the actual stimulus population consists of all $N(N-1)/2$ possibilities, there is no structure to be discovered. There are no clusters for our units to point at (unless we have one unit for each of the possible stimuli, in which case we can point a weight vector at each of the possible input stimuli). If, however, we restrict the possible dipole stimuli in certain ways, then there can be meaningful groupings of the stimulus patterns that the system can find. Consider, as an example, a case in which the stimulus lines could be thought of as forming a two-dimensional grid in which the only possible stimulus patterns were those which formed adjacent pairs in the grid. If we have an $N \times M$ grid, there are $N(M-1) + M(N-1)$ possible stimuli. Figure 4 shows one of the 24 possible adjacent dipole patterns defined on a 4×4 grid. We carried out a number of experiments employing stimulus sets of this kind. In most of these experiments we employed a two-layer system with a single inhibitory cluster of size two. Figure 5 illustrates the architecture of one of our experiments. The results of three runs with this architecture are illustrated in Figure 6, which shows the relative values of the weights for the two units. The values are shown laid out on a 4×4 grid so that weights are next to one another if the units with which they connect are next to one another. The relative values of the weights are indicated by the filling of the circles. If a circle is filled, that indicates that Unit 1 had the largest weight on that line. If the circle is unfilled, that means that Unit 2 had the largest weight on that line. The grids on the left indicate the initial configurations of the weights. The grids on the right indicate the final configurations of weights. The lines connecting the circles represent the possible stimuli. For example, the dipole stimulus pattern consisting of the upper left input line and the one immediately to the right of it is represented by the line connecting the upper-left circle in the grid with its right neighbor. The unit that wins when this stimulus is presented is indicated by the width of the line connecting the two circles. The wide line indicates

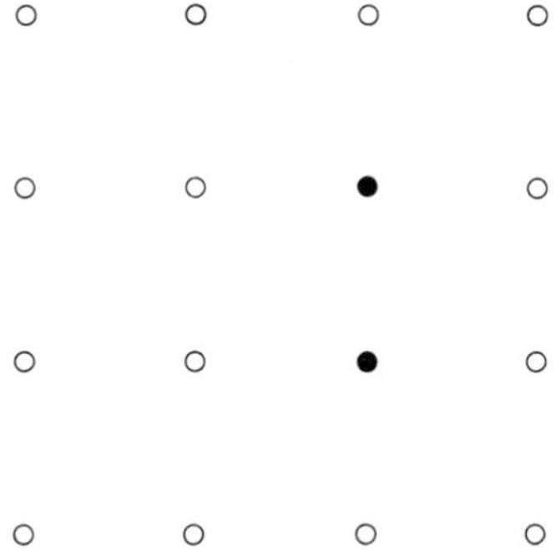

FIGURE 4. A dipole stimulus defined on a 4×4 matrix of input units. The rule for generating such stimuli is simply that any two adjacent units may be simultaneously active. Nonadjacent units may not be active and more than two units may not be simultaneously active. Active units are indicated by filled circles.

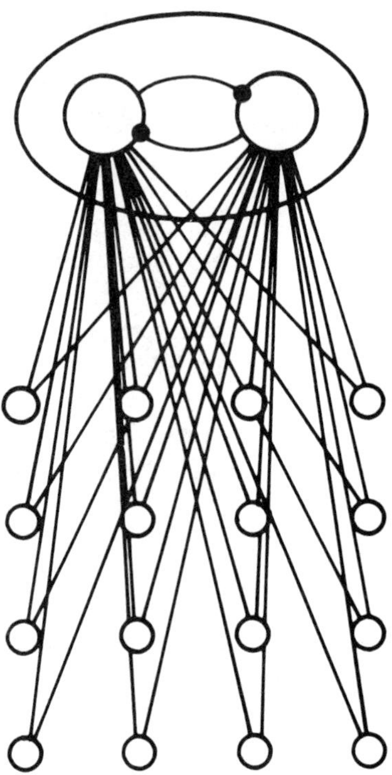

FIGURE 5. The architecture of a competitive learning system with 16 input units and one cluster of size two in the second layer.

that Unit 1 was the winner, the narrow line indicates that Unit 2 was the winner. It should be noted, therefore, that two unfilled circles must always be joined by a narrow line and two filled circles must always be joined by a wide line. The reason for this is that if a particular unit has more weight on both of the active lines then that unit *must* win the competition. The results clearly show that the weights move from a rather chaotic initial arrangement to an arrangement in which essentially all of those on one side of the grid are filled and all on the other side are unfilled. The border separating the two halves of the grid may be at any orientation, but most often it is oriented vertically and horizontally, as shown in the upper two examples. Only rarely is the orientation diagonal, as in the example in the lower right-hand grid. Thus, we have a case in which each unit has chosen a coherent half of the grid to which they respond. It is important to realize that as far as the competitive learning mechanism is concerned the sixteen input

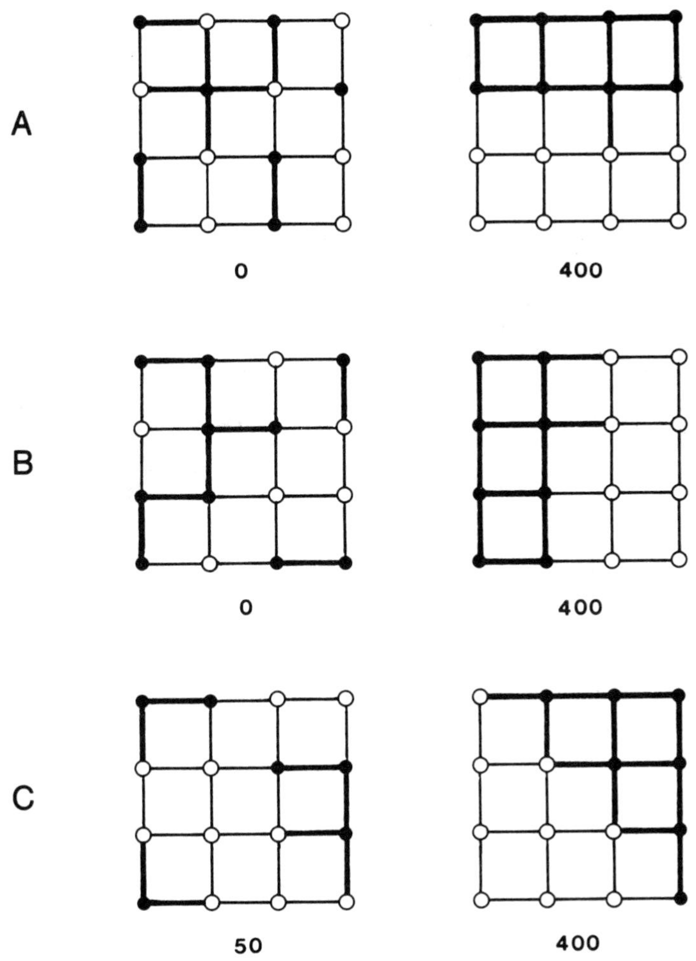

FIGURE 6. Relative weight values for the two members of the inhibitory cluster. *A*: The results for one run with the dipole stimuli defined over a two-dimensional grid. The left-hand grid shows the relative values of the weights initially and the right-hand grid shows the relative values of the weights after 400 trials. A filled circle means that Unit 1 had the larger weight on the corresponding input. An unfilled circle means that Unit 2 had the larger weight. A heavy line connecting two circles means that Unit 1 responded to the stimulus pattern consisting of the activation of the two circles, and a light line means that Unit 2 won the corresponding pattern. In this case the system has divided the grid horizontally. *B*: The results for a second run under the same conditions. In this case the system has divided the grid horizontally. *C*: The results for a third run. In this case the left-hand grid represents the state of the system after 50 trials. Here the grid was divided diagonally.

lines are unordered. The two-dimensional grid-like arrangement exists only in the statistics of the population of stimulus patterns. Thus, the system has *discovered* the dimensional structure inherent in the stimulus population and has devised binary feature detectors that tell which half of the grid contains the stimulus pattern. Note, each unit responds to roughly half of the stimulus patterns. Note also that while some units break the grid vertically, some break the grid horizontally, and some break it diagonally; a combination of several clusters offers a rather more precise classification of a stimulus pattern.

In other experiments, we tried clusters of other sizes. For example, Figure 7 shows the results for a cluster of size four. It shows the initial configuration and its sequence of evolution after 100, 200, 400, 800, and after 4000 training trials. Again, initially the regions are chaotic. After training, however, the system settles into a state in which stimuli in compact regions of the grid are responded to by the same units. It can be seen, in this case, that the trend is toward a given unit responding to a maximally compact group of stimuli. In this experiment, three of the units settled on compact square regions while the remaining one settled on two unconnected stimulus regions. It can be shown that the state into which the system settled does not quite maximize the value T, but does represent a relatively stable equilibrium state.

In the examples discussed thus far, the system, to a first approximation, settled on a highly compact representation of the input patterns in which all patterns in a region are captured by one of the units. The grids discussed above have all been two-dimensional. There is no need to restrict the analysis to a two-dimensional grid. In fact, a two-unit cluster will, essentially, pass a plane through a space of any dimensionality. There is a preference for planes perpendicular to the axes of the spaces. Figure 8 shows a typical result for the system learning a three-dimensional space. In the case of three dimensions, there are three equally good planes which can be passed through the space and, depending on the starting directions of the weight vectors and on the sequence of stimuli, different clusters will choose different ones of these planes. Thus, a system which receives input from a set of such clusters will be given information as to which *quadrant* of the space in which the pattern appears. It is important to emphasize that the coherence of the space is *entirely* in the choice of input stimuli, *not* in the architecture of the competitive learning mechanism. The system *discovers* the spatial structure in the input lines.

Formal analysis. For the dipole examples described above, it is possible to develop a rather precise characterization of the behavior of the competitive learning system. Recall our argument that the most stable equilibrium state (and therefore the one the system is *most* likely to

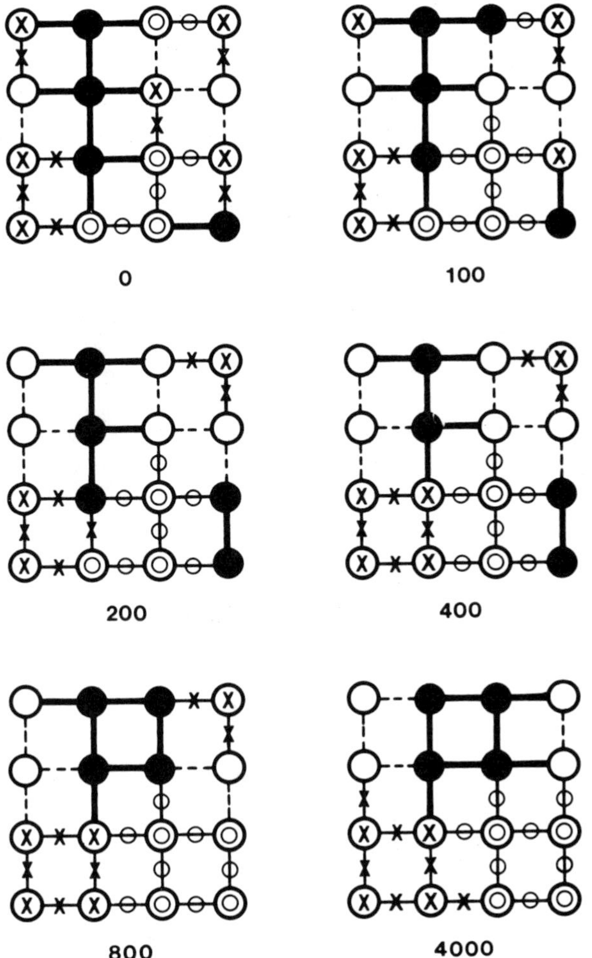

FIGURE 7. The relative weights of each of the four elements of the cluster after 0, 100, 200, 400, 800, and 4000 stimulus presentations.

end up in) is the one that maximizes the function

$$T = \sum_k p_k \sum_{j,i} v_{jk} (\alpha_{jk} - \alpha_{ik}).$$

Now, in the dipole examples, all stimulus patterns of the stimulus population are equally likely (i.e., $p_k = 1/N$), all stimulus patterns involve two active lines, and for every stimulus pattern in the population of patterns there are a fixed number of other stimulus patterns in

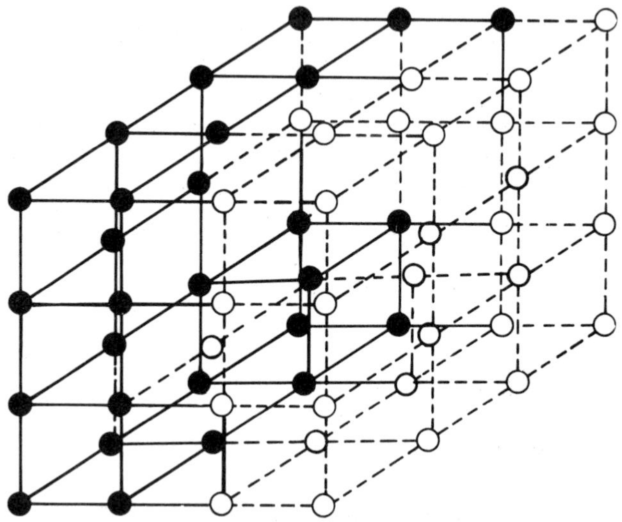

FIGURE 8. The relative weights for a system in which the stimulus patterns were chosen from a three-dimensional grid after 4000 presentations.

the population which overlap it.[6] This implies that $\sum_{k}^{N} r_{kj} = R$ for all j. With these assumptions, it is possible to show that maximizing T is equivalent to minimizing the function

$$\sum_{i}^{M} \frac{B_i}{N_i}$$

(see appendix for derivation), where N_i is the number of patterns on which unit i wins, M is the number of units in the cluster, and B_i is the number of cases in which unit i responds to a particular pattern and does not respond to a pattern which overlaps it. This is the number of *border* patterns to which unit i responds. Formally, we have

$$B_i = \sum_{j}^{N} \sum_{k}^{N} v_{ij} (1 - v_{ik}) \text{ for } r_{jk} > 0.$$

From this analysis, it is clear that the most stable states are ones in which the size of the border is minimized. Since total border region is minimized when regions are spherical, we can conclude that in a situation in which stimulus pairs are drawn from adjacent points in a

[6] Note that this latter condition does not quite hold for the examples presented above due to edge effects. It is possible to eliminate edge effects by the use of a torus. We have carried out experiments on tori as well, and the results are essentially the same.

high-dimensional hyperspace, our competitive learning mechanism will form essentially spherical regions that partition the space into one such spherical region for each element of the cluster.

Another result of our simulations which can be explained by these equations is the tendency for each element of the cluster to capture roughly equally sized regions. This results from the interconnectedness of the stimulus population. The result is easiest in the case in which $M=2$. In this case, the function we want to minimize is given by

$$\frac{B_1}{N_1} + \frac{B_2}{N_2}.$$

Now, in the case of $M=2$, we have $B_1 = B_2$, since the two regions must border on one another. Moreover, we have $N_1 + N_2 = N$, since every pattern is either responded to by Unit 1 or Unit 2. Thus, we want to minimize the function

$$B\left(\frac{1}{N_1} + \frac{1}{N-N_1}\right).$$

This function is minimized when $N_1 = N/2$. Thus, there are two pressures which determine the performance of the system in these cases:

- There is a pressure to reduce the number of border stimuli to a minimum.

- There is a pressure to divide the stimulus patterns among the units in a way that depends on the total amount of weight that unit has. If two units have the same amount of weight, they will capture roughly equal numbers of equally likely stimulus patterns.

Learning Words and Letters

It is common practice to handcraft networks to carry out particular tasks. Whenever one creates such a network that performs a task rather successfully, the question arises as to how such a network might have evolved. The word perception model developed in McClelland and Rumelhart (1981) and Rumelhart and McClelland (1982) is one such case-in-point. That model offers rather detailed accounts of a variety of word perception experiments, but it was crafted to do its job.

How could it have evolved naturally? Could a competitive learning mechanism create such a network?

Let's begin with the fact that the word perception model required a set of position-specific letter detectors. Suppose that a competitive learning mechanism is faced with a set of words—to what features would the system learn to respond? Would it create position-specific letter detectors or their equivalent? We proceeded to answer this question by again viewing the lower level units as forming a two-dimensional grid. Letters and words could then be presented by activating those units on the grid corresponding to the points of a standard CRT font. Figure 9 gives examples of some of the stimuli used in our experiments. The grid we used was a 7×14 grid. Each letter occurred in a 7×5 rectangular region on the grid. There was room for two letters with some space in between, as shown in the figure. We then carried out a series of experiments in which we presented a set of word and/or letter stimuli to the system allowing it to extract relevant features.

Before proceeding with a description of our experiments, it should be mentioned that these experiments required a slight addition to the competitive learning mechanism. The problem was that, unlike the dipole stimuli, the letter stimuli only sparsely covered the grid and many of the units in the lower level never became active at all. Therefore, there was a possibility that, by chance, one of the units would have most of its weight on input lines that were never active, whereas another unit may have had most of its weight on lines common to all of the stimulus patterns. Since a unit never learns unless it wins, it is

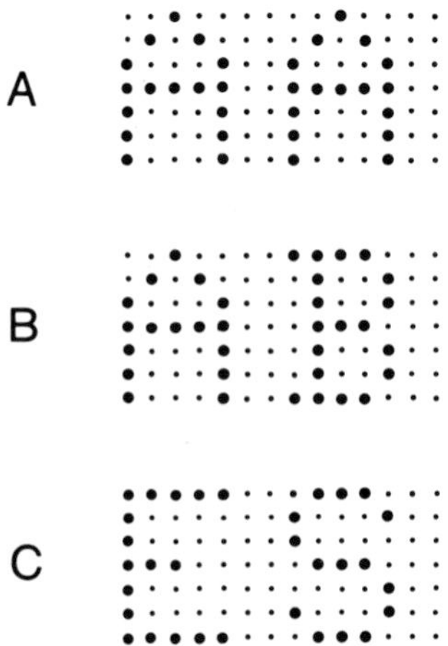

FIGURE 9. Example stimuli for the word and letter experiments.

possible that one of the units will never win, and therefore never learn. This, of course, takes the competition out of competitive learning. This situation is analogous to the situation in the geometric analogy in which all of the stimulus points are relatively close together on the hypersphere, and one of the weight vectors, by chance, points near the cluster while the other one points far from the stimuli. (See Figure 10). It is clear that the more distant vector is not closest to any stimulus and thus can never move toward the collection. We have investigated two modifications to the system which deal with the problem. One, which we call the leaky learning model, modifies the learning rule to state that *both* the winning *and* the losing units move toward the presented stimulus: the close vector simply moves much further. In symbols this suggests that

$$\Delta w_{ij} = \begin{cases} g_l \dfrac{c_{ik}}{n_k} - g_l w_{ij} & \text{if unit } j \text{ loses on stimulus } k \\ g_w \dfrac{c_{ik}}{n_k} - g_w w_{ij} & \text{if unit } j \text{ wins on stimulus } k \end{cases}$$

where g_l is the learning rate for the losing units, g_w is the learning rate for the winning unit, and where $g_l << g_w$. In our experiments we made

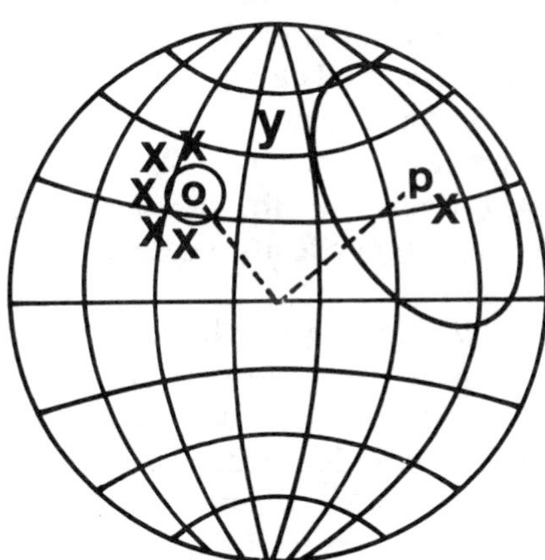

FIGURE 10. A geometric interpretation of changes in stimulus sensitivity. The larger the circle around the head of the weight vector the more sensitive the unit. The decision as to which unit wins is made on the basis of the distance from the circle rather than from the head of the weight vector. In the example, the stimulus pattern indicated by the *y* is actually closer to the head of one vector **o**, but since it is closer to the circle surrounding vector **p**, unit *p* would win the competition.

g_l an order of magnitude smaller than g_w. This change has the property that it slowly moves the losing units into the region where the actual stimuli lie, at which point they begin to capture some units and the ordinary dynamics of competitive learning take over.

The second method is similar to that employed by Bienenstock, Cooper, and Munro (1982), in which a unit modulates its own sensitivity so that when it is not receiving enough inputs, it becomes increasingly sensitive. When it is receiving too many inputs, it decreases its sensitivity. This mechanism can be implemented in the present context by assuming that there is a threshold and that the relevant activation is the degree to which the unit exceeds its threshold. If, whenever a unit fails to win it decreases its threshold and whenever it does win it increases its threshold, then this method will also make all of the units eventually respond, thereby engaging the mechanism of competitive learning. This second method can be understood in terms of the geometric analogy that the weight vectors have a circle surrounding the end of the vector. The relevant measure is not the distance to the vector itself but the distance to the circle surrounding the vector. Every time a unit loses, it increases the radius of the circle; every time it wins, it decreases the radius of the circle. Eventually, the circle on the losing unit will be large enough to be closer to some stimulus pattern than the other units.

We have used both of these mechanisms in our experiments and they appear to result in essentially similar behavior. The former, the leaky learning method, does not alter the formal analysis as long as the ratio g_l/g_w is sufficiently small. The varying threshold method is more difficult to analyze and may, under some circumstances, distort the competitive learning process somewhat. After this diversion, we can now return to our experiments on the development of word/position-specific letter detectors and other feature detectors.

Position-specific letter detectors. In our first experiment, we presented letter pairs drawn from the set: *AA, AB, BA,* and *BB*. We began with clusters of size two. The results were unequivocal. The system developed position-specific letter detectors. In some experimental runs, one of the units responded whenever *AA* or *AB* was presented, and the other responded whenever *BA* or *BB* was presented. In this case, Unit 1 represents an *A* detector in position 1 and Unit 2 represents a *B* detector for position 1. Moreover, as in the word perception model, the letter detectors are, of course, in a mutually inhibitory pool. On other experimental runs, the pattern was reversed. One of the units responded whenever there was an *A* in the second position and the other unit responded whenever there was a *B* in the second position. Figure 11 shows the final configuration of weights for one of

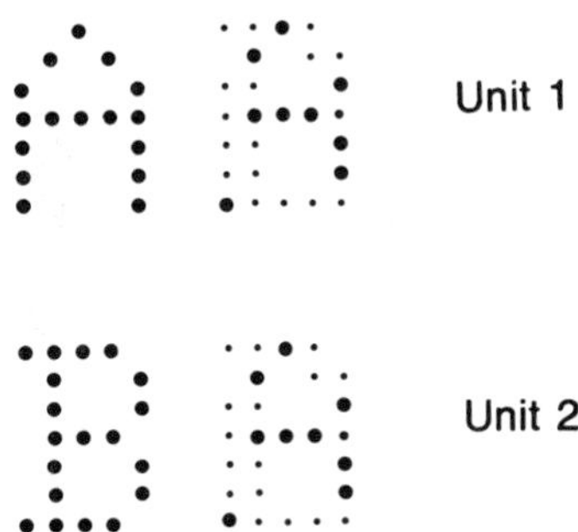

FIGURE 11. The final configuration of weights for a system trained on the stimulus patterns *A, B, C, D*.

our experimental runs. Note that although the units illustrated here respond *only* to the letter in the first position, there is still weight on the active lines in the second position. It is just that the weights on the first position differentiate between *A* and *B*, whereas those on the second position respond equally to the two letters. In particular, as suggested by our formal analysis, asymptotically the weights on a given line are proportional to the probability that that line is active when the unit wins. That is, $w_{ij} \rightarrow p(\text{unit}_i = 1 \mid \text{unit}_j \text{ wins})$. Since the lower level units unique to *A* occur equally as often as those unique to *B*, the weights on those lines are roughly equal. The input lines common to the two letters are on twice as often as those unique to either letter, and hence, they have twice as much weight. Those lines that never come on reach zero weight.

Word detection units. In another experiment, we presented the same stimulus patterns, but increased the elements in the cluster from two to four. In this case, each of the four level-two units came to respond to one of the four input patterns—in short, the system developed *word detectors*. Thus, if layer two were to consist of a number of clusters of various sizes, large clusters with approximately one unit per word pattern will develop into word detectors, while smaller clusters with approximately the number of letters per spatial position will develop into position-specific letter detectors. As we shall see below, if the number of elements of a cluster is substantially less than the number of letters per position, then the cluster will come to detect position-specific letter features.

Effects of number of elements per serial position. In another experiment, we varied the number of elements in a cluster and the number of letters per serial position. We presented stimulus patterns drawn from the set: *AA, AB, AC, AD, BA, BB, BC, BD*. In this case, we found that with clusters of size two, one unit responded to the patterns beginning with *A* and the other responded to those beginning with *B*. In our previous experiment, when we had the same number of letters in each position, we found that the clusters were indifferent as to which serial position they responded. Some responded to position 1 and others to position 2. In this experiment, we found that a two-element cluster always becomes a letter detector specific to serial position in which two letters vary. Similarly, in the case of clusters of size four we found that they always became letter detectors for the position in which four letters varied. Thus, in this case one responded to an *A* in the second position, one responded to a *B* in the second position, one responded to a *C* in the second position, and one responded to a *D* in the second position. Clearly, there are two natural ways to cluster the stimulus patterns—two levels of structure. If the patterns are to be put in two categories, then the binary feature *A* or *B* in the first position is the relevant distinction. On the other hand, if the stimuli are to be grouped into four groups, the four value feature determining the second letter is the relevant distinction. The competitive learning algorithm can discover either of the levels of structure—depending on the number of elements in a cluster.

Letter similarity effects. In another experiment, we studied the effects of letter similarity to look for units that detect letter features. We presented letter patterns consisting of a letter in the first position only. We chose the patterns so they formed two natural clusters based on the similarity of the letters to one another. We presented the letters *A, B, S,* and *E*. The letters were chosen so that they fell naturally into two classes. In our font, the letters *A* and *E* are quite similar and the letters *B* and *S* are very similar. We used a cluster of size two. Naturally, one of the units responded to the *A* or the *E* while the other unit responded to the *B* or the *S*. The weights were largest on those features of the stimulus pairs which were common among each of these similar pairs. Thus, the system developed subletter-size feature detectors for the features relevant to the discrimination.

Correlated teaching inputs. We carried out one other set of experiments with the word/letter patterns. In this case, we used clusters of size two and presented stimuli drawn from the set: *AA, BA, SB, EB*. Note that on the left-hand side, we have the same four letters as we had in the previous experiment, but on the right-hand side we have only two patterns; these two patterns are correlated with the letter in the first position. An *A* in the second position means that the first position contains either an *A* or a *B*, whereas a *B* in the second position means that the first position contains either an *S* or an *E*. Note further that those correlations between the first and second positions are in opposition to the "natural" similarity of the letters in the first serial position. In this experiment, we first trained the system on the four stimuli described above. Since the second serial position had only two letters in it, the size-two cluster became a position-specific letter detector for the second serial position. One unit responded to the *A* and one to the *B* in the second position. Notice that the units are also responding to the letters in the first serial position as well. One unit is responding to an *A* or a *B* in the first position while the other responds to an *E* or an *S*. Figure 12 shows the patterns of weights developed by the two units. After training, the system was then presented patterns containing only the first letter of the pair and, as expected, the system had learned the "unnatural" classification of the letters in the first position. Here the strong correlation between the first and second position led the competitive learning mechanism to override the strong correlation between the highly similar stimulus patterns in the first serial position. This suggests that even though the competitive learning system is an "unsupervised" learning mechanism, one can control what it learns by controlling the statistical structure of the stimulus patterns being presented to it. In this sense, we can think of the right-hand letter in this experiment as being a kind of *teaching* stimulus aimed at determining the classification learned for other aspects of the stimulus. It should also be noted that this teaching mechanism is essentially the same as the so-called errorless learning procedure used by Terrace (1963) in training pigeons to peck a certain color key by associating that color with a response situation where their pecking is determined by other factors. As we shall see below, this correlational teaching mechanism is useful in allowing the competitive learning mechanism to discover features which it otherwise would be unable to discover.

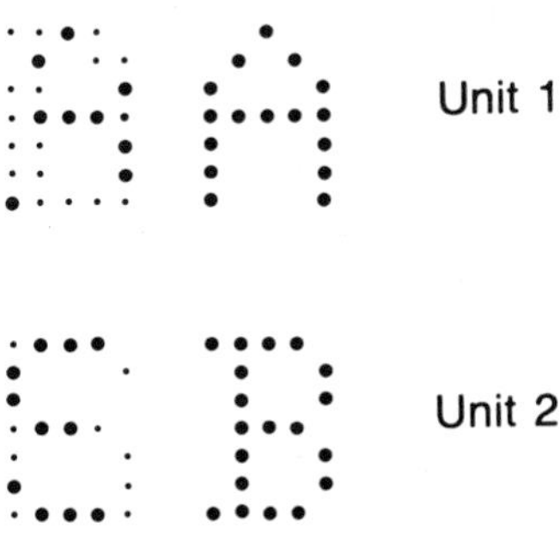

FIGURE 12. The pattern of weights developed in the correlated learning experiment.

Horizontal and Vertical Lines

One of the classically difficult problems for a linear threshold device like a perceptron is to distinguish between horizontal and vertical lines. In general, horizontal and vertical lines are not linearly separable and require a multilayer perceptron system to distinguish them. One of the goals of the competitive learning device is for it to discover features that, at a higher level of analysis, might be useful for discriminating patterns which might not otherwise be discriminable with a linear threshold-type device. It is therefore of some interest to see what kinds of features the competitive learning mechanism discovers when presented with a set of vertical and horizontal lines. In the following discussion, we chronicle a series of experiments on this problem. Several of the experiments ended in failure, but we were able to discover a way in which competitive learning systems can be put together to build a hierarchical feature detection system capable of discriminating vertical and horizontal lines. We proceed by sketching several of our failures as well as our successes because the way in which the system fails is elucidating. It should be noted at the outset that our goal is not so much to present a model of how the human learns to distinguish between vertical and horizontal lines (indeed, such a distinction is probably prewired in the human system), but rather to show how competitive learning can discover features which allow for the system to learn distinctions with multiple layers of units that cannot be learned by single-layered systems. Learning to distinguish vertical and horizontal lines is simply a paradigm case.

In this set of experiments, we represented the lower level of units as if they were on a 6×6 grid. We then had a total of 12 stimulus patterns, each consisting of turning on six Level 1 units in a row on the grid. Figure 13 illustrates the grid and several of the stimulus patterns. Ideally, one might hope that one of the units would respond whenever a vertical line is presented; the other would respond whenever a horizontal line is presented. Unfortunately, a little thought indicates that this is impossible. Since every input unit participates in exactly one vertical and one horizontal line, there is no configuration of weights which will distinguish vertical from horizontal. This is exactly why no linear threshold device can distinguish between vertical and horizontal lines in one level. Since that must fail, we might hope that some clusters in the competitive learning device will respond to vertical lines by assigning weights as illustrated in Figure 14. In this case, one unit of the pair would respond whenever the first, second, or fourth vertical line was presented, and another would respond whenever the third, fifth, or sixth vertical line was presented; since both units would

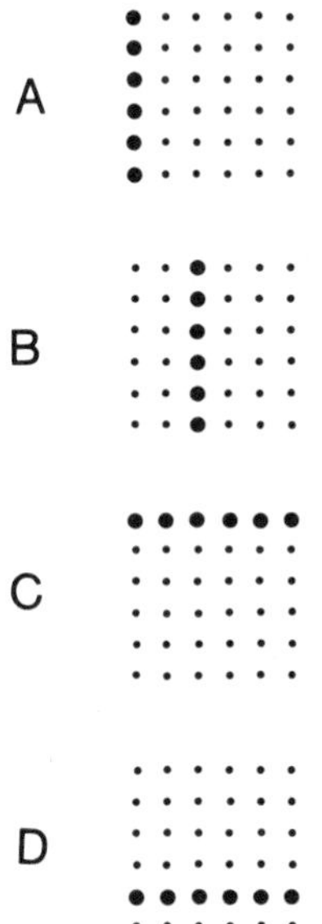

FIGURE 13. Stimulus patterns for the horizontal/vertical discrimination experiments.

receive about the same input in the face of a horizontal line, we might expect that sometimes one and sometimes the other would win the competition but that the primary response would be to vertical lines. If other clusters settled down similarly to horizontal lines, then a unit at the third level looking at the output of the various clusters could distinguish vertical and horizontal. Unfortunately, that is not the pattern of weights discovered by the competitive learning mechanism. Rather, a typical pattern of weights is illustrated in Figure 15. In this arrangement, each cluster responds to exactly three horizontal and three vertical lines. Such a cluster has lost all information that might distinguish vertical from horizontal. We have discovered a feature of absolutely no use in this distinction. In fact, such features systematically throw away the information relevant to horizontal vs. vertical. Some further thought indicates why such a result occurred. Note, in particular, that two horizontal lines have exactly *nothing* in common. The grid that we show in the diagrams is merely for our convenience. As far as the units are concerned there are 36 unordered input units; sometimes some of those units are active. Pattern similarity is determined entirely by pattern overlap. Since horizontal lines don't intersect, they have no units in common, thus they are not seen as similar at all. However, every horizontal line intersects with every vertical line and thus has much more in common with vertical lines than with other horizontal

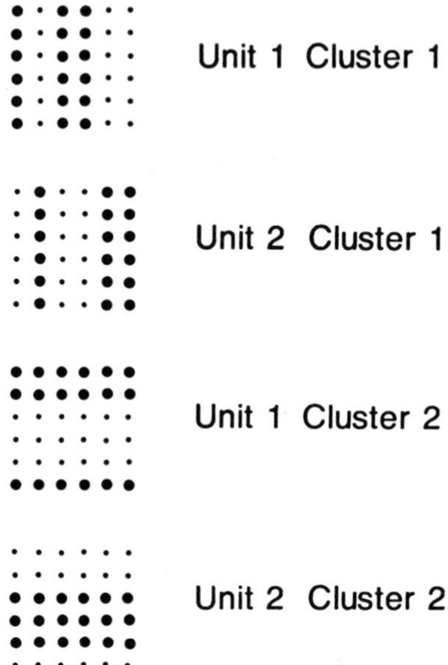

FIGURE 14. A possible weight configuration which could distinguish vertical from horizontal.

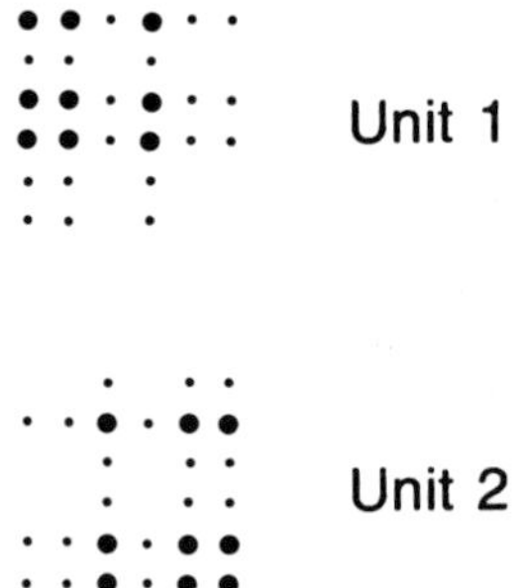

FIGURE 15. A typical configuration of weights for the vertical/horizontal discrimination.

ones. It is this similarity that the competitive learning mechanism has discovered.

Now, suppose that we change the system somewhat. Suppose that we "teach" the system the difference between vertical and horizontal (as we did in the previous experiments with letter strings). In this experiment we used a 12×6 grid. On the right-hand side of the grid we presented either a vertical or a horizontal line, as we did before. On the left-hand side of the grid we always presented the uppermost horizontal line whenever any horizontal line was presented on the right-hand grid, and we always presented the vertical line furthest to the left on the left-hand grid whenever we presented any vertical line on the right-hand side of the grid. We then had a cluster of two units receiving inputs from all $12 \times 6 = 72$ lower level units. (Figure 16 shows several of the stimulus patterns.)

As expected, the two units soon learned to discriminate between vertical and horizontal lines. One of the units responded whenever a vertical line was presented and the other responded whenever a horizontal line was presented. They were responding, however, to the pattern on the left-hand side rather than to the vertical and horizontal pattern on the right. This too should be expected. Recall that the value of the w_{ij} approaches a value which is proportional to the probability that input unit i is active, given that unit j won the competition. Now, in the case of the unit that responds to vertical lines for example, every unit on the right-hand grid occurs equally often so that all of the weights connecting to units in that grid have equal weights. The same is true for the unit responding to the horizontal line. The weights on

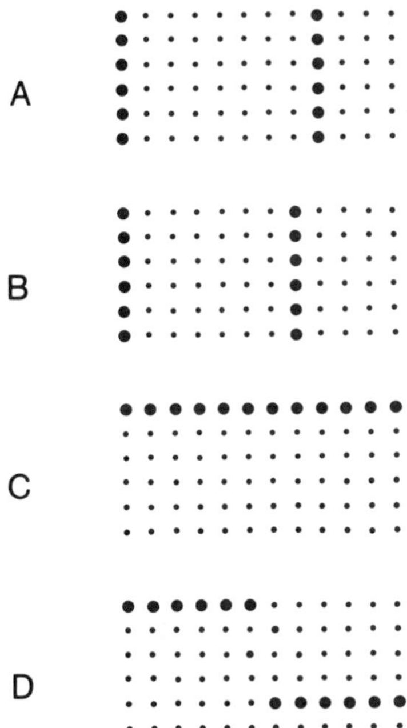

FIGURE 16. Stimulus patterns for the vertical/horizontal discrimination experiments with a correlated "teaching" input on the right-hand side.

the right-hand grid are identical for the two cluster members. Thus, when the "teacher" is turned off, and only the right-hand figure is presented, the two units respond randomly and show no evidence of having learned the horizontal/vertical distinction.

Suppose, however, that we have four, rather than two, units in the level-two clusters. We ran this experiment and found that of the four units, two of them divided up the vertical patterns and two of them divided up the horizontal patterns. Figure 17 illustrates the weight values for one of our runs. One of the units took three of the vertical line patterns; another unit took three other vertical patterns. A third unit responded to three of the horizontal line patterns, and the last unit responded to the remaining three horizontal lines. Moreover, after we took away the "teaching" pattern, the system continued to classify the vertical and horizontal lines just as it did when the left-hand "teaching" pattern was present.

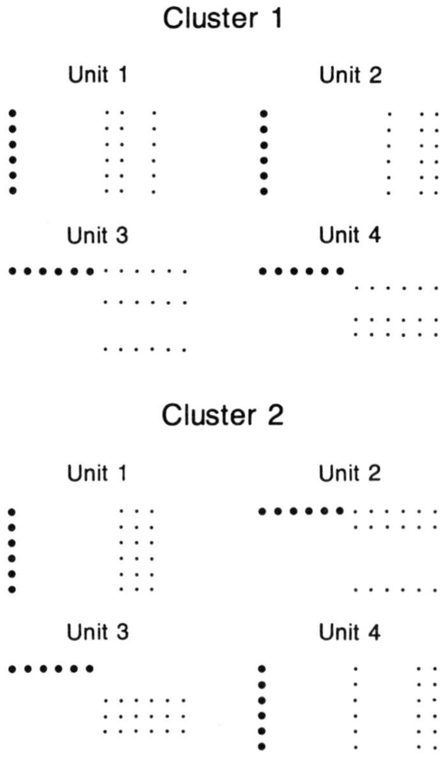

Cluster 1

Unit 1 Unit 2

Unit 3 Unit 4

Cluster 2

Unit 1 Unit 2

Unit 3 Unit 4

FIGURE 17. The weight values for the two clusters of size four for the vertical/horizontal discrimination experiment with a correlated "teaching" stimulus.

In one final experiment with vertical and horizontal lines, we developed a three-level system in which we used the same stimulus patterns as in the previous experiment; the only difference was that we had *two* clusters of four units at the second level and one cluster of two units at the third level. Figure 18 shows the architecture employed. In this case, the two four-element clusters each learned to respond to subsets of the vertical and horizontal lines as in the previous experiment. The two clusters generally responded to different subsets, however. Thus, when the upper horizontal line was presented, Unit 1 of the first cluster responded and Unit 3 of the second cluster responded. When the bottom horizontal line was presented, Unit 1 of the first cluster responded again, but Unit 4 of the second cluster also responded. Thus, the cluster of size two at the highest level was receiving a kind of dipole stimulus. It has four inputs and on any trial, two of them are active. As with our analysis of dipole stimuli, we know that stimuli that overlap are always put in the same category. Note that when a vertical line is presented, one of the two units in each of the middle layers of clusters that responds to vertical lines will become active, and that none of the units that respond to horizontal lines will ever be active; thus, this means that there are two units in each middle layer cluster that respond to vertical lines. Whenever a vertical line is presented, one of the units in each cluster will become active. None of the horizontal units will ever be active in the face of a vertical stimulus. Thus, one of the units at the highest level learns to respond whenever a vertical line is presented, and the other unit responds whenever a horizontal line is

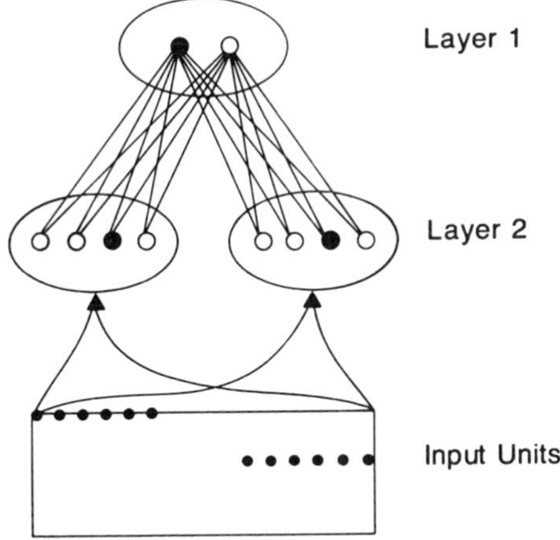

FIGURE 18. The architecture for the three-level horizontal/vertical discrimination experiment.

presented. Once the system has been trained, this occurs despite the absence of the "teaching" stimulus. Thus, what we have shown is that the competitive learning mechanism can, under certain conditions, develop feature detectors which allow the system to distinguish among patterns that are not differentiable by a simple linear unit in one level.

CONCLUSION

We have shown how a very simple competitive mechanism can discover a set of feature detectors that capture important aspects of the set of stimulus input patterns. We have also shown how these feature detectors can form the basis of a multilayer system that can serve to learn categorizations of stimulus sets that are not linearly separable. We have shown how the use of correlated stimuli can serve as a kind of "teaching" input to the system to allow the development of feature detectors which would not develop otherwise. Although we find the competitive learning mechanism a very interesting and powerful learning principle, we do not, of course, imagine that it is the only learning principle. Competitive learning is an essentially nonassociative, statistical learning scheme. We certainly imagine that other kinds of learning mechanisms will be involved in the building of associations among patterns of activation in a more complete neural network. We offer this analysis of these competitive learning mechanisms to further our understanding of how simple adaptive networks can discover features important in the description of the stimulus environment in which the system finds itself.

ACKNOWLEDGMENTS

This research was supported by grants from the System Development Foundation and by Contract N00014-79-C-0323, NR 667-437 with the Personnel and Training Research Programs of the Office of Naval Research.

APPENDIX

For the case of homogeneous *dipole* stimulus patterns, it is possible to derive an expression for the most *stable* equilibrium state of the system. We say that a set of dipole stimulus patterns is homogeneous if (a) they are equally likely and (b) for every input pattern in the set there are a fixed number of other input patterns that overlap them. These conditions were met in our simulations. Our measure of stability is given by

$$T = \sum_k p_k \sum_j \sum_i v_{jk} (\alpha_{jk} - \alpha_{ik}).$$

Since $p_k = \frac{1}{N}$, we can write

$$T = \frac{1}{N} \sum_i \sum_j \sum_k v_{jk} \alpha_{jk} - \frac{1}{N} \sum_i \sum_j \sum_k v_{jk} \alpha_{ik}.$$

Summing the first portion of the equation over i and the second over j we have

$$T = \frac{M}{N} \sum_j \sum_k v_{jk} \alpha_{jk} - \frac{1}{N} \sum_i \sum_k \alpha_{ik} \sum_j v_{jk}.$$

Now note that when $p_k = 1/N$, we have $\alpha_{ik} = \sum_j r_{kj} v_{ij} / \sum_l v_{kl}$. Furthermore, $\sum_l v_{lk} = 1$ and $\sum_k v_{lk} = N_l$, where N_l is the number of patterns captured by unit l. Thus, we have

$$T = \frac{M}{N} \sum_j \sum_k v_{jk} \alpha_{jk} - \frac{1}{N} \sum_i \sum_k \frac{\sum_l r_{kl} v_{il}}{N_i}.$$

Now, since all stimuli are the same size, we have $r_{ij} = r_{ji}$. Moreover, since all stimuli have the same number of neighbors, we have $\sum_i r_{ij} = \sum_j r_{ij} = R$, where R is a constant determined by the dimensionality of the stimulus space from which the dipole stimuli are drawn. Thus, we have

$$T = \frac{M}{N} \sum_j \sum_k v_{jk} \alpha_{jk} - \frac{R}{N} \sum_i \frac{\sum_l v_{il}}{N_i},$$

and we have

$$T = \frac{M}{N}\sum_j\sum_k v_{jk}\alpha_{jk} - \frac{RM}{N}.$$

Since R, M, and N are constants, we have that T is maximum whenever $T' = \sum_j\sum_k v_{jk}\alpha_{jk}$ is maximum. Now substituting for α_{jk}, we can write

$$T' = \sum_j \frac{1}{N_j}\sum_k\sum_l r_{kl}\, v_{jk}\, v_{jl}.$$

We can now substitute for the product $v_{jk}\, v_{jl}$ the term $v_{jk} - v_{jk}(1 - v_{jl})$. We then can write

$$T' = \sum_j \frac{1}{N_j}\sum_k\sum_l r_{kl}\, v_{jk} - \sum_j \frac{1}{N_j}\sum_k\sum_l r_{kl}\, v_{jk}(1 - v_{jl}).$$

Summing the first term of the equation first over l, then over k, and then over j, gives us

$$T' = MR - \sum_j \frac{1}{N_j}\sum_k\sum_l r_{kl}\, v_{jk}(1 - v_{jl}).$$

Now, recall that r_{kl} is given by the degree of stimulus overlap between stimulus l and stimulus k. In the case of dipoles there are only three possible values of r_{kl}:

$$r_{kl} = \begin{cases} 0 & \text{no overlap} \\ 1 & k{=}l \\ 1/2 & \text{otherwise} \end{cases}$$

Now, the second term of the equation for T' is 0 if either $r_{kl} = 0$ or if $v_{jk}(1 - v_{jl}) = 0$. Since v_{ik} is either 1 or 0, this will be zero whenever $j{=}l$. Thus, for all nonzero cases in the second term we have $r_{kl} = \frac{1}{2}$. Thus we have

$$T' = MR - \frac{1}{2}\sum_j \frac{1}{N_j}\sum_k\sum_l v_{jk}(1 - v_{jl}).$$

Finally, note that $\sum_k\sum_l v_{jk}(1 - v_{jl})$ is 1 and r_{kl} is $\frac{1}{2}$ in each case in which different units capture neighboring patterns. We refer to this as a case of *bad neighbors* and let B_j designate the number of bad neighbors for unit j. Thus, we have

$$T' = MR - \frac{1}{2}\sum_j \frac{B_j}{N_j}.$$

Finally, we can see that T' will be a maximum whenever $T'' = \sum_j \frac{B_j}{N_j}$ is minimum. Thus, minimizing T'' leads to the maximally stable solution in this case.

CHAPTER 6

Information Processing in Dynamical Systems: Foundations of Harmony Theory

P. SMOLENSKY

INTRODUCTION

The Theory of Information Processing

At this early stage in the development of cognitive science, methodological issues are both open and central. There may have been times when developments in neuroscience, artificial intelligence, or cognitive psychology seduced researchers into believing that their discipline was on the verge of discovering the secret of intelligence. But a humbling history of hopes disappointed has produced the realization that understanding the mind will challenge the power of all these methodologies combined.

The work reported in this chapter rests on the conviction that a methodology that has a crucial role to play in the development of cognitive science is *mathematical analysis*. The success of cognitive science, like that of many other sciences, will, I believe, depend upon the construction of a solid body of theoretical results: results that express in a mathematical language the conceptual insights of the field; results that squeeze all possible implications out of those insights by exploiting powerful mathematical techniques.

This body of results, which I will call the *theory of information processing*, exists because information is a concept that lends itself to mathematical formalization. One part of the theory of information processing is already well-developed. The classical theory of computation provides powerful and elegant results about the notion of *effective procedure*, including languages for precisely expressing them and theoretical machines for realizing them. This body of theory grew out of mathematical logic, and in turn contributed to computer science, physical computing systems, and the theoretical paradigm in cognitive science often called *the (von Neumann) computer metaphor.*[1]

In his paper "Physical Symbol Systems," Allen Newell (1980) articulated the role of the mathematical theory of symbolic computation in cognitive science and furnished a manifesto for what I will call *the symbolic paradigm.* The present book offers an alternative paradigm for cognitive science, the *subsymbolic paradigm*, in which the most powerful level of description of cognitive systems is hypothesized to be lower than the level that is naturally described by symbol manipulation.

The fundamental insights into cognition explored by the subsymbolic paradigm do not involve effective procedures and symbol manipulation. Instead they involve the "spread of activation," relaxation, and statistical correlation. The mathematical language in which these concepts are naturally expressed are probability theory and the theory of dynamical systems. By dynamical systems theory I mean the study of sets of numerical variables (e.g., activation levels) that evolve in time in parallel and interact through differential equations. The classical theory of dynamical systems includes the study of natural physical systems (e.g., mathematical physics) and artificially designed systems (e.g., control theory). Mathematical characterizations of dynamical systems that formalize the insights of the subsymbolic paradigm would be most helpful in developing the paradigm.

This chapter introduces *harmony theory*, a mathematical framework for studying a class of dynamical systems that perform cognitive tasks according to the account of the subsymbolic paradigm. These dynamical systems can serve as models of human cognition or as designs for artificial cognitive systems. The ultimate goal of the enterprise is to develop a body of mathematical results for the theory of information processing that complements the results of the classical theory of (symbolic) computation. These results would serve as the basis for a manifesto for the subsymbolic paradigm comparable to Newell's manifesto for the symbolic paradigm. The promise offered by this goal will, I hope, be suggested by the results of this chapter, despite their very limited scope.

---

1 Mathematical logic has recently given rise to another approach to formalizing information: *situation semantics* (Barwise & Perry, 1983). This is related to Shannon's (1948/1963) measure of information through the work of Dretske (1981). The approach of this chapter is more faithful to the probabilistic formulation of Shannon than is the symbolic approach of situation semantics. (This results from Dretske's move of identifying information with conditional probabilities of 1.)

It should be noted that harmony theory is a "theory" in the *mathematical* sense, not the *scientific* sense. By a "mathematical theory"—e.g., number theory, group theory, probability theory, the theory of computation—I mean a body of knowledge about a part of the ideal mathematical world; a set of definitions, axioms, theorems, and analytic techniques that are tightly interrelated. Such mathematical theories are distinct from scientific theories, which are of course bodies of knowledge about a part of the "real" world. Mathematical theories provide a language for expressing scientific theories; a given mathematical theory can be used to express a large class of scientific theories. Group theory, for example, provides a language for expressing many competing theories of elementary particles. Similarly, harmony theory can be used to express many alternative theories about various cognitive phenomena. The point is that without the concepts and techniques of the mathematical language of group theory, the formulation of *any* of the current scientific theories of elementary particles would be essentially impossible.

The goal of harmony theory is to provide a powerful language for expressing cognitive theories in the subsymbolic paradigm, a language that complements the existing languages for symbol manipulation. Since harmony theory is conceived as a language for using the subsymbolic paradigm to describe cognition, it embodies the fundamental scientific claims of that paradigm. But on many important issues, such as how knowledge is represented in detail for particular cases, harmony theory does not itself make commitments. Rather, it provides a language for stating alternative hypotheses and techniques for studying their consequences.

A Top-Down Theoretical Strategy

How can mathematical analysis be used to study the processing mechanisms underlying the performance of some cognitive task?

One strategy, often associated with David Marr (1982), is to characterize the task in a way that allows mathematical *derivation* of mechanisms that perform it. This *top-down* theoretical strategy is pursued in harmony theory. My claim is not that the strategy leads to descriptions that are *necessarily* applicable to all cognitive systems, but rather that the strategy leads to new insights, mathematical results, computer architectures, and computer models that fill in the relatively unexplored conceptual world of parallel, massively distributed systems that perform cognitive tasks. Filling in this conceptual world is a necessary subtask, I believe, for understanding how brains and minds are capable of intelligence and for assessing whether computers with novel architectures might share this capability.

The Centrality of Perceptual Processing

The cognitive task I will study in this chapter is an abstraction of the task of perception. This abstraction includes many cognitive tasks that are customarily regarded as much "higher level" than perception (e.g., intuiting answers to physics problems). A few comments on the role of perceptual processing in the subsymbolic paradigm are useful at this point.

The vast majority of cognitive processing lies between the highest cognitive levels of explicit logical reasoning and the lowest levels of sensory processing. Descriptions of processing at the extremes are relatively well-informed—on the high end by formal logic and on the low end by natural science. In the middle lies a conceptual abyss. How are we to conceptualize cognitive processing in this abyss?

The strategy of the symbolic paradigm is to conceptualize processing in the intermediate levels as symbol manipulation. Other kinds of processing are viewed as limited to extremely low levels of sensory and motor processing. Thus symbolic theorists climb *down* into the abyss, clutching a rope of symbolic logic anchored at the top, hoping it will stretch all the way to the bottom of the abyss.

The subsymbolic paradigm takes the opposite view, that intermediate processing mechanisms are of the same kind as perceptual processing mechanisms. Logic and symbol manipulation are viewed as appropriate descriptions only of the few cognitive processes that explicitly involve logical reasoning. Subsymbolic theorists climb *up* into the abyss on a perceptual ladder anchored at the bottom, hoping it will extend all the way to the top of the abyss.[2]

[2] There is no contradiction between working from lower level, perceptual processes up towards higher processes, and pursuing a top-down theoretical strategy. It is important to distinguish levels of *processing entities* from levels of *theoretical entities.* Higher level *processes* involve *computational* entities that are computationally distant from the peripheral, sensorimotor entities that comprise the "lowest level" of processing. These processing levels *taken together* form the processing system as a whole; they causally interact with each other through bottom-up and top-down *processing.* Higher level *theories* involve *descriptive* entities that are descriptively distant from entities that are directly part of an actual processing mechanism; these comprise the "lowest level" description. Each theoretical level *individually* describes the processing system as a whole; the interaction of descriptive levels is not *causal*, but *definitional.* (For example, changes in individual neural firing rates at the retina *cause* changes in individual firing rates in visual cortex after a delay related to causal information propagation. The same changes in individual retinal neuron firing rates *by definition* change the *average firing rates of pools* of retinal neurons; these higher level descriptive entities change instantly, without any causal information propagation from the lower level description.) Thus in harmony theory, models of higher level *processes* are derived from models of lower level, perceptual, processes, while lower level *descriptions* of these models are derived from higher level descriptions.

In this chapter, I will analyze an abstraction of the task of perception that encompasses many tasks, from low, through intermediate, to high cognitive levels. The analysis leads to a general kind of "perceptual" processing mechanism that is a powerful potential component of an information processing system. The abstract task I analyze captures a common part of the tasks of passing from an intensity pattern to a set of objects in three-dimensional space, from a sound pattern to a sequence of words, from a sequence of words to a semantic description, from a set of patient symptoms to a set of disease states, from a set of givens in a physics problem to a set of unknowns. Each of these processes is viewed as *completing an internal representation of a static state of an external world.* By suitably abstracting the task of interpreting a static *sensory* input, we can arrive at a theory of interpretation of static input *generally*, a theory of the *completion task* that applies to many cognitive phenomena in the gulf between perception and logical reasoning. An application that will be described in some detail is qualitative problem solving in circuit analysis.[3]

The central idea of the top-down theoretical strategy is that properties of the task are powerfully constraining on mechanisms. This idea can be well exploited within a perceptual approach to cognition, where the constraints on the perceptual task are characterized through the constraints operative in the external environment from which the inputs come. This permits an analysis of how internal representation of these constraints within the cognitive system itself allows it to perform its task. These kinds of considerations have been emphasized in the psychological literature prominently by Gibson and Shepard (see Shepard, 1984); they are fundamental to harmony theory.

Structure of the Chapter

The goal of harmony theory is to develop a mathematical theory of information processing in the subsymbolic paradigm. However, the theory grows out of ideas that can be stated with little or no mathematics. The organization of this chapter reflects an attempt to ensure that the central concepts are not obscured by mathematical opacity. The analysis will be presented in three parts, each part increasing in the level of formality and detail. My hope is that the slight redundancy

[3] Many cognitive tasks involve interpreting or controlling events that unfold over an extended period of time. To deal properly with such tasks, harmony theory must be extended from the interpretation of *static* environments to the interpretation of *dynamic* environments.

introduced by this expository organization will be repaid by greater accessibility.

Section 1 is a top-down presentation of how the perceptual perspective on cognition leads to the basic features of harmony theory. This presentation starts with a particular perceptual model, the letter-perception model of McClelland and Rumelhart (1981), and abstracts from it general features that can apply to modeling of higher cognitive processes. Crucial to the development is a particular formulation of aspects of schema theory, along the lines of Rumelhart (1980).

Section 2, the majority of the chapter, is a bottom-up presentation of harmony theory that starts with the primitives of the knowledge representation. Theorems are informally described that provide a competence theory for a cognitive system that performs the completion task, a machine that realizes this theory, and a learning procedure through which the machine can absorb the necessary information from its environment. Then an application of the general theory is described: a model of intuitive, qualitative problem-solving in elementary electric circuits. This model illustrates several points about the relation between symbolic and subsymbolic descriptions of cognitive phenomena; for example, it furnishes a sharp contrast between the description at these two levels of the nature and acquisition of expertise.

The final part of the chapter is an Appendix containing a concise but self-contained formal presentation of the definitions and theorems.

SECTION 1: SCHEMA THEORY AND SELF-CONSISTENCY

THE LOGICAL STRUCTURE OF HARMONY THEORY

The logical structure of harmony theory is shown schematically in Figure 1. The box labeled *Mathematical Theory* represents the use of mathematical analysis and computer simulation for drawing out the implications of the fundamental principles. These principles comprise a mathematical characterization of computational requirements of a cognitive system that performs the completion task. From these principles

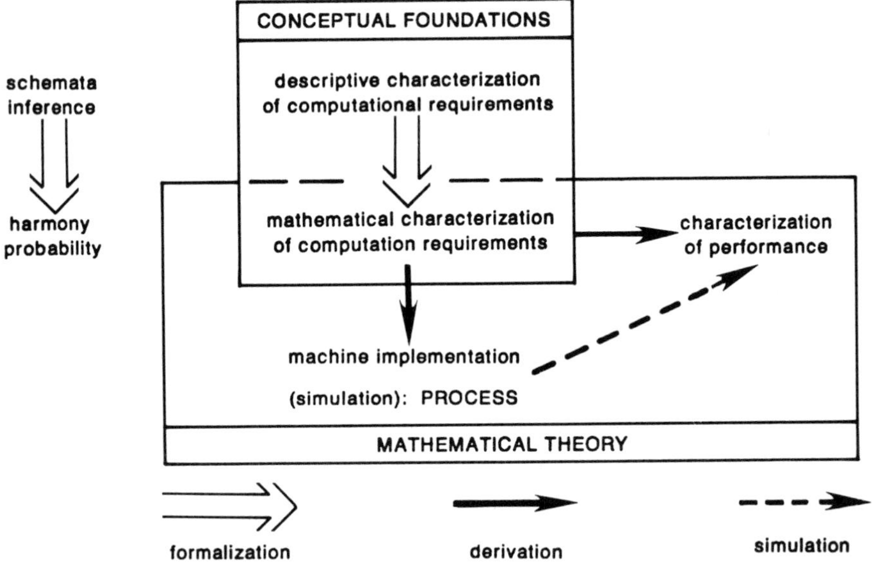

FIGURE 1. The logical structure of harmony theory.

it is possible to mathematically analyze aspects of the resulting performance as well as rigorously *derive* the rules for a machine implementing the computational requirements. The rules defining this machine have a different status from those defining most other computer models of cognition: They are not ad hoc, or post hoc; rather they are logically derived from a set of computational requirements. This is one sense in which harmony theory has a top-down theoretical development.

Where do the "mathematically characterized computational requirements" of Figure 1 come from? They are a formalization of a descriptive characterization of cognitive processing, a simple form of *schema theory*. In Section 1 of this chapter, I will give a description of this form of schema theory and show how to transform the descriptive characterization into a mathematical one—how to get from the *conceptual* box of Figure 1 into the *mathematical* box. Once we are in the formal world, mathematical analysis and computer simulation can be put to work.

Throughout Section 1, the main points of the development will be explicitly enumerated.

Point 1. The mathematics of harmony theory is founded on familiar concepts of cognitive science: inference through activation of schemata.

DYNAMIC CONSTRUCTION OF SCHEMATA

The basic problem can be posed à la Schank (1980). While eating at a fancy restaurant, you get a headache. Without effort, you ask the waitress if she could possibly get you an aspirin. How is this plan created? You have never had a headache in a restaurant before. Ordinarily, when you get a headache your plan is to go to your medicine cabinet and get yourself some aspirin. In the current situation, this plan must be modified by the knowledge that in good restaurants, the management is willing to expend effort to please its customers, and that the waitress is a liaison to that management.

The cognitive demands of this situation are schematically illustrated in Figure 2. Ordinarily, the restaurant context calls for a "restaurant script" which supports the planning and inferencing required to reach the usual goal of getting a meal. Ordinarily, the headache context calls for a "headache script" which supports the planning required to get aspirin in the usual context of home. The completely novel context of a headache in a restaurant calls for a special-purpose script integrating the knowledge that ordinarily manifests itself in two separate scripts.

What kind of cognitive system is capable of this degree of flexibility? Suppose that the knowledge base of the system does *not* consist of a set of scripts like the restaurant script and the headache script. Suppose

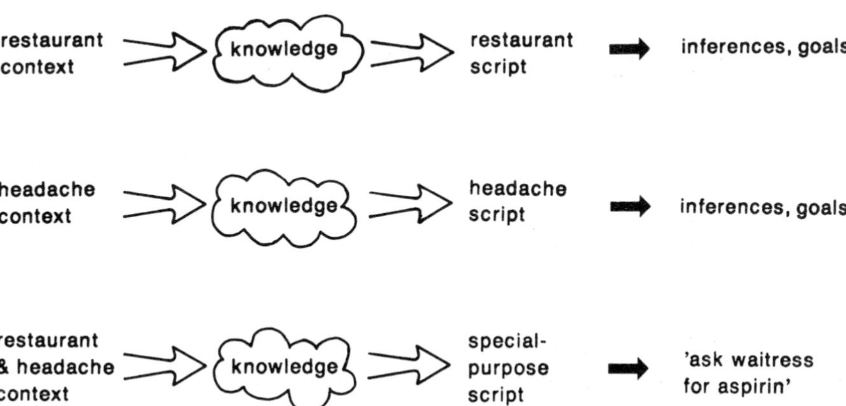

FIGURE 2. In three different contexts, the knowledge base must produce three different scripts.

instead that the knowledge base is a set of *knowledge atoms* that configure themselves dynamically in each context to form tailor-made scripts. This is the fundamental idea formalized in harmony theory.[4]

The degree of flexibility demanded of scripts is equaled by that demanded of all conceptual structures.[5] For example, metaphor is an extreme example of the flexibility demanded of word meanings; even so-called literal meaning on closer inspection actually relies on extreme flexibility of knowledge application (Rumelhart, 1979). In this chapter I will consider knowledge structures that embody our knowledge of objects, words, and other concepts of comparable complexity; these I will refer to as *schemata*. The defining properties of schemata are that they have conceptual interpretations and that they *support inference*.

For lack of a better term, I will use *knowledge atoms* to refer to the elementary constituents of which I assume schemata to be composed.[6] These atoms will shortly be given a precise description; they will be interpreted as a particular instantiation of the idea of *memory trace*.

> *Point 2. At the time of inference, stored knowledge atoms are dynamically assembled into context-sensitive schemata.*

This view of schemata was explicitly articulated in Feldman (1981). It is in part embodied in the McClelland and Rumelhart (1981) letter-perception model (see Chapter 1). One of the observed phenomena accounted for by this model is the facilitation of the perception of letters that are embedded in words. Viewing the perception of a letter as the result of a perceptual inference process, we can say that this inference is supported by a *word schema* that appears in the model as a single processing unit that encodes the knowledge of the spelling of that word. This is *not* an instantiation of the view of schemata as dynamically created entities.

---

[4] Schank (1980) describes a *symbolic* implementation of the idea of dynamic script construction; harmony theory constitutes a *subsymbolic* formalization.

[5] Hofstadter has long been making the case for the inadequacy of traditional symbolic descriptions to cope with the power and flexibility of concepts. For his most recent argument, see Hofstadter (1985). He argues for the need to admit the approximate nature of symbolic descriptions, and to explicitly consider processes that are *subcognitive*. In Hofstadter (1979, p. 324ff), this same case was phrased in terms of the need for "active symbols," of which the "schemata" described here can be viewed as instances.

[6] A physicist might call these particles *gnosons* or *sophons*, but these terms seem quite uneuphonious. An acronym for *Units for Constructing Schemata Dynamically* might serve, but would perhaps be taken as an advertising gimmick. So I have stuck with "knowledge atoms."

However, the model also accounts for the observed facilitation of letter perception within orthographically regular nonwords or *pseudowords* like *MAVE*. When the model processes this stimulus, several word units become and stay quite active, including *MAKE, WAVE, HAVE*, and other words orthographically similar to *MAVE*. In this case, the perception of a letter in the stimulus is the result of an inference process that is supported by the *collection* of activated units. This collection is a *dynamically created pseudoword schema*.

When an orthographically irregular nonword is processed by the model, letter perception is slowest. As in the case of pseudowords, many word units become active. However, none become very active, and very many are equally active, and these words have very little similarity to each other, so they do not support inference about the letters effectively. Thus the knowledge base is incapable of creating schemata for irregular nonwords.

> *Point 3. Schemata are coherent assemblies of knowledge atoms; only these can support inference.*

Note that schemata are created *simply by activating the appropriate atoms*. This brings us to what was labeled in Figure 1 the "descriptively characterized computational requirements" for harmony theory:

> *Point 4: The harmony principle. The cognitive system is an engine for activating coherent assemblies of atoms and drawing inferences that are consistent with the knowledge represented by the activated atoms.*

Subassemblies of activated atoms that tend to recur exactly or approximately are the schemata.

This principle focuses attention on the notion of *coherency* or *consistency*. This concept will be formalized under the name of *harmony*, and its centrality is acknowledged by the name of the theory.

MICRO- AND MACROLEVELS

It is important to realize that harmony theory, like all subsymbolic accounts of cognition, exists on two distinct levels of description: a microlevel involving knowledge atoms and a macrolevel involving schemata (see Chapter 14). These levels of description are completely analogous to other micro- and macrotheories, for example, in physics. The microtheory, quantum physics, is assumed to be universally valid. Part of its job as a theory is to explain why the approximate macrotheory, classical physics, works when it does and why it breaks down when it does. Understanding of physics requires understanding *both* levels of theory *and* the relation between them.

In the subsymbolic paradigm in cognitive science, it is equally important to understand the two levels and their relationship. In harmony theory, the microtheory prescribes the nature of the atoms, their interaction, and their development through experience. This description is assumed to be a universally valid description of cognition. It is also assumed (although this has yet to be explicitly worked out) that in performing certain cognitive tasks (e.g., logical reasoning), a higher level description is a valid approximation. This macrotheory describes schemata, their interaction, and their development through experience.

One of the features of the formalism of harmony theory that distinguishes it from most subsymbolic accounts of cognition is that it exploits a formal isomorphism with statistical physics. Since the main goal of statistical physics is to relate the microscopic description of matter to its macroscopic properties, harmony theory can bring the power of statistical physics concepts and techniques to bear on the problem of understanding the relation between the micro- and macro-accounts of cognition.

THE NATURE OF KNOWLEDGE

In the previous section, the letter-perception model was used to illustrate the dynamic construction of schemata from constituent atoms. However, it is only pseudowords that correspond to composite schemata; word schemata are single atoms. We can also represent words as composite schemata by using digraph units at the upper level instead of four-letter word units. A portion of this modified letter-perception model is shown in Figure 3. Now the processing of a four-letter word involves the activation of a set of digraph units, which are the knowledge atoms of this model. Omitted from the figure are the

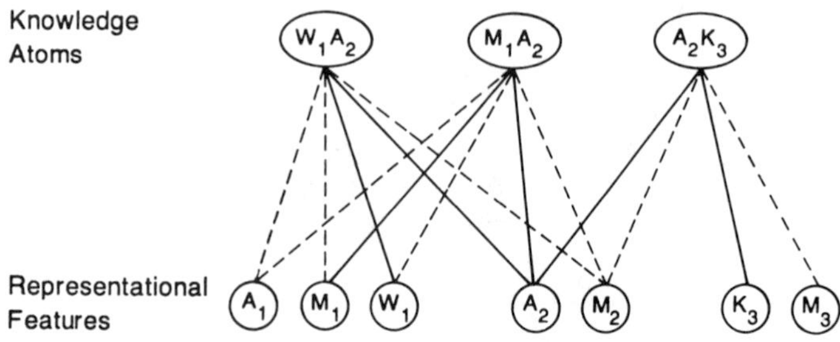

FIGURE 3. A portion of a modified reading model.

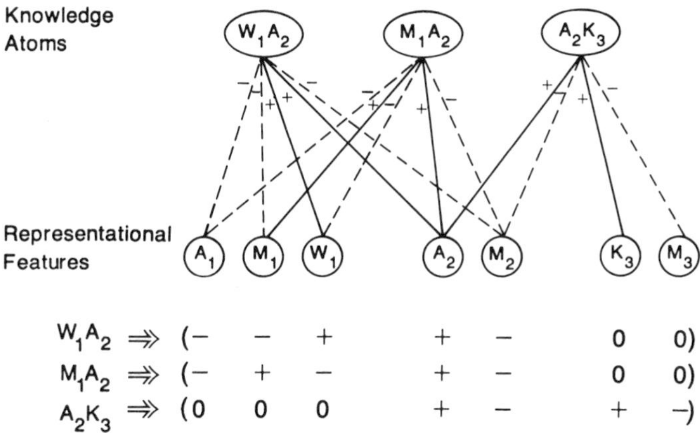

FIGURE 4. Each knowledge atom is a vector of +, −, and 0 values of the representational feature nodes.

line-segment units, which are like those in the original letter-perception model.

This simple model illustrates several points about the nature of knowledge atoms in harmony theory. The digraph unit W_1A_2 represents a pattern of values over the letter units: W_1 and A_2 on, with all other letter units for positions 1 and 2 off. This pattern is shown in Figure 4, using the labels +, −, and 0 to denote *on*, *off*, and *irrelevant*. These indicate whether there is an excitatory connection, inhibitory connection, or no connection between the corresponding nodes.[7]

Figure 4 shows the basic structure of harmony models. There are atoms of knowledge, represented by nodes in an upper layer, and a lower layer of nodes that comprises a representation of the state of the perceptual or problem domain with which the system deals. Each node is a *feature* in the representation of the domain. We can now view "atoms of knowledge" like W_1 and A_2 in several ways. Mathematically, each atom is simply a *vector* of +, −, and 0 values, one for each node in the lower, representation layer. This pattern can also be viewed as a *fragment* of a percept: The 0 values mark those features omitted in the fragment. This fragment can in turn be interpreted as a *trace* left behind in memory by perceptual experience.

[7] Omitted are the knowledge atoms that relate the letter nodes to the line segment nodes. Both line segment and letter nodes are in the lower layer, and all knowledge atoms are in the upper layer. Hierarchies in harmony theory are imbedded within an architecture of only two layers of nodes, as will be discussed in Section 2.

Point 5. Knowledge atoms are fragments of representations that accumulate with experience.

THE COMPLETION TASK

Having specified more precisely what the atoms of knowledge are, it is time to specify the task in which they are used.

Many cognitive tasks can be viewed as inference tasks. In problem solving, the role of inference is obvious; in perception and language comprehension, inference is less obvious but just as central. In harmony theory, a tightly prescribed but extremely general inferential task is studied: the *completion task.* In a problem-solving completion task, a partial description of a situation is given (for example, the initial state of a system); the problem is to complete the description to fill in the missing information (the final state, say). In a story understanding completion task, a partial description of some events and actors' goals is given; comprehension involves filling in the missing events and goals. In perception, the stimulus gives values for certain low-level features of the environmental state, and the perceptual system must fill in values for other features. In general, in the completion task some features of an environmental state are given as input, and the cognitive system must complete that input by assigning likely values to unspecified features.

A simple example of a completion task (Lindsay & Norman, 1972) is shown in Figure 5. The task is to fill in the features of the obscured portions of the stimulus and to decide what letters are present. This task can be performed by the model shown in Figure 3, as follows. The stimulus assigns values of *on* and *off* to the unobscured letter features. What happens is summarized in Table 1.

Note that which atoms are activated affects how the representation is

FIGURE 5. A perceptual completion task.

TABLE 1

A PROCEDURE FOR PERFORMING THE COMPLETION TASK

Input:	Assign values to some features in the representation
Activation:	Activate atoms that are *consistent* with the representation
Inference:	Assign values to unknown features of representation that are *consistent* with the active knowledge

filled in, and how the representation is filled in affects which atoms are activated. The activation and inference processes mutually constrain each other; these processes must run in parallel. Note also that all the decisions come out of a striving for *consistency*.

> *Point 6. Assembly of schemata (activation of atoms) and inference (completing missing parts of the representation) are both achieved by finding maximally self-consistent states of the system that are also consistent with the input.*

The completion of the stimulus shown in Figure 5 is shown in Figure 6. The consistency is high because wherever an active atom is

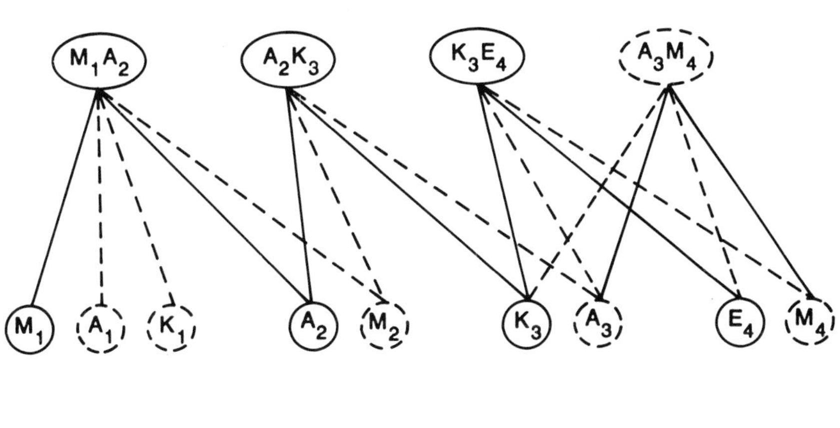

FIGURE 6. The state of the network in the completion of the stimulus shown in Figure 5.

connected to a representational feature by a + (respectively, −) connection, that feature has value *on* (respectively, *off*). In fact, we can define a very simple measure of the degree of self-consistency just by considering all active atoms, counting +1 for every agreement between one of its connections and the value of the corresponding feature, and counting −1 for every disagreement. (Here + with *on* or − with *off* constitutes agreement.) This is the simplest example of a *harmony function*—and brings us into the mathematical formulation.

THE HARMONY FUNCTION

Point 6 asserts that a central cognitive process is the construction of cognitive states that are "maximally self-consistent." To make this precise, we need only measure that self-consistency.

> *Point 7. The self-consistency of a possible state of the cognitive system can be assigned a quantitative value by a harmony function, H.*

Figure 7 displays a harmony function that generalizes the simple example discussed in the preceding paragraph. A state of the system is defined by a set of atoms which are *active* and a vector of values for all representational features. The harmony of such a state is the sum of terms, one for each active atom, weighted by the *strength* of that atom. Each weight multiplies the self-consistency between that particular atom and the vector of representational feature values. That self-consistency is the similarity between the vector of features defining the atom (the vector of its connections) and the representational feature vector. In the simplest case discussed above, the function h that measures this similarity is just the number of agreements between these vectors minus the number of disagreements. For reasons to be discussed, I have used a slightly more complicated version of h in which the simpler form is first divided by the number of (nonzero) connections to the atom, and then a fixed value κ is subtracted.

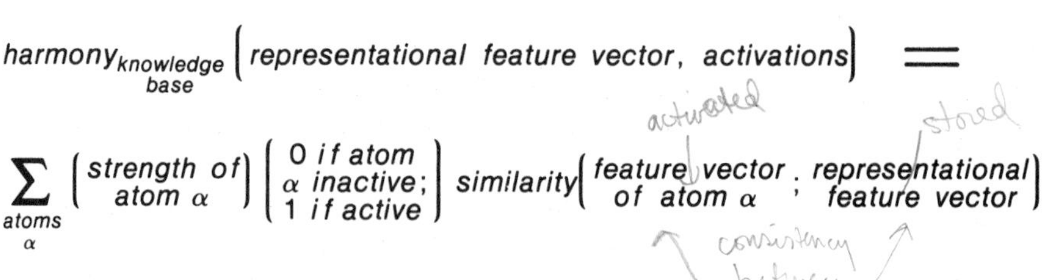

FIGURE 7. A schematic representation for a harmony function.

A PROBABILISTIC FORMULATION OF SCHEMA THEORY

The next step in the theoretical development requires returning to the higher level, symbolic description of inference, and to a more detailed discussion of schemata.

Consider a typical inference process described with schemata. A child is reading a story about presents, party hats, and a cake with candles. When asked questions, the child says that the girl getting the presents is having a birthday. In the terminology of schema theory, while reading the story, the child's *birthday party schema* becomes active and allows many inferences to be made, filling in details of the scene that were not made explicit in the story.

The birthday party schema is presumed to be a knowledge structure that contains *variables* like *birthday cake, guest of honor, other guests, gifts, location*, and so forth. The schema contains information on how to assign values to these variables. For example, the schema may specify: *default values* to be assigned to variables in the absence of any counterindicating information; *value restrictions* limiting the kind of values that can be assigned to variables; and *dependency* information, specifying how assigning a particular value to one variable affects the values that can be assigned to another variable.

A convenient framework for concisely and uniformly expressing all this information is given by *probability theory*. The default value for a variable can be viewed as its most probable value: the mode of the marginal probability distribution for that variable. The value restrictions on a variable specify the values for which it has nonzero probability: the support of its marginal distribution. The dependencies between variables are expressed by their statistical correlations, or, more completely, by their joint probability distributions.

So the birthday party schema can be viewed as containing information about the probabilities that its variables will have various possible values. These are clearly statistical properties of the particular domain or *environment* in which the inference task is being carried out. In reading the story, the child is given a partial description of a scene from the everyday environment—the values of some of the features used to represent that scene—and to understand the story, the child must *complete* the description by filling in the values for the unknown features. These values are assigned in such a way that the resulting scene has the highest possible probability. The birthday party schema contains the probabilistic information needed to carry out these inferences.

In a typical cognitive task, many schemata become active at once and interact heavily during the inference process. Each schema contains probabilistic information for its own variables, which are only a fraction of the complete set of variables involved in the task. To perform a completion, the most probable set of values must be assigned to the unknown variables, using the information in all the active schemata.

This probabilistic formulation of these aspects of schema theory can be simply summarized as follows.

> *Point 8. Each schema encodes the statistical relations among a few representational features. During inference, the probabilistic information in many active schemata are dynamically folded together to find the most probable state of the environment.*

Thus the statistical knowledge encoded in all the schemata allow the estimation of the relative probabilities of possible states of the environment. How can this be done?

At the macrolevel of schemata and variables, coordinating the folding together of the information of many schemata is difficult to describe. The inability to devise procedures that capture the flexibility displayed in human use of schemata was in fact one of the primary historical reasons for turning to the microlevel description (see Chapter 1). We therefore return to the microdescription to address this difficult problem.

At the microlevel, the probabilistic knowledge in the birthday party schema is distributed over many knowledge atoms, each carrying a small bit of statistical information. Because these atoms all tend to match the representation of a birthday party scene, they can become active together; in some approximation, they tend to function collectively, and in that sense they comprise a schema. Now, when many schemata are active at once, that means the knowledge atoms that comprise them are simultaneously active. At the microlevel, there is no real difference between the decisions required to activate the appropriate atoms to instantiate many schemata simultaneously and the decisions required to activate the atoms to instantiate a single schema. A computational system that can dynamically create a schema when it is needed can also dynamically create many schemata when they are needed. When atoms, not schemata, are the elements of computation, the problem of coordinating many schemata becomes subsumed in the problem of activating the appropriate atoms. And this is the problem that the harmony function, the measure of self-consistency, was created to solve.

HARMONY THEORY

According to Points 2, 6, and 7, schemata are collections of knowledge atoms that become active in order to maximize harmony, and inferences are also drawn to maximize harmony. This suggests that the probability of a possible state of the environment is estimated by computing its harmony: the higher the harmony, the greater the probability. In fact, from the mathematical properties of probability and harmony, in Section 2 we will show the following:

Point 9. The relationship between the harmony function H and estimated probabilities is of the form

$$\text{probability} \propto e^{H/T}$$

where T is some constant that cannot be determined a priori.

This relationship between probability and harmony is mathematically identical to the relationship between probability and (minus) energy in statistical physics: the Gibbs or Boltzmann law. This is the basis of the isomorphism between cognition and physics exploited by harmony theory. In statistical physics, H is called the *Hamiltonian function*; it measures the energy of a state of a physical system. In physics, T is the *temperature* of the system. In harmony theory, T is called the *computational temperature* of the cognitive system. When the temperature is very high, completions with high harmony are assigned estimated probabilities that are only slightly higher than those assigned to low harmony completions; the environment is treated as *more random* in the sense that all completions are estimated to have roughly equal probability. When the temperature is very low, only the completions with highest harmony are given nonnegligible estimated probabilities.[8]

Point 10. The lower the computational temperature, the more the estimated probabilities are weighted towards the completions of highest harmony.

In particular, the very best completion can be found by lowering the temperature to zero. This process, *cooling*, is fundamental to harmony theory. Concepts and techniques from thermal physics can be used to understand and analyze decision-making processes in harmony theory.

A technique for performing Monte Carlo computer studies of thermal systems can be readily adapted to harmony theory.

Point 11. A massively parallel stochastic machine can be designed that performs completions in accordance with Points 1-10.

---

[8] Since harmony corresponds to *minus* energy, at low physical temperatures only the state with the *lowest* energy (the *ground state*) has nonnegligible probability.

For a given harmony model (e.g., that of Figure 4), this machine is constructed as follows. Every node in the network becomes a simple processor, and every link in the network becomes a communication link between two processors. The processors each have two possible values (+1 and −1 for the representational feature processors; 1 = *active* and 0 = *inactive* for the knowledge atom processors). The input to a completion problem is provided by fixing the values of some of the feature processors. Each of the other processors continually updates its value by making stochastic decisions based on the harmony associated at the current time with its two possible values. It is most likely to choose the value that corresponds to greater harmony; but with some probability—greater the higher is the computational temperature T—it will make the other choice. Each processor computes the harmony associated with its possible values by a numerical calculation that uses as input the numerical values of all the other processors to which it is connected. Alternately, all the atom processors update in parallel, and then all the feature processors update in parallel. The process repeats many times, implementing the procedure of Table 1. All the while, the temperature T is lowered to zero, pursuant to Point 10. It can be proved that the machine will eventually "freeze" into a completion that maximizes the harmony.

I call this machine *harmonium* because, like the Selfridge and Neisser (1960) pattern recognition system *pandemonium*, it is a parallel distributed processing system in which many atoms of knowledge are simultaneously "shouting" out their little contributions to the inference process; but unlike pandemonium, there is an explicit method to the madness: the collective search for maximal harmony.[9]

The final point concerns the account of learning in harmony theory.

> *Point 12. There is a procedure for accumulating knowledge atoms through exposure to the environment so that the system will perform the completion task optimally.*

The precise meaning of "optimality" will be an important topic in the subsequent discussion.

This completes the descriptive account of the foundations of harmony theory. Section 2 fills in many of the steps and details omitted

---

[9] Harmonium is closely related to the *Boltzmann machine* discussed in Chapter 7. The basic dynamics of the machines are the same, although there are differences in most details. In the Appendix, it is shown that in a certain sense the Boltzmann machine is a special case of harmonium, in which knowledge atoms connected to more than two features are forbidden. In another sense, harmonium is a special case of the Boltzmann machine, in which the connections are restricted to go only between two layers.

above, and reports the results of some particular studies. The most formal matters are treated in the Appendix.

SECTION 2: HARMONY THEORY

. . . the privileged unconscious phenomena, those susceptible of becoming conscious, are those which . . . affect most profoundly our emotional sensibility . . . Now, what are the mathematic entities to which we attribute this character of beauty and elegance . . . ? They are those whose elements are harmoniously disposed so that the mind without effort can embrace their totality while realizing the details. This harmony is at once a satisfaction of our esthetic needs and an aid to the mind, sustaining and guiding. . . . Figure the future elements of our combinations as something like the unhooked atoms of Epicurus. . . . They flash in every direction through the space . . . like the molecules of a gas in the kinematic theory of gases. Then their mutual impacts may produce new combinations.

Henri Poincaré (1913)
Mathematical Creation[10]

In Section 1, a top-down analysis led from the demands of the completion task and a probabilistic formulation of schema theory to perceptual features, knowledge atoms, the central notion of harmony, and the role of harmony in estimating probabilities of environmental states. In Section 2, the presentation will be bottom-up, starting from the primitives.

KNOWLEDGE REPRESENTATION

Representation Vector

At the center of any harmony theoretic model of a particular cognitive process is a set of *representational features* $r_1, r_2, \cdots$. These

10 I am indebted to Yves Chauvin for recently pointing out this remarkable passage by the great mathematician. See also Hofstadter (1985, pp. 655-656).

features constitute the cognitive system's representation of possible states of the environment with which it deals. In the environment of visual perception, these features might include pixels, edges, depths of surface elements, and identifications of objects. In medical diagnosis, features might be symptoms, outcomes of tests, diseases, prognoses, and treatments. In the domain of qualitative circuit analysis, the features might include *increase in current through resistor x* and *increase in voltage drop across resistor x*.

The representational features are variables that I will assume take on binary values that can be thought of as *present* and *absent* or *true* and *false*. Binary values contain a tremendous amount of representational power, so it is not a great sacrifice to accept the conceptual and technical simplification they afford. It will turn out to be convenient to denote *present* and *absent* respectively by $+1$ and -1, or, equivalently, $+$ and $-$. Other values could be used if corresponding modifications were made in the equations to follow. The use of continuous numerical feature variables, while introducing some additional technical complexity, would not affect the basic character of the theory.[11]

A *representational state* of the cognitive system is determined by a collection of values for all the representational variables $\{r_i\}$. This collection can be designated by a list or vector of $+$'s and $-$'s: the *representation vector* $\mathbf{r}$.

Where do the features used in the representation vector come from? Are they "innate" or do they develop with experience? These crucial questions will be deferred until the last section of this chapter. The evaluation of various possible representations for a given environment and the study of the development of good representations through exposure to the environment is harmony theory's *raison d'être*. But a prerequisite for understanding the appropriateness of a representation is understanding how the representation supports performance on the task for which it used; that is the primary concern of this chapter. For now, we simply assume that somehow a set of representational features has already been set up: by a programmer, or experience, or evolution.

---

[11] While continuous values make the *analysis* more complex, they may well improve the performance of the simulation models. In simulations with discrete values, the system state jumps between corners of a hypercube; with continuous values, the system state crawls smoothly around inside the hypercube. It was observed in the work reported in Chapter 14 that "bad" corners corresponding to stable nonoptimal completions (local harmony maxima) were typically *not* visited by the smoothly moving continuous state; these corners typically *are* visited by the jumping discrete state and can only be escaped from through thermal stochasticity. Thus continuous values may sometimes eliminate the need for stochastic simulation.

Activation Vector

The representational features serve as the blackboard on which the cognitive system carries out its computations. The *knowledge* that guides those computations is associated with the second set of entities, the *knowledge atoms*. Each such atom α is characterized by a *knowledge vector* $\mathbf{k}_\alpha$, which is a list of +1, −1, and 0 values, one for each representation variable r_i. This list encodes a piece of knowledge that specifies what value each r_i should have: +1, −1, or unspecified (0).

Associated with knowledge atom α is its *activation variable*, a_α. This variable will also be taken to be binary: 1 will denote active; 0, inactive. Because harmony theory is probabilistic, degrees of activation are represented by varying probability of being active rather than varying values for the activation variable. (Like continuous values for representation variables, continuous values for activation variables could be incorporated into the theory with little difficulty, but a need to do so has not yet arisen.) The list of $\{0,1\}$ values for the activations $\{a_\alpha\}$ comprises the *activation vector* $\mathbf{a}$.

Knowledge atoms encode subpatterns of feature values that occur in the environment. The different frequencies with which various such patterns occur is encoded in the set of *strengths*, $\{\sigma_\alpha\}$, of the atoms.

In the example of qualitative circuit analysis, each knowledge atom records a pattern of qualitative changes in some of the circuit features (currents, voltages, etc.). These patterns are the ones that are consistent with the laws of physics, which are the constraints characterizing the circuit environment. Knowledge of the laws of physics is encoded in the set of knowledge atoms. For example, the atom whose knowledge vector contains all zeroes except those features encoding the pattern <*current decreases, voltage decreases, resistance increases*> is one of the atoms encoding qualitative knowledge of Ohm's law. Equally important is the *absence* of an atom like one encoding the pattern <*current increases, voltage decreases, resistance increases*>, which violates Ohm's law.

There is a very useful graphical representation for knowledge atoms; it was illustrated in Figure 4 and is repeated as Figure 8. The representational features are designated by nodes drawn in a lower layer; the activation variables are depicted by nodes drawn in an upper layer. The connections from an activation variable a_α to the representation variables $\{r_i\}$ show the knowledge vector $\mathbf{k}_\alpha$. When $\mathbf{k}_\alpha$ contains a + or − for r_i, the connection between a_α and r_i is labeled with the appropriate sign; when $\mathbf{k}_\alpha$ contains a 0 for r_i, the connection between a_α and r_i is omitted.

In Figure 8, all atoms are assumed to have unit strength. In general, different atoms will have different strengths; the strength of each atom

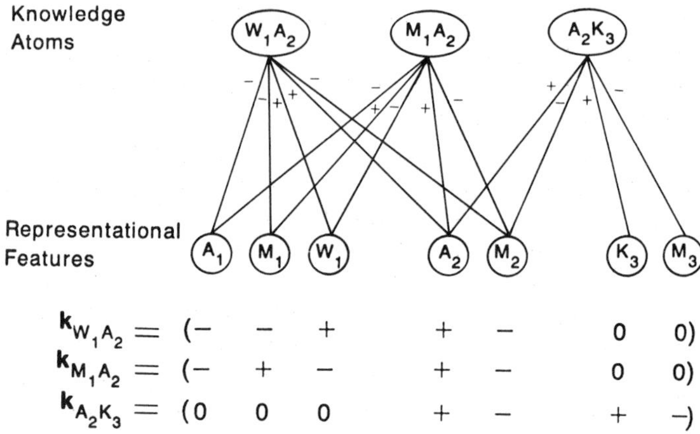

FIGURE 8. The graphical representation of a particular harmony model.

would them be indicated above the atom in the drawing. (For the completely general case, see Figure 13.)

Hierarchies and the Architecture of Harmony Networks

One of the characteristics that distinguishes harmony models from other parallel network models is that the graph *always* contains two layers of nodes, with rather different semantics. As in many networks, the nodes in the upper layer correspond to patterns of values in the lower layer. In the letter-perception model of McClelland and Rumelhart, for example, the word nodes correspond to patterns over the letter nodes, and the letter nodes in turn correspond to patterns over the line-segment nodes. The letter-perception model is typical in its *hierarchical structure*: The nodes are stratified into a sequence of several layers, with nodes in one layer being connected only to nodes in adjacent layers. Harmony models use only two layers.

The formalism could be extended to many layers, but the use of two layers has a principled foundation in the semantics of these layers. The nodes in the representation layer *support representations of the environment at all levels of abstractness*. In the case of written words, this layer could support representation at the levels of line segments, letters, and words, as shown schematically in Figure 9. The upper, knowledge, layer encodes the patterns among these representations. If information is given about line segments, then some of the knowledge atoms connect that information with the letter nodes, completing the representation to include letter recognition. Other knowledge atoms connect patterns on the letter nodes with word nodes, and these complete the representation to include word recognition.

The pattern of connectivity of Figure 9 allows the network to be redrawn as shown in Figure 10. This network shows an alternation of representation and knowledge nodes, restoring the image of a series of layers. In this sense, "vertically" hierarchical networks of many layers can be imbedded as "horizontally" hierarchical networks within a two-layer harmony network.

Figure 10 graphically displays the fact that in a harmony architecture, the nodes that encode patterns are not part of the representation; there is a firm distinction between representation and knowledge nodes. This distinction is not made in the original letter-perception model, where the nodes that detect a pattern over the line-segment features are identical with the nodes that actually represent the presence of letters. This distinction seems artificial; why is it made?

I claim that the artificiality actually resides in the original letter-perception model, in which the presence of a letter can be identified with a single pattern over the primitive graphical features (line segments). In a less idealized reading task, the presence of a letter would have to be inferable from many different combinations of primitive graphical features. In harmony theory, the idea is that there would be a set of representation nodes dedicated to the representation of the presence of letters independent of their shapes, sizes, orientations, and so forth. There would also be a set of representation nodes for graphical

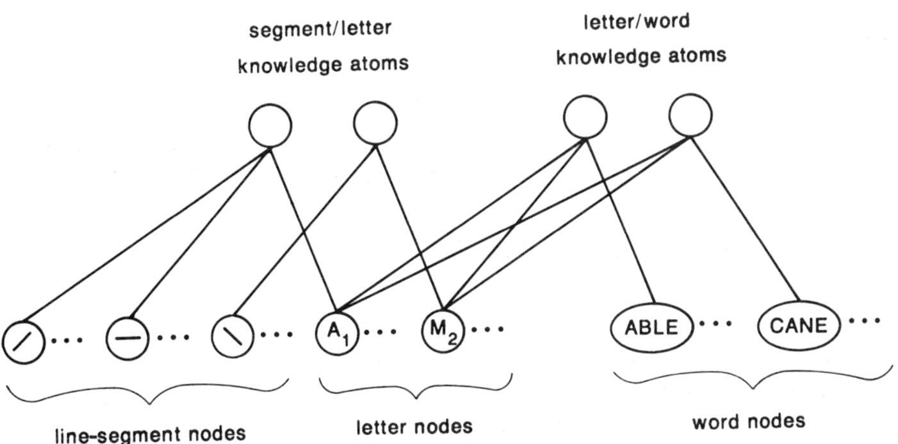

FIGURE 9. The representational features support representations at all levels of abstractness.

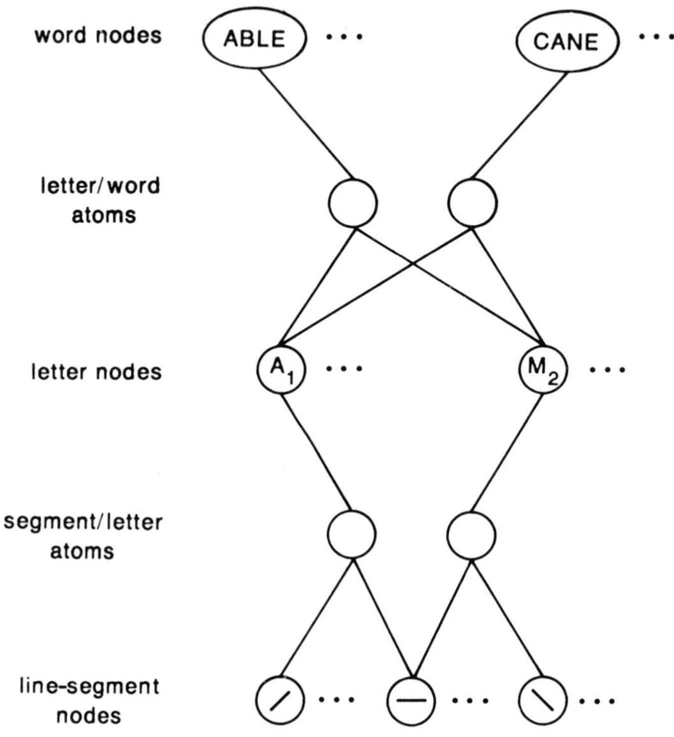

FIGURE 10. A rearrangement of the network of Figure 9.

features, and for each letter there would be *a multitude* of knowledge atoms, each relating a particular configuration of graphical features with the representation of that letter. Thus the knowledge or *schema* for that letter would be distributed over many knowledge atoms, all of which would be involved in setting up the same representation on the letter nodes. To provide a broader context, Figure 11 schematically depicts a possible model for language processing. The full representation consists of graphical features, phonological features, syntactic features, and semantic features. Some of the knowledge atoms provide connections among features within a single category, while others connect features in different categories. The nodes in the upper layer do not themselves comprise parts of the representation, but rather encode *relations between* parts of the representation.

The advantages of the two-layer scheme come from simplicity and uniformity. There are no connections within layers, only between layers. This simplifies mathematical analysis considerably and permits a

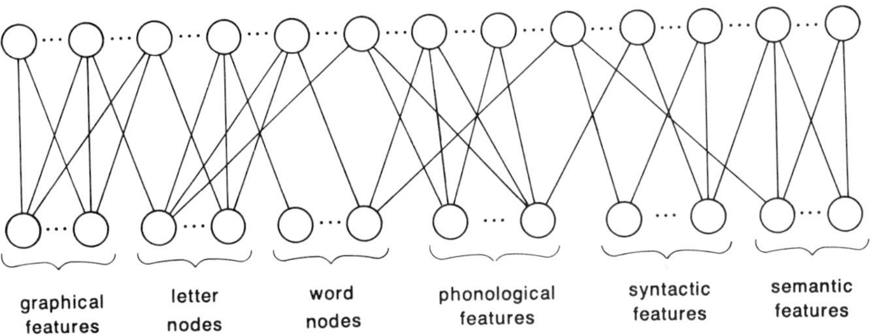

FIGURE 11. A complete model for language processing would involve representational variables of many types, and the atoms relating them.

truly parallel implementation. The uniformity means that we can imagine a system starting out with an "innate" two-layer structure and *learning* a pattern of connections like that of Figure 9, i.e., learning a hierarchical representation scheme that was in no sense put into the model in advance. The formalism is set up to analyze the environmental conditions under which certain kinds of representations (e.g., hierarchical ones) might emerge or be expedient.

The lack of within-layer connections in harmony networks is symptomatic of a major difference between the goals of harmony theory and the goals of other similar approaches. The effect of a binary connection between two representation nodes can be achieved by creating a pair of upper level nodes that connect to the two lower level nodes.[12] Thus we can dispense with lower level connections at the cost of creating upper level nodes. *Harmony theory has been developed with a systematic commitment to buy simplicity with extra upper level nodes.* The hope is that by placing all the knowledge in the patterns encoded by knowledge atoms, we will be better able to *understand* the function and structure of the models. This explains why restrictions have been placed on the network that to many would seem extraordinarily confining.

If the goal is instead to get the most "intelligent" performance out of the fewest number of nodes and connections, it is obviously wiser to

12 A negative connection between two lower level nodes means that the value pairs (+,−) and (−,+) are favored relative to the other two pairs. This effect can be achieved by creating two knowledge atoms that each encode one of the two favored patterns. A positive connection similarly can be replaced by two atoms for the patterns (+,+) and (−,−).

allow arbitrary connectivity patterns, weights, and thresholds, as in the Boltzmann machine. There are, however, theoretical disadvantages to having so many degrees of freedom, both in psychological modeling and in artificial intelligence applications. Too many free parameters in a psychological model make it too theoretically unconstrained and therefore insufficiently instructive. And as suggested in Chapter 7, networks that take advantage of all these degrees of freedom may perform their computations in ways that are completely inscrutable to the theorist. Some may take delight in such a result, but there is reason to be concerned by it. It can be argued that getting a machine to perform intelligently is more important than understanding how it does so. If a magic procedure—say for learning—did in fact lead to the level of performance desired, despite our inability to understand the resulting computation, that would of course be a landmark accomplishment. But to expect this kind of breakthrough is just the sort of naiveté referred to in the first paragraph of the chapter. We now have enough disappointing experience to expect that any particular insight is going to take us a *very small fraction* of the way to the kind of truly intelligent mechanisms we seek. The only way to reasonably expect to make progress is by chaining together many such small steps. And the only way to chain together these steps is to *understand* at the end of each one where we are, how we got there, and why we got no further, so we can make an informed guess as to how to take the next small step. A "magic" step is apt to be a *last* step; it is fine, as long as it takes you exactly where you want to go.

HARMONY AND PROBABILITY

The Harmony Function

The preceding section described how environmental states and knowledge are represented in harmony theory. The use of this knowledge in completing representations of environmental states is governed by the harmony function, which, as discussed in Section 1, measures the self-consistency of any state of a harmony model. I will now discuss the properties required of a harmony function and present the particular function I have studied.

A state of the cognitive system is determined by the values of the lower and upper level nodes. Such a state is determined by a pair $(\mathbf{r}, \mathbf{a})$ consisting of a representation vector $\mathbf{r}$ and an activation vector $\mathbf{a}$. A harmony function assigns a real number $H_{\mathbf{K}}(\mathbf{r}, \mathbf{a})$ to each such state.

The harmony function has as parameters the set of knowledge vectors and their strengths: $\{(\mathbf{k}_\alpha, \sigma_\alpha)\}$; I will call this the *knowledge base* $\mathbf{K}$.

The basic requirement on the harmony function H is that it be *additive under decompositions* of the system.[13] This means that if a network can be partitioned into two unconnected networks, as in Figure 12, the harmony of the whole network is the sum of the harmonies of the parts:

$$H(\mathbf{r}, \mathbf{a}) = H(\mathbf{r}_1, \mathbf{a}_1) + H(\mathbf{r}_2, \mathbf{a}_2).$$

In this case, the knowledge and representational feature nodes can each be broken into two subsets so that the knowledge atoms in subset 1 all have 0 connections with the representational features in subset 2, and vice versa. Corresponding to this partition of nodes there is a decomposition of the vectors $\mathbf{r}$ and $\mathbf{a}$ into the pieces $\mathbf{r}_1, \mathbf{r}_2$ and $\mathbf{a}_1, \mathbf{a}_2$.

The harmony function I have studied (recall Figure 7) is

$$H_{\mathbf{K}}(\mathbf{r}, \mathbf{a}) = \sum_\alpha \sigma_\alpha \, a_\alpha \, h_\kappa(\mathbf{r}, \mathbf{k}_\alpha). \tag{1}$$

Here, $h_\kappa(\mathbf{r}, \mathbf{k}_\alpha)$ is the harmony contributed by activating atom α, given the current representation $\mathbf{r}$. I have taken this to be

$$h_\kappa(\mathbf{r}, \mathbf{k}_\alpha) = \frac{\mathbf{r} \cdot \mathbf{k}_\alpha}{|\mathbf{k}_\alpha|} - \kappa.$$

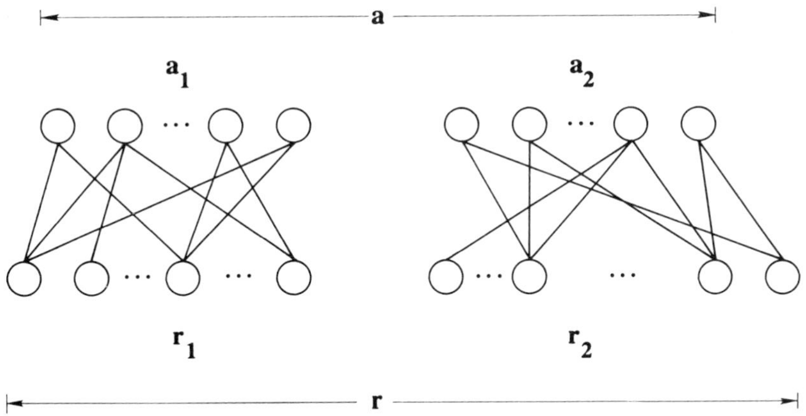

FIGURE 12. A decomposable harmony network.

13 In physics, one says that H must be an *extensive quantity*.

The vector inner product (see Chapter 9) is defined by

$$\mathbf{r}\cdot\mathbf{k}_\alpha = \sum_i r_i (\mathbf{k}_\alpha)_i$$

and the norm [14] is defined by

$$|\mathbf{k}_\alpha| = \sum_i |(\mathbf{k}_\alpha)_i|.$$

I will now comment on these definitions.

First note that this harmony function $H_\mathbf{K}$ is a sum of terms, one for each knowledge atom, with the term for atom α depending only on those representation variables r_i to which it has nonzero connection $(\mathbf{k}_\alpha)_i$. Thus $H_\mathbf{K}$ satisfies the additivity requirement.

The contribution to H of an inactive atom is zero. The contribution of an active atom α is the product of its strength and the consistency between its knowledge vector $\mathbf{k}_\alpha$ and the representation vector $\mathbf{r}$; this is measured by the function $h_\kappa(\mathbf{r}, \mathbf{k}_\alpha)$. The parameter κ always lies in the interval $(-1,1)$. When $\kappa = 0$, $h_\kappa(\mathbf{r}, \mathbf{k}_\alpha)$ is the number of representational features whose values agree with the corresponding value in the knowledge vector minus the number that disagree. This gives the simplest harmony function, the one described in Section 1. The trouble is that according to this measure, if over 50% of the knowledge vector $\mathbf{k}_\alpha$ agrees with $\mathbf{r}$, the harmony is raised by activating atom α. This is a pretty weak criterion of matching, and sometimes it is important to be able to have a more stringent criterion than 50%. As κ goes from -1 through 0 towards 1, the criterion goes from 0% through 50% towards 100%. In fact it is easy to see that the criterial fraction is $(1+\kappa)/2$. The total harmony will be raised by activating any atom for which the number of representational features on which the atom's knowledge vector agrees with the representation vector exceeds this fraction of the total number of possible agreements $(|\mathbf{k}_\alpha|)$.

An important limit of the theory is $\kappa \rightarrow 1$. In this limit, the criterion approaches perfect matching. For any given harmony model, perfect matching is required by any κ greater than some definite value less than 1 because there is a limit to how close to 100% matching one can achieve with a finite number of possible matches. Indeed it is easy to compute that if n is the largest number of nonzero connections to any atom in a model (the maximum of $|\mathbf{k}_\alpha|$), then the only way to exceed a

14 This is the so-called L_1 norm, which is different from the L_2 norm defined in Chapter 9. For each p in $(0,\infty)$ the L_p norm of a vector $\mathbf{v}$ is defined by

$$|\mathbf{v}|_p = \left[\sum_i |v_i|^p\right]^{1/p}.$$

criterion of $1 - 2/n$ is with a perfect match. Any κ value greater than this will place the model in what I will call the *perfect matching limit.* Note that since harmony theory is probabilistic, even in the perfect matching limit, atoms will sometimes become active even when they do not match the current representation perfectly; the closer the match, the more likely they will be active.

By choosing $+1$ and -1 as the binary values for representational features, we have ensured that the product $(\mathbf{k}_\alpha)_i r_i$ will be $+1$ if the knowledge vector agrees with r_i, -1 if it disagrees, and 0 if it doesn't specify a value for feature i. The maximum value that can be attained by $\mathbf{k}_\alpha \cdot \mathbf{r}$ is $|\mathbf{k}_\alpha|$, the number of nonzero connections to node α, irrespective of whether those connections are + or −.

In fact, this harmony function is *invariant under the exchange of + and − at any representation node.* That is, simultaneously flipping the signs of r_i and $(\mathbf{k}_\alpha)_i$ for all α leaves the value of $H_{\mathbf{K}}(\mathbf{r}, \mathbf{a})$ unchanged, for every $\mathbf{a}$. This symmetry was deliberately inserted into the general harmony function because I could think of no principled reason to break it. If a systematic bias in the representation variables toward one of the binary values is to be built in from the outset, how large should the bias be? It seemed reasonable to start the theory in a symmetric way, unbiased toward either value. Of course a bias *can* be inserted through the *knowledge* $\mathbf{K}$. To take an extreme example, if the value of feature i is + in all knowledge atoms, i.e., $(\mathbf{k}_\alpha)_i = +$ for all α, then the ith feature r_i will be strongly biased toward +.

There is nothing sacred about the values $+1$ and -1 in this theory. The values 1 and 0, for example, could be used as well. The preceding harmony function can easily be rewritten to give the same harmony values when $\mathbf{r}$ is changed from the $\{+1,-1\}$ form to the $\{1,0\}$ form. The underlying invariance under sign change would however be transformed into a more complicated invariance.

Estimating Probabilities With the Harmony Function

In Section 1, I suggested that a cognitive system performing the completion task could use a harmony function for estimating the probabilities of values for unknown variables. In fact, Point 9 asserted that the estimated probability of a set of values for unknown variables was an exponential function of the corresponding harmony value:

$$\text{probability} \propto e^{H/T}. \tag{2}$$

It is this relationship that establishes the mapping with statistical physics. In this section and the next, the relationship between harmony and probability is analyzed. In this section I will point out that *if* probabilities are to be estimated using H, then the exponential relationship of Equation 2 should be used. In the next section I adapt an argument of Stuart Geman (personal communication, 1984) to show that, starting from the extremely general probabilistic assumption known as the *principle of maximum missing information*, both Equation 2 and the form of the harmony function (Equation 1) can be jointly derived.

What we know about harmony functions in general is that they are additive under network decomposition. If a harmony network consists of two unconnected components, the harmony of any given state of the whole network is the *sum* of the harmonies of the states of the component networks. In the case of such a network, what is required of the *probability* assigned to the state? I claim it should be the *product* of the probabilities assigned to the states of the component networks. The meaning of the unconnectedness is that the knowledge used in the inference process does not relate the features in the two networks to each other. Thus the results of inference about these two sets of features should be *independent*. Since the probabilities assigned to the states in the two networks should be independent, the probability of their joint occurrence—the state of the network as a whole—should be the product of their individual probabilities.

In other words, *adding* the *harmonies* of the components' states should correspond to *multiplying* the *probabilities* of the components' states. The exponential function of Equation 2 establishes just this correspondence. It is a mathematical fact that the *only* continuous functions f that map addition into multiplication,

$$f(x+y) = f(x)\,f(y)$$

are the exponential functions,

$$f(x) = a^x$$

for some positive number a. Equivalently, these functions can be written

$$f(x) = e^{x/T}$$

for some value T (where $T = 1/\ln a$).

This general argument leaves undetermined the value of T, the computational temperature. However several observations about the value of T can be made.

First, the *sign* of T must be positive, for otherwise *greater* harmony would correspond to *smaller* probability.

For the second observation, consider a cognitive system a that estimates its environmental probability distribution with a certain value for

T_a and a certain harmony function H_a. Then given any other positive temperature T_b, we could hypothesize another cognitive system b using that computational temperature and the modified harmony function $H_b = (T_b / T_a)\ H_a$. Both cognitive systems would have the same estimates of environmental probabilities since $H_b / T_b = H_a / T_a$. Thus their behavior on the completion task would be indistinguishable.

Thus, the *magnitude* of T is only meaningful *once a specific scale has been set for* H. This means that if H is being *learned* by the system, rather than programmed in by the modeler, then any convenient choice of T will do; the choice simply determines the scale of H that the system will learn.

The third observation refines the second. A convenient way of expressing Equation 2 is to use the *likelihood ratio* of two states $\mathbf{s}_1$ and $\mathbf{s}_2$:

$$\frac{\text{prob}(\mathbf{s}_1)}{\text{prob}(\mathbf{s}_2)} = e^{[H(\mathbf{s}_1) - H(\mathbf{s}_2)]/T}. \tag{3}$$

Thus, *T sets the scale for those differences in harmony that correspond to significant differences in probability.* (It is understood here that "differences" in harmony are measured by *subtraction* while "differences" in probability are measured by *division.*) The smaller the value of T, the smaller the harmony differences that will correspond to significant likelihood ratios. Thus, once a scale of H has been fixed, decreasing the value of T makes the probability distribution *more sharply peaked.* In fact, Equation 3 can be rewritten

$$\frac{\text{prob}(\mathbf{s}_1)}{\text{prob}(\mathbf{s}_2)} = \left[e^{H(\mathbf{s}_1) - H(\mathbf{s}_2)}\right]^{1/T}.$$

If state $\mathbf{s}_1$ has greater harmony than $\mathbf{s}_2$, the likelihood ratio at $T = 1$ will be the number in square brackets, a number greater than one; as T goes to zero this number gets raised to higher and higher powers so that the likelihood ratio goes to infinity. In other words, compared to T, the fixed difference in harmony between the two states looks larger and larger as T gets smaller and smaller.

In the preceding argument, the exponential functions emerged as the only continuous functions mapping addition into multiplication. Of course we could consider discontinuous functions, one example being the limit as $T \to 0$ of the exponential. In this limit, the estimated probability of all states is zero, except the ones with maximal harmony. If there are several states with exactly the same maximal harmony, in the zero temperature limit they will all end up with equal, nonzero probability. This probability distribution will be called *the zero temperature distribution.* It does not correspond to an exponential distribution, but it can be obtained as the limit of exponential distributions; in fact, the zero-temperature limit plays a major role in the theory since the states of maximal harmony are the best answers to completion problems.

THE COMPETENCE, REALIZABILITY, AND LEARNABILITY THEOREMS

In this section, the mathematical results that currently form the core of harmony theory are informally described. A formal presentation may be found in the Appendix.

The Competence Theorem

In harmony theory, a cognitive system's knowledge is encoded in its knowledge atoms. Each atom represents a pattern of values for a few features describing environmental states, values that sometimes co-occur in the system's environment. The strengths of the atoms encode the frequencies with which the different patterns occur in the environment. The atoms are used to estimate the probabilities of events in the environment.

Suppose then that a particular cognitive system is capable of observing the frequency with which each pattern in some pre-existing set $\{\mathbf{k}_\alpha\}$ occurs in its environment. (The larger the set $\{\mathbf{k}_\alpha\}$, the greater is the potential power of this cognitive system.) Given the frequencies of these patterns, how should the system estimate the probabilities of environmental events? What probability distribution should the system guess for the environment?

There will generally be many possible environmental distributions that are consistent with the known pattern frequencies. How can one be selected from all these possibilities?

Consider a simple example. Suppose there are only two environmental features in the representation, r_1 and r_2, and that the system's only information is that the pattern $r_1 = +$ occurs with a frequency of 80%. There are infinitely many probability distributions for the four environmental events $(r_1,r_2) \in \{(+,+)\ (+,-)\ (-,+)\ (-,-)\}$ that are consistent with the given information. For example, we know nothing about the relative likelihood of the two events (+,+) and (+,–); all we know is that together their probability is .80 .

One respect in which the possible probability distributions differ is in their degree of homogeneity. A distribution P in which $P(+,+) = .7$

and $P(+,-) = .1$ is less homogeneous than one for which both these events have probability .4.

Another way of saying this is that the *uncertainty* associated with the second distribution is greater than that of the first. In Shannon's (1948/1963) terms, if the second, more homogeneous, distribution applies, then at any given moment there is a greater amount of *missing information* about the current state of the environment than there is if the more inhomogenous distribution applies. Shannon's formula for the missing information of a probability distribution P is

$$-\sum_x P(x)\ \ln P(x).$$

Thus the missing information in the inhomogeneous probabilities $\{.7, .1\}$ is

$$-\left[.7\ln(.7) + .1\ln(.1)\right] = .48$$

while the missing information in the homogeneous probabilities $\{.4, .4\}$ is

$$-\left[.4\ln(.4) + .4\ln(.4)\right] = .73.$$

The cognitive system's information on the frequency of patterns contains some information about any lack of homogeneity in the environmental distribution. One principle for guessing the environmental distribution is to select, of all probability distributions that are consistent with the known frequencies, the one that is most homogenous; the one that supposes the environment to have no more inhomogeneity than is needed to account for the known information. This principle can be formalized as the *principle of maximal missing information*; it is often used to extrapolate from some given statistical information to an estimate for an entire probability distribution (Christensen, 1981; Levine & Tribus, 1979).

For the simple example discussed above, the principle of maximal missing information implies that the cognitive system should estimate the environmental distribution to be $P(+,+) = P(+,-) = .40$, $P(-,+) = P(-,-) = .10$. This distribution is inhomogeneous with respect to the first feature, r_1, because it *must* be to account for the known fact that $P(r_1 = +) = .80$. It is homogeneous in the second feature, r_2, because it *can* be without violating any known information. The justification for choosing this distribution is that there is not enough given information to justify selecting any other distribution with less missing information.

In the general case, one can use the formula for missing information to derive the distribution with maximal missing information that is consistent with the observed frequencies of the patterns $\mathbf{k}_\alpha$. The result is a probability distribution I will call π:

$$\pi(\mathbf{r}) \propto e^{U(\mathbf{r})}$$

where the function U is defined by

$$U(\mathbf{r}) = \sum_\alpha \lambda_\alpha \chi_\alpha(\mathbf{r}).$$

The values of the real parameters λ_α (one for each atom) are constrained by the known pattern frequencies; they will shortly be seen to be proportional to the atom strengths, σ_α, the system should use for modeling the environment. The value of $\chi_\alpha(\mathbf{r})$ is simply 1 when the environmental state $\mathbf{r}$ includes the pattern $\mathbf{k}_\alpha$ defining atom α, and 0 otherwise.

Now that we have a formula for estimating the probability of an environmental state, we can in principle perform the completion task. An input for this task is a set of values for some of the features. The best completion is formed by assigning values to the unknown features so that the resulting vector $\mathbf{r}$ represents the most probable environment state, as estimated by π.

It turns out that the completions performed in this way are *exactly* the same as those that would be formed by using the same procedure with the different distribution

$$p(\mathbf{r},\mathbf{a}) \propto e^{H(\mathbf{r},\mathbf{a})}.$$

Here, H is the harmony function defined previously, where the strengths are

$$\sigma_\alpha = \frac{\lambda_\alpha}{1-\kappa}$$

and κ is any value satisfying

$$1 > \kappa > 1 - 2/\left[\max_\alpha |\mathbf{k}_\alpha|\right].$$

(This condition on κ is the *exact matching limit* defined earlier.)

In passing from $\pi(\mathbf{r})$ to $p(\mathbf{r},\mathbf{a})$, new variables have been introduced: the activations $\mathbf{a}$. These serve to eliminate the functions χ_α from the formula for estimating probabilities, which will be important shortly when we try to design a device to actually perform the completion computation. The result is that in addition to filling in the unknown features in $\mathbf{r}$, all the activations in $\mathbf{a}$ must be filled in as well. In other words, to perform the completion, the cognitive system must find those values of the unknown r_i and those values of the a_α that together maximize the harmony $H(\mathbf{r},\mathbf{a})$ and thereby maximize the estimated probability $p(\mathbf{r},\mathbf{a})$.

This discussion is summarized in the following theorem:

Theorem 1: Competence. Suppose a cognitive system can observe the frequency of the patterns $\{\mathbf{k}_\alpha\}$ in its environment. The probability distribution with the most Shannon missing information that is consistent with the observations is

$$\pi(\mathbf{r}) \propto e^{U(x)}$$

with U defined as above. The maximum-likelihood completions of this distribution are the same as those of

$$p(\mathbf{r},\mathbf{a}) \propto e^{H(\mathbf{r},\mathbf{a})}$$

with the harmony function defined above.

This theorem describes how a cognitive system *should* perform completions, according to some mathematical principles for statistical extrapolation and inference. In this sense, it is a *competence* theorem. The obvious next question is: Can we design a system that will really compute completions according to the specifications of the competence theorem?

The "Physics Analogy"

It turns out that designing a machine to do the required computations is a relatively straightforward application of a computational technique from statistical physics. It is therefore an appropriate time to discuss the "analogy" to physics that is exploited in harmony theory.

Why is the relation between probability and harmony expressed in the competence theorem the same as the relation between probability and energy in statistical physics? The mapping between statistical physics and inference that is being exploited is one that has been known for a long time.

The second law of thermodynamics states that as physical systems evolve in time, they will approach conditions that maximize randomness or *entropy*, subject to the constraint that a few conserved quantities like the systems' energy must always remain unchanged. One of the triumphs of statistical mechanics was the understanding that this law is the macroscopic manifestation of the underlying microscopic description of matter in terms of constituent particles. The particles will occupy various states and the macroscopic properties of a system will depend on the probabilities with which the states are occupied. The randomness or entropy of the system, in particular, is the homogeneity of this probability distribution. It is measured by the formula

$$-\sum_x P(x) \ln P(x).$$

A system evolves to maximize this entropy, and, in particular, a system that has come to equilibrium in contact with a large reservoir of heat will have a probability distribution that maximizes entropy subject to the constraint that its energy have a fixed average value.

Shannon realized that the homogeneity of a probability distribution, as measured by the microscopic formula for entropy, was a measure of the missing information of the distribution. He started the book of information theory with a page from statistical mechanics.

The competence theorem shows that the exponential relation between harmony and probability stems from maximizing missing information subject to the constraint that given information be accounted for. The exponential relation between energy and probability stems from maximizing entropy subject to a constraint on average energy. The physics analogy therefore stems from the fact that entropy and missing information share exactly the same relation to probability. It is not surprising that the theory of information processing should share formal features with the theory of statistical physics.

Shannon began a mapping between statistical physics and the theory of information by mapping entropy onto information content. Harmony theory extends this mapping by mapping self-consistency (i.e., harmony) onto energy. In the next subsection, the mapping will be further extended to map stochasticity of inference (i.e., computational temperature) onto physical temperature.

The Realizability Theorem

The mapping with statistical physics allows harmony theory to exploit a computational technique for studying thermal systems that was developed by N. Metropolis, M. Rosenbluth, A. Rosenbluth, A. Teller, and E. Teller in 1953. This technique uses stochastic or "Monte Carlo" computation to simulate the probabilistic dynamical system under study. (See Binder, 1979.)

The procedure for simulating a physical system at temperature T is as follows: The variables of the system are assigned random initial values. One by one, they are updated according to a stochastic rule: The probability of assigning a new value x to the variable is proportional to $e^{H_x/T}$, where H_x is (minus) the energy the system would have if the value x were chosen. Thus the higher T, the more random are the decisions. As the computation proceeds, the probability that the system is in state $\mathbf{s}$ at any moment becomes proportional to the desired value, $e^{H(\mathbf{s})/T}$.

Adapting this technique to the computations of harmony theory leads, through an analysis described in the Appendix, to the following theorem. It defines the machine *harmonium* that realizes the theory of completions expressed in Theorem 1.

Theorem 2: Realizability. In the graphical representation of a harmony system (see Figure 13) let each node denote a processor. Each feature node processor can have a value of $+1$ or -1, and each knowledge atom a value of 1 or 0 (its activation). Let the input to a completion problem be specified by assigning the given feature nodes their correct values; these are fixed throughout the computation. All other nodes repeatedly update their values during the computation. The features not specified in the input are assigned random initial values, and the knowledge atoms initially all have value 0. Let each node stochastically update its value according to the rule:

$$\text{prob}(\text{value} = 1) = \frac{1}{1 + e^{-I/T}}$$

where T is a global system parameter and I is the "input" to the node from the other nodes attached to it (defined below). All the

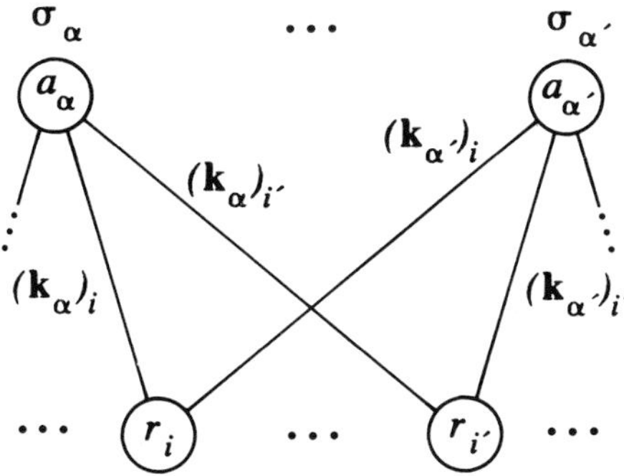

FIGURE 13. A general harmony graph.

nodes in the upper layer update in parallel, then all the nodes in the lower layer update in parallel, and so on alternately throughout the computation. During the update process, T starts out at some positive value and is gradually lowered. If T is lowered to 0 sufficiently slowly, then asymptotically, with probability 1, the system state forms the best completion (or one of the best completions if there are more than one that maximize harmony).

To define the input I to each node, it is convenient to assign to the link in the graph between atom α and feature i a weight $W_{i\alpha}$ whose sign is that of the link and whose magnitude is the strength of the atom divided by the number of links to the atom:

$$W_{i\alpha} = (\mathbf{k}_\alpha)_i \frac{\sigma_\alpha}{|\mathbf{k}_\alpha|}.$$

Using these weights, the input to a node is essentially the weighted sum of the values of the nodes connected to it. The exact definitions are

$$I_i = 2 \sum_\alpha W_{i\alpha} a_\alpha$$

for feature nodes, and

$$I_\alpha = \sum_i W_{i\alpha} r_i - \sigma_\alpha \kappa$$

for knowledge atoms.

The formulae for I_i and I_α are both derived from the fact that the input to a node is precisely the harmony the system would have if the given node were to choose the value 1 minus the harmony resulting from not choosing 1. The factor of 2 in the input to a feature node is in fact the difference $(+1) - (-1)$ between its possible values. The term κ in the input to an atom comes from the κ in the harmony function; it is a threshold that must be exceeded if activating the atom is to increase the harmony.

The stochastic decision rule can be understood with the aid of Figure 14. If the input to the node is large and positive (i.e., selecting value 1 would produce much greater system harmony), then it will almost certainly choose the value 1. If the input to the node is large and negative (i.e., selecting value 1 would produce much lower system harmony), then it will almost certainly *not* choose the value 1. If the input to the node is near zero, it will choose the value 1 with a probability near .5. The width of the zone of random decisions around zero input is larger the greater is T.

The process of gradually lowering T can be thought of as *cooling the*

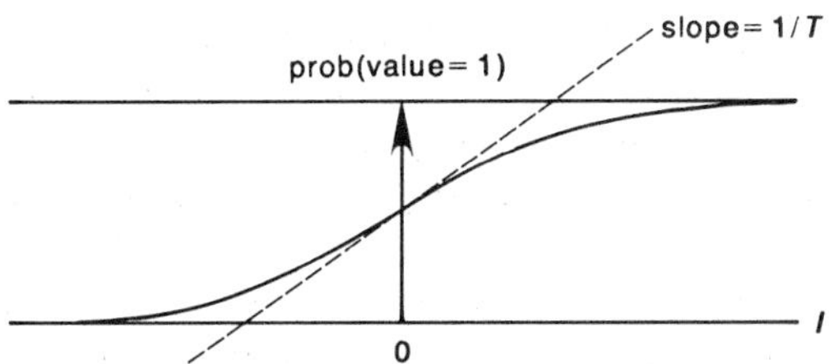

FIGURE 14. The relation between the input I to a harmonium processor node and the probability the processor will choose the value 1.

randomness out of the initial system state. In the limit that $T \rightarrow 0$, the zone of random decisions shrinks to zero and the stochastic decision rule becomes the deterministic linear threshold rule of perceptrons (Minsky & Papert, 1969; see Chapter 2). In this limit, a node will always select the value with higher harmony. At nonzero T, there is a finite probability that the node will select the value with lower harmony.

Early in a given computation, the behavior of the processors will be highly random. As T is lowered, gradually the decisions made by the processors will become more systematic. In this way, parts of the network gradually assume values that become stable; the system commits itself to decisions as it cools; it passes from fluid behavior to the rigid adoption of an answer. The decision-making process resembles the crystallization of a liquid into a solid.

Concepts from statistical physics can in fact usefully be brought to bear on the analysis of decision making in harmony theory, as we shall see in the next section. As sufficient understanding of the computational effects of different cooling procedures emerges, the hope is that harmony theory will acquire an account of how a cognitive system can regulate its own computational temperature.

Theorem 2 describes how to find the best completions by lowering to zero the computational temperature of a parallel computer—harmonium—based on the function H. Harmonium thus realizes the second half of the competence theorem, which deals with optimal completions. But Theorem 1 also states that estimates of environmental probabilities are obtained by exponentiating the function U. It is also possible to build a stochastic machine based on U that is useful for simulating the environment. I will call this the *simulation machine*.

Figure 15 shows the portion of a harmonium network involving the atom α, and the corresponding portion of the processor network for the corresponding simulation machine. The knowledge atom with strength

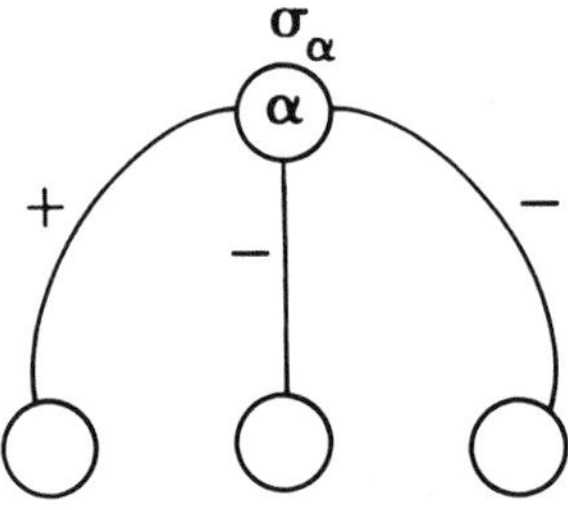

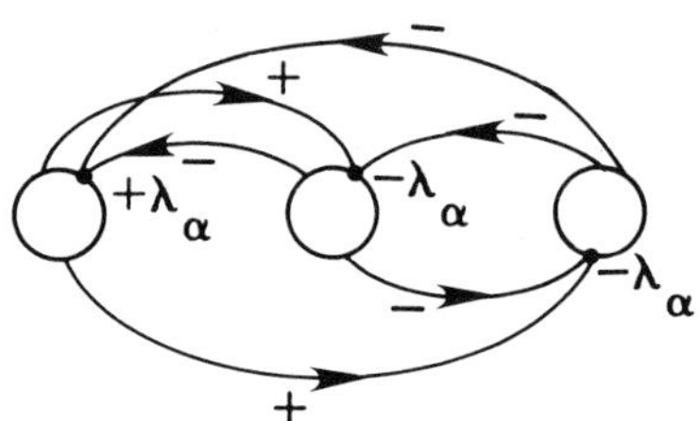

FIGURE 15. The graph for a one-atom harmony function and the graph for the corresponding U function. In the latter, there are only feature nodes. Each feature node has a single input point labeled $\pm\lambda$, where the sign is the same as that assigned to the feature by the knowledge atom. Into this input point come links from all the other features assigned values by the knowledge atom. The label on each arc leaving a feature is the same as the value assigned to that feature by the knowledge atom.

σ_α and feature pattern (+,−,−) is replaced by a set of connections between pairs of features. In accordance with Theorem 1, $\lambda_\alpha = \sigma_\alpha(1-\kappa)$. For every atom α connected to a given feature in harmonium, in the simulation machine there is a corresponding input point on that feature, labeled with λ_α.

The update rule for the simulation machine is the same as for harmonium. However, only one node can update at a time, and the definition of the input I to a node is different.[15] The input to a feature node is the sum of the inputs coming through all input points to the node. If an input point on node i is labeled $\pm\lambda_\alpha$, then the input coming to i through that point is $\pm\lambda_\alpha$ if the values of all the nodes connected to i agree with the label on the arc connecting it to i, and zero otherwise.

If the simulation machine is operated at a fixed temperature of 1, the probability that it will be found in state **r** asymptotically becomes proportional to $e^{U(\mathbf{r})/1}$. By Theorem 1, this is the cognitive system's estimate $\pi(\mathbf{r})$ of the probability that the environment will be in the state represented by **r**. Thus running this machine at temperature 1 gives a simulation of the environment. As we are about to see, this will turn out to be important for learning.

The general type of search procedure used by harmonium, with a random "thermal noise" component that is reduced during the computation, has been used to find maxima of functions other than harmony

15 Analogously to harmonium, the input to a node is the value U would have if the node adopted the value +1, minus the value U it would have if it adopted the value −1.

functions. Physicists at IBM independently applied the technique, under the name *simulated annealing*, to both practical computer design problems and classical maximization problems (Kirkpatrick, Gelatt, & Vecchi, 1983). Benchmarks of simulated annealing against other search procedures have produced mixed results (Aragon, Johnson, & McGeoch, 1985).

The contribution of harmony theory is not so much the search procedure for finding maxima of H, but rather the function H itself. Theorem 2 is important: It describes a statistical dynamical system that performs completions; it gives an implementation-level description of a kind of completion machine. But Theorem 1 is more central: It gives a high, functional-level characterization of the performance of the system—says what the machine does—and introduces the concept of harmony. More central to the theory also is Theorem 3, which says how the harmony function can be tuned with experience.

The Learnability Theorem

Performing the completion task in different environments calls for different knowledge. In the formalism of Theorem 1, a given cognitive system is assumed to be capable of observing the frequency in its environment of a predetermined set of feature patterns. What varies for a given cognitive system across environments is the *frequencies* of the patterns; this manifests itself in the variation across environments of the *strengths* of the knowledge atoms representing those patterns.

> *Theorem 3: Learnability.* Suppose states of the environment are selected according to the probability distribution defining that environment, and each state is presented to a cognitive system. Then there is a procedure for gradually modifying the strengths of the knowledge atoms that will converge to the values required by Theorem 1.

The basic idea of the learning procedure is simple. Whenever one of the patterns the cognitive system can observe is present in a stimulus from the environment, the parameter associated with that pattern is incremented. In harmonium, this means that whenever a knowledge atom matches a stimulus, its strength increases by a small amount $\Delta\sigma$. In the simulation machine, this means that the λ parameter on all the connections corresponding to that atom must be incremented by $\Delta\lambda = \Delta\sigma(1-\kappa)$. In this sense, an atom corresponds to a *memory trace* of a feature pattern, and the strength of the atom is the strength of the trace: greater the more often it has been experienced.

There is an error-correcting mechanism in the learning procedure that decrements parameters when they become too large. Intermixed with its *observation* of the environment, the cognitive system must perform *simulation* of the environment. As discussed above, this can be done by running the simulation machine at temperature 1 without input from the environment. During simulation, patterns that appear in the feature nodes produce exactly the *opposite* effect as during environmental observation, i.e., a *decrement* in the corresponding parameters.

Harmonium can be used to approximate the simulation machine. By running harmonium at temperature 1, without input, states are visited with a probability of e^H, which approximates the probabilities of the simulation machine, e^U.[16] When harmonium is used to approximately simulate the environment, every time an atom matches the feature vector its strength is *decremented* by $\Delta\sigma$.

This error-correcting mechanism has the following effect. The strength of each atom will stabilize when it gets (on the average) incremented during environmental observation as often as it gets decremented during environmental simulation. If environmental observation and simulation are intermixed in equal proportion, the strength of each atom will stabilize when its pattern appears as often in simulation as in real observation. This means the simulation is as veritical as it can be, and that is why the procedure leads to the strengths required by the competence theorem.

DECISION-MAKING AND FREEZING

The Computational Significance of Phase Transitions

Performing the completion task requires simultaneously satisfying many constraints. In such problems, it is often the case that it is easy to find "local" solutions that satisfy some of the constraints but very difficult to find a global solution that simultaneously satisfies the maximum number of constraints. In harmony theory terms, often there are *many* completions of the input that are *local* maxima of H, in which some knowledge atoms are activated, but very *few* completions that are *global* maxima, in which many atoms can be simultaneously activated.

When harmonium solves such problems, initially, at high

---

[16] Theorem 1 makes this approximation precise: These two distributions are not equal, but the maximum-probability states are the same for any possible input.

temperatures, it occupies states that are local solutions, but finally, at low temperatures, it occupies only states that are global solutions. If the problem is well posed, there is only one such state.

Thus the process of solving the problem corresponds to the passage of the harmonium dynamical system from a high-temperature phase to a low-temperature phase. An important question is: *Is there a sharp transition between these phases?* This is a "freezing point" for the system, where major decisions are made that can only be undone at lower temperatures by waiting a very long time. It is important to cool slowly through phase transitions, to maximize the chance for these decisions to be made properly; then the system will relatively quickly find the global harmony maximum without getting stuck for very long times in local maxima.

In this section, I will discuss an analysis that suggests that phase transitions *do* exist in very simple harmony theory models of decision-making. In the next section, a more complex model that answers simple physics questions will furnish another example of a harmony system that seems to possess a phase transition.[17]

The cooling process is an essentially new feature of the account of cognitive processing offered by harmony theory. To analyze the implications of cooling for cognition, it is necessary to analyze the temperature dependence of harmony models. Since the mathematical framework of harmony theory significantly overlaps that of statistical mechanics, general concepts and techniques of thermal physics can be used for this analysis. However, since the *structure* of harmony models is quite different from the structure of models of real physical systems, specific results from physics cannot be carried over. New ideas particular to cognition enter the analysis; some of these will be discussed in a later section on the macrolevel in harmony theory.

Symmetry Breaking

At high temperatures, physical systems typically have a *disordered* phase, like a fluid, which dramatically shifts to a highly *ordered* phase,

[17] It is tempting to identify freezing or "crystallization" of harmonium with the phenomenal experience of sudden "crystallization" of scattered thoughts into a coherent form. There may even be some usefulness in this identification. However, it should be pointed out that since cooling should be slow at the freezing point, in terms of iterations of harmonium, the transition from the disordered to the ordered phase may *not* be sudden. If iterations of harmonium are interpreted as real cognitive processing time, this calls into question the argument that "sudden" changes as a function of *temperature* correspond to "sudden" changes as a function of real time.

like a crystal, at a certain freezing temperature. In the low-temperature phase, a single ordered configuration is adopted by the system, while at high temperatures, parts of the system shift independently among pieces of ordered configurations so that the system as a whole is a constantly changing, disordered blend of pieces of different ordered states.

Thus we might expect that at high temperatures, the states of harmonium models will be shifting blends of pieces of reasonable completions of the current input; it will form *locally* coherent solutions. At low temperatures (in equilibrium), the model will form completions that are *globally* coherent.

Finding the best solution to a completion problem may involve fine discriminations among states that all have high harmonies. There may even be several completions that have exactly the same harmonies, as in interpreting ambiguous input. This is a useful case to consider, for in an ordered phase, harmonium must at any time construct one of these "best answers" in its pure form, without admixing parts of other best answers (assuming that such mixtures are not themselves best answers, which is typically the case). In physical terminology, *the system must break the symmetry* between the equally good answers in order to enter the ordered phase. One technique for finding phase transitions is to look for critical temperatures above which symmetry is respected, and below which it is broken.

An Idealized Decision

This suggests we consider the following idealized decision-making task. Suppose the environment is always in one of two states, A and B, with equal probability. Consider a cognitive system performing the completion task. Now for some of the system's representational features, these two states will correspond to the same feature value. These features do not enter into the decision about which state the environment is in, so let us remove them. Now the two states correspond to opposite values on all features. We can assume without loss of generality that for each feature, + is the value for A, and − the value for B (for if this were not so we could redefine the features, exploiting the symmetry of the theory under flipping signs of features). After training in this environment, the knowledge atoms of our system each have either all + connections or all − connections to the features.

To look for a phase transition, we see if the system can break symmetry. We give the system a completely ambiguous input: no input at all. It will complete this to either the all-+ state, representing A, or the all-− state, representing B, each outcome being equally likely.

Observing the harmonium model we see that for high temperatures, the states are typically blends of the all-+ and all-− states. These blends are not themselves good completions since the environment has no such states. But at low temperatures, the model is almost always in one pure state or the other, with only short-lived intrusions on a feature or two of the other state. It is equally likely to cool into either state and, given enough time, will flip from one state to the other through a sequence of (very improbable) intrusions of the second state into the first. The transition between the high- and low-temperature phases occurs over a quite narrow temperature range. At this freezing temperature, the system drifts easily back and forth between the two pure states.

The harmonium simulation gives empirical evidence that there is a critical temperature below which the symmetry between the interpretations of ambiguous input is broken. There is also analytic evidence for a phase transition in this case. This analysis rests on an important concept from statistical mechanics: the thermodynamic limit.

The Thermodynamic Limit

Statistical mechanics relates microscopic descriptions that view matter as dynamical systems of constituent particles to the macrolevel descriptions of matter used in thermodynamics. Thermodynamics provides a good approximate description of the bulk properties of systems containing an extremely large number of particles. The *thermodynamic limit* is a theoretical limit in which the number of particles in a statistical mechanical system is taken to infinity, keeping finite certain aggregate properties like the system's density and pressure. It is in this limit that the microtheory provably admits the macrotheory as a valid approximate description.

The thermodynamic limit will later be seen to relate importantly to the limit of harmony theory in which symbolic macro-accounts become valid. But for present purposes, it is relevant to the analysis of phase transitions. One of the important insights of statistical mechanics is that *qualitative* changes in thermal systems, like those characteristic of genuine phase transitions, cannot occur in systems with a finite number of degrees of freedom (e.g., particles). It is only in the thermodynamic limit that phase transitions can occur.

This means that an analysis of freezing in the idealized-decision model must consider the limit in which the number of features and knowledge atoms go to infinity. In this limit, certain approximations become valid that suggest that indeed there *is* a phase transition.

Robustness of Coherent Interpretation

To conclude this section, let me point out the significance of this simple decision-making system. Harmony theory started out to design an engine capable of constructing coherent interpretations of input and ended up with a class of thermal models realized by harmonium. We have just seen that the resulting models are capable of taking a completely ambiguous input and nonetheless constructing a completely coherent interpretation (by cooling below the critical temperature). This suggests a robustness in the drive to construct coherent interpretations that should prove adequate to cope with more typical cases characterized by less ambiguity but greater complexity. The greater complexity will surely hamper *our* attempts to analyze the models' performance; it remains to be seen whether greater complexity will hamper the models' ability to construct coherent interpretations. With this in mind, we now jump to a much more complex decision-making problem: the qualitative analysis of a simple electric circuit.

AN APPLICATION: ELECTRICITY PROBLEM SOLVING

Theoretical context of the model. In this section I show how the framework of harmony theory can be used to model the *intuition* that allows experts to answer, without any conscious application of "rules," questions like that posed in Figure 16. Theoretical conceptions of how such problems are answered plays an increasingly significant role in the design of instruction. (For example, see the new journal, *Cognition and*

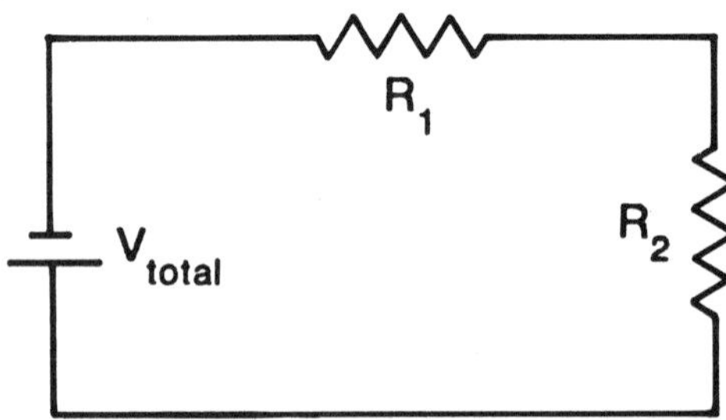

FIGURE 16. If the resistance of R_2 is increased (assuming that V_{total} and R_1 remain the same), what happens to the current and voltage drops?

Instruction, and Ginsburg, 1983.) Even such simple problems as that of Figure 16 have important instructional implications (Riley, 1984).

The model I will describe was studied in collaboration with Mary S. Riley (Riley & Smolensky, 1984) and Peter DeMarzo (1984). This model provides answers, without any symbolic manipulation of rules, to qualitative questions about the particular circuit of Figure 16. It should not be assumed that we imagine that a different harmony network like the one I will describe is created for every different circuit that is analyzed. Rather we assume that experts contain a small number of fixed networks like the one we propose, that these networks represent the effects of much cumulated experience with many different circuits, that they form the "chunks" with which the expert's *intuition* represents the circuit domain, and that complex problem solving somehow employs these networks to direct the problem solving as a whole through intuitions about chunks of the problem. At this early stage we cannot say much about the coordination of activity in complex problem solving. But we do claim that by giving an explicit example of a non-symbolic account of problem solving, our model offers insights into expertise that complement nicely those of traditional production-system models. The model also serves to render concrete many of the general features of harmony theory that have been described above.

Representational features. The first step in developing a harmony model is to select features for representing the environment. Here the environment is the set of qualitative changes in the electric circuit of Figure 16 that obey the laws of physics. What must obviously be represented are the changes in the physical components: whether R_1 goes up, goes down, or stays the same, and similarly for R_2 and the battery's voltage V_{total}. We also hypothesize that experts represent deeper features of this environment, like the current I, the voltage drops V_1 and V_2 across the two resistors, and the effective resistance R_{total} of the circuit. We claim that experts "see" these deeper features; that *perceiving* the problem of Figure 16 for experts involves filling in the deeper features just as for all sighted people—experts in vision—*perceiving* a scene involves filling in the features describing objects in three-dimensional space. Many studies of expertise in the psychological literature show that experts perceive their domain differently from novices: Their representations are much richer; they possess additional representational features that are specially developed for capturing the structure of the particular environment. (See, for example, Chase & Simon, 1973; Larkin, 1983.)

So the representational features in our model encode the qualitative changes in the seven circuit variables: R_1, R_2, R_{total}, V_1, V_2, V_{total}, and I. Our claim is that experts possess some set of features *like* these;

there are undoubtedly many other possibilities, with different sets being appropriate for modeling different experts.

Next, the three qualitative changes *up, down,* and *same* for these seven variables need to be given binary encodings. The encoding I will discuss here uses one binary variable to indicate whether there is any *change* and a second to indicate whether the change is *up*. Thus there are two binary variables, $I.c$ and $I.u$, that represent the change in the current, I. To represent no change in I, the change variable $I.c$ is set to -1; the value of $I.u$ is, in this case, irrelevant. To represent increase or decrease of I, $I.c$ is given the value $+1$ and $I.u$ is assigned a value of $+1$ or -1, respectively. Thus the total number of representational features in the model is 14: two for each of the seven circuit variables.

Knowledge atoms. The next step in constructing a harmony model is to encode the necessary knowledge into a set of atoms, each of which encodes a subpattern of features that co-occur in the environment. The environment of idealized circuits is governed by formal laws of physics, so a specification of the knowledge required for modeling the environment is straightforward. In most real-world environments, no formal laws exist, and it is not so simple to give a priori methods for directly constructing an appropriate knowledge base. However, in such environments, the fact that harmony models encode *statistical* information rather than rules makes them much more natural candidates for viable models than rule-based systems. One way that the statistical prop-erties of the environment can be captured in the strengths of knowledge atoms is given by the learning procedure. Other methods can probably be derived for directly passing from statistics about the domain (e.g., medical statistics) to an appropriate knowledge base.

The fact that the environment of electric circuits is explicitly rule-governed makes a probabilistic model of intuition, like the model under construction, a particularly interesting theoretical contrast to the obvious rule-applying models of explicit conscious reasoning.

For our model we selected a minimal set of atoms; more realistic models of experts would probably involve additional atoms. A minimal specification of the necessary knowledge is based directly on the equations constraining the circuit: Ohm's law, Kirchoff's law, and the equation for the total resistance of two resistors in series. Each of these is an equation constraining the simultaneous change in three of the circuit variables. For each law, we created a knowledge atom for each combination of changes in the three variables that does not violate the law. These are memory traces that might be left behind after experiencing many problems in this domain, i.e., after observing many states of this environment. It turns out that this process gives rise to 65 knowledge atoms,[18] all of which we gave strength 1.

A portion of the model is shown in Figure 17. The two atoms shown are respectively instances of Ohm's law for R_1 and of the formula for the total resistance of two resistors in series.

It can be shown that with the knowledge base I have described, whenever a completion problem posed has a unique correct answer, that answer will correspond to the state with highest harmony. This assumes that κ is set within the range determined by Theorem 1: the perfect matching limit.[19]

The parameter κ. According to the formula defining the perfect matching limit, κ must be less than 1 and greater than $1 - 2/6 = 2/3$ because the knowledge atoms are never connected to more than 6 features (two binary features for each of three variables). In the

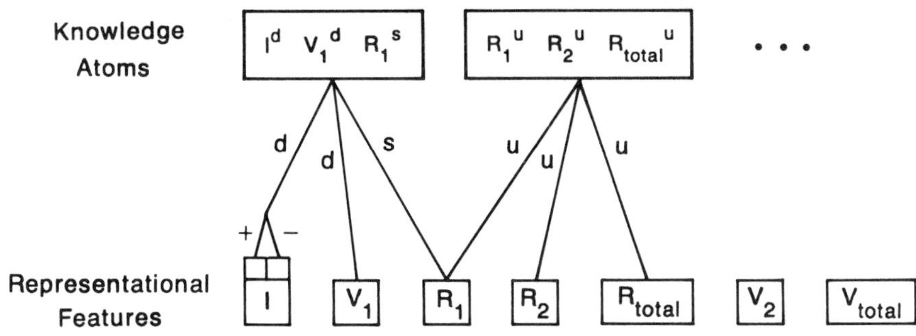

FIGURE 17. A schematic diagram of the feature nodes and two knowledge atoms of the model of circuit analysis. *u*, *d*, and *s* denote *up*, *down*, and *same*. The box labeled *I* denotes the *pair* of binary feature nodes representing *I*, and similarly for the other six circuit variables. Each connection labeled *d* denotes a *pair* of connections labeled with the binary encoding (+,−) representing *down*, and similarly for connections labeled *u* and *s*.

---

[18] Ohm's law applies three times for this circuit; once each for R_1, R_2, and R_{total}. This together with the other two laws gives five constraint equations. In each of these equations, the three variables involved can undergo 13 combinations of qualitative changes.

[19] *Proof:* The correct answer satisfies all five circuit equations, the maximum possible. Thus it exactly matches five atoms, and no possible answer can exactly match more than five atoms. In the exact matching limit, any nonexact matches cannot produce higher harmony, so the correct answer has the maximum possible harmony. If enough information is given in the problem so that there is only one correct answer, then there is only one state with this maximal harmony value.

simulations I will describe, κ was actually raised during the computation to a value of .75, as shown in Figure 18. (The model actually performs better if $\kappa = .75$ throughout: DeMarzo, 1984.)

Cooling schedule. It was not difficult to find a cooling rate that permitted the model to get the correct answer to the problem shown in Figure 16 on 28 out of 30 trials. This cooling schedule is shown in Figure 19.[20] The initial temperature (4.0) was chosen to be sufficiently high

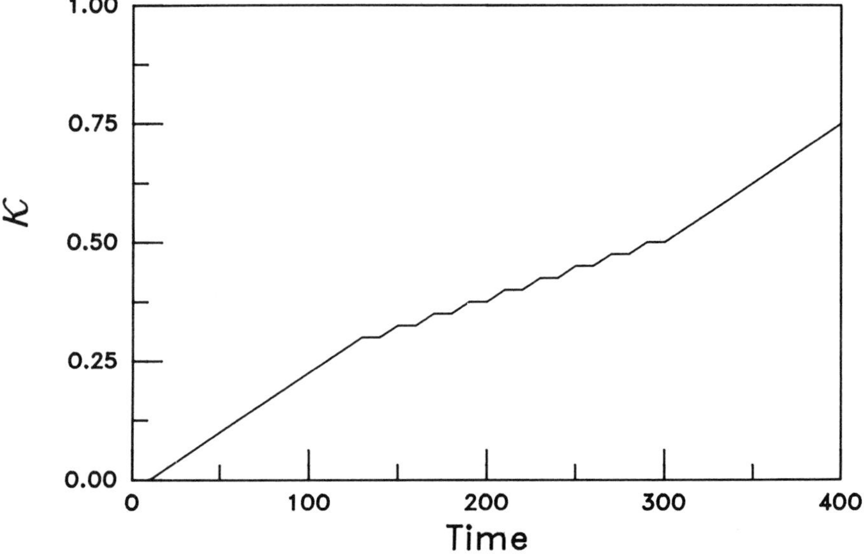

FIGURE 18. The schedule showing κ as a function of time during the computation.

[20] In the reported simulations, one node, selected randomly, was updated at a time. The computation lasted for 400 "iterations" of 100 node updates each; that is, on the average each of the 79 nodes was updated about 500 times. "Updating" a node means deciding whether to change the value of that node, regardless of whether the decision changes the value. (*Note on "psychological plausibility":* 500 updates may seem like a lot to solve such a simple problem. But I claim the model cannot be dismissed as implausible on this ground. According to current *very general* hypotheses about neural computation [see Chapter 20], each node update is a computation *comparable* to what a neuron can perform in its "cycle time" of about 10 msec. Because harmonium could actually be implemented in parallel hardware, in accordance with the realizability theorem, the 500 updates could be achieved in 500 cycles. With the cycle time of the neuron, this comes to about 5 seconds. This is clearly the correct order of magnitude for solving such problems intuitively. While it is also possible to solve such problems by firing a few symbolic productions, it is not so clear that an implementation of a production system model could be devised that would run in 500 cycles of parallel computations comparable to neural computations.)

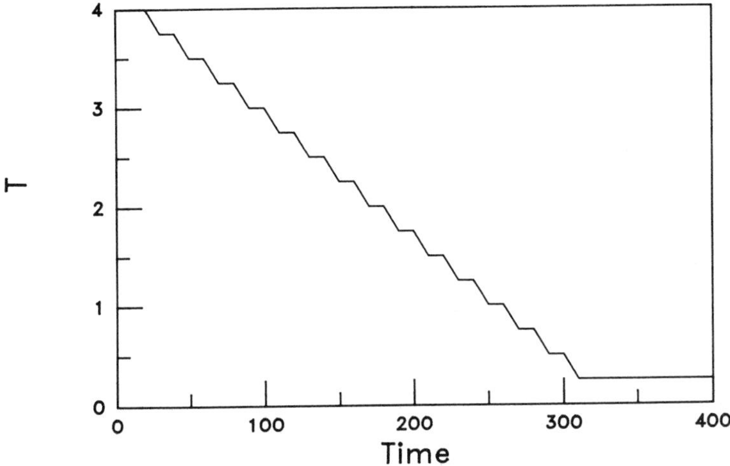

FIGURE 19. The schedule showing T as a function of time during the computation.

that nodes were flipping between their values essentially at random; the final temperature (0.25) was chosen to be sufficiently small that the representational features hardly ever flipped, so that the completion could be said to be its "final decision." Considerable computation time was probably wasted at the upper and lower ends of the cooling schedule.

The simulation. The graphical display used in the simulation provides a useful image of the computational process. On a gray background, each node was denoted by a box that was white or black depending on the current node value. Throughout the computation, the nodes encoding the given information maintain their fixed values (colors). Initially, all the atoms are black (inactive) and the unknown features are assigned random colors. When the computation starts, the temperature is high, and there is much flickering of nodes between black and white. At any moment many atoms are active. As computation proceeds and the system cools, each node flickers less and less and eventually settles into a final value.[21] The "answer" is read out by

21 It may happen that some representation variables will be connected only to knowledge atoms that are inactive towards the end of the computation; these representation variables will continue to flicker at arbitrarily low temperatures, spending 50% of the time in each state. In fact, this happens for bits of the representation (like $R_1.u$) that encode the "direction of change" of circuit variables that are in state *no change*, indicated by – on the "presence of change" bit. These bits are ignored by the active knowledge atoms (those involving *no change* for the circuit variable) and are also ignored when we "read out" the final answer produced by the network.

decoding the features for the unknowns. Ninety-three percent of the time, the answer is correct.

The microdescription of problem solving. Since the model correctly answers physics questions, it "acts as though" it knows the symbolic rules governing electric circuits. In other words, the *competence* of the harmonium model (using Chomsky's meaning of the word) could be accurately described by symbolic inference procedures (e.g., productions) that operate on symbolic representations of the circuit equations. However the *performance* of the model (including its occasional errors) is achieved without interpreting symbolic rules.[22] In fact, the process underlying the model's performance has many characteristics that are not naturally represented by symbolic computation. The answer is computed through a series of many node updates, each of which is a *microdecision* based on formal *numerical* rules and numerical computations. These microdecisions are made many times, so that the eventual values for the different circuit variables are in an important sense being computed *in parallel*. *Approximate matching* is an important part of the use of the knowledge: Atoms whose feature patterns approximately match the current feature values are more likely to become active by thermal noise than atoms that are poorer matches (because poorer matches lower the harmony by a greater amount). And all the knowledge that is active at a given moment *blends* in its effects: When a given feature updates its value, its microdecision is based on the weighted sum of the recommendations from all the active atoms.

The macrodescription of problem solving. When watching the simulation, it is hard to avoid anthropomorphizing the process. Early on, when a feature node is flickering furiously, it is clear that "the system can't make up its mind about that variable yet." At some point during the computation, however, the node seems to have stopped flickering—"it's decided that the current went down." It is reasonable to say that a *macrodecision* has been made when a node stops flickering,

---

22 The distinction between characterizing the competence and performance of dynamical systems is a common one in physics, although I know of no terminology for it. A production system expressing the circuit laws can be viewed as a *grammar for generating the high-harmony states* of the dynamical system. These laws neatly express the states into which the system will settle. However, completely different laws govern the *dynamics* through which the system enters equilibrium states. Other examples from physics of this distinction are to be found essentially everywhere. Kepler's laws, for example, neatly characterize the planetary orbits, but completely different laws, Newton's laws of motion and gravitation, describe the dynamics of planetary motion. Balmer's formula neatly characterizes the light emitted by the hydrogen atom, but utterly different laws of quantum physics describe the dynamics of the process.

although there seems to be no natural formal definition for the concept. To study the properties of macrodecisions, it is appropriate to look at how the *average values* of the stochastic node variables change during the computation. For each of the unknown variables, the node values were averaged over 30 runs of the completion problem of Figure 16, separately for each time during the computation. The resulting graphs are shown in Figure 20. The plots hover around 0 initially, indicating that values + and − are equally likely at high temperatures—lots of flickering. As the system cools, the average values of the representation variables drift toward the values they have in the correct solution to the problem (R_{total} = *up*, I = *down*, V_1 = *down*, V_2 = *up*).

Emergent seriality. To better see the macrodecisions, in Figure 21 the graphs have been superimposed and the "indecisive" band around 0 has been removed. The striking result is that out of the statistical din of parallel microdecisions emerges a *sequence* of macrodecisions.

Propagation of givens. The result is even more interesting when it is observed that in symbolic forward-chaining reasoning about this problem, the decisions are made in the order R, I, V_1, V_2. Thus not only is the *competence* of the model neatly describable symbolically, but even the *performance*, when described at the macrolevel, could be modeled by the sequential firing of productions that chain through the inferences. Of course, macrodecisions emerge first about those variables that are most directly constrained by the given inputs, but not because rules are being used that have conditions that only allow them to apply when all but one of the variables is known. Rather it is because the variables given in the input *are fixed and do not fluctuate*: They provide the information that is the most consistent over time, and therefore the knowledge consistent with the input is most consistently activated, allowing those variables involved in this knowledge to be more consistently completed than other variables. As the temperature is lowered, those variables "near" the input (with respect to the connections provided by the knowledge) stop fluctuating first, and their relative constancy of value over time makes them function somewhat like the original input to support the next wave of completion. In this sense, the stability of variables "spreads out" through the network, starting at the inputs and propagating with the help of cooling. Unlike the simple feedforward "spread of activation" through a standard activation network, this process is a spread of feedback-mediated *coherency* through a decision-making network. Like the growth of droplets or crystals, this amounts to the expansion of pockets of order into a sea of disorder.

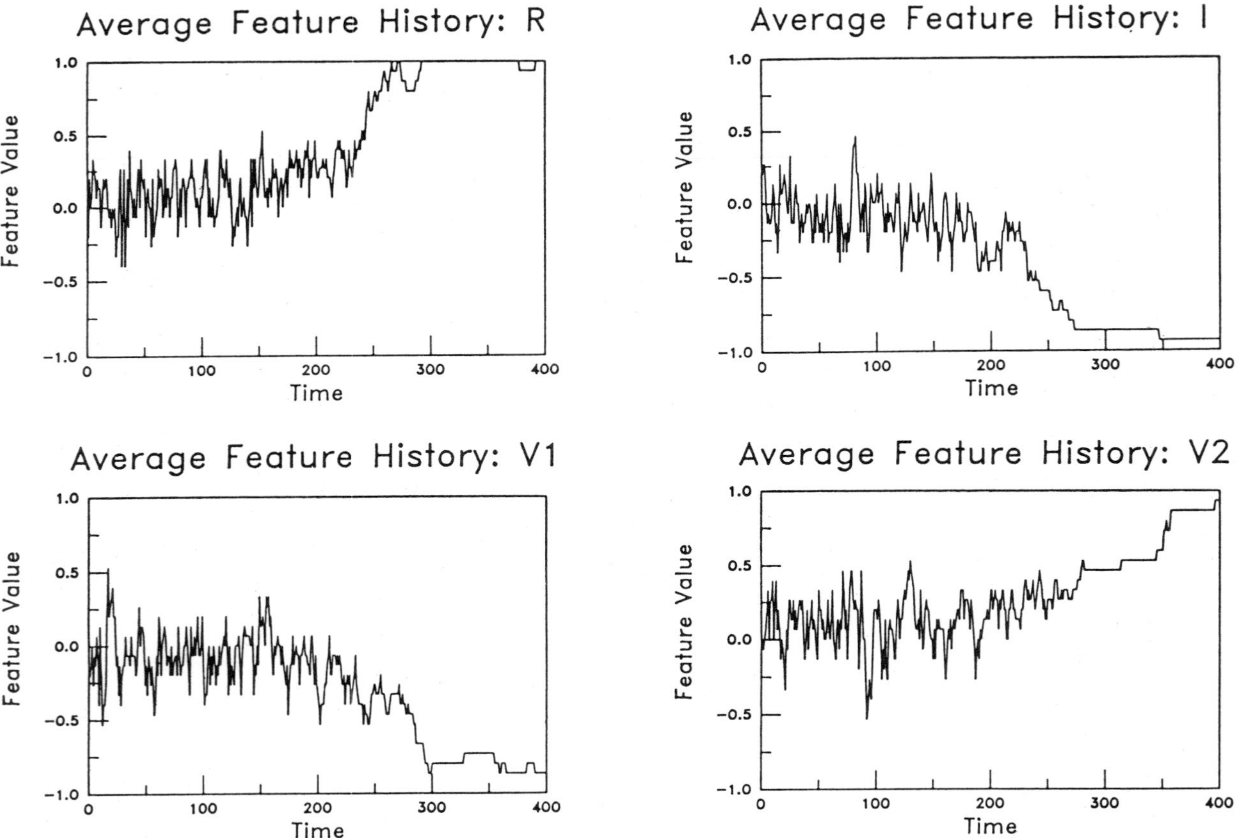

FIGURE 20. The model's hypothesized qualitative values for unknown circuit variables, averaged over 30 runs, for each iteration separately. (+ means *up*.)

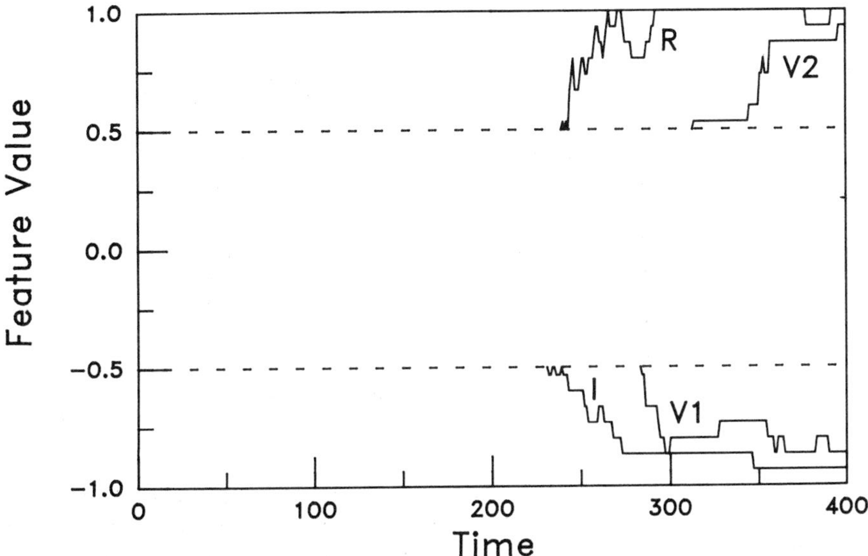

FIGURE 21. Emergent seriality: The decisions about the direction of change of the circuit variables "freeze in" in the order $R = R_{total}$, $I = I_{total}$, V_1, V_2 (R and I are very close).

Phase transition. In the previous section, a highly idealized decision-making model was seen to have a freezing temperature at which the system behavior changed from disordered (undecided) to ordered (decided). Does the same thing occur in the more complicated circuit model? As a signal for such a phase transition, physics says to look for a sharp peak in the quantity

$$C = \frac{<H^2> - <H>^2}{T^2}.$$

This is global property of the system which is proportional to the rate at which entropy—disorder—decreases as the temperature decreases; in physics, it is called the *specific heat.* If there is rapid increase in the order of the system at some temperature, the specific heat will have a peak there.

Figure 22 shows that indeed there is a rather pronounced peak. Does this macrostatistic of the system correspond to anything significant in the macrodecision process? In Figure 23, the specific heat curve is superimposed on Figure 21. The peak in the specific heat coincides remarkably with the first two major decisions about the total resistance and current.

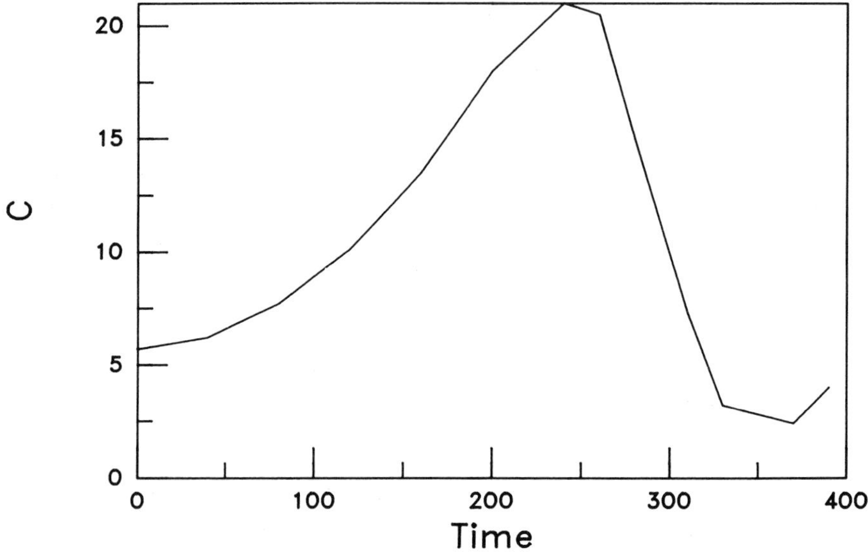

FIGURE 22. The specific heat of the circuit analysis model through the course of the computation.

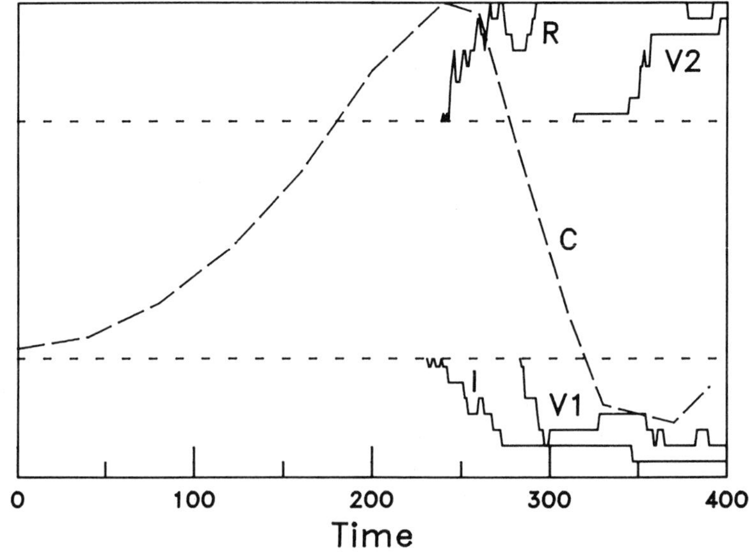

FIGURE 23. There is a peak in the specific heat at the time when the *R* and *I* decisions are being made.

MACRODESCRIPTION: PRODUCTIONS, SCHEMATA, AND EXPERTISE

Productions and Expertise

While there are similarities in the production-system account of problem solving and the macrodescription of the harmony account, there are important differences. These differences are most apparent in the accounts of how experts' knowledge is acquired and represented.

A symbolic account of expertise acquisition. A standard description within the symbolic paradigm of the acquisition of expertise is based on the idea of knowledge *compilation* (Anderson, 1982). Applied to circuit analysis, the account goes roughly like this. Novices have procedures for inspecting equations and using them to assign values to unknowns. At this stage of performance, novices consciously scan equations when solving circuit problems. As circuit problems are solved, knowledge is *proceduralized*: specialized circuit-analysis productions are stored in the knowledge base. An example of might be "IF given: R_1 and R_2 both go up, THEN conclude: R_{total} goes up" which can be abbreviated $R_1{}^u R_2{}^u \rightarrow R_{total}{}^u$. Another might be $R_{total}{}^u\, V_{total}{}^s \rightarrow I^d$. At this stage of performance, a series of logical steps is consciously experienced, but no equations are consciously searched. As the circuit productions are used together to solve problems, they are *composed* together (Lewis, 1978). The two productions just mentioned, for example, are composed into a single production, $R_1{}^u R_2{}^u\, V_{total}{}^s \rightarrow R_{total}{}^u\, I^d$. As the productions are composed, the conditions and actions get larger, more is inferred in each production firing, and so fewer productions need to fire to solve a given problem. Eventually, the compilation process has produced productions like $R_1{}^u R_2{}^u\, V_{total}{}^s \rightarrow R_{total}{}^u\, I^d\, V_1{}^d\, V_2{}^u$. Now we have an expert who can solve the problem in Figure 16 all at once, by firing this single production. The reason is that the knowledge base contains, prestored, a rule that says "whenever you are given this problem, give this answer."

A subsymbolic account. By contrast, the harmony theory account of the acquisition of expertise goes like this. (This account has not yet been tested with simulations.) Beginning physics students are novices in circuit analysis but experts (more or less) at symbol manipulation. Through experience with language and mathematics, they have built up—by means of the learning process referred to in the learnability theorem—a set of features and knowledge atoms for the perception and manipulation of symbols. These can be used to inspect the circuit equations and draw inferences from them to solve circuit problems. With experience, features dedicated to the perception of circuits evolve, and knowledge atoms relating these features develop. The final network for circuit perception contains within it something like the model described in the previous section (as well as other portions for analyzing other types of simple circuits). This final network can solve the entire problem of Figure 16 in a single cooling. Thus experts perceive the solution in a single conscious step. (Although sufficiently careful perceptual experiments that probe the internal structure of the construction of the percept should reveal the kind of sequential filling-in that was displayed by the model.) Earlier networks, however, are not sufficiently well-tuned by experience; they can only solve *pieces* of the problem in a single cooling. Several coolings are necessary to solve the problem, and the answer is derived by a series of consciously experienced steps. (This gives the symbol-manipulating network a chance to participate, offering justifications of the intuited conclusions by citing circuit laws.) The number of circuit constraints that can be satisfied in parallel during a single cooling grows as the network is learned. *Productions are higher level descriptions of what input/output pairs—completions—can be reliably performed by the network in a single cooling.* Thus, in terms of their productions, novices are described by productions with simple conditions and actions, and experts are described by complex conditions and actions.

Dynamic creation of productions. The point is, however, that in the harmony theory account, *productions are just descriptive entities; they are not stored, precompiled, and fed through a formal inference engine;* rather they are *dynamically created* at the time they are needed by the appropriate collective action of the small knowledge atoms. Old patterns that have been stored through experience can be recombined in completely novel ways, giving the appearance that productions had been precompiled even though the particular condition/action pair had never before been performed. When a familiar input is changed slightly, the network can settle down in a slightly different way, flexing the usual production to meet the new situation. Knowledge is not stored in large frozen chunks; the productions are truly context sensitive. And since the productions are created on-line by combining many small pieces of stored knowledge, the set of available productions has a size that is an exponential function of the number of knowledge atoms. The exponential explosion of compiled productions is virtual, not precompiled and stored.

Contrasts with logical inference. It should be noted that the harmonium model can answer ill-posed questions just as it can answer well-posed ones. If insufficient information is provided, there will be more than one state of highest harmony, and the model will choose one of them. It does not stop dead due to "insufficient information" for any formal inference rule to fire. If inconsistent information is given, no available state will have a harmony as high as that of the answer to a well-posed problem; nonetheless, those answers that violate as few circuit laws as possible will have the highest harmony and one of these will therefore be selected. It is not the case that "any conclusion follows from a contradiction." The mechanism that allows harmonium to solve well-posed problems allows it to find the best possible answers to ill-posed problems, with no modification whatever.

Schemata

Productions are higher level descriptions of the completion process that ignore the internal structures that bring about the input/output mapping. Schemata are higher level descriptions of chunks of the knowledge base that ignore the internal structure within the chunk. To suggest how the relation between knowledge atoms and schemata can be formalized, it is useful to begin with the idealized two-choice decision model discussed in the preceding section entitled Decision-Making and Freezing.

Two-choice model. In this model, each knowledge atom had either all + or all − connections. To form a higher level description of the knowledge, let's lump all the + atoms together into the + *schema*, and denote it with the symbol S_+. The *activation level* of this schema, $A(S_+)$, will be defined to be the average of the activations of its constituent atoms. Now let us consider all the feature nodes together as a *slot* or *variable*, s, for this schema. There are two states of the slot that occur in completions: all + and all −. We can define these to be the possible *fillers* or *values* of the slot and symbolize them by f_+ and f_-. The information in the schema S_+ is that the slot s should be filled with f_+; the proposition $s = f_+$. The "degree of truth" of this proposition, $\tau(s = f_+)$, can be defined to be the average value of all the feature nodes comprising the slot: If they are all +, this is 1 or *true*; if all − this is −1 or *false*. At intermediate points in the computation when there may be a mixture of signs on the feature nodes, the degree of truth is somewhere between 1 and −1.

Repeating the construction for the schema S_-, we end up with a higher level description of the original model depicted in Figure 24.

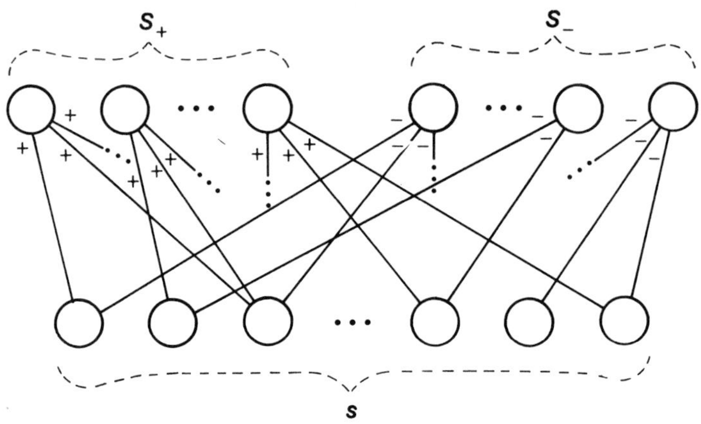

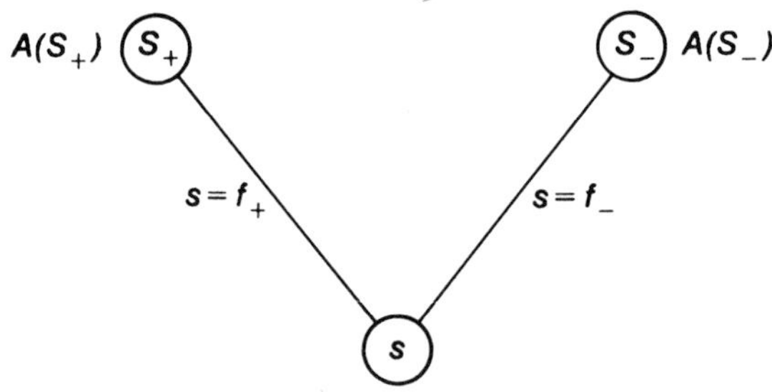

FIGURE 24. Micro- and macrodescriptions of the idealized decision model.

The interesting fact is that the harmony of any state of the original model can now be re-expressed using the higher level variables:

$$H = A(S_+)[\tau(s = f_+) - \kappa] + A(S_-)[\tau(s = f_-) - \kappa].$$

In this simple homogeneous case, the aggregate higher level variables contain sufficient information to exactly compute the harmony function.

The analysis of decision making in this model considered the limit as the number of features and atoms goes to infinity—for only in this "thermodynamic limit" can we see real phase transitions. In this limit, the set of possible values for the averages that define the aggregate variables comes closer and closer to a continuum. The central limit theorem constrains these averages to deviate less and less from their means; statistical fluctuations become less and less significant; the model's behavior becomes more and more deterministic.

Thus, just as the statistical behavior of matter disappears into the deterministic laws of thermodynamics as systems become macroscopic in size, so the statistical behavior of individual features and atoms in harmony models becomes more and more closely approximated by the higher level description in terms of schemata as the number of constituents aggregated into the schemata increases. However there are two important differences between harmony theory and statistical physics relevant here. First, the number of constituents aggregated into schemata is *nowhere near* the number—10^{23}—of particles aggregated into bulk matter. Schemata provide a useful but significantly limited description of real cognitive processing. And second, the process of aggregation in harmony theory is *much* more complex than in physics. This point can be brought out by passing from the grossly oversimplified two-choice decision model just considered to a more realistic cognitive domain.

Schemata for rooms. In a realistically complicated and large network, the schema approximation would go something like this. The knowledge atoms encode clusters of values for features that occur in the environment. Commonly recurring clusters would show up in many atoms that differ slightly from each other. (In a different language, the many exemplars of a schema would correspond to knowledge atoms that differ slightly but share many common features.) These atoms can be aggregated into a *schema*, and their average activation at any moment defines the *activation* of the schema. Now among the atoms in the cluster corresponding to a schema for a *living-room*, for example, might be a subcluster corresponding to the schema for *sofa/coffee-table*. These atoms comprise a *subschema* and the average of their activations would be the activation variable for this subschema.

The many atoms comprising the schema for *kitchen* share a set of connections to representational features relating to cooking devices. It is convenient to group together these connections into a *cooking-device slot*, $s_{cooking}$. Different atoms for different instances of *kitchen* encode various patterns of values over these representational features, corresponding to instances of *stove*, *conventional oven*, *microwave oven*, and so forth. Each of these patterns defines a possible *filler*, f_k, for the slot. The degree of truth of a proposition like $s_{cooking} = f_i$ is the number of matches minus the number of mismatches between the pattern defining f_i and the current values over the representation nodes in the slot $s_{cooking}$, all divided by the total number of features in the slot. Now the harmony obtained by activating the schema is determined by the degrees of truth of propositions specifying the possible fillers for the slots of the schema. Just like in the simple two-decision model, the harmony function, originally expressed in terms of the microscopic variables, can be re-expressed in terms of the macroscopic variables, the activations of schemata, and slot fillers. However, since the knowledge atoms being aggregated no longer have exactly the same links to features, the new expression for H in terms of aggregate variables is only *approximately* valid. The macrodescription involves fewer variables, but the structure of these variables is more complex. The objects are becoming richer, more like the structures of symbolic computation.

This is the basic idea of the analytic program of harmony theory for relating the micro- and macro-accounts of cognition. Macroscopic variables for schemata, their activations, their slots, and propositional content are defined. The harmony function is approximately rewritten in terms of these aggregate variables, and then used to study the macroscopic theory that is determined by that new function of the new variables. This theory can be simulated, defining macroscopic models. The nature of the approximation relating the macroscopic to the microscopic models is clearly articulated, and the situations and senses in which this approximation is valid are therefore specified.

The kind of variable aggregation involved in the schema approximation is in an important respect quite unlike any done in physics. The physical systems traditionally studied by physicists have *homogeneous structure*, so aggregation is done in homogeneous ways. In cognition, the distinct roles played by different schemata mean aggregates must be specially defined. The theory of the schema limit corresponds at a very general level to the theory of the thermodynamic limit, but is rather sharply distinguished by a much greater complexity.

The Schema Approximation

In this subsection I would like to briefly discuss the schema approximation in a very general information-processing context.

In harmony theory, the cognitive system fills in missing information with reference to an internal model of the environment represented as a probability distribution. Such a distribution of course contains potentially a phenomenal amount of information: the joint statistics of all combinations of all features used to represent the environment. How can we hope to encode such a distribution effectively? Schemata provide an answer. They comprise a way of breaking up the environment into modules—schemata—that can individually by represented as a miniprobability distribution. These minidistributions must then be folded together during processing to form an estimate of the whole distribution. To analyze a room scene, we don't need information about the joint probability of all possible features; rather, our schema for "chair" takes care of the joint probability of the features of chairs; the schema for "sofa/coffee-table" contains information about the joint probability of sofa and coffee-table features, and so on. Each schema *ignores* the features of the others, by and large.

This modularization of the encoding can reduce tremendously the amount of information the cognitive system needs to encode. If there are f binary features, the whole probability distribution requires 2^f numbers to specify. If we can break the features into s groups corresponding to schemata, each involving f/s features, then only $s 2^{f/s}$ numbers are needed. This can be an enormous reduction; even with such small numbers as $f = 100$ and $s = 10$, for example, the reduction factor is $10 \times 2^{-90} \approx 10^{-28}$.

The reduction in information afforded by schemata amounts to an assumption that the probability distribution representing the environment has a special, modular structure—at least, that it can be usefully so approximated. A very crude approximation would be to divide the features into disjoint groups, to separately store in schemata the probabilities of possible combinations of features within each group, and then to simply *multiply* together these probabilities to estimate the joint probability of all features. This assumes the features in the groups are completely *statistically independent*, that the values of features of a chair interact with other features of the chair but not with features of the sofa. To some extent this assumption is valid, but there clearly are limits to its validity.

A less crude approximation is to allow schemata to share features so that the shared features can be constrained simultaneously by the joint probabilities with the different sets of variables contained in the different schemata to which it relates. Now we are in the situation modeled by harmony theory. A representational feature node can be attached to many knowledge atoms and thereby participate in many schemata. The distribution $e^{H/T}$ manages to combine into a single probability distribution all the separate but interacting distributions corresponding to the separate schemata. Although the situation is not as simple as the case of nonoverlapping schemata and completely independent subdistributions, the informational savings is still there. The trick is to isolate groups of environmental features which each comprise a small fraction of the whole feature set, to use these groups to define more abstract features, and record the probability distributions using these features. The groups must be selected to capture the most important interrelationships in the environment. This is the problem of constructing new features. The last section offers a few comments on this most important issue.

LEARNING NEW REPRESENTATIONS

The Learning Procedure and Abstract Features

Throughout this chapter I have considered cognitive systems that represent states of their environment using features that were established prior to our investigation, either through programming by the modeler, or evolution, or learning. In this section I would like to make a few comments about this last possibility, the establishment of features through learning.

Throughout this chapter I have emphasized that the features in harmony models represent the environment at all levels of abstractness. In the preceding account of how expertise in circuit analysis is acquired, it was stated that through experience, experts evolve abstract features for representing the domain. So the basic notion is that the cognitive system comes into existence with a set of *exogenous features* whose values are determined completely by the state of the external environment, whenever the environment is being observed. Other *endogenous features* evolve, through a process now to be described, through experience, from an initial state of meaninglessness to a final state of abstract meaning. Endogenous features always get their values through internal completion, and never directly from the external environment.[23]

As a specific example, consider the network of Figure 9, which is repeated as Figure 25. In this network, features of several levels of

---

[23] In Chapter 7, Hinton and Sejnowski use the terms *visible* and *hidden* units. The former correspond to the exogenous feature nodes, while the latter encompass *both* the endogenous feature nodes and the knowledge atoms.

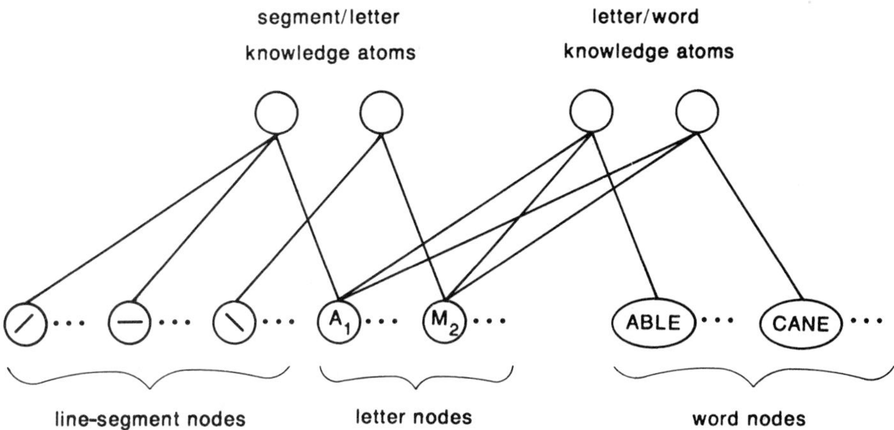

FIGURE 25. A network representing words at several levels of abstractness.

abstractness are used to represent words. Here is a *hypothetical* account of how such a network could be learned.[24]

The features representing the line segments are taken to be the exogenous features given a priori. This network comes into existence with these line-segment nodes, together with extra endogenous feature nodes which, through experience, will become the letter and word nodes.

As before, the cognitive system is assumed to come into existence with a set of knowledge atoms whose strengths will be adjusted to match the environment. Some of these atoms have connections only to exogenous features, some only to endogenous features, and some to both types of features.

The environment (in this case, a set of words) is observed. Each time a word is presented, the appropriate values for the line-segment nodes are set. The current atom strengths are used to complete the input, through the cooling procedure discussed above. The endogenous features are thus assigned values for the particular input. Initially,

[24] The issue of selecting patterns on exogenous features for use in defining endogenous features—including the word domain—is discussed in Smolensky (1983). To map the terminology of that paper on to that of this chapter, replace *schemas* by *knowledge atoms* and *beliefs* by *feature values*. That paper offers an alternative use of the harmony concept in learning. Rather than specifying a learning process, it specifies an optimality condition on the atom strengths: They should maximize the total harmony associated with interpreting all environmental stimuli. This condition is related, but not equivalent, to information-theoretic conditions on the strengths.

when the atoms' strengths have received little environmental tuning, the values assigned to the endogenous features will be highly random. Nonetheless, after the input has been completed, learning occurs: The strengths of atoms that match the feature nodes are all increased by $\Delta\sigma$.

Intermixed with this incrementing of strengths during environmental observation is a process of decrementing strengths during environmental simulation. Thus the learning process is exactly like the one referred to in the learnability theorem, except that now, during observation, not all the features are set by the environment; the endogenous features must be filled in by completion.

Initially, the values of the endogenous features are random. But as learning occurs, correlations between recurring patterns in the exogenous features and the random endogenous features will be amplified by the strengthening of atoms that encode those correlations. An endogenous feature by chance tends to be + when patterns of line segments defining the letter *A* are present and so leads to strengthening of atoms relating it to those patterns; it gradually comes to represent *A*. In this way, self-organization of the endogenous features can potentially lead them to acquire meaning.

The learnability theorem states that when no endogenous features are present, this learning process will produce strengths that optimally encode the environmental regularities, in the sense that the completions they give rise to are precisely the maximum-likelihood completions of the estimated environmental probability distribution with maximal missing information that is consistent with observable statistics. At present there is no comparable theorem that guarantees that in the presence of endogenous features this learning procedure will produce strengths with a corresponding optimality characterization.[25]

Among the most important future developments of the theory is the study of self-organization of endogenous features. These developments include a possible extension of the learnability theorem to include endogenous features as well as computer simulations of the learning procedure in specific environments.

---

[25] In Chapter 7, Hinton and Sejnowski use a different but related optimality condition. They use a function G which measures the information-theoretic difference between the true environmental probability distribution and the estimated distribution e^H. For the case of no endogenous features, the following is true (see Theorem 4 of the Appendix). The strengths that correspond to the maximal-missing-information distribution consistent with observable statistics are the same as the strengths that minimize G. That the estimated distribution is of the form e^H must be *assumed* a priori in using the minimal-G criterion; it is *entailed* by the maximal-missing-information criterion.

Learning in the Symbolic and Subsymbolic Paradigms

Nowhere is the contrast between the symbolic and subsymbolic approaches to cognition more dramatic than in learning. Learning a new concept in the symbolic approach entails creating something like a new schema. Because schemata are such large and complex knowledge structures, developing automatic procedures for generating them in original and flexible ways is extremely difficult.

In the subsymbolic account, by contrast, a new schema comes into being gradually, as the strengths of atoms slowly shifts in response to environmental observation, and new groups of coherent atoms slowly gain important influence in the processing. During learning, there need never be any decision that "now is the time to create and store a new schema." Or rather, if such a decision is made, it is by the modeler *observing* the evolving cognitive system and not by the system itself.

Similarly there is never a time when the cognitive system decides "now is the time to assign this meaning to this endogenous feature." Rather, the strengths of all the atoms that connect to the given endogenous feature slowly shift, and with it the "meaning" of the feature. Eventually, the atoms that emerge with dominant strength may create a network like that of Figure 25, and the modeler observing the system may say "this feature means the letter *A* and this feature the word *ABLE*." Then again, some completely different representation may emerge.

The reason that learning procedures can be derived for subsymbolic systems, and their properties mathematically analyzed, is that in these systems knowledge representations are extremely impoverished. It is for this same reason that they are so hard for us to program. It is therefore in the domain of learning, more than any other, that the potential seems greatest for the subsymbolic paradigm to offer new insights into cognition. Harmony theory has been motivated by the goal of establishing a subsymbolic computational environment where the mechanisms for *using* knowledge are simultaneously sufficiently powerful and analytically tractable to facilitate—rather than hinder—the study of learning.

CONCLUSIONS

In this chapter I have described the foundations of harmony theory, a formal subsymbolic framework for performing an important class of generalized perceptual computations: the completion of partial descriptions of static states of an environment. In harmony theory, knowledge is encoded as constraints among a set of well-tuned perceptual features. These constraints are numerical and are imbedded in an extremely powerful parallel constraint satisfaction machine: an informal inference engine. The constraints and features evolve gradually through experience. The numerical processing mechanisms implementing both performance and learning are derived top-down from mathematical principles. When the computation is described on an aggregate or macrolevel, qualitatively new features emerge (such as seriality). The *competence* of models in this framework can sometimes be neatly expressed by symbolic rules, but their *performance* is never achieved by explicitly storing these rules and passing them through a symbolic interpreter.

In harmony theory, the concept of self-consistency plays the leading role. The theory extends the relationship that Shannon exploited between information and physical entropy: Computational self-consistency is related to physical energy, and computational randomness to physical temperature. The centrality of the consistency or harmony function mirrors that of the energy or Hamiltonian function in statistical physics. Insights from statistical physics, adapted to the cognitive systems of harmony theory, can be exploited to relate the micro- and macrolevel accounts of the computation. Theoretical concepts, theorems, and computational techniques are being pursued, towards the ultimate goal of a subsymbolic formulation of the theory of information processing.

ACKNOWLEDGMENTS

The framework presented in this chapter grew out of an attempt to formalize approaches to understanding cognition that I have learned from Dave Rumelhart, Doug Hofstadter, and Geoff Hinton. I thank them for sharing their insights with me over several years. Thanks too to Steve Greenspan, Jay McClelland, Mary Riley, Gerhard Dirlich, Francis Crick, and especially Stu Geman for very instructive conversations. Peter DeMarzo has made important contributions to the theory and I have benefited greatly from working with him. I would like to thank the members of the UCSD Cognitive Science Lab and particularly the Parallel Distributed Processing research group for all their help and support. Special thanks go to Judith Stewart, Dan Rabin, Don Gentner, Mike Mozer, Rutie Kimchi, Don Norman, and Sondra Buffett. Thanks to Eileen Conway and Mark Wallen for excellent graphics and computer support. The work was supported by the System

Development Foundation, the Alfred P. Sloan Foundation, National Institute of Mental Health Grant PHS MH 14268 to the Center for Human Information Processing, and Personnel and Training Research Programs of the Office of Naval Research Contract N00014-79-C-0323, NR 667-437.

APPENDIX: FORMAL PRESENTATION OF THE THEOREMS

Formal relationships between parallel (or neural) computation and statistical mechanics have been exploited by several researchers. Three research groups in particular have been in rather close contact since their initially independent development of closely related ideas. These groups use names for their research which reflect the independent perspectives that they maintain: the *Boltzmann machine* (Ackley, Hinton, & Sejnowski, 1985; Fahlman, Hinton, & Sejnowski, 1983; Hinton & Sejnowski, 1983a, 1983b; Chapter 7), the *Gibbs sampler* (Geman & Geman, 1984), and *harmony theory* (Smolensky, 1983, 1984; Smolensky & Riley, 1984). In this appendix, all results are presented from the perspective of harmony theory, but ideas from the other groups have been incorporated and are so referenced.[26]

Because the ideas have been informally motivated and pursued at some length in the text, this appendix is deliberately formal and concise. The proofs are presented in the final section. In making the formal presentation properly self-contained, a certain degree of redundancy with the text is necessarily incurred; this is an inevitable consequence of presenting the theory at three levels of formality within a single, linearly ordered document.

Preliminary Definitions

Overview of the definitions. The basic theoretical framework is schematically represented in Figure 26. There is an external environment with structure that allows prediction of which events are more likely than others. This environment is passed through transducers to become represented internally in the *exogenous features* of a representational space. (Depending on the application, the transducers might include considerable perceptual and cognitive processing, so that the exogenous features might in fact be quite high level; they are just unanalyzed at the level of the particular model.) The features in the

[26] Hofstadter (1983) uses the idea of computational temperature in a heuristic rather than formal way to modulate the parallel symbolic processing in an AI system for doing anagrams. His insights into relationships between statistical mechanics and cognition were inspirational for the development of harmony theory (see Hofstadter, 1985, pp. 654-665).

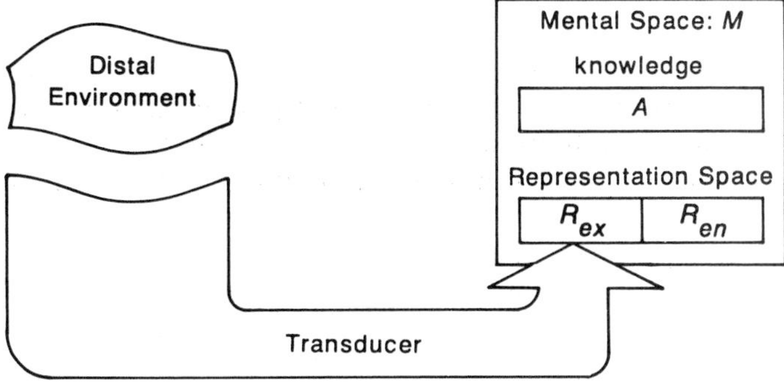

FIGURE 26. A schematic representation of the theoretical framework.

representation are taken to be binary. The prediction problem is to take some features of an environmental state as input and make best guesses about the unknown features. This amounts to extrapolating from some observed statistics of the environment to an entire probability distribution over all possible feature combinations. This extrapolation proceeds by constructing the distribution that adds minimal information (in Shannon's sense) to what is observed.

Notation. $\mathbf{B} = \{-1, +1\}$, the default *binary values*. $\mathbf{R} =$ the real numbers. $X^n = X \times X \times \cdots \times X$ (n times), where $\times$ is the cartesian product. If $\mathbf{x}, \mathbf{y} \in X^n$, then $\mathbf{x} \cdot \mathbf{y} = \sum_{m=1}^{n} x_m y_m$ and $|\mathbf{x}| = \sum_{m=1}^{n} |x_m|$. 2^X is the set of all subsets of X. $|X|$ is the number of elements of X. $\mathbf{B}^n$ is called a *binary hypercube*. The ith *coordinate function* of $\mathbf{B}^n$ ($i = 1, \ldots, n$) gives for any point (i.e., vector) in $\mathbf{B}^n$ its ith $\mathbf{B}$-valued coordinate (i.e., component).

Def. A *distal environment* $E_{distal} = (E, P)$ is a set E of *environmental events* and a probability distribution P on E.

Def. A *representational space* R is a cartesian product $R_{ex} \times R_{en}$ of two binary hypercubes. Each of the N (N_{ex}; N_{en}) binary-valued coordinate functions r_i of R (R_{ex}; R_{en}) is called an *(exogenous; endogenous) feature*.

Def. A *transduction map* T from an environment E_{distal} to a representational space $R = R_{ex} \times R_{en}$ is a map $T: E \rightarrow R_{ex}$. T induces a probability distribution p on R_{ex}: $p = P \circ T^{-1}$. This distribution is the *(proximal) environment*.

Def. Let R be a representational space. Associated with this space is the *input space* $I = \{-1, 0, +1\}^{N_{ex}}$.

Def. A point $\mathbf{r}$ in R is called a *completion* of a point ι in I if every nonzero feature of ι agrees with the corresponding feature of $\mathbf{r}$. This relationship will be designated $\mathbf{r} \supset \iota$. A *completion function* c is a map from I to 2^R (the subsets of R) for which $\mathbf{r} \in c(\iota)$ implies $\mathbf{r} \supset \iota$. The features of ι with value 0 are the "unknowns" that must be filled in by the completion function.

Def. Let p be a probability distribution on a space $X = R_{ex} \times A$. The *maximum-likelihood completion function* determined by p, $c_p: I \rightarrow 2^R$, is defined by

$$c(\iota) = \{ \mathbf{r} \in R \mid \text{for some } \mathbf{a} \in A, \text{ and all } (\mathbf{a}',\mathbf{r}') \in R \times A \text{ such that } \mathbf{r}' \supset \iota: \ p(\mathbf{r},\mathbf{a}) \geqslant p(\mathbf{r}',\mathbf{a}') \}$$

(A will be either empty or the set of possible knowledge atom activation vectors.)

Def. A *basic event* α has the form

$$\alpha: \ [r_{i_1} = b_1] \ \& \ [r_{i_2} = b_2] \ \& \ \cdots \ \& \ [r_{i_\beta} = b_\beta]$$

where $\{r_{i_1}, r_{i_2}, \ldots, r_{i_\beta}\}$ is a collection of exogenous features and $(b_1, b_2, \ldots, b_\beta) \in \mathbf{B}^\beta$. α can be characterized by the function $\chi_\alpha: R \rightarrow \{0,1\}$ defined by

$$\chi_\alpha(\mathbf{r}) = \prod_{\mu=1}^{\beta} \tfrac{1}{2} \left| r_{i_\mu}(\mathbf{r}) + b_\mu \right|$$

which is 1 if the features all have the correct values, and 0 otherwise. A convenient specification of α is as the *knowledge vector*

$$\mathbf{k}_\alpha = (0, 0, \ldots, 0, b_{i_1}, 0, \ldots, 0, b_{i_2}, 0, \ldots, 0, b_{i_\beta}, 0, \ldots, 0) \in \{-1, 0, +1\}^N$$

in which the i_μth element is b_μ and the remaining elements are all zero.

Def. A set O of *observables* is a collection of basic events.

Def. Let p be an environment and O be a set of observables. The *observable statistics* of p is the set of probabilities of all the events in O: $\{p(\alpha)\}_{\alpha \in O}$.

Def. The *entropy* (or the *missing information*; Shannon, 1948/1963) of a probability distribution p on a finite space X is

$$S(p) = - \sum_{x \in X} p(x) \ln p(x).$$

Def. The *maximum entropy estimate* $\pi_{p,O}$ of environment p with observables O is the probability distribution with maximal entropy that possesses the same observable statistics as p.

This concludes the preliminary definitions. The distal environment and transducers will play no further role in the development. They were introduced to acknowledge the important conceptual role they play: the root of all the other definitions. A truly satisfactory theory would probably include analysis of the structure of distal environments and the transformations on that structure induced by adequate transduction maps. Endogenous features will also play no further role: Henceforth, R_{en} is taken to be empty. It is an open question how to incorporate the endogenous variables into the following results. They were introduced to acknowledge the important conceptual role they must play in the future development of the theory.

Cognitive Systems and the Harmony Function H

Def. A *cognitive system* is a quintuple (R, p, O, π, c) where:

- R is a representational space,
- p is an environment,
- O is a set of statistical observables,
- π is the maximum-entropy estimate $\pi_{p,O}$ of environment p with observables O,
- c is the maximum-likelihood completion function determined by π.

Def. Let X be a finite space and $V: X \rightarrow \mathbf{R}$. The *Gibbs distribution* determined by V is

$$p_V(x) = Z^{-1} e^{V(x)}$$

where Z is the normalization constant:

$$Z = \sum_{x \in X} e^{V(x)}.$$

Theorem 1: Competence. *A*: The distribution π of the cognitive system (R, p, O, π, c) is the Gibbs distribution p_U determined by the function

$$U(\mathbf{r}) = \sum_{\alpha \in O} \lambda_\alpha \chi_\alpha(\mathbf{r})$$

for suitable parameters $\boldsymbol{\lambda} = \{\lambda_\alpha\}_{\alpha \in O}$ (S. Geman, personal communication, 1984). *B*: The completion function c is the maximum-likelihood completion function c_{p_H} of the Gibbs distribution p_H, where $H: M \rightarrow \mathbf{R}$, $M = R \times A$, $A = \{0,1\}^{|O|}$, is defined by

$$H(\mathbf{r}, \mathbf{a}) = \sum_{\alpha \in O} \sigma_\alpha a_\alpha h(\mathbf{r}, \mathbf{k}_\alpha)$$

and

$$h(\mathbf{r}, \mathbf{k}_\alpha) = \mathbf{r} \cdot \mathbf{k}_\alpha / |\mathbf{k}_\alpha| - \kappa$$

for suitable parameters $\boldsymbol{\sigma} = \{\sigma_\alpha\}_{\alpha \in O}$ and for κ sufficiently close to 1:

$$1 > \kappa > 1 - 2/\left[\max_{\alpha \in O} |\mathbf{k}_\alpha|\right].$$

Theorem 2 will describe how the variables $\mathbf{a} = \{a_\alpha\}_{\alpha \in O}$ can be used to actually compute the completion function. Theorem 3 will describe how the parameters $\boldsymbol{\sigma}$ can be learned through experience in the environment. Together, these theorems motivate the following interpretation.

Terminology. The triple $(\mathbf{k}_\alpha, \sigma_\alpha, a_\alpha)$ defines the *knowledge atom* or *memory trace* α. The vector $\mathbf{k}_\alpha$ is called *the knowledge vector of atom* α. The knowledge vector is an unchanging aspect of the atom. The real number σ_α is called *the strength of atom* α. This strength changes with experience in the environment. The $\{0,1\}$ variable a_α is called *the activation of atom* α. The activation of an atom changes during each computation of the completion function. The set $\mathbf{K} = \{(\mathbf{k}_\alpha, \sigma_\alpha)\}_{\alpha \in O}$ is the *long-term memory state* or *knowledge base* of the cognitive system. The vector $\mathbf{a}$ of knowledge atom activations $\{a_\alpha\}_{\alpha \in O}$ is the *working-memory state*. The value $h(\mathbf{r}, \mathbf{k}_\alpha)$ is a measure of the *consistency* between the representation vector $\mathbf{r}$ and the knowledge vector of atom α; it is the potential contribution (per unit strength) of atom α to H. The value $H(\mathbf{r}, \mathbf{a})$ is a measure of the overall consistency between the entire vector $\mathbf{a}$ of knowledge atom activations and the representation $\mathbf{r}$, relative to the knowledge base $\mathbf{K}$. Through $\mathbf{K}$, H internalizes within the cognitive system some of the statistical regularities of the environment. Viewing the completion of an input ι as an inference process, we can say that H allows the system to distinguish which patterns of features $\mathbf{r}$ are more *self-consistent* than others, as far as the environmental regularities are concerned. This is why H is called the *harmony function*.

Def. The cognitive system determined by a harmony function H can be represented by a *graph* which will shortly be interpreted as a network of stochastic parallel processors (see Figure 27). For each coordinate of the cognitive system's *mental space M*, that is, for each feature r_i and each atom α, there is a node. These nodes carry binary values; the node for feature r_i carries the value of $r_i \in \{+1, -1\}$, while the node for atom α carries the activation value $a_\alpha \in \{1,0\}$. If the value of $\mathbf{k}_\alpha$ for a feature r_i is $+1$ or -1, there is a link with the corresponding ± 1 label joining the nodes for a_α and r_i. Finally, each node α is labeled by its strength, σ_α. The graphs of harmony networks are *two-color*; if feature nodes are assigned one color and atom nodes another, all links go between nodes of different colors. This will turn out to permit a high degree of parallelism in the processing network.

Retrieving Information From H: Performance

Def. Let $\{p_t\}_{t=0}^{\infty}$ be a sequence of probability distributions on a binary cube $X = \mathbf{B}^n$. The paths of the *(one-variable heat bath) stochastic process* $\boldsymbol{x}$ determined by $\{p_t\}$ is defined by the following procedure. At time $t = 0$, $\boldsymbol{x}$ occupies some state $\boldsymbol{x}(0) = \mathbf{x} \in X$, described by

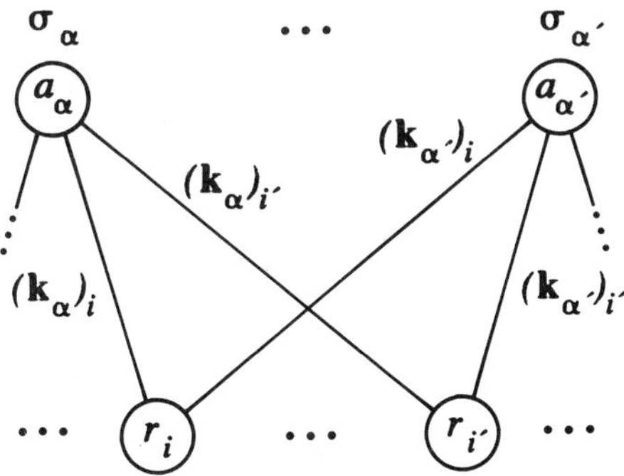

FIGURE 27. A harmony network: The graph associated with a harmony function.

some arbitrary *initial distribution*, $\mathrm{pr}(x(0) = \mathbf{x})$. Given the initial state $\mathbf{x}$, the new state at Time 1, $x(1)$, is constructed as follows. One of the n coordinates of M is selected (with uniform distribution) for *updating*. All the other $n-1$ coordinates of $x(1)$ will be the same as those of $x(0) = \mathbf{x}$. The updated coordinate can retain its previous value, leading to $x(1) = \mathbf{x}$, or it can flip to the other binary value, leading to a new state that will be denoted $\mathbf{x}'$. The selection of the value of the updated coordinate for $x(1)$ is stochastically chosen according to the likelihood ratio:

$$\frac{\mathrm{pr}(x(1) = \mathbf{x}')}{\mathrm{pr}(x(1) = \mathbf{x})} = \frac{p_0(\mathbf{x}')}{p_0(\mathbf{x})}$$

(where p_0 is the probability distribution for $t = 0$ in the given sequence $\{p_t\}_{t=0}^{\infty}$). This process—randomly select a coordinate to update and stochastically select a binary value for that coordinate—is iterated indefinitely, producing states $x(t)$ for all times $t = 1, 2, \ldots$. At each time t, the likelihood ratio of values for the stochastic choice is determined by the distribution p_t.

Def. Let p be a probability distribution. Define the one-parameter family of distributions p_T by

$$p_T = N_T^{-1} \, p^{1/T}$$

where the normalization constants are

$$N_T = \sum_{\mathbf{x} \in X} p(\mathbf{x})^{1/T}.$$

T is called the *temperature parameter*. An *annealing schedule* $\mathbf{T}$ is a sequence of positive values $\{T_t\}_{t=0}^{\infty}$ that converge to zero. The *annealing process* determined by p and $\mathbf{T}$ is the heat bath stochastic process determined by the sequence of distributions, p_{T_t}. If p is the Gibbs distribution determined by V, then

$$p_T(\mathbf{x}) = Z_T^{-1} \, e^{V(\mathbf{x})/T}$$

where

$$Z_T = \sum_{\mathbf{x} \in X} e^{V(\mathbf{x})/T}.$$

This is the same (except for the sign of the exponent) as the relationship that holds in classical statistical mechanics between the probability $p(\mathbf{x})$ of a microscopic state $\mathbf{x}$, its energy $V(\mathbf{x})$, and the temperature T. This is the basis for the names "temperature" and "annealing schedule." In the annealing process for the Gibbs distribution p_H of Theorem 1 on the space M, the graph of the harmony network has the following significance. The updating of a coordinate can be conceptualized as being performed by a processor at the corresponding node in the graph. To make its stochastic choice with the proper probabilities, a node updating at time t must compute the ratio

$$\frac{p_{T_t}(\mathbf{x}')}{p_{T_t}(\mathbf{x})} = e^{[H(\mathbf{x}') - H(\mathbf{x})]/T_t}.$$

The exponent is the difference in harmony between the two choices of value for the updating node, divided by the current computational temperature. By examining the definitions of the harmony function and its graph, this difference is easily seen to depend only on the values of nodes connected to the updating node. Suppose at times t and $t+1$ two nodes in a harmony network are updated. If these nodes are not connected, then the computation of the second node is not affected by the outcome of the first: They are statistically independent. These computations can be performed *in parallel* without changing the statistics of the outcomes (assuming the computational temperature to be the same at t and $t+1$). Because the graph of harmony networks is two-color, this means there is another stochastic process that can be used without violating the validity of the upcoming Theorem 2.[27] *All the nodes of one color can update in parallel.* To pass from $\mathbf{x}(t)$ to $\mathbf{x}(t+1)$, all the nodes of one color update in parallel; then to pass from $\mathbf{x}(t+1)$ to $\mathbf{x}(t+2)$, all the nodes of the other color update in parallel. In twice the time it takes a processor to perform an update, plus twice the time required to pass new values along the links, a cycle is completed in which an entirely new state (potentially different in all $N + |O|$ coordinates) is computed.

> *Theorem 2: Realizability. A*: The heat bath stochastic process determined by p_U converges, for any initial distribution, to the distribution π of the cognitive system (R, p, O, π, c) [Metropolis et al., 1953]. *B*: The annealing process determined by p_H converges, for any initial distribution, to the completion function of the cognitive system, for any annealing schedule that approaches zero sufficiently slowly (Geman & Geman, 1984).

Part A of this theorem means the following. Suppose an input ι is given. Those features specified in ι to have values $+1$ or -1 are

[27] This is an important respect in which harmony networks differ from the arbitrary networks allowed in the Boltzmann machine.

assigned their values, which are thereafter fixed. The remaining features are assigned random initial values; these will change through the stochastic process. Now we begin the stochastic process determined by p_U. (The state space X is now R, and the same distribution p_U is used for all times.) The nonfixed variables flip back and forth between their binary values. As time progresses, the probability of finding the system in any state $\mathbf{r} \supset \iota$ approaches the maximum-entropy estimate $\pi(\mathbf{r})$ (conditioned on ι, so that only completions of ι have nonzero probability). The meaning of Part B of Theorem 1 is this: As in Part A, we fix the features specified in the input ι and start the other features off with random values. The activation variables are assigned initial values, say, of 0. We start the annealing process determined by p_H. (The state space X is now $M = R \times A$.) The unfixed features and all the activations flip between their values. The temperature drops according to the annealing schedule. As time progresses, the probability of finding the system in a state other than a maximum-likelihood completion of ι goes to zero. (If there are multiple maximum-likelihood completions, these completions become equally likely as time progresses.)

Storing Information in *H*: Learning

Def. (After Hinton & Sejnowski, 1983a.) Let (R, p, O, π, c) be a cognitive system. The *trace learning procedure* is defined iteratively as follows. Initially, let $\lambda_\alpha = 0$ for all $\alpha \in O$. Present the system with a sample of states, $\mathbf{r}$, drawn from the environmental distribution, p (*environmental observation*). Now store an *increment* for each λ_α equal to the mean of $\chi_\alpha(\mathbf{r})$ in this sample. Next, use the current $\boldsymbol{\lambda}$ to define U as in Theorem 1 and use the stochastic process determined by p_U to generate a sample of values of $\mathbf{r}$ from the distribution p_U, following Theorem 2 (*environmental simulation*). Now store a *decrement* for each λ_α equal to the mean of $\chi_\alpha(\mathbf{r})$ in this sample. Finally, change each λ_α by the stored increment minus the decrement. Repeat this observe-environment/simulate-environment/modify-$\boldsymbol{\lambda}$ cycle. Throughout the learning, define

$$\sigma_\alpha = \frac{\lambda_\alpha}{1 - \kappa}.$$

For small $\Delta\lambda$, a good approximate way to implement this procedure is to alternately observe and simulate the environment in equal proportions, and to increment (respectively, decrement) λ_α by $\Delta\lambda$ each time the feature pattern defining α appears during observation (respectively, simulation). It is in this sense that σ_α is the strength of the memory trace for the feature pattern $\mathbf{k}_\alpha$ defining α. Note that in learning, equilibrium is established when the frequency of occurrence of each pattern $\mathbf{k}_\alpha$ during simulation equals that during observation (i.e., λ_α has no *net* change).

> *Theorem 3: Learnability.* Suppose all knowledge atoms are independent. Then if sufficient sampling is done in the trace learning procedure to produce accurate estimates of the observable statistics, $\boldsymbol{\lambda}$ and $\boldsymbol{\sigma}$ will converge to the values required by Theorem 1.

Independence of the knowledge atoms means that the functions $\{\chi_\alpha\}_{\alpha \in O}$ are linearly independent. This means no two atoms can have exactly the same knowledge vector. It also means no knowledge atom can be simply the "or" of some other atoms: for example, the atom with knowledge vector +0 is the "or" of the atoms ++ and +−, and so is not independent of them. (Indeed, $\chi_{+0} = \chi_{++} + \chi_{+-}$.) The sampling condition of this theorem indicates the tradeoff between learning speed and performance accuracy. By adding higher order statistics to O (longer patterns), we can make π a more accurate representation of p and thereby increase performance accuracy, but then learning will require greater sampling of the environment.

Second-Order Observables and the Boltzmann Machine

Consider the special case in which the observables O each involve no more than two features. The largest independent set of such observables is the set of all observables either of the form

$$\alpha_i\colon\ [r_i = +]$$

or the form

$$\alpha_{ij}\colon\ [r_i = +]\ \&\ [r_j = +]$$

with $i<j$, i.e.,

$$\alpha_{ij}\colon\ \alpha_i\ \&\ \alpha_j.$$

To see that the other first- or second-order observations are not independent of these, consider a particular pair of features r_i and r_j, and let

$$\chi_{b_1 b_2} = \chi_{[r_i = b_1] \& [r_j = b_2]}$$

and

$$\chi_{b_1 0} = \chi_{[r_i = b_1]}$$

$$\chi_{0 b_2} = \chi_{[r_j = b_2]}.$$

Then notice:

$$\chi_{+-} = \chi_{+0} - \chi_{++}$$

$$\chi_{-0} = 1 - \chi_{+0}$$

$$\chi_{--} = 1 - \chi_{++} - \chi_{+-} - \chi_{-+}$$

$$= 1 - \chi_{++} - [\chi_{+0} - \chi_{++}] - [\chi_{0+} - \chi_{++}].$$

Thus, the χ-functions for all first- and second-order observations can be linearly generated from the set

$$O = \{\chi_{ij}\}_{i<j} \cup \{\chi_i\}_i$$

which will now be taken to be the set of observables. I will abbreviate $\lambda_{\alpha_{ij}}$ as λ_{ij} and λ_{α_i} as λ_i. Next, consider the U function for this set, O:

$$U = \sum_{\alpha \in O} \lambda_\alpha \chi_\alpha = \sum_{i<j} \lambda_{ij} \chi_{ij} + \sum_i \lambda_i \chi_i$$

$$= \sum_{i<j} \lambda_{ij} \chi_i \chi_j + \sum_i \lambda_i \chi_i.$$

Here I have used

$$\chi_{ij} = \chi_i \chi_j$$

which follows from

$$\alpha_{ij} = \alpha_i \ \& \ \alpha_j.$$

Now using the formula for χ given above,

$$\chi_i = \tfrac{1}{2}(r_i + 1) = \begin{cases} 1 & \text{if } r_i = + \\ 0 & \text{if } r_i = -. \end{cases}$$

If we regard the variables of the system to be the χ_i instead of the r_i, this formula for U can be identified with minus the formula for energy, E, in the Boltzmann machine formalism (see Chapter 7). The mapping takes the harmony feature r_i to the Boltzmann node χ_i, the harmony parameter λ_{ij} to the Boltzmann weight w_{ij}, and minus the parameter λ_i to the threshold θ_i. Harmony theory's estimated probability for states of the environment, e^U, is then mapped onto the Boltzmann machine's estimate, e^{-E}. For the isomorphism to be complete, the value of $\boldsymbol{\lambda}$ that arises from learning in harmony theory must map onto the weights and thresholds given by the Boltzmann machine learning procedure. This is established by the following theorem, which also incorporates the preceding results.

> *Theorem 4.* Consider a cognitive system with the above set of first- and second-order observables, O. Then the weights $\{w_{ij}\}_{i<j}$ and thresholds $\{\theta_i\}_i$ learned by the Boltzmann machine are related to the parameters $\boldsymbol{\lambda}$ generated by the trace learning procedure by the relations $w_{ij} = \lambda_{ij}$ and $\theta_i = -\lambda_i$. It follows that the Boltzmann machine energy function, E, is equal to $-U$, and the Boltzmann machine's estimated probabilities for environmental states are the same as those of the cognitive system.

This result shows that the Boltzmann criterion of minimizing the information-theoretic distance, G, between the environmental and estimated distributions, subject to the constraint that the estimated distribution be a Gibbs distribution determined by a quadratic function, $-E$, is a consequence of the harmony theory criterion of minimizing the information of the estimated distribution subject to environmental constraints, in the special case that these constraints are no higher than second order.

Proofs of the Theorems

Theorem 1. Part A: The desired maximum-entropy distribution π is the one that maximizes $S(\pi)$ subject to the constraints

$$\sum_{\mathbf{r} \in R} \pi(\mathbf{r}) = 1$$

and

$$<\chi_\alpha>_\pi = p_\alpha$$

where $< >_\pi$ denotes the expected value with respect to the distribution π, and $\{p_\alpha\}_{\alpha \in O}$ are the observable statistics of the environment.

We introduce the Lagrange multipliers λ and λ_α (see, for example, Thomas, 1968) and solve for the values of $\pi(\mathbf{r})$ obeying

$$0 = \frac{\partial}{\partial \pi(\mathbf{r})} \left\{ \sum_{\mathbf{r}' \in R} \pi(\mathbf{r}') \ln \pi(\mathbf{r}') - \sum_{\alpha \in O} \lambda_\alpha \left[\sum_{\mathbf{r}' \in R} \chi_\alpha(\mathbf{r}') \pi(\mathbf{r}') - p_\alpha \right] - \lambda \left[\sum_{\mathbf{r}' \in R} \pi(\mathbf{r}') - 1 \right] \right\}.$$

This leads directly to A. Part B: Since χ_α can be expressed as the product of $|\mathbf{k}_\alpha|$ terms each linear in the feature variables, the function U is a polynomial in the features of degree $|\mathbf{k}_\alpha|$. By introducing new variables a_α, U will now be replaced by a quadratic function H. The trick is to write

$$\chi_\alpha(\mathbf{r}) = \begin{cases} 1 & \text{if } \mathbf{r} \cdot \mathbf{k}_\alpha / |\mathbf{k}_\alpha| = 1 \\ 0 & \text{otherwise} \end{cases}$$

as

$$\chi_\alpha(\mathbf{r}) = \max_{a_\alpha \in \{0,1\}} \left[\frac{a_\alpha}{1-\kappa} (\mathbf{r} \cdot \mathbf{k}_\alpha / |\mathbf{k}_\alpha| - \kappa) \right] = \max_{a_\alpha \in \{0,1\}} \frac{a_\alpha}{1-\kappa} h(\mathbf{r}, \mathbf{k}_\alpha)$$

where κ is chosen close enough to 1 that $\mathbf{r} \cdot \mathbf{k}_\alpha / |\mathbf{k}_\alpha|$ can only exceed κ by equaling 1. This is assured by the condition on κ of the theorem. Now U can be written

$$U(\mathbf{r}) = \sum_{\alpha \in O} \sigma_\alpha \max_{a_\alpha \in \{0,1\}} [a_\alpha h(\mathbf{r}, \mathbf{k}_\alpha)] = \max_{\mathbf{a} \in A} H(\mathbf{a}, \mathbf{r})$$

where the strengths σ_α are simply the Lagrange multipliers, rescaled:

$$\sigma_\alpha = \frac{\lambda_\alpha}{1-\kappa}.$$

Computing the maximum-likelihood completion function c_π requires maximizing $\pi(\mathbf{r}) \propto e^{U(\mathbf{r})}$ over those $\mathbf{r} \in R$ that are completions of the input ι. This is equivalent to maximizing $U(\mathbf{r})$, since the exponential function is monotonically increasing. But,

$$\max_{\mathbf{r} \supset \iota} U(\mathbf{r}) = \max_{\mathbf{r} \supset \iota} \max_{\mathbf{a} \in A} H(\mathbf{r}, \mathbf{a}).$$

Thus the maximum-likelihood completion function $c_\pi = c_{p_U}$ determined by π, the Gibbs distribution determined by U, is the same as the maximum-likelihood completion function c_{p_H} determined by p_H, the Gibbs distribution determined by H. Note that p_H is a distribution on the enlarged space $M = R \times A$. For Theorem 3, the conditions determining the Lagrange multipliers (strengths) will be examined.

Theorem 2. Part A: This classic result has, since Metropolis et al. (1953), provided the foundation for the computer simulation of thermal systems. We will prove that the stochastic process determined by any probability distribution p always converges to p. The stochastic process $\boldsymbol{x}$ is a *Markov process with a stationary transition probability matrix.* (The probability of making a transition from one state to another is time-independent. This is not true of a process in which variables are updated in a fixed sequence rather than by randomly selecting a variable according to some fixed probability distribution. For the sequential updating process, Theorem 2A still holds, but the proof is less direct [see, for example, Smolensky, 1981]). Since only one variable can change per time step, $|X|$ steps are required to completely change from one state to another. However in $|X|$ time steps, any state has a nonzero probability of changing to any other state. In the language of stochastic processes, this means that the process is *irreducible.* It is an important result from the theory of stochastic processes that in a finite state space any irreducible Markov process approaches, in the above sense, a unique limiting distribution as $t \to \infty$ (Lamperti, 1977). It remains only to show that this limiting distribution is p. The argument now is that p is a *stationary distribution* of the process. This means that if at any time t the distribution of states of the process is p, then at the next time $t+1$ (and hence at all later times) the distribution will remain p. Once p is known to be stationary, it follows that p is the unique limiting distribution, since we could always start the process with distribution p, and it would have to converge to the limiting distribution, all the while remaining in the stationary distribution p. To show that p is a stationary distribution for the process, we assume that at time t the distribution of states is p. The distribution at time $t+1$ is then

$$\begin{aligned} \mathrm{pr}(\boldsymbol{x}(t+1) = \mathbf{x}) &= \sum_{\mathbf{x}' \in X_{\mathbf{x}}} \mathrm{pr}(\boldsymbol{x}(t) = \mathbf{x}')\ \mathrm{pr}(\boldsymbol{x}(t+1) = \mathbf{x} \mid \boldsymbol{x}(t) = \mathbf{x}') \\ &= \sum_{\mathbf{x}' \in X_{\mathbf{x}}} p(\mathbf{x}')\ W_{\mathbf{x}'\mathbf{x}}. \end{aligned}$$

The sum here runs over $X_{\mathbf{x}}$, the set of states that differ from $\mathbf{x}$ in at most one coordinate; for the remaining states, the one time-step transition probability $W_{\mathbf{x}'\mathbf{x}} = \mathrm{pr}(\boldsymbol{x}(t+1) = \mathbf{x} | \boldsymbol{x}(t) = \mathbf{x}')$ is zero. Next we use the important *detailed balance condition,*

$$p(\mathbf{x}')\ W_{\mathbf{x}'\mathbf{x}} = p(\mathbf{x})\ W_{\mathbf{x}\mathbf{x}'}$$

which states that in an ensemble of systems with states distributed according to p, the number of transitions from $\mathbf{x}'$ to $\mathbf{x}$ is equal to the number from $\mathbf{x}$ to $\mathbf{x}'$. Detailed balance holds because, for the non-trivial case in which $\mathbf{x}'$ and $\mathbf{x}$ differ in the single coordinate v, the transition matrix W determined by the distribution p is

$$W_{\mathbf{x}'\mathbf{x}} = P_v \frac{p(\mathbf{x})}{p(\mathbf{x}) + p(\mathbf{x}')}$$

where P_v is the probability of selecting for update the coordinate v. Now we have

$$\begin{aligned} \mathrm{pr}(x(t+1) = \mathbf{x}) &= \sum_{\mathbf{x}' \in X_\mathbf{x}} p(\mathbf{x}')\, W_{\mathbf{x}'\mathbf{x}} = \sum_{\mathbf{x}' \in X_\mathbf{x}} p(\mathbf{x})\, W_{\mathbf{x}\mathbf{x}'} \\ &= p(\mathbf{x}) \sum_{\mathbf{x}' \in X_\mathbf{x}} W_{\mathbf{x}\mathbf{x}'} = p(\mathbf{x}). \end{aligned}$$

The last equality follows from

$$\sum_{\mathbf{x}' \in X_\mathbf{x}} W_{\mathbf{x}\mathbf{x}'} = 1$$

which simply states that the probability of a transition from $\mathbf{x}$ to *some* state $\mathbf{x}'$ is 1. The conclusion is that the probability distribution at time $t+1$ remains p, which is therefore a stationary distribution.

Part B: Part A assures us that with infinite patience we can arbitrarily well approximate the distribution p_T at any finite temperature T. It seems intuitively clear that with still further patience we could sequentially approximate in one long stochastic process a series of distributions p_{T_t} with temperatures T_t monotonically decreasing to zero. This process would presumably converge to the zero-temperature distribution that corresponds to the maximum-likelihood completion function. A proof that this is true, provided

$$T_t > C/\ln t$$

for suitable C, can be found in S. Geman and D. Geman (1984).

Theorem 3. We now pick up the analysis from the end of the proof of Theorem 1.

Lemma. (S. Geman, personal communication, 1984.) The values of the Lagrange multipliers $\boldsymbol{\lambda} = \{\lambda_\alpha\}_{\alpha \in O}$ defining the function U of Theorem 2 are those that minimize the convex function:

$$F(\boldsymbol{\lambda}) = \ln Z_V(\boldsymbol{\lambda}) = \ln \sum_{r \in R} e^{\left(\sum_{\alpha \in O} \lambda_\alpha [\chi_\alpha(\mathbf{r}) - p_\alpha] \right)}.$$

Proof of Lemma: Note that

$$p_U(\mathbf{r}) = p_V(\mathbf{r}) = Z_V(\boldsymbol{\lambda})^{-1} e^{V(\mathbf{r})}$$

where

$$V(\mathbf{r}) = \sum_{\alpha \in O} \lambda_\alpha [\chi_\alpha(\mathbf{r}) - p_\alpha] = U(\mathbf{r}) - \sum_{\alpha \in O} \lambda_\alpha p_\alpha .$$

From this it follows that the gradient of F is

$$\frac{\partial F}{\partial \lambda_\alpha} = < \chi_\alpha >_{p_U} - p_\alpha$$

The constraint that $\boldsymbol{\lambda}$ enforces is precisely that this vanish for all α; then $p_U = \pi$. Thus the correct $\boldsymbol{\lambda}$ is a critical point of F. To see that in fact the correct $\boldsymbol{\lambda}$ is a minimum of F, we show that F has a positive-definite matrix of second-partial derivatives and is therefore convex. It is straightforward to verify that the quadratic form

$$\sum_{\alpha, \alpha' \in O} q_\alpha \frac{\partial^2 F}{\partial \lambda_\alpha \partial \lambda_{\alpha'}} q_{\alpha'}$$

is the variance

$$< (Q - <Q>_{p_U})^2 >_{p_U}$$

of the random variable Q defined by $Q(\mathbf{r}) = \sum_{\alpha \in O} q_\alpha \chi_\alpha(\mathbf{r})$. This variance is clearly nonnegative definite. That Q cannot vanish is assured by the assumption that the χ_α are linearly independent. Since a Gibbs distribution p_U is nowhere zero, this means that the variance of Q is positive, so the Lemma is proved.

Proof of Theorem 3: Since F is convex, we can find its minimum, $\boldsymbol{\lambda}$, by gradient descent from any starting point. The process of learning the correct $\boldsymbol{\lambda}$, then, can proceed in time according to the gradient descent equation

$$\frac{d\lambda_\alpha}{dt} \propto -\frac{\partial F}{\partial \lambda_\alpha} = -(<\chi_\alpha>_{p_U} - p_\alpha) = <\chi_\alpha>_p - <\chi_\alpha>_{p_U}$$

where it is understood that the function U changes as $\boldsymbol{\lambda}$ changes. The two phases of the trace learning procedure generate the two terms in this equation. In the environmental observation phase, the increment

$<\chi_\alpha>_p$ is estimated; in the environmental simulation phase, the decrement $<\chi_\alpha>_{p_U}$ is estimated (following Theorem 2). By hypothesis, these estimates are accurate. (That is, this theorem treats the ideal case of perfect samples, with sample means equal to the true population means.) Thus $\boldsymbol{\lambda}$ will converge to the correct value. The proportional relation between $\boldsymbol{\sigma}$ and $\boldsymbol{\lambda}$ was derived in the proof of Theorem 1.

Theorem 4. The proof of Theorem 3 shows that the trace learning procedure does gradient descent in the function F. The Boltzmann learning procedure does gradient descent in the function G:

$$G(\boldsymbol{\lambda}) = -\sum_{\mathbf{r}} p(\mathbf{r}) \ln \frac{p_U(\mathbf{r})}{p(\mathbf{r})}$$

where, as always, the function U implicitly depends on $\boldsymbol{\lambda}$. Theorem 4 will be proved by showing that in fact F and G differ by a constant independent of $\boldsymbol{\lambda}$, and therefore they define the same gradient descent trajectories. From the above definition of V, we have

$$V(\mathbf{r}) = U(\mathbf{r}) - \sum_{\alpha \in O} \lambda_\alpha <\chi_\alpha> = U(\mathbf{r}) - <U>$$

where, here and henceforth, $< >$ denotes expectation values with respect to the environmental distribution p. This implies

$$\sum_{\mathbf{r}} e^{V(\mathbf{r})} = e^{-<U>} \sum_{\mathbf{r}} e^{U(\mathbf{r})},$$

i.e.,

$$Z_V = Z_U \, e^{-<U>}.$$

By the definition of F,

$$F = \ln Z_V = \ln Z_U - <U> = < \ln Z_U - U >.$$

To evaluate the last quantity in angle brackets, note that

$$p_U(\mathbf{r}) = Z_U^{-1} \, e^{U(\mathbf{r})}$$

implies

$$\ln p_U(\mathbf{r}) = -\ln Z_U + U(\mathbf{r})$$

so that the preceding equation for F becomes

$$F = < \ln Z_U - U > = - < \ln p_U > = - \sum_{\mathbf{r}} p(\mathbf{r}) \ln p_U(\mathbf{r}).$$

Now,

$$G = -\sum_{\mathbf{r}} p(\mathbf{r}) \ln p_U(\mathbf{r}) + \sum_{\mathbf{r}} p(\mathbf{r}) \ln p(\mathbf{r}),$$

so we have

$$G(\boldsymbol{\lambda}) = F(\boldsymbol{\lambda}) - S(p).$$

Thus, as claimed, G is just F minus a constant that is independent of $\boldsymbol{\lambda}$: the entropy of the environment.

CHAPTER 7

Learning and Relearning in Boltzmann Machines

G. E. HINTON and T. J. SEJNOWSKI

Many of the chapters in this volume make use of the ability of a parallel network to perform cooperative searches for good solutions to problems. The basic idea is simple: The weights on the connections between processing units encode knowledge about how things normally fit together in some domain and the initial states or external inputs to a subset of the units encode some fragments of a structure within the domain. These fragments constitute a problem: What is the whole structure from which they probably came? The network computes a "good solution" to the problem by repeatedly updating the states of units that represent possible other parts of the structure until the network eventually settles into a stable state of activity that represents the solution.

One field in which this style of computation seems particularly appropriate is vision (Ballard, Hinton, & Sejnowski, 1983). A visual system must be able to solve large constraint-satisfaction problems rapidly in order to interpret a two-dimensional intensity image in terms of the depths and orientations of the three-dimensional surfaces in the world that gave rise to that image. In general, the information in the image is not sufficient to specify the three-dimensional surfaces unless the interpretive process makes use of additional plausible constraints about the kinds of structures that typically appear. Neighboring pieces of an image, for example, usually depict fragments of surface that have similar depths, similar surface orientations, and the same reflectance. The most plausible interpretation of an image is the one that satisfies constraints of this kind as well as possible, and the human visual system stores enough plausible constraints and is good enough at applying them that it can arrive at the correct interpretation of most normal images.

The computation may be performed by an iterative search which starts with a poor interpretation and progressively improves it by reducing a cost function that measures the extent to which the current interpretation violates the plausible constraints. Suppose, for example, that each unit stands for a small three-dimensional surface fragment, and the state of the unit indicates the current bet about whether that surface fragment is part of the best three-dimensional interpretation. Plausible constraints about the nature of surfaces can then be encoded by the pairwise interactions between processing elements. For example, two units that stand for neighboring surface fragments of similar depth and surface orientation can be mutually excitatory to encode the constraints that each of these hypotheses tends to support the other (because objects tend to have continuous surfaces).

RELAXATION SEARCHES

The general idea of using parallel networks to perform relaxation searches that simultaneously satisfy multiple constraints is appealing. It might even provide a successor to telephone exchanges, holograms, or communities of agents as a metaphor for the style of computation in cerebral cortex. But some tough technical questions have to be answered before this style of computation can be accepted as either efficient or plausible:

- Will the network settle down or will it oscillate or wander aimlessly?

- What does the network compute by settling down? We need some characterization of the computation that the network performs other than the network itself. Ideally we would like to be able to say what *ought* to be computed (Marr, 1982) and then to show that a network can be made to compute it.

- How long does the network take to settle on a solution? If thousands of iterations are required the method becomes implausible as a model of how the cortex solves constraint-satisfaction problems.

- How much information does each unit need to convey to its neighbors? In many relaxation schemes the units communicate accurate real values to one another on each iteration. Again this is implausible if the units are intended to be like cortical neurons which communicate using all-or-none spikes. To send a real-value, accurate to within 5%, using firing rates requires about 100 ms which is about the time allowed for the whole iterative process to settle down.

- How are the weights that encode the knowledge acquired? For models of low-level vision it is possible for a programmer to decide on the weights, and evolution might do the same for the earliest stages of biological visual systems. But if the same kind of constraint-satisfaction searches are to be used for higher level functions like shape recognition or content-addressable memory, there must be some learning procedure that automatically encodes properties of the domain into the weights.

This chapter is mainly concerned with the last of these questions, but the learning procedure we present is an unexpected consequence of our attempt to answer the other questions, so we shall start with them.

Relaxation, Optimization, and Weak Constraints

One way of ensuring that a relaxation search is computing something sensible (and will eventually settle down) is to show that it is solving an optimization problem by progressively reducing the value of a cost function. Each possible state of activity of the network has an associated cost, and the rule used for updating activity levels is chosen so that this cost keeps falling. The cost function must be chosen so that low-cost states represent good solutions to problems in the domain.

Many optimization problems can be cast in a framework known as linear programming. There are some variables which take on real values and there are linear equality and inequality constraints between variables. Each combination of values for the variables has an associated cost which is the sum over all the variables of the current value times a cost-coefficient. The aim is to find a combination of values that satisfies all the constraints and minimizes the cost function. If the variables are further constrained to take on only the values 1 or 0 the problem is called zero-one programming. Hinton (1977) has shown that certain zero-one programming problems can be implemented as relaxation searches in parallel networks. This allows networks to find good solutions to problems in which there are discrete hypotheses that are true or false. Even though the allowable solutions all assign values of 1 or 0 to the hypotheses, the relaxation process works by passing through intermediate states in which hypothesis units have real-valued activity levels lying between 1 and 0. Each constraint is enforced by a feedback loop that measures the amount by which the current values violate the constraint and tries to alter the values of the variables to reduce this violation.

Linear programming and its variants make a sharp distinction between constraints (which *must* be satisfied) and costs. A solution which achieves a very low cost by violating one or two of the constraints is simply not allowed. In many domains, the distinction between constraints and costs is not so clear-cut. In vision, for example, it is usually helpful to use the constraint that neighboring pieces of surface are at similar depths because surfaces are mostly continuous and are rarely parallel to the line of sight. But this is not an absolute constraint. It doesn't apply at the edge of an object. So a visual system needs to be able to generate interpretations that violate this constraint if it can satisfy many other constraints by doing so. Constraints like these have been called "weak" constraints (Blake, 1983) and it is possible to formulate optimization problems in which all the constraints are weak and there is no distinction between constraints and costs. The optimal solution is then the one which minimizes the total constraint violation where different constraints are given different strengths depending on how reliable they are. Another way of saying this is that all the constraints have associated plausibilities, and the most plausible solution is the one which fits these plausible constraints as well as possible.

Some relaxation schemes dispense with separate feedback loops for the constraints and implement weak constraints directly in the excitatory and inhibitory interactions between units. We would like these networks to settle into states in which a few units are fully active and the rest are inactive. Such states constitute clean "digital" interpretations. To prevent the network from hedging its bets by settling into a state where many units are slightly active, it is usually necessary to use a strongly nonlinear decision rule, and this also speeds convergence. However, the strong nonlinearities that are needed to force the network to make a decision also cause it to converge on different states on different occasions: Even with the same external inputs, the final state depends on the initial state of the net. This has led many people (Hopfield, 1982; Rosenfeld, Hummel, & Zucker, 1976) to assume that the particular problem to be solved should be encoded by the initial state of the network rather than by sustained external input to some of its units.

Hummel and Zucker (1983) and Hopfield (1982) have shown that some relaxation schemes have an associated "potential" or cost function and that the states to which the network converges are local minima of this function. This means that the networks are performing optimization of a well-defined function. Unfortunately, there is no guarantee that the network will find the best minimum. One possibility is to redefine the problem as finding the local minimum which is closest to the initial state. This is useful if the minima are used to represent "items" in a memory, and the initial states are queries to memory which may contain missing or erroneous information. The network simply finds the minimum that best fits the query. This idea was used by Hopfield (1982) who introduced an interesting kind of network in which the units were always in one of two states.[1] Hopfield showed that if the units are symmetrically connected (i.e., the weight from unit i to unit j exactly equals the weight from unit j to unit i) and if they are updated one at a time, each update reduces (or at worst does not increase) the value of a cost function which he called "energy" because of the analogy with physical systems. Consequently, repeated iterations are guaranteed to find an energy minimum. The global energy of the system is defined as

$$E = -\sum_{i<j} w_{ij} s_i s_j + \sum_i \theta_i s_i \tag{1}$$

where w_{ij} is the strength of connection (synaptic weight) from the jth to the ith unit, s_i is the state of the ith unit (0 or 1), and θ_i is a threshold.

The updating rule is to switch each unit into whichever of its two states yields the lower total energy given the current states of the other units. Because the connections are symmetrical, the difference between the energy of the whole system with the kth hypothesis false and its energy with the kth hypothesis true can be determined locally by the kth unit, and is just

$$\Delta E_k = \sum_i w_{ki} s_i - \theta_k . \tag{2}$$

Therefore, the rule for minimizing the energy contributed by a unit is to adopt the true state if its total input from the other units exceeds its threshold. This is the familiar rule for binary threshold units.

[1] Hopfield used the states 1 and -1 because his model was derived from physical systems called spin glasses in which spins are either "up" or "down." Provided the units have thresholds, models that use 1 and -1 can be translated into models that use 1 and 0 and have different thresholds.

Using Probabilistic Decisions to Escape From Local Minima

At about the same time that Hopfield showed how parallel networks of this kind could be used to access memories that were stored as local minima, Kirkpatrick, working at IBM, introduced an interesting new search technique for solving hard optimization problems on conventional computers.

One standard technique is to use gradient descent: The values of the variables in the problem are modified in whatever direction reduces the cost function (energy). For hard problems, gradient descent gets stuck at *local* minima that are not globally optimal. This is an inevitable consequence of only allowing downhill moves. If jumps to higher energy states occasionally occur, it is possible to break out of local minima, but it is not obvious how the system will then behave and it is far from clear when uphill steps should be allowed.

Kirkpatrick, Gelatt, and Vecchi (1983) used another physical analogy to guide the use of occasional uphill steps. To find a very low energy state of a metal, the best strategy is to melt it and then to slowly reduce its temperature. This process is called annealing, and so they named their search method "simulated annealing." Chapter 6 contains a discussion of why annealing works. We give a simple intuitive account here.

One way of seeing why thermal noise is helpful is to consider the energy landscape shown in Figure 1. Let us suppose that a ball-bearing starts at a randomly chosen point on the landscape. If it always goes downhill (and has no inertia), it will have an even chance of ending up at A or B because both minima have the same width and so the initial

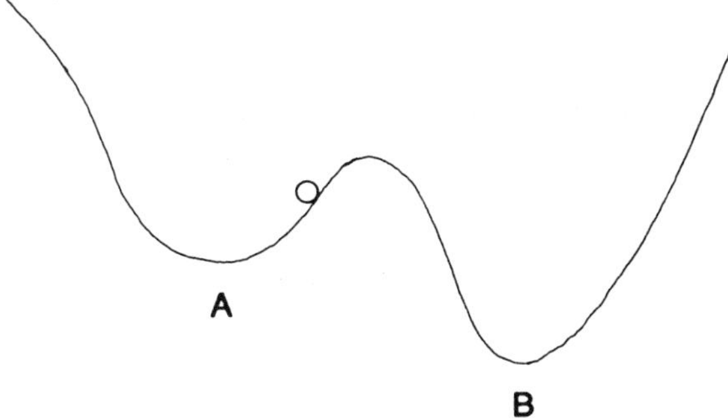

FIGURE 1. A simple energy landscape containing two local minima separated by an energy barrier. Shaking can be used to allow the state of the network (represented here by a ball-bearing) to escape from local minima.

random point is equally likely to lie in either minimum. If we shake the whole system, we are more likely to shake the ball-bearing from A to B than vice versa because the energy barrier is lower from the A side. If the shaking is gentle, a transition from A to B will be many times as probable as a transition from B to A, but both transitions will be very rare. So although gentle shaking will ultimately lead to a very high probability of being in B rather than A, it will take a very long time before this happens. On the other hand, if the shaking is violent, the ball-bearing will cross the barrier frequently and so the ultimate probability ratio will be approached rapidly, but this ratio will not be very good: With violent shaking it is almost as easy to cross the barrier in the wrong direction (from B to A) as in the right direction. A good compromise is to start by shaking hard and gradually shake more and more gently. This ensures that at some stage the noise level passes through the best possible compromise between the absolute probability of a transition and the ratio of the probabilities of good and bad transitions. It also means that at the end, the ball-bearing stays right at the bottom of the chosen minimum.

This view of why annealing helps is not the whole story. Figure 1 is misleading because all the states have been laid out in one dimension. Complex systems have high-dimensional state spaces, and so the barrier between two low-lying states is typically massively degenerate: The number of ways of getting from one low-lying state to another is an exponential function of the height of the barrier one is willing to cross. This means that a rise in the level of thermal noise opens up an enormous variety of paths for escaping from a local minimum and even though each path by itself is unlikely, it is highly probable that the system will cross the barrier. We conjecture that simulated annealing will only work well in domains where the energy barriers are highly degenerate.

Applying Simulated Annealing to Hopfield Nets

There is a simple modification of Hopfield's updating rule that allows parallel networks to implement simulated annealing. If the energy gap between the 1 and 0 states of the kth unit is ΔE_k then, regardless of the previous state set, $s_k = 1$ with probability

$$p_k = \frac{1}{\left(1+e^{-\Delta E_k / T}\right)} \tag{3}$$

where T is a parameter which acts like the temperature of a physical system. This local decision rule ensures that in thermal equilibrium the relative probability of two global states is determined solely by their energy difference, and follows a Boltzmann distribution:

$$\frac{P_\alpha}{P_\beta} = e^{-(E_\alpha - E_\beta)/T} \tag{4}$$

where P_α is the probability of being in the αth global state, and E_α is the energy of that state.

At low temperatures there is a strong bias in favor of states with low energy, but the time required to reach equilibrium may be long. At higher temperatures the bias is not so favorable, but equilibrium is reached faster. The fastest way to reach equilibrium at a given temperature is generally to use simulated annealing: Start with a higher temperature and gradually reduce it.

The idea of implementing constraints as interactions between stochastic processing elements was proposed by Moussouris (1974) who discussed the identity between Boltzmann distributions and Markov random fields. The idea of using simulated annealing to find low energy states in parallel networks has been investigated independently by several different groups. S. Geman and D. Geman (1984) established limits on the allowable speed of the annealing schedule and showed that simulated annealing can be very effective for removing noise from images. Hinton and Sejnowski (1983b) showed how the use of binary stochastic elements could solve some problems that plague other relaxation techniques, in particular the problem of learning the weights. Smolensky (1983) has been investigating a similar scheme which he calls "harmony theory." This scheme is discussed in detail in Chapter 6. Smolensky's harmony is equivalent to our energy (with a sign reversal).

Pattern Completion

One way of using a parallel network is to treat it as a pattern completion device. A subset of the units are "clamped" into their on or off states and the weights in the network then complete the pattern by determining the states of the remaining units. There are strong limitations on the sets of binary vectors that can be learned if the network has one unit for each component of the vector. These limits can be transcended by using extra units whose states do not correspond to components in the vectors to be learned. The weights of connections to these extra units can be used to represent complex interactions that cannot be expressed as pairwise correlations between the components of the vectors. We call these extra units *hidden units* (by analogy with hidden Markov processes) and we call the units that are used to specify the patterns to be learned the *visible units*. The visible units are the interface between the network and the environment that specifies vectors for it to learn or asks it to complete a partial vector. The hidden units are where the network can build its own internal representations.

Sometimes, we would like to be able to complete a pattern from any sufficiently large part of it without knowing in advance which part will be given and which part must be completed. Other times we know in advance which parts will be given as input and which parts will have to be completed as output. So there are two different completion paradigms. In the first, any of the visible units might be part of the required output. In the second, there is a distinguished subset of the visible units, called the input units, which are always clamped by the environment, so the network never needs to determine the states of these units.

EASY AND HARD LEARNING

Consider a network which is allowed to run freely, using the probabilistic decision rule in Equation 3, without having any of its units clamped by the environment. When the network reaches thermal equilibrium, the probability of finding it in any particular global state depends only on the energy of that state (Equation 4). We can therefore control the probabilities of global states by controlling their energies. If each weight only contributed to the energy of a single global state, this would be straightforward, but changing a weight will actually change the energies of many different states so it is not immediately obvious how a weight-change will affect the probability of a particular global state. Fortunately, if we run the network until it reaches thermal equilibrium, Equations 3 and 4 allow us to derive the way in which the probability of each global state changes as a weight is changed:

$$\frac{\partial \ln P_\alpha^-}{\partial w_{ij}} = \frac{1}{T}\left[s_i^\alpha s_j^\alpha - \sum_\beta P_\beta^- s_i^\beta s_j^\beta \right] \qquad (5)$$

where s_i^α is the binary state of the ith unit in the αth global state and P_α^- is the probability, at thermal equilibrium, of global state α of the network when none of the visible units are clamped (the lack of clamping is denoted by the superscript $^-$). Equation 5 shows that the effect of a weight on the log probability of a global state can be computed from purely local information because it only involves the behavior of the two units that the weight connects (the second term is just the probability of finding the ith and jth units on together). This makes it easy to manipulate the probabilities of global states provided the desired probabilities are known (see Hinton & Sejnowski, 1983a, for details).

Unfortunately, it is normally unreasonable to expect the environment or a teacher to specify the required probabilities of entire global states of the network. The task that the network must perform is defined in terms of the states of the visible units, and so the environment or teacher only has direct access to the states of these units. The difficult learning problem is to decide how to use the hidden units to help achieve the required behavior of the visible units. A learning rule which assumes that the network is instructed from outside on how to use *all* of its units is of limited interest because it evades the main problem which is to discover appropriate representations for a given task among the hidden units.

In statistical terms, there are many kinds of statistical structure implicit in a large ensemble of environmental vectors. The separate probability of each visible unit being active is the first-order structure and can be captured by the thresholds of the visible units. The $v^2/2$ pairwise correlations between the v visible units constitute the second-order structure and this can be captured by the weights between pairs of units.[2] All structure higher than second-order cannot be captured by pairwise weights *between the visible units.* A simple example may help to clarify this crucial point.

Suppose that the ensemble consists of the vectors: (1 1 0), (1 0 1), (0 1 1), and (0 0 0), each with a probability of 0.25. There is clearly some structure here because four of the eight possible 3-bit vectors never occur. However, the structure is entirely third-order. The first-order probabilities are all 0.5, and the second-order correlations are all 0, so if we consider only these statistics, this ensemble is indistinguishable from the ensemble in which all eight vectors occur equiprobably.

The Widrow-Hoff rule or perceptron convergence procedure (Rosenblatt, 1962) is a learning rule which is designed to capture second-order structure and it therefore fails miserably on the example just given. If the first two bits are treated as an input and the last bit is treated as the required output, the ensemble corresponds to the function "exclusive-or" which is one of the examples used by Minsky and Papert (1969) to show the strong limitations of one-layer perceptrons. The Widrow-Hoff

[2] Factor analysis confines itself to capturing as much of the second-order structure as possible in a few underlying "factors." It ignores all higher order structure which is where much of the interesting information lies for all but the most simple ensembles of vectors.

rule can do easy learning, but it cannot do the kind of hard learning that involves deciding how to use extra units whose behavior is not directly specified by the task.

It is tempting to think that networks with pairwise connections can never capture higher than second-order statistics. There is one sense in which this is true and another in which it is false. By introducing extra units which are not part of the definition of the original ensemble, it is possible to express the third-order structure of the original ensemble in the second-order structure of the larger set of units. In the example given above, we can add a fourth component to get the ensemble {(1101), (1010), (0110), (0000)}. It is now possible to use the thresholds and weights between all four units to express the third-order structure in the first three components. A more familiar way of saying this is that we introduce an extra "feature detector" which in this example detects the case when the first two units are both on. We can then make each of the first two units excite the third unit, and use strong inhibition from the feature detector to overrule this excitation when *both* of the first two units are on. The difficult problem in introducing the extra unit was deciding when it should be on and when it should be off—deciding what feature it should detect.[3]

One way of thinking about the higher order structure of an ensemble of environmental vectors is that it implicitly specifies good sets of underlying features that can be used to model the structure of the environment. In common-sense terms, the weights in the network should be chosen so that the hidden units represent significant underlying features that bear strong, regular relationships to each other and to the states of the visible units. The hard learning problem is to figure out what these features are, i.e., to find a set of weights which turn the hidden units into useful feature detectors that explicitly represent properties of the environment which are only implicitly present as higher order statistics in the ensemble of environmental vectors.

Maximum Likelihood Models

Another view of learning is that the weights in the network constitute a generative model of the environment—we would like to find a set of weights so that when the network is running freely, the patterns of activity that occur over the visible units are the same as they would be if the environment was clamping them. The number of units in the

[3] In this example there are six different ways of using the extra unit to solve the task.

network and their interconnectivity define a space of possible models of the environment, and any particular set of weights defines a particular model within this space. The learning problem is to find a combination of weights that gives a good model given the limitations imposed by the architecture of the network and the way it runs.

More formally, we would like a way of finding the combination of weights that is most likely to have produced the observed ensemble of environmental vectors. This is called a *maximum likelihood* model and there is a large literature within statistics on maximum likelihood estimation. The learning procedure we describe actually has a close relationship to a method called Expectation and Maximization (EM) (Dempster, Laird, & Rubin, 1976). EM is used by statisticians for estimating missing parameters. It represents probability distributions by using parameters like our weights that are exponentially related to probabilities, rather than using probabilities themselves. The EM algorithm is closely related to an earlier algorithm invented by Baum that manipulates probabilities directly. Baum's algorithm has been used successfully for speech recognition (Bahl, Jelinek, & Mercer, 1983). It estimates the parameters of a hidden Markov chain—a transition network which has a fixed structure but variable probabilities on the arcs and variable probabilities of emitting a particular output symbol as it arrives at each internal node. Given an ensemble of strings of symbols and a fixed-topology transition network, the algorithm finds the combination of transition probabilities and output probabilities that is most likely to have produced these strings (actually it only finds a local maximum).

Maximum likelihood methods work by adjusting the parameters to increase the probability that the generative model will produce the observed data. Baum's algorithm and EM are able to estimate new values for the probabilities (or weights) that are guaranteed to be better than the previous values. Our algorithm simply estimates the gradient of the log likelihood with respect to a weight, and so the magnitude of the weight change must be decided using additional criteria. Our algorithm, however, has the advantage that it is easy to implement in a parallel network of neuron-like units.

The idea of a stochastic generative model is attractive because it provides a clean quantitative way of comparing alternative representational schemes. The problem of saying which of two representational schemes is best appears to be intractable. Many sensible rules of thumb are available, but these are generally pulled out of thin air and justified by commonsense and practical experience. They lack a firm mathematical foundation. If we confine ourselves to a space of allowable stochastic models, we can then get a simple Bayesian measure of the quality of a representational scheme: How likely is the observed ensemble of environmental vectors given the representational scheme? In our networks, representations are patterns of activity in the units, and the representational scheme therefore corresponds to the set of weights that determines when those patterns are active.

THE BOLTZMANN MACHINE LEARNING ALGORITHM

If we make certain assumptions it is possible to derive a measure of how effectively the weights in the network are being used for modeling the structure of the environment, and it is also possible to show how the weights should be changed to progressively improve this measure. We assume that the environment clamps a particular vector over the visible units and it keeps it there long enough for the network to reach thermal equilibrium with this vector as a boundary condition (i.e., to "interpret" it). We also assume (unrealistically) that the there is no structure in the sequential order of the environmentally clamped vectors. This means that the complete structure of the ensemble of environmental vectors can be specified by giving the probability, $P^+(V_\alpha)$, of each of the 2^v vectors over the v visible units. Notice that the $P^+(V_\alpha)$ do not depend on the weights in the network because the environment clamps the visible units.

A particular set of weights can be said to constitute a perfect model of the structure of the environment if it leads to exactly the same probability distribution of visible vectors when the network is running freely *with no units being clamped by the environment.* Because of the stochastic behavior of the units, the network will wander through a variety of states even with no environmental input and it will therefore generate a probability distribution, $P^-(V_\alpha)$, over all 2^v visible vectors. This distribution can be compared with the environmental distribution, $P^+(V_\alpha)$. In general, it will not be possible to exactly match the 2^v environmental probabilities using the weights among the v visible and h hidden units because there are at most $(v+h-1)(v+h)/2$ symmetrical weights and $(v+h)$ thresholds. However, it may be possible to do very well if the environment contains regularities that can be expressed in the weights. An information theoretic measure (Kullback, 1959) of the distance between the environmental and free-running probability distributions is given by:

$$G = \sum_\alpha P^+(V_\alpha) \ln \frac{P^+(V_\alpha)}{P^-(V_\alpha)} \tag{6}$$

where $P^+(V_\alpha)$ is the probability of the αth state of the visible units in *phase*$^+$ when their states are determined by the environment, and $P^-(V_\alpha)$ is the corresponding probability in *phase*$^-$ when the network is running freely with no environmental input.

G is never negative and is only zero if the distributions are identical. G is actually the distance in bits *from* the free running distribution *to* the environmental distribution.[4] It is sometimes called the asymmetric divergence or information gain. The measure is not symmetric with respect to the two distributions. This seems odd but is actually very reasonable. When trying to approximate a probability distribution, it is more important to get the probabilities correct for events that happen frequently than for rare events. So the match between the actual and predicted probabilities of an event should be weighted by the actual probability as in Equation 6.

It is possible to improve the network's model of the structure of its environment by changing the weights so as to reduce G.[5] To perform gradient descent in G, we need to know how G will change when a weight is changed. But changing a single weight changes the energies of one quarter of all the global states of the network, and it changes the probabilities of all the states in ways that depend on *all* the other weights in the network. Consider, for example, the very simple network shown in Figure 2. If we want the two units at the ends of the chain to be either both on or both off, how should we change the weight $w_{3,4}$? It clearly depends on the signs of remote weights like $w_{1,2}$ because we need to have an even number of inhibitory weights in the chain.[6] So the partial derivative of G with respect to one weight depends on all the other weights and minimizing G appears to be a

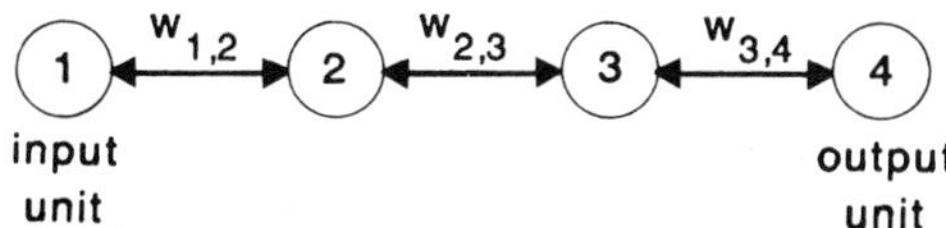

FIGURE 2. A very simple network with one input unit, one output unit, and two hidden units. The task is to make the output unit adopt the same state as the input unit. The difficulty is that the correct value for weight $w_{3,4}$ depends on remote information like the value of weight $w_{1,2}$.

---

[4] If we use base 2 logarithms.

[5] Peter Brown (personal communication) has pointed out that minimizing G is equivalent to maximizing the log of the likelihood of generating the environmental probability distribution when the network is running freely at equilibrium.

[6] The thresholds must also be adjusted appropriately.

difficult computational problem that requires nonlocal information.

Fortunately, all the information that is required about the other weights in order to change w_{ij} appropriately shows up in the behavior of the ith and jth units at thermal equilibrium. In addition to performing a search for low energy states of the network, the process of reaching thermal equilibrium ensures that the joint activity of any two units contains all the information required for changing the weight between them in order to give the network a better model of its environment. The joint activity implicitly encodes information about all the other weights in the network. The Appendix shows that

$$\frac{\partial G}{\partial w_{ij}} = -\frac{1}{T}[p_{ij}^{+} - p_{ij}^{-}] \tag{7}$$

where p_{ij}^{+} is the probability, averaged over all environmental inputs and measured at equilibrium, that the ith and jth units are both on when the network is being driven by the environment, and p_{ij}^{-} is the corresponding probability when the network is free running. One surprising feature of Equation 7 is that it does not matter whether the weight is between two visible units, two hidden units, or one of each. The same rule applies for the gradient of G.

Unlearning

Crick and Mitchison (1983) have suggested that a form of reverse learning might occur during REM sleep in mammals. Their proposal was based on the assumption that parasitic modes develop in large networks that hinder the distributed storage and retrieval of information. The mechanism that Crick and Mitchison propose is based on

> More or less random stimulation of the forebrain by the brain stem that will tend to stimulate the inappropriate modes of brain activity . . . and especially those which are too prone to be set off by random noise rather than by highly structured specific signals. (p. 112)

During this state of random excitation and free running they postulate that changes occur at synapses to decrease the probability of the spurious states.

A simulation of reverse learning was performed by Hopfield, Feinstein, and Palmer (1983) who independently had been studying ways to improve the associative storage capacity of simple networks of binary processors (Hopfield, 1982). In their algorithm an input is presented to the network as an initial condition, and the system evolves by falling into a nearby local energy minimum. However, not all local energy minima represent stored information. In creating the desired minima, they accidentally create other spurious minima, and to eliminate these they use "unlearning": The learning procedure is applied with reverse sign to the states found after starting from random initial conditions. Following this procedure, the performance of the system in accessing stored states was found to be improved.

There is an interesting relationship between the reverse learning proposed by Crick and Mitchison and Hopfield et al. and the form of the learning algorithm which we derived by considering how to minimize an information theory measure of the discrepancy between the environmental structure and the network's internal model (Hinton & Sejnowski, 1983b). The two phases of our learning algorithm resemble the learning and unlearning procedures: Positive Hebbian learning occurs in *phase*$^+$ during which information in the environment is captured by the weights; during *phase*$^-$ the system randomly samples states according to their Boltzmann distribution and Hebbian learning occurs with a negative coefficient.

However, these two phases need not be implemented in the manner suggested by Crick and Mitchison. For example, during *phase*$^-$ the average co-occurrences could be computed without making any changes to the weights. These averages could then be used as a baseline for making changes during *phase*$^+$; that is, the co-occurrences during *phase*$^+$ could be computed and the baseline subtracted before each permanent weight change. Thus, an alternative but equivalent proposal for the function of dream sleep is to recalibrate the baseline for plasticity—the break-even point which determines whether a synaptic weight is incremented or decremented. This would be safer than making permanent weight decrements to synaptic weights during sleep and solves the problem of deciding how much "unlearning" to do.

Our learning algorithm refines Crick and Mitchison's interpretation of why two phases are needed. Consider a hidden unit deep within the network: How should its connections with other units be changed to best capture regularity present in the environment? If it does not receive direct input from the environment, the hidden unit has no way to determine whether the information it receives from neighboring units is ultimately caused by structure in the environment or is entirely a result of the other weights. This can lead to a "folie a deux" where two parts of the network each construct a model of the other and ignore the external environment. The contribution of internal and external sources can be separated by comparing the co-occurrences in *phase*$^+$ with similar information that is collected in the absence of environmental input. *phase*$^-$ thus acts as a control condition. Because of the special properties of equilibrium it is possible to subtract off this purely internal contribution and use the difference to update the weights. Thus, the role of the two phases is to make the system maximally responsive to regularities present in the environment and to prevent the system from using its capacity to model internally-generated regularities.

Ways in Which the Learning Algorithm Can Fail

The ability to discover the partial derivative of G by observing p_{ij}^+ and p_{ij}^- does not completely determine the learning algorithm. It is still necessary to decide how much to change each weight, how long to collect co-occurrence statistics before changing the weight, how many weights to change at a time, and what temperature schedule to use during the annealing searches. For very simple networks in very simple environments, it is possible to discover reasonable values for these parameters by trial and error. For more complex and interesting cases, serious difficulties arise because it is very easy to violate the assumptions on which the mathematical results are based (Derthick, 1984).

The first difficulty is that there is nothing to prevent the learning algorithm from generating very large weights which create such high energy barriers that the network cannot reach equilibrium in the allotted time. Once this happens, the statistics that are collected will not be the equilibrium statistics required for Equation 7 to hold and so all bets are off. We have observed this happening for a number of different networks. They start off learning quite well and then the weights become too large and the network "goes sour"—its performance deteriorates dramatically.

One way to ensure that the network gets close to equilibrium is to keep the weights small. Pearlmutter (personal communication) has shown that the learning works much better if, in addition to the weight changes caused by the learning, every weight continually decays towards a value of zero, with the speed of the decay being proportional to the absolute magnitude of the weight. This keeps the weights small and eventually leads to a relatively stable situation in which the decay rate of a weight is balanced by the partial derivative of G with respect to the weight. This has the satisfactory property that the absolute magnitude of a weight shows how important it is for modeling the environmental structure.

The use of weight-decay has several other consequences which are not so desirable. Because the weights stay small, the network cannot construct very deep minima in the energy landscape and so it cannot make the probability ratios for similar global states be very different.

This means that it is bound to give a significant number of errors in modeling environments where very similar vectors have very different probabilities. Better *performance* can be achieved by annealing the network to a lower final temperature (which is equivalent to making all the weights larger), but this will make the *learning* worse for two separate reasons. First, with less errors there is less to drive the learning because it relies on the difference between the *phase*$^+$ and *phase*$^-$ statistics. Second, it will be harder to reach thermal equilibrium at this lower temperature and so the co-occurrence statistics will be unreliable. One way of getting good statistics to drive the learning and also getting very few overt errors is to measure the co-occurrence statistics at a temperature higher than the final one.

Another way of ensuring that the network approaches equilibrium is to eliminate deep, narrow minima that are often not found by the annealing process. Derthick (1984) has shown that this can be done using a longer gentler annealing schedule in *phase*$^-$. This means that the network is more likely to occupy the hard-to-find minima in *phase*$^-$ than in *phase*$^+$, and so these minima will get filled in because the learning rule raises the energies of states that are occupied more in *phase*$^-$ than in *phase*$^+$.

AN EXAMPLE OF HARD LEARNING

A simple example which can only be solved by capturing the higher order statistical structure in the ensemble of input vectors is the "shifter" problem. The visible units are divided into three groups. Group V_1 is a one-dimensional array of 8 units, each of which is clamped on or off at random with a probability of 0.3 of being on. Group V_2 also contains 8 units and their states are determined by shifting and copying the states of the units in group V_1. The only shifts allowed are one to the left, one to the right, or no shift. Wrap-around is used so that when there is a right shift, the state of the right-most unit in V_1 determines the state of the left-most unit in V_2. The three possible shifts are chosen at random with equal probabilities. Group V_3 contains three units to represent the three possible shifts, so at any one time one of them is clamped on and the others are clamped off.

The problem is to learn the structure that relates the states of the three groups. One facet of this problem is to "recognize" the shift—i.e., to complete a partial input vector in which the states of V_1 and V_2 are clamped but the units in V_3 are left free. It is fairly easy to see why this problem cannot possibly be solved by just adding together a lot of pairwise interactions between units in V_1, V_2, and V_3. If you know that a particular unit in V_1 is on, it tells you nothing whatsoever about what the shift is. It is only by finding *combinations* of active units in V_1 and V_2 that it is possible to predict the shift, so the information required is of at least third-order. This means that extra hidden units are required to perform the task.

The obvious way to recognize the shift is to have extra units which detect informative features such as an active unit in V_1 and an active unit one place to the right in V_2 and then support the unit V_3 that represents a right shift. The empirical question is whether the learning algorithm is capable of turning some hidden units into feature detectors of this kind, and whether it will generate a set of detectors that work well together rather than duplicating the same detector. The set of weights that minimizes G defines the *optimal* set of detectors but it is not at all obvious what these detectors are, nor is it obvious that the learning algorithm is capable of finding a good set.

Figure 3 shows the result of running a version of the Boltzmann machine learning procedure. Of the 24 hidden units, 5 seem to be doing very little but the remainder are sensible looking detectors and most of them have become spatially localized. One type of detector which occurs several times consists of two large negative weights, one above the other, flanked by smaller excitatory weights on each side. This is a more discriminating detector of no-shift than simply having two positive weights, one above the other. It interesting to note that the various instances of this feature type all have different locations in V_1 and V_2, even though the hidden units are not connected to each other. The pressure for the feature detectors to be different from each other comes from the gradient of G, rather than from the kind of lateral inhibition among the feature detectors that is used in "competitive learning" paradigms (Fukushima, 1980; Rumelhart & Zipser, 1985).

The Training Procedure

The training procedure alternated between two phases. In *phase*$^+$, all the units in V_1, V_2, and V_3 were clamped into states representing a pair of 8-bit vectors and their relative shift. The hidden units were then allowed to change their states until the system approached thermal equilibrium at a temperature of 10. The annealing schedule is described below. After annealing, the network was assumed to be close to thermal equilibrium and it was then run for a further 10 iterations during which time the frequency with which each pair of connected units were both on was measured. This was repeated 20 times with

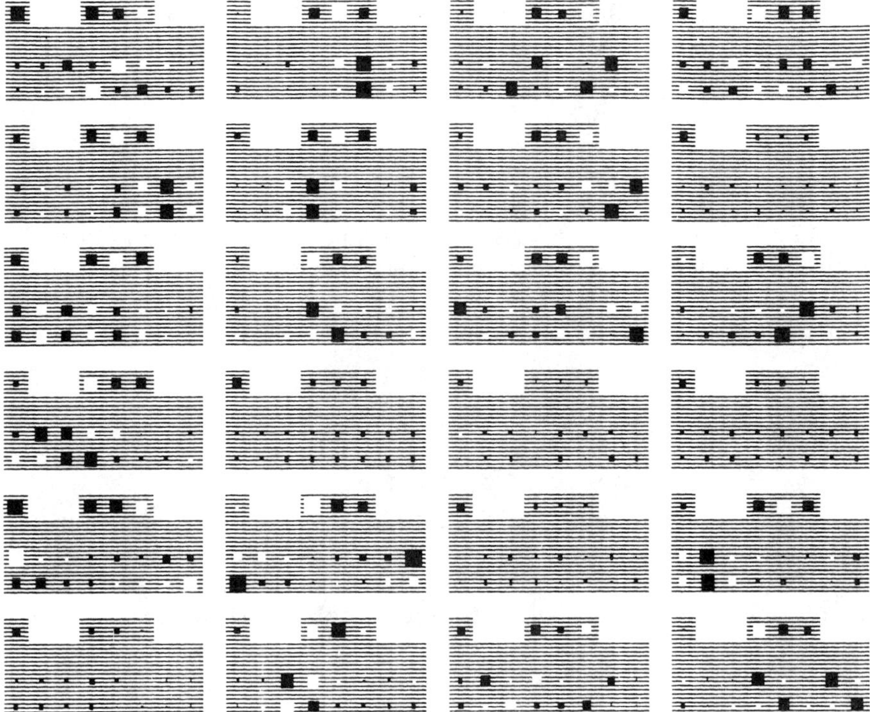

FIGURE 3. The weights of the 24 hidden units in the shifter network. Each large region corresponds to a unit. Within this region the black rectangles represent negative weights and the white rectangles represent positive ones. The size of a rectangle represents the magnitude of the weight. The two rows of weights at the bottom of each unit are its connections to the two groups of input units, V_1 and V_2. These weights therefore represent the "receptive field" of the hidden unit. The three weights in the middle of the top row of each unit are its connections to the three output units that represent shift-left, no-shift, and shift-right. The solitary weight at the top left of each unit is its threshold. Each hidden unit is directly connected to all 16 input units and all 3 output units. In this example, the hidden units are not connected to each other. The top-left unit has weights that are easy to understand: Its optimal stimulus is activity in the fourth unit of V_1 and the fifth unit of V_2, and it votes for shift-right. It has negative weights to make it less likely to come on when there is an alternative explanation for why its two favorite input units are active.

different clamped vectors and the co-occurrence statistics were averaged over all 20 runs to yield an estimate, for each connection, of p_{ij}^{+} in Equation 7. In *phase*$^-$, none of the units were clamped and the network was annealed in the same way. The network was then run for a further 10 iterations and the co-occurrence statistics were collected for all connected pairs of units. This was repeated 20 times and the co-occurrence statistics were averaged to yield an estimate of p_{ij}^{-}.

The entire set of 40 annealings that were used to estimate p_{ij}^+ and p_{ij}^- was called a sweep. After each sweep, every weight was incremented by $5(p_{ij}^+ - p_{ij}^-)$. In addition, every weight had its absolute magnitude decreased by 0.0005 times its absolute magnitude. This weight decay prevented the weights from becoming too large and it also helped to resuscitate hidden units which had predominantly negative or predominantly positive weights. Such units spend all their time in the same state and therefore convey no information. The *phase*$^+$ and *phase*$^-$ statistics are identical for these units, and so the weight decay gradually erodes their weights until they come back to life (units with all zero weights come on half the time).

The Annealing Schedule

The annealing schedule spent the following number of iterations at the following temperatures: 2 at 40, 2 at 35, 2 at 30, 2 at 25, 2 at 20, 2 at 15, 2 at 12, 2 at 10. One iteration is defined as the number of random probes required so that each unit is probed one time on average. When it is probed, a unit uses its energy gap to decide which of its two states to adopt using the stochastic decision rule in Equation 3. Since each unit gets to see the most recent states of all the other units, an iteration cannot be regarded as a single parallel step. An truly parallel asynchronous system must tolerate time delays. Units must decide on their new states without being aware of very recent changes in the states of other units. It can be shown (Sejnowski, Hinton, Kienker, & Schumacher, 1985) that first-order time delays act like added temperature and can therefore be tolerated by networks of this kind.

The Performance of the Shifter Network

The shifter network is encouraging because it is a clear example of the kind of learning of higher order structure that was beyond the capability of perceptrons, but it also illustrates several weaknesses in the current approach.

- The learning was very slow. It required 9000 learning sweeps, each of which involved reaching equilibrium 20 times in *phase*$^+$ with vectors clamped on V_1, V_2, and V_3, and 20 times in *phase*$^-$ with no units clamped. Even for low-level perceptual learning, this seems excessively slow.

- The weights are fairly clearly not optimal because of the 5 hidden units that appear to do nothing useful. Also, the performance is far from perfect. When the states of the units in V_1 and V_2 are clamped and the network is annealed gently to half the final temperature used during learning, the units in V_3 quite frequently adopt the wrong states. If the number of *on* units in V_1 is 1,2,3,4,5,6,7, the percentage of correctly recognized shifts is 50%, 71%, 81%, 86%, 89%, 82%, and 66% respectively. The wide variation in the number of active units in V_1 naturally makes the task harder to learn than if a constant proportion of the units were active. Also, some of the input patterns are ambiguous. When all the units in V_1 and V_2 are off, the network can do no better than chance.

ACHIEVING RELIABLE COMPUTATION WITH UNRELIABLE HARDWARE

Conventional computers only work if all their individual components work perfectly, so as systems become larger they become more and more unreliable. Current computer technology uses extremely reliable components and error-correcting memories to achieve overall reliability. The brain appears to have much less reliable components, and so it must use much more error-correction. It is conceivable that the brain uses the kinds of representations that would be appropriate given reliable hardware and then superimposes redundancy to compensate for its unreliable hardware.

The reliability issue is typically treated as a tedious residual problem to be dealt with after the main decisions about the form of the computation have been made. A more direct approach is to treat reliability as a serious design constraint from the outset and to choose a basic style of computation that does not require reliable components. Ideally, we want a system in which *none* of the individual components are critical to the ability of the whole system to meet its requirements. In other words, we want some high-level description of the behavior of the system to remain valid even when the low-level descriptions of the behavior of some of the individual components change. This is only possible if the high-level description is related to the low level descriptions in a particular way: Every robust high-level property must be implemented by the combined effect of many local components, and no single component must be crucial for the realization of the high-level property. This makes distributed representations (see Chapter 3) a natural choice when designing a damage-resistant system.

Distributed representations tend to behave robustly because they have an internal coherence which leads to an automatic "clean-up" effect. This effect can be seen in the patterns of activity that occur within a group of units and also in the interactions between groups. If a group of units, A, has a number of distinct and well-defined energy minima then these minima will remain even if a few units are removed or a little noise is added to many of the connections within A. The damage may distort the minima slightly and it may also change their relative probabilities, but minor damage will not alter the gross topography of the energy landscape, so it will not affect higher level descriptions that depend only on this gross topography.

Even if the patterns of activity in A are slightly changed, this will often have *no* effect on the patterns caused in other groups of units. If the weights between groups of units have been fixed so that a particular pattern in A regularly causes a particular pattern in B, a small variation in the input coming from A will typically make no difference to the pattern that gets selected in B, because this pattern has its own internal coherence, and if the input from A is sufficiently accurate to select approximately the right pattern, the interactions among the elements in B will ensure that the details are right.

Damage resistance can be achieved by using a simple kind of representation in which there are many identical copies of each type of unit and each macroscopic item is encoded by activity in all the units of one type. In the undamaged system all these copies behave identically and a lot of capacity is therefore wasted. If we use distributed representations in which each unit may be used for representing many different items we can achieve comparable resistance to damage without wasting capacity. Because all the units behave differently from each other, the undamaged system can implement many fine distinctions in the fine detail of the energy landscape. At the macroscopic level, these fine distinctions will appear as somewhat unreliable probabilistic tendencies and will be very sensitive to minor damage.

The fine details in the current energy landscape may contain the seeds of future changes in the gross topography. If learning novel distinctions involves the progressive strengthening of regularities that are initially tentative and unreliable, then it follows that learning may well suffer considerably when physical damage washes out these minor regularities. However, the simulations described below do not bear on this interesting issue.

AN EXAMPLE OF THE EFFECTS OF DAMAGE

To show the effects of damage on a network, it is necessary to choose a task for the network to perform. Since we are mainly concerned with properties that are fairly domain-independent, the details of the task are not especially relevant here. For reasons described in Chapter 3, we were interested in networks that can learn an *arbitrary* mapping between items in two different domains, and we use that network to investigate the effects of damage. As we shall see, the fact that the task involves purely arbitrary associations makes it easier to interpret some of the interesting transfer effects that occur when a network relearns after sustaining major damage.

The Network

The network consisted of three groups or layers of units. The *grapheme* group was used to represent the letters in a three-letter word. It contained 30 units and was subdivided into three groups of 10 units each. Each subgroup was dedicated to one of the three letter positions within a word, and it represented one of the 10 possible letters in that position by having a single active unit for that letter. The three-letter grapheme strings were not English words. They were chosen randomly, subject to the constraint that each of the 10 possible graphemes in each position had to be used at least once. The *sememe* group was used to encode the semantic features of the "word."[7] It contained 30 units, one for each possible semantic feature. The semantic features to be associated with a word were chosen randomly, with each feature having a probability of 0.2 of being chosen for each word. There were connections between all pairs of units in the sememe group to allow the network to learn familiar combinations of semantic features. There were no direct connections between the grapheme and sememe groups. Instead, there was an intermediate layer of 20 units, each of which was connected to all the units in both the grapheme and the sememe groups. Figure 4 is an artist's impression of the network. It uses English letters and words to convey the functions of the units in the various layers. Most of the connections are missing.

The Training Procedure

The network was trained to associate each of 20 patterns of activity in the grapheme units with an arbitrarily related pattern in the sememe

[7] The representation of meaning is clearly more complicated than just a set of features, so the use of the word "semantic" here should not be taken too literally.

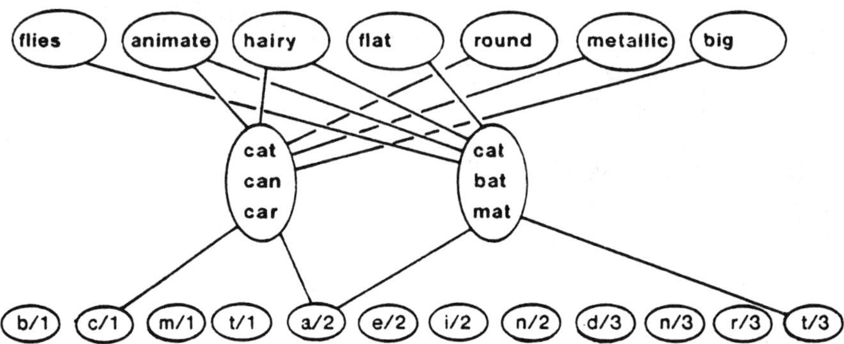

FIGURE 4. Part of the network used for associating three-letter words with sets of semantic features. English words are used in this figure to help convey the functional roles of the units. In the actual simulation, the letter-strings and semantic features were chosen randomly.

units. As before, the training procedure alternated between two phases. In *phase*$^+$ all the grapheme and sememe units were clamped in states that represented the physical form and the meaning of a single word, and the intermediate units were allowed to change their states until the system approached thermal equilibrium at a temperature of 10. The annealing schedule was: 2 at 30, 2 at 26, 2 at 22, 2 at 20, 2 at 18, 2 at 16, 2 at 15, 2 at 14, 2 at 13, 4 at 12, 4 at 11, 8 at 10. After annealing, the network was assumed to be close to thermal equilibrium and it was then run for a further 5 iterations during which time the frequency with which each pair of connected units were both on was measured. This was repeated twice for each of the 20 possible grapheme/sememe associations and the co-occurrence statistics were averaged over all 40 annealings to yield an estimate, for each connection, of p_{ij}^+. In *phase*$^-$, only the grapheme units were clamped and the network settled to equilibrium (using the same schedule as before) and thus decided for itself what sememe units should be active. The network was then run for a further 5 iterations and the co-occurrence statistics were collected for all connected pairs of units. This was repeated twice for each of the 20 grapheme strings and the co-occurrence statistics were averaged to yield an estimate of p_{ij}^-. Each learning sweep thus involved a total of 80 annealings.

After each sweep, every weight was either incremented or decremented by 1, with the sign of the change being determined by the sign of $p_{ij}^+ - p_{ij}^-$.[8] In addition, some of the weights had their absolute

[8] See Hinton, Sejnowski, and Ackley (1984) for a discussion of the advantages of discrete weight increments over the more obvious steepest descent technique in which the weight increment is proportional to $p_{ij}^+ - p_{ij}^-$.

magnitude decreased by 1. For each weight, the probability of this happening was 0.0005 times the absolute magnitude of the weight.

We found that the network performed better if there was a preliminary learning stage which just involved the sememe units. In this stage, the intermediate units were not yet connected. During *phase*$^+$ the required patterns were clamped on the sememe units and p_{ij}^+ was measured (annealing was not required because all the units involved were clamped). During *phase*$^-$ no units were clamped and the network was allowed to reach equilibrium 20 times using the annealing schedule given above. After annealing, p_{ij}^- was estimated from the co-occurrences as before, except that only 20 *phase*$^-$ annealings were used instead of 40. There were 300 sweeps of this learning stage and they resulted in weights between pairs of sememe units that were sufficient to give the sememe group an energy landscape with 20 strong minima corresponding to the 20 possible "word meanings." This helped subsequent learning considerably, because it reduced the tendency for the intermediate units to be recruited for the job of modeling the structure *among* the sememe units. They were therefore free to model the structure *between* the grapheme units and the sememe units.[9] The results described here were obtained using the preliminary learning stage and so they correspond to learning to associate grapheme strings with "meanings" that are already familiar.

The Performance of the Network

Using the same annealing schedule as was used during learning, the network can be tested by clamping a grapheme string and looking at the resulting activities of the sememe units. After 5000 learning sweeps, it gets the semantic features exactly correct 99.3% of the time. A performance level of 99.9% can be achieved by using a "careful" annealing schedule that spends twice as long at each temperature and goes down to half the final temperature.

The Effect of Local Damage

The learning procedure generates weights which cause each of the units in the intermediate layer to be used for many different words.

---

9 There was no need to have a similar stage for learning the structure among the grapheme units because in the main stage of learning the grapheme units are always clamped and so there is no tendency for the network to try to model the structure among them.

This kind of distributed representation should be more tolerant of local damage than the more obvious method of using one intermediate unit per word. We were particularly interested in the pattern of errors produced by local damage. If the connections between sememe units are left intact, they should be able to "clean up" patterns of activity that are close to familiar ones. So the network should still produce perfect output even if the input to the sememe units is slightly disrupted. If the disruption is more severe, the clean-up effect may actually produce a *different* familiar meaning that happens to share the few semantic features that were correctly activated by the intermediate layer.

To test these predictions we removed each of the intermediate units in turn, leaving the other 19 intact. We tested the network 25 times on each of the 20 words with each of the 20 units removed. In all 10,000 tests, using the careful annealing schedule, it made 140 errors (98.6% correct). Many errors consisted of the correct set of semantic features with one or two extra or missing features, but 83 of the errors consisted of the precise meaning of some other grapheme string. An analysis of these 83 errors showed that the hamming distance between the correct meanings and the erroneous ones had a mean of 9.34 and a standard deviation of 1.27 which is significantly lower ($p < .01$) than the complete set of hamming distances which had a mean of 10.30 and a standard deviation of 2.41. We also looked at the hamming distances between the grapheme strings that the network was given as input and the grapheme strings that corresponded to the erroneous familiar meanings. The mean was 3.95 and the standard deviation was 0.62 which is significantly lower ($p < .01$) than the complete set which had mean 5.53 and standard deviation 0.87. (A hamming distance of 4 means that the strings have one letter in common.)

In summary, when a single unit is removed from the intermediate layer, the network still performs well. The majority of its errors consist of producing exactly the meaning of some other grapheme string, and the erroneous meanings tend to be similar to the correct one and to be associated with a grapheme string that has one letter in common with the string used as input.

The Speed of Relearning

The original learning was very slow. Each item had to be presented 5000 times to eliminate almost all the errors. One reason for the slowness is the shape of the *G*-surface in weight-space. It tends to have long diagonal ravines which can be characterized in the following way: In the direction of steepest descent, the surface slopes steeply down for a short distance and then steeply up again (like the cross-section of a ravine).[10] In most other directions the surface slopes gently upwards. In a relatively narrow cone of directions, the surface slopes gently down with very low curvature. This narrow cone corresponds to the floor of the ravine and to get a low value of G (which is the definition of good performance) the learning must follow the floor of the ravine without going up the sides. This is particularly hard in a high-dimensional space. Unless the gradient of the surface is measured very accurately, a step in the direction of the *estimated* gradient will have a component along the floor of the ravine and a component up one of the many sides of the ravine. Because the sides are much steeper than the floor, the result of the step will be to raise the value of G which makes performance worse. Once out of the bottom of the ravine, almost all the measurable gradient will be down towards the floor of the ravine instead of along the ravine. As a result, the path followed in weight space tends to consist of an irregular sloshing across the ravine with only a small amount of forward progress. We are investigating ways of ameliorating this difficulty, but it is a well-known problem of gradient descent techniques in high-dimensional spaces, and it may be unavoidable.

The ravine problem leads to a very interesting prediction about relearning when random noise is added to the weights. The original learning takes the weights a considerable distance along a ravine which is slow and difficult because most directions in weight space are up the sides of the ravine. When a lot of random noise is added, there will typically be a small component along the ravine and a large component up the sides. Performance will therefore get much worse (because height in this space *means* poor performance), but relearning will be fast because the network can get back most of its performance by simply descending to the floor of the ravine (which is easy) without making progress along the ravine (which is hard).

The same phenomenon can be understood by considering the energy landscape rather than the weight-space (recall that one point in weight-space constitutes a whole energy landscape). Good performance requires a rather precise balance between the relative depths of the 20 energy minima and it also requires that all the 20 minima have considerably lower energy than other parts of the energy landscape. The balance between the minima in energy-space is the cross-section of the ravine in weight-space (see Figure 5) and the depth of all the minima compared with the rest of the energy landscape corresponds to the direction along the ravine. Random noise upsets the precise balance

---

10 The surface is never very steep. Its gradient parallel to any weight axis must always lie between 1 and -1 because it is the difference of two probabilities.

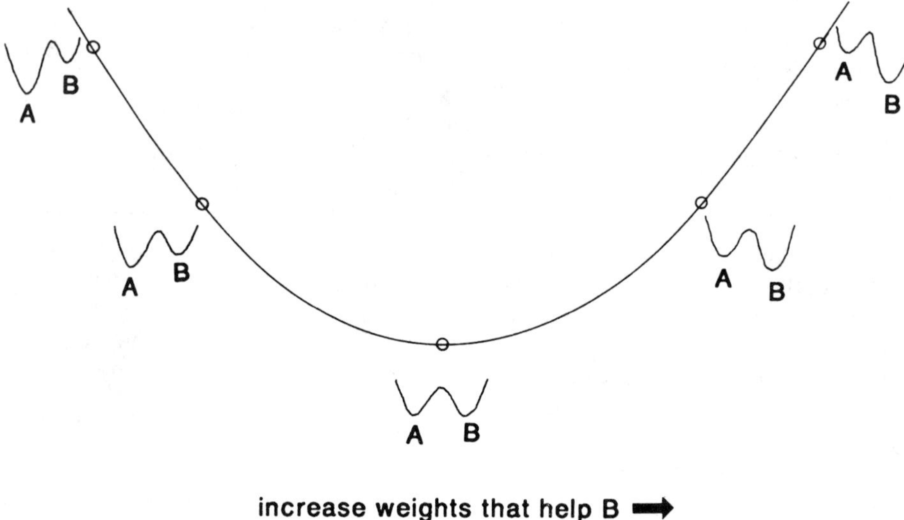

FIGURE 5. One cross-section of a ravine in weight-space. Each point in weight space corresponds to a whole energy landscape. To indicate this, we show how a very simple landscape changes as the weights are changed. Movement to the right along the x-axis corresponds to increasing the weights between pairs of units that are both on in state B and not both on in state A. This increases the depth of A. If the task requires that A and B have about the same depth, an imbalance between them will lower the performance and thus raise *G*.

between the various minima without significantly affecting the gross topography of the energy landscape. Relearning can then restore most of the performance by restoring the balance between the existing minima.

The simulation behaved as predicted. The mean absolute value of the weights connecting the intermediate units to the other two groups was 21.5. These weights were first perturbed by adding uniform random noise in the range −2 to +2. This had surprisingly little effect, reducing the performance using the normal annealing schedule from 99.3% to 98.0%. This shows that the network is robust against slight noise in the weights. To cause significant deterioration, uniform random noise between −22 and +22 was added. On average, this perturbs each weight by about half its magnitude which was enough to reduce normal performance to 64.3% correct. Figure 6 shows the course of the relearning and compares it with the speed of the original learning when performance was at this level. It also shows that other kinds of damage produce very similar relearning curves.

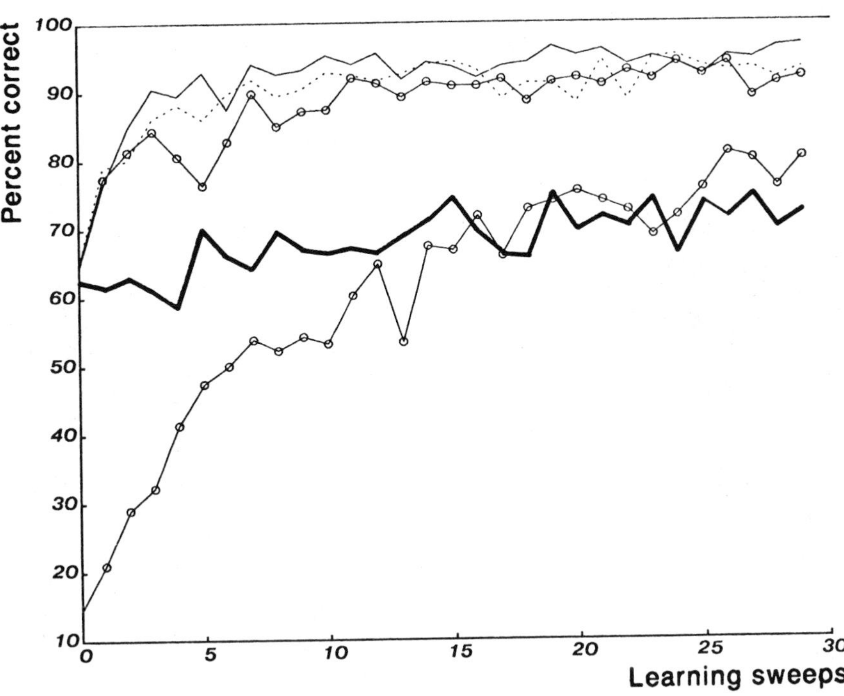

FIGURE 6. The recovery of performance after various types of damage. Each data-point represents 500 tests (25 with each word). The heavy line is a section of the original learning curve after a considerable number of learning sweeps. It shows that in the original learning, performance increases by less than 10% in 30 learning sweeps. All the other lines show recovery after damaging a net that had very good performance (99.3% correct). The lines with open circles show the rapid recovery after 20% or 50% of the weights to the hidden units have been set to zero (but allowed to relearn). The dashed line shows recovery after 5 of the 20 hidden units have been permanently ablated. The remaining line is the case when uniform random noise between −22 and +22 is added to all the connections to the hidden units. In all cases, a successful trial was defined as one in which the network produced *exactly* the correct semantic features when given the graphemic input.

Spontaneous Recovery of Unrehearsed Items

When it learns the associations, the network uses distributed representations among the intermediate units. This means that many of the weights are involved in encoding several different associations, and each association is encoded in many weights. If a weight is changed, it will affect several different energy minima and all of them will require the same change in the weight to restore them to their previous depths. So, in relearning any one of the associations, there should be a positive transfer effect which tends to restore the others. This effect is actually rather weak and is easily masked so it can only be seen clearly if we retrain the network on most of the original associations and watch what happens to the remaining few. As predicted, these showed a marked improvement even though they were only randomly related to the associations on which the network was retrained.

We took exactly the same perturbed network as before (uniform random noise between +22 and −22 added to the connections to and from the intermediate units) and retrained it on 18 of the associations for 30 learning sweeps. The two associations that were not retrained were selected to be ones where the network made frequent minor errors even when the careful annealing schedule was used. As a result of the retraining, the performance on these two items rose from 30/100 correct to 90/100 correct with the careful schedule, but the few errors that remained tended to be completely wrong answers rather than minor perturbations of the correct answer. We repeated the experiment selecting two associations for which the error rate was high and the errors were typically large. Retraining on the other 18 associations caused an improvement from 17/100 correct to 98/100 correct. Despite these impressive improvements, the effect disappeared when we retrained on only 15 of the associations. The remaining 5 actually got slightly worse. It is clear that the fraction of the associations which needs to be retrained to cause improvement in the remainder depends on how distributed the representations are, but more analysis is required to characterize this relationship properly.

The spontaneous recovery of unrehearsed items seems paradoxical because the set of 20 associations was randomly generated and so there is no way of generalizing from the 18 associations on which the network is retrained to the remaining two. During the original learning, however, the weights capture regularities in the whole set of associations. In this example, the regularities are spurious but the network doesn't know that—it just finds whatever regularities it can and expresses the associations in terms of them. Now, consider two different regularities that are equally strong among 18 of the associations. If one regularity also holds for the remaining two associations and the other doesn't, the first regularity is more likely to be captured by the weights. During retraining, the learning procedure restores the weights to the values needed to express the regularities it originally chose to capture and it therefore tends to restore the remaining associations.

It would be interesting to see if any of the neuro-psychological data on the effects of brain damage could be interpreted in terms of the kinds of qualitative effects exhibited by the simulation when it is damaged and relearns. However, we have not made any serious attempt to fit the simulation to particular data.

CONCLUSION

We have presented three ideas:

- Networks of symmetrically connected, binary units can escape from local minima during a relaxation search by using a stochastic decision rule.

- The process of reaching thermal equilibrium in a network of stochastic units propagates exactly the information needed to do credit assignment. This makes possible a *local* learning rule which can modify the weights so as to create new and useful feature detectors. The learning rule only needs to observe how often two units are both active (at thermal equilibrium) in two different phases. It can then change the weight between the units to make the spontaneous behavior of the network in one phase mimic the behavior that is forced on it in the other phase.

- The learning rule tends to construct distributed representations which are resistant to minor damage and exhibit rapid relearning after major damage. The relearning process can bring back associations that are not practiced during the relearning and are only randomly related to the associations that are practiced.

These three ideas can be assessed separately. In particular, resistance to damage, rapid relearning, and spontaneous recovery of unrehearsed items can be exhibited by other kinds of parallel network that use distributed representations. The use of stochastic units, annealing search, and the two-phase learning algorithm are not crucial for these properties, though they are a convenient testbed in which to investigate them. Hogg and Huberman (1984) have demonstrated self-repair effects in nonstochastic, layered networks similar to those used by Fukushima (1980).

We have left many loose ends, some of which are discussed elsewhere. Sejnowski and Hinton (in press) give a detailed example of a search problem where annealing helps, and they also discuss the relationship between between these networks and the mammalian cortex. Ackley, Hinton, and Sejnowski (1985) give a different example of learning in which the network constructs efficient internal codes for communicating information across narrow bandwidth channels. At present, the learning algorithm is too slow to be tested properly on large networks and future progress hinges on being able to speed it up.

ACKNOWLEDGMENTS

This research was supported by grants from the System Development Foundation. We thank David Ackley, Peter Brown, Francis Crick, Mark Derthick, Scott Fahlman, Stuart Geman, John Hopfield, Paul Kienker, Jay McClelland, Barak Pearlmutter, David Rumelhart, Tim Shallice, and Paul Smolensky for helpful discussions.

APPENDIX: DERIVATION OF THE LEARNING ALGORITHM

When a network is free-running at equilibrium the probability distribution over the visible units is given by

$$P^{-}(V_\alpha) = \sum_\beta P^{-}(V_\alpha \wedge H_\beta) = \frac{\sum_\beta e^{-E_{\alpha\beta}/T}}{\sum_{\lambda\mu} e^{-E_{\lambda\mu}/T}} \tag{8}$$

where V_α is a vector of the states of the visible units, H_β is a vector of states of the hidden units, and $E_{\alpha\beta}$ is the energy of the system in state $V_\alpha \wedge H_\beta$

$$E_{\alpha\beta} = -\sum_{i<j} w_{ij}\, s_i^{\alpha\beta}\, s_j^{\alpha\beta}.$$

Hence,

$$\frac{\partial e^{-E_{\alpha\beta}/T}}{\partial w_{ij}} = \frac{1}{T} s_i^{\alpha\beta}\, s_j^{\alpha\beta}\, e^{-E_{\alpha\beta}/T}.$$

Differentiating (8) then yields

$$\frac{\partial P^{-}(V_\alpha)}{\partial w_{ij}} = \frac{\frac{1}{T}\sum_\beta e^{-E_{\alpha\beta}/T} s_i^{\alpha\beta} s_j^{\alpha\beta}}{\sum_{\alpha\beta} e^{-E_{\alpha\beta}/T}} - \frac{\sum_\beta e^{-E_{\alpha\beta}/T}\frac{1}{T}\sum_{\lambda\mu} e^{-E_{\lambda\mu}/T} s_i^{\lambda\mu} s_j^{\lambda\mu}}{\left(\sum_{\lambda\mu} e^{-E_{\lambda\mu}/T}\right)^2}$$

$$= \frac{1}{T}\left[\sum_\beta P^{-}(V_\alpha \wedge H_\beta) s_i^{\alpha\beta} s_j^{\alpha\beta} - P^{-}(V_\alpha)\sum_{\lambda\mu} P^{-}(V_\lambda \wedge H_\mu) s_i^{\lambda\mu} s_j^{\lambda\mu}\right].$$

This derivative is used to compute the gradient of the G-measure

$$G = \sum_\alpha P^{+}(V_\alpha) \ln \frac{P^{+}(V_\alpha)}{P^{-}(V_\alpha)}$$

where $P^{+}(V_\alpha)$ is the clamped probability distribution over the visible units and is independent of w_{ij}. So

$$\frac{\partial G}{\partial w_{ij}} = -\sum_\alpha \frac{P^{+}(V_\alpha)}{P^{-}(V_\alpha)} \frac{\partial P^{-}(V_\alpha)}{\partial w_{ij}}$$

$$= -\frac{1}{T}\left[\sum_{\alpha} \frac{P^{+}(V_{\alpha})}{P^{-}(V_{\alpha})} \sum_{\beta} P^{-}(V_{\alpha} \wedge H_{\beta}) s_i^{\alpha\beta} s_j^{\alpha\beta} - \right.$$

$$\left. \sum_{\alpha} \frac{P^{+}(V_{\alpha})}{P^{-}(V_{alpha})} P^{-}(V_{\alpha}) \sum_{\lambda\mu} P^{-}(V_{\lambda} \wedge H_{\mu}) s_i^{\lambda\mu} s_j^{\lambda\mu} \right].$$

Now,

$$P^{+}(V_{\alpha} \wedge H_{\beta}) = P^{+}(H_{\beta} \mid V_{\alpha}) P^{+}(V_{\alpha}),$$

$$P^{-}(V_{\alpha} \wedge H_{\beta}) = P^{-}(H_{\beta} \mid V_{\alpha}) P^{-}(V_{\alpha}),$$

and

$$P^{-}(H_{\beta} \mid V_{\alpha}) = P^{+}(H_{\beta} \mid V_{\alpha}). \tag{9}$$

Equation 9 holds because the probability of a hidden state given some visible state must be the same in equilibrium whether the visible units were clamped in that state or arrived there by free-running. Hence,

$$P^{-}(V_{\alpha} \wedge H_{\beta}) \frac{P^{+}(V_{\alpha})}{P^{-}(V_{\alpha})} = P^{+}(V_{\alpha} \wedge H_{\beta}).$$

Also,

$$\sum_{\alpha} P^{+}(V_{\alpha}) = 1.$$

Therefore,

$$\frac{\partial G}{\partial w_{ij}} = -\frac{1}{T}[p_{ij}^{+} - p_{ij}^{-}]$$

where

$$p_{ij}^{+} \equiv \sum_{\alpha\beta} P^{+}(V_{\alpha} \wedge H_{\beta}) s_i^{\alpha\beta} s_j^{\alpha\beta}$$

and

$$p_{ij}^{-} \equiv \sum_{\lambda\mu} P^{-}(V_{\lambda} \wedge H_{\mu}) s_i^{\lambda\mu} s_j^{\lambda\mu}.$$

The Boltzmann machine learning algorithm can also be formulated as an input-output model. The visible units are divided into an input set I and an output set O, and an environment specifies a set of conditional probabilities of the form $P^{+}(O_{\beta} \mid I_{\alpha})$. During *phase*$^{+}$ the environment clamps both the input and output units, and the p_{ij}^{+}s are estimated. During *phase*$^{-}$ the input units are clamped and the output units and hidden units free-run, and the p_{ij}^{-}s are estimated. The appropriate G measure in this case is

$$G = \sum_{\alpha\beta} P^{+}(I_\alpha \wedge O_\beta) \ln \frac{P^{+}(O_\beta \mid I_\alpha)}{P^{-}(O_\beta \mid I_\alpha)}.$$

Similar mathematics apply in this formulation and $\partial G / \partial w_{ij}$ is the same as before.

CHAPTER 8

Learning Internal Representations by Error Propagation

D. E. RUMELHART, G. E. HINTON, and R. J. WILLIAMS

THE PROBLEM

We now have a rather good understanding of simple two-layer associative networks in which a set of input patterns arriving at an input layer are mapped directly to a set of output patterns at an output layer. Such networks have no *hidden* units. They involve only *input* and *output* units. In these cases there is no *internal representation.* The coding provided by the external world must suffice. These networks have proved useful in a wide variety of applications (cf. Chapters 2, 17, and 18). Perhaps the essential character of such networks is that they map similar input patterns to similar output patterns. This is what allows these networks to make reasonable generalizations and perform reasonably on patterns that have never before been presented. The similarity of patterns in a PDP system is determined by their overlap. The overlap in such networks is determined outside the learning system itself—by whatever produces the patterns.

The constraint that similar input patterns lead to similar outputs can lead to an inability of the system to learn certain mappings from input to output. Whenever the representation provided by the outside world is such that the similarity structure of the input and output patterns are very different, a network without internal representations (i.e., a network without hidden units) will be unable to perform the necessary mappings. A classic example of this case is the *exclusive-or* (XOR) problem illustrated in Table 1. Here we see that those patterns which overlap least are supposed to generate identical output values. This problem and many others like it cannot be performed by networks without hidden units with which to create their own internal representations of the input patterns. It is interesting to note that had the input patterns contained a third input taking the value 1 whenever the first two have value 1 as shown in Table 2, a two-layer system would be able to solve the problem.

Minsky and Papert (1969) have provided a very careful analysis of conditions under which such systems are capable of carrying out the required mappings. They show that in a large number of interesting cases, networks of this kind are incapable of solving the problems. On the other hand, as Minsky and Papert also pointed out, if there is a layer of simple perceptron-like hidden units, as shown in Figure 1, with which the original input pattern can be augmented, there is always a recoding (i.e., an internal representation) of the input patterns in the hidden units in which the similarity of the patterns among the hidden units can support any required mapping from the input to the output units. Thus, if we have the right connections from the input units to a large enough set of hidden units, we can always find a representation that will perform any mapping from input to output through these hidden units. In the case of the XOR problem, the addition of a feature that detects the conjunction of the input units changes the similarity

TABLE 1

Input Patterns		Output Patterns
00	→	0
01	→	1
10	→	1
11	→	0

TABLE 2

Input Patterns		Output Patterns
000	→	0
010	→	1
100	→	1
111	→	0

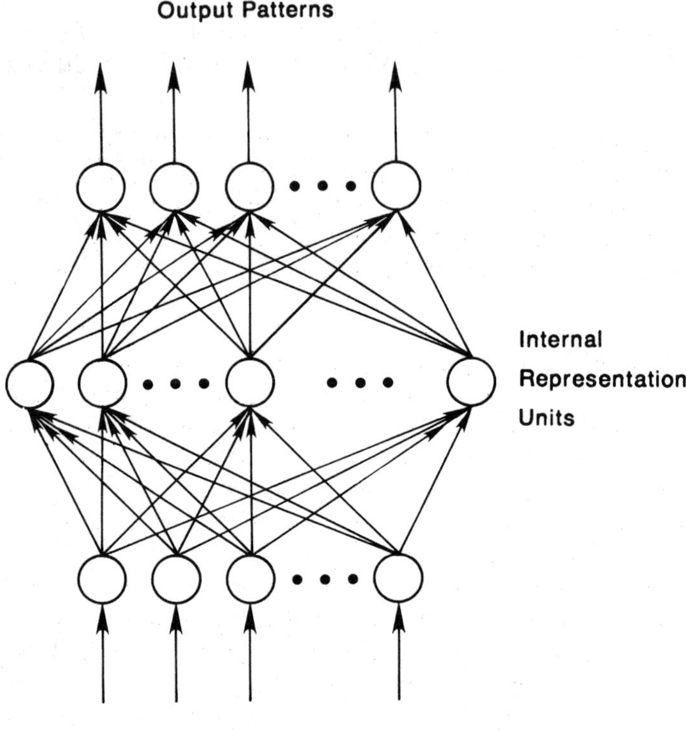

FIGURE 1. A multilayer network. In this case the information coming to the input units is *recoded* into an internal representation and the outputs are generated by the internal representation rather than by the original pattern. Input patterns can always be encoded, if there are enough hidden units, in a form so that the appropriate output pattern can be generated from any input pattern.

structure of the patterns sufficiently to allow the solution to be learned. As illustrated in Figure 2, this can be done with a single hidden unit. The numbers on the arrows represent the strengths of the connections among the units. The numbers written in the circles represent the thresholds of the units. The value of +1.5 for the threshold of the hidden unit insures that it will be turned on only when both input units are on. The value 0.5 for the output unit insures that it will turn on only when it receives a net positive input greater than 0.5. The weight of −2 from the hidden unit to the output unit insures that the output unit will not come on when both input units are on. Note that from the point of view of the output unit, the hidden unit is treated as simply another input unit. It is as if the input patterns consisted of three rather than two units.

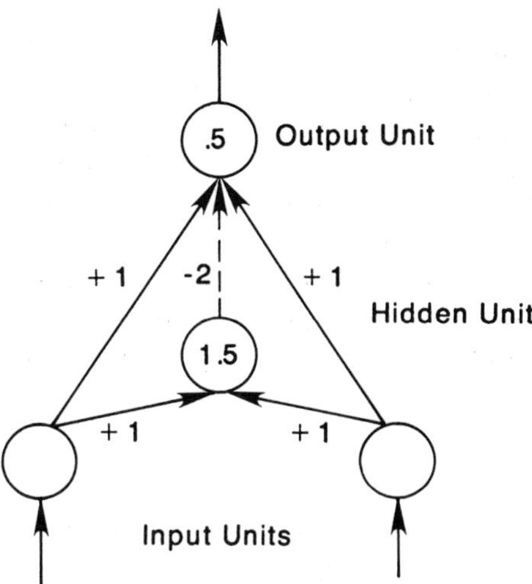

FIGURE 2. A simple XOR network with one hidden unit. See text for explanation.

The existence of networks such as this illustrates the potential power of hidden units and internal representations. The problem, as noted by Minsky and Papert, is that whereas there is a very simple guaranteed learning rule for all problems that can be solved without hidden units, namely, the perceptron convergence procedure (or the variation due originally to Widrow and Hoff, 1960, which we call the delta rule; see Chapter 11), there is no equally powerful rule for learning in networks with hidden units. There have been three basic responses to this lack. One response is represented by competitive learning (Chapter 5) in which simple *unsupervised* learning rules are employed so that useful hidden units develop. Although these approaches are promising, there is no external force to *insure* that hidden units appropriate for the required mapping are developed. The second response is to simply *assume* an internal representation that, on some a priori grounds, seems reasonable. This is the tack taken in the chapter on verb learning (Chapter 18) and in the interactive activation model of word perception (McClelland & Rumelhart, 1981; Rumelhart & McClelland, 1982). The third approach is to attempt to *develop* a learning procedure capable of learning an internal representation adequate for performing the task at hand. One such development is presented in the discussion of Boltzmann machines in Chapter 7. As we have seen, this procedure involves the use of stochastic units, requires the network to reach equilibrium in two different phases, and is limited to symmetric networks. Another recent approach, also employing stochastic units, has been developed by Barto (1985) and various of his colleagues (cf. Barto

& Anandan, 1985). In this chapter we present another alternative that works with deterministic units, that involves only local computations, and that is a clear generalization of the delta rule. We call this the *generalized delta rule.* From other considerations, Parker (1985) has independently derived a similar generalization, which he calls *learning-logic.* Le Cun (1985) has also studied a roughly similar learning scheme. In the remainder of this chapter we first derive the generalized delta rule, then we illustrate its use by providing some results of our simulations, and finally we indicate some further generalizations of the basic idea.

THE GENERALIZED DELTA RULE

The learning procedure we propose involves the presentation of a set of pairs of input and output patterns. The system first uses the input vector to produce its own output vector and then compares this with the *desired output*, or *target* vector. If there is no difference, no learning takes place. Otherwise the weights are changed to reduce the difference. In this case, with no hidden units, this generates the standard delta rule as described in Chapters 2 and 11. The rule for changing weights following presentation of input/output pair p is given by

$$\Delta_p w_{ji} = \eta (t_{pj} - o_{pj})\, i_{pi} = \eta \delta_{pj} i_{pi} \tag{1}$$

where t_{pj} is the target input for jth component of the output pattern for pattern p, o_{pj} is the jth element of the actual output pattern produced by the presentation of input pattern p, i_{pi} is the value of the ith element of the input pattern, $\delta_{pj} = t_{pj} - o_{pj}$, and $\Delta_p w_{ij}$ is the change to be made to the weight from the ith to the jth unit following presentation of pattern p.

The delta rule and gradient descent. There are many ways of deriving this rule. For present purposes, it is useful to see that for linear units it minimizes the squares of the differences between the actual and the desired output values summed over the output units and all pairs of input/output vectors. One way to show this is to show that the derivative of the error measure with respect to each weight is proportional to the weight change dictated by the delta rule, with negative constant of proportionality. This corresponds to performing steepest descent on a surface in weight space whose height at any point in weight space is equal to the error measure. (Note that some of the following sections are written in italics. These sections constitute informal derivations of the claims made in the surrounding text and can be omitted by the reader who finds such derivations tedious.)

To be more specific, then, let

$$E_p = \frac{1}{2}\sum_j (t_{pj} - o_{pj})^2 \tag{2}$$

be our measure of the error on input/output pattern p *and let* $E = \sum E_p$ *be our overall measure of the error. We wish to show that the delta rule implements a gradient descent in* E *when the units are linear. We will proceed by simply showing that*

$$-\frac{\partial E_p}{\partial w_{ji}} = \delta_{pj} i_{pi},$$

which is proportional to $\Delta_p w_{ji}$ *as prescribed by the delta rule. When there are no hidden units it is straightforward to compute the relevant derivative. For this purpose we use the chain rule to write the derivative as the product of two parts: the derivative of the error with respect to the output of the unit times the derivative of the output with respect to the weight.*

$$\frac{\partial E_p}{\partial w_{ji}} = \frac{\partial E_p}{\partial o_{pj}} \frac{\partial o_{pj}}{\partial w_{ji}}. \tag{3}$$

The first part tells how the error changes with the output of the j*th unit and the second part tells how much changing* w_{ji} *changes that output. Now, the derivatives are easy to compute. First, from Equation 2*

$$\frac{\partial E_p}{\partial o_{pj}} = -(t_{pj} - o_{pj}) = -\delta_{pj}. \tag{4}$$

Not surprisingly, the contribution of unit u_j *to the error is simply proportional to* δ_{pj}*. Moreover, since we have linear units,*

$$o_{pj} = \sum_i w_{ji} i_{pi}, \tag{5}$$

from which we conclude that

$$\frac{\partial o_{pj}}{\partial w_{ji}} = i_{pi}.$$

Thus, substituting back into Equation 3, we see that

$$-\frac{\partial E_p}{\partial w_{ji}} = \delta_{pj} i_{pi} \tag{6}$$

as desired. Now, combining this with the observation that

$$\frac{\partial E}{\partial w_{ji}} = \sum_p \frac{\partial E_p}{\partial w_{ji}}$$

should lead us to conclude that the net change in w_{ji} *after one complete cycle of pattern presentations is proportional to this derivative and hence that the delta rule implements a gradient descent in* E. *In fact, this is strictly true only if the values of the weights are not changed during this cycle. By changing the weights after each pattern is presented we depart to some extent from a true gradient descent in* E. *Nevertheless, provided the learning rate (i.e., the constant of proportionality) is sufficiently small, this departure will be negligible and the delta rule will implement a very close approximation to gradient descent in sum-squared error. In particular, with small enough learning rate, the delta rule will find a set of weights minimizing this error function.*

The delta rule for semilinear activation functions in feedforward networks. We have shown how the standard delta rule essentially implements gradient descent in sum-squared error for linear activation functions. In this case, without hidden units, the error surface is shaped like a bowl with only one minimum, so gradient descent is guaranteed to find the best set of weights. With hidden units, however, it is not so obvious how to compute the derivatives, and the error surface is not concave upwards, so there is the danger of getting stuck in local minima. The main theoretical contribution of this chapter is to show that there is an efficient way of computing the derivatives. The main empirical contribution is to show that the apparently fatal problem of local minima is irrelevant in a wide variety of learning tasks.

At the end of the chapter we show how the generalized delta rule can be applied to arbitrary networks, but, to begin with, we confine ourselves to *layered feedforward* networks. In these networks, the input units are the bottom layer and the output units are the top layer. There can be many layers of hidden units in between, but every unit must send its output to higher layers than its own and must receive its input from lower layers than its own. Given an input vector, the output vector is computed by a forward pass which computes the activity levels of each layer in turn using the already computed activity levels in the earlier layers.

Since we are primarily interested in extending this result to the case with hidden units and since, for reasons outlined in Chapter 2, hidden units with linear activation functions provide no advantage, we begin by generalizing our analysis to the set of nonlinear activation functions which we call *semilinear* (see Chapter 2). A semilinear activation function is one in which the output of a unit is a nondecreasing and differentiable function of the net total output,

$$net_{pj} = \sum_i w_{ji} o_{pi}, \tag{7}$$

where $o_i = i_i$ if unit i is an input unit. Thus, a semilinear activation function is one in which

$$o_{pj} = f_j(net_{pj}) \tag{8}$$

and f is differentiable and nondecreasing. The generalized delta rule works if the network consists of units having semilinear activation functions. Notice that linear threshold units do not satisfy the requirement because their derivative is infinite at the threshold and zero elsewhere.

To get the correct generalization of the delta rule, we must set

$$\Delta_p w_{ji} \propto -\frac{\partial E_p}{\partial w_{ji}},$$

where E is the same sum-squared error function defined earlier. As in the standard delta rule it is again useful to see this derivative as resulting from the product of two parts: one part reflecting the change in error as a function of the change in the net input to the unit and one part representing the effect of changing a particular weight on the net input. Thus we can write

$$\frac{\partial E_p}{\partial w_{ji}} = \frac{\partial E_p}{\partial net_{pj}} \frac{\partial net_{pj}}{\partial w_{ji}}. \tag{9}$$

By Equation 7 we see that the second factor is

$$\frac{\partial net_{pj}}{\partial w_{ji}} = \frac{\partial}{\partial w_{ji}} \sum_k w_{jk} o_{pk} = o_{pi}. \tag{10}$$

Now let us define

$$\delta_{pj} = -\frac{\partial E_p}{\partial net_{pj}}.$$

(By comparing this to Equation 4, note that this is consistent with the definition of δ_{pj} used in the original delta rule for linear units since $o_{pj} = net_{pj}$ when unit u_j is linear.) Equation 9 thus has the equivalent form

$$-\frac{\partial E_p}{\partial w_{ji}} = \delta_{pj} o_{pi}.$$

This says that to implement gradient descent in E we should make our weight changes according to

$$\Delta_p w_{ji} = \eta \delta_{pj} o_{pi}, \tag{11}$$

just as in the standard delta rule. The trick is to figure out what δ_{pj} should be for each unit u_j in the network. The interesting result, which we now derive, is that there is a simple recursive computation of these δ's which can be implemented by propagating error signals backward through the network.

To compute $\delta_{pj} = -\frac{\partial E_p}{\partial net_{pj}}$, we apply the chain rule to write this partial derivative as the product of two factors, one factor reflecting the change in error as a function of the output of the unit and one reflecting the change in the output as a function of changes in the input. Thus, we have

$$\delta_{pj} = -\frac{\partial E_p}{\partial net_{pj}} = -\frac{\partial E_p}{\partial o_{pj}} \frac{\partial o_{pj}}{\partial net_{pj}}. \tag{12}$$

Let us compute the second factor. By Equation 8 we see that

$$\frac{\partial o_{pj}}{\partial net_{pj}} = f'_j(net_{pj}),$$

which is simply the derivative of the squashing function f_j for the jth unit, evaluated at the net input net_{pj} to that unit. To compute the first factor, we consider two cases. First, assume that unit u_j is an output unit of the network. In this case, it follows from the definition of E_p that

$$\frac{\partial E_p}{\partial o_{pj}} = -(t_{pj} - o_{pj}),$$

which is the same result as we obtained with the standard delta rule. Substituting for the two factors in Equation 12, we get

$$\delta_{pj} = (t_{pj} - o_{pj}) f'_j(net_{pj}) \tag{13}$$

for any output unit u_j. If u_j is not an output unit we use the chain rule to write

$$\sum_k \frac{\partial E_p}{\partial net_{pk}} \frac{\partial net_{pk}}{\partial o_{pj}} = \sum_k \frac{\partial E_p}{\partial net_{pk}} \frac{\partial}{\partial o_{pj}} \sum_i w_{ki} o_{pi} = \sum_k \frac{\partial E_p}{\partial net_{pk}} w_{kj} = -\sum_k \delta_{pk} w_{kj}.$$

In this case, substituting for the two factors in Equation 12 yields

$$\delta_{pj} = f'_j(net_{pj}) \sum_k \delta_{pk} w_{kj} \tag{14}$$

whenever u_j is not an output unit. Equations 13 and 14 give a recursive procedure for computing the δ's for all units in the network, which are then used to compute the weight changes in the network according to Equation 11. This procedure constitutes the generalized delta rule for a feedforward network of semilinear units.

These results can be summarized in three equations. First, the generalized delta rule has exactly the same form as the standard delta rule of Equation 1. The weight on each line should be changed by an amount proportional to the product of an error signal, δ, available to the unit receiving input along that line and the output of the unit sending activation along that line. In symbols,

$$\Delta_p w_{ji} = \eta \delta_{pj} o_{pi}.$$

The other two equations specify the error signal. Essentially, the determination of the error signal is a recursive process which starts with the output units. If a unit is an output unit, its error signal is very similar to the standard delta rule. It is given by

$$\delta_{pj} = (t_{pj} - o_{pj}) f'_j (net_{pj})$$

where $f'_j(net_{pj})$ is the derivative of the semilinear activation function which maps the total input to the unit to an output value. Finally, the error signal for hidden units for which there is no specified target is determined recursively in terms of the error signals of the units to which it directly connects and the weights of those connections. That is,

$$\delta_{pj} = f'_j (net_{pj}) \sum_k \delta_{pk} w_{kj}$$

whenever the unit is not an output unit.

The application of the generalized delta rule, thus, involves two phases: During the first phase the input is presented and propagated forward through the network to compute the output value o_{pj} for each unit. This output is then compared with the targets, resulting in an error signal δ_{pj} for each output unit. The second phase involves a backward pass through the network (analogous to the initial forward pass) during which the error signal is passed to each unit in the network and the appropriate weight changes are made. This second, backward pass allows the recursive computation of δ as indicated above. The first step is to compute δ for each of the output units. This is simply the difference between the actual and desired output values times the derivative of the squashing function. We can then compute weight changes for all connections that feed into the final layer. After this is done, then compute δ's for all units in the penultimate layer. This propagates the errors back one layer, and the same process can be repeated for every layer. The backward pass has the same computational complexity as the forward pass, and so it is not unduly expensive.

We have now generated a gradient descent method for finding weights in any feedforward network with semilinear units. Before reporting our results with these networks, it is useful to note some further observations. It is interesting that not all weights need be variable. Any number of weights in the network can be fixed. In this case, error is still propagated as before; the fixed weights are simply not modified. It should also be noted that there is no reason why some output units might not receive inputs from other output units in earlier layers. In this case, those units receive two different kinds of error: that from the direct comparison with the target and that passed through the other output units whose activation it affects. In this case, the correct procedure is to simply add the weight changes dictated by the direct comparison to that propagated back from the other output units.

SIMULATION RESULTS

We now have a learning procedure which could, in principle, evolve a set of weights to produce an arbitrary mapping from input to output. However, the procedure we have produced is a gradient descent procedure and, as such, is bound by all of the problems of any hill climbing procedure—namely, the problem of local maxima or (in our case) minima. Moreover, there is a question of how long it might take a system to learn. Even if we could guarantee that it would eventually find a solution, there is the question of whether our procedure could learn in a reasonable period of time. It is interesting to ask what hidden units the system actually develops in the solution of particular problems. This is the question of what kinds of internal representations the system actually creates. We do not yet have definitive answers to these questions. However, we have carried out many simulations which lead us to be optimistic about the local minima and time questions and to be surprised by the kinds of representations our learning mechanism discovers. Before proceeding with our results, we must describe our simulation system in more detail. In particular, we must specify an activation function and show how the system can compute the derivative of this function.

A useful activation function. In our above derivations the derivative of the activation function of unit u_j, $f'_j(net_j)$, always played a role. This implies that we need an activation function for which a derivative exists. It is interesting to note that the linear threshold function, on which the perceptron is based, is discontinuous and hence will not suffice for the generalized delta rule. Similarly, since a linear system achieves no advantage from hidden units, a linear activation function will not suffice either. Thus, we need a continuous, nonlinear activation function. In most of our experiments we have used the *logistic* activation function in which

$$o_{pj} = \frac{1}{1 + e^{-(\sum_i w_{ji} o_{pi} + \theta_j)}} \tag{15}$$

where θ_j is a bias similar in function to a threshold.[1] In order to apply our learning rule, we need to know the derivative of this function with respect to its total input, net_{pj}, where $net_{pj} = \sum w_{ji} o_{pi} + \theta_j$. It is easy to show that this derivative is given by

$$\frac{\partial o_{pj}}{\partial net_{pj}} = o_{pj}(1 - o_{pj}).$$

Thus, for the logistic activation function, the error signal, δ_{pj}, for an output unit is given by

$$\delta_{pj} = (t_{pj} - o_{pj}) o_{pj}(1 - o_{pj}),$$

and the error for an arbitrary hidden u_j is given by

$$\delta_{pj} = o_{pj}(1 - o_{pj}) \sum_k \delta_{pk} w_{kj}.$$

It should be noted that the derivative, $o_{pj}(1 - o_{pj})$, reaches its maximum for $o_{pj} = 0.5$ and, since $0 \leqslant o_{pj} \leqslant 1$, approaches its minimum as o_{pj} approaches zero or one. Since the amount of change in a given weight is proportional to this derivative, weights will be changed most for those units that are near their midrange and, in some sense, not yet committed to being either on or off. This feature, we believe, contributes to the stability of the learning of the system.

One other feature of this activation function should be noted. The system can not actually reach its extreme values of 1 or 0 without infinitely large weights. Therefore, in a practical learning situation in which the desired outputs are binary $\{0,1\}$, the system can never actually achieve these values. Therefore, we typically use the values of 0.1 and 0.9 as the targets, even though we will talk as if values of $\{0,1\}$ are sought.

The learning rate. Our learning procedure requires only that the change in weight be proportional to $\partial E_p / \partial w$. True gradient descent requires that infinitesimal steps be taken. The constant of proportionality is the learning rate in our procedure. The larger this constant, the larger the changes in the weights. For practical purposes we choose a

---

[1] Note that the values of the bias, θ_j, can be learned just like any other weights. We simply imagine that θ_j is the weight from a unit that is always on.

learning rate that is as large as possible without leading to oscillation. This offers the most rapid learning. One way to increase the learning rate without leading to oscillation is to modify the generalized delta rule to include a *momentum* term. This can be accomplished by the following rule:

$$\Delta w_{ji}(n+1) = \eta(\delta_{pj} o_{pi}) + \alpha \Delta w_{ji}(n) \tag{16}$$

where the subscript n indexes the presentation number, η is the learning rate, and α is a constant which determines the effect of past weight changes on the current direction of movement in weight space. This provides a kind of momentum in weight space that effectively filters out high-frequency variations of the error-surface in the weight space. This is useful in spaces containing long ravines that are characterized by sharp curvature across the ravine and a gently sloping floor. The sharp curvature tends to cause divergent oscillations across the ravine. To prevent these it is necessary to take very small steps, but this causes very slow progress along the ravine. The momentum filters out the high curvature and thus allows the effective weight steps to be bigger. In most of our simulations α was about 0.9. Our experience has been that we get the same solutions by setting $\alpha = 0$ and reducing the size of η, but the system learns much faster overall with larger values of α and η.

Symmetry breaking. Our learning procedure has one more problem that can be readily overcome and this is the problem of symmetry breaking. If all weights start out with equal values and if the solution requires that unequal weights be developed, the system can never learn. This is because error is propagated back through the weights in proportion to the values of the weights. This means that all hidden units connected directly to the output inputs will get identical error signals, and, since the weight changes depend on the error signals, the weights from those units to the output units must always be the same. The system is starting out at a kind of *local maximum,* which keeps the weights equal, but it is a maximum of the error function, so once it escapes it will never return. We counteract this problem by starting the system with small random weights. Under these conditions symmetry problems of this kind do not arise.

The XOR Problem

It is useful to begin with the exclusive-or problem since it is the classic problem requiring hidden units and since many other difficult problems involve an XOR as a subproblem. We have run the XOR problem many times and with a couple of exceptions discussed below, the system has always solved the problem. Figure 3 shows one of the solutions to the problem. This solution was reached after 558 sweeps through the four stimulus patterns with a learning rate of $\eta = 0.5$. In this case, both the hidden unit and the output unit have *positive biases* so they are on unless turned off. The hidden unit turns on if neither input unit is on. When it is on, it turns off the output unit. The connections from input to output units arranged themselves so that they turn off the output unit whenever both inputs are on. In this case, the network has settled to a solution which is a sort of mirror image of the one illustrated in Figure 2.

We have taught the system to solve the XOR problem hundreds of times. Sometimes we have used a single hidden unit and direct connections to the output unit as illustrated here, and other times we have allowed two hidden units and set the connections from the input units to the outputs to be zero, as shown in Figure 4. In only two cases has the system encountered a *local minimum* and thus been unable to solve the problem. Both cases involved the two hidden units version of the

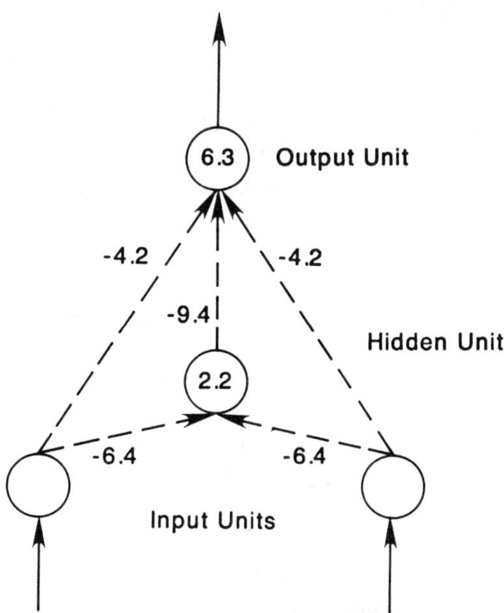

FIGURE 3. Observed XOR network. The connection weights are written on the arrows and the biases are written in the circles. Note a positive bias means that the unit is on unless turned off.

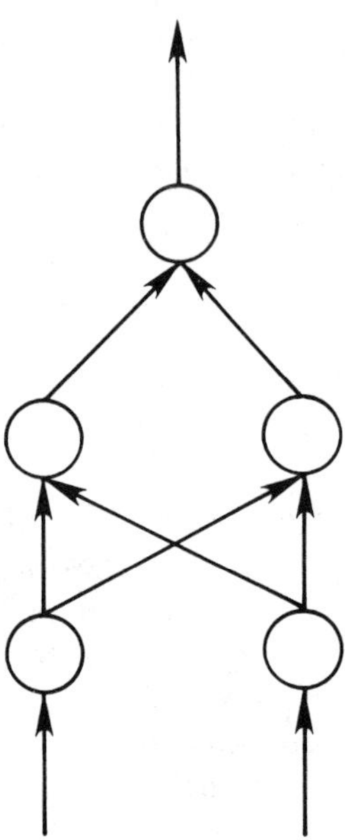

FIGURE 4. A simple architecture for solving XOR with two hidden units and no direct connections from input to output.

problem and both ended up in the same local minimum. Figure 5 shows the weights for the local minimum. In this case, the system correctly responds to two of the patterns—namely, the patterns 00 and 10. In the cases of the other two patterns 11 and 01, the output unit gets a net input of zero. This leads to an output value of 0.5 for both of these patterns. This state was reached after 6,587 presentations of each pattern with η=0.25.[2] Although many problems require more presentations for learning to occur, further trials on this problem merely increase the magnitude of the weights but do not lead to any improvement in performance. We do not know the frequency of such local minima, but our experience with this and other problems is that they are quite rare. We have found only one other situation in which a local minimum has occurred in many hundreds of problems of various sorts. We will discuss this case below.

The XOR problem has proved a useful test case for a number of other studies. Using the architecture illustrated in Figure 4, a student in our laboratory, Yves Chauvin, has studied the effect of varying the

[2] If we set $\eta = 0.5$ or above, the system escapes this minimum. In general, however, the best way to avoid local minima is probably to use very small values of η.

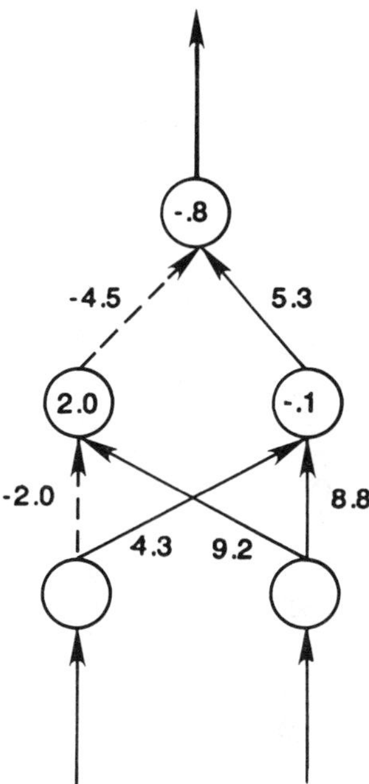

FIGURE 5. A network at a local minimum for the exclusive-or problem. The dotted lines indicate negative weights. Note that whenever the right most input unit is on it turns on *both* hidden units. The weights connecting the hidden units to the output are arranged so that when both hidden units are on, the output unit gets a net input of zero. This leads to an output value of 0.5. In the other cases the network provides the correct answer.

number of hidden units and varying the learning rate on time to solve the problem. Using as a learning criterion an error of 0.01 per pattern, Yves found that the average number of presentations to solve the problem with $\eta = 0.25$ varied from about 245 for the case with two hidden units to about 120 presentations for 32 hidden units. The results can be summarized by $P = 280 - 33\log_2 H$, where P is the required number of presentations and H is the number of hidden units employed. Thus, the time to solve XOR is reduced linearly with the logarithm of the number of hidden units. This result holds for values of H up to about 40 in the case of XOR. The general result that the time to solution is reduced by increasing the number of hidden units has been observed in virtually all of our simulations. Yves also studied the time to solution as a function of learning rate for the case of eight hidden units. He found an average of about 450 presentations with $\eta = 0.1$ to about 68 presentations with $\eta = 0.75$. He also found that learning rates larger than this led to unstable behavior. However, within this range larger learning rates speeded the learning substantially. In most of our problems we have employed learning rates of $\eta = 0.25$ or smaller and have had no difficulty.

Parity

One of the problems given a good deal of discussion by Minsky and Papert (1969) is the parity problem, in which the output required is 1 if the input pattern contains an odd number of 1s and 0 otherwise. This is a very difficult problem because the most similar patterns (those which differ by a single bit) require different answers. The XOR problem is a parity problem with input patterns of size two. We have tried a number of parity problems with patterns ranging from size two to eight. Generally we have employed layered networks in which direct connections from the input to the output units are not allowed, but must be mediated through a set of hidden units. In this architecture, it requires at least N hidden units to solve parity with patterns of length N. Figure 6 illustrates the basic paradigm for the solutions discovered by the system. The solid lines in the figure indicate weights of $+1$ and the dotted lines indicate weights of -1. The numbers in the circles represent the biases of the units. Basically, the hidden units arranged

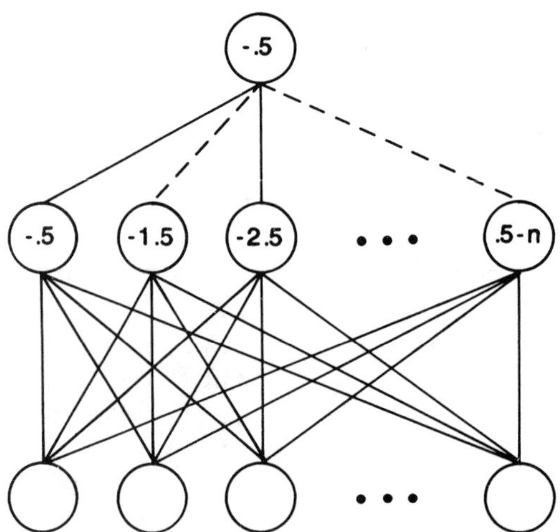

FIGURE 6. A paradigm for the solutions to the parity problem discovered by the learning system. See text for explanation.

themselves so that they count the number of inputs. In the diagram, the one at the far left comes on if one or more input units are on, the next comes on if two or more are on, etc. All of the hidden units come on if all of the input lines are on. The first m hidden units come on whenever m bits are on in the input pattern. The hidden units then connect with alternately positive and negative weights. In this way the net input from the hidden units is zero for even numbers and +1 for odd numbers. Table 3 shows the actual solution attained for one of our simulations with four input lines and four hidden units. This solution was reached after 2,825 presentations of each of the sixteen patterns with $\eta = 0.5$. Note that the solution is roughly a mirror image of that shown in Figure 6 in that the number of hidden units turned on is equal to the number of zero input values rather than the number of ones. Beyond that the principle is that shown above. It should be noted that the internal representation created by the learning rule is to arrange that the number of hidden units that come on is equal to the number of zeros in the input and that the particular hidden units that come on depend *only* on the number, not on which input units are on. This is exactly the sort of recoding *required* by parity. It is not the kind of representation readily discovered by unsupervised learning schemes such as competitive learning.

The Encoding Problem

Ackley, Hinton, and Sejnowski (1985) have posed a problem in which a set of orthogonal input patterns are mapped to a set of orthogonal output patterns through a small set of hidden units. In such cases the internal representations of the patterns on the hidden units must be rather efficient. Suppose that we attempt to map N input patterns onto N output patterns. Suppose further that $\log_2 N$ hidden units are provided. In this case, we expect that the system will learn to use the

TABLE 3

Number of *On* Input Units		Hidden Unit Patterns		Output Value
0	→	1111	→	0
1	→	1011	→	1
2	→	1010	→	0
3	→	0010	→	1
4	→	0000	→	0

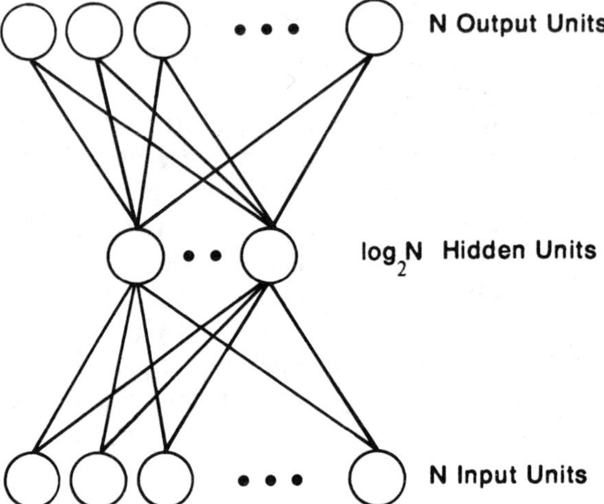

FIGURE 7. A network for solving the encoder problem. In this problem there are N orthogonal input patterns each paired with one of N orthogonal output patterns. There are only $\log_2 N$ hidden units. Thus, if the hidden units take on binary values, the hidden units must form a binary number to encode each of the input patterns. This is exactly what the system learns to do.

hidden units to form a binary code with a distinct binary pattern for each of the N input patterns. Figure 7 illustrates the basic architecture for the encoder problem. Essentially, the problem is to learn an encoding of an N bit pattern into a $\log_2 N$ bit pattern and then learn to decode this representation into the output pattern. We have presented the system with a number of these problems. Here we present a problem with eight input patterns, eight output patterns, and three hidden units. In this case the required mapping is the identity mapping illustrated in Table 4. The problem is simply to turn on the same bit in the

TABLE 4

Input Patterns		Output Patterns
10000000	→	10000000
01000000	→	01000000
00100000	→	00100000
00010000	→	00010000
00001000	→	00001000
00000100	→	00000100
00000010	→	00000010
00000001	→	00000001

output as in the input. Table 5 shows the mapping generated by our learning system on this example. It is of some interest that the system employed its ability to use intermediate values in solving this problem. It could, of course, have found a solution in which the hidden units took on only the values of zero and one. Often it does just that, but in this instance, and many others, there are solutions that use the intermediate values, and the learning system finds them even though it has a bias toward extreme values. It is possible to set up problems that *require* the system to make use of intermediate values in order to solve a problem. We now turn to such a case.

Table 6 shows a very simple problem in which we have to convert from a *distributed representation* over two units into a *local representation* over four units. The similarity structure of the distributed input patterns is simply not preserved in the local output representation.

We presented this problem to our learning system with a number of constraints which made it especially difficult. The two input units were only allowed to connect to a single hidden unit which, in turn, was allowed to connect to four more hidden units. Only these four hidden units were allowed to connect to the four output units. To solve this problem, then, the system must first convert the distributed

TABLE 5

Input Patterns		Hidden Unit Patterns				Output Patterns
10000000	→	.5	0	0	→	10000000
01000000	→	0	1	0	→	01000000
00100000	→	1	1	0	→	00100000
00010000	→	1	1	1	→	00010000
00001000	→	0	1	1	→	00001000
00000100	→	.5	0	1	→	00000100
00000010	→	1	0	.5	→	00000010
00000001	→	0	0	.5	→	00000001

TABLE 6

Input Patterns		Output Patterns
00	→	1000
01	→	0100
10	→	0010
11	→	0001

representation of the input patterns into various intermediate values of the singleton hidden unit in which different activation values correspond to the different input patterns. These continuous values must then be converted back through the next layer of hidden units—first to another distributed representation and then, finally, to a local representation. This problem was presented to the system and it reached a solution after 5,226 presentations with $\eta = 0.05$.[3] Table 7 shows the sequence of representations the system actually developed in order to transform the patterns and solve the problem. Note each of the four input patterns was mapped onto a particular activation value of the singleton hidden unit. These values were then mapped onto distributed patterns at the next layer of hidden units which were finally mapped into the required local representation at the output level. In principle, this trick of mapping patterns into activation values and then converting those activation values back into patterns could be done for any number of patterns, but it becomes increasingly difficult for the system to make the necessary distinctions as ever smaller differences among activation values must be distinguished. Figure 8 shows the network the system developed to do this job. The connection weights from the hidden units to the output units have been suppressed for clarity. (The sign of the connection, however, is indicated by the form of the connection—e.g., dashed lines mean inhibitory connections). The four different activation values were generated by having relatively large weights of opposite sign. One input line turns the hidden unit full on, one turns it full off. The two differ by a relatively small amount so that when both turn on, the unit attains a value intermediate between 0 and 0.5. When neither turns on, the near zero bias causes the unit to attain a value slightly over 0.5. The connections to the second layer of hidden units is likewise interesting. When the hidden unit is full on,

TABLE 7

Input Patterns		Singleton Hidden Unit		Remaining Hidden Units		Output Patterns
10	→	0	→	1 1 1 0	→	0010
11	→	.2	→	1 1 0 0	→	0001
00	→	.6	→	.5 0 0 .3	→	1000
01	→	1	→	0 0 0 1	→	0100

[3] Relatively small learning rates make units employing intermediate values easier to obtain.

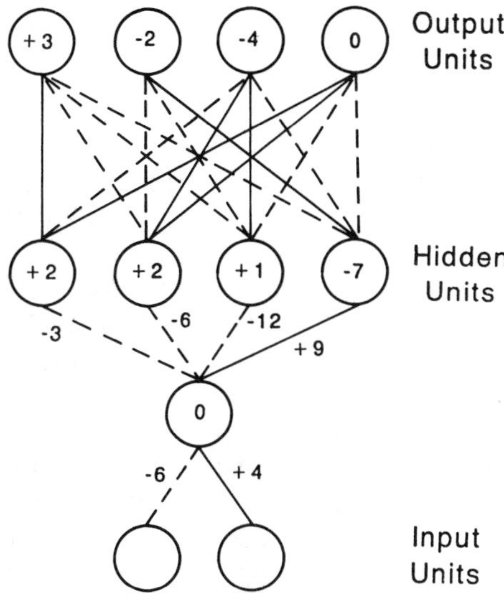

FIGURE 8. The network illustrating the use of intermediate values in solving a problem. See text for explanation.

the right-most of these hidden units is turned on and all others turned off. When the hidden unit is turned off, the other three of these hidden units are on and the left-most unit off. The other connections from the singleton hidden unit to the other hidden units are graded so that a distinct pattern is turned on for its other two values. Here we have an example of the flexibility of the learning system.

Our experience is that there is a propensity for the hidden units to take on extreme values, but, whenever the learning problem calls for it, they can learn to take on graded values. It is likely that the propensity to take on extreme values follows from the fact that the logistic is a sigmoid so that increasing magnitudes of its inputs push it toward zero or one. This means that in a problem in which intermediate values are required, the incoming weights must remain of moderate size. It is interesting that the derivation of the generalized delta rule does not depend on all of the units having identical activation functions. Thus, it would be possible for some units, those required to encode information in a graded fashion, to be linear while others might be logistic. The linear unit would have a much wider dynamic range and could encode more different values. This would be a useful role for a linear unit in a network with hidden units.

Symmetry

Another interesting problem we studied is that of classifying input strings as to whether or not they are symmetric about their center. We used patterns of various lengths with various numbers of hidden units. To our surprise, we discovered that the problem can always be solved with only two hidden units. To understand the derived representation, consider one of the solutions generated by our system for strings of length six. This solution was arrived at after 1,208 presentations of each six-bit pattern with $\eta = 0.1$. The final network is shown in Figure 9. For simplicity we have shown the six input units in the center of the diagram with one hidden unit above and one below. The output unit, which signals whether or not the string is symmetric about its center, is shown at the far right. The key point to see about this solution is that for a given hidden unit, weights that are symmetric about the middle are equal in magnitude and opposite in sign. That means that if a symmetric pattern is on, both hidden units will receive a net input of zero from the input units, and, since the hidden units have a negative bias, both will be off. In this case, the output unit, having a positive bias,

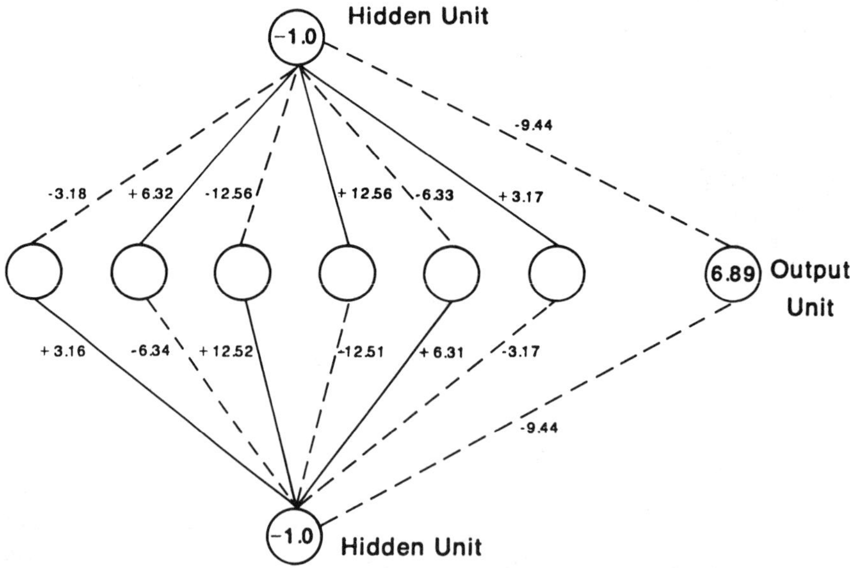

FIGURE 9. Network for solving the symmetry problem. The six open circles represent the input units. There are two hidden units, one shown above and one below the input units. The output unit is shown to the far right. See text for explanation.

will be on. The next most important thing to note about the solution is that the weights on each side of the midpoint of the string are in the ratio of 1:2:4. This insures that each of the eight patterns that can occur on each side of the midpoint sends a unique activation sum to the hidden unit. This assures that there is no pattern on the left that will exactly balance a non-mirror-image pattern on the right. Finally, the two hidden units have identical patterns of weights from the input units except for sign. This insures that for every nonsymmetric pattern, at least one of the two hidden units will come on and turn on the output unit. To summarize, the network is arranged so that both hidden units will receive exactly zero activation from the input units when the pattern is symmetric, and at least one of them will receive positive input for every nonsymmetric pattern.

This problem was interesting to us because the learning system developed a much more elegant solution to the problem than we had previously considered. This problem was not the only one in which this happened. The parity solution discovered by the learning procedure was also one that we had not discovered prior to testing the problem with our learning procedure. Indeed, we frequently discover these more elegant solutions by giving the system more hidden units than it needs and observing that it does not make use of some of those provided. Some analysis of the actual solutions discovered often leads us to the discovery of a better solution involving fewer hidden units.

Addition

Another interesting problem on which we have tested our learning algorithm is the simple binary addition problem. This problem is interesting because there is a very elegant solution to it, because it is the one problem we have found where we can reliably find local minima and because the way of avoiding these local minima gives us some insight into the conditions under which local minima may be found and avoided. Figure 10 illustrates the basic problem and a minimal solution to it. There are four input units, three output units, and two hidden units. The output patterns can be viewed as the binary representation of the sum of two two-bit binary numbers represented by the input patterns. The second and fourth input units in the diagram correspond to the low-order bits of the two binary numbers and the first and third units correspond to the two higher order bits. The hidden units correspond to the *carry bits* in the summation. Thus the hidden unit on the far right comes on when both of the lower order bits in the input pattern are turned on, and the one on the left comes

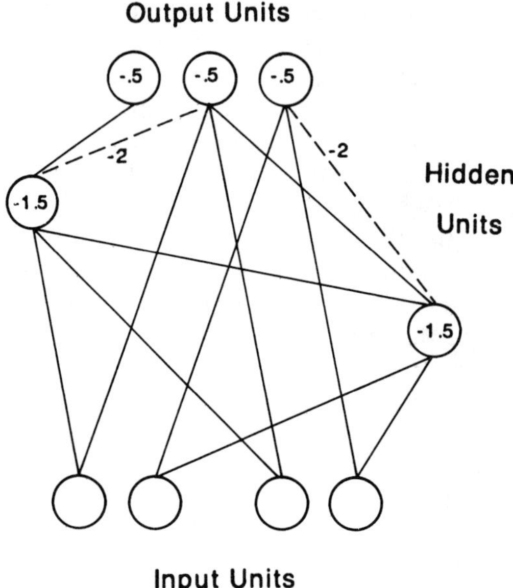

FIGURE 10. Minimal network for adding two two-bit binary numbers. There are four input units, three output units, and two hidden units. The output patterns can be viewed as the binary representation of the sum of two two-bit binary numbers represented by the input patterns. The second and fourth input units in the diagram correspond to the low-order bits of the two binary numbers, and the first and third units correspond to the two higher order bits. The hidden units correspond to the carry bits in the summation. The hidden unit on the far right comes on when both of the lower order bits in the input pattern are turned on, and the one on the left comes on when both higher order bits are turned on or when one of the higher order bits and the other hidden unit is turned on. The weights on all lines are assumed to be +1 except where noted. Negative connections are indicated by dashed lines. As usual, the biases are indicated by the numbers in the circles.

on when both higher order bits are turned on or when one of the higher order bits and the other hidden unit is turned on. In the diagram, the weights on all lines are assumed to be +1 except where noted. Inhibitory connections are indicated by dashed lines. As usual, the biases are indicated by the numbers in the circles. To understand how this network works, it is useful to note that the lowest order output bit is determined by an exclusive-or among the two low-order input bits. One way to solve this XOR problem is to have a hidden unit come on when both low-order input bits are on and then have it inhibit the output unit. Otherwise either of the low-order input units can turn on the low-order output bit. The middle bit is somewhat more difficult. Note that the middle bit should come on whenever an odd number of the set containing the two higher order input bits and the lower order carry bit is turned on. Observation will confirm that the network shown performs that task. The left-most hidden unit receives inputs from the two higher order bits and from the carry bit. Its bias is such that it will come on whenever two or more of its inputs are turned on. The middle output unit receives positive inputs from the same three units and a negative input of -2 from the second hidden unit. This insures that whenever just one of the three are turned on, the second hidden unit will remain off and the output bit will come on. Whenever exactly two of the three are on, the hidden unit will turn on and counteract the two units exciting the output bit, so it will stay off. Finally, when all three are turned on, the output bit will receive -2 from its carry bit and $+3$ from its other three inputs. The net is positive, so the middle unit will be on. Finally, the third output bit should turn on whenever the second hidden unit is on—that is, whenever there is a carry from the second bit. Here then we have a minimal network to carry out the job at hand. Moreover, it should be noted that the concept behind this network is generalizable to an arbitrary number of input and output bits. In general, for adding two m bit binary numbers we will require $2m$ input units, m hidden units, and $m+1$ output units.

Unfortunately, this is the one problem we have found that reliably leads the system into local minima. At the start in our learning trials on this problem we allow any input unit to connect to any output unit and to any hidden unit. We allow any hidden unit to connect to any output unit, and we allow one of the hidden units to connect to the other hidden unit, but, since we can have no loops, the connection in the opposite direction is disallowed. Sometimes the system will discover essentially the same network shown in the figure.[4] Often, however, the system ends up in a local minimum. The problem arises when the XOR problem on the low-order bits is not solved in the way shown in the diagram. One way it can fail is when the "higher" of the two hidden units is "selected" to solve the XOR problem. This is a problem because then the other hidden unit cannot "see" the carry bit and therefore cannot finally solve the problem. This problem seems to stem from the fact that the learning of the second output bit is always dependent on learning the first (because information about the carry is necessary to learn the second bit) and therefore lags behind the learning of the first bit and has no influence on the selection of a hidden unit to

[4] The network is the same except for the highest order bit. The highest order bit is always on whenever three or more of the input units are on. This is always learned first and always learned with direct connections to the input units.

solve the first XOR problem. Thus, about half of the time (in this problem) the wrong unit is chosen and the problem cannot be solved. In this case, the system finds a solution for all of the sums except the 11+11 → 110 (3+3 = 6) case in which it misses the carry into the middle bit and gets 11+11 → 100 instead. This problem differs from others we have solved in as much as the hidden units are not "equipotential" here. In most of our other problems the hidden units have been equipotential, and this problem has not arisen.

It should be noted, however, that there is a relatively simple way out of the problem--namely, add some extra hidden units. In this case we can afford to make a mistake on one or more selections and the system can still solve the problems. For the problem of adding two-bit numbers we have found that the system always solves the problem with one extra hidden unit. With larger numbers it may require two or three more. For purposes of illustration, we show the results of one of our runs with three rather than the minimum two hidden units. Figure 11 shows the state reached by the network after 3,020 presentations of each input pattern and with a learning rate of $\eta = 0.5$. For convenience, we show the network in four parts. In Figure 11A we show the connections to and among the hidden units. This figure shows the internal representation generated for this problem. The "lowest" hidden unit turns off whenever either of the low-order bits are on. In other words it detects the case in which no low-order bit is turn on. The "highest" hidden unit is arranged so that it comes on whenever the sum is less than two. The conditions under which the middle hidden unit comes on are more complex. Table 8 shows the patterns of hidden units which occur to each of the sixteen input patterns. Figure 11B shows the connections to the lowest order output unit. Noting that the relevant hidden unit comes on when neither low-order input unit is on, it is clear how the system computes XOR. When both low-order inputs are off, the output unit is turned off by the hidden unit. When both low-order input units are on, the output is turned off directly by the two input units. If just one is on, the positive bias on the output unit keeps it on. Figure 11C gives the connections to the middle output unit, and in Figure 11D we show those connections to the left-most, highest order output unit. It is somewhat difficult to see how these connections always lead to the correct output answer, but, as can be verified from the figures, the network is balanced so that this works.

It should be pointed out that most of the problems described thus far have involved hidden units with quite simple interpretations. It is much more often the case, especially when the number of hidden units exceeds the minimum number required for the task, that the hidden units are not readily interpreted. This follows from the fact that there is very little tendency for *localist* representations to develop. Typically

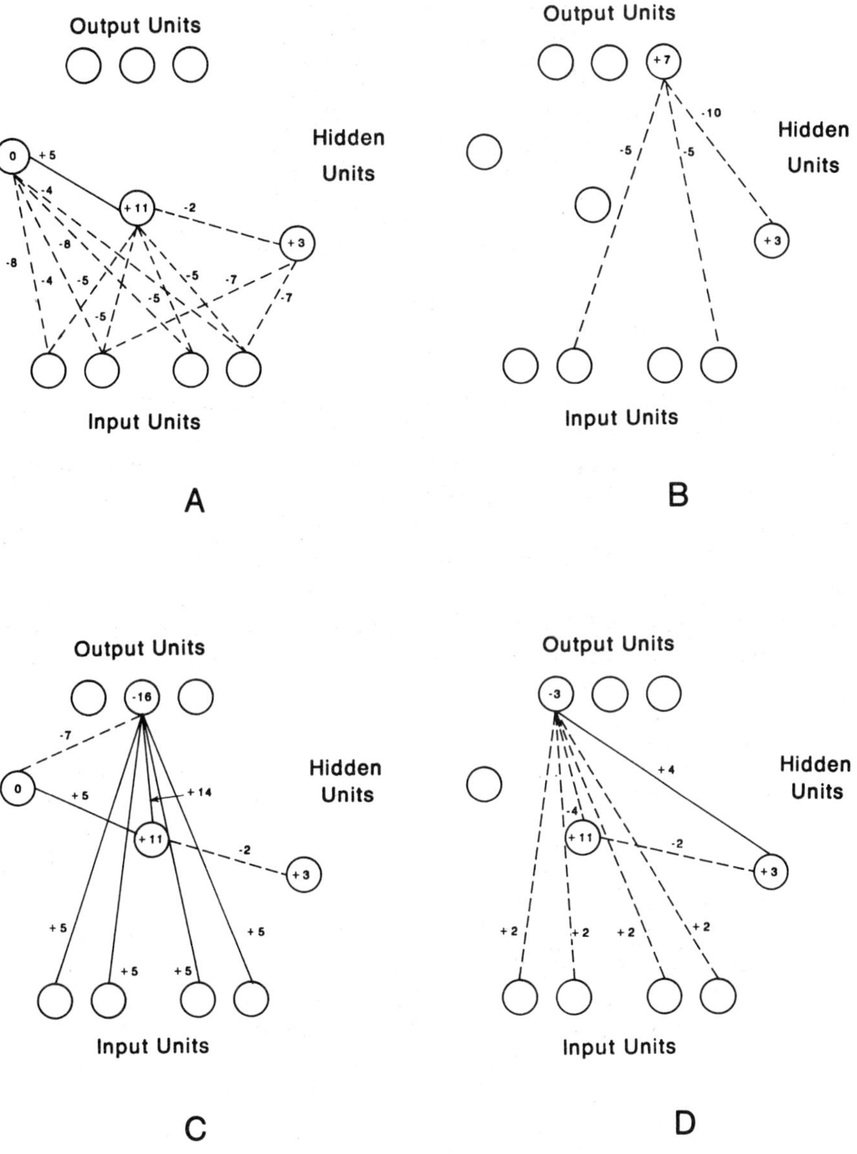

FIGURE 11. Network found for the summation problem. *A*: The connections from the input units to the three hidden units and the connections among the hidden units. *B*: The connections from the input and hidden units to the lowest order output unit. *C*: The connections from the input and hidden units to the middle output unit. *D*: The connections from the input and hidden units to the highest order output unit.

TABLE 8

Input Patterns		Hidden Unit Patterns		Output Patterns
00 + 00	→	111	→	000
00 + 01	→	110	→	001
00 + 10	→	011	→	010
00 + 11	→	010	→	011
01 + 00	→	110	→	001
01 + 01	→	010	→	010
01 + 10	→	010	→	011
01 + 11	→	000	→	100
10 + 00	→	011	→	010
10 + 01	→	010	→	011
10 + 10	→	001	→	100
10 + 11	→	000	→	101
11 + 00	→	010	→	011
11 + 01	→	000	→	100
11 + 10	→	000	→	101
11 + 11	→	000	→	110

the internal representations are distributed and it is the *pattern* of activity over the hidden units, not the meaning of any particular hidden unit that is important.

The Negation Problem

Consider a situation in which the input to a system consists of patterns of $n+1$ binary values and an output of n values. Suppose further that the general rule is that n of the input units should be mapped directly to the output patterns. One of the input bits, however, is special. It is a negation bit. When that bit is off, the rest of the pattern is supposed to map straight through, but when it is on, the complement of the pattern is to be mapped to the output. Table 9 shows the appropriate mapping. In this case the left element of the input pattern is the negation bit, but the system has no way of knowing this and must learn which bit is the negation bit. In this case, weights were allowed from any input unit to any hidden or output unit and from any hidden unit to any output unit. The system learned to set all of the weights to zero except those shown in Figure 12. The basic structure of the problem and of the solution is evident in the figure. Clearly the problem was reduced to a set of three XORs between the negation bit

TABLE 9

Input Patterns		Output Patterns
0000	→	000
0001	→	001
0010	→	010
0011	→	011
0100	→	100
0101	→	101
0110	→	110
0111	→	111
1000	→	111
1001	→	110
1010	→	101
1011	→	100
1100	→	011
1101	→	010
1110	→	001
1111	→	000

and each input. In the case of the two right-most input units, the XOR problems were solved by recruiting a hidden unit to detect the case in which *neither* the negation unit *nor* the corresponding input unit was on. In the third case, the hidden unit detects the case in which *both* the negation unit *and* relevant input were on. In this case the problem was solved in less than 5,000 passes through the stimulus set with $\eta = 0.25$.

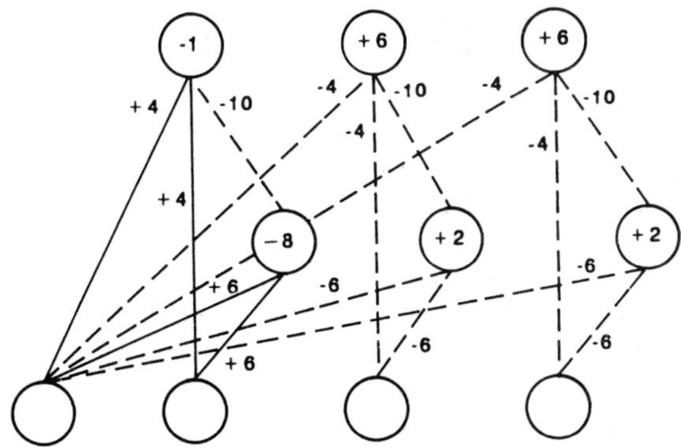

FIGURE 12. The solution discovered for the negation problem. The left-most unit is the negation unit. The problem has been reduced and solved as three exclusive-ors between the negation unit and each of the other three units.

The T-C Problem

Most of the problems discussed so far (except the symmetry problem) are rather abstract mathematical problems. We now turn to a more geometric problem—that of discriminating between a *T* and a *C*—independent of translation and rotation. Figure 13 shows the stimulus patterns used in these experiments. Note, these patterns are each made of five squares and differ from one another by a single square. Moreover, as Minsky and Papert (1969) point out, when considering the set of patterns over all possible translations and rotations (of 90°, 180°, and 270°), the patterns do not differ in the set of distances among their pairs of squares. To see a difference between the sets of patterns one must look, at least, at configurations of triplets of squares. Thus Minsky and Papert call this a problem of *order three.*[5] In order to facilitate the learning, a rather different architecture was employed for this problem. Figure 14 shows the basic structure of the network we employed. Input patterns were now conceptualized as two-dimensional patterns superimposed on a rectangular grid. Rather than allowing each input unit to connect to each hidden unit, the hidden units themselves were organized into a two-dimensional grid with each unit receiving input from a square 3×3 region of the input space. In this sense, the overlapping square regions constitute the predefined *receptive field* of the hidden units. Each of the hidden units, over the entire field, feeds into a single output unit which is to take on the value

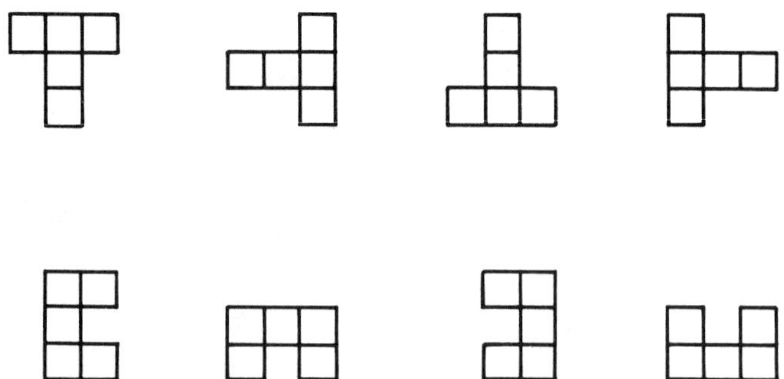

FIGURE 13. The stimulus set for the T-C problem. The set consists of a block *T* and a block *C* in each of four orientations. One of the eight patterns is presented on each trial.

[5] Terry Sejnowski pointed out to us that the T-C problem was difficult for models of this sort to learn and therefore worthy of study.

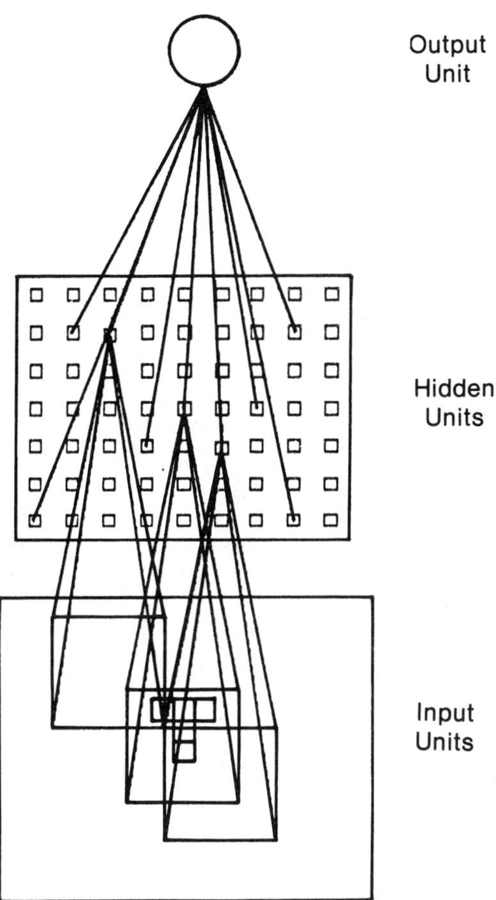

FIGURE 14. The network for solving the T-C problem. See text for explanation.

1 if the input is a *T* (at any location or orientation) and 0 if the input is a *C*. Further, in order that the learning that occurred be independent of where on the field the pattern appeared, we constrained all of the units to learn exactly the same pattern of weights. In this way each unit was constrained to compute exactly the same function over its receptive field—the receptive fields were constrained to all have the same shape. This guarantees translation independence and avoids any possible "edge effects" in the learning. The learning can readily be extended to arbitrarily large fields of input units. This constraint was accomplished by simply adding together the weight changes dictated by the delta rule for each unit and then changing all weights exactly the same amount. In

this way, the whole field of hidden units consists simply of replications of a single feature detector centered on different regions of the input space, and the learning that occurs in one part of the field is automatically generalized to the rest of the field.[6]

We have run this problem in this way a number of times. As a result, we have found a number of solutions. Perhaps the simplest way to understand the system is by looking at the form of the receptive field for the hidden units. Figure 15 shows several of the receptive fields we have seen.[7] Figure 15A shows the most local representation developed. This *on-center–off-surround* detector turns out to be an excellent *T* detector. Since, as illustrated, a *T* can extend into the on-center and achieve a net input of +1, this detector will be turned on for a *T* at any orientation. On the other hand, any *C* extending into the center must cover at least *two* inhibitory cells. With this detector the bias can be set so that only one of the whole field of inhibitory units will come on whenever a *T* is presented and none of the hidden units will be turned on by any *C*. This is a kind of *protrusion* detector which differentiates between a *T* and *C* by detecting the protrusion of the *T*.

The receptive field shown in Figure 15B is again a kind of *T* detector. Every *T* activates one of the hidden units by an amount +2 and none of the hidden units receives more than +1 from any of the *C*'s. As shown in the figure, *T*'s at 90° and 270° send a total of +2 to the hidden units on which the crossbar lines up. The *T*'s at the other two orientations receive +2 from the way it detects the vertical protrusions of those two characters. Figure 15C shows a more distributed representation. As illustrated in the figure, each *T* activates five different hidden units whereas each *C* excites only three hidden units. In this case the system again is differentiating between the characters on the basis of the protruding end of the *T* which is not shared by the *C*.

Finally, the receptive field shown in Figure 15D is even more interesting. In this case every hidden unit has a positive bias so that it is on unless turned off. The strength of the inhibitory weights are such that if a character overlaps the receptive field of a hidden unit, that unit turns off. The system works because a *C* is more compact than a *T* and therefore the *T* turns off more units that the *C*. The *T* turns off 21 hidden units, and the *C* turns off only 20. This is a truly distributed

---

6 A similar procedure has been employed by Fukushima (1980) in his *neocognitron* and by Kienker, Sejnowski, Hinton, and Schumacher (1985).

7 The ratios of the weights are about right. The actual values can be larger or smaller than the values given in the figure.

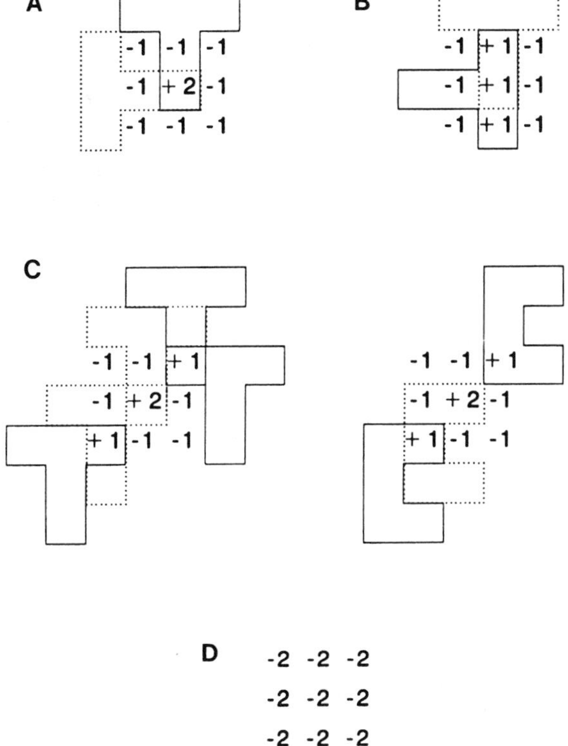

FIGURE 15. Receptive fields found in different runs of the T-C problem. *A*: An on-center-off-surround receptive field for detecting *T*'s. *B*: A vertical bar detector which responds to *T*'s more strongly than *C*'s. *C*: A diagonal bar detector. A *T* activates five such detectors whereas a *C* activates only three such detectors. *D*: A compactness detector. This inhibitory receptive field turns off whenever an input covers any region of its receptive field. Since the *C* is more compact than the *T* it turns off 20 such detectors whereas the *T* turns off 21 of them.

representation. In each case, the solution was reached in from about 5,000 to 10,000 presentations of the set of eight patterns.[8]

It is interesting that the inhibitory type of receptive field shown in Figure 15D was the most common and that there is a predominance of inhibitory connections in this and indeed all of our simulations. This can be understood by considering the trajectory through which the learning typically moves. At first, when the system is presented with a

[8] Since translation independence was built into the learning procedure, it makes no difference *where* the input occurs; the same thing will be learned wherever the pattern is presented. Thus, there are only eight distinct patterns to be presented to the system.

difficult problem, the initial random connections are as likely to mislead as to give the correct answer. In this case, it is best for the output units to take on a value of 0.5 than to take on a more extreme value. This follows from the form of the error function given in Equation 2. The output unit can achieve a constant output of 0.5 by turning off those units feeding into it. Thus, the first thing that happens in virtually every difficult problem is that the hidden units are turned off. One way to achieve this is to have the input units inhibit the hidden units. As the system begins to sort things out and to learn the appropriate function some of the connections will typically go positive, but the majority of the connections will remain negative. This *bias* for solutions involving inhibitory inputs can often lead to nonintuitive results in which hidden units are often on unless turned off by the input.

More Simulation Results

We have offered a sample of our results in this section. In addition to having studied our learning system on the problems discussed here, we have employed back propagation for learning to multiply binary digits, to play tic-tac-toe, to distinguish between vertical and horizontal lines, to perform sequences of actions, to recognize characters, to associate random vectors, and a host of other applications. In all of these applications we have found that the generalized delta rule was capable of generating the kinds of internal representations required for the problems in question. We have found local minima to be very rare and that the system learns in a reasonable period of time. Still more studies of this type will be required to understand precisely the conditions under which the system will be plagued by local minima. Suffice it to say that the problem has not been serious to date. We now turn to a pointer to some future developments.

SOME FURTHER GENERALIZATIONS

We have intensively studied the learning characteristics of the generalized delta rule on feedforward networks and semilinear activations functions. Interestingly these are not the most general cases to which the learning procedure is applicable. As yet we have only studied a few examples of the more fully generalized system, but it is relatively easy to apply the same learning rule to sigma-pi units and to recurrent networks. We will simply sketch the basic ideas here.

The Generalized Delta Rule and Sigma-Pi Units

It will be recalled from Chapter 2 that in the case of sigma-pi units we have

$$o_j = f_j\left(\sum_i w_{ji} \prod_k o_{i_k}\right) \tag{17}$$

where i varies over the set of conjuncts feeding into unit j and k varies over the elements of the conjuncts. For simplicity of exposition, we restrict ourselves to the case in which no conjuncts involve more than two elements. In this case we can notate the weight from the conjunction of units i and j to unit k by w_{kij}. The weight on the direct connection from unit i to unit j would, thus, be w_{jii}, and since the relation is multiplicative, $w_{kij} = w_{kji}$. We can now rewrite Equation 17 as

$$o_j = f_j\left(\sum_{i,h} w_{jhi}\, o_h\, o_i\right).$$

We now set

$$\Delta_p w_{kij} \propto -\frac{\partial E_p}{\partial w_{kij}}.$$

Taking the derivative and simplifying, we get a rule for sigma-pi units strictly analogous to the rule for semilinear activation functions:

$$\Delta_p w_{kij} = \delta_k\, o_i\, o_j.$$

We can see the correct form of the error signal, δ, for this case by inspecting Figure 16. Consider the appropriate value of δ_i for unit u_i in the figure. As before, the correct value of δ_i is given by the sum of the δ's for all of the units into which u_i feeds, weighted by the amount of effect due to the activation of u_i times the derivative of the activation function. In the case of semilinear functions, the measure of a unit's effect on another unit is given simply by the weight w connecting the first unit to the second. In this case, the u_i's effect on u_k depends not only on w_{kij}, but also on the value of u_j. Thus, we have

$$\delta_i = f'_i(net_i) \sum_{j,k} \delta_k\, w_{kij}\, o_j$$

if u_i is not an output unit and, as before,

$$\delta_i = f'_i(net_i)(t_i - o_i)$$

if it is an output unit.

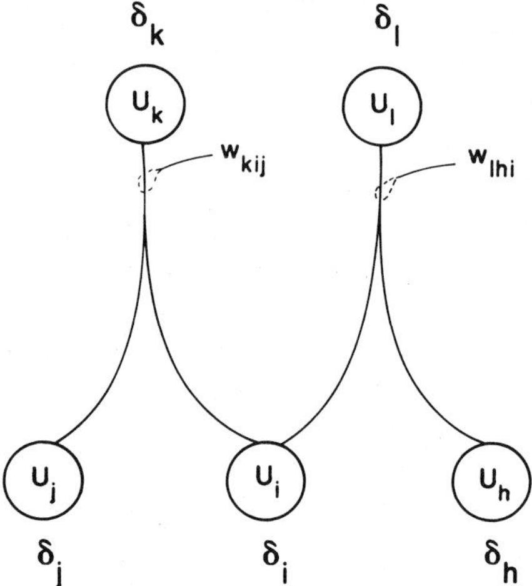

FIGURE 16. The generalized delta rule for sigma-pi units. The products of activation values of individual units activate output units. See text for explanation of how the δ values are computed in this case.

Recurrent Nets

We have thus far restricted ourselves to *feedforward* nets. This may seem like a substantial restriction, but as Minsky and Papert point out, there is, for every recurrent network, a feedforward network with identical behavior (over a finite period of time). We will now indicate how this construction can proceed and thereby show the correct form of the learning rule for the recurrent network. Consider the simple recurrent network shown in Figure 17A. The same network in a feedforward architecture is shown in Figure 17B. The behavior of a recurrent network can be achieved in a feedforward network at the cost of duplicating the hardware many times over for the feedforward version of the network.[9] We have distinct units and distinct weights for each point in time. For naming convenience, we subscript each unit with its unit number in the corresponding recurrent network and the time it represents. As long as we constrain the weights at each level of the feedforward network to be the same, we have a feedforward network which performs identically with the recurrent network of Figure 17A.

---

[9] Note that in this discussion, and indeed in our entire development here, we have assumed a discrete time system with synchronous update and with each connection involving a unit delay.

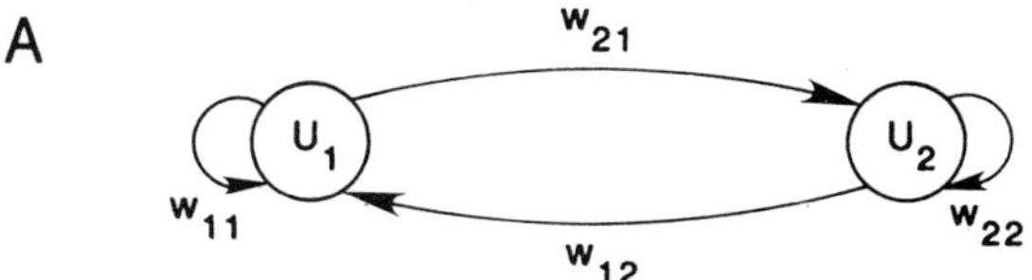

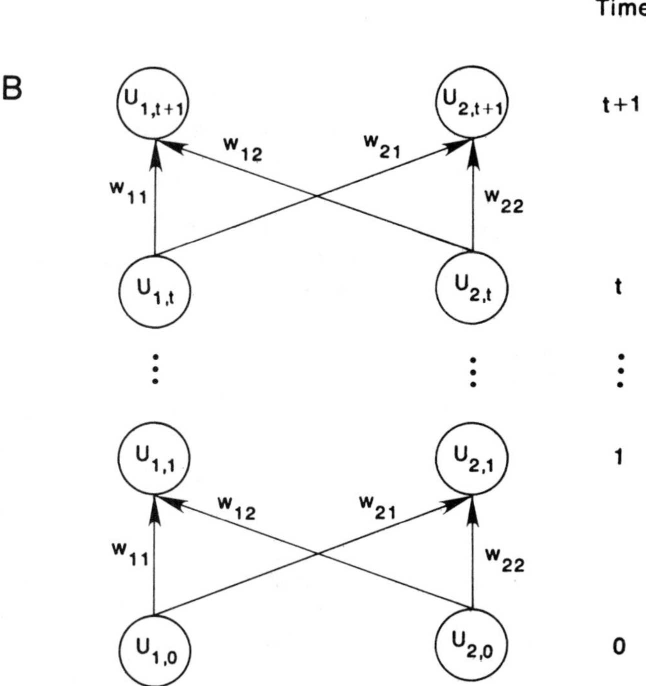

FIGURE 17. A comparison of a recurrent network and a feedforward network with identical behavior. *A*: A completely connected recurrent network with two units. *B*: A feedforward network which behaves the same as the recurrent network. In this case, we have a separate unit for each time step and we require that the weights connecting each layer of units to the next be the same for all layers. Moreover, they must be the same as the analogous weights in the recurrent case.

The appropriate method for maintaining the constraint that all weights be equal is simply to keep track of the changes dictated for each weight at each level and then change each of the weights according to the *sum* of these individually prescribed changes. Now, the general rule for determining the change prescribed for a weight in the system for a particular time is simply to take the product of an appropriate error measure δ and the input along the relevant line both for the appropriate times. Thus, the problem of specifying the correct learning rule for recurrent networks is simply one of determining the appropriate value of δ for each time. In a feedforward network we determine δ by multiplying the derivative of the activation function by the sum of the δ's for those units it feeds into weighted by the connection strengths. The same process works for the recurrent network—except in this case, the value of δ associated with a particular unit changes in time as a unit passes error back, sometimes to itself. After each iteration, as error is being passed back through the network, the change in weight for that iteration must be added to the weight changes specified by the preceding iterations and the sum stored. This process of passing error through the network should continue for a number of iterations equal to the number of iterations through which the activation was originally passed. At this point, the appropriate changes to all of the weights can be made.

In general, the procedure for a recurrent network is that an input (generally a sequence) is presented to the system while it runs for some number of iterations. At certain specified times during the operation of the system, the output of certain units are compared to the target for that unit at that time and error signals are generated. Each such error signal is then passed back through the network for a number of iterations equal to the number of iterations used in the forward pass. Weight changes are computed at each iteration and a sum of all the weight changes dictated for a particular weight is saved. Finally, after all such error signals have been propagated through the system, the weights are changed. The major problem with this procedure is the memory required. Not only does the system have to hold its summed weight changes while the error is being propagated, but each unit must somehow record the sequence of activation values through which it was driven during the original processing. This follows from the fact that during each iteration while the error is passed back through the system, the current δ is relevant to a point earlier in time and the required weight changes depend on the activation levels of the units at that time. It is not entirely clear how such a mechanism could be implemented in the brain. Nevertheless, it is tantalizing to realize that such a procedure is potentially very powerful, since the problem it is attempting to solve amounts to that of finding a sequential program (like that for a digital computer) that produces specified input-sequence/output-sequence pairs. Furthermore, the interaction of the teacher with the system can be quite flexible, so that, for example, should the system get stuck in a local minimum, the teacher could introduce "hints" in the form of desired output values for intermediate stages of processing. Our experience with recurrent networks is limited, but we have carried out some experiments. We turn first to a very simple problem in which the system is induced to invent a shift register to solve the problem.

Learning to be a shift register. Perhaps the simplest class of recurrent problems we have studied is one in which the input and output units are one and the same and there are no hidden units. We simply present a pattern and let the system process it for a period of time. The state of the system is then compared to some target state. If it hasn't reached the target state at the designated time, error is injected into the system and it modifies its weights. Then it is shown a new input pattern and restarted. In these cases, there is no constraint on the connections in the system. Any unit can connect to any other unit. The simplest such problem we have studied is what we call the *shift register* problem. In this problem, the units are conceptualized as a circular shift register. An arbitrary bit pattern is first established on the units. They are then allowed to process for two time-steps. The target state, after those two time-steps, is the original pattern shifted two spaces to the left. The interesting question here concerns the state of the units between the presentation of the start state and the time at which the target state is presented. One solution to the problem is for the system to become a shift register and shift the pattern exactly one unit to the left during each time period. If the system did this then it would surely be shifted two places to the left after two time units. We have tried this problem with groups of three or five units and, if we constrain the biases on all of the units to be negative (so the units are off unless turned on), the system always learns to be a shift register of this sort.[10] Thus, even though in principle any unit can connect to any other unit, the system actually learns to set all weights to zero except the ones connecting a unit to its left neighbor. Since the target states were determined on the assumption of a circular register, the left-most unit developed a strong connection to the right-most unit. The system learns this relatively quickly. With $\eta = 0.25$ it learns perfectly in fewer than 200 sweeps through the set of possible patterns with either three- or five-unit systems.

The tasks we have described so far are exceptionally simple, but they do illustrate how the algorithm works with unrestricted networks. We have attempted a few more difficult problems with recurrent networks.

[10] If the constraint that biases be negative is not imposed, other solutions are possible. These solutions can involve the units passing through the complements of the shifted pattern or even through more complicated intermediate states. These trajectories are interesting in that they match a simple shift register on all even numbers of shifts, but do not match following an odd number of shifts.

One of the more interesting involves learning to complete sequences of patterns. Our final example comes from this domain.

Learning to complete sequences. Table 10 shows a set of 25 sequences which were chosen so that the first two items of a sequence uniquely determine the remaining four. We used this set of sequences to test out the learning abilities of a recurrent network. The network consisted of five input units (A, B, C, D, E), 30 hidden units, and three output units (1, 2, 3). At Time 1, the input unit corresponding to the first item of the sequence is turned on and the other input units are turned off. At Time 2, the input unit for the second item in the sequence is turned on and the others are all turned off. Then all the input units are turned off and kept off for the remaining four steps of the forward iteration. The network must learn to make the output units adopt states that represent the rest of the sequence. Unlike simple feedforward networks (or their iterative equivalents), the errors are not only assessed at the final layer or time. The output units must adopt the appropriate states *during* the forward iteration, and so during the back-propagation phase, errors are injected at each time-step by comparing the remembered actual states of the output units with their desired states.

The learning procedure for recurrent nets places no constraints on the allowable connectivity structure.[11] For the sequence completion problem, we used one-way connections from the input units to the hidden units and from the hidden units to the output units. Every hidden unit had a one-way connection to every other hidden unit and to itself,

TABLE 10

25 SEQUENCES TO BE LEARNED

AA1212	AB1223	AC1231	AD1221	AE1213
BA2312	BB2323	BC2331	BD2321	BE2313
CA3112	CB3123	CC3131	CD3121	CE3113
DA2112	DB2123	DC2131	DD2121	DE2113
EA1312	EB1323	EC1331	ED1321	EE1313

[11] The constraint in feedforward networks is that it must be possible to arrange the units into layers such that units do not influence units in the same or lower layers. In recurrent networks this amounts to the constraint that during the forward iteration, future states must not affect past ones.

and every output unit was also connected to every other output unit and to itself. All the connections started with small random weights uniformly distributed between -0.3 and $+0.3$. All the hidden and output units started with an activity level of 0.2 at the beginning of each sequence.

We used a version of the learning procedure in which the gradient of the error with respect to each weight is computed for a whole set of examples before the weights are changed. This means that each connection must accumulate the sum of the gradients for all the examples and for all the time steps involved in each example. During training, we used a particular set of 20 examples, and after these were learned almost perfectly we tested the network on the remaining examples to see if it had picked up on the obvious regularity that relates the first two items of a sequence to the subsequent four. The results are shown in Table 11. For four out of the five test sequences, the output units all have the correct values at all times (assuming we treat values above 0.5 as 1 and values below 0.5 as 0). The network has clearly captured the rule that the first item of a sequence determines the third and fourth, and the second determines the fifth and sixth. We repeated the simulation with a different set of random initial weights, and it got all five test sequences correct.

The learning required 260 sweeps through all 20 training sequences. The errors in the output units were computed as follows: For a unit that should be on, there was no error if its activity level was above 0.8, otherwise the derivative of the error was the amount below 0.8. Similarly, for output units that should be off, the derivative of the error was the amount above 0.2. After each sweep, each weight was decremented by .02 times the total gradient accumulated on that sweep plus 0.9 times the previous weight change.

We have shown that the learning procedure can be used to create a network with interesting sequential behavior, but the particular problem we used can be solved by simply using the hidden units to create "delay lines" which hold information for a fixed length of time before allowing it to influence the output. A harder problem that cannot be solved with delay lines of fixed duration is shown in Table 12. The output is the same as before, but the two input items can arrive at variable times so that the item arriving at time 2, for example, could be either the first or the second item and could therefore determine the states of the output units at either the fifth and sixth or the seventh and eighth times. The new task is equivalent to requiring a buffer that receives two input "words" at variable times and outputs their "phonemic realizations" one after the other. This problem was solved successfully by a network similar to the one above except that it had 60 hidden units and half of their possible interconnections were omitted at random. The

TABLE 11

PERFORMANCE OF THE NETWORK ON FIVE NOVEL TEST SEQUENCES

Input Sequence	A	D	–	–	–	–
Desired Outputs	–	–	1	2	2	1
Actual States of:						
Output Unit 1	0.2	0.12	0.90	0.22	0.11	0.83
Output Unit 2	0.2	0.16	0.13	0.82	0.88	0.03
Output Unit 3	0.2	0.07	0.08	0.03	0.01	0.22
Input Sequence	B	E	–	–	–	–
Desired Outputs	–	–	2	3	1	3
Actual States of:						
Output Unit 1	0.2	0.12	0.20	0.25	0.48	0.26
Output Unit 2	0.2	0.16	0.80	0.05	0.04	0.09
Output Unit 3	0.2	0.07	0.02	0.79	0.48	0.53
Input Sequence	C	A	–	–	–	–
Desired Outputs	–	–	3	1	1	2
Actual States of:						
Output Unit 1	0.2	0.12	0.19	0.80	0.87	0.11
Output Unit 2	0.2	0.16	0.19	0.00	0.13	0.70
Output Unit 3	0.2	0.07	0.80	0.13	0.01	0.25
Input Sequence	D	B	–	–	–	–
Desired Outputs	–	–	2	1	2	3
Actual States of:						
Output Unit 1	0.2	0.12	0.16	0.79	0.07	0.11
Output Unit 2	0.2	0.16	0.80	0.15	0.87	0.05
Output Unit 3	0.2	0.07	0.20	0.01	0.13	0.96
Input Sequence	E	C	–	–	–	–
Desired Outputs	–	–	1	3	3	1
Actual States of:						
Output Unit 1	0.2	0.12	0.80	0.09	0.27	0.78
Output Unit 2	0.2	0.16	0.20	0.13	0.01	0.02
Output Unit 3	0.2	0.07	0.07	0.94	0.76	0.13

learning was much slower, requiring thousands of sweeps through all 136 training examples. There were also a few more errors on the 14 test examples, but the generalization was still good with most of the test sequences being completed perfectly.

TABLE 12

SIX VARIATIONS OF THE SEQUENCE EA1312 PRODUCED BY PRESENTING THE FIRST TWO ITEMS AT VARIABLE TIMES

EA−−1312	E−A−1312	E−−A1312
−EA−1312	−E−A1312	−−EA1312

Note: With these temporal variations, the 25 sequences shown in Table 10 can be used to generate 150 different sequences.

CONCLUSION

In their pessimistic discussion of perceptrons, Minsky and Papert (1969) finally discuss multilayer machines near the end of their book. They state:

> The perceptron has shown itself worthy of study despite (and even because of!) its severe limitations. It has many features that attract attention: its linearity; its intriguing learning theorem; its clear paradigmatic simplicity as a kind of parallel computation. There is no reason to suppose that any of these virtues carry over to the many-layered version. Nevertheless, we consider it to be an important research problem to elucidate (or reject) our intuitive judgement that the extension is sterile. Perhaps some powerful convergence theorem will be discovered, or some profound reason for the failure to produce an interesting "learning theorem" for the multilayered machine will be found. (pp. 231-232)

Although our learning results do not *guarantee* that we can find a solution for all solvable problems, our analyses and results have shown that as a practical matter, the error propagation scheme leads to solutions in virtually every case. In short, we believe that we have answered Minsky and Papert's challenge and *have* found a learning result sufficiently powerful to demonstrate that their pessimism about learning in multilayer machines was misplaced.

One way to view the procedure we have been describing is as a parallel computer that, having been shown the appropriate input/output exemplars specifying some function, programs itself to compute that function in general. Parallel computers are notoriously difficult to program. Here we have a mechanism whereby we do not actually have to know how to write the program in order to get the system to do it. Parker (1985) has emphasized this point.

On many occasions we have been surprised to learn of new methods of computing interesting functions by observing the behavior of our learning algorithm. This also raised the question of generalization. In most of the cases presented above, we have presented the system with the entire set of exemplars. It is interesting to ask what would happen if we presented only a subset of the exemplars at training time and then watched the system generalize to remaining exemplars. In small problems such as those presented here, the system sometimes finds solutions to the problems which do not properly generalize. However, preliminary results on larger problems are very encouraging in this regard. This research is still in progress and cannot be reported here. This is currently a very active interest of ours.

Finally, we should say that this work is not yet in a finished form. We have only begun our study of recurrent networks and sigma-pi units. We have not yet applied our learning procedure to many very complex problems. However, the results to date are encouraging and we are continuing our work.

PART III

FORMAL ANALYSES

Part III is focused on the formal tools employed in the study of PDP models and their application in the analysis of several specific aspects of PDP mechanisms.

In Chapter 9, Jordan provides a very accessible introduction to linear algebra and its applications to the analysis of PDP models. This chapter is designed to be a tutorial for those who are not familiar with the basics of linear algebra. Most of the book can be read and understood without knowledge of linear algebra, but an understanding of this important tool will greatly enhance a reader's understanding of the mathematical discussions that can be found in several chapters of the book.

In Chapter 10, Williams provides a useful analysis of *activation functions*. Throughout the book we employ several different activation functions. There is a question as to whether we will need to look for more complex activation functions to carry out some of the more complex computations. Williams shows that we will never have to consider activation functions more complex than the *sigma pi* function.

In Chapter 11, Stone provides a useful analysis of the *delta rule*, which plays an important role throughout the book. Stone shows how a change of basis can be employed to reveal the internal workings of the delta rule. He shows that when there is no deterministic relationship between inputs and targets, the delta rule leads to a system whose outputs match the central tendencies of the target patterns. Finally, he shows how the delta rule is related to linear regression.

In Chapter 12, McClelland analyzes the capacity limitations of two kinds of networks. He studies the effects of limitations of fan-in and fan-out on the capacities of standard pattern-association networks, and he explores the costs in units and connections of using programmable networks of the kind outlined in Chapter 16.

Finally, in Chapter 13, Zipser and Rabin describe a computer simulation system, called P3, for building computer simulations of PDP models. P3 provides both a language for describing networks and an interface for interacting with these networks and observing their behavior. Chapter 13 gives as an example a description of how the competitive learning algorithm can be built in P3.

In general, the chapters in this section are useful for two reasons. First, they describe several useful basic results—results that lie behind many of the simulation models described in other sections of the book. Second, and perhaps more importantly, they indicate some of the formal tools that are available for analyzing parallel networks, and show through example how these tools can be used to produce useful results.

CHAPTER 9

An Introduction to Linear Algebra in Parallel Distributed Processing

M. I. JORDAN

Many of the properties of the models described in this book are captured by the mathematics of linear algebra. This chapter serves as a introduction to linear algebra and is a good starting place for the reader who wishes to delve further into the models presented in other parts of the book. I will focus on the aspects of linear algebra most essential for the analysis of parallel distributed processing models, particularly the notions of a vector space, the inner product, and linearity. I will also discuss some simple PDP models, and show how their workings correspond to operations on vectors.

VECTORS

A vector is a useful way to describe a pattern of numbers. Consider for example the pattern of numbers that describe the age, height, and weight of an average person. Suppose that Joe is 37 years old, 72 inches tall, and weighs 175 pounds. This information can be summarized in a vector or ordered list of numbers. For each person, there is a corresponding vector, as in Figure 1A. Each vector has three components: age, height, and weight. There is no reason to limit ourselves

A

$$\textbf{Joe} \begin{bmatrix} 37 \\ 72 \\ 1\,75 \end{bmatrix} \qquad \textbf{Mary} \begin{bmatrix} 1\,0 \\ 30 \\ 61 \end{bmatrix}$$

$$\textbf{Carol} \begin{bmatrix} 25 \\ 65 \\ 1\,21 \end{bmatrix} \qquad \textbf{Brad} \begin{bmatrix} 66 \\ 67 \\ 1\,55 \end{bmatrix}$$

B

$$\textbf{Joe} \begin{bmatrix} 37 \\ 72 \\ 1\,75 \\ 8 \\ 1\,946 \end{bmatrix}$$

FIGURE 1.

to only three components, however. If, for example, we also wanted to keep track of Joe's shoe size and year of birth, then we would simply make a vector with five components, as in Figure 1B.

One important reason for the great utility of linear algebra lies in the simplicity of its notation. We will use bold, lower-case letters such as **v** to stand for vectors. With this notation, an arbitrarily long list of information can be designated by a single symbol.

When a vector has no more than three components, it can be represented graphically by a point or an arrow in three-dimensional space. An example with three components is given in Figure 2 for the vector corresponding to Mary. Each axis in the figure corresponds to one of the three components of the vector.

It will prove helpful to try and visualize vectors as points or arrows in two- and three-dimensional space in proceeding through this chapter in order to develop geometric intuition for the operations on vectors. Notice, however, that there is no fundamental distinction between such vectors and vectors with more than three components. All of the operations upon vectors described in later sections apply equally well to vectors with any finite number of components.

In a parallel distributed processing model, many quantities are best represented by vectors. The pattern of numbers representing the activations of many processing units is one example. Other examples are the set of weights on the input lines to a particular processing unit, or the set of inputs to a system.

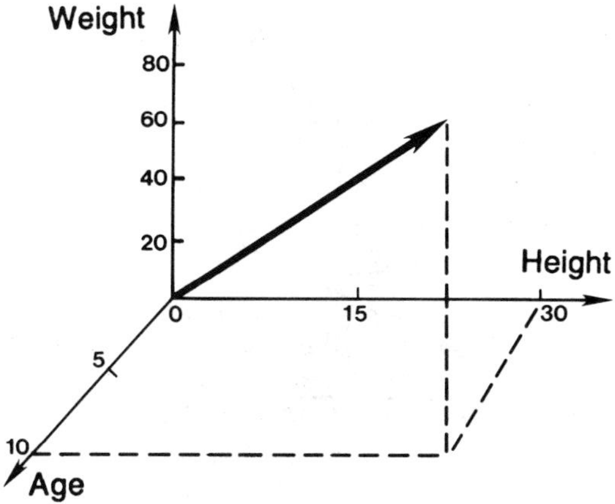

FIGURE 2.

BASIC OPERATIONS

Multiplication by Scalars

In linear algebra, a single real number is referred to as a *scalar*. A vector can be multiplied by a scalar by multiplying every component of the vector by the scalar.

Examples:

$$2\begin{bmatrix} 2 \\ 1 \end{bmatrix} = \begin{bmatrix} 4 \\ 2 \end{bmatrix} \qquad 5\begin{bmatrix} -3 \\ 4 \\ 1 \end{bmatrix} = \begin{bmatrix} -15 \\ 20 \\ 5 \end{bmatrix}$$

Geometrically, scalar multiplication corresponds to lengthening or shortening the vector, while leaving it pointing in the same or opposite direction. As can be seen in Figure 3, multiplying a vector by 2 leaves it pointing in the same direction but twice as long. In general, multiplying a vector by a positive scalar produces a new vector that is longer or shorter by an amount corresponding to the magnitude of the scalar. Multiplication by a negative scalar produces a vector pointing in the opposite direction. It, too, is longer or shorter depending on the magnitude of the scalar. Two vectors that are scalar multiples of one another are said to be *collinear*.

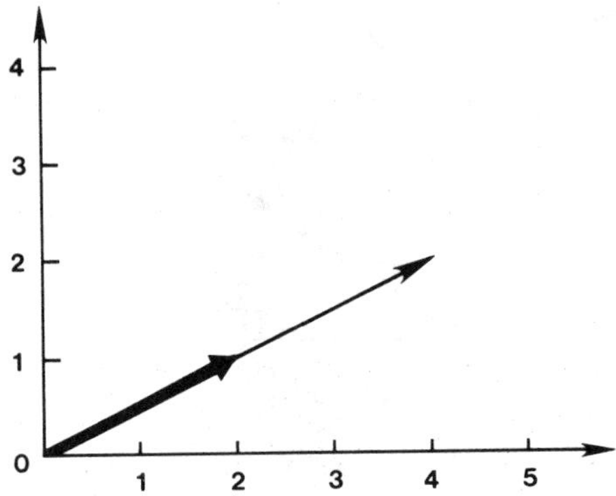

FIGURE 3.

Addition of Vectors

Two or more vectors can be added by adding their components. The vectors must have the same number of components to be added; otherwise the operation is undefined.

Examples:

$$\begin{bmatrix}1\\2\\1\end{bmatrix}+\begin{bmatrix}2\\1\\3\end{bmatrix}=\begin{bmatrix}3\\3\\4\end{bmatrix} \qquad \begin{bmatrix}2\\1\end{bmatrix}+\begin{bmatrix}0\\1\end{bmatrix}+\begin{bmatrix}3\\-3\end{bmatrix}=\begin{bmatrix}5\\-1\end{bmatrix}$$

Vector addition is associative (the vectors can be grouped in any manner) and commutative (the order of addition is unimportant) just like addition in ordinary algebra. This is true because if we consider one component at a time, vector addition *is* just addition in ordinary algebra.

How can vector addition be represented graphically? Consider Figure 4, where the vectors $\mathbf{v}_1 = \begin{bmatrix}1\\2\end{bmatrix}$ and $\mathbf{v}_2 = \begin{bmatrix}3\\1\end{bmatrix}$ are being added. It can be seen that the sum $\mathbf{v}_1 + \mathbf{v}_2$ is a vector $\begin{bmatrix}4\\3\end{bmatrix}$ which lies between $\mathbf{v}_1$ and $\mathbf{v}_2$. Forming the parallelogram with sides $\mathbf{v}_1$ and $\mathbf{v}_2$, we see that the sum of

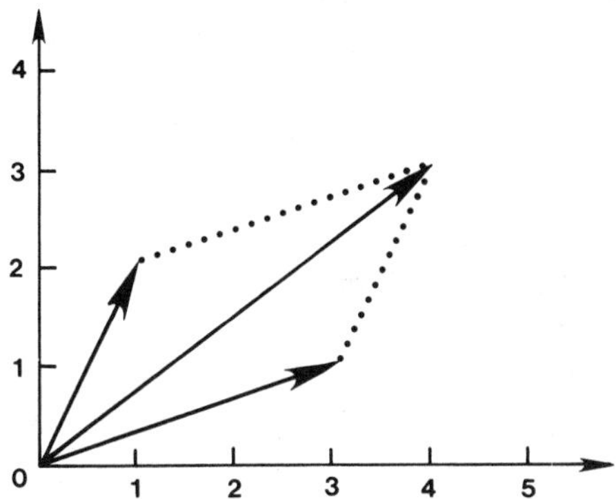

FIGURE 4.

the two vectors is the diagonal of this parallelogram. In two and three dimensions this is easy to visualize, but not when the vectors have more than three components. Nevertheless, it will be useful to imagine vector addition as forming the diagonal of a parallelogram. One implication of this view, which we will find useful, is that the sum of two vectors is a vector that lies in the same plane as the vectors being added.

Example: Calculating averages. We can demonstrate the use of the two operations thus far defined in calculating the average vector. Suppose we want to find the average age, height, and weight of the four individuals in Figure 1A. Clearly this involves summing the components separately and then dividing each sum by 4. Using vectors, this corresponds to adding the four vectors and then multiplying the resulting sum by the scalar 1/4. Using **u** to denote the average vector,

$$\mathbf{u} = \frac{1}{4}\left\{\begin{bmatrix} 37 \\ 72 \\ 175 \end{bmatrix} + \begin{bmatrix} 10 \\ 30 \\ 61 \end{bmatrix} + \begin{bmatrix} 25 \\ 65 \\ 121 \end{bmatrix} + \begin{bmatrix} 66 \\ 67 \\ 155 \end{bmatrix}\right\} = \begin{bmatrix} 34.5 \\ 58.5 \\ 128 \end{bmatrix}.$$

Using vector notation, if we denote the four vectors by $\mathbf{v}_1$, $\mathbf{v}_2$, $\mathbf{v}_3$, and $\mathbf{v}_4$, then we can write the averaging operation as

$$\mathbf{u} = \frac{1}{4}(\mathbf{v}_1 + \mathbf{v}_2 + \mathbf{v}_3 + \mathbf{v}_4).$$

The vector **u**, then, is a vector whose components are the averages of the components of the four individual vectors. Notice that the same result is obtained if each vector is first multiplied by 1/4, and the resulting vectors are added. This shows that multiplication by scalars and vector addition obey a distributive law, as in ordinary algebra.

LINEAR COMBINATIONS AND LINEAR INDEPENDENCE

Linear Combinations of Vectors

The average vector calculated in the last section is an example of a *linear combination* of vectors. In this section, we pursue this idea further.

Consider the vectors $\mathbf{v}_1 = \begin{bmatrix} 1 \\ 2 \end{bmatrix}$, $\mathbf{v}_2 = \begin{bmatrix} 3 \\ 2 \end{bmatrix}$, and $\mathbf{u} = \begin{bmatrix} 9 \\ 10 \end{bmatrix}$. Can **u** be written as the sum of scalar multiples of $\mathbf{v}_1$ and $\mathbf{v}_2$? That is, can scalars c_1 and c_2 be found such that **u** can be written in the form

$$\mathbf{u} = c_1\mathbf{v}_1 + c_2\mathbf{v}_2\ ?$$

If so, then **u** is said to be a linear combination of the vectors $\mathbf{v}_1$ and $\mathbf{v}_2$. The reader can verify that $c_1 = 3$ and $c_2 = 2$ will work, and thus **u** is a linear combination of $\mathbf{v}_1$ and $\mathbf{v}_2$.

This can also be seen directly in Figure 5, where these vectors are plotted. Remembering that multiplication by a scalar shortens or

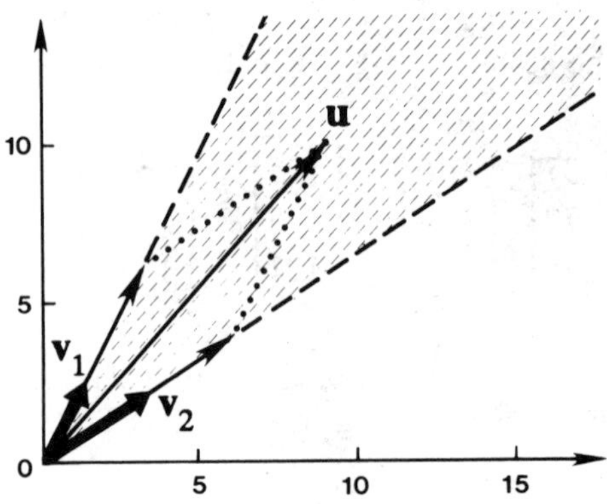

FIGURE 5.

lengthens a vector and that vector addition corresponds to forming the diagonal of a parallelogram, it seems clear that we can find scalars to adjust $\mathbf{v}_1$ and $\mathbf{v}_2$ to form a parallelogram that yields $\mathbf{u}$. This is indicated in the figure. It also seems clear that, using positive scalars, any vector in the shaded area of the figure can be generated this way. By using both negative and positive scalars, any vector in the plane can be written as a linear combination of $\mathbf{v}_1$ and $\mathbf{v}_2$. This is true because multiplication by a negative scalar reverses the direction of a vector as well as shortening or lengthening it. The vectors $\mathbf{v}_1$ and $\mathbf{v}_2$ are said to *span* the plane, because any vector in the plane can be generated from these two vectors.

In general, given a set $\mathbf{v}_1, \mathbf{v}_2, \ldots, \mathbf{v}_n$ of vectors, a vector $\mathbf{v}$ is said to be a linear combination of the $\mathbf{v}_i$ if scalars $c_1, c_2, \ldots, c_n$ can be found such that

$$\mathbf{v} = c_1\mathbf{v}_1 + c_2\mathbf{v}_2 + \cdots + c_n\mathbf{v}_n. \tag{1}$$

The set of *all* linear combinations of the $\mathbf{v}_i$ is called the set *spanned* by the $\mathbf{v}_i$.

Example. The three vectors $\begin{bmatrix}1\\0\\0\end{bmatrix}$, $\begin{bmatrix}0\\1\\0\end{bmatrix}$ and $\begin{bmatrix}0\\0\\1\end{bmatrix}$ span all of three-dimensional space since any vector $\mathbf{v} = \begin{bmatrix}a\\b\\c\end{bmatrix}$ can be written as a linear combination $\mathbf{v} = a\begin{bmatrix}1\\0\\0\end{bmatrix} + b\begin{bmatrix}0\\1\\0\end{bmatrix} + c\begin{bmatrix}0\\0\\1\end{bmatrix}$ The vectors are referred to as the standard basis for three-dimensional space (more on the idea of a basis in the next section).

Linear Independence

To say that a set of vectors span a space is to say that all vectors in the space can be generated from the original set by linear combination. We have shown examples in which two vectors span two-dimensional space and three vectors span three-dimensional space. We might be led to expect that, in general, n vectors suffice to span n-dimensional space. In fact, we have been using the term "dimension" without defining what it means; it would seem that a good definition of n-dimensional space is the set of vectors spanned by n vectors.

To make this definition work, we would require that the same size space be generated by any set of n vectors. However, this is not the case, as can be easily shown. Consider any pair of collinear vectors, for example. Such vectors lie along a single line, thus any linear combination of the vectors will lie along the same line. The space spanned by these two vectors is therefore only a one-dimensional set. The collinear vectors $\begin{bmatrix} 1 \\ 1 \end{bmatrix}$ and $\begin{bmatrix} 2 \\ 2 \end{bmatrix}$ are a good example. Any linear combination of these vectors will have equal components, thus they do not span the plane.

Another example is a set of three vectors that lie on a plane in three-dimensional space. Any parallelograms that we form will be in the same plane, thus all linear combinations will remain in the plane and we can't span all of three-dimensional space.

The general rule arising from these examples is that of a set of n vectors, if at least one can be written as a linear combination of the others, then the vectors span something less than a full n-dimensional space. We call such a set of vectors *linearly dependent.* If, on the other hand, none of the vectors can be written as a linear combination of the others, then the set is called *linearly independent.* We now revise the definition of dimensionality as follows: n-dimensional space is the set of vectors spanned by a set of n linearly independent vectors. The n vectors are referred to as a *basis* for the space.

Examples:

1. $\begin{bmatrix} 1 \\ 1 \end{bmatrix}$ and $\begin{bmatrix} 2 \\ 2 \end{bmatrix}$ are linearly dependent. They span only a one-dimensional space.

2. $\begin{bmatrix} 1 \\ 1 \end{bmatrix}$ and $\begin{bmatrix} 2 \\ 1 \end{bmatrix}$ are linearly independent. Thus they span the plane, a two-dimensional space.

3. $\begin{bmatrix} 1 \\ 1 \end{bmatrix}$, $\begin{bmatrix} 2 \\ 1 \end{bmatrix}$, and $\begin{bmatrix} -1 \\ 3 \end{bmatrix}$ are linearly dependent since 7 times the first vector minus 4 times the second vector is equal to the third vector.

4. $\begin{bmatrix} 1 \\ 2 \\ 0 \end{bmatrix}$, $\begin{bmatrix} 3 \\ 2 \\ 0 \end{bmatrix}$, and $\begin{bmatrix} 9 \\ 10 \\ 0 \end{bmatrix}$ are linearly dependent. Clearly they cannot span all of three-dimensional space, because no vector with a nonzero third component can be generated from this set.

Notice the relationship between examples (2) and (3). The vectors in example (2) are linearly independent, therefore they span the plane. Thus any other vector with two components is a linear combination of these two vectors. In example (3), then, we know that the set will be linearly dependent before being told what the third vector is. This suggests the following rule: There can be no more than n linearly independent vectors in n-dimensional space.

A linearly independent set of vectors has the important property that a vector can be written as a linear combination of the set in only one way. In other words, the coefficients c_i in Equation 1 are unique if the vectors $\mathbf{v}_i$ are linearly independent. This fact can be easily seen, for example, in the case of the standard basis, for there is only one vector in the basis which has a nonzero entry for any given component.

For linearly dependent vectors, however, the situation is different. If a vector can be written as a linear combination of a linearly dependent set of vectors, then there are an infinite number of sets of coefficients that will work. Let us attempt to demonstrate this fact with the aid of geometric intuition. Suppose that we wish to write vector $\mathbf{v}$ as a linear combination of three vectors $\mathbf{v}_1$, $\mathbf{v}_2$, and $\mathbf{v}_3$ in the plane. Let us choose any arbitrary coefficient c_1 for the vector $\mathbf{v}_1$. As shown in Figure 6, there must be a vector $\mathbf{w}$ such that $\mathbf{v} = c_1\mathbf{v}_1 + \mathbf{w}$. Thus, if we can write $\mathbf{w}$ as a linear combination of $\mathbf{v}_2$ and $\mathbf{v}_3$, i.e., $\mathbf{w} = c_2\mathbf{v}_2 + c_3\mathbf{v}_3$, then we have succeeded in writing $\mathbf{v}$ as a linear combination of $\mathbf{v}_1$, $\mathbf{v}_2$, and $\mathbf{v}_3$. But clearly we can do this, because $\mathbf{w}$ is a vector in the plane, and $\mathbf{v}_2$ and $\mathbf{v}_3$ together span the plane.

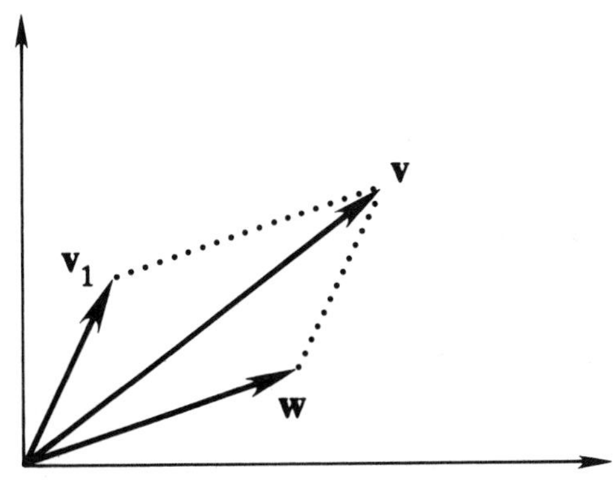

FIGURE 6.

VECTOR SPACES

Let us pause to reflect for a moment upon what a vector is. I have implied that a vector is a list of numbers, and I have also used the term to refer to a point or an arrow in space. Are both of these objects vectors, or is one just a heuristic representation for the other? Are there other objects that should be called vectors? Just what is a vector?

As is often the case in mathematics, these kinds of questions are solved by being avoided. Consider the following definition of an abstract vector space, and try to decide what a vector is.

A *vector space* is a set V of elements, called vectors, with the following properties:

- To every pair, $\mathbf{u}$ and $\mathbf{v}$, of vectors in V, there corresponds a vector $\mathbf{u} + \mathbf{v}$ also in V, called the sum of $\mathbf{u}$ and $\mathbf{v}$, in such a way that addition is commutative and associative.

- For any scalar c and any vector $\mathbf{v}$ in V, there is a vector $c\mathbf{v}$ in V, called the product of c and $\mathbf{v}$, in such a way that multiplication by scalars is associative and distributive with respect to vector addition.[1]

The answer to the question is that a vector is an undefined object in linear algebra, much like a line in geometry. The definition of a vector space simply lists the properties that vectors must have, without specifying what a vector must be. Thus, any set of objects that obey these properties can be called a vector space. Lists of numbers are vectors when addition is defined as adding components separately and scalar multiplication is defined as multiplying all the components by the scalar, because these operations fill all the requirements of a vector space. Arrows or points in space are also vectors when addition is defined geometrically as taking the diagonal of a parallelogram and scalar multiplication is defined as lengthening or shortening the arrow, because again, these operations fill the requirements of a vector space. A seemingly unrelated example of a vector space is the set of polynomials of order n, with addition and scalar multiplication defined in the obvious way.

This sort of abstraction is common in mathematics. It is useful because any theorem that is true about a general vector space must be

[1] I have left out certain technicalities usually included as axioms for a vector space. These include the axiom that there must be a zero vector, and for every vector, there is an additive inverse.

true about any instantiation of a vector space. We can therefore discuss general properties of vector spaces without being committed to choosing a particular representation such as a list of numbers. Much of the discussion about linear combinations and linear independence was of this nature.

When we do choose numbers to represent vectors, we use the following scheme. First we choose a basis for the space. Since every vector in the space can be written as a linear combination of the basis vectors, each vector has a set of coefficients $c_1, c_2, \ldots, c_n$ which are the coefficients in the linear combination. These coefficients are the numbers used as the components of the vector. As was shown in the previous section, the coefficients of a given vector are unique because basis vectors are linearly independent.

There is a certain arbitrariness in assigning the numbers, since there are infinitely many sets of basis vectors, and each vector in the space has a different description depending on which basis is used. That is, the coefficients, which are referred to as *coordinates*, are different for different choices of basis. The implications of this fact are discussed further in a later section where I also discuss how to relate the coordinates of a vector in one basis to the coordinates of the vector in another basis. Chapter 22 contains a lengthy discussion of several issues relating to the choice of basis.

INNER PRODUCTS

As of yet, we have no way to speak of the length of a vector or of the similarity between two vectors. This will be rectified with the notion of an inner product.

The inner product of two vectors is the sum of the products of the vector components. The notation for the inner product of vectors $\mathbf{v}$ and $\mathbf{w}$ is $\mathbf{v} \cdot \mathbf{w}$. As with vector addition, the inner product is defined only if the vectors have the same number of components.

Example:

$$\mathbf{v} = \begin{bmatrix} 3 \\ -1 \\ 2 \end{bmatrix} \qquad \mathbf{w} = \begin{bmatrix} 1 \\ 2 \\ 1 \end{bmatrix}$$

$$\mathbf{v} \cdot \mathbf{w} = (3 \cdot 1) + (-1 \cdot 2) + (2 \cdot 1) = 3.$$

The inner product is a kind of multiplication between vectors, although somewhat of a strange sort of multiplication, since it produces a single number from a pair of vectors. What does this single number "measure"?

Length

As a special case, consider taking the inner product of a vector with itself. An example is the vector $\mathbf{v} = \begin{bmatrix} 3 \\ 4 \end{bmatrix}$ in Figure 7. The inner product of $\mathbf{v}$ with itself is

$$\mathbf{v} \cdot \mathbf{v} = 3^2 + 4^2 = 25.$$

Consider the right triangle in Figure 7 with sides corresponding to the components of $\mathbf{v}$, and hypotenuse $\mathbf{v}$ itself. The Pythagorean theorem tells us that the square of the length of $\mathbf{v}$ is equal to the sum of the squares of the sides. Since this is exactly what is calculated by the inner product $\mathbf{v} \cdot \mathbf{v}$, it appears that a reasonable definition of the *length* of a vector is the square root of the inner product of the vector with itself. Thus we define the length of a vector $\mathbf{v}$, denoted by $\|\mathbf{v}\|$, as

$$\|\mathbf{v}\| = (\mathbf{v} \cdot \mathbf{v})^{1/2}.$$

Although the definition was motivated by an example in two dimensions, it can be applied to any vector. Notice that many of the

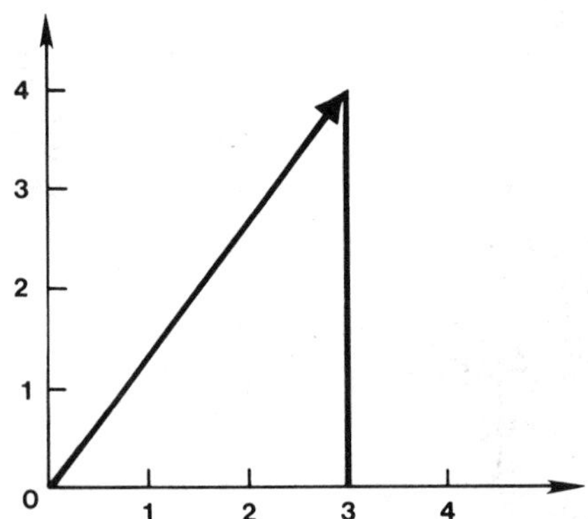

FIGURE 7.

properties we intuitively associate with length are included in this definition. For example, if a vector has larger components than another vector, it will be longer, because the squared components will contribute to a larger inner product. Multiplying a vector by a scalar produces a new vector whose length is the absolute value of the scalar times the length of the old vector:

$$\|c\mathbf{v}\| = |c|\,\|\mathbf{v}\|.$$

This is a property that can be easily proved. Somewhat harder to prove is the so-called triangle inequality, which states that the length of the sum of two vectors is less than or equal to the sum of the lengths of the two vectors:

$$\|\mathbf{v}_1 + \mathbf{v}_2\| \leqslant \|\mathbf{v}_1\| + \|\mathbf{v}_2\|.$$

Geometrically, the triangle inequality corresponds to the statement that one side of a triangle is no longer than the sum of the lengths of the other two sides.

Thus, in the special case where the operands are the same vector, the inner product is closely related to the idea of length. What if the operands are different vectors?

Angle

The angle between two vectors $\mathbf{v}$ and $\mathbf{w}$ is defined in terms of the inner product by the following definition:

$$\cos\theta = \frac{\mathbf{v}\cdot\mathbf{w}}{\|\mathbf{v}\|\,\|\mathbf{w}\|} \tag{2}$$

where θ is the angle between $\mathbf{v}$ and $\mathbf{w}$. Note that all of the quantities on the right hand side of the equation are easily calculated for n-dimensional vectors. At the end of this section, I will show geometrically why this formula is correct in two-dimensional space, using the ordinary geometrical definition of angle.

Example. Find the angle θ between the vectors $\mathbf{v}_1 = \begin{bmatrix}0\\1\end{bmatrix}$ and $\mathbf{v}_2 = \begin{bmatrix}1\\1\end{bmatrix}$. First, we calculate the necessary inner product and lengths:

$$\mathbf{v}_1\cdot\mathbf{v}_2 = 1 \qquad \|\mathbf{v}_1\| = 1 \qquad \|\mathbf{v}_2\| = \sqrt{2},$$

and then substitute these values in Equation 2:

$$\cos\theta = \frac{1}{1 \cdot \sqrt{2}} = 0.707.$$

Thus,

$$\theta = \cos^{-1}(0.707) = 45°.$$

This result could also have been found using basic trigonometry, but clearly the inner product method is superior in general (consider finding the angle between vectors with forty components!).

The inner product is often said to measure the "match" or "similarity" between two vectors. In a vague sense, this seems to be the case from the definition of the inner product as the sum of products. Equation 2, however, shows this in a clearer way: Writing out the equation in terms of the components of the vectors gives

$$\cos\theta = \frac{\sum_{i=1}^{n} v_i\, w_i}{(\sum_{i=1}^{n} v_i^2)^{1/2} (\sum_{i=1}^{n} w_i^2)^{1/2}}.$$

This is the formula for the correlation between two sets of numbers with zero means.

We can use our geometrical intuitions about angles and our understanding of correlation to turn Equation 2 around and gain a better understanding of the inner product. This understanding is important for the analysis of PDP models, because as will be seen, PDP models often compute inner products. Let us imagine moving two vectors around in space like the hands on a clock. If we hold the lengths of the vectors constant, then Equation 2 says that the inner product is proportional to the cosine of the angle: $\mathbf{v} \cdot \mathbf{w} = \|\mathbf{v}\|\,\|\mathbf{w}\| \cos\theta$. For example, if the angle between the vectors is zero, where the cosine is at a maximum, the inner product must therefore be at a maximum. As the two vectors move farther apart, the cosine decreases, thus the inner product decreases. It reaches zero when the angle is 90° , and its most negative value when the angle between the vectors is 180°, that is, when the vectors point in opposite directions. Thus, the closer the two vectors are, the larger the inner product. The more the vectors point in opposite directions, the more negative the inner product.

We must be careful, however, in claiming that two vectors are closer together than two others because they have a larger inner product. We must remember to divide the inner product by the lengths of the vectors involved to make such comparative statements.

An important special case occurs when the inner product is zero. In this case, the two vectors are said to be *orthogonal.* Plugging zero into the right side of Equation 2 gives

$$\cos\theta = 0.$$

which implies that the angle between the vectors is 90°. Thus, orthogonal vectors are vectors which lie at right angles to one another.

We will often speak of a set of orthogonal vectors. This means that every vector in the set is orthogonal to every other vector in the set. That is, every vector lies at a right angle to every other vector. A good example in three-dimensional space is the standard basis referred to earlier. Although we will skip the proof, it is probably clear that any orthogonal set is linearly independent. Indeed, orthogonality is stronger than linear independence: whereas every orthogonal set is linearly independent, there are very many linearly independent sets of vectors that are not orthogonal. An example in two-dimensional space is the pair $\begin{bmatrix} 1 \\ 1 \end{bmatrix}$ and $\begin{bmatrix} 2 \\ 1 \end{bmatrix}$. When we choose a basis for a space, we typically choose an orthogonal basis. In fact, in much of classical physics and mathematics, there is not the slightest hint that a basis should be anything but orthogonal.

Projections

A further application of the inner product, closely related to the ideas of length and angle, is the notion of a projection of one vector onto another. An example is given in Figure 8. The distance x is the projection of $\mathbf{v}$ on $\mathbf{w}$. In two dimensions, we readily know how to calculate the projection. It is

$$x = \|\mathbf{v}\| \cos\theta \tag{3}$$

where θ is the angle between $\mathbf{v}$ and $\mathbf{w}$. This formula generalizes, and for any vectors $\mathbf{v}$ and $\mathbf{w}$, the projection of $\mathbf{v}$ on $\mathbf{w}$ is given by Equation 3. It is a scalar which can be thought of as indicating how much $\mathbf{v}$ is pointing in the direction of $\mathbf{w}$.

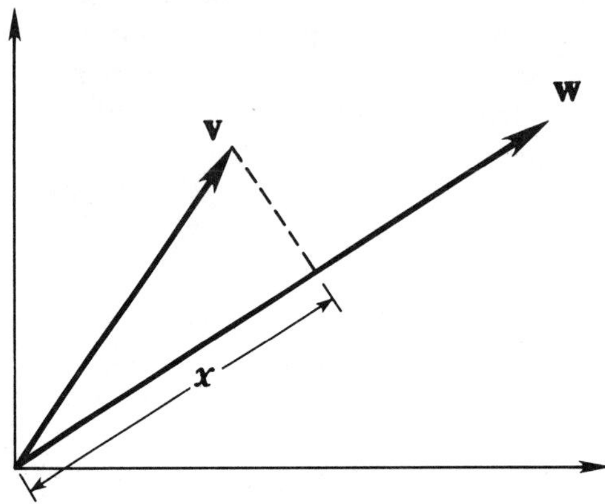

FIGURE 8.

There is a close relationship between the inner product and the projection. Using Equation 2, we can rewrite the formula for the projection:

$$
\begin{aligned}
x &= \|\mathbf{v}\| \cos \theta \\
&= \|\mathbf{v}\| \frac{\mathbf{v} \cdot \mathbf{w}}{\|\mathbf{v}\| \, \|\mathbf{w}\|} \\
&= \frac{\mathbf{v} \cdot \mathbf{w}}{\|\mathbf{w}\|}.
\end{aligned}
$$

Thus, the projection is the inner product divided by the length of **w**. In particular, if **w** has length one, then $\|\mathbf{w}\| = 1$, and the projection of **v** on **w** and the inner product of **v** and **w** are the same thing. This way of thinking about the inner product is consistent with our earlier comments. That is, if we hold the lengths of **v** and **w** constant, then we know that the inner product gets larger as **v** moves toward **w**. From the picture, we see that the projection gets larger as well. When the two vectors are orthogonal, the projection as well as the inner product are zero.

Inner Products in Two Dimensions

Equation 2 can be shown to be correct in two-dimensional space with the help of some simple geometry. Let **v** and **w** be two vectors in the plane, and θ be the angle between them, as shown in Figure 9. Denote the x and y coordinates of **v** and **w** by v_x, v_y and w_x, w_y, respectively.

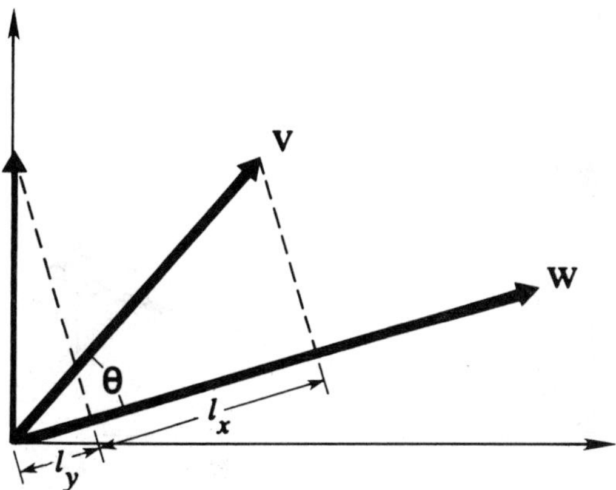

FIGURE 9.

Let l denote the projection of $\mathbf{v}$ on $\mathbf{w}$. We have $l = \|\mathbf{v}\| \cos\theta$ from geometry. We can break l into two pieces l_x and l_y as shown in the figure. l_y can be computed from the diagram by noticing that triangles OAD and COB, in Figure 10, are similar triangles. Thus, the ratio of corresponding sides is constant:

$$\frac{l_y}{v_y} = \frac{w_y}{\|\mathbf{w}\|},$$

giving

$$l_y = \frac{v_y\, w_y}{\|\mathbf{w}\|}.$$

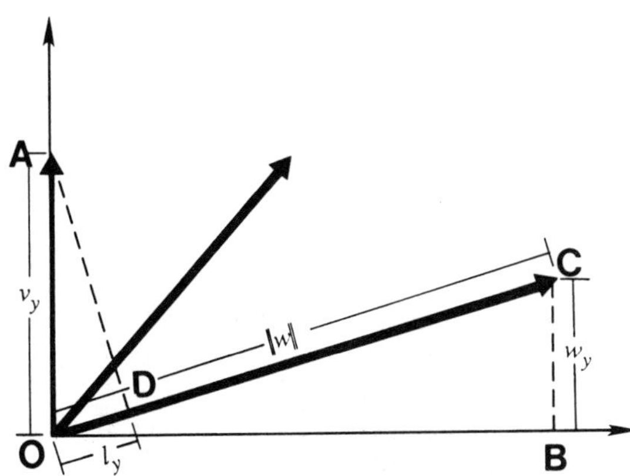

FIGURE 10.

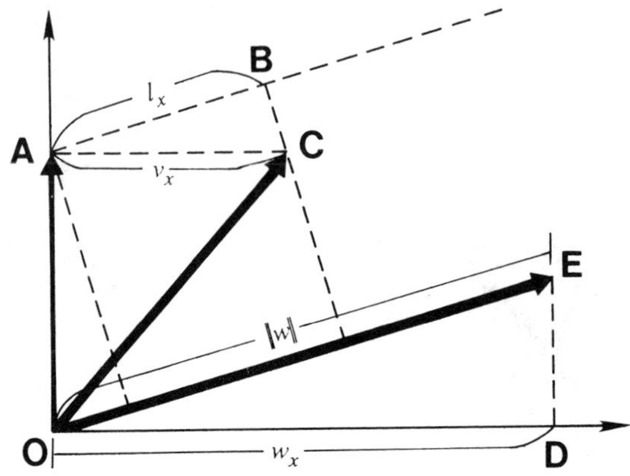

FIGURE 11.

In Figure 11, we see how to compute l_x, by observing that triangles EOD and CAB are similar. Thus,

$$\frac{l_x}{v_x} = \frac{w_x}{\|\mathbf{w}\|},$$

giving

$$l_x = \frac{v_x\, w_x}{\|\mathbf{w}\|}.$$

We can now write $l = l_x + l_y$, which yields

$$l = \|\mathbf{v}\| \cos \theta = l_x + l_y = \frac{v_x\, w_x}{\|\mathbf{w}\|} + \frac{v_y\, w_y}{\|\mathbf{w}\|} = \frac{\mathbf{v} \cdot \mathbf{w}}{\|\mathbf{w}\|}.$$

Thus,

$$\cos \theta = \frac{\mathbf{v} \cdot \mathbf{w}}{\|\mathbf{v}\|\, \|\mathbf{w}\|}.$$

Algebraic Properties of the Inner Product

In this section, we collect together some useful algebraic theorems concerning inner products. Most of these theorems can be easily proved using the definition of the inner product and properties of real numbers. In what follows, c and c_i will be any scalars, and the $\mathbf{v}$ and $\mathbf{w}$ will be n-dimensional vectors.

$$\mathbf{v} \cdot \mathbf{w} = \mathbf{w} \cdot \mathbf{v} \tag{4}$$

$$c\,(\mathbf{v} \cdot \mathbf{w}) = (c\,\mathbf{v}) \cdot \mathbf{w} = \mathbf{v} \cdot (c\,\mathbf{w}) \tag{5}$$

$$\mathbf{w} \cdot (\mathbf{v}_1 + \mathbf{v}_2) = \mathbf{w} \cdot \mathbf{v}_1 + \mathbf{w} \cdot \mathbf{v}_2 \tag{6}$$

The first theorem says simply that order is unimportant; the inner product is commutative. The second and third theorems show that the inner product is a *linear* function, as we will discuss at length in a later section. We can combine these two equations to get $\mathbf{w} \cdot (c_1\mathbf{v}_1 + c_2\mathbf{v}_2) = c_1\,(\mathbf{w} \cdot \mathbf{v}_1) + c_2\,(\mathbf{w} \cdot \mathbf{v}_2)$. It is also well worth our while to use mathematical induction to generalize this formula, giving us

$$\mathbf{w} \cdot (c_1\mathbf{v}_1 + c_2\mathbf{v}_2 + \cdots + c_n\mathbf{v}_n) =$$

$$c_1\,(\mathbf{w} \cdot \mathbf{v}_1) + c_2\,(\mathbf{w} \cdot \mathbf{v}_2) + \cdots + c_n\,(\mathbf{w} \cdot \mathbf{v}_n). \tag{7}$$

This important result tells us how to calculate the inner product of $\mathbf{w}$ and a linear combination of vectors.

Another useful theorem is

$$|\mathbf{v} \cdot \mathbf{w}| \leqslant \|\mathbf{v}\|\,\|\mathbf{w}\| \tag{8}$$

This is known as the Cauchy-Schwartz inequality. It gives an upper bound on the inner product.

ONE UNIT IN A PARALLEL DISTRIBUTED PROCESSING SYSTEM

In this section, we show how some of the concepts we have introduced can be used in analyzing a very simple PDP model. Consider the processing unit in Figure 12 which receives inputs from the n units below. Associated with each of the $n+1$ units there is a scalar *activation value*. We shall use the scalar u to denote the activation of the output unit and the vector $\mathbf{v}$ to denote the activations of the n input units. That is, the ith component of $\mathbf{v}$ is the activation of the ith input unit. Since there are n input units, $\mathbf{v}$ is an n-dimensional vector.

Associated with each link between the input units and the output unit, there is a scalar weight value, and we can think of the set of n

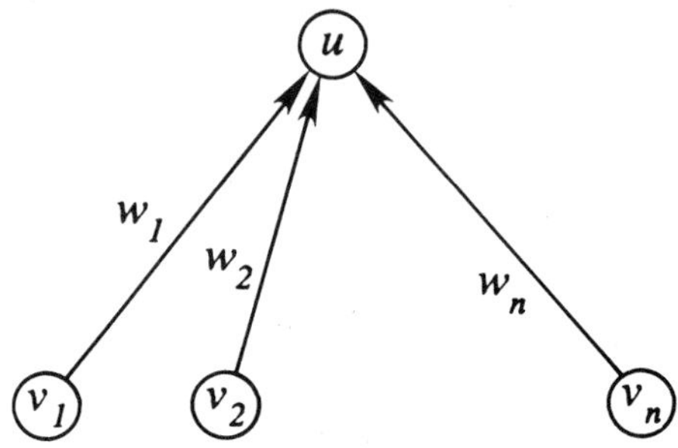

FIGURE 12.

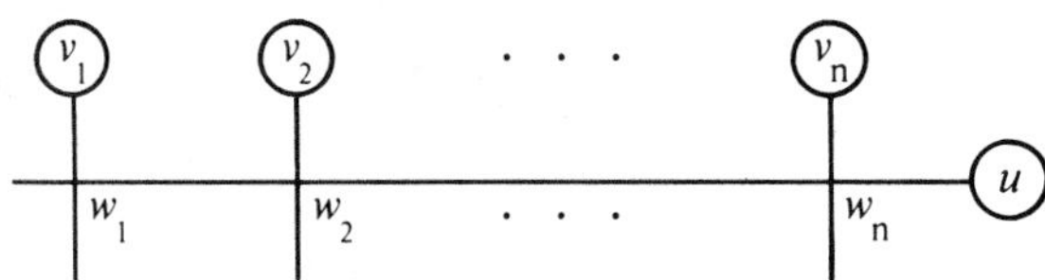

FIGURE 13.

weights as an n-dimensional vector $\mathbf{w}$. This is the *weight vector* corresponding to the output unit. Later we will discuss a model with many output units, each of which will have its own weight vector.

Another way to draw the same model is shown in Figure 13. Here we have drawn the n input units at the top with the output unit on the right. The components of the weight vector are stored at the junctions where the vertical input lines meet the horizontal output line. Which diagram is to be preferred (Figure 12 or Figure 13) is mostly a matter of taste, although we will see that the diagram in Figure 13 generalizes better to the case of many output units.

Now to the operation of the model: Let us assume that the activation of each input unit is multiplied by the weight on its link, and that these products are added up to give the activation of the output unit. Using the definition of the inner product, we translate that statement into mathematics as follows:

$$u = \mathbf{w} \cdot \mathbf{v}.$$

The activation of the output unit is the inner product of its weight vector with the vector of input activations.

The geometric properties of the inner product give us the following picture to help in understanding what the model is computing. We imagine that the set of possible inputs to the model is a vector space. It is an n-dimensional space, where n is the number of input lines. The weight vector also has n components, thus we can plot the weight vector in the input space. The advantage of doing this is that we can now state how the system will respond to the various inputs. As we have seen, the inner product gives an indication of how close two vectors are. Thus, in this simple PDP model, the output activation gives an indication or measurement of how close the input vector is to the stored weight vector. The inputs lying close to the weight vector will yield a large positive response, those lying near $90°$ will yield a zero response, and those pointing in the opposite direction will yield a large negative response. If we present a succession of input vectors of constant length, the output unit will respond most strongly to that input vector which is closest to its weight vector, and will drop off in response as the input vectors move away from the weight vector.

One way to describe the functioning of the processing unit is to say that it splits the input space into two parts, the part where the response is negative and the part where the response is positive. We can easily imagine augmenting the unit in the following way: if the inner product is positive, output a 1; if the inner product is negative, output a 0. This unit, referred to as a *linear threshold unit*, explicitly computes which part of the space the input lies in.

In some models, the weight vector is assumed to be normalized, that is, $\|\mathbf{w}\| = 1$. As we have seen, in this case, the activation of the output unit is simply the projection of the input vector on the weight vector.

MATRICES AND LINEAR SYSTEMS

The first section introduced the concepts of a vector space and the inner product. We have seen that vectors may be added together and multiplied by scalars. Vectors also have a length, and there is an angle between any pair of vectors. Thus, we have good ways of describing the structure of a set of vectors.

The usefulness of vectors can be broadened considerably by introducing the concept of a matrix. From an abstract point of view, matrices are a kind of "operator" that provide a mapping from one vector space to another vector space. They are at the base of most of the models in this book which take vectors as inputs and yield vectors as outputs.

First, we will define matrices and show that they have an algebra of their own which is analogous to that of vectors. In particular, matrices can be added together and multiplied by scalars.

MATRICES

A matrix is simply an array of real numbers. If the array has m rows and n columns, then we will refer to the matrix as an $m \times n$ matrix. Capital letters will be used to denote matrices.

Examples:

$$\mathbf{M} = \begin{bmatrix} 3 & 4 & 5 \\ 1 & 0 & 1 \end{bmatrix} \qquad \mathbf{N} = \begin{bmatrix} 3 & 0 & 0 \\ 0 & 7 & 0 \\ 0 & 0 & 1 \end{bmatrix} \qquad \mathbf{P} = \begin{bmatrix} 10 & -1 \\ -1 & 27 \end{bmatrix}$$

$\mathbf{M}$ is a 2×3 matrix, $\mathbf{N}$ is a 3×3 matrix, and $\mathbf{P}$ is a 2×2 matrix.

Some special matrices. There are several classes of matrices that are useful to identify. A *square* matrix is a matrix with the same number of rows and columns. The matrices **N** and **P** are examples of square matrices. A *diagonal* matrix is a square matrix that is zero everywhere except on its main diagonal. An example is matrix **N**. A *symmetric* matrix is a square matrix whose i,jth element is equal to its j,ith element. Any diagonal matrix is symmetric. Matrix **P** is an example of a symmetric matrix that is not diagonal. Finally, the diagonal matrix that has all ones on its main diagonal is referred to as the identity matrix, and is denoted **I**.

Multiplication by Scalars

A matrix can be multiplied by a scalar by multiplying every element in the matrix by that scalar.

Example:

$$3\,\mathbf{M} = 3 \begin{bmatrix} 3 & 4 & 5 \\ 1 & 0 & 1 \end{bmatrix} = \begin{bmatrix} 9 & 12 & 15 \\ 3 & 0 & 3 \end{bmatrix}$$

Addition of Matrices

Matrices are added together by adding corresponding elements. Only matrices that have the same number of rows and columns can be added together.

Example:

$$\mathbf{M} + \mathbf{N} = \begin{bmatrix} 3 & 4 & 5 \\ 1 & 0 & 1 \end{bmatrix} + \begin{bmatrix} -1 & 0 & 2 \\ 4 & 1 & -1 \end{bmatrix} = \begin{bmatrix} 2 & 4 & 7 \\ 5 & 1 & 0 \end{bmatrix}$$

Notice that there is a close relationship between these definitions and the corresponding definitions for vectors. In fact, for fixed integers m and n, the set of all $m \times n$ matrices is another example of a vector space. However, we will not exploit this fact, rather, we will think about matrices in another way, in terms of functions from one vector space to another. This is the subject of the next section.

Multiplication of a Vector by a Matrix

We now link up vectors and matrices by showing how a vector can be multiplied by a matrix to produce a new vector. Consider the matrix $\mathbf{W} = \begin{bmatrix} 3 & 4 & 5 \\ 1 & 0 & 1 \end{bmatrix}$ and the vector $\mathbf{v} = \begin{bmatrix} 1 \\ 0 \\ 2 \end{bmatrix}$. We wish to define a vector $\mathbf{u}$ which is the product of $\mathbf{W}$ and $\mathbf{v}$, and denoted

$$\mathbf{u} = \mathbf{W}\,\mathbf{v} = \begin{bmatrix} 3 & 4 & 5 \\ 1 & 0 & 1 \end{bmatrix} \begin{bmatrix} 1 \\ 0 \\ 2 \end{bmatrix}.$$

To define this operation, first imagine breaking the matrix into its rows. Each row of the matrix is a list of three numbers. We can think of the row as a three-dimensional vector and speak of the *row vectors* of the matrix. There are two such row vectors. Now consider forming the inner products of each of these row vectors with the vector $\mathbf{v}$. This will yield two numbers. These two numbers can be thought of as a two-dimensional vector $\mathbf{u}$, which is defined to be the product $\mathbf{W}\,\mathbf{v}$.

Example:

$$\mathbf{u} = \mathbf{W}\mathbf{v} = \begin{bmatrix} 3 & 4 & 5 \\ 1 & 0 & 1 \end{bmatrix} \begin{bmatrix} 1 \\ 0 \\ 2 \end{bmatrix} = \begin{bmatrix} 3\cdot 1 + 4\cdot 0 + 5\cdot 2 \\ 1\cdot 1 + 0\cdot 0 + 1\cdot 2 \end{bmatrix} = \begin{bmatrix} 13 \\ 3 \end{bmatrix}$$

The components of $\mathbf{u}$ are the inner products of $\mathbf{v}$ with the row vectors of $\mathbf{W}$.

For a general $m \times n$ matrix $\mathbf{W}$ and an n-dimensional vector $\mathbf{v}$,[2] the product $\mathbf{W}\mathbf{v}$ is an m-dimensional vector $\mathbf{u}$, whose elements are the inner products of $\mathbf{v}$ with the row vectors of $\mathbf{W}$. As suggested by Figure 14, the ith component of $\mathbf{u}$ is the inner product of $\mathbf{v}$ with the ith row vector of $\mathbf{W}$. Thus, the multiplication of a vector by a matrix can be thought of as simply a shorthand way to write down a series of inner products of a vector with a set of other vectors. The vector $\mathbf{u}$ tabulates the results. This way of thinking about the multiplication operation is a good way to conceptualize what is happening in a PDP model with many output units, as we will see in the next section.

There is another way of writing the multiplication operation that gives a different perspective on what is occurring. If we imagine breaking the matrix up into its columns, then we can equally well speak of the *column vectors* of the matrix. It can then be easily shown that the multiplication operation $\mathbf{W}\mathbf{v}$ produces a vector $\mathbf{u}$ that is a linear combination of the column vectors of $\mathbf{W}$. Furthermore, the coefficients of the linear combination are the components of $\mathbf{v}$. For example, letting $\mathbf{w}_1, \mathbf{w}_2, \mathbf{w}_3$ be the column vectors of $\mathbf{W}$, we have

$$\mathbf{u} = v_1\mathbf{w}_1 + v_2\mathbf{w}_2 + v_3\mathbf{w}_3 = \left[1\begin{bmatrix} 3 \\ 1 \end{bmatrix} + 0\begin{bmatrix} 4 \\ 0 \end{bmatrix} + 2\begin{bmatrix} 5 \\ 1 \end{bmatrix} \right] = \begin{bmatrix} 13 \\ 3 \end{bmatrix}$$

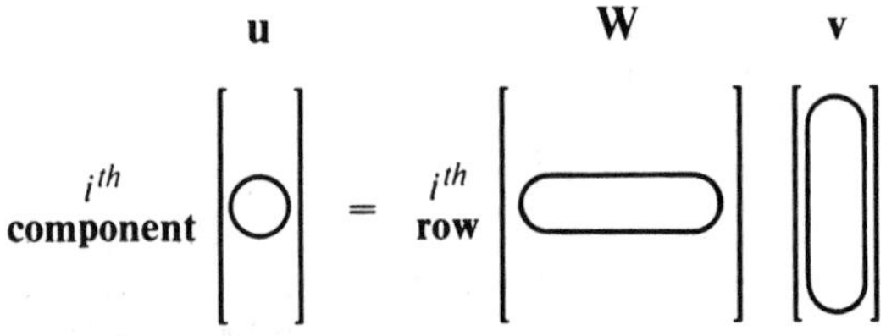

FIGURE 14.

[2] The dimensionality of $\mathbf{v}$ must be equal to the number of columns of $\mathbf{W}$ so that the inner products can be defined.

where the v_i are the components of $\mathbf{v}$. This way of viewing the multiplication operation is suggested in Figure 15 for a matrix with n columns.

If we let the term *column space* refer to the space spanned by the column vectors of a matrix, then we have the following interesting result: The vector $\mathbf{u}$ is in the column space of $\mathbf{W}$.

Finally, it is important to understand what is happening on an abstract level. Notice that for each vector $\mathbf{v}$, the operation $\mathbf{Wv}$ produces another vector $\mathbf{u}$. The operation can thus be thought of as a mapping or function from one set of vectors to another set of vectors. That is, if we consider an n-dimensional vector space $\mathbf{V}$ (the domain) and an m-dimensional vector space U (the range), then the operation of multiplication by a fixed matrix $\mathbf{W}$ is a function from $\mathbf{V}$ to U, as shown in Figure 16. It is a function whose domain and range are both vector spaces.

Algebraic Properties of Matrix Mapping

Several properties of matrix-vector multiplication follow directly from the properties of the inner product. In all cases, the number of

$$\underset{\mathbf{W}}{\begin{bmatrix} | & & | \\ \mathbf{w}_1 & \cdots & \mathbf{w}_n \\ | & & | \end{bmatrix}} \underset{\mathbf{v}}{\begin{bmatrix} v_1 \\ \vdots \\ v_n \end{bmatrix}} = \underset{\mathbf{u}}{\begin{bmatrix} & | & \\ v_1\mathbf{w}_1 + & \cdots & + v_n\mathbf{w}_n \\ & | & \end{bmatrix}}$$

FIGURE 15.

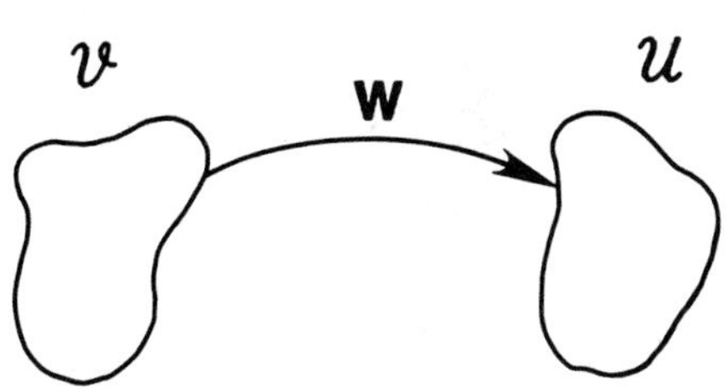

FIGURE 16.

components of the vector must be the same as the number of columns of the matrix.

$$\mathbf{W}\,(a\mathbf{v}) = a\mathbf{W}\mathbf{v} \tag{9}$$

$$\mathbf{W}\,(\mathbf{u} + \mathbf{v}) = \mathbf{W}\mathbf{u} + \mathbf{W}\mathbf{v} \tag{10}$$

These equations are the counterparts to Equations 5 and 6. As in that section, they can be combined and generalized to general linear combinations:

$$\mathbf{W}\,(c_1\mathbf{v}_1 + c_2\mathbf{v}_2 + \cdots + c_n\mathbf{v}_n) = c_1\,(\mathbf{W}\mathbf{v}_1) + c_2(\mathbf{W}\mathbf{v}_2) + \cdots + c_n\,(\mathbf{W}\mathbf{v}_n) \tag{11}$$

In the next theorem, the matrices **M** and **N** must have the same number of rows and columns.

$$\mathbf{M}\mathbf{v} + \mathbf{N}\mathbf{v} = (\mathbf{M} + \mathbf{N})\mathbf{v} \tag{12}$$

ONE LAYER OF A PARALLEL DISTRIBUTED PROCESSING SYSTEM

I now generalize the simple model presented earlier to show how matrices can be used in analyzing PDP models. Consider Figure 17, which is the generalization of Figure 12 to the case of many output units. Suppose that there are m output units, each one connected to all of the n input units. Denote the activation of the output units by $u_1, u_2, \ldots, u_m$. Each output unit has its own weight vector $\mathbf{w}_i$, separate from the other output units. As before, the activation rule

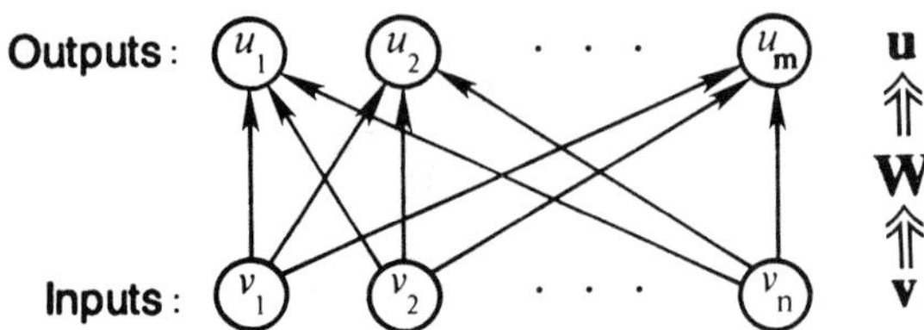

FIGURE 17.

says that the activation of an output unit is given by the inner product of its weight vector with the input vector, thus,

$$u_i = \mathbf{w}_i \cdot \mathbf{v}.$$

If we form a matrix **W** whose row vectors are the $\mathbf{w}_i$, then we can use the rule for matrix-vector multiplication to write all of the computations at once. Let **u** be the vector whose components are the u_i. Then

$$\mathbf{u} = \mathbf{W}\mathbf{v}.$$

This is a very succinct expression of the computation performed by the network. It says that for each input vector **v**, the network produces an output vector **u** whose components are the activations of the output units.

Another way to draw the network is shown in Figure 18, which is the generalization of Figure 13 to the case of many output units. At each junction in the diagram there is a weight connecting an input unit with an output unit.[3] The weight vectors associated with each output unit appear on the horizontal lines. When drawn this way, it is clear why a matrix appears in the equation linking the output vector to the input vector: The array of junctions in the diagram is exactly the weight matrix **W**.

Now let us attempt to understand geometrically what is being computed by the model. Each output unit is computing the inner product

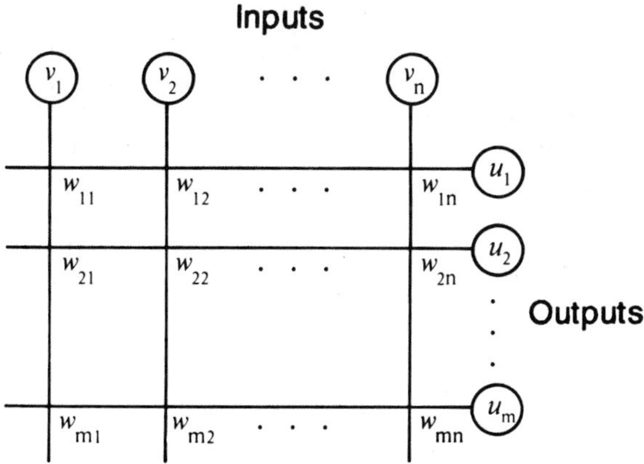

FIGURE 18.

[3] Note that the weight in the *i*th row and *j*th column connects the *j*th input unit to the *i*th output unit.

of its weight vector and the input vector (which is common to all output units). Thus, each unit can be thought of as computing how close its weight vector is to the input vector. A larger activation is attained the closer the two vectors are. If all of the weight vectors have the same length, then that output unit with the largest activation will be the unit whose weight vector is closest to the input vector.

In the model with only one output unit, we imagined plotting the weight vector in the input vector space. This enabled us to see directly which input vectors led to a large response and which input vectors led to a small response. In the model with several output units, we can generalize by plotting each weight vector in the input space. Now we can see for each unit which inputs it responds to. If the weight vectors are spread around in the space, then every input will lead to some response. Also, the different units will respond to different inputs. If the weight vectors are assumed to have unit length, then the activation of the ith output unit is just the projection of $\mathbf{v}$ on the ith weight vector. For a given input, we can draw the projections of the input on the weight vectors. This gives us a graphic representation of the output of the network. It should be emphasized, however, that this representation is useful mostly as a conceptual tool. The graphic approach cannot be used in most systems, which can have hundreds or thousands of input lines.

Another perspective on the operation of the model can be obtained by focusing on the columns of the weight matrix rather than on its rows. Whereas the rows of the matrix are the weights on the lines coming *in* to the processing units, the columns correspond to the weights on the lines going *out* from the processing units. Each unit on the lower row in Figure 17 is associated with such a vector: The components of the vector are the weights linking that unit with the output units above. These vectors are referred to as the *outgoing weight vectors*, as contrasted with the *incoming weight vectors* which are the rows of the weight matrix. [4] In the previous section, it was seen that when a matrix multiplies a vector, the resulting vector is a linear combination of the columns of the matrix. This view applies to the PDP model as follows: The output vector $\mathbf{u}$ is a linear combination of the outgoing weight vectors from the input units. The coefficients in the linear combination are the activations of the input units. Thus, in this perspective, each input unit multiplies its outgoing weight vector by its activation, and the resulting vectors are added to yield the output vector of the system.

In general, as will be discussed further in a later section, a unit can

[4] This is not standard terminology, and I will continue to use the term *weight vector* to refer to the incoming weight vectors.

appear in a multilayer system and thus have both an incoming weight vector and an outgoing weight vector, as shown in Figure 19. In this case, both views of matrix-vector multiplication can be useful: The unit can be thought of as matching its incoming weight vector to the current input using the inner product, and sending the result of this match multiplied by the outgoing weight vector to the next level.

LINEARITY

A distinction is often made between a *linear* system and a *nonlinear* system. In general, linear systems are relatively easy to analyze and understand, whereas nonlinear systems can be difficult. In this section, I will characterize linear systems. Nonlinear systems are defined simply as everything else. In a later section, I will give some specific examples of nonlinear systems.

Suppose that there is a function f which represents a system in that for each input x to the system, the output y is given by

$$y = f(x).$$

The x and y might be scalars or they might be vectors, depending on the particular system. The function f is said to be *linear* if for any inputs x_1 and x_2, and any real number c, the following two equations hold:

$$f(cx) = c f(x). \tag{13}$$

$$f(x_1 + x_2) = f(x_1) + f(x_2). \tag{14}$$

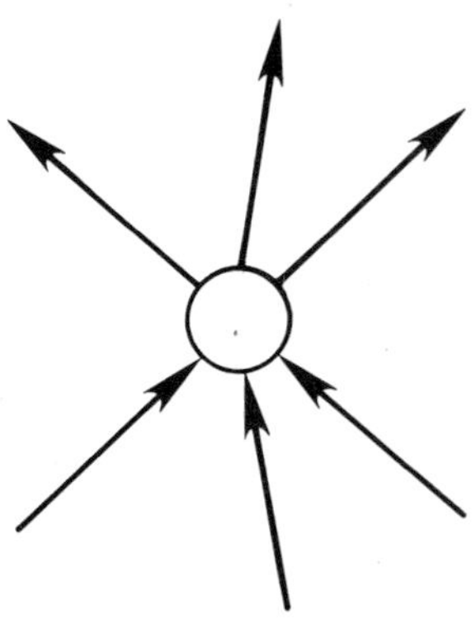

FIGURE 19.

The first of these two equations implies that if we multiply the input by some constant, then the output is multiplied by the same constant. The second equation is more important. Consider presenting the inputs x_1 and x_2 separately to the system and measuring the outputs. In a linear system, knowing how the system responds separately to the inputs is all we need to predict the output of the system when the sum $x_1 + x_2$ is presented. We simply add the outputs found separately to obtain the response to the sum. In a nonlinear system, on the other hand, we might find that the response to the sum is much larger or smaller than would be expected based on the inputs taken separately. The response to the sum might be zero even when strong responses are obtained separately.

If we restrict ourselves to scalar functions of a scalar variable, then the only linear functions are those in which the output is proportional to the input, i.e., for some real number c:

$$y = cx.$$

However, many systems are scalar or vector functions of a vector input. For example, for a fixed vector $\mathbf{w}$, the function

$$u = \mathbf{w} \cdot \mathbf{v}$$

is a scalar function of a vector input $\mathbf{v}$. This function is a linear function because

$$\mathbf{w} \cdot (c\,\mathbf{v}) = c\,(\mathbf{w} \cdot \mathbf{v})$$

and

$$\mathbf{w} \cdot (\mathbf{v}_1 + \mathbf{v}_2) = \mathbf{w} \cdot \mathbf{v}_1 + \mathbf{w} \cdot \mathbf{v}_2.$$

The PDP model with one output unit is an example of such a linear system.

A system in which the output is obtained from the input by matrix multiplication is also a linear system, according to Equations 9 and 10. It turns out that these are the only linear vector functions. That is, if a function f which maps from one vector space to another vector space is linear, then it can be represented by matrix multiplication.[5]

The PDP model discussed in the previous section is an example of a linear system because it is represented by matrix multiplication. In such a system, because of linearity, we know what the output will be when the sum of two vectors is presented if we know the outputs when

[5] Let $\mathbf{v}_i$ be the ith standard basis vector and let $\mathbf{w}_i = f(\mathbf{v}_i)$. Then if $\mathbf{W}$ is a matrix whose columns are the $\mathbf{w}_i$, $f(\mathbf{v}_i) = \mathbf{W}\mathbf{v}$ for all $\mathbf{v}$.

the vectors are presented separately. We also know what the output will be to scalar multiples of a vector. These properties imply that if we know the output to all of the vectors in some set $\{\mathbf{v}_i\}$, then we can calculate the output to any linear combination of the $\mathbf{v}_i$. That is, if $\mathbf{v} = c_1\mathbf{v}_1 + c_2\mathbf{v}_2 + \cdots + c_n\mathbf{v}_n$, then the output when $\mathbf{v}$ is presented to the system is

$$\mathbf{W}\mathbf{v} = \mathbf{W}\,(c_1\mathbf{v}_1 + c_2\mathbf{v}_2 + \cdots + c_n\mathbf{v}_n) =$$

$$c_1\,(\mathbf{W}\mathbf{v}_1) + c_2\,(\mathbf{W}\mathbf{v}_2) + \cdots + c_n\,(\mathbf{W}\mathbf{v}_n) \qquad (15)$$

The terms in the parentheses on the right are known vectors: They are the outputs to the vectors $\mathbf{v}_i$. Thus, we simply multiply these vectors by the c_i to calculate the output when $\mathbf{v}$ is presented. If the $\mathbf{v}_i$ are a basis for some vector space, then every vector in the space is a linear combination of the $\mathbf{v}_i$. Therefore, knowing the outputs of the system to the basis vectors allows us to calculate immediately the output to any other vector in the vector space without reference to the system matrix $\mathbf{W}$. The preceding statement should be studied carefully, because it expresses an extremely important defining property of linear systems. Another way to say the same thing is as follows: Imagine that we are studying some physical system by measuring its responses to various inputs. The system might be electronic or physiological, for example. If it is a linear system, then we should first measure the responses to a set of inputs that constitute a basis for the input space. We then have no need to make any further measurements. The responses of the system to any other input vector can be immediately calculated based on the measurements that we have already made.

MATRIX MULTIPLICATION AND MULTILAYER SYSTEMS

The systems considered until now have been *one-layer* systems. That is, the input arrives at a set of input units, is passed through a set of weighted connections described by a matrix, and appears on a set of output units. Let us now arrange two such systems in *cascade*, so that the output of the first system becomes the input to the next system, as shown in Figure 20. The composite system is a *two-layer* system and is described by two matrix-vector multiplications. An input vector $\mathbf{v}$ is first multiplied by the matrix $\mathbf{N}$ to produce a vector $\mathbf{z}$ on the set of intermediate units:

$$\mathbf{z} = \mathbf{N}\mathbf{v},$$

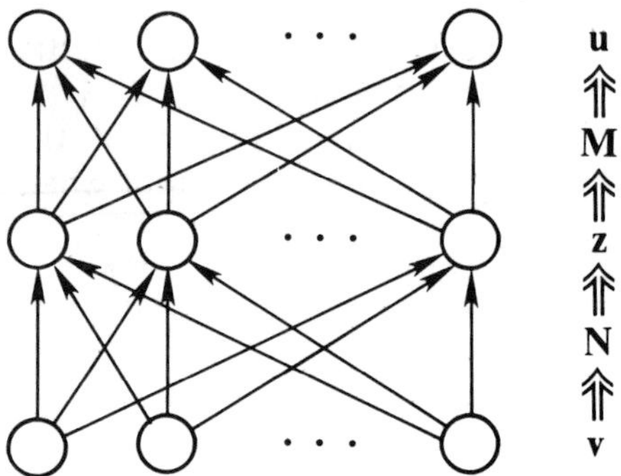

FIGURE 20.

and then $\mathbf{z}$ is multiplied by $\mathbf{M}$ to produce a vector $\mathbf{u}$ on the uppermost set of units:

$$\mathbf{u} = \mathbf{M}\mathbf{z}.$$

Substituting $\mathbf{N}\mathbf{v}$ for $\mathbf{z}$ yields the response for the composite system:

$$\mathbf{u} = \mathbf{M}\,(\mathbf{N}\mathbf{v}). \tag{16}$$

This equation relates the input vectors $\mathbf{v}$ to the output vectors $\mathbf{u}$.

We will now define an operation on matrices, called *matrix multiplication*, which will simplify the analysis of cascaded systems, allowing us to replace the two matrices $\mathbf{M}$ and $\mathbf{N}$ in Equation 16 by a single matrix $\mathbf{P}$. Matrices $\mathbf{M}$ and $\mathbf{N}$ can be multiplied to produce a matrix $\mathbf{P} = \mathbf{MN}$ as follows: The i,jth element of $\mathbf{P}$ is the inner product of the ith row of $\mathbf{M}$ with the jth column of $\mathbf{N}$. Note that the order of multiplication is important—the product $\mathbf{MN}$ is generally not equal to the product $\mathbf{NM}$. This is to be expected from the asymmetric treatment of $\mathbf{M}$ and $\mathbf{N}$ in the definition.

Example:

$$\begin{bmatrix} 3 & 4 & 5 \\ 1 & 0 & 1 \\ 0 & 1 & 2 \end{bmatrix} \begin{bmatrix} 1 & 2 \\ 2 & 0 \\ -1 & 1 \end{bmatrix} = \begin{bmatrix} (3+8-5) & (6+0+5) \\ (1+0-1) & (2+0+1) \\ (0+2-2) & (0+0+2) \end{bmatrix} = \begin{bmatrix} 6 & 11 \\ 0 & 3 \\ 0 & 2 \end{bmatrix}$$

Another way to think about matrix multiplication follows from the definition of matrix-vector multiplication. Each column vector of $\mathbf{P}$ is the product of the matrix $\mathbf{M}$ with the corresponding column vector of $\mathbf{N}$. For example, the first column of $\mathbf{P}$ is computed by multiplying the first column of **N** by the matrix **M**. This is shown in Figure 21, where we have explicitly shown the column vectors of **N** and **P**.

The product of two matrices is defined only if the number of columns of the first matrix is equal to the number of rows of the second matrix. Otherwise, the inner products cannot be formed. A handy rule is the following: Multiplying an $r \times s$ matrix and an $s \times t$ matrix yields an $r \times t$ matrix.

Let us return to Figure 20 and Equation 16, which describes the system. I make the claim that the matrices **M** and **N** in the equation can be replaced by the matrix **P**, if **P** is the matrix product of **M** and **N**. In other words,

$$\mathbf{u} = \mathbf{M}(\mathbf{N}\mathbf{v}) = (\mathbf{M}\mathbf{N})\mathbf{v} = \mathbf{P}\mathbf{v}.$$

What this equation says is that the two-layer system in Figure 20 is equivalent to a one-layer system with weight matrix **P**. For every input vector **v**, the two systems will produce the same output vector **u**. Thus, for linear systems at least, the distinction between two-layer systems and one-layer systems is more apparent than real.[6]

We can attempt to justify our claim and, in so doing, get a better understanding of matrix multiplication if we examine the system in Figure 20 more closely. Let us assume that a matrix **P** exists which can replace the cascaded pair **M**, **N**, and consider what the element in the first row and the first column of **P** should be. This element gives the strength of the connection between the first component of the input vector **v** and the first component of the output vector **u**. In the cascaded system, there are s paths through which this connection can occur, as shown in Figure 22. We must multiply the weights along each path and add the values for the paths to get the strength of the connection in the equivalent one-layer system. This is calculated as

$$p_{11} = m_{11}n_{11} + m_{12}n_{21} + \cdots + m_{1s}n_{s1}.$$

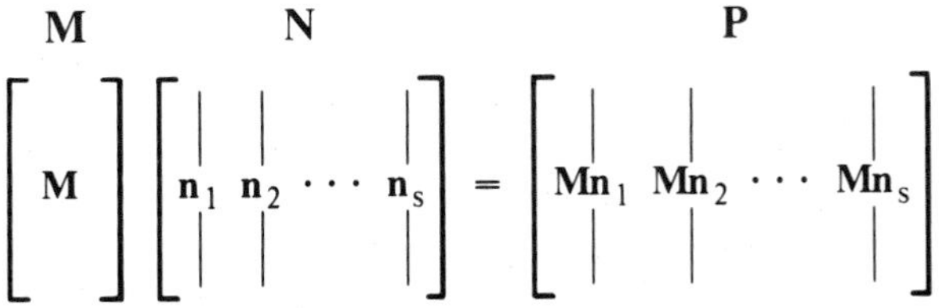

$$\overset{\mathbf{M}}{\begin{bmatrix} \quad \mathbf{M} \quad \end{bmatrix}} \overset{\mathbf{N}}{\begin{bmatrix} | & | & & | \\ \mathbf{n}_1 & \mathbf{n}_2 & \cdots & \mathbf{n}_s \\ | & | & & | \end{bmatrix}} = \overset{\mathbf{P}}{\begin{bmatrix} | & | & & | \\ \mathbf{M}\mathbf{n}_1 & \mathbf{M}\mathbf{n}_2 & \cdots & \mathbf{M}\mathbf{n}_s \\ | & | & & | \end{bmatrix}}$$

FIGURE 21.

[6] The two systems are identical in the sense that they compute the same function. Of course, they may have different internal dynamics and therefore take different amounts of time to compute their outputs.

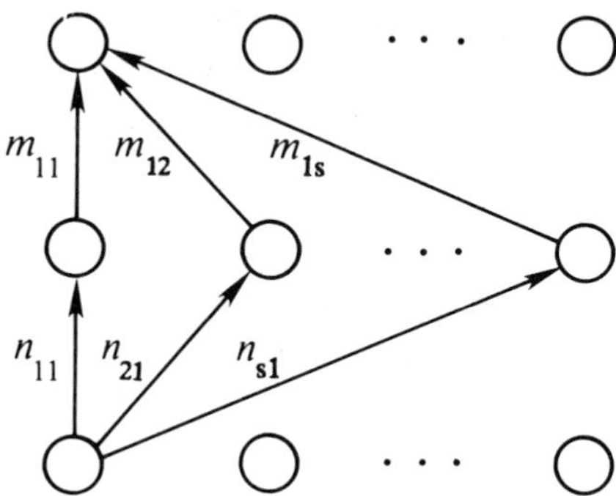

FIGURE 22.

This equation can be easily generalized to give the strength of the connection between the jth element of **v** and the ith element of **u**:

$$p_{ij} = m_{i1} n_{1j} + m_{i2} n_{2j} + \cdots + m_{is} n_{sj}.$$

This formula calculates the inner product between the ith row of **M** and the jth column of **N**, which shows that **P** is equal to the product **MN**.

This result can be extended to systems with more than two layers by induction. For example, in a three-layer system, the first two layers can be replaced with a matrix (as we have just seen), and then that matrix can be multiplied by the matrix of the remaining layer to get a single matrix for the whole system. In general, the cascaded matrices of any n-layer linear system can be replaced by a single matrix which is the product of the n matrices.

As a final comment, the definition of matrix multiplication may seem somewhat odd, especially since it would seem more straightforward to define it by analogy with matrix addition as the element-wise product. In fact, it would be perfectly acceptable to define multiplication as the element-wise product, and then to use another name for the operation we have discussed in this section. However, element-wise multiplication has never found much of an application in linear algebra. Therefore, the term multiplication has been reserved for the operation described in this section, which proves to be a useful definition, as the application to multilayer systems demonstrates.

Algebraic Properties of Matrix Multiplication

The following properties are identical to the corresponding properties of matrix-vector multiplication. This is to be expected given the relationship between matrix multiplication and matrix-vector multiplication (cf. Figure 21).

$$\mathbf{M}(c\mathbf{N}) = c\mathbf{MN} \tag{17}$$

$$\mathbf{M}(\mathbf{N} + \mathbf{P}) = \mathbf{MN} + \mathbf{MP} \tag{18}$$

$$(\mathbf{N} + \mathbf{P})\mathbf{M} = \mathbf{NM} + \mathbf{PM} \tag{19}$$

EIGENVECTORS AND EIGENVALUES

The next two sections develop some of the mathematics important for the study of *learning* in PDP networks. First, I will discuss *eigenvectors* and *eigenvalues* and show how they relate to matrices. Second, I will discuss *outer products*. Outer products provide one way of constructing matrices from vectors. In a later section, I will bring these concepts together in a discussion of learning.

Recall the abstract point of view of matrices and vectors that was discussed earlier: The equation $\mathbf{u} = \mathbf{Wv}$ describes a *function* or *mapping* from one space, called the *domain*, to another space, called the *range*. In such vector equations, both the domain and the range are vector spaces, and the equation associates a vector $\mathbf{u}$ in the range with each vector $\mathbf{v}$ in the domain.

In general, a function from one vector space to another can associate an arbitrary vector in the range with each vector in the domain. However, knowing that $\mathbf{u} = \mathbf{Wv}$ is a linear function highly constrains the form the mapping between the domain and range can have. For example, if $\mathbf{v}_1$ and $\mathbf{v}_2$ are close together in the domain, then the vectors $\mathbf{u}_1 = \mathbf{Wv}_1$ and $\mathbf{u}_2 = \mathbf{Wv}_2$ must be close together in the range. This is known as a *continuity* property of linear functions. Another important constraint on the form of the mapping is the following, which has already been discussed. If $\mathbf{v}_3$ is a linear combination of $\mathbf{v}_1$ and $\mathbf{v}_2$, and the vectors $\mathbf{u}_1 = \mathbf{Wv}_1$ and $\mathbf{u}_2 = \mathbf{Wv}_2$ are known, then $\mathbf{u}_3 = \mathbf{Wv}_3$ is completely determined—it is the same linear combination of $\mathbf{u}_1$ and $\mathbf{u}_2$. Furthermore, if we have a set of basis vectors for the domain, and it is known which vector in the range each basis vector maps to, then the mappings of all other vectors in the domain are determined (cf. Equation 15).

In this section, let us specialize to the case of square matrices, that is, matrices with the same number of rows as columns. In this case, the domain and the range will have the same number of dimensions (because the vectors **v** and **u** must have the same number of components), and the vectors in the domain and the range can be plotted in the same space. This is done in Figure 23, where we have shown two vectors before and after multiplication by a matrix.

In general, vectors in this space will change direction as well as length when multiplied by a matrix. However, as demonstrated by one of the vectors in Figure 23, there will be some vectors that will change only in length, not direction. In other words, for these vectors, multiplication by the matrix is no different than multiplication by a simple scalar. Such vectors are known as *eigenvectors*. Each eigenvector **v** of a matrix obeys the equation

$$\mathbf{W}\mathbf{v} = \lambda\mathbf{v} \tag{20}$$

where λ is a scalar. λ is called an *eigenvalue*, and indicates how much **v** is shortened or lengthened after multiplication by **W**.

Example:

$$\begin{bmatrix} 4 & -1 \\ 2 & 1 \end{bmatrix} \begin{bmatrix} 1 \\ 2 \end{bmatrix} = 2 \begin{bmatrix} 1 \\ 2 \end{bmatrix} \qquad \begin{bmatrix} 3 & 0 \\ 0 & 4 \end{bmatrix} \begin{bmatrix} 1 \\ 0 \end{bmatrix} = 3 \begin{bmatrix} 1 \\ 0 \end{bmatrix}$$

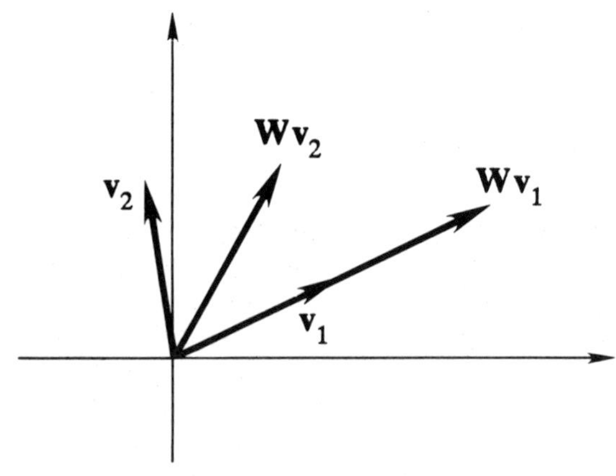

FIGURE 23.

A matrix can have more than one eigenvector, which, geometrically, means that it is possible to have eigenvectors in more than one direction. For example, the leftmost matrix above also has the eigenvector $\begin{bmatrix} 1 \\ 1 \end{bmatrix}$ with eigenvalue 3, and the diagonal matrix on the right also has the eigenvector $\begin{bmatrix} 0 \\ 1 \end{bmatrix}$ with eigenvalue 4.

There is another, more trivial, sense in which a matrix can have multiple eigenvectors: Each vector that is collinear with an eigenvector is itself an eigenvector. If $\mathbf{v}$ is an eigenvector with eigenvalue λ, and if $\mathbf{y} = c\,\mathbf{v}$, then it is easy to show that $\mathbf{y}$ is also an eigenvector with eigenvalue λ. For the ensuing discussion, the collinear eigenvectors will just confuse things, so I will adopt the convention of reserving the term eigenvector only for vectors of length 1. This is equivalent to choosing a representative eigenvector for each direction in which there are eigenvectors.

Let us now return to the diagonal matrix $\begin{bmatrix} 3 & 0 \\ 0 & 4 \end{bmatrix}$. We have seen that this matrix has two eigenvectors, $\begin{bmatrix} 1 \\ 0 \end{bmatrix}$ and $\begin{bmatrix} 0 \\ 1 \end{bmatrix}$, with eigenvalues 3 and 4. The fact that the eigenvalues are the same as the diagonal elements of the matrix is no coincidence: This is true for all diagonal matrices, as can be seen by multiplying any diagonal matrix by one of its eigenvectors—a vector in the standard basis. It is also true that this matrix has only two eigenvectors. This can be seen by considering any vector of the form $\begin{bmatrix} a \\ b \end{bmatrix}$, where a and b are both nonzero. Then we have

$$\begin{bmatrix} 3 & 0 \\ 0 & 4 \end{bmatrix} \begin{bmatrix} a \\ b \end{bmatrix} = \begin{bmatrix} 3a \\ 4b \end{bmatrix}.$$

Such a vector is not an eigenvector, because the components are multiplied by different scalars. The fact that the matrix has distinct eigenvalues is the determining factor here. If the diagonal elements had been identical, then any two-dimensional vector would indeed have been an eigenvector. This can also be seen in the case of the $n \times n$ identity matrix $\mathbf{I}$, for which every n-dimensional vector is an eigenvector with eigenvalue 1.

In general, an $n \times n$ matrix can have up to, but no more than, n distinct eigenvalues. Furthermore, distinct eigenvalues correspond to distinct directions. To be more precise, if a matrix has n distinct eigenvalues, then the n associated eigenvectors are *linearly independent*. Although the conditions under which a matrix has a full set of distinct eigenvalues are beyond the scope of this chapter, it is quite possible to have matrices with fewer than n eigenvalues, as in the case of the identity matrix.

I will not discuss how to find eigenvectors and eigenvalues for a particular matrix, but refer the reader to the books on linear algebra listed at the end of the chapter. There are several methods, all of which can be computationally expensive for large matrices. In a later section I will discuss how to construct a certain class of matrices given a set of desired eigenvectors.

The goal now is to show how eigenvectors can be used. To do so, let us begin by assuming that we are dealing with the most favorable case: an $n \times n$ matrix $\mathbf{W}$ with n distinct eigenvalues $\lambda_1, \lambda_2, \ldots, \lambda_n$. Denote the associated linearly independent eigenvectors by $\mathbf{v}_1, \mathbf{v}_2, \ldots, \mathbf{v}_n$. Recall that if we have a set of basis vectors for the domain of a matrix, and if we know the vectors in the range associated with each basis vector, then the mapping of all other vectors in the domain are determined. The eigenvectors of $\mathbf{W}$ form such a basis. This is because there are n eigenvectors, and they are linearly independent. Furthermore, we know the vectors in the range associated with each eigenvector $\mathbf{v}_i$; they are simply the scalar multiples given by $\mathbf{W}\mathbf{v} = \lambda\mathbf{v}$.

To show how to take advantage of these observations, pick an arbitrary vector $\mathbf{v}$ in the domain of $\mathbf{W}$. It can be written as a linear combination of the eigenvectors, because the eigenvectors form a basis:

$$\mathbf{v} = c_1\mathbf{v}_1 + c_2\mathbf{v}_2 + \cdots + c_n\mathbf{v}_n.$$

We can now write:

$$\mathbf{u} = \mathbf{W}\mathbf{v}$$

$$\mathbf{u} = \mathbf{W}\ (c_1\mathbf{v}_1 + c_2\mathbf{v}_2 + \cdots + c_n\mathbf{v}_n).$$

Using linearity,

$$\mathbf{u} = c_1(\mathbf{W}\mathbf{v}_1) + c_2(\mathbf{W}\mathbf{v}_2) + \cdots + c_n(\mathbf{W}\mathbf{v}_n).$$

If we next substitute for each of the quantities $\mathbf{W}\mathbf{v}_i$, using Equation 20:

$$\mathbf{u} = c_1\lambda_1\mathbf{v}_1 + c_2\lambda_2\mathbf{v}_2 + \cdots + c_n\lambda_n\mathbf{v}_n. \tag{21}$$

Notice that there are no matrices in this last equation. Each term $c_i\lambda_i$ is a scalar; thus we are left with a simple linear combination of vectors after having started with a matrix multiplication.

This equation should give some idea of the power and utility of the eigenvectors and eigenvalues of a matrix. If we know the eigenvectors and eigenvalues, then, in essence, we can throw away the matrix. We simply write a vector as a linear combination of eigenvectors, then multiply each term by the appropriate eigenvalue to produce Equation 21, which can be recombined to produce the result. Eigenvectors turn matrix multiplication into simple multiplication by scalars.

It is also revealing to consider the magnitudes of the eigenvalues for a particular matrix. In Equation 21, all of the vectors $\mathbf{v}_i$ are of unit length, thus the length of the vector $\mathbf{u}$ depends directly on the product of the magnitudes of the c_i and the eigenvalues λ_i. Consider the vectors that tend to point in the directions of the eigenvectors with large eigenvalues. These are the vectors with large c_i for those eigenvectors. Equation 21 says that after multiplication by the matrix they will be longer than vectors of the same initial length that point in other directions. In particular, of all unit length vectors, the vector that will be the longest after multiplication by the matrix is the eigenvector with the largest eigenvalue. In other words, knowledge of the eigenvectors and eigenvalues of a system tells which input vectors the system will give a large response to. This fact can be useful in the analysis of linear models.

TRANSPOSES AND THE OUTER PRODUCT

The transpose of an $n \times m$ matrix $\mathbf{W}$ is an $m \times n$ matrix denoted $\mathbf{W}^T$. The i,jth element of $\mathbf{W}^T$ is the j,ith element of $\mathbf{W}$.

Example:

$$\begin{bmatrix} 3 & 4 & 5 \\ 1 & 0 & 2 \end{bmatrix}^T = \begin{bmatrix} 3 & 1 \\ 4 & 0 \\ 5 & 2 \end{bmatrix}$$

Another way to describe the transpose is as follows: The row vectors of $\mathbf{W}^T$ are the column vectors of $\mathbf{W}$, and the column vectors of $\mathbf{W}^T$ are the row vectors of $\mathbf{W}$.

Algebraic Properties of the Transpose

$$(\mathbf{W}^T)^T = \mathbf{W}$$

$$(c\mathbf{W})^T = c\mathbf{W}^T$$

$$(\mathbf{M} + \mathbf{N})^T = \mathbf{M}^T + \mathbf{N}^T$$

$$(\mathbf{MN})^T = \mathbf{N}^T\mathbf{M}^T$$

If a matrix is its own transpose, that is if $\mathbf{W}^T = \mathbf{W}$, then the matrix is symmetric.

Outer Products

Before discussing outer products, let me attempt to ward off what could be a confusing aspect of the notation we are using. Consider, for example, the entity below. Is it a matrix with one column or is it a vector?

$$\begin{bmatrix} 3 \\ 1 \\ 2 \end{bmatrix}$$

The answer is that it could be either—there is no way of distinguishing one from the other based on the notation. There is nothing wrong with this failure to distinguish between vectors and $n \times 1$ matrices for the following reason. In equations involving vectors and matrices, the same results will be obtained whether entities such as the one above are treated as vectors or as matrices. This is true because the algebra for vectors and matrices is exactly the same, as a review of the relevant earlier sections will show. Thus, as long as we are simply interested in calculating values and manipulating equations, there is no need to distinguish between vectors and $n \times 1$ matrices. Rather, by treating them as the same thing, we have a uniform set of procedures for dealing with all equations involving vectors and matrices.

Nevertheless, on the conceptual level, it is important to distinguish between vectors and matrices. The way we are using the terms, a vector is an element in a vector space, whereas a matrix can be used to define a linear mapping from one vector space to another. These are very different concepts.

With this caveat in mind, we will continue to take advantage of the uniformity of notation, blurring the distinction between a vector and an

$n \times 1$ matrix. For example, for every n-dimensional vector $\mathbf{v}$, we can form the transpose $\mathbf{v}^T$, which is simply a matrix with one row. We can then form the product $\mathbf{v}^T\mathbf{u}$, where $\mathbf{u}$ is any n-dimensional vector, as in the following example.

Example:

$$\mathbf{v} = \begin{bmatrix} 3 \\ 1 \\ 2 \end{bmatrix} \qquad \mathbf{u} = \begin{bmatrix} 0 \\ 4 \\ 1 \end{bmatrix}$$

$$\mathbf{v}^T\mathbf{u} = \begin{bmatrix} 3 & 1 & 2 \end{bmatrix} \begin{bmatrix} 0 \\ 4 \\ 1 \end{bmatrix} = \begin{bmatrix} 6 \end{bmatrix}$$

Notice that the result has only a single component, and that this component is calculated by taking the inner product of the vectors $\mathbf{v}$ and $\mathbf{u}$. In many applications, there is no need to distinguish between vectors with one component and scalars, thus the notation $\mathbf{v}^T\mathbf{u}$ is often used for the inner product.

Let us next consider the product $\mathbf{u}\mathbf{v}^T$. This is a legal product because the number of columns in $\mathbf{u}$ and the number of rows in $\mathbf{v}^T$ are the same, namely one. Following the rule for matrix multiplication, we find that there are n^2 inner products to calculate and that each inner product involves vectors of length one.

Example:

$$\mathbf{u}\mathbf{v}^T = \begin{bmatrix} 1 \\ 4 \\ 0 \end{bmatrix} \begin{bmatrix} 3 & 1 & 2 \end{bmatrix} = \begin{bmatrix} 3 & 1 & 2 \\ 12 & 4 & 8 \\ 0 & 0 & 0 \end{bmatrix}$$

The i,jth element of the resulting matrix is equal to the product $u_i v_j$.

For those who may have forgotten the noncommutativity of matrix multiplication, this serves as a good reminder: Whereas the product $\mathbf{v}^T\mathbf{u}$ has a single component, a simple change in the order of multiplication yields an $n \times n$ matrix.

Products of the form $\mathbf{u}\mathbf{v}^T$ are referred to as *outer products*, and will be discussed further in the next section. Note that the rows of the resulting matrix are simply scalar multiples of the vector $\mathbf{v}$. In other words, if we let $\mathbf{W}$ be the matrix $\mathbf{u}\mathbf{v}^T$, and let $\mathbf{w}_i$ be the ith row of $\mathbf{W}$, then we have

$$\mathbf{w}_i = u_i\mathbf{v}$$

where u_i is the ith component of the vector $\mathbf{u}$.

OUTER PRODUCTS, EIGENVECTORS, AND LEARNING

In this section, I discuss two example PDP systems that bring together several of the concepts discussed previously, including eigenvectors and outer products. These systems are described in J. A. Anderson, Silverstein, Ritz, and Jones (1977) and Kohonen (1977).

We have seen that simple linear PDP systems can be modeled with the equation $\mathbf{u} = \mathbf{W}\mathbf{v}$, where $\mathbf{W}$ is a weight matrix. The rows of $\mathbf{W}$ are the weight vectors associated with each of the units in the upper level of the system. Until now, we have taken the matrix $\mathbf{W}$ to be a given, and have discussed how it maps input vectors to output vectors. Let us now consider a simple scheme, referred to as a Hebbian learning rule, whereby we can choose a matrix that associates a particular output vector $\mathbf{u}$ with a particular input vector $\mathbf{v}$. A system that can autonomously implement such a scheme is capable of a rudimentary form of associative learning.

The scheme will only work with input vectors of unit length, so let us begin by making that assumption. Thus, we have $\mathbf{v} \cdot \mathbf{v} = 1$. Let us consider the simplest case, in which the output vector $\mathbf{u}$ has only one component, which we will denote by u. This is the system discussed in Figure 13. We wish a weight vector $\mathbf{w}$ such that when $\mathbf{v}$ is present as the input, the output is u: $u = \mathbf{w} \cdot \mathbf{v}$. Note that u and $\mathbf{v}$ are the given here, and $\mathbf{w}$ is the unknown. To make a choice for $\mathbf{w}$, we can use the following logic. We wish to convert the vector $\mathbf{v}$ into a scalar u. If we were to choose $\mathbf{v}$ itself as the weight vector, then we would have $\mathbf{v} \cdot \mathbf{v} = 1$. Since we wish the scalar u, not 1, we choose $\mathbf{v}$ multiplied by u, which gives the desired result. This can be seen using simple algebra as follows:

$$\begin{aligned}\mathbf{w} \cdot \mathbf{v} &= (u\mathbf{v}) \cdot \mathbf{v} \\ &= u(\mathbf{v} \cdot \mathbf{v}) \\ &= u.\end{aligned}$$

Geometrically, the problem of finding $\mathbf{w}$ corresponds to finding a vector whose projection on $\mathbf{v}$ is u. As shown in Figure 24, any vector along the dotted line will work, because each such vector projects to the same place on $\mathbf{v}$. Our solution involved making the simple choice of the vector that points in the same direction as $\mathbf{v}$.

It is not difficult to generalize to the case of an output vector $\mathbf{u}$ with more than one component. To do so, let us consider the PDP system of Figure 18. Each output unit has a weight vector, and these weight vectors form the rows of the weight matrix $\mathbf{W}$. As discussed earlier, each unit calculates the inner product between its weight vector and the

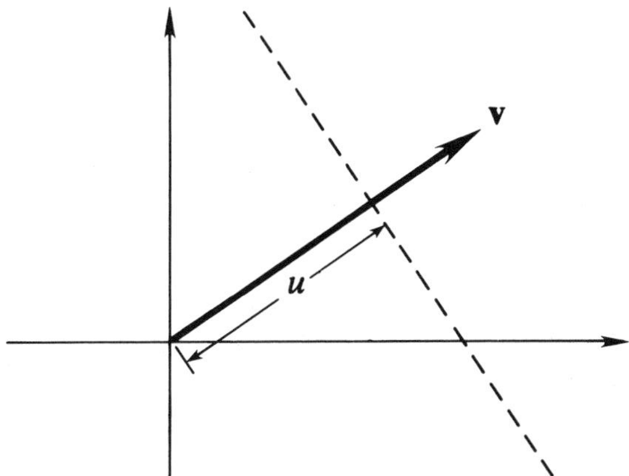

FIGURE 24.

input vector **v**, and these inner products are the components of the output vector **u**. To implement a learning scheme, we need to be able to choose weight vectors that produce the desired components of **u**. Clearly, for each component, we can use the scheme already described for the single unit model above. In other words, the *i*th weight vector should be given by

$$\mathbf{w}_i = u_i \mathbf{v}. \tag{22}$$

The *i*th unit will then produce the *i*th component of **u** when presented with **v**. Thus, the system as a whole will produce the vector **u** when presented with **v**. We now would like a way to write a matrix **W** whose rows are given by Equation 22. This is done by noting that Equation 22 is a set of equations calculating the outer product of **u** and **v**. Thus, **W** can be written as follows:

$$\mathbf{W} = \mathbf{u}\mathbf{v}^T.$$

We can check the correctness of this choice for **W** as follows:

$$\begin{aligned} \mathbf{W}\mathbf{v} &= (\mathbf{u}\mathbf{v}^T)\mathbf{v} \\ &= \mathbf{u}\,(\mathbf{v}^T\mathbf{v}) \\ &= \mathbf{u} \end{aligned}$$

using the fact that **v** is of length one in making the last step.

The fact that **W** is an outer product has important implications for the implementation of Hebbian learning in PDP networks. As discussed in the previous section, the i,jth element of $\mathbf{W}$ is equal to the product $u_i v_j$, which is the product of the activation of the jth input unit and the ith output unit. Both of these quantities are available in a physically circumscribed area on the link joining these two units. Thus, the weight on that link can be changed by autonomous local processes. The Hebb rule is often referred to as a *local* learning rule for this reason.

To summarize, we have established a procedure for finding a matrix $\mathbf{W}$ which will associate any particular pair of input and output vectors. Clearly for every pair of vectors, we can find a different weight matrix to perform the association. What is less obvious is that the same matrix can be used for several pairs of associations. Let us assume that we are given n n-dimensional output vectors $\mathbf{u}_1, \mathbf{u}_2, \ldots, \mathbf{u}_n$ which we want to associate with n n-dimensional input vectors $\mathbf{v}_1, \mathbf{v}_2, \ldots, \mathbf{v}_n$. In other words, for each i, we wish to have

$$\mathbf{u}_i = \mathbf{W}\mathbf{v}_i.$$

Let us further assume that the vectors $\mathbf{v}_i$ form a mutually orthogonal set and that each vector $\mathbf{v}_i$ is of unit length. That is, we assume

$$\mathbf{v}_i{}^T\mathbf{v}_j = \begin{cases} 1 & \text{if } i = j \\ 0 & \text{otherwise.} \end{cases}$$

We now form a set of matrices $\mathbf{W}_i$ using the learning scheme developed above:

$$\mathbf{W}_i = \mathbf{u}_i\mathbf{v}_i^T$$

Finally, we form a composite weight matrix $\mathbf{W}$ which is the sum of the $\mathbf{W}_i$:

$$\mathbf{W} = \mathbf{W}_1 + \cdots + \mathbf{W}_i + \cdots + \mathbf{W}_n.$$

We already know that, for example, $\mathbf{W}_1$ above will associate $\mathbf{v}_1$ and $\mathbf{u}_1$. It is also true that $\mathbf{W}$ will perform all such associations. Thus, for arbitrary i:

$$\begin{aligned}
\mathbf{W}\mathbf{v}_i &= (\mathbf{W}_1 + \cdots + \mathbf{W}_i + \cdots + \mathbf{W}_n)\mathbf{v}_i \\
&= (\mathbf{u}_1\mathbf{v}_1^T + \cdots + \mathbf{u}_i\mathbf{v}_i^T + \cdots + \mathbf{u}_n\mathbf{v}_n^T)\mathbf{v}_i \\
&= (\mathbf{u}_1\mathbf{v}_1^T)\mathbf{v}_i + \cdots + (\mathbf{u}_i\mathbf{v}_i^T)\mathbf{v}_i + \cdots + (\mathbf{u}_n\mathbf{v}_n^T)\mathbf{v}_i \\
&= \mathbf{u}_1(\mathbf{v}_1^T\mathbf{v}_i) + \cdots + \mathbf{u}_i(\mathbf{v}_i^T\mathbf{v}_i) + \cdots + \mathbf{u}_n(\mathbf{v}_n^T\mathbf{v}_i) \\
&= 0 + \cdots + \mathbf{u}_i(\mathbf{v}_i^T\mathbf{v}_i) + \cdots + 0 \\
&= \mathbf{u}_i.
\end{aligned}$$

The property of orthogonality was crucial here, because it forced the disappearance of all terms involving vectors other than $\mathbf{u}_i$ in the next to last step. The reader may find it useful to justify the steps in this derivation.

When the set of input vectors is not orthogonal, the Hebb rule will not correctly associate output vectors with input vectors. However, a modification of the Hebb rule, known as the *delta rule*, or the *Widrow-Hoff rule*, can make such associations. The requirement for the delta rule to work is that the input vectors be linearly independent. The delta rule is discussed further in Chapter 11, and at length in Kohonen (1977).

Earlier it was discussed how, at least for square matrices, knowledge of the eigenvectors of a matrix permits an important simplification to be made. The matrix multiplication of a vector can be replaced by scalar multiplication (cf. Equation 21). I will now show that the Hebbian learning scheme fits nicely with the notion of eigenvectors. Suppose that we wish to associate vectors with scalar copies of themselves. This is what is done, for example, in an auto-associator like those discussed in J. A. Anderson et al. (1977); see Chapters 2 and 17. In other words, we want the vectors $\mathbf{u}_i$ to be of the form $\lambda_i \mathbf{v}_i$ where $\mathbf{v}_i$ are the input vectors. Let us further assume that the n scalars λ_i are distinct. Using the outer product learning rule, we have

$$\mathbf{W} = \mathbf{W}_1 + \cdots + \mathbf{W}_i + \cdots + \mathbf{W}_n$$

where

$$\mathbf{W}_i = \mathbf{u}_i \mathbf{v}_i^T = \lambda_i \mathbf{v}_i \mathbf{v}_i^T.$$

If we now present the vector $\mathbf{v}_i$ to the matrix $\mathbf{W}$ thus formed, we have

$$\begin{aligned}\mathbf{W}\mathbf{v}_i &= (\mathbf{W}_1 + \cdots + \mathbf{W}_i + \cdots + \mathbf{W}_n)\mathbf{v}_i \\ &= (\lambda_1 \mathbf{v}_1 \mathbf{v}_1^T + \cdots + \lambda_i \mathbf{v}_i \mathbf{v}_i^T + \cdots + \lambda_n \mathbf{v}_n \mathbf{v}_n^T)\mathbf{v}_i \\ &= 0 + \cdots + \lambda_i \mathbf{v}_i (\mathbf{v}_i^T \mathbf{v}_i) + \cdots + 0 \\ &= \lambda_i \mathbf{v}_i.\end{aligned}$$

This equation shows that $\mathbf{v}_i$ is an eigenvector of $\mathbf{W}$ with eigenvalue λ_i.

Let me summarize. When we calculate a weight matrix $\mathbf{W}$ using the Hebbian learning rule and associate input vectors to scalar multiples of themselves, then those input vectors are the eigenvectors of $\mathbf{W}$. It is important to note that the matrix $\mathbf{W}$ need not even be calculated—as was stated in the section on eigenvectors, once we have the eigenvectors and eigenvalues of a matrix, we can throw away the matrix. All input-output computations can be done by using Equation 21. This approach is in contrast to a scheme in which we first calculate a matrix **W** from the input vectors, and then calculate the eigenvectors from the matrix **W**. Here, the eigenvectors are available in the statement of the problem.

Why should one want to associate vectors with scalar copies of themselves? Essentially, the answer is that a system which learns in this way will exhibit the desirable property of *completion*. That is, when partial versions of previously learned vectors are presented to the system, it will be able to produce the whole vector. Readers desiring more details on how this is done should consult Anderson et al. (1977).

MATRIX INVERSES

Throughout this chapter, I have discussed the linear vector equation $\mathbf{u} = \mathbf{W}\mathbf{v}$. First, I discussed the situation in which $\mathbf{v}$ was a known vector and $\mathbf{W}$ a known matrix. This corresponds to knowing the input to a system and its matrix, and wanting to know the output of the system. Next, I discussed the situation in which $\mathbf{v}$ and $\mathbf{u}$ were known vectors, and a matrix $\mathbf{W}$ was desired to associate the two vectors. This is the learning problem discussed in the previous section. Finally, in this section, I discuss the case in which both $\mathbf{u}$ and $\mathbf{W}$ are known, but $\mathbf{v}$ is unknown. There are many situations in which this problem arises, including the change of basis discussed in the next section.

As we will see, the solution to this problem involves the concept of a *matrix inverse*. Let us first assume that we are dealing with square matrices. The inverse of a matrix $\mathbf{W}$, if it exists, is another matrix denoted $\mathbf{W}^{-1}$ that obeys the following equations:

$$\mathbf{W}^{-1}\mathbf{W} = \mathbf{I}$$

$$\mathbf{W}\mathbf{W}^{-1} = \mathbf{I}$$

where $\mathbf{I}$ is the identity matrix.

Example:

$$\mathbf{W} = \begin{bmatrix} 1 & \frac{1}{2} \\ -1 & 1 \end{bmatrix} \qquad \mathbf{W}^{-1} = \begin{bmatrix} \frac{2}{3} & -\frac{1}{3} \\ \frac{2}{3} & \frac{2}{3} \end{bmatrix}$$

$$\mathbf{W}\mathbf{W}^{-1} = \begin{bmatrix} 1 & \frac{1}{2} \\ -1 & 1 \end{bmatrix} \begin{bmatrix} \frac{2}{3} & -\frac{1}{3} \\ \frac{2}{3} & \frac{2}{3} \end{bmatrix} = \begin{bmatrix} 1 & 0 \\ 0 & 1 \end{bmatrix}$$

$$\mathbf{W}^{-1}\mathbf{W} = \begin{bmatrix} \frac{2}{3} & -\frac{1}{3} \\ \frac{2}{3} & \frac{2}{3} \end{bmatrix} \begin{bmatrix} 1 & \frac{1}{2} \\ -1 & 1 \end{bmatrix} = \begin{bmatrix} 1 & 0 \\ 0 & 1 \end{bmatrix}$$

A good discussion of how to calculate a matrix inverse can be found in Strang (1976).

Let us now show that the matrix inverse is the tool we need to solve the equation $\mathbf{u} = \mathbf{W}\mathbf{v}$, where $\mathbf{v}$ is the unknown. We multiply both sides of the equation by $\mathbf{W}^{-1}$, which yields

$$\begin{aligned} \mathbf{W}^{-1}\mathbf{u} &= \mathbf{W}^{-1}\mathbf{W}\mathbf{v} \\ &= \mathbf{I}\mathbf{v} \\ &= \mathbf{v}. \end{aligned}$$

Thus the solution of the equation simply involves multiplying $\mathbf{u}$ by the matrix $\mathbf{W}^{-1}$.

Example. We wish to find the vector $\mathbf{v}$ that satisfies the equation

$$\begin{bmatrix} 1 & \frac{1}{2} \\ -1 & 1 \end{bmatrix} \mathbf{v} = \begin{bmatrix} 3 \\ 3 \end{bmatrix}.$$

To do so, we use the matrix $\mathbf{W}^{-1}$ given above:

$$\mathbf{v} = \begin{bmatrix} \frac{2}{3} & -\frac{1}{3} \\ \frac{2}{3} & \frac{2}{3} \end{bmatrix} \begin{bmatrix} 3 \\ 3 \end{bmatrix} = \begin{bmatrix} 1 \\ 4 \end{bmatrix}.$$

We can now check the result as follows:

$$\begin{bmatrix} 1 & \frac{1}{2} \\ -1 & 1 \end{bmatrix} \begin{bmatrix} 1 \\ 4 \end{bmatrix} = \begin{bmatrix} 3 \\ 3 \end{bmatrix}.$$

It is important to realize that $\mathbf{W}^{-1}$, despite the new notation, is simply a matrix like any other. Furthermore, the equation $\mathbf{v} = \mathbf{W}^{-1}\mathbf{u}$ is nothing more than a linear mapping of the kind we have studied throughout this chapter. The domain of this mapping is the range of

W, and the range of the mapping is the domain of **W**. This inverse relationship is shown in Figure 25. The fact that $\mathbf{W}^{-1}$ represents a function from one vector space to another has an important consequence. For every **u** in the domain of $\mathbf{W}^{-1}$, there can be only one **v** in the range such that $\mathbf{v} = \mathbf{W}^{-1}\mathbf{u}$. This is true because of the definition of a function. Now let us look at the consequence of this fact from the point of view of the mapping represented by **W**. If **W** maps any two distinct points $\mathbf{v}_1$ and $\mathbf{v}_2$ in its domain to the same point **u** in its range, that is, if **W** is not one-to-one, then there can be no $\mathbf{W}^{-1}$ to represent the inverse mapping.

We now wish to characterize matrices that can map distinct points in the domain to a single point in the range, for these are the matrices that do not have inverses. To do so, first recall that one way to view the equation $\mathbf{u} = \mathbf{W}\mathbf{v}$ is that **u** is a linear combination of the column vectors of **W**. The coefficients of the linear combination are the components of **v**. Thus, there is more than one **v** which maps to the same point **u** exactly in the case in which there is more than one way to write **u** as a linear combination of the column vectors of **W**. These are completely equivalent statements. As discussed earlier, we know that a vector **u** can be written as a unique linear combination of a set of vectors only in the case where the vectors are linearly independent. Otherwise, if the vectors are linearly dependent, then there are an infinite number of ways to write **u** as a linear combination. Therefore, we have the result that a matrix has an inverse only if its column vectors are linearly independent.

For square matrices with linearly dependent column vectors and for non-square matrices, it is possible to define an inverse called the *generalized inverse*, which performs part of the inverse mapping. In the case in which an infinite number of points map to the same point, there will be an infinite number of generalized inverses for a particular matrix, each of which will map from the point in the range to one of the points in the domain.

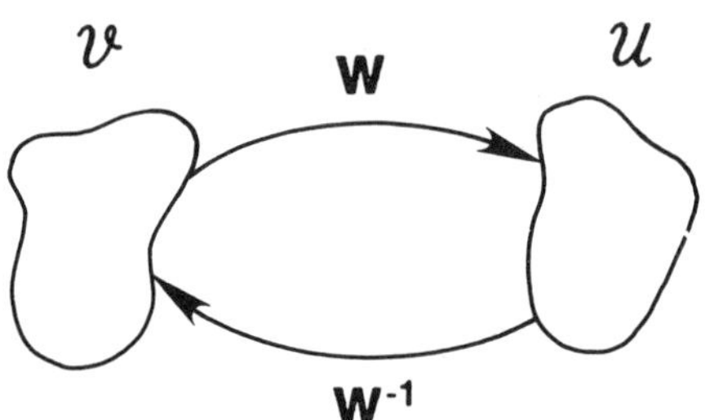

FIGURE 25.

In summary, the matrix inverse $\mathbf{W}^{-1}$ can be used to solve the equation $\mathbf{u} = \mathbf{W}\mathbf{v}$, where $\mathbf{v}$ is the unknown, by multiplying $\mathbf{u}$ by $\mathbf{W}^{-1}$. The inverse exists only when the column vectors of $\mathbf{W}$ are linearly independent. Let me mention in passing that the maximum number of linearly independent column vectors of a matrix is called the *rank* of the matrix.[7] An $n \times n$ matrix is defined to have *full rank* if the rank is equal to n. Thus, the condition that a matrix have an inverse is equivalent to the condition that it have full rank.

CHANGE OF BASIS

As was discussed earlier, a basis for a vector space is a set of linearly independent vectors that span the space. Although we most naturally tend to think in terms of the standard basis, for a variety of reasons it is often convenient to change the basis. For example, some relationships between vectors or operations on vectors are easier to describe when a good choice of basis has been made. To make a change of basis, we need to be able to describe the vectors and matrices we are using in terms of the new basis. In this section, I use the results of the previous section to discuss the problems that arise under a change of basis. I also discuss some of the implications of a change of basis for linear PDP models.

The numbers that are used to represent a vector, it should be remembered, are relative to a particular choice of basis. When we change the basis, these numbers, which we refer to as *coordinates*, change. Our first task, then, is to find a way to relate the coordinates in a new basis to the coordinates in the old basis. Let me begin with an example. In Figure 26, there is a vector $\mathbf{v}$, which in the standard basis has the coordinates $\begin{bmatrix} 2 \\ 1 \end{bmatrix}$. We now change basis by choosing two new basis vectors, $\mathbf{y}_1 = \begin{bmatrix} 1 \\ -1 \end{bmatrix}$ and $\mathbf{y}_2 = \begin{bmatrix} 1/2 \\ 1 \end{bmatrix}$. As shown in Figure 27, $\mathbf{v}$ can be written as a linear combination of $\mathbf{y}_1$ and $\mathbf{y}_2$. It turns out, as we shall see below, that the coefficients 1 and 2 are the correct coefficients of $\mathbf{y}_1$ and $\mathbf{y}_2$ in the linear combination. Let the symbol $\mathbf{v}^*$ represent $\mathbf{v}$ in the new basis. Thus, $\mathbf{v}^* = \begin{bmatrix} 1 \\ 2 \end{bmatrix}$.

7 An important theorem in linear algebra establishes that, for any matrix, the maximum number of linearly independent column vectors is equal to the maximum number of linearly independent row vectors. Thus, the rank can be taken as either.

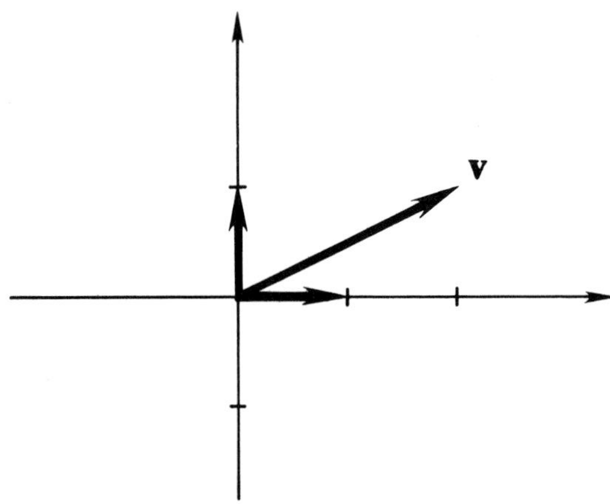

FIGURE 26.

We now want to show how to find the coordinates of a vector $\mathbf{v}$ in a new basis $\mathbf{y}_1, \mathbf{y}_2, \ldots, \mathbf{y}_n$. These coordinates are simply the coefficients c_i in the equation

$$\mathbf{v} = c_1\mathbf{y}_1 + c_2\mathbf{y}_2 + \cdots + c_n\mathbf{y}_n. \tag{23}$$

Let us form a matrix $\mathbf{Y}$ whose columns are the new basis vectors $\mathbf{y}_i$, and let $\mathbf{v}^*$ be the vector whose components are the c_i. Then Equation 23 is equivalent to the following equation:

$$\mathbf{v} = \mathbf{Y}\mathbf{v}^* \tag{24}$$

where $\mathbf{v}^*$ is the unknown. The solution to the problem is now clear: we use the inverse matrix $\mathbf{Y}^{-1}$ to calculate the unknown vector as in the previous section:

$$\mathbf{v}^* = \mathbf{Y}^{-1}\mathbf{v}.$$

Example. Letting $\mathbf{y}_1 = \begin{bmatrix} 1 \\ -1 \end{bmatrix}$ and $\mathbf{y}_2 = \begin{bmatrix} \frac{1}{2} \\ 1 \end{bmatrix}$, we have $\mathbf{Y} = \begin{bmatrix} 1 & \frac{1}{2} \\ -1 & 1 \end{bmatrix}$ and $\mathbf{Y}^{-1} = \begin{bmatrix} \frac{2}{3} & -\frac{1}{3} \\ \frac{2}{3} & \frac{2}{3} \end{bmatrix}$.

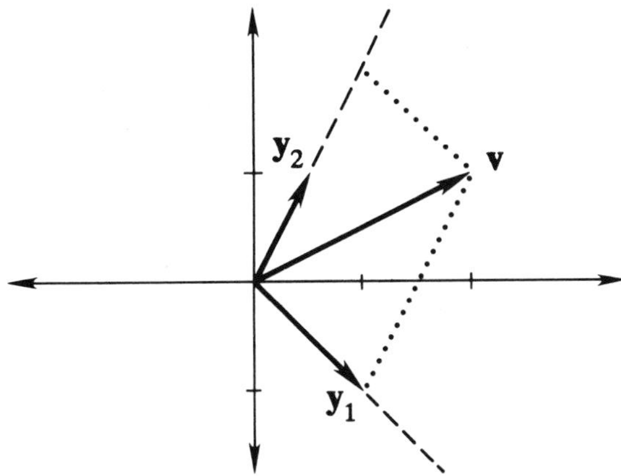

FIGURE 27.

Thus,

$$\mathbf{v}^* = \mathbf{Y}^{-1}\mathbf{v} = \begin{bmatrix} \frac{2}{3} & -\frac{1}{3} \\ \frac{2}{3} & \frac{2}{3} \end{bmatrix} \begin{bmatrix} 2 \\ 1 \end{bmatrix} = \begin{bmatrix} 1 \\ 2 \end{bmatrix}.$$

Notice that we have also solved the inverse problem along the way. That is, suppose that we know the coordinates $\mathbf{v}^*$ in the new basis, and we wish to find the coordinates $\mathbf{v}$ in the old basis. This transformation is that shown in Equation 24: We simply multiply the vector of new coordinates by $\mathbf{Y}$.

We have shown how to represent vectors when the basis is changed. Now, let us accomplish the same thing for matrices. Let there be a square matrix $\mathbf{W}$ that transforms vectors in accordance with the equation $\mathbf{u} = \mathbf{W}\mathbf{v}$. Suppose we now change basis and write $\mathbf{v}$ and $\mathbf{u}$ in the new basis as $\mathbf{v}^*$ and $\mathbf{u}^*$. We want to know if there is a matrix that does the same thing in the new basis as $\mathbf{W}$ did in the original basis. In other words, we want to know if there is a matrix $\mathbf{W}^*$ such that $\mathbf{u}^* = \mathbf{W}^*\mathbf{v}^*$. This is shown in the diagram in Figure 28, where it should be remembered that $\mathbf{v}$ and $\mathbf{v}^*$ (and $\mathbf{u}$ and $\mathbf{u}^*$) are really the same vector, just described in terms of different basis vectors.

To see how to find $\mathbf{W}^*$, consider a somewhat roundabout way of solving $\mathbf{u}^* = \mathbf{W}^*\mathbf{v}^*$. We can convert $\mathbf{v}^*$ back to the original basis, then map from $\mathbf{v}$ to $\mathbf{u}$ using the matrix $\mathbf{W}$, and finally convert $\mathbf{u}$ to $\mathbf{u}^*$.

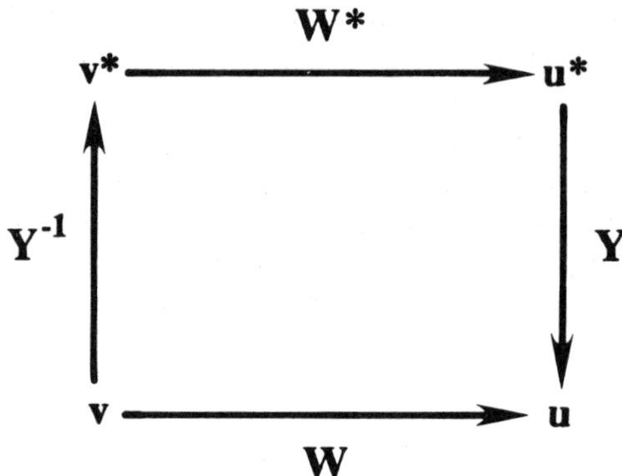

FIGURE 28.

Luckily, we already know how to make each of these transformations—they are given by the equations:

$$\mathbf{v} = \mathbf{Y}\mathbf{v}^*$$

$$\mathbf{u} = \mathbf{W}\mathbf{v}$$

$$\mathbf{u}^* = \mathbf{Y}^{-1}\mathbf{u}.$$

Putting these three equations together, we have

$$\begin{aligned} \mathbf{u}^* &= \mathbf{Y}^{-1}\mathbf{u} \\ &= \mathbf{Y}^{-1}\mathbf{W}\mathbf{v} \\ &= \mathbf{Y}^{-1}\mathbf{W}\mathbf{Y}\mathbf{v}^*. \end{aligned}$$

Thus, $\mathbf{W}^*$ must be equal to $\mathbf{Y}^{-1}\mathbf{W}\mathbf{Y}$. Matrices related by an equation of the form $\mathbf{W}^* = \mathbf{Y}^{-1}\mathbf{W}\mathbf{Y}$ are called *similar*.

One aspect of this discussion needs further elaboration. We have been treating matrices as linear operators on a vector space. However, as the results of this section make clear, a matrix is tied to a particular basis. That is, the numbers in the matrix are just as arbitrary as the numbers used for representing vectors. When the basis changes, the numbers change according to the equation $\mathbf{W}^* = \mathbf{Y}^{-1}\mathbf{W}\mathbf{Y}$. The underlying mapping, which remains the same when the matrix $\mathbf{W}$ is used in the original basis and the matrix $\mathbf{W}^*$ is used in the new basis, is called a *linear transformation*. The same linear transformation is represented by different matrices in different bases.

It is interesting to recast the results on eigenvectors in terms of a change of basis. For some matrix $\mathbf{W}$, let us consider changing basis to the eigenvectors of $\mathbf{W}$. Let us find the matrix $\mathbf{W}^*$ in the new basis. For each eigenvector $\mathbf{y}_i$, by definition

$$\mathbf{W}\mathbf{y}_i = \lambda_i \mathbf{y}_i. \tag{25}$$

If $\mathbf{Y}$ is a matrix whose columns are the $\mathbf{y}_i$, then we can write Equation 25 for all of the eigenvectors at once as follows (cf. Figure 21):

$$\mathbf{WY} = \mathbf{Y}\Lambda$$

where Λ is a diagonal matrix whose entries on the main diagonal are the eigenvalues λ_i. You should try to convince yourself of the correctness of this equation, particularly the placement of Λ. Now premultiply both sides by $\mathbf{Y}^{-1}$ to give

$$\mathbf{Y}^{-1}\mathbf{WY} = \Lambda.$$

Thus, the matrix $\mathbf{W}^*$ is equal to Λ. In other words, when we use the eigenvectors of $\mathbf{W}$ as the new basis, the matrix corresponding to $\mathbf{W}$ in the new basis is a diagonal matrix whose entries are the eigenvalues. This is really nothing more than a restatement of the earlier results on eigenvectors, but seen in a different perspective.

It is worthwhile to consider the implications of a change of basis for PDP models. How does the behavior of the model depend on the basis that is chosen? This question is discussed in depth in Chapter 22. For now, let us simply note that the linear structure of a set of vectors remains the same over a change of basis. That is, if a vector can be written as a linear combination of a set of vectors in one basis, then it can be written as the same linear combination of those vectors in all bases. For example, let $\mathbf{w} = a\mathbf{v}_1 + b\mathbf{v}_2$. Let $\mathbf{Y}$ be the matrix of a change of basis. Then we have

$$\begin{aligned}\mathbf{w}^* &= \mathbf{Y}^{-1}\mathbf{w} \\ &= \mathbf{Y}^{-1}(a\mathbf{v}_1 + b\mathbf{v}_2) \\ &= a\mathbf{Y}^{-1}\mathbf{v}_1 + b\mathbf{Y}^{-1}\mathbf{v}_2 \\ &= a\mathbf{v}_1^* + b\mathbf{v}_2^*.\end{aligned}$$

The coefficients in the linear combination are the same in the old and in the new basis. The equations show that this result holds because change of basis is a *linear* operation.

The behavior of a linear PDP model depends entirely on the linear structure of the input vectors. That is, if $\mathbf{w} = a\mathbf{v}_1 + b\mathbf{v}_2$, then the response of the system to $\mathbf{w}$ is determined by its response to $\mathbf{v}_1$ and $\mathbf{v}_2$ and the coefficients a and b. The fact that a change of basis preserves the linear structure of the vectors shows that it is this linear structure that is relevant to the behavior of the model, and not the particular basis chosen to describe the vectors.

NONLINEAR SYSTEMS

The use of nonlinearity occurs throughout this book and throughout the literature on parallel distributed processing systems (Anderson et al., 1977; Grossberg, 1978; Hopfield, 1982; Kohonen, 1977). In this section, I will indicate some of the reasons why nonlinearities are deemed necessary.[8] Although these reasons are based on the desire for behaviors outside the domain of linear models, it should be stated that linear systems have a great deal of power in themselves, and that many of the nonlinearities represent comparatively small changes to underlying models which are linear. Other models are more fundamentally nonlinear. Further discussions of nonlinear mathematics can be found in Chapters 10 and 22.

One simple nonlinearity has already arisen in the discussion of a PDP system with one output unit. Such a system computes the inner product of its weight vector and the input vector. This is a linear system, given the linearity of the inner product. The geometrical properties of the inner product led us to picture the operation of this system as computing the closeness of input vectors to the weight vector in space.

Suppose we draw a line perpendicular to the weight vector at some point, as in Figure 29. Since all vectors on this line project to the same point on the weight vector, their inner products with the weight vector are equal. Furthermore, all vectors to the left of this line have a smaller inner product, and all vectors to the right have a larger inner product. Let us choose a fixed number as a *threshold* for the unit by requiring that if the inner product is greater than the threshold, the unit outputs a 1, otherwise it outputs a 0. Such a unit breaks the space into two parts by producing a different response to vectors in the two parts.

This use of a threshold is natural in using the unit to classify patterns as belonging to one group or another. The essential point is that the threshold permits the unit to make a *decision*. Other units in a larger

[8] Since nonlinear systems in general are systems that are defined as "not linear," it is important to understand clearly what "linear" means. A review of the section on linearity may be necessary before proceeding.

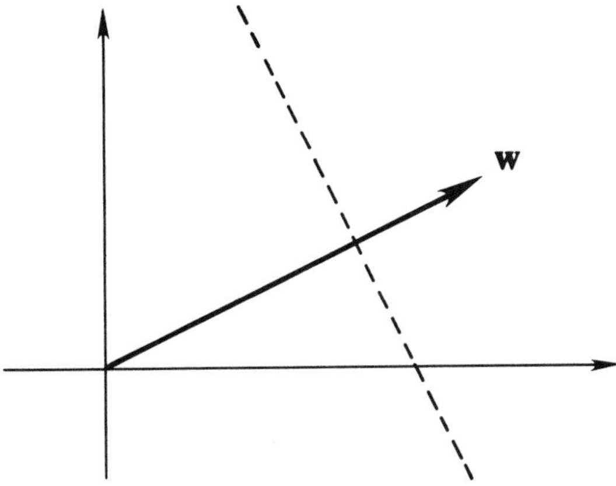

FIGURE 29.

system that take their input from this unit could choose completely different behaviors based on the decision. Notice also that the unit is a categorizer: All input vectors that are on the same side of the space lead to the same response.

To introduce a threshold into the mathematical description of the processing unit, it is necessary to distinguish between the activation of the unit and its output. A function relating the two quantities is shown in Figure 30. It produces a one or a zero based on the magnitude of the activation. It is also possible to have a probabilistic threshold. In this case, the farther the activation is above the threshold, the more

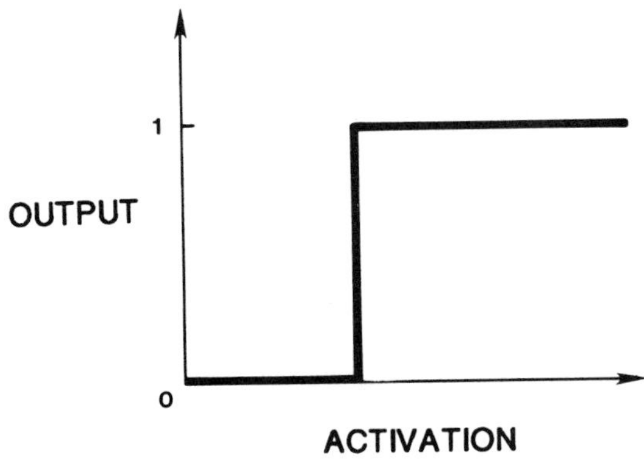

FIGURE 30.

likely the unit is to have an output of one, and the farther the activation is below the threshold, the more likely the unit is to have an output of zero. Units such as these are discussed in Chapters 6 and 7.

The threshold unit is a good example of many of the nonlinearities that are to be found in PDP models. An underlying linear model is modified with a nonlinear function relating the output of a unit to its activation. Another related example of such a nonlinearity is termed *subthreshold summation.* It is often observed in biological systems that two stimuli presented separately to the system provoke no response, although when presented simultaneously, a response is obtained. Furthermore, once the system is responding, further stimuli are responded to in a linear fashion. Such a system can be modeled by endowing a linear PDP unit with the nonlinear output function in Figure 31. Note that only if the sum of the activations produced by vectors exceeds T will a response be produced. Also, there is a *linear range* in which the system responds linearly. It is often the case in nonlinear systems that there is such a linear range, and the system can be treated as linear provided that the inputs are restricted to this linear range.

One reason why subthreshold summation is desirable is that it suppresses noise. The system will not respond to small random inputs that are assumed to be noise.

All physical systems have a limited *dynamic range.* That is, the response of the system cannot exceed a certain maximum response. This fact can be modeled with the output function in Figure 32, which shows a linear range followed by a cutoff. The system will behave linearly until the output reaches **M**, at which point no further increase can occur. In Figure 33, a nonlinear function is shown which also has a

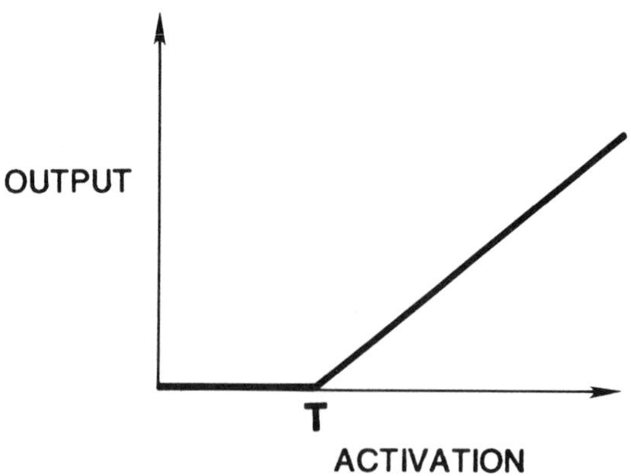

FIGURE 31.

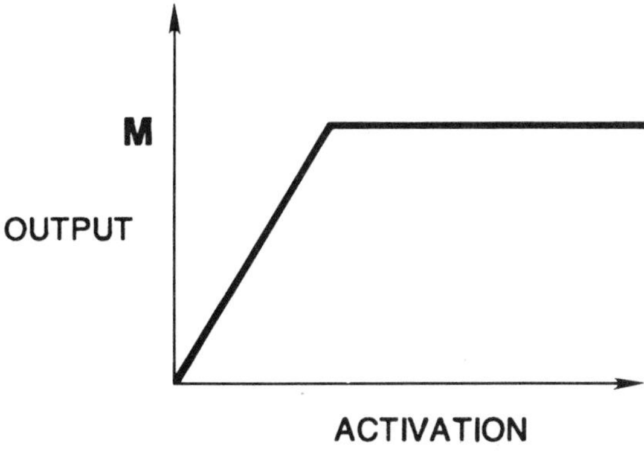

FIGURE 32.

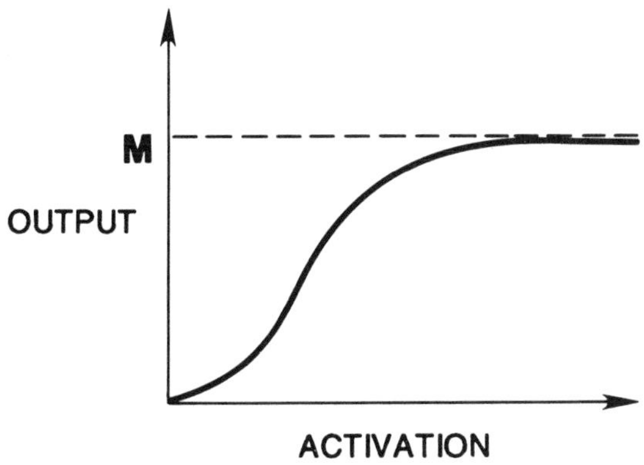

FIGURE 33.

maximum output M. This curve, called a *sigmoid*, is a sort of hybrid between Figure 31 and Figure 32. It combines noise suppression with a limited dynamic range. Chapter 8 shows how such units are necessary for certain kinds of interesting behavior to arise in layered networks.

To summarize, I have described some of the ways in which linear systems are modified to produce nonlinear systems that exhibit certain desired behaviors. All of these systems have an important linear component and are sometimes referred to as *semilinear*. Furthermore, several of the systems have a linear range in which the nonlinearities can be ignored. The next chapter discusses more fundamentally nonlinear systems.

FURTHER READING

Halmos, P. R. (1974). *Finite-dimensional vector spaces.* New York: Springer-Verlag. For the more mathematically minded. An excellent account of linear algebra from an abstract point of view.

Kohonen, T. (1977). *Associative memory: A system theoretic approach.* Berlin: Springer-Verlag. This book has a short tutorial on linear algebra. The discussion of associative memory depends heavily on the mathematics of linear algebra.

Strang, G. (1976). *Linear algebra and its applications.* New York: Academic Press. A general textbook treating most of the essentials of linear algebra. It is especially good in its treatment of computational topics. A good place to find out about calculating matrix inverses and eigenvalues.

CHAPTER 10

The Logic of Activation Functions

R. J. WILLIAMS

The notion of logical computation, in some form or other, seems to provide a convenient language for describing the operation of many of the networks we seek to understand. Digital computers are built out of such constituents as AND and OR gates. Feature-detecting neurons in biological sensory systems are often idealized as signaling the presence or absence of their preferred features by becoming highly active or inactive, respectively. It seems a relatively simple extension of this concept to allow the activity of units in the network to range over some interval rather than over just two values; in this case the activity of a unit is regarded as signaling its *degree of confidence* that its preferred feature is present, rather than just the presence or absence of this feature. There are several ways one might attempt to formalize this degree-of-confidence notion. For example, if the activation values range over the closed unit interval [0,1], one might treat such an activation value as a conditional probability; alternatively, it might be viewed as a measure of truth in some unit-interval-valued logic, such as fuzzy logic (Zadeh, 1965).

There is at least one alternative to the notion of activation as degree of confidence which sometimes provides a convenient language for discussing the role of, for example, neural feature detectors in sensory systems. In this view, the activation of a unit encodes (within finite limits) the *amount* of its preferred feature present. This rival view seems advantageous particularly when the computation performed is described in the language of linear systems or linear signal processing;

examples of this are the concepts of spatial filtering and spatial Fourier analysis in the visual system and the concept of correlational processing in matrix models of associative memory (Kohonen, 1977). Chapter 9 describes the relevant mathematics for this approach, that of *linear algebra*.

This chapter explores some ideas motivated by the first of these two views of a PDP unit's computation (i.e., as some generalization of the notion of a Boolean function), but the approach is implicitly based on a very liberal interpretation of what this means. Essentially, the only structure assumed for the set of confidence values is that it be a totally ordered set with a Boolean interpretation of its endpoints. While a fully developed mathematical theory along these lines would deal with those properties that are invariant under any transformations preserving this structure, the ideas presented here do not go this far.

The specific program to be embarked upon here is probably best described as an exploratory interweaving of several threads, all related to these notions of logical computation and their potential applicability to the study of activation functions. First, the point of view is taken that any function whatsoever is a candidate for being an activation function. From this perspective, the traditional linear and thresholded linear activation functions may be viewed as very isolated examples from a much larger range of possibilities. Next, several ways to shrink this vast space of possibilities are suggested. One way proposed here is the imposition of a constraint based on the requirement that the notion of excitatory or inhibitory input be meaningful. Another way is the introduction of an equivalence relation on activation functions based on invariance under transformations preserving the logical and ordinal structure. Finally, an investigation is carried out to determine just where certain familiar types of activation functions, built out of the more traditional ingredients such as additive, subtractive, and multiplicative interactions among input values and weights, fit into this scheme. As a by-product of this development, some elementary results concerning implementation of Boolean functions via real-valued functions are also obtained.

This last aspect is closely related to what is historically one of the oldest formal approaches to the theory of neural computation, in which neurons are treated as Boolean devices. This approach was pioneered by McCulloch and Pitts (1943); an introductory overview of this whole subject can be found in the text by Glorioso and Colón Osorio (1980). An important influence on much of the work done in this area has been the perceptron research of Rosenblatt (1962; Minsky & Papert, 1969).

In what follows, several simplifying assumptions will be made. The first is that the range of values over which each input to a unit may vary is the same as the range of values over which the output of the unit (its *activation*) may vary. Another is that time may be ignored as a variable. The activation function of a unit will be taken to be a function that computes the output of the unit (at a fixed but unspecified time) as a function of its inputs (at a presumably slightly earlier but unspecified time). Thus, given a unit with n inputs whose activation values range over the set $\mathbf{A}$, the activation function α for this unit is just a function from $\mathbf{A}^n$ (the set of ordered n-tuples of elements of $\mathbf{A}$) to $\mathbf{A}$, denoted $\alpha : \mathbf{A}^n \rightarrow \mathbf{A}$.

In order to avoid cluttering the presentation, detailed proofs of the results have been omitted; in their place are short sketches indicating the key steps. A more rigorous and abstract formulation of the basic concepts introduced here, along with detailed proofs of the results, may be found in Williams (1983).

EXAMPLES OF ACTIVATION RULES

The following are some examples of activation functions from which models have been constructed.

Example 1. $\mathbf{A} = \{0,1\}$ (the two-point set), $\alpha = f \circ g$, where g is linear into $\mathbb{R}$ and $f : \mathbb{R} \rightarrow \mathbf{A}$ is a thresholding function. (The operator $\circ$ between two functions here denotes composition in a right-to-left manner.) A unit using this activation function is called a *threshold logic unit* or a *linear threshold unit* and is the basis of the simple perceptron (Rosenblatt, 1962; Minsky & Papert, 1969).

Example 2. $\mathbf{A} = \mathbb{R}$, α linear (Kohonen, 1977).

Example 3. $\mathbf{A} = \mathbf{I}$ (the closed unit interval $[0,1]$), $\alpha = f \circ g$, where g is linear into $\mathbb{R}$ and f is nondecreasing into $\mathbf{I}$. This is a commonly used variant of Example 1. Let us call this a *quasi-linear activation function*. The function f is sometimes called a *squashing function* for obvious reasons.

Example 4. $\mathbf{A} = \mathbf{I}$, $\alpha = f \circ g$, where f is nondecreasing into $\mathbf{I}$ and g is a multilinear function into $\mathbb{R}$ of the form

$$g(x_1, \ldots, x_n) = x_1 x_2 + x_3 x_4 + \cdots + x_{n-1} x_n$$

(where n is assumed to be even). Such an activation function is suggested by Hinton (1981b). Note that this is similar to Example 3 except that the coefficients have now become explicit inputs. This type of activation function will be called a *gating activation function* because the odd-numbered inputs gate the even-numbered ones (and vice-versa).

Example 5. $\mathbf{A} = \mathbf{I}$, $\alpha = f \circ g$, where f is nondecreasing into $\mathbf{I}$ and g is an arbitrary multilinear function into $\mathbb{R}$. That is, g is of the form

$$g(x_1, \ldots, x_n) = \sum_{S_j \in \mathbf{P}} w_j \prod_{i \in S_j} x_i ,$$

where $\mathbf{P}$ is the power set (i.e., set of subsets) of $\{1, \ldots, n\}$. Such an activation function is called a *sigma-pi activation function*, with the coefficients w_j being called *weights*. (We might also call this a *quasi-multilinear activation function* to emphasize its relationship to Example 3.) Note that Examples 3 and 4 are just special cases of this activation function.

THE MAIN CONCEPTS

Henceforth in this chapter the set of activation values will be assumed to be the closed unit interval [0,1], denoted $\mathbf{I}$. An *activation function* is then simply a function $\alpha : \mathbf{I}^n \rightarrow \mathbf{I}$. It will be convenient to identify $0 \in \mathbf{I}$ with the Boolean value *false* and $1 \in \mathbf{I}$ with the Boolean value *true*.

Now we introduce a key concept of this chapter by considering the extension of the familiar notion of a monotonic function to the multidimensional case in two different ways. In order to get a feeling for the precise definitions to be given below, first consider what it means for an input to a unit to have an excitatory influence on the output of that unit. Such an input must have the property that an increase in its value must result in an increase in the output of the unit, as long as all other inputs are held constant. Furthermore, this should be true regardless of the values of the other inputs. A similar property should hold for an inhibitory input, where the output of the unit must decrease as the value of the input is increased in this case. This is the basic idea behind the notion of *uniform monotonicity*, as defined below. The weaker notion of *monotonicity-in-context* corresponds to the situation in which an input may be sometimes excitatory and sometimes inhibitory, depending on the values taken on by the other inputs.

Now we make these concepts rigorous. Let $\alpha : \mathbf{I}^n \rightarrow \mathbf{I}$. Pick one of the coordinates, say the kth, and fix all coordinates but this one, which is allowed to vary. This defines a function of a single variable which is parameterized by the remaining coordinates. Such a function is called a *section* of the original function α along the kth coordinate. Note that there is one such section along the kth coordinate for each possible combination of values for the remaining $n-1$ coordinates. Now make the following definitions:[1]

1. α is *monotonic-in-context along the* kth *coordinate* if all its sections along the kth coordinate are monotonic.

2. α is *uniformly monotonic in the* kth *coordinate* if all sections along the kth coordinate are monotonic and have the same sense (i.e., all are nondecreasing or all are nonincreasing).

3. α is *monotonic-in-context* if it is monotonic-in-context along all its coordinates.

4. α is *uniformly monotonic* if it is uniformly monotonic along all its coordinates.

One special case of a uniformly monotonic function is a *uniformly nondecreasing* function, which has the property that all its sections along all coordinates are nondecreasing. This special case will be used later.

Note that if α is uniformly monotonic then it is monotonic-in-context, but the converse need not be true, unless α is a function of a single variable, in which case both definitions collapse onto the usual notion of monotonicity. The key distinction between uniformly monotonic and monotonic-in-context is that the sense of monotonicity of the sections of α along the kth coordinate must be fixed for each k in order for α to be uniformly monotonic.

It is important to emphasize the significance of these monotonicity concepts for activation functions. An activation function is uniformly monotonic if and only if each input may be classified as solely excitatory or solely inhibitory, independently of the values actually taken on by any other inputs. Thus the usual sense of excitatory or inhibitory input to a unit is meaningful exactly when the unit's activation function is uniformly monotonic. If a unit's activation function is monotonic-in-context, then it may not be possible to categorize its inputs as solely excitatory or solely inhibitory, but the following may be a useful conceptualization of such a unit's operation: Certain inputs to the unit are

[1] The reader should be warned that the names introduced here for these concepts are not standard; these terms were chosen because it was felt that they helped to clarify the important distinctions being made in the current context.

used to set the context for the computation of its output as a function of the remaining inputs, and each input in this latter group has purely excitatory or purely inhibitory effect on the unit's output in this particular context. Whether this turns out to be a useful way to view the monotonic-in-context activation function and its possible role in activation models will not be explored here. The main reason for introducing the concept is simply that it appears to be the strongest variant on monotonicity satisfied by any activation function capable of computing an arbitrary Boolean function (such as the multilinear and sigma-pi activation functions, as will be seen later).

In order to capture the notion of an activation function being simply an extension of a Boolean function, define an activation function $\alpha : \mathbf{I}^n \rightarrow \mathbf{I}$ to be *Boolean-like* if $\alpha(x_1, \ldots, x_n) = 0$ or 1 whenever all the x_i are 0 or 1. In other words, an activation function is Boolean-like if and only if it can be viewed as a Boolean function when restricted to the vertices of $\mathbf{I}^n$. It is also useful to say that such an activation function *realizes* the Boolean function obtained by restricting to vertices.

In order to capture the notion of two activation functions agreeing for Boolean input values, define two activation functions $\alpha_1, \alpha_2 : \mathbf{I}^n \rightarrow \mathbf{I}$ to be *vertex-equivalent* if $\alpha_1(x_1, \ldots, x_n) = \alpha_2(x_1, \ldots, x_n)$ whenever all the x_i are 0 or 1. In other words, two activation functions are vertex-equivalent if and only if they agree on the vertices of $\mathbf{I}^n$. It is clear that vertex-equivalence is indeed an equivalence relation.

The reason for introducing this notion is the suggestion that there may be a certain interchangeability between different activation functions that are vertex-equivalent, in that the logic of a unit's computation might be considered to reside solely in what it does when all input lines are set to their extreme values (corresponding to *true* or *false*). If two vertex-equivalent activation functions are additionally monotonic-in-context and continuous, then an even stronger case can be made for their interchangeability in certain models, but these ideas will not be pursued here.

ILLUSTRATION OF THESE CONCEPTS

A number of examples of activation functions $\alpha : \mathbf{I}^2 \rightarrow \mathbf{I}$ will now be presented to clarify the definitions given in the previous section. The figure corresponding to each example consists of three different graphical representations for that particular function: (a) a three-dimensional plot of $\alpha(x_1, x_2)$ versus (x_1, x_2); (b) a contour plot showing at which points (x_1, x_2) certain values of $\alpha(x_1, x_2)$ are attained; and (c) various sections of α along x_1 superimposed on a single two-dimensional plot. The activation function being displayed in each figure is defined in the caption of that figure.

Figures 1, 2, and 3 show three different activation functions that realize the Boolean AND function at the vertices, while Figures 4, 5, and 6 show three different activation functions realizing the Boolean OR function at the vertices. These functions are all Boolean-like and uniformly monotonic.

Figure 7 shows a realization of the Boolean XOR (*exclusive or*) function. The activation function depicted is Boolean-like and monotonic-in-context, but not uniformly monotonic. In fact, no realization of XOR can be uniformly monotonic. Figure 8 shows an activation function that is uniformly monotonic but not Boolean-like. Its restriction to vertices thus does not have a straightforward Boolean interpretation; this activation function might be viewed as a unit-interval confidence measure based on the number of active inputs. Finally, Figure 9 shows a rather pathological example of an activation function. It is Boolean-like and vertex-equivalent to the constant function 1, but intuition suggests that any unit in a PDP network which performs such a computation will behave very differently from one which puts out the constant value 1. This essential difference in behavior is formalized here in terms of the observation that such an activation function fails to be monotonic-in-context while the constant function 1 is uniformly monotonic.

SOME RESULTS

Before stating the main results, it will be helpful to define two functions, the first of which maps vertices of $\mathbf{I}^n$ to Boolean expressions in formal variables $X_1, \ldots, X_n$, and the second of which maps such Boolean expressions to real algebraic expressions in formal variables $x_1, \ldots, x_n$. In our notation for Boolean expressions we will use "+" to denote disjunction and juxtaposition to denote conjunction but it will always be clear from the context whether Boolean or real operations are intended.

The mapping from vertices to Boolean expressions is defined by assigning to a vertex $(v_1, \ldots, v_n)$ the conjunction in which each X_i appears once, with the negation operator applied to X_i if and only if $v_i = 0$. For example, applying this function to the vertex (0,1,1,0) of $\mathbf{I}^4$ yields the expression $\bar{X}_1 X_2 X_3 \bar{X}_4$.

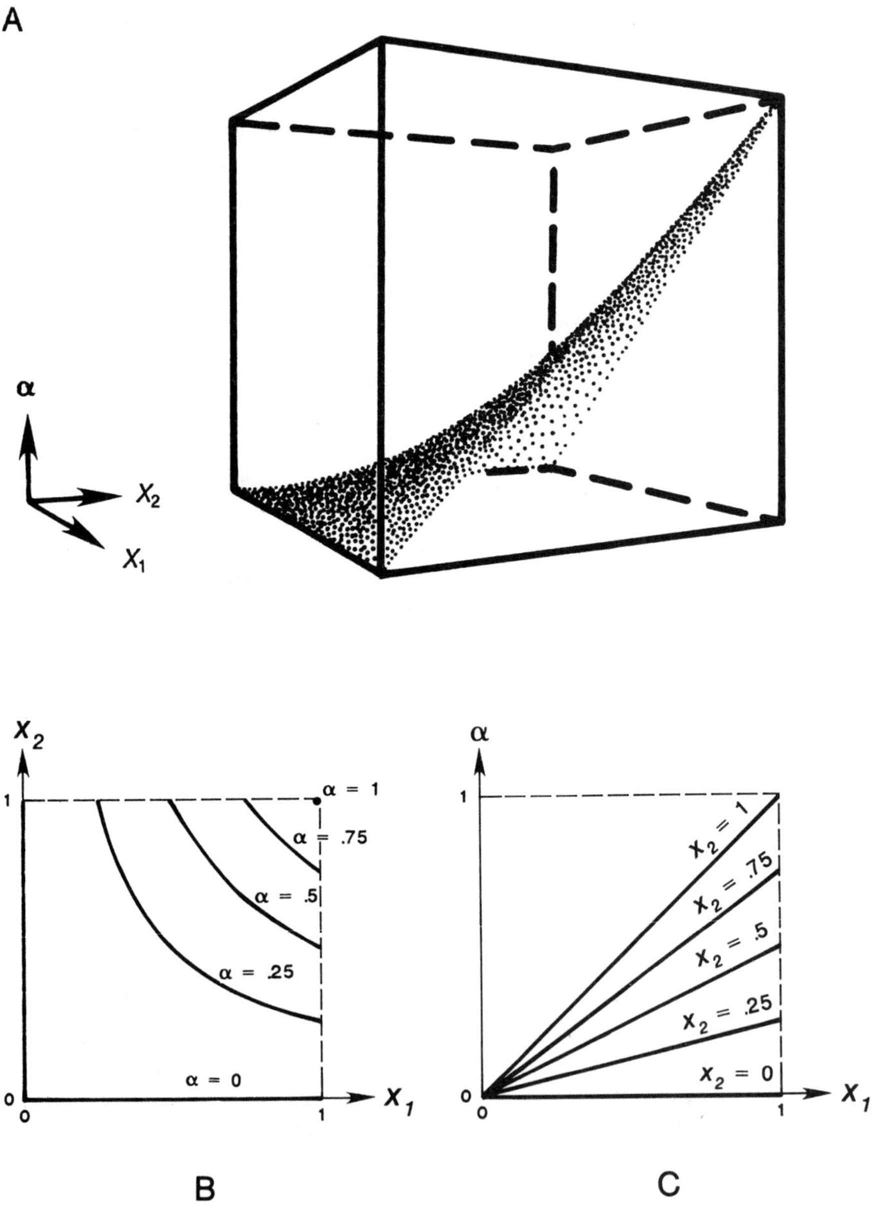

FIGURE 1. $\alpha(x_1,x_2) = x_1x_2$. *A*: Three-dimensional plot. The cube is bounded by the planes where each coordinate is 0 or 1. *B*: Contour plot. *C*: Some sections along x_1. Note that each section along x_1 is a linear function with nonnegative slope; by symmetry the same is true of each section along x_2. Thus this function is uniformly nondecreasing.

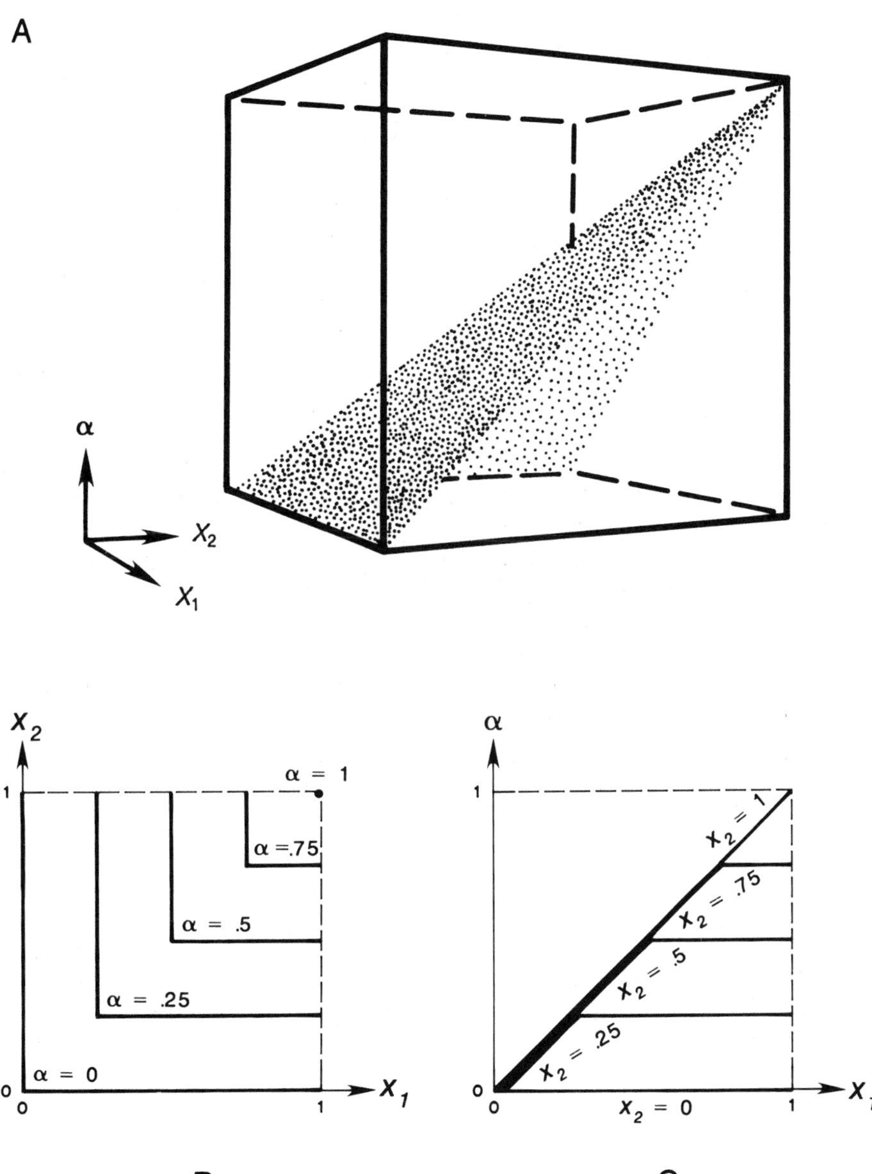

FIGURE 2. $\alpha(x_1,x_2) = \min(x_1,x_2)$. *A*: Three-dimensional plot. The cube is bounded by the planes where each coordinate is 0 or 1. *B*: Contour plot. *C*: Some sections along x_1. Note that the three-dimensional plot of this function consists of two planar surfaces. Evidently, each section along x_1 is a nondecreasing function; by symmetry the same is true of each section along x_2. Thus this function is uniformly nondecreasing.

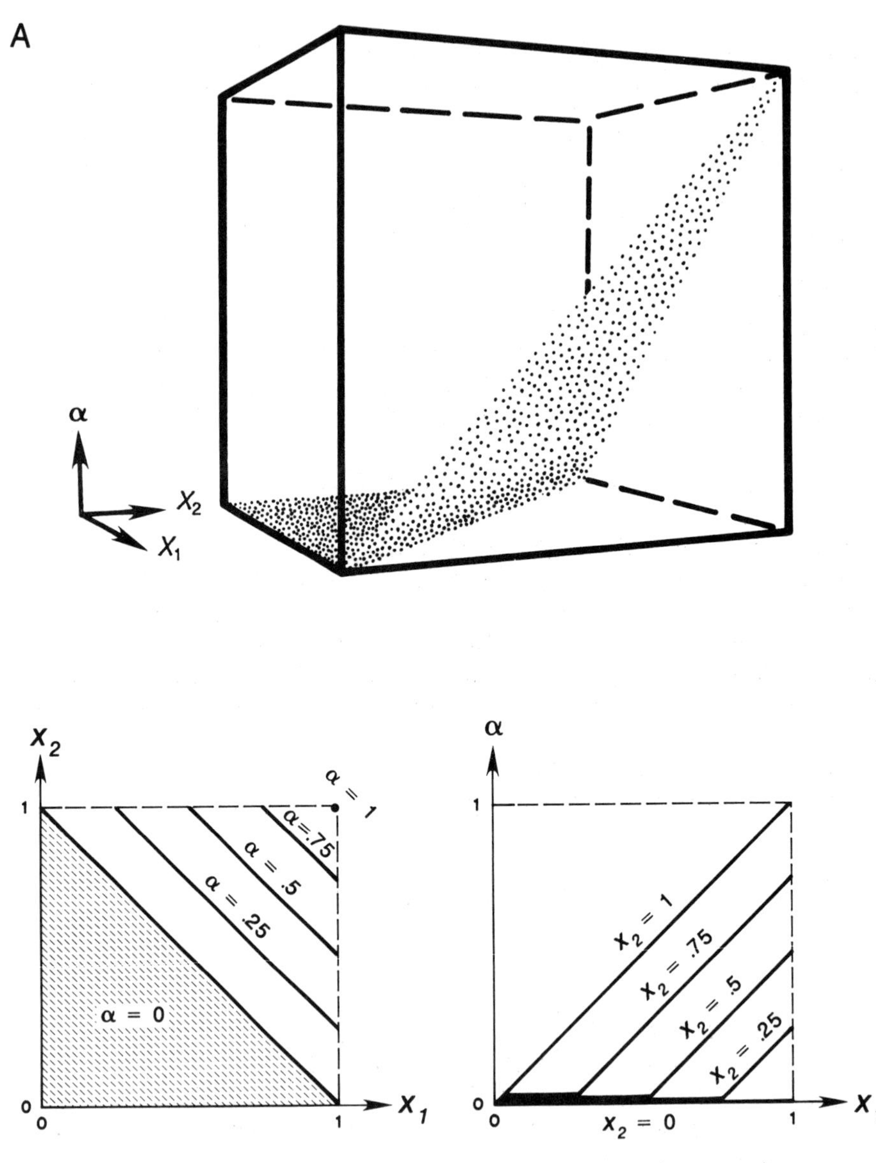

FIGURE 3. $\alpha(x_1,x_2) = \max(0,x_1+x_2-1)$. *A*: Three-dimensional plot. The cube is bounded by the planes where each coordinate is 0 or 1. *B*: Contour plot. *C*: Some sections along x_1. Note that the three-dimensional plot of this function consists of two planar surfaces. Clearly, each section along x_1 is a nondecreasing function; by symmetry the same is true of each section along x_2. Thus this function is uniformly nondecreasing.

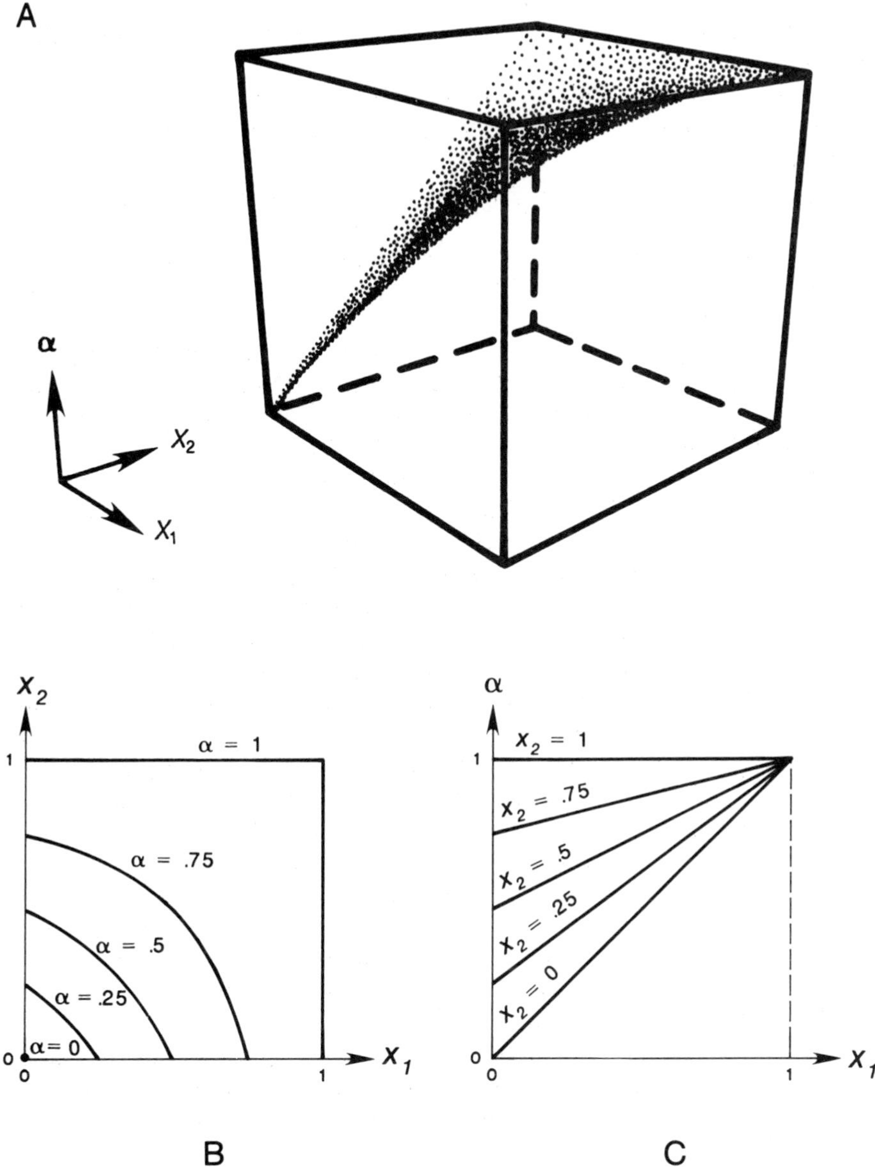

FIGURE 4. $\alpha(x_1,x_2) = x_1+x_2-x_1x_2$. *A*: Three-dimensional plot. The cube is bounded by the planes where each coordinate is 0 or 1. *B*: Contour plot. *C*: Some sections along x_1. Note that each section along x_1 is a linear function with nonnegative slope; by symmetry the same is true of each section along x_2. Thus this function is uniformly nondecreasing.

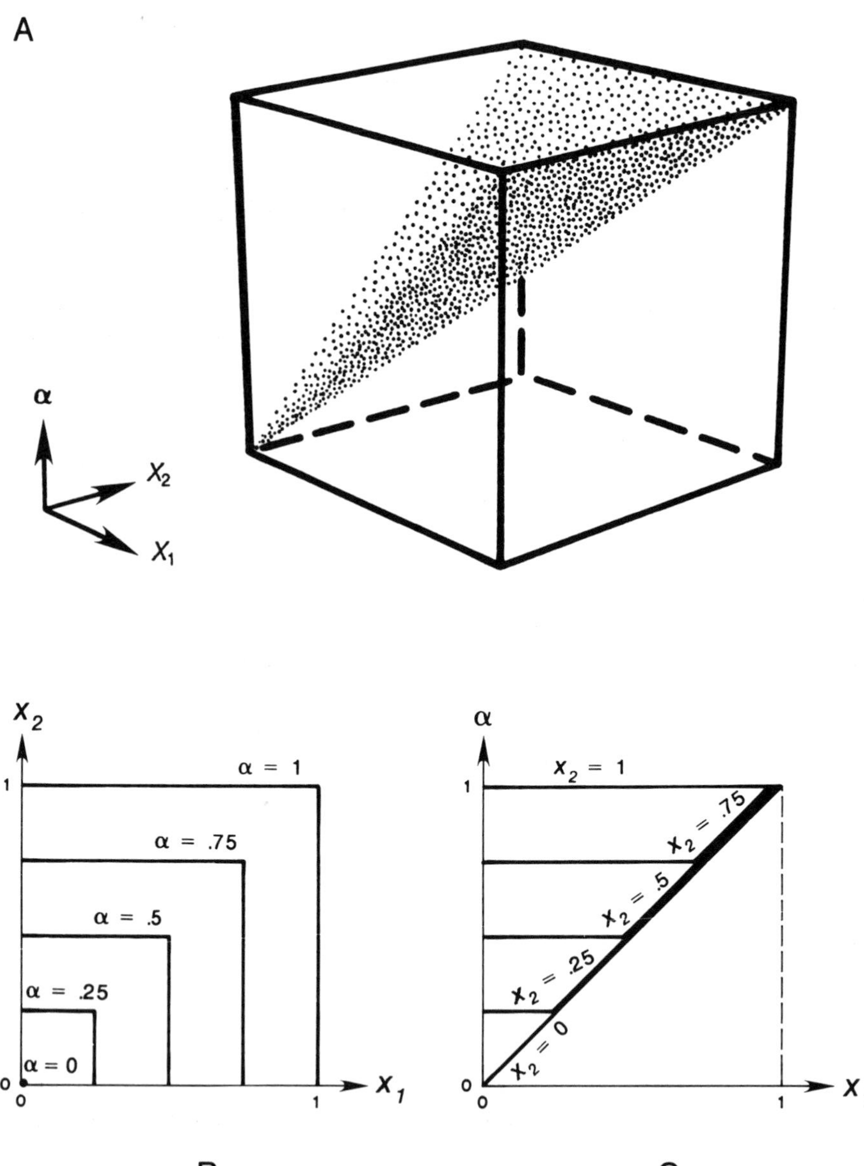

FIGURE 5. $\alpha(x_1,x_2) = \max(x_1,x_2)$. *A*: Three-dimensional plot. The cube is bounded by the planes where each coordinate is 0 or 1. *B*: Contour plot. *C*: Some sections along x_1. Note that the three-dimensional plot of this function consists of two planar surfaces. Note also that each section along x_1 is a nondecreasing function; by symmetry the same is true of each section along x_2. Thus this function is uniformly nondecreasing.

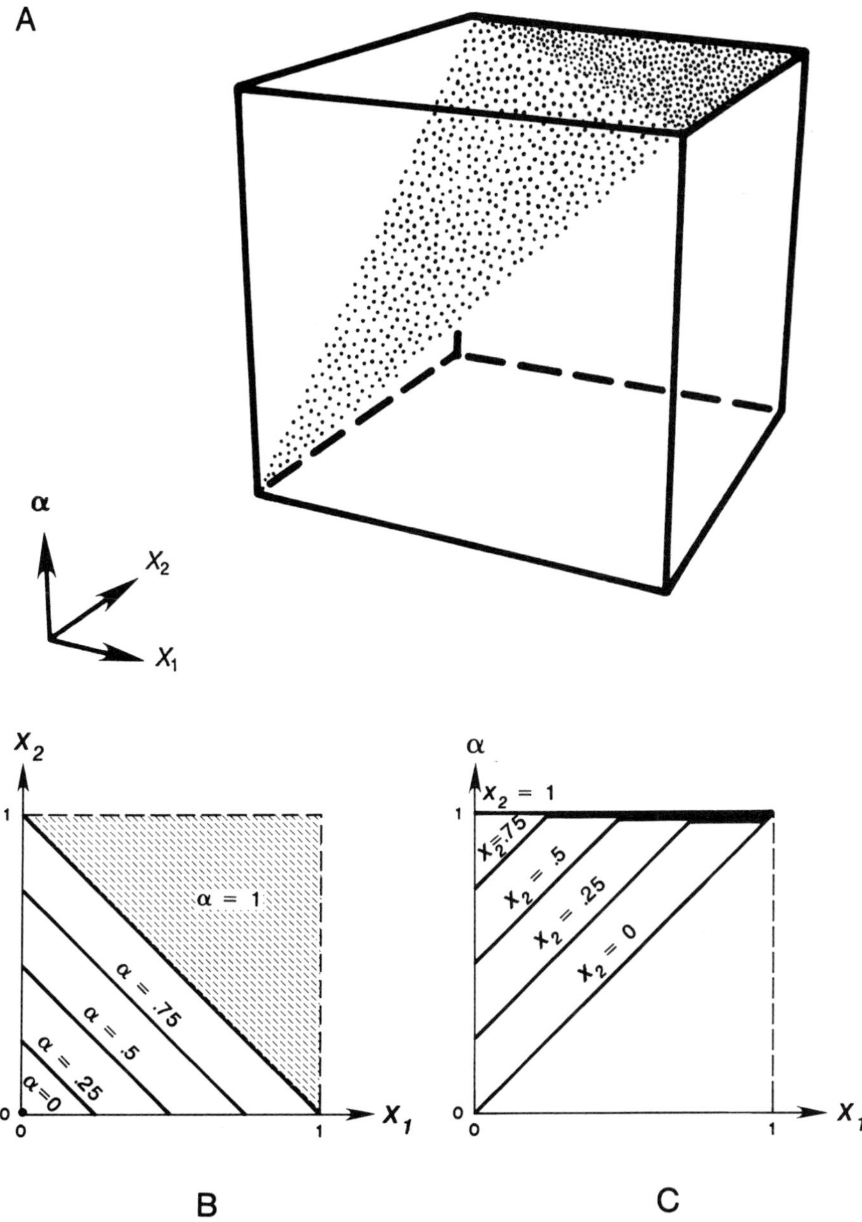

FIGURE 6. $\alpha(x_1,x_2) = \min(1,x_1+x_2)$. *A*: Three-dimensional plot. The cube is bounded by the planes where each coordinate is 0 or 1. *B*: Contour plot. *C*: Some sections along x_1. Note that the three-dimensional plot of this function consists of two planar surfaces. Evidently, each section along x_1 is a nondecreasing function; by symmetry the same is true of each section along x_2. Thus this function is uniformly nondecreasing.

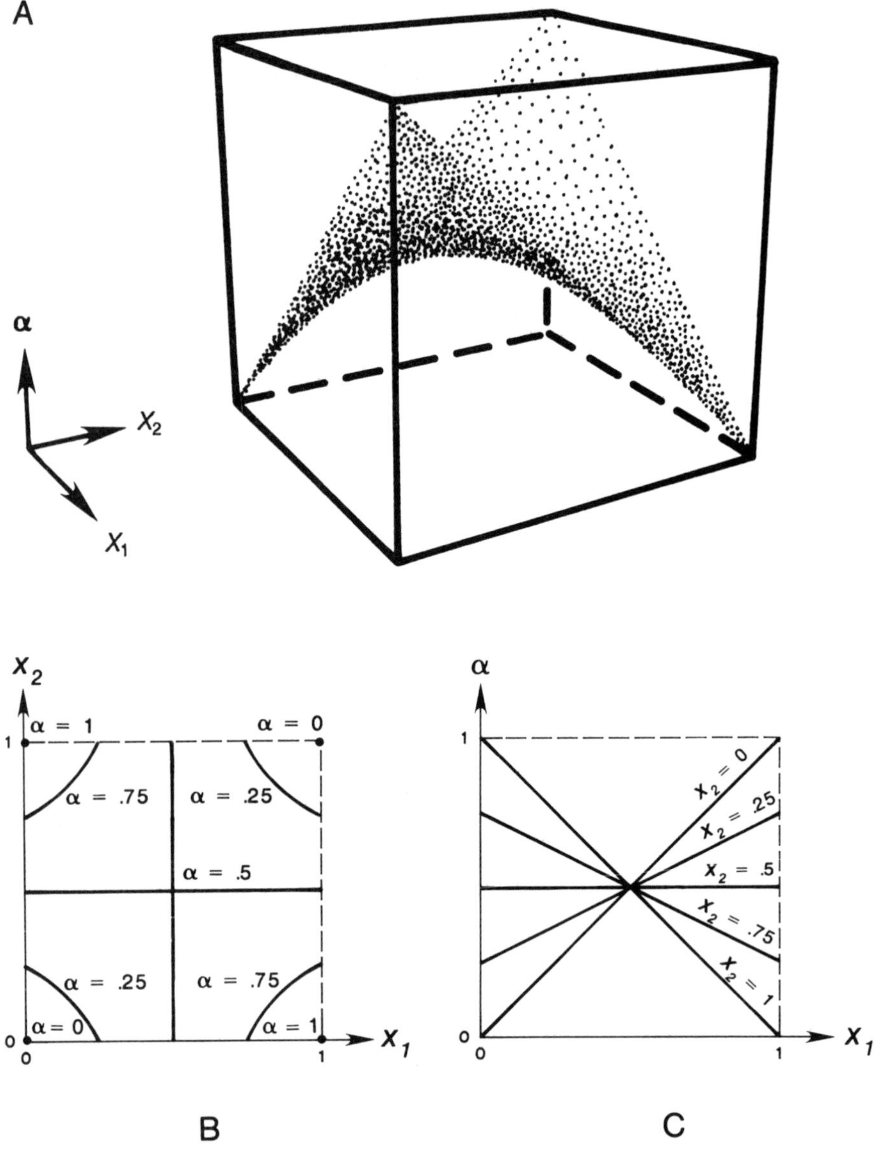

FIGURE 7. $\alpha(x_1,x_2) = x_1+x_2-2x_1x_2$. *A*: Three-dimensional plot. The cube is bounded by the planes where each coordinate is 0 or 1. *B*: Contour plot. *C*: Some sections along x_1. Note the saddle shape of the three-dimensional plot of this function. Also note that the sections along x_1 are linear functions with slopes ranging from 1 to -1; by symmetry the same is true of the sections along x_2. Thus this function is monotonic-in-context but not uniformly monotonic.

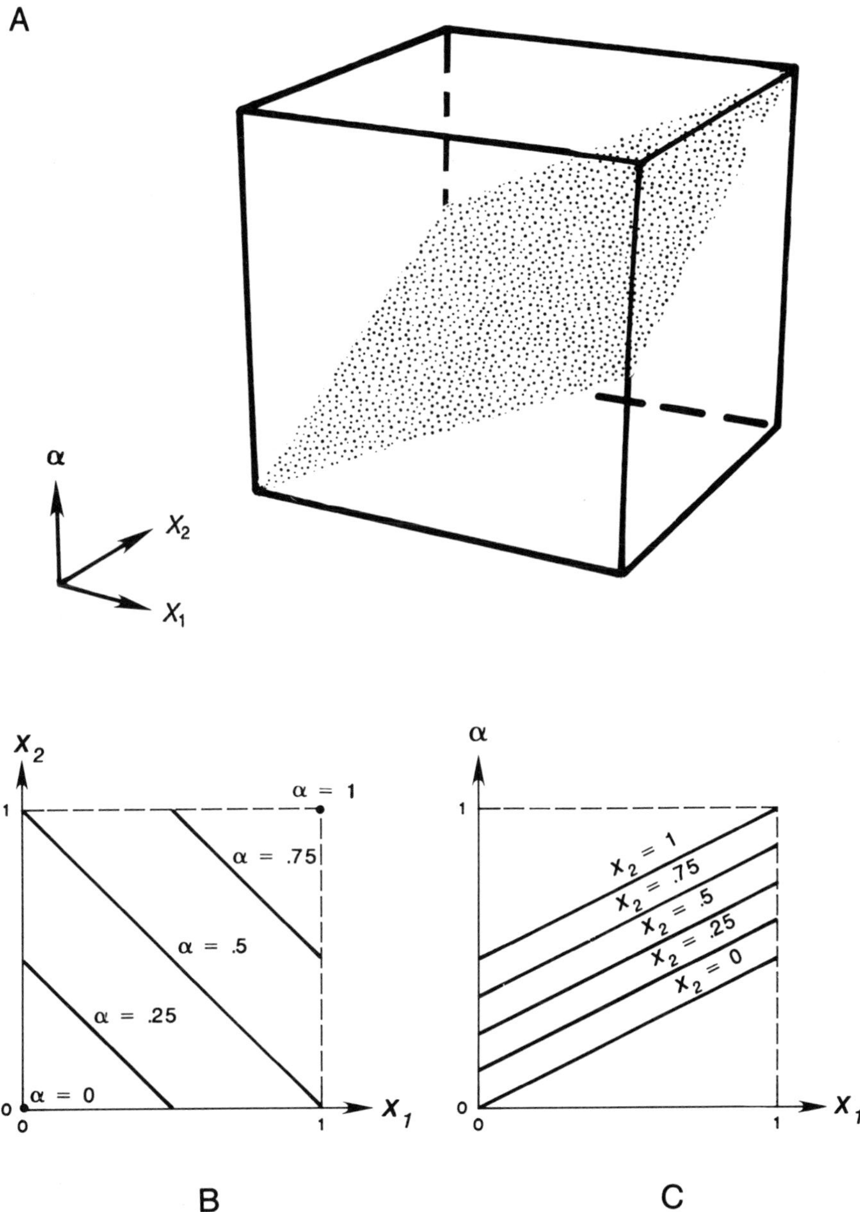

FIGURE 8. $\alpha(x_1,x_2) = \frac{1}{2}(x_1+x_2)$. *A*: Three-dimensional plot. The cube is bounded by the planes where each coordinate is 0 or 1. *B*: Contour plot. *C*: Some sections along x_1. Note that the three-dimensional plot of this function consists of a single planar surface. Each section along x_1 is a linear function with slope ½, as is each section along x_2, by symmetry. Thus this function is uniformly nondecreasing.

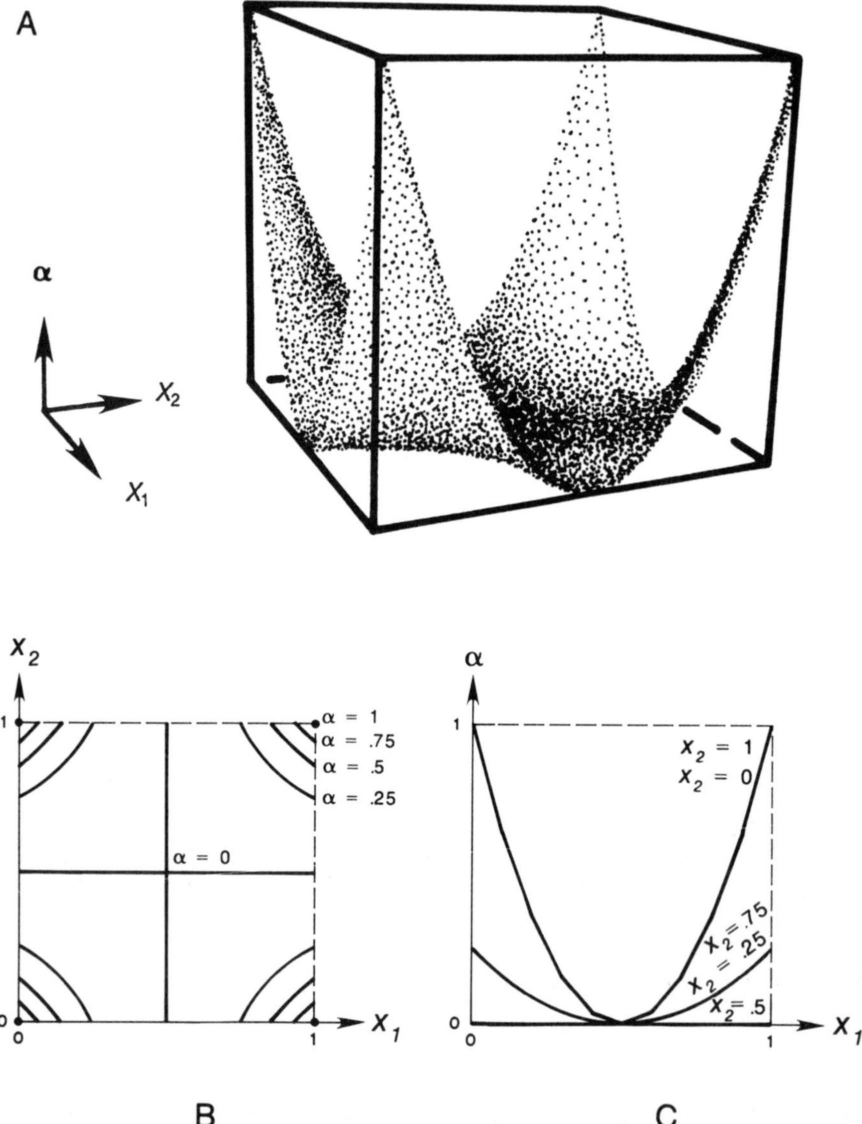

FIGURE 9. $\alpha(x_1,x_2) = (2x_1-1)^2(2x_2-1)^2$. *A*: Three-dimensional plot. The cube is bounded by the planes where each coordinate is 0 or 1. *B*: Contour plot. *C*: Some sections along x_1. Note that the sections along x_1 are parabolas of varying widths. Evidently, this function is not monotonic-in-context since, for example, when $x_2 = 0$, α first decreases and then increases as x_1 increases.

The mapping from Boolean expressions to real algebraic expressions is defined by replacing:

1. *True* by 1.
2. *False* by 0.
3. The disjunction operator by addition.
4. The conjunction operator by multiplication.
5. The negation operator by subtraction from 1.
6. X_i by x_i, for each i.

For example, applying this function to the Boolean expression $X_1\bar{X}_2+\bar{X}_1$ yields the real expression $x_1(1-x_2)+(1-x_1)$. It should be emphasized that this is a function defined only on formal expressions; two expressions that are equivalent under Boolean algebra will not, in general, be mapped to the same real algebraic expression or even equivalent real algebraic expressions. In other words, it is not a mapping from Boolean functions to real functions.

A standard result from Boolean algebra is that any Boolean function may be expressed in a certain canonical form, called the *disjunctive normal form*. A simple prescription for this form is as follows: Form a disjunction of terms, each of which is the result of applying the vertices-to-Boolean-expressions function described above to those vertices of $\mathbf{I}^n$ for which the function takes on the value *true*. For example, the disjunctive normal form for the Boolean function $\beta(X_1,X_2) = X_1+X_2$ is $X_1\bar{X}_2+\bar{X}_1X_2+X_1X_2$.

A closely related result for multilinear functions is the following:

> *Lemma.* For any function assigning arbitrary real numbers to the vertices of $\mathbf{I}^n$ there is a unique multilinear function agreeing with the given function on these vertices.

This function is formed in a manner generalizing the prescription given above for the disjunctive normal form: For each vertex of $\mathbf{I}^n$, form the corresponding Boolean conjunct; then apply the other function described above to turn each of these conjuncts into a real expression; finally, form the sum of these individual expressions with each one weighted by the value of the given function at the corresponding vertex. It will be convenient to dub the result the *vertex normal form* for the given function. For example, the vertex normal form for a multilinear function α of two variables is

$$\alpha(x_1,x_2) = \alpha(0,0)(1-x_1)(1-x_2)+\alpha(0,1)(1-x_1)x_2$$
$$+\alpha(1,0)x_1(1-x_2)+\alpha(1,1)x_1x_2.$$

This lemma has the following immediate consequence:

> *Theorem 1.* Given any Boolean function, there is a unique multilinear activation function realizing it.

In contrast, not every Boolean function can be realized by a quasi-linear activation function. Those Boolean functions that can be so realized are called *linearly separable.* It is easily shown that any linearly separable Boolean function is necessarily uniformly monotonic, but the converse is not true. A simple example of a function that is not linearly separable is the XOR function $\beta_1(X_1,X_2) = X_1\bar{X}_2 + \bar{X}_1X_2$. The easiest way to see that it is not linearly separable is to observe that it is not uniformly monotonic. An example of a function that is uniformly monotonic but not linearly separable is

$$\beta_2(X_1,X_2,X_3,X_4) = X_1X_2 + X_3X_4.$$

Our next result, also a consequence of the lemma, shows that the very general class of all activation functions may be represented up to vertex-equivalence by the narrower class of multilinear activation functions.

> *Theorem 2.* Every activation function is vertex-equivalent to a unique multilinear activation function.

The next result suggests that monotonicity-in-context is enjoyed by a fairly wide variety of activation functions.

> *Theorem 3.* Every sigma-pi activation function is monotonic-in-context.

This is an easy consequence of three facts: (a) that a multilinear function is linear in each variable when the other variables are held constant; (b) that a linear function is monotonic; and (c) that the composition of monotonic functions is monotonic.

The following result characterizes uniform monotonicity for multilinear activation functions.

> *Theorem 4.* A multilinear activation function is uniformly monotonic if and only if its restriction to vertices is uniformly monotonic.

The key step in the proof of this result is the observation that a multilinear function may be built up inductively through linear interpolation, starting with the values at the vertices. This follows from the fact that a multilinear function is linear in each variable when the other variables are held constant. The remainder of the proof consists of verifying that each step of this inductive construction preserves uniform monotonicity. This result may be extended to the sigma-pi case as well, under certain mild restrictions, using the fact that a strictly increasing function has a monotonic inverse.

Corollary. Let $\alpha = f \circ g$ be a sigma-pi activation function, where g is multilinear and f is a squashing function. If f is strictly increasing, then α is uniformly monotonic if and only if its restriction to vertices is uniformly monotonic.

The results presented up to this point would seem to suggest that the class of multilinear activation functions provides us with sufficient power that we need not consider the more general class of sigma-pi activation functions. However, from the standpoint of uniform monotonicity, there may be some drawbacks in restricting ourselves to multilinear activation functions. One such potential drawback is that a uniformly nondecreasing multilinear activation function may have some negative weights. For example, the Boolean function $\beta(X_1,X_2) = X_1 + X_2$ corresponds, by Theorem 1, to the multilinear activation function $\alpha(x_1,x_2) = x_1 + x_2 - x_1 x_2$, which requires a negative weight even though it is uniformly nondecreasing. But what if a more general sigma-pi activation function were to be used? Is there a sigma-pi realization of this same Boolean function for which all weights are nonnegative? Of course there is in this case: The sigma-pi activation function $\alpha(x_1,x_2) = \min(x_1 + x_2, 1)$ is one such realization; many others could be devised. (These two realizations of the OR function are displayed in Figures 4 and 6.) It seems reasonable to suspect that the following is true:

Conjecture. Every uniformly nondecreasing activation function is vertex-equivalent to a sigma-pi activation function with nonnegative weights.

Note that any sigma-pi activation function with nonnegative weights is certainly uniformly nondecreasing. The conjecture is that the converse is true (up to vertex equivalence). Under the assumption that the uniformly nondecreasing activation function is Boolean-like (as in the preceding example), the conjecture is indeed valid, as the following theorem shows. In fact, the conclusion may be made even stronger in this case.

Theorem 5. Every uniformly nondecreasing Boolean-like activation function is vertex-equivalent to a sigma-pi activation function whose weights are all 0 or 1.

The essential step in the proof of this result is showing that any uniformly nondecreasing Boolean function may be expressed as a disjunction of conjunctions containing no negated factors. Once such an expression is available, the desired sigma-pi activation function is obtained by converting this Boolean expression to a real expression and then composing this with the function $f(z) = \min(z,1)$.

This theorem may be generalized to cover arbitrary senses of uniform monotonicity by running any inputs for which the activation function is nonincreasing through the "inverter" $f(x) = 1-x$. Thus the general class of all uniformly monotonic Boolean-like activation functions may be represented up to vertex-equivalence by a narrower class of sigma-pi activation functions of a certain form.

It is instructive to contrast the sigma-pi activation functions which result from applying Theorems 1 and 5 to a particular uniformly monotonic activation function. Consider the Boolean function of six variables $\beta(X_1,X_2,X_3,X_4,X_5,X_6) = X_1X_2 + X_3X_4 + X_5X_6$. Theorem 1 realizes this using the vertex normal form, which, after simplification, becomes

$$\begin{aligned}\alpha_1(x_1,x_2,x_3,x_4,x_5,x_6) = {} & x_1x_2 + x_3x_4 + x_5x_6 \\ & - x_1x_2x_3x_4 - x_1x_2x_5x_6 - x_3x_4x_5x_6 \\ & + x_1x_2x_3x_4x_5x_6 .\end{aligned}$$

In contrast, Theorem 5 implies a realization of this same function by the gating activation function

$$\alpha_2(x_1,x_2,x_3,x_4,x_5,x_6) = \min(x_1x_2 + x_3x_4 + x_5x_6, 1).$$

CONCLUSION

As suggested in the introduction, the ideas and results presented here represent an exploratory set of concepts intended to help in understanding PDP networks. There is a clear need for a general language and set of concepts for describing and understanding PDP computation, both at the local, individual unit level, as explored here, and at the level of whole networks. (In fact, the greatest need is for a means of describing and understanding the relationship between computation at these two levels.) Whether the ideas contained in this chapter can extend naturally to become a useful framework for understanding the behavior of whole networks is difficult to foresee. One way that this gap between local and global computation might be bridged is by dealing with questions of *learning* in such networks. The goal of learning is generally to cause the network to have a particular global behavior, but the learning should be implemented locally. An example of how the requirement that the network be capable of learning might interact with the ideas explored here can be found by considering the recently discovered *back-propagation* learning algorithm, described in Chapter 8. To be able to apply such a learning algorithm requires imposing the constraint on activation functions that they be differentiable, a property not satisfied by all the examples considered here. As our understanding of learning in PDP networks progresses, we may find still further restrictions useful or even necessary.

ACKNOWLEDGMENTS

This research was supported by a grant to David Zipser from the System Development Foundation. I am also grateful to James McClelland and David Zipser for their many helpful comments and suggestions.

CHAPTER 11

An Analysis of the Delta Rule and the Learning of Statistical Associations

G. O. STONE

The development of parallel distributed processing models involves two complementary enterprises: first, the development of complete models with desired operating characteristics; and second, the in-depth analysis of component mechanisms and basic principles. The primary objective in modeling is the development and testing of complete systems. In general these models are complex and their behavior cannot be fully deduced directly from their mathematical description. In such cases, simulation plays an important role in understanding the properties of a model. Although simulations are useful in determining the properties of a specific model, they do not, on their own, indicate how a model should be modified when a desired behavior is not achieved. An understanding of basic principles and a collection of potential mechanisms with known properties provide the best guides to the development of complex models.

This chapter provides an analysis of one of the most popular components—namely, the error correction learning rule developed by Widrow and Hoff (1960). This learning rule which has been analyzed and employed by a number of authors (Amari, 1977a, 1977b; Kohonen, 1974, 1977; Sutton & Barto, 1981), has been called the Widrow-Hoff rule by Sutton and Barto (1981) and is generally referred to as the delta rule in this book. This rule is introduced in Chapter 2, discussed extensively and generalized in Chapter 8, and employed in models discussed in a number of chapters—most notably Chapters 17 and 18. In the present chapter I show how concepts from linear algebra and vector spaces can provide insight into the operation of this learning mechanism. I then show how this mechanism can be used for learning statistical relationships between patterns, and finally show how the delta rule relates to multiple linear regression. Concepts from linear algebra are used extensively; for explanation of these concepts, especially as applied to PDP models, the reader is referred to Chapter 9.

The Delta Rule in Vector Notation

The delta rule is typically applied to the case in which pairs of patterns, consisting of an input pattern and a target output pattern, are to be associated so that when an input pattern is presented to an input layer of units, the appropriate output pattern will appear on the output layer of units. It is possible to represent the patterns as *vectors* in which each element of the vector corresponds to the activation value of a corresponding unit. Similarly, we can represent the connections from input units to the output units by the cells of a weight matrix. For linear units, the output vector can be computed by multiplying the input vector by the weight matrix. In the present chapter our analysis is restricted to linear units. (See Chapter 8 for a discussion of the delta rule for nonlinear units.)

Now we imagine a learning situation in which the set of input/output pairs are presented (possibly repeatedly) to the system. If the set of input vectors are orthogonal (i.e., at right angles to each other), a simple pattern associator can be constructed using a *product* learning rule in which the change in weight w_{ji} following the presentation of pattern p is given by the product of the ith input element and the jth target element, that is,

$$\Delta_p w_{ji} = t_{pj} i_{pi}$$

where t_{pj} represents the value of the desired or target output for the jth element of pattern p and i_{pi} is the activation value of the ith element of the input for that pattern.[1] In vector notation, we can write the change for the entire weight matrix as

$$\Delta_p = \mathbf{t}_p \mathbf{i}_p^T$$

[1] Note this is essentially the *Hebbian* learning rule. In the Hebbian rule it is assumed that the product of the activation levels of the input and output units determine the weight change. If we assume that the activation of the output unit is entirely determined by the target input the product rule described here is identically the Hebbian rule.

where, as usual, bold letters indicate vectors, uppercase indicates matrices and the superscript T indicates the transpose of a vector or matrix. This learning rule was described in some detail in Chapter 9 and that discussion will not be repeated here. It was shown there that if the input vectors are normalized in length so that $i_p \cdot i_p = 1$ and are orthogonal, the product rule will, after the presentation of all of the input/output patterns, lead to the following weight matrix:

$$\mathbf{W} = \sum_{p=1}^{P} \mathbf{t}_p \mathbf{i}_p^T.$$

If the input vectors are orthogonal, there will be no interference from storing one vector on others already stored so that the presentation of input $\mathbf{i}_p$ will lead to the desired output $\mathbf{t}_p$, that is,

$$\mathbf{W}\mathbf{i}_p = \mathbf{t}_p$$

for all patterns p from 1 to P. Unfortunately, we cannot always insure that the input vectors are orthogonal. Generally, the storage of one input/output pair can interfere with the storage of another and cause crosstalk. For this case a more sophisticated learning rule is required.

Fortunately, as we saw in Chapter 8, the delta rule is a rule that will work when the input patterns are *not* orthogonal. This rule will produce perfect associations so long as the input patterns are merely *linearly independent* (see Chapter 9) and will find a weight matrix which will produce a "least squares" solution for the weight matrix when an exact solution is not possible (i.e., the input patterns are not linearly independent). In matrix notation the rule can be written as

$$\mathbf{W}(n) = \mathbf{W}(n-1) + \eta\delta(n)\mathbf{i}^T(n) \tag{1}$$

where $\mathbf{W}(n)$ is the state of the connection matrix after n presentations, $\mathbf{i}(n)$ is the input presented on the nth presentation, η is a scalar constant which determines the rate of learning, and $\delta(n)$ is the difference between the desired and actual output on trial n, such that

$$\delta(n) = \mathbf{t}(n) - \mathbf{W}(n-1)\mathbf{i}(n) \tag{2}$$

where $\mathbf{t}(n)$ is the desired output (or *target*) for presentation n and $\mathbf{W}(n-1)\mathbf{i}(n) = \mathbf{o}(n)$ is the output actually produced on that presentation. $\mathbf{W}(0)$ is assumed to be the matrix with all zero entries. In other words, the weight matrix is updated by adding the outer product of the response error and the input. (See Chapter 9 for discussion of outer product.) Proofs concerning the convergence of this recursion to the optimum weight matrix (in the sense outlined above) are provided by Kohonen (1974, 1977, 1984).

The Delta Rule in Pattern-Based Coordinates

To this point we have discussed the delta rule for what Smolensky (Chapter 22) has called the *neural* or *unit* level of representation. Before proceeding, it is useful to consider the form that the rule takes in the *conceptual* level of representation in which there is one vector component for each concept. In general, the input and output patterns correspond to an arbitrary set of vectors. Interestingly, it is possible to show that the delta rule applies only to the "structure" of the input and output vectors and not to other details of the representation. In a linear system, it is only the pattern of correlations among the patterns that matter, not the contents of the specific patterns themselves.

We can demonstrate this by deriving the same learning rule following a *change of basis* from the *unit basis* to the *pattern basis*. Since a detailed discussion of the process whereby bases can be changed is given in Chapter 9 and, in more detail, in Chapter 22, I will merely sketch the concept here. Each pattern over a set of units corresponds to a vector. If there are N units, then the vector is of dimension N. In the unit basis, each element of the vector corresponds to the activation value of one of the units. Geometrically, we can think of each unit as specifying a value on a dimension and the entire vector as corresponding to the coordinates of a point in N-dimensional space. Thus, the dimensions of the space correspond directly to the units (this is why it is called the unit basis). Now, a change of basis amounts essentially to a change in coordinate system. This can be accomplished through rotation, as well as other linear transformations. Converting to the pattern basis merely involves transforming the coordinate system so that the patterns line up with the axes. Figure 1 illustrates a simple case of this process. In Figure 1A we give the geometric representation of the patterns. Pattern 1, $\mathbf{p}_1$, involves two units, each with activation value +1. Pattern 2, $\mathbf{p}_2$, has activation values $<+1,-1>$. The patterns described in the unit basis are

$$\mathbf{p}_1 = \begin{bmatrix} +1 \\ +1 \end{bmatrix} \quad \text{and} \quad \mathbf{p}_2 = \begin{bmatrix} +1 \\ -1 \end{bmatrix}.$$

Figure 1B shows the same two vectors, but now expressed with respect to a new coordinate system, the *pattern* coordinate system. In this case the axes correspond to the *patterns* not the *units*. The vectors corresponding to patterns 1 and 2 now become

$$\mathbf{p^*}_1 = \begin{bmatrix} 0 \\ 1 \end{bmatrix} \quad \text{and} \quad \mathbf{p^*}_2 = \begin{bmatrix} 1 \\ 0 \end{bmatrix}.$$

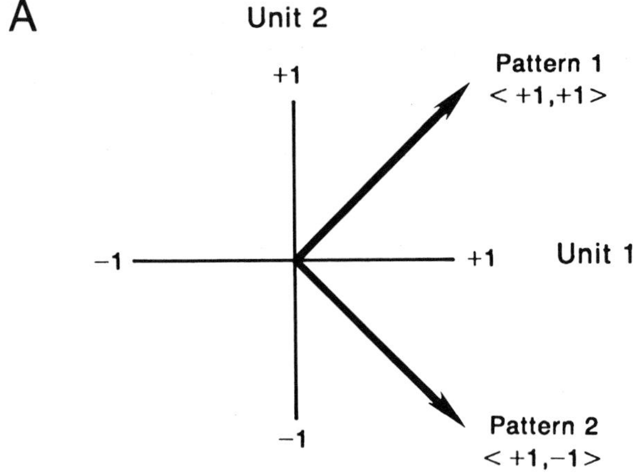

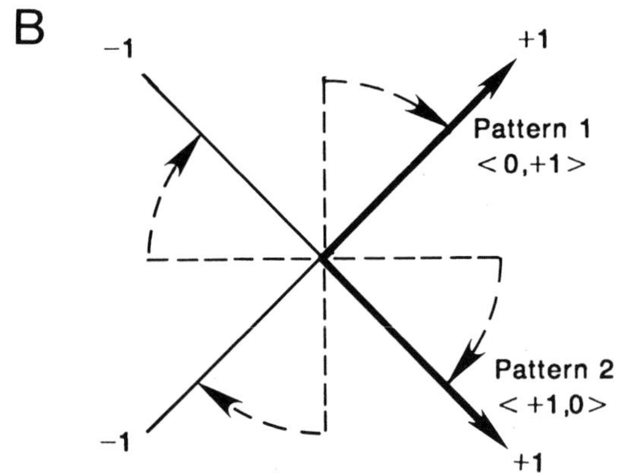

FIGURE 1. An example of conversion from unit-based coordinates into pattern-based coordinates.

In general, conversion to a new basis requires a matrix **P** which specifies the relationship between the new and old coordinate systems. For each vector, $\mathbf{p}_i$, we write the new vector $\mathbf{p}^*_i$ as $\mathbf{p}^*_i = \mathbf{P}\mathbf{p}_i$. If all of the vectors and matrices of the original system are converted into the new basis, we simply have a new way to describe the same system. For present purposes we have two transformation matrices, one that transforms the input patterns into a coordinate space based on the input patterns, which we denote $\mathbf{P}_I$, and one that transforms the target patterns into a coordinate space based on the target patterns, $\mathbf{P}_T$. In this case, we have $\mathbf{i}^*_i = \mathbf{P}_I \mathbf{i}_i$ for the input vectors and $\mathbf{t}^*_i = \mathbf{P}_T \mathbf{t}_i$ for the target vectors. Moreover, since the output vectors must be in the same space as the target vectors we have $\mathbf{o}^*_i = \mathbf{P}_T \mathbf{o}_i$. We must also transform the weight matrix $\mathbf{W}$ to the new basis. Since the weight matrix maps the input space onto the output space, both transformations must be involved in transforming the weight matrix. We can see what this transformation must be by considering the job that the weight matrix must do. Suppose that in the old bases $\mathbf{Wi} = \mathbf{o}$ for some input $\mathbf{i}$ and output $\mathbf{o}$. In the new bases we should be able to write $\mathbf{W}^*\mathbf{i}^* = \mathbf{o}^*$. Thus, $\mathbf{W}^*\mathbf{P}_I\mathbf{i} = \mathbf{P}_T\mathbf{o}$ and $\mathbf{P}_T^{-1}\mathbf{W}^*\mathbf{P}_I\mathbf{i} = \mathbf{o} = \mathbf{Wi}$. From this we can readily see that $\mathbf{P}_T^{-1}\mathbf{W}^*\mathbf{P}_I = \mathbf{W}$ and finally, we can write the appropriate transformation matrix for $\mathbf{W}$ as

$$\mathbf{W}^* = \mathbf{P}_T\mathbf{W}\mathbf{P}_I^{-1}.$$

We can multiply both sides of Equation 1 by $\mathbf{P}_T$ on the right and $\mathbf{P}_I^{-1}$ on the left. This leads to

$$\mathbf{P}_T\mathbf{W}\mathbf{P}_I^{-1}(n) = \mathbf{P}_T\mathbf{W}\mathbf{P}_I^{-1}(n-1) + \mathbf{P}_T \eta \delta(n)\mathbf{i}^T(n)\mathbf{P}_I^{-1}$$

which, by substitution, can be written as

$$\mathbf{W}^*(n) = \mathbf{W}^*(n-1) + \eta\delta^*(n)\left[\mathbf{P}_I^{-1}\mathbf{i}^*(n)\right]^T\mathbf{P}_I^{-1},$$

where

$$\delta^*(n) = \mathbf{t}^*(n) - \mathbf{W}^*(n-1)\mathbf{i}^*(n). \tag{3}$$

Finally, by rearranging we have

$$\mathbf{W}^*(n) = \mathbf{W}^*(n-1) + \eta\,\delta^*(n)\mathbf{i}^*(n)^T\mathbf{C} \tag{4}$$

where the matrix $\mathbf{C}$, given by $\mathbf{C} = (\mathbf{P}_I^{-1})^T\mathbf{P}_I^{-1}$, is a matrix which holds the correlational information among the original input patterns. To see this, recall that we are changing the input patterns into their pattern basis and the target patterns into their pattern basis. Therefore, the vector $\mathbf{i}^*_j$ consists of a 1 in the jth cell and zeros everywhere else. Thus, since $\mathbf{i}_j = \mathbf{P}_I^{-1}\mathbf{i}^*_j$, we see that $\mathbf{P}_I^{-1}$ must be a matrix whose jth column is the jth original input vector. Therefore, $\mathbf{C}$ is a matrix with the inner product of the input vectors $\mathbf{i}_i$ and $\mathbf{i}_j$ occupying the ith row and jth column. This inner product is the vector correlation between the two patterns.

We have finally constructed a new description which, as we shall see, allows many insights into the operation of the delta rule which are normally obscured by the internal structure of the patterns themselves. Instead, we have isolated the critical interpattern structure in the matrix **C**.

One advantage of this new description is that the output the system actually produces—even when it does not match any target exactly—can easily be interpreted as the weighted average of the various target patterns. The value in each cell of the output vector is the coefficient determining the amount of that target in the output. In this case the sum squared error for input/output pattern p, given by

$$E_p = \sum_j (t^*_j - o^*_j)^2,$$

measures the error directly in terms of the degree to which each *target pattern* is present in the output, rather than the degree to which each *unit* is present. It should be noted, of course, that this new pattern-based error function is related to the old unit-based error by the same change of basis matrices discussed above.

It might be observed further that under this description, the perfect associator—which results when the input and output patterns are linearly independent—will be the identity matrix, **I**, in which the main diagonal has a 1 in each entry and all other entries are 0. It should be noted, however, that the preceding analysis of this new description has assumed the input and target output patterns were linearly independent. If they are not, no such pattern basis exists. However, there is an analogous, but somewhat more complex, development for the case in which these vectors cannot form a legitimate basis.

I will now demonstrate some of the useful insights which can be gained through this analysis by comparing the unit and pattern basis descriptions for a sample learning problem. The upper portion of Figure 2 gives the representations of the four input/output patterns to be learned in the unit basis. These patterns are all linearly independent and were generated under the constraint that each pattern has unit length and that the input patterns have the correlation structure given in the matrix shown in the figure.

Figure 3 shows the states of **W** and **W*** after one, four, and eight sweeps through the four input/output patterns. While inspection of the unit-based representations gives no direct information about the degree of learning and crosstalk between targets, this information is explicit in the pattern-based representation. For example, one can discern that the error for the pairs with highly correlated inputs (pairs 1 and 2) is greater at each stage than that for the pairs with slightly correlated input

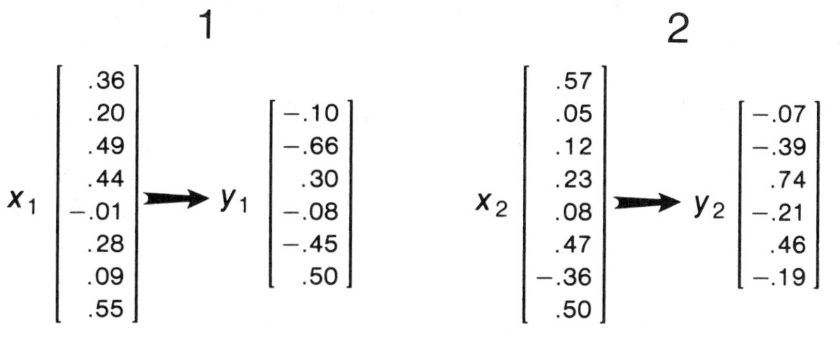

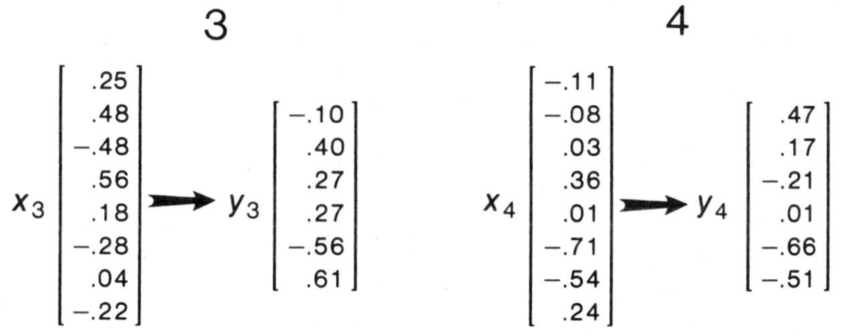

$$\mathbf{C} = \begin{bmatrix} 1.00 & .75 & 0 & 0 \\ .75 & 1.00 & 0 & 0 \\ 0 & 0 & 1.00 & .25 \\ 0 & 0 & .25 & 1.00 \end{bmatrix}$$

FIGURE 2. Key-target pairs and the key correlation structure.

patterns (pairs 3 and 4). Moreover, there is no intrusion of targets associated with orthogonal inputs. In addition, the intrusion of targets from correlated pairs is least for the pair most recently learned, pairs 2 and 4. (The patterns were presented in order 1-2-3-4 on each sweep.) Finally, it is clear from inspection of the pattern-based weight matrix that after eight sweeps the patterns have been almost perfectly learned.

The pattern-based formulation also allows a more detailed analysis of the general effect of a learning trial on the error. We can define the "potential error" to pattern j, $\delta_j{}^*$ as

Learning **with g** = **1.20**

AFTER 1 Learning Cycle

Pattern Based: mse=0.09

0.39	-0.18	0.00	0.00
0.90	1.20	0.00	0.00
0.00	0.00	1.11	-0.06
0.00	0.00	0.30	1.20

Unit Based: mse=0.049

-0.12	-0.13	0.02	0.10	-0.01	-0.42	-0.35	0.12
-0.03	0.08	-0.59	0.00	0.12	-0.29	-0.18	-0.40
0.57	0.28	0.08	0.35	0.10	0.52	0.03	0.33
-0.04	0.13	-0.23	0.07	0.05	-0.14	0.10	-0.23
0.30	-0.33	0.17	-0.59	-0.04	0.94	-0.13	0.23
0.05	0.50	-0.17	0.20	0.06	0.20	0.81	-0.42

AFTER 4 Learning Cycles

Pattern Based: mse=0.00

0.98	-0.01	0.00	0.00
0.03	1.01	0.00	0.00
0.00	0.00	1.00	0.00
0.00	0.00	0.00	1.00

Unit Based: mse=0.00

-0.15	-0.18	0.07	0.01	-0.04	-0.34	-0.31	0.13
-0.07	0.02	-0.57	-0.08	0.10	-0.28	-0.20	-0.41
0.59	0.13	-0.30	0.11	0.16	0.50	-0.29	0.13
-0.05	0.16	-0.10	0.14	0.02	-0.15	0.17	-0.16
0.36	-0.42	-0.47	-0.81	0.08	0.86	-0.53	-0.12
0.06	0.66	0.16	0.53	0.02	0.09	1.01	-0.19

AFTER 8 Learning Cycles

Pattern Based: mse=0.00

1.00	0.00	0.00	0.00
0.00	1.00	0.00	0.00
0.00	0.00	1.00	0.00
0.00	0.00	0.00	1.00

Unit Based: mse=0.00

-0.15	-0.18	0.07	0.01	-0.04	-0.34	-0.31	0.13
-0.07	0.02	-0.57	-0.08	0.10	-0.28	-0.20	-0.41
0.59	0.13	-0.32	0.10	0.16	0.50	-0.30	0.12
-0.05	0.16	-0.10	0.14	0.02	-0.15	0.18	-0.15
0.35	-0.43	-0.49	-0.82	0.08	0.85	-0.54	-0.13
0.06	0.66	0.17	0.54	0.02	0.10	1.01	-0.18

FIGURE 3. Comparison of unit-based and pattern-based weight matrices after one, four, and eight learning cycles.

$$\delta_j{}^*(n) = t^*_j - \mathbf{W}^*(n) i^*_j. \tag{5}$$

Substituting for $\mathbf{W}^*(n)$ from Equation 1, gives

$$\delta_j{}^*(n) = t^*_j - \mathbf{W}^*(n-1) i_j - \eta \delta_k{}^* i^{*T}_k \mathbf{C} i^*_j$$

where k is the index of the pattern presented on trial $n-1$. Simplifying further, we have the recursive form:

$$\delta_j{}^*(n) = \delta_j{}^*(n-1) - \eta \delta_k{}^*(n-1) \mathbf{i}^{*T}_k \mathbf{C} \mathbf{i}^*_j. \tag{6}$$

Since the vectors $\mathbf{i}^*_j$ and $\mathbf{i}^{*T}_k$ consist of a 1 and the rest zeros, the entire expression $\mathbf{i}^{*T}_k \mathbf{C} \mathbf{i}^*_j$ reduces to c_{kj}, the entry in the kth row and jth column of matrix $\mathbf{C}$. Thus, Equation 6 becomes simply

$$\delta_j{}^*(n) - \delta_j{}^*(n-1) = -\eta c_{kj} \delta_k{}^*(n-1). \tag{7}$$

In other words, the decrease in error to the jth input/output pair due to a new learning trial is a constant times the error pattern on the new learning trial. The constant is given by the learning rate, η, times the correlation of the currently tested input and input from the learning trial. Thus, the degree to which learning affects performance on each test input is proportional to its correlation with the pattern just used in learning. Note that if η is small enough, the error to the presented pattern always decreases. In this case Equation 7 can be rewritten

$$\delta_k{}^*(n) = \delta_k{}^*(n-1)(1 - \eta c_{kk}).$$

Recalling that c_{kk} is given by $\mathbf{i}_k^T \mathbf{i}_k$, the length of the kth input vector, we can see that the error will always decrease provided $|1 - \eta \mathbf{i}_k^T \mathbf{i}_k| < 1$.

To summarize, this exercise has demonstrated that a mechanism can often be made more conceptually tractable by a judicious transformation. In this case, expressing the possible input and output representations in the appropriate pattern bases clarified the importance, indeed the sufficiency, of the input "structure" (i.e., the pattern of inner products among the input vectors) in determining the role of the input representations in learning. Furthermore, converting the weight matrix into a form from which the errors at any stage of learning can be read directly allowed us to "see" the learning more obviously. The result has been a clearer understanding of the operation of the delta rule for learning.

STATISTICAL LEARNING

In this section we extend our analysis of the delta rule from the case in which there is a fixed target output pattern for each input pattern to the case in which sets of input patterns are associated with sets of output patterns. We can think of the sets as representing *categories* of input and outputs. Thus, rather than associate particular input patterns with particular output patterns, we analyze the case in which *categories* of input patterns are associated with *categories* of output patterns. This, for example, might be the case if the system is learning that dogs bark. The representation for dog might differ on each learning trial with respect to size, shagginess, etc. while the representation for the bark might vary with regard to pitch, timbre, etc. In this case, the system is simultaneously learning the categories of *dog* and *bark* at the same time it is learning the association between the two concepts.

In addition, when we have category associations, statistical relationships between the input and output patterns within a category can be picked up. For example, the system could learn that small dogs tend to have high-pitched barks whereas large dogs may tend to have low-pitched barks.

In order to analyze the case of statistical learning, we now treat the input/output pairs of patterns as random variables. In other words, each time pattern i_j is selected as input, its entries can take different values. Similarly, the target output for pair j, t_j will have variable entries. The probability distributions of these random variables may take any form whatsoever, but they are assumed not to change over time. Moreover, we can consider the entire set of input/output pairs to form a single probability distribution. We then assume that on each trial an input/output pair is randomly sampled from this overall probability distribution.

We proceed with our analysis of statistical learning by computing the *expected* or *average* change in the weight matrix following a presentation. From Equations 1 and 2 we get the following form of the delta rule:

$$\mathbf{W}(n) = \mathbf{W}(n-1) + \eta[\mathbf{t}(n) - \mathbf{W}(n-1)\mathbf{i}(n)]\mathbf{i}^T(n).$$

Simplifying and taking the expected value of each side we have

$$E[\mathbf{W}(n)] = E[\mathbf{W}(n-1)](\mathbf{I} - \eta E[\mathbf{i}(n)\mathbf{i}^T(n)]) + \eta E[\mathbf{t}(n)\mathbf{i}^T(n)]. \quad (8)$$

Note, we may take

$$E[\mathbf{W}(n-1)\mathbf{i}(n)\mathbf{i}^T(n)] = E[\mathbf{W}(n-1)]E[\mathbf{i}(n)\mathbf{i}^T(n)]$$

since each trial is assumed to be statistically independent of all preceding trials, upon which $\mathbf{W}(n-1)$ depends. Letting $\mathbf{R}_I = E[\mathbf{i}\mathbf{i}^T]$ be the pattern of statistical correlations among the input patterns and $\mathbf{R}_{IO} = E[\mathbf{t}\mathbf{i}^T]$ be the statistical correlations between the input and target patterns, we can rewrite Equation 7 as

$$E[\mathbf{W}(n)] = E[\mathbf{W}(n-1)](\mathbf{I} - \eta\mathbf{R}_I) + \eta\mathbf{R}_{IO}.$$

If we solve the recursion by replacing $\mathbf{W}(n-1)$ with an expression in terms of $\mathbf{W}(n-2)$ etc. down to $\mathbf{W}(0)$ and assuming that $\mathbf{W}(0) = 0$, the matrix of all 0 entries, we can write the expected value of the weight matrix after n trials as

$$E[\mathbf{W}(n)] = \eta \mathbf{R}_{IO} \sum_{j=0}^{j=n} (\mathbf{I} - \eta \mathbf{R}_I)^j. \tag{9}$$

Fortunately, in the limit, this matrix reduces to a simpler form. To see this, we must introduce the concept of the *pseudo-inverse* of a matrix. This is a matrix which, unlike the inverse, is certain to exist for all matrices, but which has a number of properties in common with an true inverse. (See Chapter 9 for a discussion of matrix inverses and the conditions under which they exist.) In particular, it *is* the true inverse, if the true inverse exists. The *pseudo-inverse* of a matrix $\mathbf{B}$, designated $\mathbf{B}^+$, is given by

$$\mathbf{B}^+ = \eta \mathbf{B}^T \sum_{j=1}^{\infty} (\mathbf{I} - \eta \mathbf{B}\mathbf{B}^T)^j$$

provided η is sufficiently small. (See Rao & Mitra, 1971, and Kohonen, 1977, 1984, for a full discussion of the pseudo-inverse.)

In order to convert Equation 9 into a form that includes the expression for the pseudo-inverse, we observe that since the square matrix $\mathbf{R}_I = E[\mathbf{i}\mathbf{i}^T]$ has independent rows and columns, we can select a matrix $\mathbf{P}$ such that $\mathbf{P}\mathbf{P}^T = \mathbf{R}_I$ and $\mathbf{P}$ also has linearly independent rows and columns. Since the generalized inverse of $\mathbf{P}$, $\mathbf{P}^+$, is also the true inverse of $\mathbf{P}$, it satisfies $(\mathbf{P}^T)^{-1}\mathbf{P}^T = \mathbf{I}$. Thus, taking the limit as $n \rightarrow \infty$ of Equation 9 and substituting $\mathbf{P}$, we can write

$$\lim_{n\rightarrow\infty} E[\mathbf{W}(n)] = E[\mathbf{W}_\infty] = \mathbf{R}_{IO} (\mathbf{P}^T)^{-1} [\eta \mathbf{P}^T \sum_{j=1}^{\infty} (\mathbf{I} - \eta \mathbf{P}\mathbf{P}^T)^j]. \tag{10}$$

Now, by substituting in for the pseudo-inverse of $\mathbf{P}$ and simplifying we get

$$E[\mathbf{W}_\infty] = \mathbf{R}_{IO} (\mathbf{P}^T)^{-1} \mathbf{P}^+ = \mathbf{R}_{IO} (\mathbf{P}\mathbf{P}^T)^{-1} = \mathbf{R}_{IO} \mathbf{R}_I^{-1}. \tag{11}$$

Since the rows and columns of $\mathbf{R}_I$ are linearly independent, $\mathbf{R}_I^{-1} = \mathbf{R}_I^+$. So we finally get

$$E[\mathbf{W}_\infty] = \mathbf{R}_{IO} \mathbf{R}_I^+. \tag{12}$$

Now we wish to show that, after training, the system will respond appropriately. Without further restrictions, we can demonstrate a minimal appropriateness of the response, namely, we can show that $E[\mathbf{W}_\infty \mathbf{i}] = E[\mathbf{t}]$. In other words, we can show that the mean output of the system, after learning, is the mean target. Since the test trials and learning trials are statistically independent we can write

$$E[\mathbf{W}_\infty \mathbf{i}] = E[\mathbf{W}_\infty] E[\mathbf{i}].$$

Now, substituting in from Equation 9 we have

$$E[\mathbf{W}_\infty \mathbf{i}] = \mathbf{R}_{IO}\mathbf{R}_I^+ E[\mathbf{i}] = E[\mathbf{t}\mathbf{i}^T(\mathbf{i}\mathbf{i}^T)^+]E[\mathbf{i}].$$

Although it is not generally true that $(\mathbf{BC})^+ = \mathbf{C}^+\mathbf{B}^+$, this relation does hold for $\mathbf{B} = \mathbf{i}$ and $\mathbf{C} = \mathbf{i}^T$, where $\mathbf{i}$ is a column vector. Thus, we have

$$E[\mathbf{W}_\infty \mathbf{i}] = E[\mathbf{t}(\mathbf{i}^+\mathbf{i})^T(\mathbf{i}^+\mathbf{i})].$$

Finally, since $\mathbf{i}$ has only one column, its columns are linearly independent and $\mathbf{i}^+\mathbf{i} = 1$. We have therefore obtained the desired result.

Thus far we have only shown that the mean response to inputs is equivalent to the mean of the target patterns. This result says nothing about the appropriateness of the response to a particular pattern. Ideally we would want the expected response to a particular pattern to yield the expected value of our target given the input. We can show that the input will produce this result as long as $\mathbf{i}$ and $\mathbf{t}$ are distributed normally with zero means. Although this seems to be a strong assumption, it is not a difficult situation to obtain. First, we can easily arrange that the input patterns have zero means by simply having a *bias* feeding into each unit equal to minus the mean of the value for that cell of the pattern. This is not especially difficult, but we will not dwell on the process here. (See Chapter 8 for a discussion of *biases* and the learning of biases.) Suffice it to say that it is not very difficult to convert a set of input vectors into a set of patterns with zero mean.

The requirement of normal distributions is often not as restrictive as it appears. When input patterns being associated are themselves the output of a linear system, each entry in the pattern will be a linear combination of the original input's entries. If the patterns have large dimensionality (i.e., there are many components to the vectors), one obtains an approximation to an infinite series of random variables. A powerful central-limit theorem due to Lyapunov (Eisen, 1969, Ch. 13) shows that such a series will converge to a normal distribution so long as several weak assumptions hold (most importantly, the means and variances of each random variable must exist and none of the random variables may be excessively dominant).

Under these conditions, it can be shown that the expected value of the target $\mathbf{t}$ given the input $\mathbf{i}$, takes the form $E[\mathbf{t}|\mathbf{i}] = \mathbf{R}_{IO}\mathbf{R}_I^{-1}\mathbf{i}$ (Meditch, 1969, chap. 3). Since $E[\mathbf{W}_\infty] = \mathbf{R}_{IO}\mathbf{R}_I^{-1}$, we have shown that

$$E[\mathbf{W}_\infty \mathbf{i}] = E[\mathbf{t}\,|\,\mathbf{i}], \tag{13}$$

so that after a sufficient number of learning trials, the law of large numbers and the convergence of the delta rule learning process imply that, given a particular input, the system will produce an output equal to the average of the targets paired with that input. In this sense, systematic covariation of input/output pairs will be learned.

The Delta Rule and Multiple Linear Regression

Some readers may have already noticed the similarity of the learning task we have been analyzing to the problem encountered in multiple linear regression. In a linear regression problem the objective is to predict, to the degree possible, one variable, say y, from a set of variables $\mathbf{x}$. In these problems we typically wish to find a set of coefficients, $\mathbf{b}$, such that

$$\hat{y}_j = b_0 x_{0j} + b_1 x_{1j} + b_2 x_{2j} \cdots b_n x_{nj} = \mathbf{b}^T \mathbf{x}_j$$

(where x_0 is taken to be 1) and the sum-squared error

$$\sum_{j=1}^{n} (y_j - \hat{y}_j)^2$$

is minimized. This is precisely the problem that the delta rule seeks to solve. In this case, each element of the target vector for input/output pair $(p\ \mathbf{t}_p)$ is analogous to a to-be-predicted observation y_j; our prediction variables $\mathbf{x}_j$ are analogous to our input vectors i_p; our regression coefficients $\mathbf{b}$ correspond to a row of the weight matrix $\mathbf{W}$; and the intercept of the regression line, b_0, corresponds to the *bias* often assumed for our units (cf. Chapter 8). In our typical case the target vectors have many components, so we are simultaneously solving a multiple regression problem for each of the components of the target vectors. Now, the standard result from linear regression, for zero-mean random variables, is that our estimate for the vector $\mathbf{b}$, $\hat{\mathbf{b}}$ is given by

$$\hat{\mathbf{b}} = (\mathbf{X}^T \mathbf{X})^{-1} \mathbf{X}^T \mathbf{y}$$

where $\mathbf{X}$ is the matrix whose columns represent the values of the predictors and whose rows represent the individual observations. (Again, we take the first column to be all 1s.) Now, note from Equation 12 that the delta rule converges to

$$E[\mathbf{W}_\infty] = (E[\mathbf{i}^T \mathbf{i}])^+ E[\mathbf{i}^T \mathbf{t}].$$

This equation is the strict analog of that from linear regression theory.[2] If we assume that each output unit has a bias corresponding to the intercept b_0 of the regression line, we can see that the delta rule is, in effect, an iterative method of computing the best, in the sense of least squares, linear regression coefficients for our problems.

SUMMARY

To summarize, this chapter has shown that close examination of the delta rule reveals a number of interesting and useful properties. When fixed patterns are being learned, the rule's operation can be elucidated by converting from a unit-based description to a pattern-based description. In particular, the analysis showed that the correlations between the input patterns, and not the specific patterns used, determined their effect on the learning process. Thus, any alteration of the specific input patterns that does not alter the correlations will have no effect on learning by a linear delta rule. It was also shown that expressing the inputs and outputs in terms of the patterns being learned facilitated analysis of the learning process by allowing one to read directly from the output produced the degree to which each target was present in the output generated by a given input pattern.

When the patterns being learned are variable, it was noted that the final weight matrix could be expressed simply in terms of the intercorrelations among the input patterns, $\mathbf{R}_I$, and the correlations between the input and output patterns, $\mathbf{R}_{IO}$. It was also shown that when several reasonable requirements for the distribution of the input/output random variables are met, the delta rule will learn the pattern of covariation between the inputs and targets. Finally, we showed that the delta rule carries out the equivalent of a multiple linear regression from the input patterns to the targets. Those familiar with linear regression should conclude from this both the power of the rule and its weaknesses. In particular, wherever a linear regression is insufficient to provide a good account of the relationship between input and target patterns, the system will perform poorly. The solution to this problem is to have nonlinear units and intermediate layers of hidden units. Chapter 8 is a detailed discussion of the generalized delta rule and its application to these situations.

---

[2] Actually, there is a slight difference in convention between our development and that typical of linear regression. In our case, the stimulus vectors are the column vectors, whereas in linear regression the predictor variables are the rows of the matrix $\mathbf{X}$. Thus this equation differs by a transposition from Equation 12. This has no consequences for the points made here.

The preceding discussion does not, by any means, provide a complete analysis of the delta rule. Rather, it illustrates two important ideas. First, that a basic principle (in this case, the use of pattern-based, rather than unit-based representations) can provide valuable insights into the operation of a useful mechanism; and second, that the analysis of component mechanisms which were designed for one use can often reveal new applications.

CHAPTER 12

Resource Requirements of Standard and Programmable Nets

J. L. McCLELLAND

In several places in this book we have examined the capabilities of various models of parallel distributed processing. We have considered models that are guaranteed to do one thing or another—to learn, say, up to some criterion of optimality or to settle into global states with probabilities proportional to the goodness of the states. In later chapters, we describe various models of psychological or neurophysiological processes and consider how well they account for the data. The models, then, are held up against various criteria of computational, psychological, and sometimes physiological adequacy.

In this chapter I raise another question about PDP models. I consider the resources they require, in terms of units and connections, to carry out a particular amount of work. This issue is touched on in various other places in the book, particularly Chapter 3. There we showed that a distributed model can often perform even an arbitrary mapping with less hardware than a local model would require to do the same task.

In this chapter I continue this line of thinking and extend it in various ways, drawing on the work of several other researchers, particularly Willshaw (1971, 1981). The analysis is far from exhaustive, but it focuses on several fairly central questions about the resource requirements of PDP networks. In the first part of the chapter, I consider the resource requirements of a simple pattern associator. I review the analysis offered by Willshaw (1981) and extend it in one or two small ways, and I consider how it might be possible to overcome some limitations that arise in networks consisting of units with limited connectivity. In the second part of the chapter, I consider the resource requirements of a distributed version of the dynamically programmable networks described in Chapter 16.

THE STANDARD PATTERN ASSOCIATOR

In this section, we will consider pattern associator models similar to the models studied by J. A. Anderson (e.g., Anderson, 1983) and Kohonen (1977, 1984), and to the past-tense learning model described in Chapter 18. A small pattern associator is illustrated in Figure 1. A pattern associator consists of two sets of units, called *input* and *output* units, and a connection from each input unit to each output unit. The associator takes as input a pattern of activation on its input units and produces in response a pattern on the output units based on the connections between the input and output units.

Different pattern associators make slightly different assumptions about the processing characteristics of the units. We will follow Willshaw's (1981) analysis of a particular, simple case; he used binary units and binary connections between units. Thus, units could take on activation values of 0 or 1. Similarly, the connections between the units could take on only binary values of 0 and 1.

In Willshaw nets, processing is an extremely simple matter. A pattern of activation is imposed on the input units, turning each one either on or off. Each active input unit then sends a quantum of activation to each of the output units it has a switched-on connection to. Output units go on if the number of quanta they receive exceeds a threshold; otherwise they stay off.

The learning rule Willshaw studied is equally simple. Training amounts to presenting each input pattern paired with the corresponding output pattern, and turning on the connection from each active input unit to each active output unit. This is, of course, a simple variant of Hebbian learning. Given this learning rule, it follows that when the input pattern of a known association is presented to the network, each of the activated input units will send one quantum of activation to all of the correct output units. This means that the number of quanta of activation each correct output unit will receive will be equal to the number of active input units.

In examining the learning capacity of this network, Willshaw made several further assumptions. First, he assumed that all of the associations (or pairs of patterns) to be learned have the same number of active input units and the same number of active output units. Second,

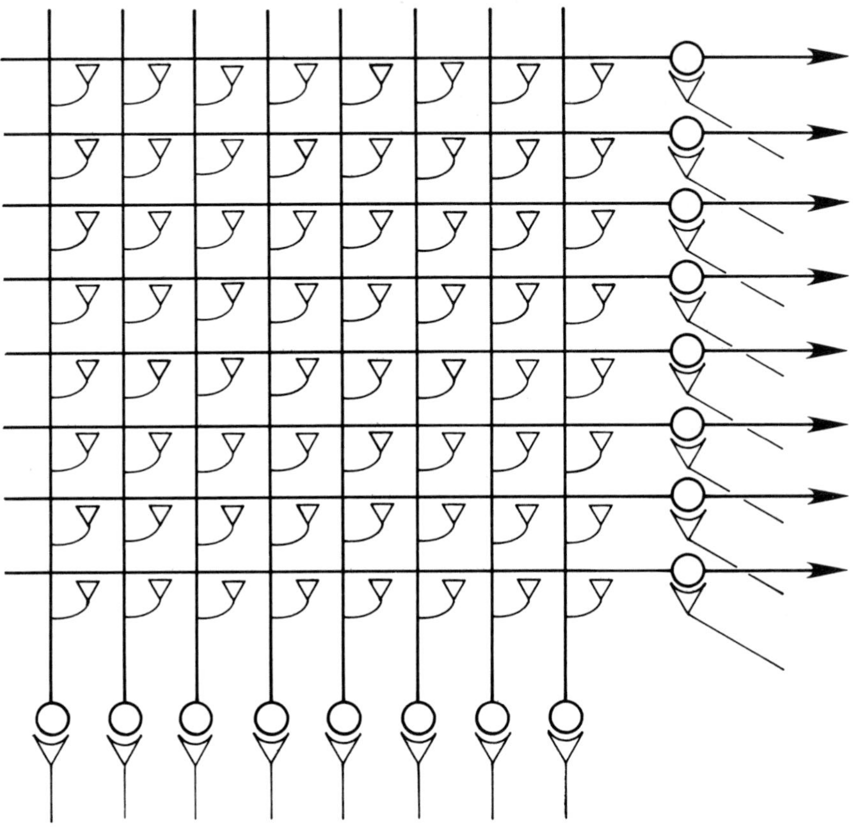

FIGURE 1. A pattern associator consisting of a set of input units (across the bottom) and output units (along the right side), with a connection from each input unit to each output unit.

he assumed that the threshold of each output unit is set equal to the number of active input units. Given this assumption, only those output units with switched-on connections from *all* of the active input units will reach threshold.

Now we can begin to examine the capacity of these networks. In particular, we can ask questions like the following. How many input units (n_i) and output units (n_o) would be needed to allow retrieval of the correct mate of each of r different input patterns?

The answer to such a question depends on the criterion of correct retrieval used. For present purposes, we can adopt the following criterion: All of the correct output units should be turned on, and, on the average, no more than one output unit should be turned on spuriously.

Since the assumptions of the model guarantee that all the correct output units will be turned on when the correct input is shown, the analysis focuses on the number of units needed to store r patterns without exceeding the acceptable number of spurious activations.

The answer to our question also depends on the number of units active in the input and output patterns in each pattern pair and on the similarity relations among the patterns. A very useful case that Willshaw considered is the case in which each of the r associations involves a random selection of m_i input units and m_o output units. From the assumption of randomness, it is easy to compute the probability that any given junction will be turned on after learning all r associations. From this it is easy to compute the average number of spurious activations. We will now go through these computations.

First we consider the probability p_{on} that any given junction will end up being turned on, for a particular choice of the parameters n_i, n_o, m_i, m_o, and r. Imagine that the r patterns are stored, one after the other, in the $n_i n_o$ connections between the n_i input units and the n_o output units. As each pattern is stored, it turns on $m_i m_o$ of the $n_i n_o$ connections, so each junction in the network is turned on with probability $m_i m_o / n_i n_o$. The probability that a junction is not turned on by a single association is just 1 minus this quantity. Since each of the r associations is a new random sample of m_i of the n_i input units and m_o of the n_o output units, the probability that a junction has not been turned on—or 1 minus the probability that it has been turned on—after r patterns have been stored is

$$1 - p_{on} = \left(1 - \frac{m_i m_o}{n_i n_o}\right)^r .$$

Rearranging to solve for p_{on} we obtain

$$p_{on} = 1 - \left(1 - \frac{m_i m_o}{n_i n_o}\right)^r .$$

Now that we know p_{on}, it is easy to calculate the number of spurious activations of output units. First, any output unit that should not be activated will be turned on if and only if all of its junctions from the m_i active input units happen to be on. Given the assumption of randomness, this will occur with probability $p_{on}^{m_i}$, since each junction is on with probability p_{on}. Since there are $n_o - m_o$ output units that are candidates for spurious activation, the average number of spuriously activated units is

$$(n_o - m_o) p_{on}^{m_i}.$$

We want to keep this number less than 1. Adopting a slightly more stringent criterion to simplify the calculations, we can set

$$1 \geqslant n_o p_{on}{}^{m_i} ,$$

or

$$\left(\frac{1}{n_o}\right)^{\frac{1}{m_i}} \geqslant p_{on}$$

$$\geqslant 1 - \left(1 - \frac{m_i m_o}{n_i n_o}\right)^r .$$

Rearranging, we get

$$1-\left(\frac{1}{n_o}\right)^{\frac{1}{m_i}} \leqslant \left(1 - \frac{m_i m_o}{n_i n_o}\right)^r .$$

For small positive x, $\log(1-x) = -x$. If we restrict ourselves to cases where $m_i m_o / n_i n_o < .1$—that is, reasonably sparse patterns in the sense that $m < n/\sqrt{10}$—the approximation will hold for the right-hand side of the equation, so that taking logs we get

$$\log\left[1-\left(\frac{1}{n}\right)^{\frac{1}{m_i}}\right] \leqslant -r\frac{m_i m_o}{n_i n_o} .$$

We can solve this for r, the number of patterns, to obtain

$$r \leqslant -\frac{n_i n_o}{m_i m_o} \log\left[1-\left(\frac{1}{n_o}\right)^{\frac{1}{m_i}}\right] . \quad (1)$$

Now, $-\log\left[1-\left(\frac{1}{n_o}\right)^{\frac{1}{m_i}}\right]$ ranges upward from .69 for very sparse patterns where $m_i = \log_2 n_o$. Using .69 as a lower bound, we are safe if we say:

$$r \leqslant .69\frac{n_i n_o}{m_i m_o}$$

or

$$n_i n_o \geqslant 1.45 r m_i m_o .$$

This result tells us that the number of storage elements (that is, connections, $n_i n_o$) that we need is proportional to the number of associations we wish to store times the number of connections $(m_i m_o)$ activated in storing each association. This seems about right, intuitively. In fact, this is an upper bound rather greater than the true number of storage elements required for less sparse patterns, as can be seen by plugging values of m_i greater than $\log_2 n_o$ into Equation 1.

It is interesting to compare Willshaw nets to various kinds of local representation. One very simple local representation would associate a single, active input unit with one or more active output units. Obviously, such a network would have a capacity of only n_i patterns. We can use the connections of a Willshaw net more effectively with a distributed input if the input and output patterns are reasonably sparse. For instance, in a square net with the same number n of input and output units and the same number m of active elements in each, if $n = 1000$ and $m = 10$, we find that we can store about 7,000 associations instead of the 1,000 we could store using local representation over the input units.

Another scheme to compare to the Willshaw scheme would be one that encodes each pattern to be learned with a single hidden unit between the input and output layers. Obviously a net that behaved perfectly in performing r associations between m_i active input elements and m_o active output units could be handcrafted using r hidden units, each having m_i input connections and m_o output connections. Such a network can be economical once it is wired up exactly right: It only needs $r(m_i+m_o)$ connections. However, there are two points to note. First, it is not obvious how to provide enough hardware in advance to handle an arbitrary r patterns of m_i active input units and m_o active output units. The number of such patterns possible is approximately $(n_i^{m_i}/m_i!)(n_o^{m_o}/m_o!)$, and if we had to provide a unit in advance for each of these our hardware cost would get out of hand very fast. Second, the economy of the scheme is not due to the use of local representation, but to the use of hidden units. In many cases even more economical representation can be achieved with coarse-coded hidden units (see Chapter 3 and Kanerva, 1984).

Randomly Connected Nets

Returning to the standard Willshaw net, there are several minor difficulties with Willshaw's scheme. First, it assumes that each input unit sends one and only one connection to each output unit. In a neural network, we might assume each input unit sends out a randomly distributed array of connections to the set of output units without any guarantee that each output unit actually receives a connection. Second, the analysis depends on a rather strict and sharp threshold for output unit activation. In a random net rather than a fully connected net, we could not actually guarantee that a given output unit would in fact receive m_i inputs; and in realistic nets, we would expect there to be some inherent variability in the activations of the units. Thus, we would not be able to guarantee that all correct units would exceed the sharp threshold, nor that all incorrect units would fall below it.

However, it turns out that we can reformulate the problem just slightly and get a handle on networks that have these properties. Assume that we have a square network of n input and n output units and that we wish to store associations between m active input units and m active output units. Suppose each input unit has f output connections which fall where they may among the n output units so that the output units have an average of f inputs each. Note again that the connections are randomly distributed without restriction so that there is no guarantee that input unit i projects to output unit j.

To study the performance of this net, imagine storing some number r of patterns using the Willshaw learning scheme. During testing, we will examine the number of active inputs each output unit that should be turned on will receive and the number of active inputs each unit that should not be turned on will receive, and we will then calculate the signal-detection measure of sensitivity d' (Green & Swets, 1966) as an index of the ability of inputs reaching each output unit to distinguish between units that should be on and units that should not be on. Since d' is independent of the threshold, this measure allows us to bypass the question of the threshold itself.

Let us first consider what happens in our random network as we train it with pairs of patterns using Willshaw's scheme. Pick an arbitrary connection in our net between an arbitrary input unit and an arbitrary output unit. Now, consider learning an arbitrary pattern. The probability that a particular input unit will be on is m/n. Similarly, the probability that a particular output unit will be on is m/n. The probability that the units joined by the particular connection we are considering will be one of the ones turned on in learning a particular pattern, then, is m^2/n^2 just as before. The rest of the earlier analysis still applies, and we get

$$p_{on} = 1 - \left(1 - \frac{m^2}{n^2} \right)^r .$$

This is exactly the same value that we had before in the original Willshaw model, and it is independent of f, the number of connections each unit makes. This factor will become important soon, but it does not affect the probability that a particular connection will be on after learning r patterns.

Now consider what happens during the testing of a particular learned association. We activate the correct m input units and examine the mean number of quanta of activation that each output unit that should be on will receive. The m active input units each have f outputs, so there are mf total "active" connections. A particular one of these connections reaches a particular output unit with probability $1/n$, since each connection is assumed to fall at random among the n output units. Thus, the average number of active connections each output unit receives will simply be mf/n. For output units that should be on, each of these connections will have been turned on during learning, so mf/n is the average number of quanta that unit will receive. Assuming that n is reasonably large, the distribution of this quantity is approximately Poisson, so its variance is also given by mf/n.

Units that should not be on also receive an arbitrary connection from an active input unit with probability $1/n$, but each such connection is only on with probability p_{on}. Thus, the average number of quanta such units receive is $(mf/n)p_{on}$. This quantity is also approximately Poisson, so its variance is also equal to its mean.

Our measure of sensitivity, d', is the difference between these means divided by the square root of the average of the variances. That is,

$$d' = \frac{mf/n\,(1 - p_{on})}{\sqrt{(mf/n)(1 + p_{on})/2}}.$$

Simplifying, this becomes

$$d' = \sqrt{mf/n}\,\frac{1 - p_{on}}{\sqrt{(1 + p_{on})/2}}. \tag{2}$$

We can get bounds on the true value of d' by noting that the denominator above cannot be greater than 1 or less than $\sqrt{1/2}$. The largest value of the denominator sets a lower bound on d', so we find that

$$d' \geqslant \sqrt{mf/n}\,(1 - p_{on}).$$

Substituting for $1 - p_{on}$, we obtain

$$d' \geqslant \sqrt{mf/n}\left(1 - \frac{m^2}{n^2}\right)^r. \tag{3}$$

Taking logs of both sides, invoking the $\log(1-x) = -x$ approximation, and solving for r, we obtain

$$r \leqslant .5 \frac{n^2}{m^2}\Big[\log(mf/n) - 2\log(d')\Big].$$

One of the first things to note from this expression is its similarity to the expression we had for the case of Willshaw's fully connected net. In particular, if we let $f = n$, so that each unit sends an average of one connection to reach another unit, we get

$$r \leqslant .5 \frac{n^2}{m^2}\Big[\log(m) - 2\log(d')\Big]. \tag{4}$$

The expression in brackets on the right expresses the fact that the capacity of the net goes down as the sensitivity we want to achieve goes up and captures the fact that there is a slight benefit as we increase m, independent of its effect on the ratio of total connections to connections activated per association. This is due to the fact that the distributions of activations of correct and spurious units pull apart as m gets larger. These are relatively small factors for moderate values of m and d'. More important, as before, is the ratio of the number of connections (n^2) relative to the average number of connections each pattern takes up (m^2).

Effects of Limited Fan-Out

A new result emerges when we consider other possible values for f: Equation 3 indicates that d' is directly proportional to the square root of f. Thus, we can achieve any degree of fidelity we require by increasing f though returns diminish as f gets bigger and bigger. Alternatively, the performance of our network will degrade gracefully as fan-out is reduced.

We can also see that increases in n are no longer uniformly beneficial. The term $\log(mf/n)$ decreases a n increases; we can no longer increase the capacity indefinitely simply by increasing n.

Figure 2 indicates a discovery of Mitchison (personal communication, 1984) concerning the capacity r of a network as a function of n for several values of m and f, with $d' = 5$. Capacity depends roughly on n^2/m^2 and is relatively insensitive to f as long as $\sqrt{mf/n} >> d'$. However, as n increases we reach a point where $\sqrt{mf/n}$ approaches d';

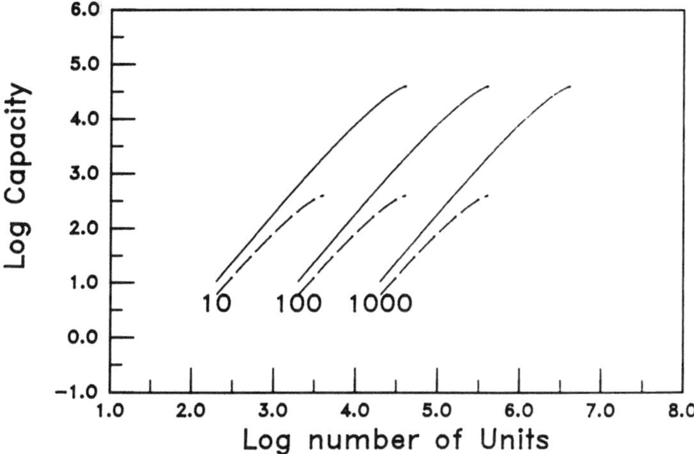

FIGURE 2. Effects of limited fan-out in a randomly connected associative net as a function of the log of n, the number of input and output units; for different values of m, the number of active units in each input and output pattern, indicated below each pair of curves. The upper member of each pair of curves is for fan-out of 10,000; the lower member is for fan-out of 1,000. In all cases, the y-axis reflects the log of the maximum number of patterns that can be stored while maintaining a d' of 5. Calculations are based on Equation 2 (Equation 3 gives misleading results for $\sqrt{mf/n}$ near d').

here capacity levels off and further increases in n result in no further increase in sensitivity. The maximal capacity achievable by increasing n is invariant, regardless of the value of m, and depends only on d' and f. Thus, if we were to pick a fixed value of d', we would find that the maximum number of patterns we could store would be strictly limited by f.

Biological limits on storage capacity of neural nets. With these analyses in mind, we can now consider what limits biological hardware might place on the storage capacity of a neural net. Of course, we must be clear on the fact that we are considering a very restricted class of distributed models and there is no guarantee that our results will generalize. Nevertheless, it is reasonably interesting to consider what it would take to store a large body of information, say, a million different pairs of patterns, with each pattern consisting of a 1,000 active input units and 1,000 active output units.

To be on the safe side, let's adopt a d' of 5. With this value, if the units have an unbiased threshold, the network will miss less than 1% of the units that should be on and false alarm to less than 1% of the units that should be off.[1]

How big would a net have to be to meet these specifications? Assuming a fully connected net, and consulting Equation 4, we find that we need to set n equal to a value near about 10^6 to get r large enough.

This number of units is not a serious problem since estimates of the number of units in the brain generally range upward from 10^{10} (see Chapter 20). However, individual units are not generally assumed to have enough connections for this scheme to work as stated. If there are 1,000 to 10,000 connections per unit, as suggested in Chapter 20, we are off by two to three orders of magnitude in the number of connections per unit.

Given this limitation on fan-out, we had better consult Figure 2. The figure indicates that the maximum capacity of a net with a fan-out of 1,000 and a d' of 5 is only about 150 patterns. With $f = 10{,}000$ we get up to a capacity of about 15,000 patterns, but we are still well short of the mark. It seems, then, that the fan-out of neurons drastically limits the capacity of a distributed network.

A simple method for overcoming the fan-out limitation. But all is not completely lost. It turns out that it is a relatively simple matter to overcome the fan-out limitation. The trick is simply to use multiple layers of units. Let each input unit activate a set of what we might call *dispersion* units, and let each output unit receive input from a set of *collection* units. Let the f outgoing connections of each of the dispersion units be randomly distributed among the "dendrites" of the collection units. A miniature version of this scheme is illustrated in Figure 3. Note that it is assumed that each dispersion unit is driven by a *single* input unit, and each collection unit projects to a *single* output unit. Collection units are assumed to be perfectly linear so that the net input to each output unit is just the sum of the net inputs to the collector units that project to it. Assuming each input unit and each dispersion unit has a fan-out of f, the effective fan-out of the input and dispersion layers together becomes f^2. Similarly, the set of collection units feeding into each output unit collect an average of f^2 connections. To construct an associator of 1 million input units by 1 million output units assuming each unit has a fanout of 1,000, we will need 1 billion dispersion units and 1 billion collection units. The number of connections between the dispersion units and the collection units would be on the order of 10^{12}, or 1 trillion connections.

[1] It should be pointed out that any intrinsic noise in the units would reduce the actual observed sensitivity.

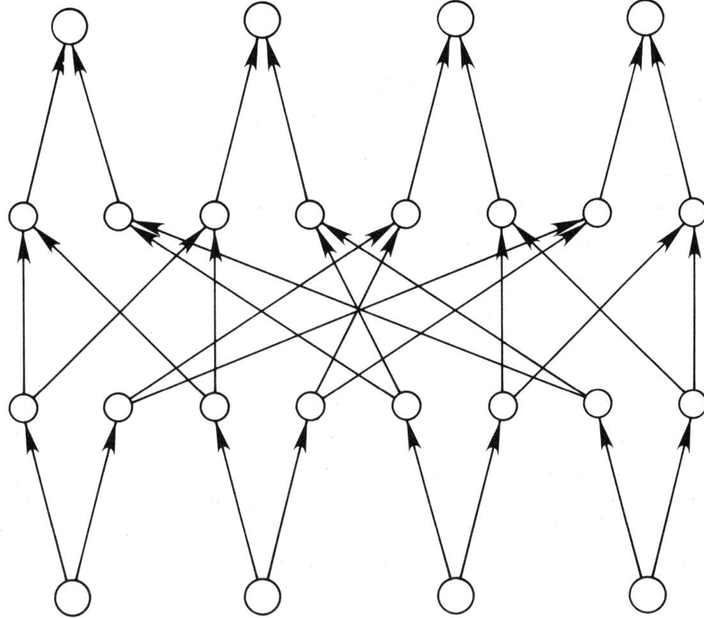

FIGURE 3. A diagram of a multilayer network consisting of an input layer, a dispersion layer, a collection layer, and an output layer. The network serves to square the effective fan-out of each input unit, relative to the simple two-layer case.

The network would require about 20% of human cortex, based on the estimate that there are 10^5 neurons under each square millimeter of the brain and that there are about 10^5 square millimeters of cortical surface. This might be a little tight, but if the fan-out were 10,000, the network would fit handily. In that case, it would only require about 2 percent of the 10^{10} units.

There are, of course, a lot of reasons to doubt that these figures represent anything more than a first-order estimate of the capacity of real associative networks. There are several oversimplifications, including for example the assumption that the dispersion units are each driven by a single connection. We must also note that we have assumed a two-layer net along with an extremely simple learning rule. The intermediate layers postulated here merely serve to provide a way of overcoming the fan-out limits of individual units. However, as was pointed out in Chapters 7 and 8, a multilayer net can often learn to construct its own coding schemes that are much more efficient than the random coding schemes used here. Even simple two-layer nets can profit if there are some regularities in the network and if they use a sensible learning rule, as shown in Chapter 18. Thus random nets like the ones that have been analyzed in this section probably represent a lower limit on efficiency that we can use as a benchmark against which to measure "smarter" PDP mechanisms.

Effects of Degradation and the Benefits of Redundancy

One virtue of distributed models is their ability to handle degradation, either of the input pattern or of the network itself. The d' analysis allows us to tell a very simple story about the effects of degradation. In this section I will just consider the effects of degradation by removal, either of a random fraction of the pattern or of a random fraction of the connections in the network; effects of added noise will be considered later on. In the case of removal, we can think of it either in terms of presenting an incomplete pattern or actually destroying some of the input units so that parts of the pattern are simply no longer represented. Consider the case of a network that has already been trained with some number of patterns so that p_{on} can be treated as a constant. Then we can write the equation relating d' to m, f, and n as

$$d' \geqslant k\sqrt{mf/n}.$$

Now, suppose that during testing we turn on only some proportion p_t of the m units representing a pattern. The m in the above equation becomes mp_t, so we see that the sensitivity of the network as indexed by d' falls off as the *square root* of the fraction of the probe that is presented. Similarly, suppose some of the connections leading out of each unit are destroyed, leaving a random intact proportion p_i of the mf active connections. Again, the sensitivity of the network will be proportional to the square root of the number of remaining connections. Thus, performance degrades gracefully under both kinds of damage.

Another frequently noted virtue of distributed memories is the redundancy they tend naturally to provide. The ability of simple distributed memories to cope with degraded input patterns is really just a matter of their redundancy, as Willshaw (1981) pointed out. For, if a network is fully loaded, in the sense that it can hold no more associations and still meet some predetermined standard of accuracy with complete patterns, it will not be able to meet that same criterion with degradation. The only way to guard against this problem is to load the network lightly enough so that the criterion can still be met after subjecting the network or the inputs to the specified degree of degradation.

PROGRAMMABLE PATTERN ASSOCIATORS

In this section, I extend the sort of analysis we have performed on simple associator models to the resource requirements of connection information distribution (CID) networks of the type discussed in Chapter 16.

The mechanism shown in Figure 4 is a distributed CID mechanism. The purpose of this network is to allow connection information stored in a central associative network to be used to set connections in several *local* or *programmable* networks in the course of processing so that more

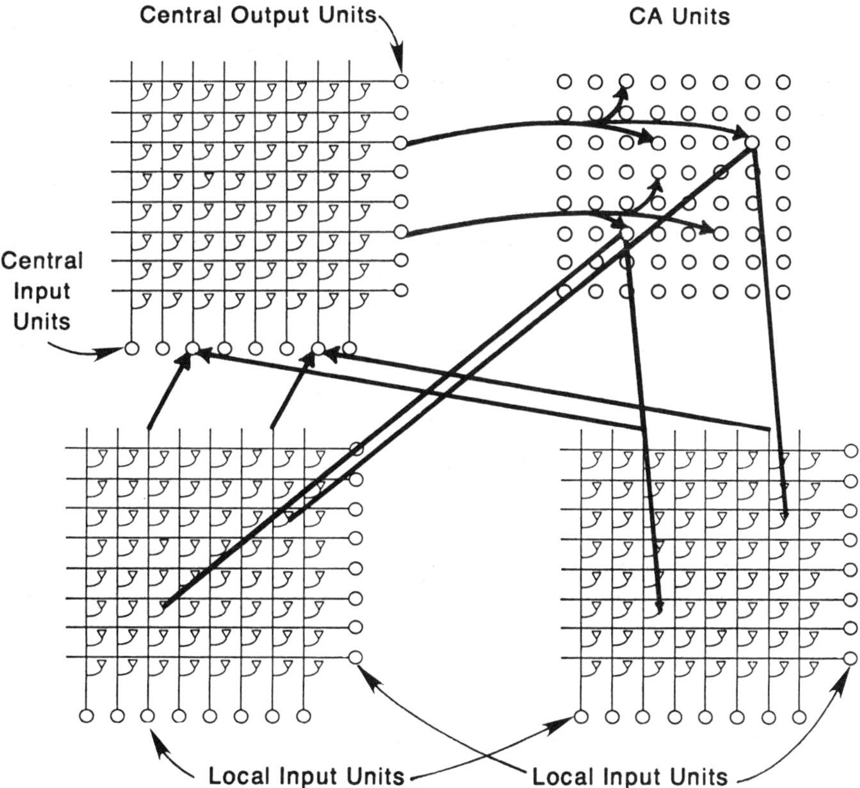

FIGURE 4. A connection information distribution (CID) network consisting of two local, programmable networks; a central, standard network; and a set of connection activation (CA) units. Each local input unit projects to the corresponding central input unit, and each CA unit projects to the corresponding connection in both local networks. Central output units turn on CA units relevant to processing the patterns they program the local modules to process. The connections drawn in are a few examples of each type.

than one input pattern can be processed at one time. The mechanism works as follows: One or more patterns to be processed are presented as inputs, with each pattern going to the input units in a different programmable network. The input pattern to each local net is also transmitted to the input units of the central associative network. When more than one pattern is presented at a time, the input to the central network is just the pattern that results from superimposing all of the input patterns. This pattern, via the connections in the central associative network, causes a pattern of activation over the central output units. The central output pattern, of course, is a composite representation of all of the input patterns. It is not itself the desired output of the system, but is the pattern that serves as the basis for programming (or turning on connections) in the local, programmable networks. The local networks are programmed via a set of units called the connection activation (CA) units. The CA units act essentially as switches that turn on connections in the programmable networks. In the version of the model we will start with, each CA unit projects to the one specific connection it corresponds to in each programmable network, so there are as many CA units as there are connections in a single programmable net. In the figure, the CA units are laid out so that the location of each one corresponds to the location of the connection it commands in each of the programmable networks.

To program the local networks, then, central output units activate the CA units corresponding to the connections needed to process the patterns represented on the central output units. The CA units turn on the corresponding connections. This does not mean that the CA units actually cause activation to pass to the local output units. Rather, they simply enable connections in the programmable nets. Each active local input unit sends a quantum of activation to a given local output unit if the connection between them is turned on.

The question we will be concerned with first is the number of CA units required to make the mechanism work properly. In a later section, we will consider the effect of processing multiple items simultaneously on the resource requirements of the central network.

Connection Activation Unit Requirements

Consider a CID mechanism containing programmable networks of n_i by n_o units in which we wish to be able to associate each of s different output patterns with each of s different input patterns arising at the same time in different local networks. Input and output patterns consist of m_i by m_o active units, respectively. Following the assumptions for Willshaw nets, we assume binary units and connections, and we assume that output units are turned on only if they receive m quanta of activation.

Now, let us consider how many CA units are needed to implement this mechanism. For now we bypass the bottom-up activation of CA units and assume instead that we know in advance which connections need to be turned on. If each local network must be as complex as a standard network capable of processing r different patterns, we are in serious trouble. In the previous analysis of Willshaw networks, we found that the number of connections we needed to process r associations of m by m active units was

$$n_c = n_i n_o = 1.45 r m_i m_o .$$

It looks as though the number of connections required in each local network grows linearly with the number of known patterns times the content of each. If we had one CA unit for each programmable connection, a programmable version of our square 1-million-pattern associator would require 10^{12} CA units, a figure which is one or two orders of magnitude larger than conventional estimates of the number of units in the brain. Just putting the matter in terms of the cost we must bear to use programmable connections, it appears that we need n^2 CA units just to specify the connections needed for a standard net that could do the same work with just the connections between n input and n output units.[2]

However, things are not nearly as bad as this argument suggests. The computation I just gave misses the very important fact that it is generally not necessary to pinpoint only those connections that are relevant to a particular association. We can do very well if we allow each CA unit to activate a whole *cohort* of connections, as long as (a) we activate all the connections that we need to process any particular pattern of interest, and (b) we do not activate so many that we give rise to an inordinate number of spurious activations of output units.

The idea of using one CA unit for a whole cohort of programmable connections is a kind of coarse coding. In this case, we will see that we can reap a considerable benefit from coarse coding, compared to using one CA unit per connection. A simple illustration of the idea is shown in Figure 5. The figure illustrates CA units projecting to a single one

[2] Many readers will observe that the CA units are not strictly necessary. However, the specificity of their connections to connections in local networks is an issue whether CA units are used as intermediaries or not. Thus, even if the CA units were eliminated, it would not change the relevance of the following results. In a later section, the CA units and central output units will be collapsed into one set of units; in that case, this analysis will apply directly to the number of such units that will be required.

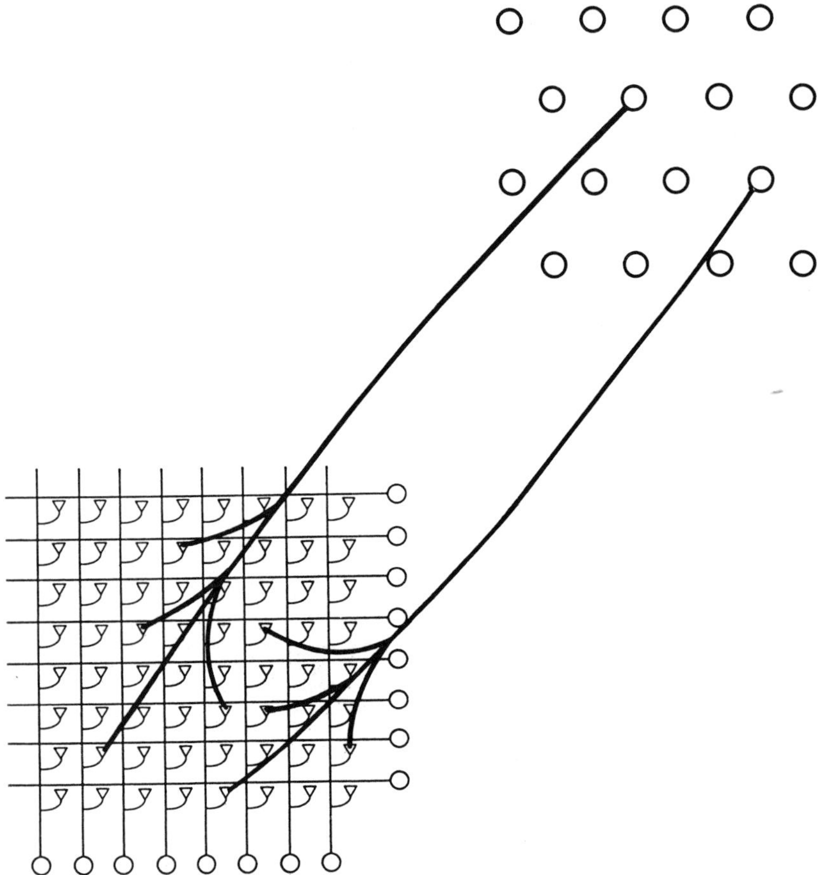

FIGURE 5. A programmable network with 8 input units and 8 output units and 64 programmable connections. Each of the 16 connection activation units is assumed to project to a random set of 4 programmable connections. These connections are only drawn in for two of the CA units. The sets of connections are chosen without replacement so that each connection is programmed by one and only one CA unit. Whenever a CA unit is on it turns on all of the connections it projects to.

of two programmable networks. Note that a given CA unit must activate the same connections in each programmable net when there is more than one.

One Pattern at a Time

To see how much this scheme can buy us, I will start by considering the case in which we want to program some local nets to process a single pattern. We ask, how small a number n_{ca} of CA units can we get by with, assuming that each one activates a distinct, randomly selected set of $n_i n_o / n_{ca}$ connections?

First of all, the number of CA units that must be activated may have to be as large as $m_i m_o$, in case each of the different connections required to process the pattern is a member of a distinct cohort. Second, for comparability to our analysis of the standard network, we want the total fraction of connections turned on to allow no more than an average of 1 output unit to be spuriously activated. As before, this constraint is represented by

$$p_{on} \leqslant \left(\frac{1}{n_i}\right)^{\frac{1}{m_i}}.$$

As long as $m_i \geqslant \log_2 n_i$, .5 will be less than the right-hand side of the expression, so we will be safe if we keep p_{on} less than or equal to .5. Since we may have to activate $m_i m_o$ CA units to activate all the right connections and since we do not want to activate more than half of the connections in all, we conclude that

$$n_{ca} \geqslant 2 m_i m_o .$$

From this result we discover that the number of CA units required *does not depend at all* on the number of connections in each programmable network. Nor in fact does it depend on the number of different known patterns. The number of known patterns does of course influence the complexity of the central network, but it does not affect the number of CA units. The number of CA units depends on $m_i m_o$, the number of connections that need to be turned on per pattern. Obviously, this places a premium on the sparseness of the patterns. Regardless of this, we are much better off than before.

Several Patterns at a Time

So far we have considered the case in which only one item is presented for processing at a time. However, the whole point of the connection information distribution scheme is that it permits simultaneous processing of several different patterns. There is, however, a cost associated with simultaneous processing, since for each pattern we need to turn on all the connections needed to process it. In this situation, we will need to increase the total number of CA units to increase the specificity of the set of connections each association requires if we are to keep the total fraction of connections that have been turned on below .5. Formally, assume that we know which s patterns we want to process. Each one will need to turn on its own set of $m_i m_o$ CA units out of the total number n_{ca} of CA units. The proportion of connections turned on will then be

$$p_{on} = 1 - \left(1 - \frac{m_i m_o}{n_{ca}} \right)^s .$$

This formula is, of course, the same as the one we saw before for the number of connections activated in the standard net with s, the number of different patterns to be processed simultaneously, replacing r, the number of patterns stored in the memory, and with n_{ca}, the number of connection activation units, replacing $n_i n_o$, the total number of connections. Using $p_{on} = .5$ and taking the log of both sides we get

$$-.69 = s \log \left(1 - \frac{m_i m_o}{n_{ca}} \right).$$

Invoking the $\log(1 - x) = -x$ approximation, we obtain

$$n_{ca} \geqslant 1.45 s m^2.$$

This formula underestimates n_{ca} slightly for $s < 3$. With this caveat, the number of CA units required is roughly proportional to the number of patterns to be processed at one time, times the number of connections needed to process each pattern.

Overlapping the Programmable Networks

In Chapter 16, the CID scheme we have been considering thus far was generalized to the case where the programmable networks overlapped with each other. This allowed strings of letters starting in any of a large number of input locations to correctly activate units for the corresponding word at the appropriate location at the next higher level. Here I will consider a more general overlapping scheme using distributed representations in the overlapping local networks. A set of three overlapping local networks is illustrated in Figure 6. In this scheme, both the input and the output units can play different roles depending on the alignment of the input pattern with the input units. In consequence, some of the connections also play more than one role. These connections are assumed to be programmable by a number of different CA units, one for each of the connection's different roles. Obviously, this will tend to increase the probability that a connection will be turned

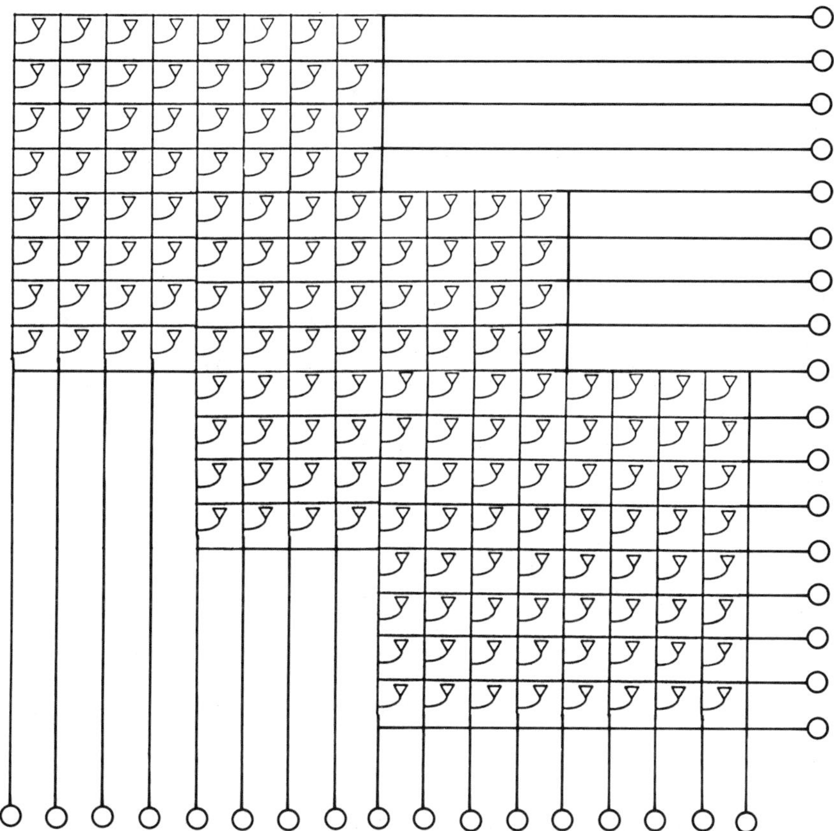

FIGURE 6. Three overlapping programmable networks of 8×8 units each. The networks overlap every four units, so the input and output units can participate in two different, partially overlapping networks.

on, and therefore will require a further revision of our estimate of the number of CA units required.

Unfortunately, an exact mathematical analysis is a bit tricky due to the fact that different junctions have different numbers of opportunities to be turned on. In addition, input patterns in adjacent locations will tend to cross-activate each other's output units. If the patterns to be processed are well separated, this will not be a problem. Restricting our attention to the well-separated case, we can get an upper bound on the cost in CA units of allowing overlapping modules by considering the case where *all* of the connections are assumed to play the maximum number of roles. This number is equivalent to the step size or grain, g, of the overlap, relative to the size of the pattern as a whole. For example, for four-letter words, if the increments in starting places of successive overlapping networks were one letter wide, g would be 4. Assuming that the connections turned on for each slice of a pattern are independent of those turned on by each other slice, it is easy to show that the formula for p_{on} becomes

$$p_{on} \leqslant 1 - \left(1 - \frac{m_i m_o}{n_{ca}}\right)^{sg},$$

and the number of CA units required to keep p_{on} less than .5 is approximated by

$$n_{ca} \geqslant 1.45\, s\, g\, m_i m_o .$$

The cost goes up with the number of patterns to be processed simultaneously times the grain of the overlap.

Summary of CA Unit Requirements

In summary, the number of CA units required to program a programmable network depends on different variables than the number of connections required in a standard associator. We can unify the two analyses by noting that both depend on the number of patterns the net must be ready to process at any given time. For the standard associator, the number is r, the number of known patterns; for the programmable net, the number is sg, the number of patterns the net is programmed for times the grain of overlap allowed in the starting locations of input patterns.

This analysis greatly increases the plausibility of the CID scheme. For we find that the "initial investment" in CA units needed to program a set of networks to process a single association is related to the content of the association or the number of connections required to allow each of the active input elements to send a quantum of activation to each of the active output elements. Incorporating a provision for overlapping networks, we find that the investment required for processing one association is related to the content of the association times the grain of the overlap. This cost is far more reasonable than it looked like it might be at first, and, most importantly, it does not depend on the number of patterns known.

An additional important result is that the cost of programming a set of networks grows with the number of patterns we wish to program for at one time. This cost seems commensurate with the linear speedup we would get by being able to process several patterns simultaneously.

The somewhat intangible benefit to be derived from mutual constraint among the patterns would come over and above the simple linear throughput effect. However, this benefit, as we shall see in the next section, is balanced by the extra cost associated with the possibility that there might be spurious patterns in the intersection of input elements of the presented patterns.

The Cost of Simultaneous Access

So far, we have proceeded as though we already knew what patterns to prepare each local module for. However, the CID mechanism was intended to allow several inputs to access the central network simultaneously and thereby program the local networks in the course of processing. This simultaneous access costs something; in this section we consider how much. The discussion here is relevant to the general issue of the costs of simultaneous access to a PDP network, as well as to the specific question of the capacity requirements of CID.

For simplicity I will begin by considering local representations at the central output level. That is, I will assume that each central output unit represents a different pattern and that it is switched on only when all of the central input units corresponding to its pattern are active.

Now, recall that a central input unit is switched on if the corresponding unit is active in any of the programmable nets. Thus, what the central output units actually see is the pattern of activation that results from the superimposition of the input patterns presented for simultaneous processing. The effect of this is that there is some possibility that ghosts of patterns not actually presented will show up in the result. This is just the kind of situation that is described in Chapter 16 when similar words such as *SAND* and *LANE* are presented to each of two programmable networks for simultaneous processing. When the activation patterns of the two words are superimposed, the central word units for *LAND* and *SANE* get turned on just as strongly as the central word units for *SAND* and *LANE.* Thus, the programmable networks end up being programmed to process any one of these four words, rather than just any one of the two actually presented.

Is there anything that can be done to control the number of different patterns that show up when several patterns are superimposed? In fact, there is. If we increase the number of input units in each programmable network or if we reduce the number of input units active in each pattern, we will reduce the possibility of spurious patterns showing up in the superposition.

To get a quantitative grip on this matter, assume that the input patterns are random selections of m out of the n input units as we have been assuming throughout. The probability that a spurious pattern is present in the superposition of s patterns can now be easily calculated. First, we calculate the probability that a randomly selected unit will be on; this is just

$$1-(1-m/n)^s.$$

The probability that a particular spurious pattern is fully represented in the set of units activated by the s patterns is just this number to the power m, and the average number of such patterns out of r known patterns is just this probability times $r-s$. Thus, the average number of spurious patterns present in the superposition is

$$(r-s)[1-(1-m/n)^s]^m.$$

Assuming $r >> s$, we can simplify by replacing $r-s$ with r. If we take acceptable performance to be an average of one or fewer spurious patterns present and therefore of spurious CP units active, we get

$$1=r[1-(1-m/n)^s]^m.$$

Rearranging and taking logs,

$$\log\left[1-\left(\frac{1}{r}\right)^{\frac{1}{m}}\right]=s\log(1-m/n).$$

Several things are apparent from this equation. First, the number of patterns that can be processed at one time increases with the number of input units. The effect is approximately linear as long as $m/n \leqslant .1$. Second, though it is not quite as straightforward, s tends to increase with a decrease in m. For example, suppose $n = 5{,}000$ and $r = 10{,}000$. In this case, when m drops from 1,000 to 500, s increases from 21 to about 37; if m drops to 100, s goes up to about 120. Third, for a fixed m and n, especially for large m, we can make very large changes in r with only minimal impact on s. Thus, if we have, say, $n = 10{,}000$ and $m = 1{,}000$ with $r = 10^6$, we get $s = 43$; if we reduce r to 10^5, we only get an increase of 2 in s, to 45.

If we allow overlapping local networks, and we assume that the patterns are random with independent subparts, we need only replace s in the preceeding equation with sg. While this is a fairly steep cost, it is still the case that reasonably moderate values of n (about 2.5×10^5) would be sufficient to process 10 out of 10^6 known patterns of size 1,000 simultaneously with a grain of 100.

Simultaneous Access to Distributed Representations

The results just described, it must be remembered, depend on the use of *local* representations at the central output level. What happens if we consider simultaneously accessing distributed representations instead? Obviously this question remains relevant to general questions about simultaneous access, as well as to the situation that would arise using distributed central output units in CID. Furthermore, we should note that the central output units in Figure 4 simply mediate a mapping from one distributed representation—on the central input units—to another—on the CA units. The present analysis describes what would happen if we simply collapsed these two sets of units into one, activating the connections directly from the central output units.

We consider a case exactly like the one we were just considering, except that now the output representation is not a single unit per pattern, but m_o active units on out of n_o central output units. We consider two somewhat separate questions. First, if we superimpose several input patterns, what effect does this have on d' at the central output level, relative to the case where only a single pattern is shown? Second, what is the probability that ghosts of whole patterns not presented will show up in the *output* of the central network?

To begin our analysis of the first question, recall from Equation 2 the expression for d' in random nets with full fan-out ($n = f$):

$$d' = \sqrt{m_i}\,\frac{1 - p_{on}}{\sqrt{(1 + p_{on})/2}}.$$

We first ask, what is the effect on d' of turning on spurious input units with probability ρ, in addition to the m units representing a particular pattern to be processed? The number M_i of input units that will then be on is

$$M_i = m_i + (n_i - m_i)\rho.$$

Consider first, output units that should not be on. These will receive M_i active inputs, and each of these connections will be on with probability p_{on}. The output units that should be on will receive m_i inputs on the input lines whose connections were turned on in learning the presented pattern plus $(n_i - m_i)\rho$ inputs to connections that will have been turned on in learning other patterns with probability p_{on}. The numerator for our revised expression will then simply reduce to its old value, with the $(n_i - m_i)\rho$ term canceling out. However, there will be an increase in variance, and hence a decrease in d'. The denominator is as before the square root of the average of the variances of the two means, which are, also as before, equal to the means. The expression for d' therefore becomes

$$d' = m \frac{(1 - p_{on})}{\sqrt{[m_i + m_i p_{on} + 2(n_i - m_i)\rho]/2}}.$$

We get a simpler expression if we approximate by replacing p_{on} in the denominator with its maximum value of 1; this gives us a slight overestimate of the variance and therefore a slight underestimate of d':

$$d' \geqslant m \frac{(1 - p_{on})}{\sqrt{m_i + (n_i - m_i)\rho}}.$$

The variance goes up with the mean number of spuriously activated units, and d' goes down with the effect of this on the square root of the variance.

To determine the effect of presenting several patterns on d', we note that from the point of view of the units that belong to one of the patterns, all the units activated by the other patterns are spurious. The number of such units is

$$1 - (1 - m_i/n_i)^{s-1}$$

Inserting this for ρ in the previous equation gives

$$d' = m \frac{(1 - p_{on})}{\sqrt{m_i + (n_i - m_i)[1 - (1 - m_i/n_i)^{s-1}]}}.$$

Using this equation we can examine the effects of increasing s on the value of d'. Not too surprisingly, d' does go down as s goes up, but the effect is relatively benign. For example, with $n = 10^6$, $r = 10^6$, $m = 1{,}000$, and $s = 1$, d' is about 11.6. It drops to half that value at $s = 4$, and drops much more gradually thereafter. With $n = 2 \times 10^6$ units and the same values of r and m, we can get an acceptable value of d' ($\geqslant 6$) with s as high as 16.

The final issue we will consider is the possibility that new spurious output patterns have been introduced in the superposition of the s output patterns simultaneously activated in processing the s input patterns. For simplicity, we will just consider the probability of a "ghost," given that all and only the correct m_o units are active for each of the s patterns. The analysis is entirely the same as the one we gave before for the probability of ghosts showing up in the input patterns. We get an average of one ghost when

$$1 \geqslant r[1 - (1 - m/n)^s]^m.$$

As before, the number of simultaneous patterns we can tolerate increases with n and decreases with m and is relatively insensitive to the value of r.

In general, it appears that the probability of ghosts occurring can be kept small with sufficiently large dedication of resources, but these trade off approximately linearly with s. With fixed n, we must simply make the patterns sparser or tolerate some loss of sensitivity.

Discussion

This analysis of the resource requirements of networks like the CID model has discovered a number of basic results. In essence, the picture is really a very simple one. The resource requirements of CID depend on the number of programmable networks one wants to program for at once. The number of connections needed in each local network depends on the number of patterns to be programmed for and is independent of r, the number of known patterns. In the central network, the number of units required to keep spurious activations under control grows with s, as does the number of units required to keep ghosts from emerging in the input and output patterns. It is worth noting, also, that the probability of ghosts *increases* as we increase m.

The fact that the resource requirements of the local networks are independent of the number of patterns known is obviously important. Relative to the central network, it means that the local networks are very cheap. The number of distinct inputs that are needed to program them is quite reasonable, and, as I will explain, we can even get by with far fewer units in the local networks than we need at the central level.

On the other hand, the results concerning the costs of simultaneous access to the central network are much less encouraging for the CID scheme. Using local or distributed representations in the central module, the unit requirements grow with the product of s and r—a very expensive proposition since the number of central connections will then grow as sr^2.

However, there are several important further observations. One is that, at fixed numbers of units and patterns known, the degradation of sensitivity as a function of s is rather gradual. And, given a lightly loaded network, one can take s up to reasonable values without catastrophe. Simultaneous access by multiple patterns is very much like degradation: a network can handle it without a noticeable decrement of function if it is lightly loaded. A second observation concerns the limits of coarse coding. For fixed n, the choice of m essentially amounts to a question of how coarse the code is: Large m corresponds to very coarse coding, and small m corresponds to very fine coding. As we saw in Chapter 3, the ability to represent several patterns at a time goes down as the coding gets coarser. For simultaneous processing we need sparse patterns, with each unit serving as a rather sharply tuned conjunctive detector.

The final observation is that large costs are associated with simultaneous access to the central network. This fact has lead me to the view that it is probably most reasonable to imagine that we must probably restrict simultaneous access, except perhaps in the case of small, compact and well-differentiated subpatterns like letters. I incorporated this idea of restricted access in the programmable blackboard model of reading by assuming that we program successive parts of the programmable blackboard sequentially, using only the contents of the spotlight of attention to access the central network; but that the local networks so programmed continue to process and hold patterns of activation and to allow those patterns to interact with one and other after the spotlight of attention has moved on. In this way we get the best of both worlds: sequential access to central knowledge, combined with interactive parallel processing of several stimuli in the programmable nets. Another point is that it may be a good idea to dissociate the inputs to the local networks and the inputs to the central networks. Throughout this chapter and Chapter 16, I have assumed that the units in each local network would be isomorphic to units in the central network. However, there is no reason for them to be. The central network needs much higher "resolution" (n proportional to r) than the local networks (n proportional to s). Thus, the units in the programmable modules need only provide a few primitive clues to which of the s patterns are to be represented in their outputs, while the units in the central network would require a much higher-resolution representation.

CONCLUSION

This chapter has indicated how Willshaw's fruitful analysis of simple pattern associator models can be extended in several directions. These extensions have lead to several interesting observations, particularly into the effects of limited connectivity (Mitchison, personal communication, 1984) and into the capacity requirements of programmable networks. A large number of issues remain to be explored. I hope that this discussion and elaboration of Willshaw's analysis will aid in this continuing exploration.

ACKNOWLEDGMENTS

This work was supported by Contract N-00014-82-C-0374, NR 667-483 with the Personnel and Training Research Programs of the Office of Naval Research, by a grant from the System Development Foundation to the Institute for Cognitive Science at UCSD, and by an NIMH Research Scientist Career Development Award (MH-00385). This chapter was developed in response to a number of questions raised by Geoff Hinton and Scott Fahlman about the resource requirements of programmable nets. I thank Dave Rumelhart for several useful discussions and for encouraging me to pursue the issues described herein. The material described in the section entitled "Randomly Connected Nets" was developed in collaboration with Dave, and the application of the d' analysis to the problem of simultaneous access to a distributed memory network was Dave's suggestion.

CHAPTER 13

P3: A Parallel Network Simulating System

D. ZIPSER and D. RABIN

Research on parallel distributed processing is to a large extent dependent upon the use of computer simulation, and a good deal of the researcher's time is spent writing programs for this purpose. Virtually all the PDP systems described in this book require special-purpose computer programs to emulate the networks under study. In writing programs of this type, it is usually found that the basic algorithms of the PDP network are easy to program but that these rather simple "core" programs are of little value unless they are embedded in a system that lets the researcher observe and interact with their functions. These user interface programs are generally tedious and very time consuming to write. What is more, when they are directed toward one particular system they can be quite inflexible, making it difficult to easily modify the PDP network being studied. Also, because of the time involved, particularly for interactive graphics programs, the researcher often makes do with very limited facilities for analyzing the performance of the network. In this chapter we will describe a general-purpose parallel system simulator called P3. It was developed with PDP research explicitly in mind and its major goal is to facilitate simulation by providing both the tools for network description and a powerful user interface that can be used with any network described using the tools. There are many problems to be faced and tradeoffs to be made in designing such a system but in the process of doing this we feel that not only has a useful system been developed, but also that we have learned a great deal about the whole problem of PDP simulations.

In P3 networks, each computing element, called a *unit,* contains a computer program that reads inputs from connections and sets outputs on other connections, possibly also modifying some local state parameters. The major components of P3 are:

- The *plan language*, which describes the collection of units in a model and specifies the connections between them. This description is called a "plan."
- The *method language,* an extension to LISP, which implements the internal computational behaviors of the units in a model.
- The *constructor*, which transforms the plan and associated methods into a computer program and, when run, simulates the network.
- The *simulation environment*, which provides an interactive display-oriented facility for observing and testing P3 models.

Input to units described in a P3 plan can come only from other units in the plan. That is, there is no "outside world" in a P3 plan language description of a network. This means that at the level of description of the P3 plan language, the P3 network is closed. Access to the *outside* world must occur *inside* a unit through its method. Methods may access the world outside the P3 system through any available computer peripheral. The only thing that methods are not allowed to do is to reconfigure with the P3 system itself or communicate with other methods through "underground connections" not mentioned in the P3 plan.

In any simulation, the relationship between real and modeled time is of key importance. A real unit, such as a neuron, would read inputs continuously and update its outputs asynchronously, but this cannot be simulated exactly on a digital computer. Many simulations use a simple synchronous approximation to real time. However, sometimes this produces unwanted artifacts and a closer approximation of asynchrony is required. Often, in fact, what the investigator really wants to do is to experiment with the effect of different kinds of time simulation on the network under study. Since there is no way for the system designer to know in advance all the possible ways that the investigator will want to handle time, some strategy has to be used that allows great flexibility. The approach taken by P3 is that this flexibility can come through the methods that can use conditional updating. The P3 system itself is completely synchronous and updates all units on each cycle. Since updating a unit involves invoking its method, the question of whether or not the outputs of a unit actually change on any P3 cycle can be decided by the method. For example, to model asynchronous updating, each unit can have an additional input that controls whether or not it is updated on a cycle. Then the decision as to which units are to be updated can be given to a control unit that is connected by a separate line to the update inputs of all the other units. The method program inside this control unit decides which units in the network will be updated on each cycle. Note that this approach is very flexible since small changes in the method program of the control unit can implement a large range of possible update time schemes.

A typical P3 plan might contain a large number of simple neuron-like units forming the core of the network together with a few special purpose units to generate input to the core network and control its function. The master control unit, used above to implement asynchronous updating, is an example of this kind of special-purpose unit. They can also be used to sequence simulated experiments and to interpret output of other units. How all this can be done will become clearer as we describe the use of P3 in detail. They key point here is that the P3 "style" is to include *within* the P3 plan all aspects of the simulation including input to and control of the core network. This approach simplifies the problem of constantly having to interfere special-purpose routines to a general-purpose modeling environment.

It often happens that networks are modular, that is, made up of distinct subnetworks. P3 facilitates the use of modularity by allowing subnetworks to be treated as single processing units. This feature is of particular use when several P3 units are used to simulate a single object such as a "realistic" neuron. The modular feature also facilitates "top-down" and "structured" definition of the plan even when the underlying networks are not particularly modular.

The P3 plan language has an additional feature that is not directly concerned with describing the functional aspects of a parallel network. Every unit in a P3 plan has a location in a three-dimensional Euclidean reference frame call *P3 space*. This means that every P3 plan not only describes a network, but it also describes a geometrical structure. Since the functioning of a P3 network does not depend on its geometrical structure, it might seem odd to go to all the trouble of describing the geometry. There are two main reasons for locating P3 units in space. The first reason is to facilitate visualizing a P3 network while observing its function during the simulation of a model. The units can be placed so that they appear at the same relative positions on the computer display during simulation as they have in the investigator's conceptual image of the model. The second reason to give each unit a position in space is to make it possible to specify connections between units implicitly on the basis of their spatial locations rather than explicitly. This latter feature is of particular importance when modeling systems in which the connectivity is described in terms of geometrical relations. This is often the case when dealing with realistic neuronal modeling, especially of primary sensory processing structures.

The P3 Plan Language

The job of the P3 plan language is to describe the units and connections that constitute the network being simulated. To do this, the language uses a small but rich set of statements that make it possible to succinctly describe large groups of complex, connected units. The three fundamental constituents of the plan language are the UNIT TYPE, UNIT, and CONNECT statements. The UNIT TYPE statement names and describes a kind of unit. The UNIT statement instantiates and names actual units. This statement can instantiate either a single unit or a whole array of units of the same type. The CONNECT statement makes connections. Since the statement can be used inside of loops, a single connect statement can make an arbitrarily large number of connections using the available array features.

A unit in P3 can have any number of inputs and outputs together with any number of parameters. Before the start of a simulation, values must be given to all parameters and to all outputs. Each value is always a single computer word in length. The interpretation of this word depends on how the methods use it. As the simulation proceeds, these initial values are continuously updated. Taken together, the values of the parameters and the outputs constitute the state of the system at any time during simulation. The major difference between parameter values and output values is that outputs are available to other units in a network through connections, while the value of parameters can only be read by the unit to which they belong. P3 units can have two classes of parameters: *unit parameters* and *terminal parameters*. The unit parameters apply to the whole unit, for example, the threshold in a linear threshold unit. The terminal parameters are associated with individual inputs or outputs and correspond, for example, to weights.

An important function of the P3 plan language is to describe the connections between units. Since units can have multiple inputs and outputs there has to be some way to name them so that the CONNECT statements will know which connections to make. These names are also used within the method programs to read inputs and set outputs. The basic form of the CONNECT statement is

```
(CONNECT < unit-name > OUTPUT < output-name >
   TO < unit-name >  INPUT < input-name >)
```

For units with only a few inputs or outputs each input or output can be given a separate name. When a unit has a large number of inputs or outputs it is more convenient to group them together in input or output arrays. The individual items in these arrays are referenced by giving the array name and a set of subscript values. These arrays can be used in iterative statements in plans and methods.

An output value can serve as input to any number of units, i.e., the fan-out is arbitrarily large. Each individual input can receive only one value. This is easy to enforce as long as it is known that just one connection is to be made to each input. This works well in many cases but it often happens that it is very hard or impossible for the programmer to know exactly how many connections will be made. This is the case, for example, when connection decisions are being made implicitly by some computational procedure such as "connection by location" or random connection. To overcome this, P3 secretly treats each individual input as an array and automatically adjusts its size to fit the number of inputs. This process is transparent to the programmer which means that multiple connections can be made freely to a single input. There is a special iteration statement in the method language to access these multiple inputs. Each individual input that actually gets generated is called a TERMINAL and there are procedures for associating parameters with terminals and initializing their values.

The method programs that implement the internal functionings of units are written in the form of ordinary computer programs in an appropriate language. In the current implementation, which runs on the Symbolics 3600, the language is LISP. In order to allow the methods to use the values of inputs and parameters in their computations, a set of special access statements is incorporated into this system and is available to LISP programs. These statements make it possible for methods to read and set inputs, outputs, and parameters more or less as if they are ordinary variables.

In order to illustrate how P3 works, we will describe a model of a simple competitive learning network of the type described in Chapter 5. The basic network contains two types of units: a pattern generator to supply stimuli and a cluster of competitive learners connected to it, which spontaneously discover some features of the patterns. Since learning is spontaneous and does not require a teacher, the functioning of the network is simple and straightforward. The pattern generators sequentially produce output patterns that serve as input stimuli to the cluster units. Each pattern is an activation vector specifying which of the inputs are active and which are not. Each cluster unit produces an output indicating its response to the current stimulus which is transmitted to all other members of the cluster to create a "winner take all" network. The cluster unit which wins is the only one that learns and it uses the weight redistribution procedure described in the competitive learning chapter, that is,

$$\Delta\omega_{ij} = \begin{cases} 0 & \text{if unit } j \text{ loses on stimulus } k \\ g\dfrac{c_{ik}}{n_k} - g\omega_{ij} & \text{if unit } j \text{ wins on stimulus } k \end{cases}$$

where c_{ik} is equal to 1 if in stimulus pattern S_k, element i in the lower layer is active and zero otherwise, and n_k is the number of active elements in pattern S_k (thus $n_k = \sum_i c_{ik}$).

The first step in creating a P3 plan is to supply the UNIT TYPE statements. The UNIT TYPE statement for the pattern generator is given below:

```
(unit type dipole
    parameters flag i1 j1 i2 j2
    outputs (d array i j)
    method <update routine code in lisp>)
```

In this, and all our other examples, words in italics are part of the P3 plan language while the nonitalicized words are supplied by the user. The UNIT TYPE statement gives the type a name that will be used throughout the plan. The name for the pattern generator type is "dipole." There are five parameters that are used internally for pattern generation. The technicalities of the use of these parameters is irrelevant here. The UNIT TYPE statement describes the output of the unit. This output is a two-dimensional array of lines called "d." This array of outputs is the retina on which stimulus patterns are generated which serves as an input to the competitive learning cluster units. The "i" and "j" that follow the word *array* are dummy variables that tell P3 how many dimensions the array has. The actual size of the array is variable and is initialized when we instantiate units of the type dipole. Note that the unit type dipole had no inputs since it is itself the source of patterns.

The second basic unit type is the competitive learning unit, which in our plan we call "competitor." The unit type statement for it is given below:

```
(unit type competitor
    parameters p g flag
    inputs (C array i j terminal parameters W)
        (i-A)
    outputs (o-A)
    method <lisp code>)
```

Note that the input array "C" of this unit corresponds exactly in form to the output array "d" of the dipole unit described previously. This correspondence will make it possible to make one-to-one connections between the output of dipole type units and the input of competitor type units. Also notice that a terminal parameter "W" has been associated with the input array "C." The competitor unit needs an additional input called "i-A" which will receive information from the outputs of all the other members of the cluster.

We have described the two unit types we will need. We can now go ahead and instantiate units of these types. The statement that creates a pattern generator unit of type dipole is shown below:

```
(unit stimulus of type dipole
    at (@ 0 0 0)
    outputs (d array (i 0 5) (j 0 5))))
```

The unit statement names the unit it is creating. This is the name of a real unit that is actually going to exist in our model and it is the name that will be referred to when this unit is connected to other units. For P3 to build such a unit, it has to be told the type. There can be any number of units of the same type and they can all have different names. Since every real unit in P3 has a location in P3 space, we must specify it in the unit statement that instantiates the unit. The *at* clause is used for this. The *at* is followed by a location specifier that simply evaluates to the x-, y-, and z-coordinates of the unit in P3 space. For simplicity we locate the pattern generator at the origin of P3 space which will initially be located at the center of the display window when we simulate the model. Since we are building a real unit, we have to give a size to its array of output lines. This is done in the *outputs* clause of the UNIT statement. Each subscript specifier consists of a subscript name and initial value, which in the current implementation must be 0, and final value, which in this example is 5 for both the "i" and the "j" subscripts. This statement will generate a 6×6 array of output lines on connector "d."

Now that we have a source of patterns, we need to create a cluster of units that will receive these patterns. The statement that instantiates these units is given below:

```
(unit cluster array (k 0 – cluster-size 1) of type competitor
   at (@ ( * k (+ cluster-size 4))(+ cluster-size 10) 0)
   initialize (g = 0.05)
   inputs (C array (i 0 (– stimulus-size 1))(j 0 (– stimulus-size 1)))
```

In this case, we are not instantiating a single unit but an array of units. In the competitive learning model, the learning cluster always consists of two or more units, so we want a way to vary the number of units in a cluster. In the first line of the unit statement we give the name cluster to the array and then we indicate the size of the array with a subscript specifier. The name of this subscript is "k"; its initial value is 0. Its final value is one less than the global constant "cluster-size." The value of cluster-size, which will occur at various points in the plan, is set by a statement at the beginning of the P3 plan that determines the value of global constants. This feature means that we can change the parameters such as cluster-size globally throughout the plan by only fiddling with a single value. The upper bound of the stimulus input line array has also been set with the use of a global constant "stimulus-size" rather than with an integer as was done previously. Also notice that the variable "k" is used in an *at* clause to place each unit of the array at a different place in P3 space.

Our next task is to connect the units together in the appropriate fashion. We have two classes of connections: those that go from the stimulus generator to the learning cluster and those that interconnect the units within the learning cluster. Each of these classes of connections has many individual connections within it, but these individual connections can be specified algorithmically in such a way that only a few CONNECT statements are needed to generate the entire network. What is more, the algorithmic specification of these connections makes it possible to change the size of the cluster or the size of the stimulus array without altering the CONNECT statements at all. The code required to connect the stimulus to the learning cluster is given below:

```
(for (k 0 (+ 1 k))
   exit when (> k cluster-size) do
   (for (i 0 (+ 1 i))
      exit when (> i stimulus-size) do
      (for (j 0 (+ 1 j))
         exit when (> j stimulus-size) do
         (connect unit stimulus output d i j
            to unit (cluster k) input C i j
            terminal initialize (W = (si:random-in-range
               0.0 (// 2.0 (expt (+ stimulus-size 1) 2))))))))
```

There are three nested loops. The first ranges over each member of the cluster, and the next two range over each dimension of the stimulus array. Inside these three nested loops is a single CONNECT statement. The CONNECT statement has the job of initializing the value of any terminal parameters. In our model we have a very important terminal parameter, "W," the weight between a stimulus line and a cluster unit, which we want to initialize to a random value which sums to one for the whole input array. This is accomplished by setting the initial value of "W" with a LISP function that evaluates to the required quantity. In general, in a P3 plan wherever a number is required, a function (in our case a LISP function) that evaluates to a number can replace the number itself. The sum of the random numbers generated by our simple LISP function is not exactly one, but only averages one. This is satisfactory for the competitive learning algorithm because it is self-normalizing and will force the sum to one in the course of learning.

The connections that link the members of a cluster are a bit more complex. Each member of the cluster must receive input from all other members except itself. The code for doing this in a completely general way for clusters of any size is given below:

```
(for (k 0 (+ 1 k))
    exit when (> k cluster-size) do
    (for (j 0 (+ 1 j))
        exit when (= j k) do
        (connect unit cluster k output o-A
            to unit cluster j input i-A))
    (for (j (+ k 1) (+ 1 j))
        exit when (> j cluster-size) do
        (connect unit cluster k output o-A
            to unit cluster j input i-A)))
```

The idea here is that we first connect each unit to those units whose subscripts are lower than it and then to each unit whose subscript is higher than it. This requires two separate loops, each with its own CONNECT statement, both nested within an outer loop that ranges over all units in the cluster. Note that this is a case of making multiple connections to a single input line. We don't have to know how many connections there are because within the method there is code that will examine all connections on this line to decide if the unit has won. This feature is very useful and can be applied whenever a method needs to know the value of an input but not its originating unit.

We have now specified all the features of a plan that describes the basic competitive learning network. Of course, this plan can only be used to construct a running model if we have available the appropriate method programs. Since these are ordinary computer programs written in LISP, we won't analyze them in detail. The code for the methods used here is given in the appendix of this chapter, which shows a complete plan for a simulation of competitive learning. It is worthwhile, however, to see how the method language accesses the inputs and outputs of the units about which we have been saying so much in the development of the plan.

The only difference between the arguments to a P3 method and the arguments to a normal LISP function is that the P3 arguments are accessed by special access functions. For example, to get the value of a parameter, the following form is used:

(*read-unit-parameter* flag)

This form returns the current value of flag. To read an input from an array of input lines the following form can be used:

(*read-input* (C i j))

In this case the value of "i" and "j" must be bound at the point in the program where an expression using them occurs. There are corresponding forms for reading terminal parameters, setting outputs, and setting parameter values.

The P3 Simulation System

The P3 simulation system is the environment in which models in P3 are simulated. It is highly interactive and makes extensive use of the window system and the "mouse" pointer of the Symbolics 3600. The first step in simulating a model is to compile the methods and construct the plan. The constructor is a program similar in purpose to a compiler. However, the input is a P3 description of a network, rather than a computer language description of a program. The output of the constructor is a data structure containing all the relevant information about the network that can be used by the P3 simulation system to run a simulation of the model. As with any form of computer programming, a model must be debugged before it can be simulated. There are really two levels of debugging for network models. First, the user wants to know that the network that has been created is connected up in the way intended. Once this has been established, the actual functioning of the network can be debugged. P3 provides tools for both of these phases of the debugging process.

To check the correctness of connections, P3 provides a display that shows each unit in the model at its location in P3 space. The user interacts with this display with a mouse pointing device. Clicking on a particular unit provides a menu that enables the user to trace out any of the connections emanating from that unit. This facility for tracing out connections, one at a time, has proved much more useful than simply presenting a user with the wiring diagram of the model. Once the user is convinced that the constructed model corresponds to the envisioned network, the job of analyzing the function of the model can begin.

Analyzing the running of a complex simulation is a demanding task. It is in this analysis that we have found that all the features of the P3 system come together and begin to justify their existence. Because every object in the model has a location in P3 space that corresponds to the user's mental image of the network, the simulation system can display values representing the state of the system at locations on the screen that have meaning to the user. This means that during the course of a simulation, meaningful patterns of P3 variables can be displayed. This approach is widely used in analyzing the function of parallel systems. What P3 has done is to standardize it and relieve the user of the need to implement the details of this display strategy for each new model.

In the current implementation of P3, each object in the model is represented at its designated location by a small rectangular icon. By the use of a mouse pointer driven menu system, the user can assign the icon representing a unit the variable whose value is to be displayed. Thus, for example, the icons representing the input terminals of a cluster unit in our example can be assigned either the value of the input to that terminal or the value of the weight on that terminal. These assignments can be made or changed at any time during a simulation run. They can be set to be updated continually as a simulation proceeds, or they can be examined in detail when the simulation is temporarily interrupted. The current P3 implementation displays the relevant state values at two possible levels of precision. The approximate value of the state value is indicated by the degree of darkening of the icon. There are five levels of intensity. Their range is under user control and can be changed at any time. This enables the user to adjust the range so that the difference between the lightest and the darkest icons will optimize the information content of the display. There is also a high precision display that permits the exact value of any P3 variable to be examined.

Figure 1 shows how the screen of the Symbolics 3600 looks after 588 P3 cycles of simulation of a competitive learning model with a 6×6 stimulus array and a dipole stimulus. There are six windows displayed and each shows a different aspect of the simulation. Window A shows the three units in the model at their respective positions in P3 space. The upper narrow rectangle is the pattern generator. It is not displaying any value. The lower two rectangles represent the two cluster units. They are displaying the approximate value of their outputs by the size of the contained black rectangle. Clearly the unit on the left has a lower output value than the one on the right. Window B shows the output of the pattern generator unit, which was called "stimulus" in the plan. The lines form a square array because that is the way they were specified in the plan. The two dark rectangles show the current dipole

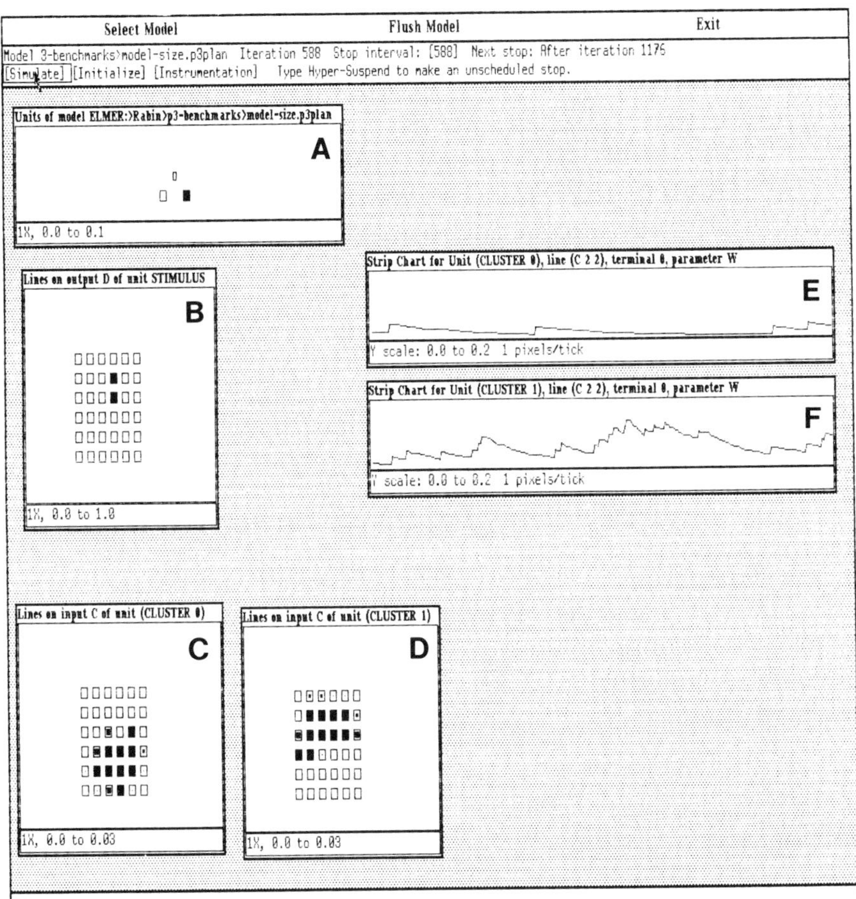

FIGURE 1. Display of Symbolics 3600 during P3 session. The mouse arrow is pointing to the "simulate" command in the upper left. Clicking a mouse button will start simulation.

pattern. Windows C and D show the approximate values of the weights on the input line arrays of each of the two cluster units. The fact that competition has pretty well separated the weights along a horizontal line is clearly visible from these two windows. Windows E and F are "strip chart" records that produce a graphical record of any P3 variable. The strip charts have been set up to record the value of a pair of corresponding weights, one from each unit in the cluster. Time increases to the right so the initial state is at the extreme left side of the strip charts. It is interesting to note that one of the weights became dominant for a while but at later times seems to have lost its dominance.

In addition to the special functions of P3, the user also has available all the powerful program development tools of the Symbolics 3600. For example, suppose that the user believes that an observed bug is due to an error in the code of a method. It is possible to interrupt the simulation, go directly to the editor buffer that contains the method code, alter it, recompile the alteration, and then return to the simulation at exactly the point at which it was interrupted. This facility has proved invaluable in debugging.

As we work with the P3 simulation system, we constantly find new features that are useful in the analytical process. We view the implementation of each of these new analytical techniques as analogous to adding a new instrument to a laboratory. Thus, we call the features of P3 that enable the user to analyze a functioning model "instruments." Each of these instruments can be called up at any time. Every instrument has a window that displays the results of the instrument's analysis. For example, one instrument is the "strip chart recorder" used in Figure 1. The strip chart recorder has a probe that can be connected to any particular state variable of any unit. Since multiple instances of any instrument can be created, any number of strip charts can be running at the same time. In addition to instruments that display the values of variables, we also envision a class of instruments that record these variables. Clearly, it is very important for a serious modeler to be able to record the results of a simulation. The instrument concept will enable the modeler to record just those variables required. This is a very important feature since simply recording the entire state of the model as it develops in time would produce an overwhelming flow of data.

Performance

So far we have said nothing about the speed at which simulations run. This is a problem of tremendous importance for PDP models. Big models inherently run slowly on serial computers. Generally, parallel programming systems like P3 stress ease of model definition and simulation. How much penalty must we pay in model performance? There is always some performance penalty for a general-purpose system. For any given piece of computer hardware, it is generally possible to write a specially tailored program that will run some particular model faster than any general system will run it. However, this special tailoring itself takes considerable time and makes it much harder to change the details of the model structure. Thus, we envision that programs like P3 will be useful in the early stages of model development when the size of the models are modest and there is frequent need for changes in structure. When the structure and parameters of a model have been decided upon and it is necessary to scale the model up and have it run extremely rapidly, it may in some cases be advantageous to write a special program to implement the model.

The general-purpose systems, however, have several things going for them with respect to model performance. First of all, since the data structure has the same form for models, it is possible to put a lot of effort into optimizing running speed for the particular hardware on which the system is implemented. This optimization only has to be done once rather than for each model. A second way in which general-purpose systems can improve performance is through the use of special-purpose hardware. The models generated by the P3 system are inherently parallel models and map well to some parallel computer architectures. The one way to get blinding speed from parallel models is to implement real parallelism in parallel computers. In some cases, array processors can also be highly beneficial. Since all the P3 models are of the same sort, a constructor can be made that will provide the appropriate data structures to run any P3 model on these kinds of hardware. This will make the hardware transparently available to the user of systems like P3. This, we believe, is a significant plus, since it is notoriously difficult to program any particular application for array processors or truly parallel hardware.

In conclusion, the P3 system illustrates some of the general issues that arise in any attempt to simulate PDP models, and provides a number of useful tools that can greatly facilitate model development. General-purpose systems like P3 have promise for speeding and facilitating the programming of parallel models and the ultimate ability to run these models very fast using specialized hardware.

APPENDIX A

```
;;;
;;;           -----------------------------------------------------
;;;
;;;                  P3 Plan for Competitive Learning
;;;   (NOTE the use of the "plan constant" and "include" statements.)
;;;           -----------------------------------------------------
;;;
;;;*******************************************************************
;;;                             Unit types
;;;*******************************************************************


;;;******** Dipole pattern generator ********
(unit type dipole
   parameters flag i1 j1 j1 i2 j2
   outputs (d array i j)
   include dipole-generator) . . . (see code file on p. 506)


;;;******** Learning unit ********
(unit type competitor
   parameters p q flag
   inputs (C array i j terminal parameters W)
      (i-A)
   outputs (o-A)
   include comp-learn) . . . (code on p. 504)


;;;*******************************************************************
;;;                           Unit instances
;;;*******************************************************************


   (plan constant stimulus-size = 6) (plan constant cluster-size = 2)


;;;******** Dipole pattern generator********
(unit stimulus of type dipole
   at (@ 0 0 0)
   outputs(d array(i 0stimulus-size)(j 0stimulus-size)linesat(@ i j 0)))
```

```
;;;******** Learning units ********
(unit cluster array (k 0 (- cluster-size 1)) of type competitor
   at (@ (* 1 (+ cluster-size 4)) (+ cluster-size 10) 0)
   initialize (q = 0.05)
   inputs (C array (i 0 (- stimulus-size 1)) (j 0 stimulus-size)))


;;;*****************************************************************
;;;                       Connections
;;;*****************************************************************


;;;******** Stimulus to both clusters ********
(for (k 0 (+ 1 k))
   exit when (= k cluster-size) do
   (for (i 0 (+ 1 i))
      exit when (= i stimulus-size ) do
      (for (j 0 (+ 1 j))
         exit when (= j stimulus-size) do
            (connect unit stimulus output d i j
               to unit cluster k input C i j
               terminal initialize
               (W = (si:random-in-range
                  0.0 (// 2.0 (expt (+ stimulus-size 1) 2))))))))


;;;******* Interconnect the clusters to implement competition ********
(for (k 0 (+ 1 k))
   exit when (= k cluster-size 1) do
   (for (j 0 (+ 1 j))
      exit when (= j k) do
      (connect unit cluster k output o-A
         to unit cluster j input i-A))
   for (j (+ k 1) (+ 1 j))
      exit when (= j cluster-size 1) do
      (connect unit cluster k output o-A
         to unit cluster j input i-A)))
```

APPENDIX B

```
;;;
;;;          -----------------------------------------------------
;;;
;;;                    Competitive Learning:  Methods
;;;
;;;          -----------------------------------------------------
;;;
;;;*************************************************************************
;;;
;;;          Method for unit in cluster of competitive learners
;;;*************************************************************************
;;;

method
   (let ((imax (input-dimension-n C 1))
      (jmax (input-dimension-n C 2))
      (win t)
   (N 0))

   ;; ******** Is this a learning iteration? ********
   (cond

      ;; ******** No ********
      ;; Accumulate the weighted sum of the pattern inputs into
      ;; unit parameter p, and set the competition output p-A to
      ;; that value
      ((> (read-unit-parameter flag) 0)
         (loop initially (set-unit-parameter p 0)
         for i from 0 below imax do
            (loop for j from 0 below jmax do
               (set-unit-parameter p
                  (+ (read-unit-parameter p)
                     (* read-terminal-parameter (C i j) W)
                     (read-input (C i j))))))
            finally (set-output o-A (read-unit-parameter p)))

   ;;******** Flip the iteration-parity flag ********
   (set-unit-parameter flag 0))
```

```
;;******** Yes ********
;; Figure out whether this unit wins on this cycle.  Winning
;; requires that this unit's parameter p be greater than those
;; for the other units of this type.  Those values are available
;; on the terminals of input i-A.
;; NOTE:  On iteration 0, everything is 0, so no unit thinks it
;; wins, and hence all avoid learning.
(t


;; ******** Find out whether we won ********
;; Win was initialized to t in the let at the top level of this method.
(for-terminals k of input i-A
   (if (<= (read-unit-parameter p)
         (read-input (i-A terminal k)))
   (setq win nil)))
(when win


   ;; ******** Accumulate sum of all inputs into N ********
   ;; This will become a normalizing constant.
      (loop for i from 0 below imax do
         (loop for j from 0 below jmax do
            (setq N (+ N (read-input (C i j))))))


;; ********Compute new weights ********
;; But only if the total input was greater than 0.
(if (> N 0)
   (loop with q-factor = (read-unit-parameter g)
      for i from 0 below imax do
      (loop for j from 0 below jmax do


         ;; ******** Compute one new weight ********
         (let* (old-weight
            (read-terminal-parameter
               (C i j) W))
            (new-weight
               (+ old-weight
                  (* g-factor
                     (- (// (read-input (C i j)) (float N))
                        old-weight)))))
```

```
            ;; Update the terminal parameter to the new weight
            (set-terminal-parameter
               (C i j ) W
               new-weight))))))

    ;; ******** Flip the iteration-parity flag ********
    (set-unit-parameter flag 1))))

;;;*******************************************************************
;;;               Dipole pattern generator method
;;;*******************************************************************

method

;;******** Do we need a new pattern on this iteration? ********
(cond

  ;; ******** Yes. Erase old dipole and make new one. ********
  ((< (read-unit-parameter flag) 1)
     (let (( imax (- (output-dimension-n d 1) 2))
        ( jmax (- (output-dimension-n d 1) 2)))
     (set-output (d (read-unit-parameter i1) (read-unit-parameter i1)) 0)
     (set-output (d (read-unit-parameter i2) (read-unit-parameter i2)) 0)
     (set-unit-parameter i1 (+ (random imax) 1))
     (set-unit-parameter j1 (+ (random jmax 1))
     (cond ((> (random 2) 0.5
        (cond ((> (random 2 0.5)
           (set-unit-parameter i2 (+ (read-unit-parameter i1) 1)))
           (t
           (set-unit-parameter i2 (- (read-unit-parameter i1 1))))
        (set-unit-parameter i2 (read-unit-parameter j1)))
        (t
        (cond ((> (random 2) 0.5)
           (set-unit-parameter i2 (+ (read-unit-parameter j1) 1)))
           (t
           (set-unit-parameter i2 (- (read-unit-parameter j1) 1))))
        (set-unit-parameter i2 (read-unit-parameter i1))))
  (set-output (d (read-unit-parameter i1) (read-unit-parameter j1)) 1)
  (set-output (d (read-unit-parameter i2) (read-unit-parameter j2)) 1)
  (set-unit-parameter flag 1)))
  (t
  (set-unit-parameter flag 0)))
```

References

Ackley, D. H., Hinton, G. E., & Sejnowski, T. J. (1985). A learning algorithm for Boltzmann machines. *Cognitive Science*, *9*, 147-169.

Amari, S. A. (1977a). A mathematical approach to neural systems. In J. Metzler (Ed.), *Systems neuroscience* (pp. 67-117). New York: Academic Press.

Amari, S. A. (1977b). Neural theory of association and concept formation. *Biological Cybernetics*, *26*, 175-185.

Anderson, J. A. (1970). Two models for memory organization using interacting traces. *Mathematical Biosciences*, *8*, 137-160.

Anderson, J. A. (1973). A theory for the recognition of items from short memorized lists. *Psychological Review*, *80*, 417-438.

Anderson, J. A. (1977). Neural models with cognitive implications. In D. LaBerge & S. J. Samuels (Eds.), *Basic processes in reading perception and comprehension* (pp. 27-90). Hillsdale, NJ: Erlbaum.

Anderson, J. A. (1983). Cognitive and psychological computation with neural models. *IEEE Transactions on Systems, Man, and Cybernetics*, *13*, 799-815.

Anderson, J. A., & Mozer, M. C. (1981). Categorization and selective neurons. In G. E. Hinton & J. A. Anderson (Eds.), *Parallel models of associative memory* (pp. 213-236). Hillsdale, NJ: Erlbaum.

Anderson, J. A., Silverstein, J. W., Ritz, S. A., & Jones, R. S. (1977). Distinctive features, categorical perception, and probability learning: Some applications of a neural model. *Psychological Review*, *84*, 413-451.

Anderson, J. R. (1982). Acquisition of cognitive skill. *Psychological Review*, *89*, 369-406.

Anderson, J. R. (1983). *The architecture of cognition.* Cambridge, MA: Harvard University Press.

Aragon, C. R., Johnson, D. S., & McGeoch, L. A. (1985). *Optimization by simulated annealing: An experimental evaluation.* Unpublished manuscript.

Bahl, L. R., Jelinek, F., & Mercer, R. L. (1983). A maximum likelihood approach to continuous speech recognition. *IEEE Transactions on Pattern Analysis and Machine Intelligence*, *5*, 179-190.

Ballard, D. H. (in press). Cortical connections and parallel processing: Structure and function. *Behavioral and Brain Sciences.*

Ballard, D. H., Hinton, G. E., & Sejnowski, T. J. (1983). Parallel visual computation. *Nature*, *306*, 21-26.

Bartlett, F. C. (1932). *Remembering.* Cambridge, England: Cambridge University Press.

Barto, A. G. (1985). *Learning by statistical cooperation of self-interested neuron-like computing elements* (COINS Tech. Rep. 85-11). Amherst: University of Massachusetts, Department of Computer and Information Science.

Barto, A. G., & Anandan, P. (1985). Pattern recognizing stochastic learning automata. *IEEE Transactions on Systems, Man, and Cybernetics*, *15*, 360-375.

Barto, A. G., & Sutton, R. S. (1981). Landmark learning: An illustration of associative search. *Biological Cybernetics*, *42*, 1-8.

Barwise, J., & Perry, J. (1983). *Situations and attitudes.* Cambridge, MA: MIT Press/Bradford.

Berko, J. (1958). The child's learning of English morphology. *Word*, *14*, 150-177.

Bernstein, J. (1981, December 14). Profiles: AI, Marvin Minsky. *The New Yorker*, pp. 50-126.

Bienenstock, E. L., Cooper, L. N., & Munro, P. W. (1982). Theory for the development of neuron activity: Orientation specificity and binocular interaction in visual cortex. *Journal of Neuroscience*, *2*, 32-48.

Binder, K. (1979). *Monte Carlo methods in statistical physics.* Berlin: Springer-Verlag.

Blake, A. (1983). The least disturbance principle and weak constraints. *Pattern Recognition Letters*, *1*, 393-399.

Blakemore, C. (1977). *Mechanics of the mind.* Cambridge, England: Cambridge University Press.

Broadbent, D. (1985). A question of levels: Comment on McClelland and Rumelhart. *Journal of Experimental Psychology: General*, *114*, 189-192.

Chase, W. G., & Simon, H. A. (1973). Perception in chess. *Cognitive Psychology*, *4*, 55-81.

Chomsky, N. (1957). *Syntactic structures.* The Hague: Mouton.

Chomsky, N. (1965). *Aspects of the theory of syntax.* Cambridge, MA: MIT Press.

Chomsky, N., & Halle, M. (1968). *The sound pattern of English.* New York: Harper & Row.

Christensen, R. (1981). *Entropy minimax sourcebook* (Vols. 1-4). Lincoln, MA: Entropy Limited.

Collins, A. M., & Loftus, E. F. (1975). A spreading-activation theory of semantic processing. *Psychological Review*, *82*, 407-425.

Coltheart, M., Patterson, K., & Marshall, J. C. (1980). *Deep dyslexia.* London: Routledge & Kegan.

Crick, F., & Mitchison, G. (1983). The function of dream sleep. *Nature*, *304*, 111-114.

DeMarzo, P. M. (1984). *Gibbs potentials, Boltzmann machines, and harmony theory.* Unpublished manuscript.

Dempster, A. P., Laird, N. M., & Rubin, D. B. (1976). Maximum likelihood from incomplete data via the EM algorithm. *Proceedings of the Royal Statistical Society*, 1-38.

Derthick, M. (1984). *Variations on the Boltzmann machine learning algorithm* (Tech. Rep. No. CMU-CS-84-120). Pittsburgh: Carnegie-Mellon University, Department of Computer Science.

Dretske, F. (1981). *Knowledge and the flow of information.* Cambridge, MA: MIT Press/Bradford.

Eisen, M. (1969). *Introduction to mathematical probability theory.* Englewood Cliffs, NJ: Prentice Hall.

Fahlman, S. E. (1979). *NETL: A system for representing and using real-world knowledge.* Cambridge, MA: MIT Press.

Fahlman, S. E. (1980). *The Hashnet interconnection scheme* (Tech. Rep. CMU-CS-80-125). Pittsburgh: Carnegie-Mellon University, Department of Computer Science.

Fahlman, S. E., Hinton, G. E., & Sejnowski, T. J. (1983). Massively parallel architectures for AI: NETL, Thistle, and Boltzmann machines. *Proceedings of the National Conference on Artificial Intelligence AAAI-83.*

Farley, B. G., & Clark, W. A. (1954). Simulation of self-organizing systems by digital computer. *IRE Transactions of Information Theory*, *4*, 76-84.

Feldman, J. A. (1981). A connectionist model of visual memory. In G. E. Hinton & J. A. Anderson (Eds.), *Parallel models of associative memory* (pp. 49-81). Hillsdale, NJ: Erlbaum.

Feldman, J. A. (1982). Dynamic connections in neural networks. *Biological Cybernetics*, *46*, 27-39.

Feldman, J. A. (1985). Connectionist models and their applications: Introduction. *Cognitive Science*, *9*, 1-2.

Feldman, J. A., & Ballard, D. H. (1982). Connectionist models and their properties. *Cognitive Science*, *6*, 205-254.

Fodor, J. A. (1983). *Modularity of mind: An essay on faculty psychology.* Cambridge, MA: MIT Press.

Fukushima, K. (1975). Cognitron: A self-organizing multilayered neural network. *Biological Cybernetics*, *20*, 121-136.

Fukushima, K. (1980). Neocognitron: A self-organizing neural network model for a mechanism of pattern recognition unaffected by shift in position. *Biological Cybernetics*, *36*, 193-202.

Gallistel, C. R. (1980). *The organization of action: A new synthesis.* Hillsdale, NJ: Erlbaum.

Geman, S., & Geman, D. (1984). Stochastic relaxation, Gibbs distributions, and the Bayesian restoration of images. *IEEE Transactions on Pattern Analysis and Machine Intelligence*, *6*, 721-741.

Ginsburg, H. P. (1983). *The development of mathematical thinking.* New York: Academic Press.

Glorioso, R. M., & Colón Osorio, F. C. (1980). *Engineering intelligent systems.* Bedford, MA: Digital Press.

Glushko, R. J. (1979). The organization and activation of orthographic knowledge in reading words aloud. *Journal of Experimental Psychology: Human Perception and Performance, 5,* 674-691.

Green, D. M., & Swets, J. A. (1966). *Signal detection theory and psychophysics.* New York: Wiley.

Grossberg, S. (1976). Adaptive pattern classification and universal recoding: Part I. Parallel development and coding of neural feature detectors. *Biological Cybernetics, 23,* 121-134.

Grossberg, S. (1978). A theory of visual coding, memory, and development. In E. L. J. Leeuwenberg & H. F. J. M. Buffart (Eds.), *Formal theories of visual perception.* New York: Wiley.

Grossberg, S. (1980). How does the brain build a cognitive code? *Psychological Review, 87,* 1-51.

Halmos, P. R. (1974). *Finite-dimensional vector spaces.* New York: Springer-Verlag.

Hebb, D. O. (1949). *The organization of behavior.* New York: Wiley.

Hewitt, C. (1975). Stereotypes as an ACTOR approach towards solving the problem of procedural attachment in FRAME theories. In *Proceedings of Theoretical Issues in Natural Language Processing: An interdisciplinary workshop.* Cambridge, MA: Bolt, Beranek, & Newman.

Hinton, G. E. (1977). *Relaxation and its role in vision.* Unpublished doctoral dissertation, University of Edinburgh.

Hinton, G. E. (1981a). Implementing semantic networks in parallel hardware. In G. E. Hinton & J. A. Anderson (Eds.), *Parallel models of associative memory* (pp. 161-188). Hillsdale, NJ: Erlbaum.

Hinton, G. E. (1981b). A parallel computation that assigns canonical object-based frames of reference. *Proceedings of the 7th International Joint Conference on Artificial Intelligence.*

Hinton, G. E. (1984). Parallel computations for controlling an arm. *Journal of Motor Behavior, 16,* 171-194.

Hinton, G. E., & Anderson, J. A. (Eds.). (1981). *Parallel models of associative memory.* Hillsdale, NJ: Erlbaum.

Hinton, G. E., & Lang, K. (1985). Shape recognition and illusory conjunctions. *Proceedings of the Ninth International Joint Conference on Artificial Intelligence.*

Hinton, G. E., & Sejnowski, T. J. (1983a). Analyzing cooperative computation. *Proceedings of the Fifth Annual Conference of the Cognitive Science Society.*

Hinton, G. E., & Sejnowski, T. J. (1983b). Optimal perceptual inference. *Proceedings of the IEEE Computer Society Conference on Computer Vision and Pattern Recognition,* 448-453.

Hinton, G. E., Sejnowski, T. J., & Ackley, D. H. (1984). *Boltzmann machines: Constraint satisfaction networks that learn* (Tech. Rep. No. CMU-CS-84-119). Pittsburgh, PA: Carnegie-Mellon University, Department of Computer Science.

Hofstadter, D. R. (1979). *Gödel, Escher, Bach: An eternal golden braid.* New York: Basic Books.

Hofstadter, D. R. (1983). The architecture of Jumbo. *Proceedings of the International Machine Learning Workshop.*

Hofstadter, D. R. (1985). *Metamagical themas.* New York: Basic Books.

Hogg, T., & Huberman, B. A. (1984). Understanding biological computation. *Proceedings of the National Academy of Sciences, USA, 81,* 6871-6874.

Hopfield, J. J. (1982). Neural networks and physical systems with emergent collective computational abilities. *Proceedings of the National Academy of Sciences, USA, 79,* 2554-2558.

Hopfield, J. J. (1984). Neurons with graded response have collective computational properties like those of two-state neurons. *Proceedings of the National Academy of Sciences, USA, 81,* 3088-3092.

Hopfield, J. J., Feinstein, D. I., & Palmer, R. G. (1983). "Unlearning" has a stabilizing effect in collective memories. *Nature, 304,* 158-159.

Hummel, R. A., & Zucker, S. W. (1983). On the foundations of relaxation labeling processes. *IEEE Transactions on Pattern Analysis and Machine Intelligence, 5,* 267-287.

Isenberg, D., Walker, E. C. T., Ryder, J. M., & Schweikert, J. (1980, November). *A top-down effect on the identification of function words.* Paper presented at the Acoustical Society of America, Los Angeles.

Jackson, J. H. (1958). On localization. In *Selected writings* (Vol. 2). New York: Basic Books. (Original work published 1869)

Julesz, B. (1971). *Foundations of cyclopean perception.* Chicago: University of Chicago Press.

Kanerva, P. (1984). *Self-propagating search: A unified theory of memory* (Rep. No. CSLI-84-7). Stanford, CA: Stanford University, Center for the Study of Language and Information.

Kawamoto, A. H., & Anderson, J. A. (1984). Lexical access using a neural network. *Proceedings of the Sixth Annual Conference of the Cognitive Science Society,* 204-213.

Kienker, P. K., Sejnowski, T. J., Hinton, G. E., & Schumacher, L. E. (1985). *Separating figure from ground with a parallel network.* Unpublished.

Kirkpatrick, S., Gelatt, C. D. Jr., & Vecchi, M. P. (1983). Optimization by simulated annealing. *Science, 220,* 671-680.

Kohonen, T. (1974). An adaptive associative memory principle. *IEEE Transactions, C-23,* 444-445.

Kohonen, T. (1977). *Associative memory: A system theoretical approach.* New York: Springer.

Kohonen, T. (1982). Clustering, taxonomy, and topological maps of patterns. In M. Lang (Ed.), *Proceedings of the Sixth International Conference on Pattern Recognition* (pp. 114-125). Silver Spring, MD: IEEE Computer Society Press.

Kohonen, T. (1984). *Self-organization and associative memory.* Berlin: Springer-Verlag.

Kullback, S. (1959). *Information theory and statistics.* New York: Wiley.

Lamperti, J. (1977). *Lecture notes in applied mathematical sciences: Stochastic processes.* Berlin: Springer-Verlag.

Larkin, J. H. (1983). The role of problem representation in physics. In D. Gentner & A. L. Stevens (Eds.), *Mental models* (pp. 75-98). Hillsdale, NJ: Erlbaum.

Lashley, K. S. (1950). In search of the engram. In *Society of Experimental Biology Symposium No. 4: Psychological mechanisms in animal behavior* (pp. 478-505). London: Cambridge University Press.

Le Cun, Y. (1985, June). Une procedure d'apprentissage pour reseau a seuil assymetrique [A learning procedure for assymetric threshold network]. *Proceedings of Cognitiva 85*, 599-604. Paris.

Levin, J. A. (1976). *Proteus: An activation framework for cognitive process models* (Tech. Rep. No. ISI/WP-2). Marina del Rey, CA: University of Southern California, Information Sciences Institute.

Levine, R. D., & Tribus, M. (1979). *The maximum entropy formalism.* Cambridge, MA: MIT Press.

Lewis, C. H. (1978). *Production system models of practice effects.* Unpublished doctoral dissertation, University of Michigan.

Lindsay, P. H., & Norman, D. A. (1972). *Human information processing: An introduction to psychology.* New York: Academic Press.

Luria, A. R. (1966). *Higher cortical functions in man.* New York: Basic Books.

Luria, A. R. (1973). *The working brain.* London: Penguin.

Marr, D. (1982). *Vision.* San Francisco: Freeman.

Marr, D., & Poggio, T. (1976). Cooperative computation of stereo disparity. *Science*, *194*, 283-287.

Marr, D., & Poggio, T. (1979). A computational theory of human stereo vision. *Proceedings of the Royal Society of London, Series B*, *204*, 301-328.

Marslen-Wilson, W. D., & Welsh, A. (1978). Processing interactions and lexical access during word recognition in continuous speech. *Cognitive Psychology*, *10*, 29-63.

McCarthy, J. (1959). Comments. In *Mechanisation of thought processes: Proceedings of a symposium held at the National Physical Laboratory, November 1958. Vol. 1* (p. 464). London: Her Majesty's Stationery Office.

McClelland, J. L. (1979). On the time-relations of mental processes: An examination of systems of processes in cascade. *Psychological Review*, *86*, 287-330.

McClelland, J. L. (1981). Retrieving general and specific information from stored knowledge of specifics. *Proceedings of the Third Annual Meeting of the Cognitive Science Society*, 170-172.

McClelland, J. L., & Rumelhart, D. E. (1981). An interactive activation model of context effects in letter perception: Part 1. An account of basic findings. *Psychological Review*, *88*, 375-407.

McClelland, J. L., & Rumelhart, D. E. (1985). Distributed memory and the representation of general and specific information. *Journal of Experimental Psychology: General*, *114*, 159-188.

McCulloch, W. S., & Pitts, W. (1943). A logical calculus of the ideas immanent in nervous activity. *Bulletin of Mathematical Biophysics*, *5*, 115-133.

Meditch, J. S. (1969). *Stochastic optimal linear estimation and control.* New York: McGraw-Hill.

Metropolis, N., Rosenbluth, A. W., Rosenbluth, M. N., Teller, A. H., & Teller, E. (1953). Equation of state calculations for fast computing machines. *Journal of Chemical Physics*, *6*, 1087.

Minsky, M. (1954). *Neural nets and the brain-model problem.* Unpublished doctoral dissertation, Princeton University.

Minsky, M. (1959). Some methods of artificial intelligence and heuristic programming. In *Mechanisation of thought processes: Proceedings of a symposium held at the National Physical Laboratory, November 1958. Vol. 1* (pp. 3-28). London: Her Majesty's Stationery Office.

Minsky, M. (1975). A framework for representing knowledge. In P. H. Winston (Ed.), *The psychology of computer vision* (pp. 211-277). New York: McGraw-Hill.

Minsky, M., & Papert, S. (1969). *Perceptrons.* Cambridge, MA: MIT Press.

Morton, J. (1969). Interaction of information in word recognition. *Psychological Review*, *76*, 165-178.

Moussouris, J. (1974). Gibbs and Markov random systems with constraints. *Journal of Statistical Physics*, *10*, 11-33.

Mozer, M. C. (1984). *The perception of multiple objects: A parallel, distributed processing approach.* Unpublished manuscript, University of California, San Diego, Institute for Cognitive Science.

Neisser, U. (1967). *Cognitive psychology.* New York: Appleton-Century-Crofts.

Neisser, U. (1981). John Dean's memory: A case study. *Cognition*, *9*, 1-22.

Newell, A. (1980). Physical symbol systems. *Cognitive Science*, *4*, 135-183.

Norman, D. A., & Bobrow, D. G. (1975). On data-limited and resource-limited processes. *Cognitive Psychology*, *7*, 44-64.

Norman, D. A., & Bobrow, D. G. (1976). On the role of active memory processes in perception and cognition. In C. N. Cofer (Ed.), *The structure of human memory* (pp. 114-132). Freeman: San Francisco.

Norman, D. A., & Bobrow, D. G. (1979). Descriptions: An intermediate stage in memory retrieval. *Cognitive Psychology*, *11*, 107-123.

Palmer, S. E. (1980). What makes triangles point: Local and global effects in configurations of ambiguous triangles. *Cognitive Psychology*, *9*, 353-383.

Parker, D. B. (1985). *Learning-logic* (TR-47). Cambridge, MA: Massachusetts Institute of Technology, Center for Computational Research in Economics and Management Science.

Pillsbury, W. B. (1897). A study in apperception. *American Journal of Psychology*, *8*, 315-393.

Poggio, T., & Torre, V. (1978). A new approach to synaptic interactions. In R. Heim & G. Palm (Eds.), *Approaches to complex systems.* Berlin: Springer-Verlag.

Poincaré, H. (1913). *Foundations of science* (G. B. Halstead, Trans.). New York: Science Press.

Quillian, M. R. (1968). Semantic memory. In M. Minsky (Ed.), *Semantic information processing* (pp. 227-270). Cambridge, MA: MIT Press.

Rao, C. R., & Mitra, S. K. (1971). Generalized inverse of a matrix and applications. *Sixth Berkeley Symposium on Mathematical Statistics and Probability*, *1*, 601-620.

Riley, M. S. (1984). *Structural understanding in performance and learning.* Unpublished doctoral dissertation, University of Pittsburgh.

Riley, M. S., & Smolensky, P. (1984). A parallel model of (sequential) problem solving. *Proceedings of the Sixth Annual Conference of the Cognitive Science Society.*

Rock, I. (1973). *Orientation and form.* New York: Academic Press.

Rosenblatt, F. (1959). Two theorems of statistical separability in the perceptron. In *Mechanisation of thought processes: Proceedings of a symposium held at the National Physical Laboratory, November 1958. Vol. 1* (pp. 421-456). London: HM Stationery Office.

Rosenblatt, F. (1962). *Principles of neurodynamics.* New York: Spartan.

Rosenfeld, A., Hummel, R. A., & Zucker, S. W. (1976). Scene labeling by relaxation operations. *IEEE Transactions on Systems, Man, and Cybernetics, 6,* 420-433.

Rumelhart, D. E. (1975). Notes on a schema for stories. In D. G. Bobrow & A. Collins (Eds.), *Representation and understanding* (pp. 211-236). New York: Academic Press.

Rumelhart, D. E. (1977). Toward an interactive model of reading. In S. Dornic (Ed.), *Attention & Performance VI.* Hillsdale, NJ: Erlbaum.

Rumelhart, D. E. (1979). Some problems with the notion of literal meanings. In A. Ortony (Ed.), *Metaphor and thought.* Cambridge, England: Cambridge University Press.

Rumelhart, D. E. (1980). Schemata: The building blocks of cognition. In R. Spiro, B. Bruce, & W. Brewer (Eds.), *Theoretical issues in reading comprehension* (pp. 33-58). Hillsdale, NJ: Erlbaum.

Rumelhart, D. E., & McClelland, J. L. (1982). An interactive activation model of context effects in letter perception: Part 2. The contextual enhancement effect and some tests and extensions of the model. *Psychological Review, 89,* 60-94.

Rumelhart, D. E., & McClelland, J. L. (1985). Levels indeed! A response to Broadbent. *Journal of Experimental Psychology: General, 114,* 193-197.

Rumelhart, D. E., & Norman, D. A. (1982). Simulating a skilled typist: A study of skilled cognitive-motor performance. *Cognitive Science, 6,* 1-36.

Rumelhart, D. E., & Zipser, D. (1985). Feature discovery by competitive learning. *Cognitive Science, 9,* 75-112.

Schank, R. C. (1973). Identification of conceptualizations underlying natural language. In R. C. Schank & K. M. Colby (Eds.), *Computer models of thought and language* (pp. 187-247). San Francisco: Freeman.

Schank, R. C. (1976). The role of memory in language processing. In C. N. Cofer (Ed.), *The structure of human memory* (pp. 162-189). Freeman: San Francisco.

Schank, R. C. (1980). Language and memory. *Cognitive Science, 4,* 243-284.

Schwartz, M. F., Marin, O. S. M., & Saffran, E. M. (1979). Dissociations of language function in dementia: A case study. *Brain and Language, 7,* 277-306.

Sejnowski, T. J. (1981). Skeleton filters in the brain. In G. E. Hinton & J. A. Anderson (Eds.), *Parallel models of associative memory* (pp. 49-82). Hillsdale, NJ: Erlbaum.

Sejnowski, T. J., & Hinton, G. E. (in press). Separating figure from ground with a Boltzmann machine. In M. A. Arbib & A. R. Hanson (Eds.), *Vision, brain, and cooperative computation.* Cambridge, MA: MIT Press/Bradford.

Sejnowski, T. J., Hinton, G. E., Kienker, P., & Schumacher, L. E. (1985). *Figure-ground separation by simulated annealing.* Unpublished manuscript.

Selfridge, O. G. (1955). Pattern recognition in modern computers. *Proceedings of the Western Joint Computer Conference.*

Selfridge, O. G., & Neisser, U. (1960). Pattern recognition by machine. *Scientific American, 203,* 60-68.

Shannon, C. E. (1963). The mathematical theory of communication. In C. E. Shannon & W. Weaver (Eds.), *The mathematical theory of communication* (pp. 29-125). Urbana: University of Illinois Press. (Reprinted from *Bell System Technical Journal,* 1948, July and October)

Shepard, R. N. (1984). Ecological constraints on internal representation: Resonant kinematics of perceiving, imagining, thinking, and dreaming. *Psychological Review, 91,* 417-447.

Smith, P. T., & Baker, R. G. (1976). The influence of English spelling patterns on pronounciation. *Journal of Verbal Learning and Verbal Behavior, 15,* 267-286.

Smolensky, P. (1981). *Lattice renormalization of ϕ^4 theory.* Unpublished doctoral dissertation, Indiana University.

Smolensky, P. (1983). Schema selection and stochastic inference in modular environments. *Proceedings of the National Conference on Artificial Intelligence AAAI-83,* 109-113.

Smolensky, P. (1984). The mathematical role of self-consistency in parallel computation. *Proceedings of the Sixth Annual Conference of the Cognitive Science Society.*

Smolensky, P., & Riley, M. S. (1984). *Harmony theory: Problem solving, parallel cognitive models, and thermal physics* (Tech. Rep. No. 8404). La Jolla: University of California, San Diego, Institute for Cognitive Science.

Spoehr, K., & Smith, E. (1975). The role of orthographic and phonotactic rules in perceiving letter patterns. *Journal of Experimental Psychology: Human Perception and Performance, 1,* 21-34.

Sternberg, S. (1969). Memory scanning: Mental processes revealed by reaction-time experiments. *American Scientist, 57,* 421-457.

Strang, G. (1976). *Linear algebra and its applications.* New York: Academic Press.

Sutton, R. S., & Barto, A. G. (1981). Toward a modern theory of adaptive networks: Expectation and prediction. *Psychological Review, 88,* 135-170.

Teitelbaum, P. (1967). The biology of drive. In G. Quarton, T. Melnechuk, & F. O. Schmitt (Eds.), *The neurosciences: A study program.* New York: Rockefeller Press.

Terrace, H. S. (1963). Discrimination learning with and without errors. *Journal of the Experimental Analysis of Behavior, 6,* 1-27.

Thomas, G. B. Jr. (1968). *Calculus and analytic geometry* (4th ed.). Reading, MA: Addison-Wesley.

Venesky, R. L. (1970). *The structure of English orthography.* The Hague: Mouton.

von der Malsberg, C. (1973). Self-organizing of orientation sensitive cells in the striate cortex. *Kybernetik*, *14*, 85-100.

Warren, R. M. (1970). Perceptual restoration of missing speech sounds. *Science*, *167*, 393-395.

Widrow, G., & Hoff, M. E. (1960). Adaptive switching circuits. *Institute of Radio Engineers, Western Electronic Show and Convention, Convention Record, Part 4*, 96-104.

Williams, R. J. (1983). *Unit activation rules for cognitive network models* (Tech. Rep. No. ICS 8303). La Jolla: University of California, San Diego, Institute for Cognitive Science.

Willshaw, D. J. (1971). *Models of distributed associative memory.* Unpublished doctoral dissertation, University of Edinburgh.

Willshaw, D. J. (1981). Holography, associative memory, and inductive generalization. In G. E. Hinton & J. A. Anderson (Eds.), *Parallel models of associative memory* (pp. 83-104). Hillsdale, NJ: Erlbaum.

Winston, P. H. (1975). Learning structural descriptions from examples. In P. H. Winston (Ed.), *The psychology of computer vision* (pp. 157-209). New York: McGraw-Hill.

Wood, C. C. (1978). Variations on a theme by Lashley: Lesion experiments on the neural model of Anderson, Silverstein, Ritz, & Jones. *Psychological Review*, *85*, 582-591.

Woods, W. (1973). An experimental parsing system for transition network grammars. In R. Rustin (Ed.), *Natural language processing.* New York: Algorithmics Press.

Woods, W., & Kaplan, R. (1971). *The lunar sciences natural language information system* (Rep. No. 2265). Cambridge, MA: Bolt, Beranek, and Newman.

Zadeh, L. A. (1965). Fuzzy sets. *Information and Control*, *8*, 338-353.

Index

Page numbers in roman type refer to Volume 1; page numbers in italic type refer to Volume 2.

Abeles, M., *367*, *369*, *385*, *553*
Abelson, R. P., *18*, *19*, *574*
Abrams, T. W., *552*, *561*
Abramson, A. S., *94*, *560*
Abstraction models of memory, *199-206*
  comparison of experimental and simulation results, *203-205*
  other findings on, *205-206*
  summary of training and test stimuli, *202-203*
  Whittlesea's experiments on, *201-202*
Ackley, D. H., 264, 306, 313, 317, 335, 507, 510, *393*, *562*
ACT* model, 32, 124, 127
Activation functions
  examples of
    gating activation function, 426
    semilinear, 52, 324-328
    quasi-linear, 425
    quasi-multilinear, 426
    squashing function, 425
    threshold logic or linear threshold unit, 425
  logic of
    conclusions on, 442-443
    description of, 363
    examples of, 428-429
    main concepts of, 426-428
    as major aspect of PDP models, 51-52
    results of, 429, 439-442
    rules, examples of, 425-426
    three-dimensional plots, 429, 430-438 (*Figs.*)
    views of, 423-425
Activation rule. *See* Activation functions
Activation vector of harmony theoretical model, 215-216
Active representation in PDP models. *See* PDP models, active representation in
Addition problem, simple binary, 341-346. *See also* Delta rule, generalized
Albright, T. D., *368*, *558*

Algebra, linear. *See* Linear algebra
Algebraic properties of inner products, 382-383. *See also* Vectors
Allman, J., *347*, *374*, *375*, *553*, *554*
Alternative activity patterns, 82-83
AM. *See* Monocular occlusion
Amari, S. A., 42, 45, 444, 507, *489*, *495*, *553*
Ambiguity
  lexical, *302-304*
  structural, *304-305*
  and shading of feature patterns, *305-306*
Ambiguous characters, 8, *155-157*. *See also* Reading, programmable blackboard model of
Amnesia. *See also* Memory, a distributed model of
  anterograde, *504*, *505-506*, *512-513*
  bitemporal, basic aspects of, *505-506*
  conclusions on, *527*
  description of, *503-505*
  neurochemistry of synaptic change, hypothetical account of, *507-509*
  paradox of, resolution to, *506-507*
  quantitative model, formulation of, *509*
  relation to other accounts of, *510-511*
  residual learning in, *518-524*
  simulations, *511-518*
    anterograde amnesia, *512-513*
    lost memories, recovery of, *515-516*
    retrograde amnesia, *513-515*
    retrograde and anterograde amnesia, correlation of, *513*
    studies on, *516-518*
    summary of, *518*
  spared learning in, *207-208*, *518*, *524-526*
Anandan, P., 322, 508, *550*, *554*
AND function, 429. *See also* Boolean function
Andén, N. E., *350*, *553*
Andersen, P., *336*, *553*
Anderson, C. W., *539*, *554*
Anderson, J. A., 33, 42, 56, 62, 66, 68, 80, 82, 101, 406, 409, 410, 418, 507, 510, 511, *8*, *173*, *183*, *200*, *226*, *277*, *311*, *380*, *389*, *394*, *399*, *432*, *551*, *553*, *554*, *562*, *564*
Anderson, J. R., 32, 124, 127, 251, 461, 507, *173*, *206*, *209*, *524*, *549*, *554*, *558*
Anlezark, G. M., *477*, *554*
Annealing, simulated. *See* Simulated annealing
Aragon, C. R., 235, 508
Arbib, M. A., *362*, *577*
Arbitrary mapping, implementing, 96-104
  grapheme strings, 97-99, 102
  sememe units, 97-98, 99, 101-102
  three-layer network, 97-98. *See also* Boltzmann machines
Arguments, missing, filling in, *301-302*. *See also* Case role assignment, model of
Ary, M., *477*, *564*
Asanuma, H., *357*, *554*
Asynchronous update vs. synchronous update, 61
ATN. *See* Augmented transition network parsers
Attention
  networks for focusing, 114-118
  shifting focus of, *147-151*
Augmented transition network parsers (ATN), 119
Auto-associative paradigm. *See also* Memory, a distributed model of
  definition of, 55, 161
  modification of, *211-212*

Back-propagation simulator, description of, 328-330
Bagley, W. C., *58*, *98*, *106*, 554
Bahl, L. R., 293, 508
Baker, J. F., *347*, *554*
Baker, R. G., 24, 515
Ballard, D. H., 12, 43, 45, 72, 117, 124, 133, 282, 508, 509, *128*,

373, *381*, *554*, *559*
Banerjee, S. P., *477*, *561*
Barber, R. P., *351*, *562*
Bard, P., *352*, *579*
Barlow, H. B., *373*, *554*
Barnes, C. A., *448*, *568*
Barrow, H. G., *63*, *554*
Bartlett, F. C., 81, 508, *17*, *19*, *554*
Barto, A. G., 43, 53, 57, 321-322, 444, 508, 515, *383*, *539*, *550*, *554*, *576*
Barwise, J., 195, 508
Basket cells, *363-364*
Bates, E., *217*, *273*, *274*, *554*, *567*
Baumgartner, G., *376*, *578*
β-coefficient constants, (*App.*), *467-468*. *See also* β-coefficient model
β-coefficient model, *460-466*. *See also* Place recognition and goal location, biologically plausible models of
  concept, network using, *461-462*
  constants (*App.*), *467-468*
  description of, *460-461*
  issue in, *463*
  performance of, *464*
  programming, *463*
  simulation of, *469-470*
  testing, *463-464*
BD. *See* Binocular deprivation
Bear, M. F., *477*, *554*
Becker, J. T., *435*, *554*
Benoit, R., *364*, *569*
Bentivoglio, M., *350*, *567*
Berko, J., 40, 508, *219*, *220*, *265*, *555*
Berman, N., *475*, *478*, *558*
Bernstein, J., 153, 159, 508
Best, P., *435*, *571*
Bever, T. G., *274*, *555*, *559*
Bienenstock, E. L., 42, 180, 508, *480*, *487*, *489*, *495*, *555*
Binder, K., 230, 508
Binding problem, 88-90
  of neurons, *377-378*
Binocular deprivation (BD), *474*, *475*
Bipolar cells, *363*
Bishop, P. O., *480*, *574*
Bitemporal amnesia. *See* Amnesia, bitemporal
Bixby, J. L., *345*, *577*
Blake, A., 285, 508
Blakemore, C., 11, 508, *475*, *489*, *490*, *491*, *497*, *500*, *555*, *571*, *577*
Blanchard, H. E., *161*, *568*
Blank, M. A., *79*, *111*, *559*
Blasdel, G. G., *487*, *490*, *555*
Blends of memory traces, *208*. *See also* Memory, a distributed model of
Bloom, F. E., *364*, *385*, *569*
Bloom, M. J., *385*, *560*
Blumstein, S., *62*, *576*
Bobillier, P., *350*, *555*
Bobrow, D. G., 9, 79, 133, 513, *18*, *19*, *536*, *555*, *570*
Boltzmann machines
  damage, example of effects of, 304-313
  description of, 43, 148-149
  hard learning, example of, 299-303
    annealing schedule, 302
    shifter network performance, 302-303
    training procedure, 300
  learning algorithm, 294-303, *209*
    conclusions on, 313-314
    derivation of (*App.*), 315-317
    failure of algorithm, 298-299
    hardware, unreliable, achieving reliable computation with, 303-304
  learning, easy and hard, 290-294
  relaxation searches, use of to perform, 283-290
  research with, 264
  second-order observables and, 273-275
  unlearning, 296-298
Bond, Z. S., *61*, *555*
Bonds, A. B., *476*, *478*, *560*
Boolean function, 428, 429, 439-442
  activation function as extension of, 428
  AND function, 429
  disjunctive normal form, 439

Boolean function *(continued)*
linearly separable functions, 440
mapping from expressions, 439
neurons treated as devices, 424-425
XOR function, 429
Bottom-up approach to analysis of information processing systems, 123
Bottom-up presentation of harmony theory, 199, 213-261. *See also* Harmony theory
Bottom-up processing system, 51
matrix representation of, 57-58
Boycott, B. B., *336*, *558*
Brachman, R. J., *313*, *555*
Brain. *See* Cerebral cortex, anatomy and physiology of; Cerebral cortex, questions about computation in
Brain damage. *See also* Amnesia; Damage, effects of on a network
graceful degradation and, 29, 134
neuropsychological investigation of patients with, 134-135
simulated effects of, *304-313*
Brain state in a box model (BSB), 66-68
Branch, M., *435*, *571*
Brayton, R. K., *381*, *382*, *575*
Bresnan, J., *274*, *559*, *564*
Brightman, M. W., *336*, *572*
Broadbent, D. E., 121, 508, *97*, *532*, *555*
Brock, L. G., *367*, *555*
Brodmann, K., *345*, *346*, *555*
Brodmann's areas of the neocortex, *345-346*. *See also* Cerebral cortex, anatomy and physiology of
Brooks, C. McC., *336*, *553*
Brooks, L. R., *171*, *556*
Brown, P., 295
Brown, R., *219*, *241*, *556*
Bruce, C. J., *368*, *556*, *558*
Brugge, J. F., *356*, *563*
BSB model. *See* Brain state in a box model
Buisseret, P., *476*, *478*, *556*
β units, simulations of (*App.*), *469-470*. *See also* β-coefficient model
Bunt, A. H., *357*, *566*
Bybee, J. L., *221*, *247*, *249*, *250*, *251*, *254*, *255*, *256*, *556*

CA. *See* Connection activation unit
Caan, W., *368*, *571*
Cajal, S. Ramon y, *336*, *350*, *358*, *359*, *361*, *363*, *367*, *556*
Caminiti, R., *377-378*, *560*
Canonical feature detectors, 114
Caplan, C. J., *478*, *570*
Carew, T. J., *552*, *561*
Carlson, M., *275*, *573*
Carman, J. B., *350*, *556*
Carnes, K. M., *477*, *554*
Carpenter, P. A., *153*, *161*, *549*, *564*, *577*
Carroll, Lewis, 97
Cascade model, 42
Case role assignment, model of
architecture of, *277-289*
case role representation, *286-288*
semantic microfeatures, *278-283*
sentence processing and learning, details of, *288-289*
sentence-structure units, *283-286*
descriptions of, *3-4*
discussion of, *313-325*
context-sensitive coding, iteration, and center embedding, *323-325*
fixed-length, *320-322*
limitation myths, *322-323*
meaning, representation of, *315-316*
model, basic features of, *314-315*
parsers, conventional interfacing with, *317-318*
recursion, *318-320*
goals of, *276-277*
studies on, *277*
multiple constraints on, *272-275*
studies on, *273*, *275*, *277*
simulation experiments of, *289-292*
basic results of, *292-293*

feature patterns, shading of, *305-306*
lexical ambiguity resolution, *302-304*
missing arguments, filling in, *301-302*
novel words, generalization to, *307-310*
other creative errors, *306-307*
roles, distributed representation of, *312-313*
semantic and word-order cues, use of in, *293-300*
straightforward extensions, *310-312*
structural ambiguity of, *304-305*
verb-frame selection, *300-301*
Central module, *130-131*
Cerebral cortex, anatomy and physiology of
cortex inputs, *346-356*
irregularities within, *353-356*
topographic representation of, *352-353*
cortical areas of, *345*
cortical outputs, *356-357*
feature detection of, *367-371*
firing, rates of, *366-367*
general organization of, *340-345*
main layers, *341-345*
general points on, *333-335*
group neuron behavior in, *365-366*
neocortical neurons, nature of
cell types in, *358-360*
excitatory vs. inhibitory neurons, *362*
experimental methods, *357-358*
neurons without many spines, *361*
neurons with spines, *360-361*
special cell types, *362*
neuron behavior in, *364-365*
neuron, classical, *335-337*
peptides, *339*
synapses, types of, *338-339*
Cerebral cortex, questions about computation in
computational models, role of in, *387-389*
neuronal plasticity in, *385-387*
neuronal processing in, *378-382*
nonlinear computations, *381*
single-shot algorithms, *380-381*
timing problem, *378-380*
representing information in, *373-377*
binding problem, *377*
surround effects, *374-377*
temporal binding, *383-385*
Chace, P., *513*, *576*
Chandelier cells, *362-363*
Changeux, J. -P., *387*, *556*
Chapman, R. A., *485*, *556*
Charniak, E., *324*, *556*
Chase, W. G., 241, 508
Chauvin, Y., 213, 332-334,
Chomsky, N., 24, 119, 123, 246, 508
Christen, W. G., *478*, *570*
Christensen, R., 227, 508
CID. *See* Connection information distribution mechanism
Clark, W. A., 154, 509
Class C′ perceptron (Rosenblatt), 155-156
Classification paradigm, 161
Coarse coding, 91-96. *See also* Conjunctive encoding; Distributed representations
limitations on, 92-94
principle underlying, 94-96
Cognition and parallel distributed processing. *See* PDP approach, introduction to
Cognition, microstructure of, 12-13
Cognitive science. *See* PDP approach and cognitive science
Cognitive theories, constraints on, 129-130
Cohen, M. A., *389*, *556*
Cohen, M. M., *81*, *86*, *568*
Cohen, N. J., *510*, *519*, *520*, *521-522*, *524*, *525*, *527*, *556*, *576*
COHORT model (Marslen-Wilson), *77*, *97-106*
basic assumptions of, *98-99*
dilemma for, *99-100*, *101*

COHORT model *(continued)*
resolution of, *101-106*
Cole, K. S., *364*, *556*
Cole, R. A., *58*, *61*, *98*, *99*, *100*, *107*, *111*, *556*, *557*
Collins, A. M., 85, 508
Colonnier, M., *348*, *361*, *557*, *571*
Colón Osorio, F. C., 424, 510
Coltheart, M., 102, 508
Competence theorem, 226-229
Competitive inhibition, 21. *See also* Phoneme identification, factors influencing
effect of at phoneme level, *89-90*
Competitive learning
architecture of competitive learning system, 162-166
basic components of, 151-152
characteristics of, 166-167
conclusions on, 190
definition of, 147
dipole experiments, results of, 170-177
correlated teaching inputs, 182-183
letter similarity effects, 182
number of elements, effect of per serial position, 181-182
position-specific letter detectors, 180-181
word detection units, 181
word perception model, 177-180
formal analysis of, 168-170
geometric interpretation of, 164-166
history of, 152-159
horizontal and vertical lines, experiments with, 184-190
mechanism of, 159
neural-like processing systems, 160-161
in P3 simulation system
methods (*App. B*), 504-506
plans for (*App. A*), 502-503
Completion task, example of, 206-208
Computational level, 121
Computational models, role of
cerebral cortex in, *387-389*
Computational temperature (*T*), 211
Computational viewpoint on PDP models, *397-398*
Conel, J. LeRoy, *358*, *557*
Confabulation, as a stable pattern, 81
Conjunctive encoding, 90-91, 96. *See also* Coarse coding; Distributed representations
CONNECT statements for P3 system, 495-496. *See also* P3 system
Connection activation system, *130-134*
Connection activation unit (CA). *See also* Connection information distribution mechanism
definition of, *132-134*
multiple pattern processing, 477-478
requirements of, 474-476
single pattern processing, 476-477
summary of requirements, 480-481
Connection information distribution (CID) mechanism, 473-486, *129-134*, *137*, *139-140*
benefits of, *164-166*
central knowledge store in, *130-134*
computer simulation of word recognition using, *134-136*
extensions of, *167-168*
resource requirements of, 473-486, *166-167*
Connectionist models, 72
Connolly, M., *353*, *355*, *566*
Connors, B. W., *364*, *369*, *557*
Constructor, as major component of P3 system, 489. *See also* P3 system
Content-addressable memory, 79-80
Continuity and uniqueness constraints in depth perception, 19-20
Cooling schedule, 244-245. *See also* Electricity problem-solving; Simulated annealing
Coombs, J. S., *367*, *555*
Cooper, F. S., *92*, *94*, *495*, *566*, *576*

Cooper, L. N., 42, 180, 508, *480*, *487*, *489*, *499*, *555*, *557*, *573*
Corkin, S., *519*, *524*, *556*
Cortical areas of the neocortex,
  Brodmann's cortical parcellation scheme, 345
  input systems, 346
    irregularities within, 353-356
    thalamus, as gateway to cerebral cortex, 349-352
    topographic representation, 352-353
  output systems, 356-357
Cortical plasticity, processes that modulate, *476-478*
Cotton, S., *99*, *105*, *557*
Cottrell, G., *165*, *277*, *311*, *314*, *557*
Coulter, J. D., *357*, *570*
Cowan, J. D., *381*, *389*, *578*
Cowan, W. M., *350*, *351*, *556*, *572*
Cowey, A., *363*, *576*
Crain, S., *274*, *557*
Crane, A. M., *350*, *572*
Crick, F. H. C., 296, 297, 509, *351*, *384*, *387*, *557*
Critical or sensitive period of plasticity, *473-484*
  cortical plasticity, processes that modulate, *476-477*
  effect of environment on, *478*
  hypothesis for, *483-484*
  ocular dominance statistics, *474-476*
  other examples of, *477-478*
Crosstalk, *139-142*. *See also* Reading, programmable blackboard model of
Crow, T. J., *476*, *477*, *554*, *557*
Crowder, R. G., *64*, *94*, *209*, *557*
Cynader, M., *475*, *476*, *478*, *492*, *498*, *557*, *558*

Dahlström, A., *350*, *553*
Damage, effects of on a network, 29, 134, 472. *See also* Amnesia; Boltzmann machines; Brain damage; Graceful degradation
  in Boltzmann machines, 304-313
Daniel, P. M., *354*, *558*
Daniels, J. D., *477*, *554*
Darien-Smith, J., *480*, *574*
Davis, E., *432*, *558*
Daw, N. W., *497*, *500*, *558*, *577*
Deacedo, B. S., *519*, *524*, *556*
Decay process in increments to weights, *181*. *See also* Memory, a distributed model of
Decision-making and freezing in harmony theory
  coherent interpretation, robustness of, 240
  idealized task, 238-239
  phase transitions, computational significance of, 236-237
  symmetry breaking, 237-238
  thermodynamic limit, 239
Deep dyslexia, 102
Degradation, effects of and benefits of redundancy, 472. *See also* Standard pattern associators
Deliberate conscious control (DCC), *543-545*. *See also* PDP approach, reflections on
Delta rule, 43, 53, 62, 63, 363, *417-418*
Delta rule, analysis of. *See also* Delta rule, generalized
  and multiple linear regression, 457-458
  in pattern-based coordinates, 447-453
  statistical learning and, 453-457
  summary of, 458-459
  in vector notation, 445-447
Delta rule, generalized, 149
  application of, 327-328
  conclusions on, 361-362
  general cases, 352-361
    recurrent nets, 354-361
  and gradient descent, 322-324
  problem of, 318-323
    XOR problem, 319-321
  for semilinear activation functions in feedforward networks, 324-328
  and sigma-pi units, 353

Delta rule, generalized *(continued)*
simulation results, 328-330, 352
encoding problem, 335-339
negation problem, 346-347
parity, 334-335
simple binary addition problem, 341-346
symmetry, 340-341
T-C problem, 348-352
XOR problem, 330-334
use of to determine size and direction of changes in connections, *179-181*
generalized, *209*
DeMarzo, P. M., 241, 242, 509
Dempster, A. P., 293, 509
Dendrites, studies on, *381-382. See also* Cerebral cortex, questions about computation in
Denes, P., *87*, *558*
de Riboupierre, F., *385*, *553*
de Riboupierre, Y., *385*, *553*
Derthick, M., 298, 299, 509, *313*
Desimone, R., *368*, *374*, *556*, *558*
Dipole experiments for competitive learning mechanisms, 170-174
formal analysis of, 174-177
homogeneous stimulus patterns, 191-193
Distal landmarks for biologically plausible models of place recognition and goal location, *445*
Distributed representations. *See also* Memory, a distributed model of; Schemata, concept of
features of
generalization effects, 82-85
memory, 79-81
new concepts, 86-87
status of, 78-79
structure in representations and processes, 104-108
constituent structure, representing, 105-106
sequential symbol processing, 106-108
summary on, 108-109
technical details of, 87-104
arbitrary pairing, implementing, 96-104
binding problem, 88-90
coarse coding, 91-96
conjunctive encoding, 90-91
Distributed view-field model for goal location, *449-460*. *See also* Place recognition and goal location, biologically plausible models of
description of, *451-453*
network used in, *450-451*
P3 simulation of, *453-454*
Symbolics 3600 LISP machine, use of for, *454-456*
problems of, *451*
properties of, *453*
testing of, *453*
Dobson, V., 97, 100
Dostrovsky, J., *435*, *571*
Dowling, J. E., *336*, *558*, *578*
Dräger, U. C., *490*, *558*
Dretske, F., 195, 509
Duckrow, R. B., *477*, *561*
Duda, R. O., *380*, *558*
Dukes, K., *61*, *110*, *570*
Durham, D., *500*, *558*
Dynamic functional system, 41
Dynamical systems, perspective of PDP models as, *397-398*

Eccles, J. C., *336*, *367*, *370*, *553*, *555*, *558*
Edelman, G. M., *387*, *558*
Edmonds, D., 153,
Ehrlich, S., *163*, *573*
Eichenbaum, H., *385*, *519*, *524*, *556*, *565*
Eigenvalues. *See* Eigenvectors and eigenvalues
Eigenvectors and eigenvalues, 399-403. *See also* Matrices and linear systems
Eimas, P. D., *94*, *473*, *558*, *560*
Eisen, M., 456, 509
Elbaum, C., *499*, *573*
Electricity problem-solving, 240-250
Electroencephalography (EEG), *335*

Elio, R., *172*, *558*
Elman, J. L., *58*, *63*, *69*, *71*, *80*, *81*, *119*, *558*, *559*, *568*
EM. *See* Expectation and maximization method
Empiricism vs. nativism, 139-142
Emson, P. C., *364*, *559*
Encoding problem, 335-339. *See also* Delta rule, generalized
Equilibrium states of the competitive learning system, 168-170
Erman, L. D., *63*, *122*, *559*, *573*
Error correction rule. *See* Delta rule
Error propagation, learning internal representations by. *See* Delta rule, generalized
Ervin, S., *219*, *220*, *254*, *559*
Espinosa, I. E., *385*, *560*
Evanczuk, S., *385*, *560*
Exclusive or (XOR) problem, 64-65, 96, 319-321, 330-334. *See also* Delta rule, generalized
Executive-driven processing, 134
Expectation and maximization (EM) method, 293
Explicit inaccessible rule, *217*. *See also* Verbs, learning past tenses of
Explicit rule formulation, tradition, 32

Fahlman, S. E., 85, 86, 264, 509
Fairén, A., *363*, *559*
Famiglietti, E. V., *336*, *559*
Fan-in. *See* Fan-out
Fan-out
  definition of, 51
  limited, effects of, 468-472
  method for overcoming limitation, 470-472
  neural nets, biological limits on storage capacity of, 469-470
Fanty, M., *320*, *321*, *322*, *559*
Farley, B. G., 154, 509
Feature discovery by competitive learning. *See* Competitive learning
Feedback, effects of display length on amount of, *159-161*. *See also* Reading, programmable blackboard model of
Feedforward networks, delta rule for semilinear activation functions in, 324-328. *See also* Delta rule, generalized
Feinstein, D. J., 296, 511
Feirtag, M., *334*, *342*, *570*
Feldman, J. A., 12, 43, 45, 72, 75, 86, 117, 124, 130, 181, 509, *9*, *128*, *559*
Feldman, M. L., *363*, *377*, *559*
Feldman and Ballard units, 72
  conjunctive units, 72
  relation to sigma-pi units, 72
Felleman, D. J., *352*, *354*, *385*, *569*, *570*
Fennell, R. D., *63*, *122*, *573*
Feustel, T. C., *197*, *198*, *559*, *574*
Fillmore, C. J., *273*, *559*
Finlay, B. L., *367*, *574*
Firing, rates of in neocortical neurons, *366-367*. *See also* Neocortical neurons, nature of
First formant onset frequency (F1OF), *84*, *85*. *See also* Phoneme identification, factors influencing
Fixations. *See also* Reading, programmable blackboard model of
  sequences of, *161-164*
  single and multiple, *153-155*
Fodor, J. A., 141, 509, *274*, *559*
Foley, J. D., *467*, *559*
Ford, M., *274*, *559*
Foss, D. J., *79*, *111*, *559*
Fowler, C. A., *60*, *73*, *77*, *95*, *118*, *559*
Fox, R. A., *79*, *559*, *560*
Frames, use of as knowledge structure, 9. *See also* Schemata, concept of
Francis, W., *74*, *240*, *565*
Frazier, L., *275*, *560*, *573*
Freeman, R. D., *475*, *476*, *478*, *481*, *492*, *560*, *567*, *571*

Freezing and decision-making in harmony theory. *See* Decision-making and freezing in harmony theory
Freund, T. F., *363*, *576*
Friedlander, M. J., *351*, *560*
Fry, D. B., *94*, *560*
Fuchs, A. F., *357*, *566*
Fujimura, O., *62*, *473*, *560*, *569*
Fujisaki, H., *77*, *94*, *560*
Fukushima, K., 42, 152, 162, 300, 313, 350, 509
Future directions for PDP, *547-552*
Fuxe, K., *350*, *364*, *553*, *560*
Fuzzy map theory, *432-433*. *See also* Place recognition and goal location, biologically plausible models of

Gallistel, C. R., 141, 509
Gamma factor in bitemporal amnesia, *507*
Ganong, W. F., *60*, *78*, *560*
Garey, L. J., *348*, *497*, *500*, *555*, *560*, *577*
Garnes, S., *61*, *555*
Garrett, M. F., *274*, *559*
Garrud, P., *434*, *466*, *569*
Gary-Bobo, E., *476*, *478*, *556*
Gati, I., *499*, *560*
Gating activation function, 426. *See also* Activation functions
Gee, J., *60*, *63*, *107*, *115*, *561*
Gelatt, C. D., Jr., 48, 235, 287, 511
Geman, D., 148, 264, 271, 278, 289, 509
Geman, S., 148, 264, 268, 271, 278, 289, 509
Generalization, 30, 85. *See also* Memory, a distributed model of
Georgopoulos, A. P., *377-378*, *560*
Gernsbacher, M. A., *79*, *559*
Gerstein, G. L., *385*, *560*
Gibbs sampler, research with, 264
Gibson, E. J., 198
Gilbert, C. D., *356*, *358*, *366*, *385*, *480*, *560*, *561*, *577*, *578*
Ginsburg, H. P., 241, 509
Glaser, E. M., *366*, *577*
Glass, L., *494*, *571*
Glorioso, R. M., 424, 510
Gluck, M. A., *383*, *552*, *561*
Glushko, R. J., 43, 510, *171*, *561*
Goal location. *See* Place recognition and goal location, biologically plausible models of
Goldman-Rakic, P. S., *350*, *572*
Goodness-of-fit function, *14-16*, *31*, *32-33*, *35-36*. *See also* Schemata, concept of
Graceful degradation, 29, 134. *See also* Damage, effects of on a network
Gradient descent
  and delta rule, 322-324
  use of to solve hard optimizing problems on conventional computers, 287-288
Grapheme strings, 97-99, 102. *See also* Arbitrary mapping, implementing
Gray, E. G., *339*, *361*, *561*
Green, D. M., 466, 510, *225*, *561*
Green, K., *96*, *569*
Greenberg, Z., *254*
Greenway, A. P., *477*, *554*
Grinvald, A., *385*, *561*
Grosjean, F., *60*, *63*, *99*, *100*, *105*, *107*, *114*, *115*, *557*, *561*
Gross, C. G., *368*, *556*, *558*
Grossberg, S., 42, 53, 70, 116, 146, 152, 162, 164, 167, 418, 510, *90*, *389*, *494*, *535*, *556*, *561*
Grossberg's models, 70-71
Guillery, R. W., *351*, *561*
Gutnick, M. J., *364*, *369*, *557*

Haggard, M., *85*, *576*
Hale, B. L., *159*, *563*
Halle, M., 24, 508, *168*, *561*
Halmos, P. R., 422, 510
Hamiltonian function (*H*), 211
Hámori, J., *351*, *577*
Hard learning, example of, 299-303. *See also* Boltzmann machines

Harik, S. J., *477*, *561*
Harmonium machine, 212
Harmony function (*H*). *See also* Harmony theory
basic requirements of, 220-223
cognitive systems and, 267-268
mathematic formulation of, 208, 211
retrieving information from, 269-272
terminology, 268-269
Harmony theory, 213-220
conclusions on, 261-262
decision-making and freezing, 236-240
definition of, 148
electricity, problem-solving of, 240-250
goal of, 198-199
learning new representations, 258-261
macrodescription, 251-258
mathematical results, description of, 226-236
competence theorem, 226-229
learnability theorem, 235-236
physics analogy, 229-230
realizability theorem, 230-235
perceptual processing centrality, 197-198
and probability, 220-226
research with, 264
schema theory and self-consistency of, 199-213
theorems on, formal presentation of, 264-281
top-down strategy pursued in, 196
Harris, K. S., *92*, *576*
Hart, P. E., *380*, *558*
Hash coding, 80
Hawken, M. J., *490*, *555*
Hawkins, R. D., *552*, *561*
HEARSAY model of speech understanding, 43, *119*, *122-123*, *124*
BLACKBOARD, *123*
Hebb, D. O., 36, 41, 53, 152-153, 510
Hebbian learning rule, 36, 37, 38, 53, 69-70, 297
Heggelund, P., *497*, *564*
Heidmann, T., *387*, *556*
Hein, A., *475*, *478*, *558*
Heise, G., *63*, *569*
Hendrickson, A. E., *344*, *357*, *566*, *572*
Henneberg, R., *341*, *561*
Hewitt, C., 132, 510
Hidden units, augmenting memory with, *209-214*. *See also* Memory, a distributed model of
Hidden units, definition of, 48
Hierarchy, kinds of, 105-106
Hinton, G. E., 17, 20, 33, 42, 80, 82, 83, 84, 96, 107, 114, 115, 127, 133, 264, 272, 282, 283, 289, 297, 302, 306, 313, 317, 335, 350, 507, 508, 510, 511, 515, *8*, *23*, *24*, *63*, *68*, *128*, *129*, *151*, *173*, *175*, *209*, *210*, *277*, *278*, *312*, *313*, *314*, *318*, *322*, *373*, *377*, *381*, *389*, *393*, *394*, *533*, *539*, *548*, *554*, *562*, *575*, *577*
Hinton's scheme for mapping patterns, 114-115, 117, 118. *See also* Attention, networks for focusing
Hintzman, D., *171*, *172*, *200*, *562*
Hiorns, R. W., *344*, *573*
Hirst, G., *321*, *575*
Hoff, M. E., 321, 444, 516
Hofstadter, D. R., 43, 132, 202, 213, 264, 511, *20*, *562*
Hogg, T., 313, 511, *389*, *562*
Hökfelt, T., *350*, *364*, *560*, *577*
Homogeneous dipole stimulus patterns (*App.*), 191-193
Hopfield, J. J., 43, 61, 81, 133, 148, 285, 286, 296, 297, 418, 511, *13*, *14*, *389*, *394*, *562*
Hopfield nets, applying simulated annealing to, 288-289. *See also* Simulated annealing
Hopkins, W. F., *477*, *562*
Horizontal and vertical lines, experiments with, 184-190

Horizontally hierarchical networks, 217
Houde, J., *353*, *355*, *566*
Houser, C. R., *351*, *562*
Hubel, D. H., *340*, *353*, *356*, *367*, *373*, *474*, *475*, *483*, *497*, *500*, *562*, *563*, *566*, *578*
Huberman, B. A., 313, 511, *389*, *562*
Hughlings-Jackson, J., 41, 141-142
Human information processing. *See also* PDP approach, reflections on
  essential properties of, *537*
  new understanding of, *545-546*
Human memory. *See* Memory, a distributed model of; Memory, retrieving information from
Hummel, R. A., 285, 286, 511, 514
Hunt, S. P., *364*, *559*
Huppert, F. A., *516*, *517*, *563*
6-hydroxydopamine (6-OHDA), *477-496*

Identity/role combinations, 106. *See also* Case role assignment, model of; Distributed representations
Imbert, M., *476*, *478*, *556*
Imig, T. J., *356*, *563*
Implementational (physiological) level of distributed memory, 121
Inner products. *See also* Vectors
  algebraic properties of, 382-383
  in two-dimensional space, 380-382
Input units, definition of, 48
Interactive activation model of word perception, 43, 71-72, 177-180, 216-217, *125-129*, *137-138*
Interactive model of reading (Rumelhart), 43, *122*
Interactive models, representation of in matrix form, 57, 59-61. *See also* Interactive activation model of word perception
  layered systems, 60
  one-step system, 60
  single-level, 60
  three-level, 59
Interference of patterns, *139-142*. *See also* Programmable pattern associators; Reading, programmable blackboard model of; Standard pattern associators
Interference of memories, *208-209*. *See also* Memory, a distributed model of
Internal representations. *See* Delta rule, generalized; Representation, learning of
IS-A hierarchy, 105
Isenberg, D., 7, 511
Isomorphism hypothesis. *See also* PDP models, neural and conceptual interpretation of
  of conceptual and neural levels, *395-396*
  failure of in nonlinear models, *422-424*
  levels and localized damage, *413-416*
  levels, learning of connections and, *416-418*
  in linear systems, *411-413*
Iverson, L. L., *340*, *563*

Jackson, J. H., 41, 141, 511
Jacoby, L. L., *171*, *172*, *192*, *193*, *556*, *563*
Jakimik, J., *61*, *98*, *99*, *100*, *107*, *111*, *557*
Jelinek, F., 293, 508
Jenkins, J. J., *473*, *569*
Jenkins, W. M., *385*, *563*
Johnson, D. S., 235, 508
Johnson, E., *324*, *563*
Johnston, D., *477*, *562*
Johnston, J. C., *159*, *160*, *563*, *574*
Jones, E. G., *351*, *352*, *357*, *363*, *563*, *564*
Jones, R. S., 56, 406, 409, 410, 418, 507, *173*, *226*, *311*, *551*, *554*
Jouvet, M., *350*, *555*
Julesz, B., 18, 511
Just, M. A., *153*, *161*, *549*, *564*, *577*

Kaas, J. H., *345*, *352*, *354*, *385*, *386*, *387*, *569*, *570*, *578*
Kahneman, D., *536*, *564*

Kaiserman-Abramof, I. R., *336*, *361*, *365*, *571*
Kalaska, J. F., *378*, *560*
Kandel, E. R., *333*, *364*, *507*, *552*, *561*, *564*, *576*
Kanerva, P., 76, 465, 511
Kant, E., *17*, *19*, *564*
Kaplan, R. M., 119, 516, *274*, *559*, *564*
Kasamatsu, T., *476*, *477*, *492*, *497*, *564*
Kawamoto, A. H., 101, 511, *277*, *311*, *564*
Kawashima, T., *77*, *94*, *560*
Keele, S. W., *171*, *183*, *200*, *203*, *572*
Kelly, J. P., *480*, *560*
Kewley-Port, D., *85*, *564*
Kienker, P. K., 302, 350, 511, 515
Kinematics of the dynamical system, *398-399*, *400-403*. *See also* PDP models, neural and conceptual interpretation of
Kirkpatrick, S., 148, 235, 287, 511
Kisvárdy, Z. F., *363*, *576*
Klatt, D. H., *59*, *60*, *62*, 564
Kliegl, R., *273*, *567*
Knapp, A., *173*, *200*, *564*
Knowledge atoms
  definition of, 202
  and electricity problem-solving, 242
Koch, C., *365*, *381*, *383*, *564*, *565*
Kohonen, T., 42, 45, 62, 63, 152, 406, 409, 418, 422, 424, 425, 444, 446, 455, 461, 511, *222*, *226*, *380*, *565*
Konishi, M., *473*, *565*
Kratz, K. E., *490*, *565*
Krnjević, K., *339*, *565*
Kubie, J. L., *435*, *441*, *445*, *447*, *565*, *570*
Kucera, H., *74*, *240*, *565*
Kuczaj, S. A., *219*, *220*, *221*, *253*, *257*, *258*, *565*
Kuffler, S. W., *367*, *565*
Kuipers, B., *433*, *565*
Kullback, S., 294, 511
Kuno, M., *336*, *565*
Kuperstein, M., *385*, *565*
Kupperman, B., *478*, *572*
Kurtzman, H. S., *275*, *565*
Kuypers, H. G. J. M., *352*, *571*

Laird, N. M., 293, 509
Lakoff, G., 97
LaManna, J. C., *477*, *561*
Lamperti, J., 277, 511
Lane, H. L., *91*, *565*
Lang, K., 127, 510
Lang, M., 511
Language acquisition device (LAD), *217*. *See also* Verbs, learning past tenses of
Larkin, J. H., 241, 512
Larsson, K., *350*, *553*
Lashley, K. S., 41, 512
Law of mass action, *509-510*. *See also* Amnesia
Layered systems in interactive models, 60
Lazarus, J. H., *94*, *572*
LC. *See* Locus coeruleus
Leaky learning model, 179
Learnability theorem, 235-236, 260
Learning. *See also* Boltzmann machines; Delta rule, generalized; Memory, a distributed model of; Neural plasticity and learning
  in Boltzmann machines
    easy and hard, 290-299
    hard, example of, 299-303
    learning algorithm, derivation of, 315-318
  establishing features through, 258-260
  in symbolic and subsymbolic paradigms, 261-262
Learning machine (Minsky and Edmonds), 153-154
Learning paradigms, 54-57
Learning rule, general form of, 52-53
Leavitt, R. Y., *351*, *563*
Le Cun, Y., 322, 512
Lehiste, I., *61*, *565*
Lenneberg, E. H., *473*, *565*
Lesser, U. R., *63*, *559*

Letter-perception model. *See* Interactive activation model of word perception
LeVay, S., *350*, *353*, *355*, *361*, *374*, *497*, *500*, *563*, *565*, *566*
Levels of analysis, 121-129. *See also* Isomorphism hypothesis
  Marr's levels, 122-124
  other notions of levels, 124-127
  reductionism and emergent properties, 127-129
Levin, J. A., 43, 85, 512, *90*, *566*
Levin's proteus model, 43
Levine, R. D., 227, 512
Lewis, B., *341*, *566*
Lewis, C. H., 251, 512
LGN cells, *480*
Liberman, A. M., *61*, *62*, *73*, *92*, *94*, *95*, *473*, *560*, *566*, *569*, *573*, *576*
Lichten, W., *63*, *569*
Licklider, J. C. R., *106*, *566*
Lieberman, F., *489*, *557*
Limited fan-out. *See* Fan-out, limited; Standard pattern associators
Limited increment hypothesis, *520*. *See also* Amnesia
Lin, C. S., *351*, *560*
Lindsay, P. H., 8, 206, 512
Linear algebra
  matrices and linear systems
    basis for vector space, change of, 413
    description of, 385-386
    eigenvectors and eigenvalues, 399-403
    linearity, 393
    matrices, 386-390
    matrix inverses, 410-413
    matrix multiplication and multilayer systems, 395-399
    one-layer PDP system, 390-393
    PDP systems, 2 examples, 406-410
    transposes and the outer product, 403-405
  nonlinear systems, 418-420
  vectors
    basic operations of, 367-370
    concepts, use of in analysis of simple PDP model, 383-385
    description of, 365-366
    inner products, 375
    linear combinations and independence, 370-373
    vector spaces, 374-375
Linear models, simple, 61-63. *See also* Linear algebra
  auto-associator version of, 63
  pattern associator, 63
  simple linear associator, 62
  weaknesses of, 63
Linear threshold units, 63-66, 425, *224*. *See also* Activation functions
  perceptron, 65
  XOR function, 64-65
LISP programming language, 124
  use of in P3 system, 492, 496-497
Llinás, R., *364*, *370*, *558*, *566*
Local representations, 77, 85, 96
Locus coeruleus (LC), *476-477*, *493*
Loeb, G. E., *383*, *566*
Loftus, E. F., 85, 508, *208*, *566*
Logical computation, notion of. *See* Activation functions
Logogen model, 43, *192-193*
Loomis, L. H., *402*, *566*
Lorente de Nó, R., *344*, *358*, *566*
Lovins, J. B., *62*, *560*
Luce, R. D., *75*, *93*, *195*, 566
Luce choice rule, application of, *90-91*, *195*
Lund, J. S., *357*, *358*, *361*, *366*, *374*, *566*, *573*
Lund, R. D., *336*, *357*, *566*
Luria, A. R., 41, 79, 135, 512
Luria's dynamic functional system, 41
Lynch, J. C., *366*, *567*

Ma, S. -K., *388*, *567*
Macchi, G., *350*, *567*
Macrodescription of harmony mechanism, 246-258

problem solving for, 246-247
productions and expertise, 251-253
schemata, 253
approximation, 256-258
for rooms, 255-256
two-choice model, 253-255
MacWhinney, B., *273*, *274*, *554*, *567*
Macy, A., *481*, *567*
Magistretti, P. J., *364*, *569*
Mann, V. A., *95*, *118*, *567*
Mapping from expressions, 439. *See also* Boolean function
Marcus, M. P., *317*, *324*, *567*
Marin, O. S. M., 134, 514
Marin-Padilla, M., *363*, *567*
Mark, R. F., *490*, *555*
Marr, D., 18, 19, 20, 42, 113, 116, 117, 121-122, 123, 196, 283, 512, *63*, *119*, *378*, *567*
Marr's levels of analysis, 122-124. *See also* Levels of analysis
Marrocco, R. T., *480*, *567*
Marshall, J. C., 102, 508
Marshall, W. H., *352*, *579*
Marslen-Wilson, W. D., 43, 512, *63*, *77*, *79*, *80*, *97*, *98*, *99*, *275*, *567*
Martin, K. A. C., *363*, *567*, *576*
Massaro, D. W., *77*, *81*, *86*, *94*, *567*, *568*, *571*
Massey, T., *378*, *560*
Matrices and linear systems. *See also* Linear algebra
basis for vector space, change of, 413-418
descriptions of, 385-386
eigenvectors and eigenvalues, 399-403
examples of PDP systems, 406-410
linearity, 393-395
matrices, 386
addition of, 387-389
matrix mapping, algebraic properties of, 389-390
scalars, multiplication by, 386
matrix inverses, 410-413
multiplication and multilayer systems, 395-398
algebraic properties of, 399
one-layer PDP system, 390-393
transposes and outer product, 403-405
Matrix inverses, 410-413. *See also* Matrices and linear systems
Matrix mapping, algebraic properties of, 389-390. *See also* Matrices and linear systems
Maunsell, J. H. R., *345*, *352*, *353*, *356*, *500*, *568*, *577*
Maximum-likelihood model, 292-294
McCarthy, J., 157-158, 512
McClelland, J. L., 20, 22, 24, 27, 28, 42, 43, 71, 79, 85, 120, 121, 133, 177, 199, 202, 216, 321, 512, 514, *8*, *58*, *59*, *63*, *69*, *71*, *75*, *77*, *80*, *90*, *119*, *123*, *126*, *127*, *130*, *131*, *135*, *138*, *140*, *141*, *142*, *170*, *172*, *195*, *217*, *370*, *380*, *381*, *383*, *394*, *532*, *558*, *559*, *568*, *574*
McClurkin, J. W., *480*, *567*
McConkie, G. W., *161*, *163*, *568*, *573*
McCulloch, W. S., 152, 424, 512
McDermott, D., *432*, *568*
McGeoch, L. A., 235, 508
McGill, J., *145*, *575*
McGuinness, E., *374*, *375*, *553*
McNaughton, B. L., *448*, *568*
MD. *See* Monocular deprivation
Medin, D. L., *171*, *181*, *200*, *205*, *536*, *568*
Meditch, J. S., 456, 512
Memory, a distributed model of. *See also* Distributed representations; Memory, retrieving information from
conclusions on, *214-215*
detailed assumptions of, *176-182*
experimental results of simulations
repetition and familiarity effects, *192-199*
representation of general and specific information, *199-206*
extensions of model
amnesia, spared learning in, *207-208*

Memory, a distributed model of
extensions of model *(continued)*
interference and fan effects, *208-209*
memory blends, *208*
regularities of behavior, emergence of, *207*
semantic memory, emergence of from episodic traces, *206*
general properties of, *173-175*
modular structure, *174-175*
pattern of activation, *175*
hidden units, augmenting model with, *209-214*
model's behavior, key aspects of, *182-192*
relation to basic concept in, *176*
theories of, *2-3*, *170-171*
Memory, retrieving information from. *See also* Distributed representations, features of; Memory, a distributed model of
content addressability, 25-29
default assignment, 29-30
graceful degradation, 29
spontaneous generalization, 30-31
Mercer, R. L., 293, 508
Merzenich, M. M., *385*, *386*, *387*, *563*, *569*
Mesulam, M. M., *350*, *569*
Metropolis, N., 230, 277, 513
Meyer, D. R., *352*, *579*
Michael, C. R., *367*, *368*, *569*
Micro- and macrolevels of harmony theory, 203-204, 210
Microdescription, problem-solving of, 246. *See also* Electricity problem-solving
Microfeature, 80-81
Microfeatures, semantic. *See* Semantic microfeatures
Microstructure of cognition, 12-13
Miezin, J., *374*, *375*, *553*
Miller, D. T., *536*, *564*
Miller, G. A., *63*, *106*, *323*, *566*, *569*
Miller, J. L., *62*, *96*, *569*
Miller, J. P., *381*, *382*, *569*, *575*
Miller, P., *515*, *576*
Miller, W., *254*
Milner, B., *504*, *506*, *510*, *514*, *569*
Minciacchi, D., *350*, *567*
Minsky, M., 65, 76, 96, 111-113, 153, 154, 157-158, 160, 233, 291, 319, 321, 334, 348, 354, 361, 424, 513, *18*, *19*, *535*, *569*
Mitchell, D. E., *475*, *558*
Mitchinson, G., 296, 297, 468, 486, 509
Mitra, S. K., 455, 513
Miyuwaki, K., *473*, *569*
Models, similarities and differences between, *4-5*
Modifications of patterns of interconnectivity in PDP models, 52-53. *See also* Learning
Modular structure of memory, 79, *174-175*. *See also* Memory, a distributed model of
Molinari, M., *35*, *567*
Monocular deprivation (MD), *474*, *475*
OD shift under, *487*
rearing, *489*
Monocular occlusion (AM), *474*
Monotonicity concepts for activation functions, 427-428. *See also* Activation functions
Monotonicity-in-context, 426-428
Montero, V. M., *351*, *569*
Moran, J., *374*, *558*
Morrell, F., *379*, *569*
Morris, R. G. M., *434*, *466*, *569*
Morrison, J. H., *364*, *569*
Morton, J., 43, 513, *97*, *106*, *192*, 570
Moser, M. G., *313*, *570*
Motor control
example of multiple constraints in, 4-6
PDP models for, examples of, 13-18
finger movements in skilled typing, 14-16
reaching for objects, 16-18
Mountcastle, V. B., *356*, *366*, *373*, *385*, *567*, *570*

Moussouris, J., 289, 513
Mower, G. D., *478*, *570*
Mozer, M. C., 68, 127, 507, 513, *125*, *139*, *140*, *142*, *570*
Muller, R. U., *435*, *441*, *445*, *447*, *565*, *570*
Multiple linear regression and the delta rule, 457-458. *See also* Delta rule, analysis of
Multiple simultaneous constraints, 4-9, *58*, *124*, *272-275*
  mutual constraints, 7
  operation of in syntax and semantics, 6-7
  duplication of connection information, need for to exploit, *124*
  role assignment, use of in, *272-275*
  simultaneous mutual constraints in word recognition, 7-9
  speech perception, role of in, *124*
Munro, P. W., 42, 180, 508, *480*, *487*, *489*, *495*, *496*, *555*, *570*
Murray, E. A., *357*, *570*
Mutt, V., *364*, *560*

Nadel, L., *435*, *445*, *510*, *527*, *571*, *576*
Nakatani, L., *61*, *110*, *570*
Nathan, P. W., *514*, *515*, *574*
Nativism vs. empiricism, 139-142
Nauta, W. J. H., *334*, *342*, *570*
NE. *See* Norepinephrine
Necker cube, *11*, *13*, *16*, *28*. *See also* Schemata, concept of
Neely, R. B., *63*, *122*, *573*
Negation problem, 346-348. *See also* Delta rule, generalized
Neisser, U., 81, 113, 116, 212, 513, 515
Nelson, R. J., *352*, *354*, *385*, *477*, *569*, *570*
Nelson, S. B., *477*, *554*
Neocortical neurons, nature of
  cell types in, *358-360*
  experimental methods, *357-358*
  feature detection, *367-371*
  firing, rates of, *366-367*
  groups of neurons behavior in cerebral cortex, *365-366*
  neurons without many spines, *361*
  neurons with spines, *360-361*
  single-neuron behavior in cerebral cortex, *364-365*
  special cell types, *362-364*
Network damage. *See* Damage, effects of on a network; Graceful degradation
Neural and conceptual interpretation of PDP models. *See* PDP models, neural and conceptual interpretation of
Neural-like processing systems, common learning paradigms in, 160-161
Neural modeling, 130
Neural nets, biological limits on storage capacity of, 469-470. *See also* Fan-out, limited
Neural or unit level of representation. *See* Pattern-based coordinates, delta rule in
Neural plasticity in cerebral cortex, *385-387*. *See also* Cerebral cortex, questions about computation in
Neural plasticity and learning
  critical period, effect of environment on, *478*
  critical period of, *473-478*
    ocular dominance, measuring changes in, *474-476*
    plasticity-modulating processes, *476-478*
  discussion of, *471-473*, *494-499*
    existing modification rules, state dependence and, *494-496*
    global modulators as dynamic variables, *496-497*
    predictions for, *497-499*
  experimental data on, comparison with, *489-494*
  ocularity state and its effect on, *478-489*
    model neuron, *479-480*
    ocularity plane, *480-484*

Neural plasticity and learning *(continued)*
state dependencies of plasticity, *484-489*
PDP models, learning rate as factor in, *472*
single-unit learning, focus on, *472*
summary of, *501*
terminology, *473*
visual cortex, ideas described with respect to ocular dominance in, *499-501*
Neural processing in cerebral cortex, *378-382*. *See also* Cerebral cortex, questions about computation in
Neural realism, lack of in PDP models, 136-138
Neurons. *See also* Cerebral cortex, anatomy and physiology of; Neocortical neurons, nature of
behavior in the cerebral cortex
groups of neurons, *365-366*
single neuron, *364-365*
classical description of, *335-337*
connections between, in brain, 132-133
communication among, 132
continuous output of, 133-134
graceful degradation of, 134
neocortical, *358-365*
number of, 131
speed of, 130-131
systems, 131-132
treated as devices, 424-425 (*see also* Boolean function)
without many spines, *361*
with spines, *360-361*
Newell, A., 108, 195, 513
Newsome, W. T., *347*, *356*, *554*, *568*
Newtonian mechanics, 125
Nicholson, C., *364*, *566*
Ninteman, F. W., *493*, *572*
Nonlinear systems. *See also* PDP models, neural and conceptual interpretation of
distributed, natural competition in, *424-428*
isomorphism, failure of in, *422-424*
quasi-linear systems with, *418-422*
use of, 418-421
limited dynamic range and, 420-421
subthreshold summation, 420
Nonpyramidal cells, *358-360*. *See also* Neocortical neurons, nature of
Norepinephrine (NE), *476-477*, *478*, *480*, *493*
as potential modulator of neural plasticity, *476-477*, *492-494*, *497*
Normal rearing (NR), *474*
Norman, D. A., 8, 9, 14, 15, 79, 116, 133, 206, 512, 513, 514, *18*, *19*, *537*, *539*, *540*, *543*, *545*, *555*, *570*, *574*
Norris, D., *63*, *100*, *571*
NR. *See* Normal rearing
Nusbaum, H. C., *120*, *571*

Ochs, M. T., *385*, *563*
Ocular dominance (OD)
class, *484*
histograms, *475*, *479*, *489*, *490*
shift, under MD, *487*
statistics, *474-476*
Ocular dominance index, *481-483*, *484*, *490*
vs. responsivity plot, *492*
Ocularity plane, power of as tool in theoretical analyses of ocular dominance plasticity, *483-484*
Ocularity state and its effect on plasticity, *478-480*. *See also* Neural plasticity and learning
ideal neuron, *479-480*
ocularity plane, *480-484*
plasticity, state dependence of, *484-489*
OD. *See* Ocular dominance
Oden, G. C., *77*, *275*, *568*, *571*
ODH. *See* Ocular dominance, histogram
ODI. *See* Ocular dominance index
6-OHDA. *See* 6-hydroxydopamine
Ohzawa, I., *481*, *492*, *560*, *567*

Oja, E., *489*, *557*
O'Keefe, J., *434*, *435*, *445*, *448*, *466*, *568*, *569*, *571*
O'Kusky, J., *348*, *571*
Olson, C. R., *475*, *571*
Olson, L., *350*, *553*
Olton, D. S., *435*, *522*, *554*, *571*
One-layer PDP systems, use of matrices in analyzing, 390-393. *See also* Matrices and linear systems
One-layer perceptron, 111-113
limitations of, 112-113
One-step system in interactive models, 60
Optimization problems, use of linear programming for, 284-286
Organization of Behavior, 53, 152
Ortony, A., *19*, *32*, *574*
Output units
definition of, 48
as major aspect of PDP models, 46, 48-49

P3 system. *See* Parallel process programmer
PABLO. *See* Reading, programmable blackboard model of
Palay, S. L., *338*, *571*
Palmer, R. G., 296, 511, 513
Palmer, S. E., 117, 513
Pandemonium, 42
Pandya, D. N., *352*, *571*, *573*
Papert, S., 65, 76, 96, 111-113, 158, 160, 233, 291, 319, 321, 334, 348, 354, 361, 424, 513, *535*, *569*
Paradigms of learning
associative, 54-55
regularity discovery, 55
Paradiso, M. A., *477*, *554*
Parallel distributed processing. *See* PDP.
Parallel Models of Associative Memory, 33, *533*
Parallel network simulating system. *See* Parallel process programmer
Parallel process programmer (P3 system), *453-454*
competitive learning methods (*App. B*), 504-506
description of, 364, 488-489
major components of, 489-490
performance of, 500-501
plan for competitive learning, (*App. A*), 502-503
plan language of, 490, 491-497
simplified diagrams of, *454-455*, *464*
simulation system, 497-500
typical plan for, 490
Parity networks, 159, 160
Parity problem, 334-335 *See also* Delta rule, generalized
Parker, D. B., 322, 361, 513
PARSIFAL (Marcus), *317*
Parsing in PDP models, *317-323*
Part/whole hierarchy, 105
Past-tense acquisition, three stages of, *219-221*. *See also* Verbs, learning past tenses of
Patte, P., *387*, 556
Pattern of activation, in distributed model of memory, *175*
memory traces as change in weights, *176*
mental state as, *176*
prior, retrieval as reinstatement of, *176*
and response strength, *194-195*
Pattern association paradigm, definition of, 55
Pattern associators. *See also* Programmable pattern associators; Standard pattern associators; Verbs, learning past tenses of
basic properties of, 33-37, *226-228*
definition of, 161
learning regular and exceptional patterns in, *226*
models, attractive properties of, 38
restrictions of, *228-233*
Pattern-based coordinates, delta rule in, 447-453
in conceptual interpretation of PDP models, *406-411*

Pattern completion device, use of Boltzmann machine as, 289-290. *See also* Boltzmann machines
Pattern of connectivity as major aspect of PDP models, 46, 49-51
Patterson, K., 102, 508
PDP approach and cognitive science
conclusions on, 145-146
natural applications of, 144
objections to
analysis, wrong level of, 121-127
cognitive approach, lack of, 120-121
cognitive theories, constraints of, 129-136
conscious knowledge and explicit reasoning, 143-145
human vs. rat intelligence, 143
lack of neural realism in, 136-138
Marr's levels, 122-124
nativism vs. empiricism, 139-142
other notions of levels, 124-127
reductionism and emergent properties, 127-129
weaknesses of, 111-120
status of various models, 144-145
PDP approach, introduction to
active representation in, 31-40
as alternative to serial models, 12-13
appeal of, 3-4, 10-12
examples of
memory retrieval, 25-31
motor control, 13-17
perception, 18-24
history of, 41-44
local vs. distributed representation, 32-33
pattern associator models
attractive properties of, 38
ensemble of patterns, extracting structure from, 39-40
learning multiple patterns, 37-38
learning rules of, 36-37
workings of, 33-36
PDP approach, reflections on
computer metaphor and, *533-535*
learning and consciousness,
problems of, *543-545*
new directions in, *545-546*
strengths of, *535-539*
description, levels of, *538-539*
human information processing, essential properties of, *537*
schema, *536-537*
useful result of, *537-538*
weaknesses of, *539-543*
evaluative structure, need for, *541-542*
multiple systems, required for, *542-543*
type-token problem, *539-540*
variables, *540-541*
PDP models, active representation in, 31-40, *175-176*
local vs. distributed, 32
pattern associator models attractive properties of, 38
pattern associators, 33-37
structure of ensemble of patterns, extracting, 39-40
PDP models and the brain. *See also* Cerebral cortex, anatomy and physiology of; Cerebral cortex, questions about computation in
relationship between, *328-330*
models of neural mechanisms, *330-331*
neurophysiology relevant to, *327-328*
PDP models, future directions for, *547-552*
PDP models, general framework for
bottom-up processing, 57-59
conclusions on, 74-76
hierarchical organizations, 57
interactive models, 59-60
learning paradigms, 54-57
major aspects of, 46-54
activation rule, 51-52
learning rule, 52-54
propagation rule, 51
sigma-pi units, 73-74
synchronous vs. asynchronous update, 61
top-down processing, 59

versions, specific
brain state in a box model (BSB), 66-68
Feldman and Ballard's units, 72
Grossberg's units, 70-71
interactive activation model, 71
linear threshold units, 63-66
simple linear models, 61-63
thermodynamic models, 68-70
PDP models, learning rate as factor in, *472-473*. *See also* Neural plasticity and learning
PDP models, neural and conceptual interpretation of
conclusions on, *429-431*
consideration of, *390-391*
distributed nonlinear models, natural competition in, *424-429*
as dynamical systems, *397-398*
interpretations, *391-396*
isomorphism hypothesis, failure of in nonlinear models, *422-424*
kinematics, *400-403*
kinematics and dynamics, *398-399*
learning connections and isomorphism of levels, *416-418*
linear systems, isomorphism of levels in, *411-413*
localized damage and, *413-416*
nonlinearity, quasi-linear systems with, *418-422*
pattern coordinates, *406-411*
vector space, structure of, *403-406*
Pearlmutter, B., 298
Pearson, J. C., *385*, *575*
Peck, C. K., *475*, *571*
Peptides in the cerebral cortex, *340*
Perez, R., *494*, *571*
Perception, examples of for PDP models
familiar patterns and, 20-23
novel patterns, completion of, 23-25
stereoscopic vision, 18-20
Perceptrons (Rosenblatt), 154-158
convergence procedure, 41-42, 65, *225-226*
class C′, 157-158
learning rule, 53, 154-157
parallel reorganizing elements, 158-159
Perceptual processing, centrality of, 197-198. *See also* Harmony theory
Perkel, D. H., *381*, *571*
Perkel, D. J., *381*, *571*
Perrett, D. I., *368*, *571*
Perry, J., 195, 508
Peterhans, E., *376*, *578*
Peters, A., *336*, *338*, *361*, *363*, *365*, *559*, *571*, *572*
Petersen, S. E., *347*, *554*
Petitjean, F., *350*, *555*
Pettigrew, J. D., *476*, *477*, *487*, *490*, *492*, *555*, *564*
Phase transitions, computational significance of, 236-237
Phillis, J. W., *339*, *565*
Phoneme identification, factors influencing
categorical perception, *84*, *88-95*
detectors, retuning of by context, *95-97*
lexical effects on, *77-78*
factors influencing, *78-80*
simulations, summary of, *97*
trading relations, *84-88*
use of phonotactic rules in, *81-83*
Phonemic restoration effect, 20
Piaget, J., *17*, *19*, *572*
Piercy, M., *516*, *517*, *563*
Pillsbury, W. B., 20, 513
Pinker, S., *217*, *572*
Pinto-Hamuy, T., *352*, *579*
Pisoni, D. B., *60*, *77*, *92*, *94*, *100*, *572*, *574*
Pitts, W, 152, 424, 512
Place-field model. *See also* Place recognition and goal location, biologically plausible models of
description of, *436-441*
goal location, *449*
properties of, *439-440*
scope of, *448*
shape and size, *445-446*

Place recognition and goal location, biologically plausible models of
- β-coefficient constants (*App.*), *467-468*
- β-coefficient model, *460-466*
- β units (*App.*), *469-470*
- conclusions on, *466*
- distal landmarks, *445*
- distributed view-field model, *449-460*
- goal location, *449*
- location parameters, *441-443*
- model, description of, *436-441*
  - properties of, *439-440*
- place-field location, *446-448*
- place-field model, scope of, *448*
- place-field shape and size, *445-446*
- place recognition, *434-436*
- simulated experiments, *443-445*

Plan language, as major component of P3 system, 489, 490, 491-497
- creating P3 plan for, 493-497
- features of, 490
- functions of, 491-493

Plasticity, neural. *See* Neural plasticity

Podgorny, P., *501*, *575*

Poggio, T., 18, 19, 20, 42, 117, 512, 513, *129*, *365*, *381*, *383*, *564*, *565*, *572*

Poincaré, H., 213, 513

Pollack, J. B., *277*, *278*, *311*, *314*, *578*

Porrino, L. J., *350*, *572*

Poschel, B. P. H., *493*, *572*

Posner, M. I., *171*, *183*, *200*, *203*, *572*

Powell, T. P. S., *344*, *348*, *350*, *351*, *352*, *556*, *560*, *563*, *564*, *572*, *573*

Prince, D. A., *364*, *369*, *557*

Principles of Neurodynamics, 41-42, 154

Probability theory, 209-210

Processing units, set of for PDP model, 46-48
- vs. one-unit-one-concept representational system, 47

Programmable blackboard model of reading. *See* Reading, programmable blackboard model of

Programmable pattern associators. *See also* Connection information distribution mechanism; Reading, programmable blackboard model of
- CA units, requirements of, 474-476
- CID networks, requirements of, 473-474
- conclusions on, 486
- discussion of, 485-486
- distributed representations, simultaneous access to, 483-485
- multiple pattern processing, 477-478
- overlapping, 478-480
- simultaneous access, cost of, 481-482
- single pattern processing, 476-477
- summary of CA requirements, 480-481

Proskauer, C. C., *336*, *361*, *363*, *571*, *572*

Prototypes
- coexistence of and repeated exemplars, *189-192*
- learning from exemplars, *182-184*
- multiple, nonorthogonal, *184-188*

Pyramidal cells, *358-360*. *See also* Neocortical neurons, nature of

Quasi-linear activation function, 52, 425. *See also* Activation functions

Quasi-linear systems with nonlinearity, *418-422*. *See also* Nonlinear systems; PDP models, neural and conceptual interpretation of

Quasi-local interpretations, *394-395*. *See also* PDP models, neural and conceptual interpretation of

Quasi-multilinear activation function, 426. *See also* Activation functions

Quillan, M. R., 85, 513

Rader, R. K., *497*, *577*
Rall, W., *336*, *381*, *382*, *569*, *572*, *575*
Ralston, H. J., *336*, *572*
Ramachandran, V. S., *478*, *572*
Ranck, J. B., Jr., *435*, *441*, *445*, *447*, *565*, *570*
Random-dot stereograms, 18
Rao, C. R., 455, 513
Rauschecker, J. P., *476*, *478*, *576*
Rawlins, J. N. P., *434*, *466*, *569*
Rayner, K., *153*, *161*, *163*, *164*, *275*, *560*, *572*, *573*
Reading, programmable blackboard model of (PABLO)
  ambiguous characters, *155-157*
  amount of feedback, effect of display length on, *159-161*
  CID computer simulation, results of, *136-141*
  conclusions on, *168-169*
  connection information distribution,
    benefits of, *164-166*
    computer simulation of word recognition using, *134-136*
    cost of, *166-167*
    extensions of, *167-168*
    mechanism, details of, *129-136* (*see also* Programmable pattern associators)
  description of, *2*, *125*
  fixations, sequences of, *161-164*
  fixations, single and multiple, *153-155*
  interactive activation model, bottom-up activations of word units in CID version of, *137-138*
  interference and crosstalk, *139-141*
  PABLO simulation model
    coarse coding, *146-147*
    details of, *151-153*
    feedback, *147*
    focus of attention, shifting, *147-151*
    overlapping slots in, *143-147*
    role-specific letter units, *145-146*
  words of different lengths, conspiracies of, *157-159*
Realizability theorem, 230-235
Receptor, cartoon of, *508-509*. *See also* Amnesia
Recurrent networks, 354-360. *See also* Delta rule, generalized
  performance of, 359-360
  sequence completion, learning of, 358-359
  shift register problem and, 357-358
Recursion, 119-120, *318-320*
Reddy, D. R., *63*, *107*, *122*, *573*
Reductionism, PDP models as exercise in, 127-129
Redundancy, benefits of, 472. *See also* Standard pattern associators
Reese, T. S., *336*, *572*
Regularity detector paradigm, 161
Reich, P. A., *323*, *573*
Reilly, D. L., *499*, *573*
Reitboek, H. J. P., *385*, *573*
Relaxation searches, use of parallel networks to perform, 283-290
  learning, difficult and easy, 290-292
  maximum likelihood models, 292-294
  optimization problems and, 284-286
  pattern completion, 289-290
  probabilistic decisions, use of to escape from local minima, 287-288
  simulated annealing, application of to Hopfield nets, 288-289
Relaxation system, 135-136
Relearning, speed of in Boltzmann machines, 308-310
Repetition and familiarity effects, *192-199*
  alternative interpretation of, *193-194*
    pattern action and response strength, *194-195*
    time-accuracy curves, effects of experimental variables on, *195-199*
  traditional interpretation of, *192-193*

Repp, B. H., *95*, *118*, *567*, *573*
Representation, distributed. *See* Distributed representation
Representation of environment as major aspect of PDP models, 53-54
Representation vector of harmony theory, 213-214
Representational features of harmony theoretical model, 213-214
Representation, learning of. *See* Boltzmann machines; Competitive learning; Delta rule, generalized
Representation, learning of new in harmony theory
  procedure and abstract features, 258-260
  in symbolic and subsymbolic paradigms, 261
Reproduction trials, *520*. *See also* Amnesia
Residual learning skills in amnesia, *518-524*.
Retinocentric feature detectors, 114
Retrograde amnesia, *505-506*, *513-515*
Reverse learning, occurrence of, 296-298
Reverse suture (RS), *474*, *487-488*, *489*
Reverse suture paradigm, time course of, *489-490*. *See also* Visual cortex, developmental models of
Ribak, C. E., *363*, *572*
Riley, M. S., 241, 264, 514, 515
Rinzel, J., *381*, *382*, *569*, *575*
Ritz, S. A., 56, 406, 409, 410, 418, 507, *173*, *226*, *311*, *399*, *551*, *554*
Roberts, E., *351*, *562*
Rock, I., 117, 514
Rockel, A. J., *344*, *573*
Rockland, K. S., *352*, *366*, *374*, *573*
Role-assignment model. *See* Case role assignment, model of
Role-specific letter units, *145-146*. *See also* Reading, programmable blackboard model of
Rolls, E. T., *368*, *571*
Rosch, E., *171*, *573*
Rose, J. E., *345*, *573*
Rosén, I., *357*, *554*
Rosenblatt, F., 41, 111, 152, 153-154, 155-157, 158, 291, 424, 514, *226*, *289*, *535*, *573*
Rosenbluth, A. W., 230, 277, 513
Rosenbluth, M. N., 230, 277, 513
Rosenfeld, A., 285, 514
Rosenthal, M., *477*, *561*
Ross, B. H., *206*, *554*
RS. *See* Reverse suture
Rubin, D. S., 293, 509
Rudnicky, A., *58*, *557*
Rule of propagation as major aspect of PDP models, 46, 51
Rumelhart, D. E., 6, 9, 14, 15, 20, 22, 24, 43, 71, 116, 120, 121, 130, 133, 177, 199, 202, 216, 300, 321, 512, 514, *7*, *18*, *19*, *31*, *59*, *71*, *75*, *77*, *90*, *170*, *195*, *217*, *316*, *380*, *394*, *532*, *539*, *540*, *545*, *568*, *573*, *574*
Russell, W. R., *514*, *515*, *574*
Ryder, J. M., 7, 511

Sachs, M. B., *383*, *574*
Saffran, E. M., 134, 514
Said, S., *364*, *560*
Sakaski, K., *370*, *558*
Salasoo, A., *60*, *100*, *197*, *198*, *559*, *574*
Salvert, D., *350*, *555*
Samuel, A. G., *95*, *160*, *574*
Sanderson, K. J., *480*, *574*
Sayers, F. C., *324*, *563*
Scalars, multiplication by, 367, 386. *See also* Matrices and linear systems; Vectors
Schacter, D., *519*, *574*
Schaffer, M. M., *171*, *200*, *536*, *568*
Schank, R. C., 6, 9, 201, 202, 514, *18*, *19*, *324*, *574*
Scheibel, A. B., *351*, *574*
Scheibel, M. E., *351*, *574*

Schein, S. J., *374*, *558*
Schemata, concept of, 9, 78-79, 199-213, *1*, *7-37*, *536-537*
account of mental processing, *38-53*
consciousness, content of, *39*
control, problem of, *39-40*
conversations and, *42-44*
external representations and formal reasoning, *44-48*
mental models and, *40-42*
mental stimulation and practice, *42*
assumptions made about, *30-31*
conclusions on, *53-57*
constraint satisfaction and, *17*
description of, *1*, *7-8*
example of, *22-25*
examples of processing of, *25-31*
goodness-of-fit landscapes of, *15*, *16*, *28*, *29*, *30*, *31*, *32-33*, *35*
in harmony theory, 199-213
completion task, 206-208
construction of, 201-203
formulation of, 209-210
function of, 208
knowledge atoms, nature of in, 205-206
logical structure of, 199-200
mathematical properties of probability and, 211-213
micro- and microlevels of, 203-204
modified letter perception model, 204-205
history of, *17-19*
important features of, *19-20*
interpretation differences and, *21*
PDP models as constraint networks, *8-17*
properties of
active processes, *36*
additional features, *36-37*
goodness-of-fit evaluation to data, *36*
knowledge representation, *36*
subschema, *35*
variables, *33-34*
summary of, *31*, *48*
thinking, goal direction in, *48*
use of as knowledge structures, 9
Schermer, T. M., *96*, *569*
Schiller, P. H., *367*, *574*
Schmolze, J. G., *313*, *555*
Schneider, W., 126, *549*, *575*
Schumacher, L. E., 302, 350, 511, 515
Schwanenflugel, P. J., *181*, *205*, *568*
Schwartz, J. H., *333*, *507*, *552*, *564*
Schwartz, M. F., 134, 514
Schwartz, M., *477*, *554*
Schweikert, J., 7, 511
Sclar, G., *492*, *560*
Scott, G. L., *351*, *569*
Scott, J. P., *473*, *575*
Scripts, use of as knowledge structure, 9
Sears, T. A., *336*, *553*
Segev, I., *381*, *382*, *575*
Seguin, S., *350*, *555*
Sejnowski, T. J., 118, 264, 272, 282, 289, 297, 302, 306, 313, 317, 335, 348, 350, 507, 508, 509, 510, 511, 514, 515, *23*, *24*, *63*, *128*, *373*, *377*, *379*, *380*, *393*, *554*, *562*, *575*
Selfridge, O. G., 8, 41, 212, 515
Selman, B., *321*, *575*
Semantic cues. *See* Word-order and semantic cues to role assignment
Semantic memory, emergence of from episodic traces, *206*. *See also* Memory, a distributed model of
Semantic microfeatures, *278-283*. *See also* Case role assignment, model of
Sememe units, 97-98, 99, 101-102, 305-310. *See also* Arbitrary mapping; Damage, effects of on a network
Semilinear activation functions. *See* Activation functions, semilinear
Sencer, W., *352*, *579*

Sentence processing in PDP networks. *See* Case role assignment, model of
Sentence-structure (SS) representation, *283-286*. *See also* Case role assignment, model of
Sequential symbol processing, 106-108
Sequential thought processes in PDP models. *See also* Recurrent networks; Sequential symbol processing; Seriality, emergent
  account of mental processing, development of, *38-39*
  conclusions on, *53-57*
  consciousness, contents of, *39*
  control, problem of, *39-40*
  conversations, *42-44*
  external representations and formal reasoning, *44-48*
    important aspects of, *47*
    role of language in, *47*
  mental models and, *40-42*
  mental simulations and practice, *42*
  summary of, *48*
  thinking, goal direction in, *48*
  tic-tac-toe example of, *48-53*, *54*
Seriality, emergent, 247, 249. *See also* Electricity problem-solving
Settlage, P. H., *352*, *579*
Shallice, T., *145*, *543*, *570*, *575*
Shankweiler, D., *92*, *94*, *566*
Shannon, C. E., 195, 267, 515
Sharma, V. K., *477*, *561*
Shaw, G. L., *385*, *575*
Shepard, R. N., 198, 515, *501*, *536*, *575*
Shepherd, G. M., *336*, *381*, *382*, *572*, *575*
Sherk, H., *350*, *374*, *566*
Sherman, S. M., *351*, *560*
Shiffrin, R. M., *197*, *198*, *559*, *574*
Shlaer, R., *494*, *571*
Sickels, E. R., *324*, *563*
Sigma-pi units, 72, 73-74, 426
  generalized delta rule for, 353
Silverman, D. J., *385*, *575*
Silverstein, J. W., 56, 406, 409, 410, 418, 507, *173*, *226*, *311*, *399*, *551*, *554*
Simon, H. A., 241, 508
Simple binary addition problem, 341-346. *See also* Delta rule, generalized
Simulated annealing, 287, 288-289, 313. *See also* Cooling schedule; Harmony theory
Simulation system environment, as major component of P3 system, 489, 497-500
Singer, W., *476*, *478*, *575*, *576*
Single-level interactive model, 60
Single-shot algorithms, *380*. *See also* Cerebral cortex, questions about computation in
Single-unit learning, focus on, *472*. *See also* Neural plasticity and learning
Singley, *209*
Skirboll, L. R., *350*, *577*
Slater, P. C., *513*, *515*, *576*
Slobin, D. I., *221*, *247*, *249*, *250*, *251*, *254*, *255*, *256*, *556*
Slowiaczek, L. M., *120*, *571*
Small, S. L., *277*, *314*, *557*, *576*
Smith, D. C., *490*, *565*
Smith, E., 24, 515
Smith, P. T., 24, 515
Smolensky, P., 125, 241, 259, 264, 277, 289, 447, 514, 515
Sokolov, J. L., *274*, *567*
Somogyi, P., *362*, *363*, *567*, *576*
Spared learning in amnesia, *518-519*, *521-524*. *See also* Amnesia
Spear, P. D., *490*, *565*
Speech, fundamental aspects for development of TRACE model
  architecture for TRACE model, importance of, *63-64*
  context effects, left and right, *60*
  cues, sensitivity of, *62*
  lack of boundaries, *60*, *61*
  speech signal, noise and indeterminacy in, *62-63*
  stimulus, temporal nature of, *59-60*
  temporal overlap, *60-61*

Spencer, W. A., *364*, *576*
Spoehr, K., 24, 515
Spoken word recognition, study of, *97-98*
Spontaneous learning (Rosenblatt), 155-156
Squashing function, 425, *485-489*. *See also* Activation functions; Ocularity state and its effect on plasticity
Squire, L. R., *505*, *510*, *513*, *515*, *516*, *517*, *525*, *527*, *556*, *576*
Standard pattern associators. *See also* Programmable pattern associators
conclusions on, 486
degradation, effects of, 472
limited fan-out, effects of, 468-472
programmable nets, resource requirements, 465-468
redundancy, benefits of, 472
resource requirements of, 460, 461-465
computations of, 463-465
Stanford, L. R., *351*, *560*
State of activation as major aspect of PDP model, 46, 48
State space (*S*), *398-399*. *See also* Kinematics of the dynamical system
coordinate system for, *400*
of general nonlinear activation model, *402*
pattern view of, *406*
unit coordinates for, *400-401*
Statistical learning, analyzing case of, 453-457. *See also* Delta rule, analysis of
Steedman, M., *274*, *557*
Stemberger, J. P., *248*, *576*
Sternberg, S., 133, 515, *402*, *566*
Stevens, K. N., *62*, *168*, *561*, *576*
Stimulus equivalence, problem of, 113-114
Stochastic generative model, 293-294, 313
Stochastic units, 81
Strang, G., 411, 422, 515
Strange, W., *473*, *569*
Structure in representations and processes, 104-108
constituent structure, 105-106
sequential symbol processing, 106-108
Studdert-Kennedy, M., *92*, *94*, *566*, *576*
Subsymbolic and symbolic paradigms, learning in, 261-262
Subthreshold summation, 420. *See also* Nonlinear systems, use of
Summerfield, Q., *85*, *576*
Sur, M., *352*, *354*, *385*, *569*, *570*
Surround effects in visual cortex, *374-377*. *See also* Cerebral cortex, questions about computation in
Sutton, R. S., 43, 53, 57, 444, 508, 515, *383*, *539*, *554*, *576*
Swanson, L. W., *350*, *576*
Swets, J. A., 466, 510, *225*, *561*
Swinney, D. A., *109*, *577*
Symbolic and subsymbolic paradigms, learning in, 261-262
Symmetry problem, 340-341. *See also* Delta rule, generalized
Synapses in the cerebral cortex, basic types, *338-339*
Synaptic change, neurochemistry of, *507-509*. *See also* Amnesia
Synchronous update vs. asynchronous update, 61
Syntactic processing in PDP models, *317-323*
Szentágothai, J., *351*, *362*, *577*

T-C problem, 348-352. *See also* Delta rule, generalized
Tabula rasa, 139, 141
Takeuchi, A., *489*, *495*, *553*
Talbot, W. H., *366*, *567*
Tank, D., *389*, *562*
Tash, J., *92*, *572*
Teitelbaum, P., 142, 515
Teller, A. H., 230, 277, 513
Teller, E., 230, 277, 513
Tenenbaum, J. M., *63*, *554*

Terminal parameters, 491. *See also* P3 system
Terrace, H. S., 183, 515
Theorems, harmony, (*App.*)
Boltzmann machines, second-order observables and, 273-275
harmony function *H*, cognitive systems and, 267-268
terminology, 268-269
overview of definitions, 264-267
proofs of, 275-281
retrieving information from *H*, 269-272
storing information in *H*, 272-273
Thermal equilibrium of network, 290-291, 313
Thermodynamic limit, 239
Thermodynamic models, 68-70
Boltzmann machines, 68, 69
harmony theory, 68
Thibadeau, R., *161*, *549*, *577*
Thomas, G. B., Jr., 276, 515
Thompson, H., *60*, *63*, *84*, *107*, *577*
Thompson, R. F., *383*, *552*, *561*
Three-dimensional plots, 429, 430-438. *See also* Activation functions
Three-layer network, 97-98. *See also* Arbitrary mapping, implementing
Three-level interactive model, 59
Three-stage learning curve, *240-245*. *See also* Verbs, learning past tenses of
Threshold logic unit, 425. *See also* Activation functions
Tic-tac-toe, as example of sequential thought processes in PDP models, *48-53*, *54*
Tigges, J., *348*, *577*
Tigges, M., *348*, *577*
Timing
problem of, *378-380*
of sensory stimulation, *383-384*
temporal binding, *383-385*
Timney, B. N., *475*, *558*
Tömböl, T., *351*, *361*, *363*, *577*
Top-down approach, 123
Top-down processing system, 51, 57-59
Top-down theoretical strategy pursued in harmony theory, 196, 199-213
Torre, V., 117, 513, *129*, *365*, *381*, *565*, *572*
Touret, M., *350*, *555*
Touretzky, D., *322*, *548*, *577*
TRACE model of speech perception
compared to Fanty's parser, *321-322*
conclusions on, *120-121*
deficiencies of, *119-120*
description of, *2*, *58-59*, *64-68*, *123-124*, *143*, *153-154*
phoneme identification, factors influencing
categorical perception, *84*, *88-95*
lexical effects of on, *77-81*
phoneme detectors, retuning of by context, *95-97*
simulations, summary of, *97*
trading relations, *84-88*
use of phonotactic rules in, *81-83*
phoneme units, context-sensitive tuning of, *68-69*
programmable version of, *167-168*
speech, fundamental aspects for, *59-63*
spoken word recognition, study of,
COHORT model, *98-101*, *102*, *103*
word segmentation, lexical basis of, *106-115*
word segmentation simulations, summary of, *115-117*
successes, summary of, *117-119*
TRACE I model, *69*, *70-71*, *75*, *76*
TRACE II model, *69*, *70*, *71-75*, *76*, *102*, *110*
Travis, A. M., *352*, *579*
Tribus, M., 227, 512
T'so, D. Y., *385*, *577*
Turner, M. R., *385*, *560*
Tversky, A., *499*, *560*
Two-dimensional space, inner products in, 380-382. *See also* Vectors

Two-layer scheme in harmony theory, advantages of, 218-219
Tyler, L. K., *97*, *98*, *99*, *104*, *275*, *567*, *577*
Type-token problem, as weakness of PDP approach to cognition, *539-540*

Uchizono, K., *339*, *577*
Ungerleider, L. G., *374*, *558*
Ungerstredt, U., *350*, *553*
Uniform monotonicity, 426-428
Uniformly nondecreasing function, as special case of uniformly monotonic function, 427
Uniqueness and continuity constraints, 19-20
Unit parameters, 491. *See also* P3 system
UNIT TYPE statement for pattern generator in P3, 493-494
Unlearning, 296-298. *See also* Boltzmann machines

Valverde, F., *363*, *559*
Van Dam, A., *467*, *559*
Van der Loos, H., *366*, *577*
Van Essen, D. C., *352*, *353*, *355*, *356*, *368*, *500*, *566*, *568*, *577*
Van Hoesen, G. W., *350*, *569*
van Santen, J. P. H., *159*, *160*, *563*, *574*
Van Sluyters, R. C., *489*, *490*, *491*, *555*
Variable translational mappings, 116
Vaughn, J. E., *351*, *562*
Vecchi, M. P., 148, 235, 287, 511
Vector notation, delta rule in, 445-447. *See also* Delta rule, analysis of
Vectors. *See also* Linear algebra
  basic operations of
    calculating averages, 369
    scalars, multiplication by, 367
    vectors, addition of 368-369
  concepts, use of to analyze simple PDP model, 383-385.
  description of, 365-366
  inner products, 375-376
    algebraic properties of inner product, 382-383
    angle, 377-379
    length, 376-377
    projections, 379-380
    two-dimensional space, inner products in, 380-382
  linear combinations and independence
    combinations of vectors, 370-371
    linear independence, 371-373
  vector spaces, 374-375
    structure of, *403-406*
Venesky, R. L., 24, 515
Verb-frame selection for role-assignment models, *300-301*
Verbs, irregular, types of, *245-246*, *247-254*. *See also* Verbs, learning past tenses of
Verbs, learning past tenses of
  binding networks for (*App.*), *269-271*
  conclusions on, *266-268*
  example of model based on LAD approach, *217-219*
  issue of, *3*, *216-217*
  model of
    learning and, *225-226*
    operation of, *223-225*
    phonological patterns, featural representations of, *233-239*
    simple pattern associator model, *226-233*
    structure of, *221-223*
    summary of structure of, *239-240*
  novel verbs, transfer to, *261-266*
  simulations, main points of
    irregular verbs, types of, *245-246*, *247-254*
    regularization, types of, *257-260*
    regular verbs, types of, *245-246*, *247*
    three-stage learning curve, *240-245*
    vowel-change verbs, *254-257*
  stages, sequence of in acquisition of use of, *219-221*

Verbs, regular, *245-246*, *247*, *254-257*, *258-260*. *See also* Verbs, learning past tenses of
Verbrugge, R., *473*, *569*
Vertical and horizontal lines, experiments with, 184-190
Vertically hierarchical networks, 217
Videen, T. O., *497*, *577*
View-field model, distributed. *See* Distributed view-field model
Vincent, S. R., *350*, *577*
Visual cortex, developmental models of, *489-494*
  alternating monocular occlusion, *490*, *491*
  norepinephrine, role of, *492-494*
  responsivity, relation of to connectivity, *490*, *492*
  reverse suture paradigm, time course of, *489-490*
Visual system, 282-283. *See also* Boltzmann machines
Vital-Durand, F., *497*, *500*, *555*, *577*
Voight, H. F., *383*, *574*
Volman, S. F., *367*, *574*
von der Heydt, R., *376*, *578*
von der Malsberg, C., 42, 147, 152, 162, 164, 516, *384*, *489*, *494*, *578*
Von Neumann architecture, *534-535*. *See also* PDP approach, reflections on
Von Neumann computer metaphor, 195
Vygotsky, L. S., *43*, *47*, *578*

Walker, A. E., *349*, *578*
Walker, E. C. T., 7, 511
Walker, J. A., *435*, *554*
Wall, J. T., *385*, *569*
Waltz, D. L., *277*, *278*, *311*, *314*, *578*
Warren, R. M., 20, 516
Webster, H. de F., *338*, *571*
Weight-decay, use of in Boltzmann machine, 298-299.
Weller, R. E., *345*, *578*
Welsh, A., 43, 512, *63*, *77*, *79*, *80*, *98*, *99*, *567*
Werblin, F. S., *336*, *578*
Wessels, J., *99*, *104*, *577*
Westrum, L. E., *336*, *578*
Whitteridge, D., *354*, *363*, *558*, *567*, *576*
Whittlesea, B. W. A., *171*, *172*, *200*, *201*, *202*, *203*, *204*, *556*, *578*
Wickelfeature representation (Wickelgren)
  blurring, *238-239*
  details of, *234-239*
Wickelgren, W. A., *62*, *181*, *233*, *510*, *511*, *527*, *578*
Wickelphones, *233-234*, *236-238*
Widrow, G., 321, 516
Widrow-Hoff rule, 53, 291-292. *See also* Delta rule
Wiener, *534*
Wiesel, T. N., *340*, *353*, *356*, *358*, *366*, *367*, *373*, *374*, *385*, *474*, *475*, *483*, *497*, *500*, *561*, *562*, *563*, *566*, *577*, *578*
Williams, R. J., 425, 516
Willshaw, D. J., 42, 97, 100, 460, 461, 465-466, 468, 472, 475, 516
Willshaw nets, 461-465
  comparison of to various kinds of local representation, 465
  difficulties with, 465-468
Wilson, H. R., *381*, *389*, *578*
Winston, P. H., 32, 516, *524*, *578*
Wise, R. A., *493*, *578*
Wise, S. P., *357*, *564*
Wolverton, G. S., *161*, *568*
Wood, C. C., 102, 516, *551*, *578*
Woods, W., 119, 516, *322*, *578*
Woolsey, C. N., *352*, *579*
Woolsey, T. A., *355*, *500*, *558*, *579*
Word identification simulations in TRACE, summary of, *115-117*
Word-order and semantic cues to role assignment, *293-300*. *See also* Case role assignment, model of
Word perception model (McClelland & Rumelhart). *See* Interactive activation model of word perception

Word segmentation, lexical basis of
for TRACE, *106-115*
identification, word, *112-115*
nonwords, end of, *111-112*
short sentence example, *115*
word inputs, single and multiple, *107-111*
Wu, T. Y., *350*, *577*
Wyatt, H. J., *500*, *558*

XOR problem, 319-321, 330-334. *See also* Delta rule, generalized

Yin, T. C. T., *366*, *567*
Young, E. D., *383*, *574*

Zadeh, L. A., 423, 516
Zeki, S. M., *368*, *374*, *577*, *579*
Zipser, D., 97, 300, 514, *432*, *437*, *438*, *440*, *442*, *443*, *444*, *447*, *579*
Zola, D., *161*, *568*
Zucker, S. W., 285, 286, 511, 514

It's been
It can be
It might be

prove
eat
shaken
woken